Advance_
Professional Chef

LEVEL 3 DIPLOMA

Gary Hunter & Terry Tinton

CENGAGE
Learning·

Australia · Brazil · Japan · Korea · Mexico · Singapore · Spain · United Kingdom · United States

Advanced Professional Chef: Level 3 Diploma, 2nd Edition
Gary Hunter and Terry Tinton

Publishing Director: Linden Harris

Commissioning Editor: Lucy Mills

Development Editor: Claire Napoli

Editorial Assistant: Lauren Darby

Project Editor: Alison Cooke

Production Controller: Eyvett Davis

Marketing Manager: Lauren Mottram

Typesetter: MPS Limited

Cover design: HCT Creative

Text design: Design Deluxe

© 2013, Cengage Learning EMEA

While the publisher has taken all reasonable care in the preparation of this book, the publisher makes no representation, express or implied, with regard to the accuracy of the information contained in this book and cannot accept any legal responsibility or liability for any errors or omissions from the book or the consequences thereof.

Products and services that are referred to in this book may be either trademarks and/or registered trademarks of their respective owners. The publishers and author/s make no claim to these trademarks. The publisher does not endorse, and accepts no responsibility or liability for, incorrect or defamatory content contained in hyperlinked material.

For product information and technology assistance,
contact **emea.info@cengage.com**.

For permission to use material from this text or product,
and for permission queries,
email **emea.permissions@cengage.com**.

British Library Cataloguing-in-Publication Data
A catalogue record for this book is available from the British Library.

ISBN: 978-1-4080-6421-4

Cengage Learning EMEA
Cheriton House, North Way, Andover, Hampshire, SP10 5BE
United Kingdom

Cengage Learning products are represented in Canada by Nelson Education Ltd.

For your lifelong learning solutions, visit **www.cengage.co.uk**

Purchase your next print book, e-book or e-chapter at **www.cengagebrain.com**

Printed in the United Kingdom by Ashford Colour Press
Print Number: 03   Print Year: 2017

Contents

About the authors

Gary Hunter *Head of Culinary Arts, Hospitality, Food and Beverage Service at Westminster Kingsway College*

Gary has many years of education and training experience within the further, higher and vocational education sectors. He continues to travel the world as a culinary and hospitality consultant and as a leading chocolatier with Barry Callebaut, giving seminars in Europe, Korea and the USA.

Gary is an experienced international culinary competition judge and competitor and has won numerous awards and medals. He is a Fellow of the Master Chefs of Great Britain and continues to work with and train many of today's successful chefs in the UK.

Leading the education sector for culinary and hospitality training, Gary was part of the team to produce the City & Guilds Diploma in Professional Cookery qualifications at levels 1, 2 and 3. He was recognized in 2012 by the Craft Guild of Chefs for his contribution to culinary arts with the Education Chef of the Year Award.

As an award winning author with books endorsed by Jamie Oliver and Heston Blumenthal, Gary has published a second edition to the popular Professional Chef Level 2 book.

Terry Tinton is the Senior Chef and Programme Manager for Culinary Arts and has recently been made an Academician with the Academy of Culinary Arts. Specializing in Culinary Science and managing over 25 staff in 14 working kitchens; provenance, sustainability and green issues are a passion. Supporting local producers and working with exemplary ingredients are paramount.

Travelling abroad frequently to work with leading chefs in countries such as USA, Switzerland, France and Germany, Terry also works to a large extent throughout the UK providing specialist culinary demonstrations and training to the wider industry. He has a strong practical background with international and Michelin restaurant experience.

Finding the time to write is a strong passion and he has now written and had published seven educational professional cookery books for students and training chefs. These books have been endorsed by Jamie Oliver and Heston Blumenthal, who have both written forewords for the series. Terry has recently published a second edition to his much-loved Professional Chef Level 2 book.

Acknowledgements

The authors would like to thank the following:

Sarah-Jane Hunter
Estelle Hunter
Phillip Hunter
Patricia Long

Charlotte Hunter
Hilary Hunter
Paul Hunter
John Long

Dom Healy, Jimmy Mair and Martin Jermy for their inspiration.

Margaret Tinton
Terence Tinton
Rosaleen Lane
Lewis Tinton

Kate Tinton
Andy Tinton
Ava - Grace Tinton
Malachy Lane

Oisin Lane
Paul Lane
Claire Lane

The authors would like to dedicate this book to Maeve Mitchell.

College acknowledgements:

Andy Wilson
Barry Jones

Geoff Booth
Jose Souto

Ian Wild

Contributors to the book:

Dr Rachel Edwards-Stuart graduated from the University of Cambridge with a degree in Biochemistry. She then moved to Paris where she worked with Herve This in his Molecular Gastronomy Research team. While in Paris, Rachel became involved in chef consultancy and training, and in 2005 she moved back to the UK where she studied a PhD in Food and Flavour Science sponsored by Heston Blumenthal. She then spent some time working for Sainsbury's as a Food technologist before moving to Westminster Kingsway College, where she helped set up their Culinary Science and Kitchen Innovation Laboratory and where she currently teaches Culinary Science to the students.

Paul Jervis studied at Westminster Kingsway College and graduated after three years. He spent the next years working at prestige contract catering units before being a head chef at a unit catering for 1500 people per day. Each establishment had a strong emphasis in training so Paul developed his teaching experience whilst at work. Paul returned to Westminster Kingsway college to teach in 2009.

Jonathon Warner has been working as a lecturer for four years at Westminster Kingsway college and previously two years at a private cooking school. Before teaching as a chef Jonathon worked for 18 years in hotels and restaurants.

The Publisher wishes to thank the following for granting permission to use images:

istockphoto; Shutterstock; Dreamstime Photos; Russum's; Nisbetts.

In addition we would like to thank Nathan Allan and Laura Pinnell of Nathan Allan Photography for providing commissioned photography.
Web Address: **www.nathanallanphotography.com**
Video Content provided by Ken Franklin and Video 4 Ltd.
Web Address: **www.video4.co.uk**
Photo Research and Video/Photo Project Management was provided by Jason Newman, Annalisa de Hassek, Bradley Hearn and Alexander Goldberg of Media Selectors Ltd. Web Address: **www.mediaselectors.com**

This book is endorsed by:

British Culinary Federation

BRITISH CULINARY FEDERATION
National Member of the
World Association of Chefs' Societies

PATRON: HIS ROYAL HIGHNESS THE PRINCE OF WALES

Academy of Culinary Arts

Craft Guild of Chefs

The Master Chefs of Great Britain

For providing the Nutritional Information for the Recipes:

KitMan

Olympus Associates specializes in providing consultancy and management services to the catering industry. With a unique kitchen management system called The *KitMan System* – the company is able to assist operations in controlling food costs and managing their food service operations more effectively.

The KitMan System is a food cost control and kitchen management system used by many leading catering establishments throughout the UK in hospitality, healthcare and education markets.

The company has a specialist version for the education sector, and has working partnerships with many catering colleges and universities throughout the United Kingdom and Ireland using the program, including the authors of this book, not only for controlling their own food costs, but also as a teaching tool for the catering and hospitality students.

KitMan provides valuable detailed analysis of costs per class, per student and is ideal for use for the commercial activities of a college including refectory and restaurant services.

We are pleased to be associated with Cengage Learning and to continue our relationships with the Hospitality & Catering departments of colleges.

For more information please visit **www.kitman.com**

Notes on Nutritional Information and recipe processing

Please note the Nutritional Information is for guidance only and may not necessarily match the final result. The sample ingredients are based on average contents. The Nutritional Information is calculated **per portion**.

The final nutritional content can be effected by any of the following factors: seasonality; storage method; storage time; brand, breed, variety; cooking method; cooking time; regeneration method. Wastage and yield may also result in the final nutritional content being lower than the results shown.

Where two alternative ingredients have been listed, the first has been used wherever possible.

If an ingredient is listed as optional it has been included if it appears in the main ingredient listing, where possible, but has not if it appears in the method or Chef's Tips part of the original recipe.

Foreword

If you're reading this, you're thinking about pushing the envelope to Level 3 standard. Congratulations – it means you've already got some determination and culinary skill, both things you'll definitely need to make it as a chef. Because mastering the techniques is the foundation of good cookery.

I wanted to be a chef after being taken to a three-star French restaurant when I was 16. I taught myself to cook, preparing the dishes of the classical repertoire over and over, perfecting the techniques they demanded and endeavouring to understand the principles behind them. In the process I acquired a body of knowledge and a 'feel' for cooking that has underpinned everything I've done since. In our modern, techno-savvy world there's a tremendous pressure to look for the fast track, and cooking's no exception. It's tempting to ignore tradition and focus only on what's new and revolutionary. But, for me, cooking's about evolution not revolution: exploring and understanding the foundations of cuisine is the best springboard for taking a leap forward, for taking food in new and exciting directions.

Teaching myself to cook had its benefits, but it was a solitary and often frustrating way to learn. Taking a diploma, on the other hand, must be one of the best ways of getting exposure to every aspect of cooking: the techniques, the teamwork, the time pressure – all the things you'll need to get under your belt in order to progress. *Professional Chef Level 3 Diploma* is the secret weapon that can help you excel on such a course. It's clear, practical and informative, giving you exactly the kind of grounding you need to become a versatile, consistent and creative chef.

And that's where the fun really starts.

Heston Blumenthal

A quick reference guide to the qualification

When people previously qualified as chefs there would have been a wide range of routes and options that could have been taken to achieve this. Some may have followed the NVQ curriculum and that could have been as a full-time college student, part-time college student or through an industry based apprenticeship. Others may never have followed a formal training path at all and reached the qualification by using work-based learning.

The National Vocational Qualification has provided the main curriculum route for industry and College-based training for many years. Historically, the ways in which these qualifications were structured meant that students or trainees would complete a variety of compulsory – or mandatory units and then could choose from other options or additional units in order to complete their qualification.

That has now changed. There are now two types of accredited qualification:

1 the VRQ

2 the NVQ.

The VRQ Diploma or vocationally related qualification is specifically designed for college-based delivery on either a full or part-time basis. There are a variety of qualifications designed to meet the VRQ criteria and these can provide students with practical experience and an insight to what happens in this diverse hospitality industry. The philosophy behind this Diploma is the principle that a chef needs to have a sound foundation of high quality skills and to be able to apply these skills across a wide range of kitchen activities using a broad variety of commodities.

The NVQ Diploma, as it is now called, is a qualification that provides the learner with a 'job ready' experience. That currently means that for students who want to be trained in an apprenticeship; this will be the only option available to them. However, many colleges have chosen the VRQ Diploma as the preferred route and any students enrolled on this type of programme, can expect that at least part of the course will be on a work placement out in industry.

The other main changes relate to the value or weighting of the individual units that make up the professional cookery qualification at all NVQ and VRQ Diploma levels. Now, both VRQs and NVQs are required to meet the Qualifications and Credit Framework (QCF).

The different units currently have a varying amount of credit values. In order to complete an NVQ Diploma the learner will complete all mandatory units and make up the outstanding balance of credits by choosing from optional units that will make up at least the minimum number of credits that are required to gain full certification. The VRQ Diploma requires the student to complete all units to achieve the full qualification.

People 1st, the Sector Skills Council, are the representative organization responsible for defining the standards for the hospitality industry. The National Occupational Standards (NOS) that they produce are then taken and used by awarding bodies such as City & Guilds or EDI to create the qualifications that you take part in. So in simple terms People 1st produce the standards that you work towards and the awarding bodies define the conditions and specifications against which you are assessed.

All NOS have a common structure and design. That is to say they all follow a particular format for all vocational sectors. Each vocational qualification is structured in the same way and is made up from a number of grouped components; called units and elements. The units are structured in a standard format and comprise the Unit reference number and title, which you will find aligned to each chapter in this book to help you navigate the information you need. The learning outcomes specify the practical skills and underpinning knowledge to be covered in the range, which will provide you with the detail of each learning outcome.

PROFESSIONAL COOKERY LEVEL 3 QUALIFICATIONS

		SUPERVISORY SKILLS	FOOD SAFETY	PRACTICAL GASTRONOMY	COLD LARDER	SOUPS, SAUCES AND DRESSINGS	VEGETABLES AND VEGETARIAN	MEAT	POULTRY AND GAME	FISH AND SHELLFISH	PASTRY AND PATISSERIE	DOUGH AND FERMENTED	DESSERTS	CAKES AND SPONGES	CHOCOLATE	SUGAR	FOOD PRODUCT DEVELOPMENT	HEALTHIER DISHES
		1	2	3	4	5	6	7	8	9	10	11	12	13	14	15	16	17
VRQ	Supervisory skills in the hospitality industry	✓																
	Practical gastronomy			✓														
	Advanced skills and techniques in producing vegetable and vegetarian dishes				✓	✓	✓											
	Advanced skills and techniques in producing meat dishes				✓	✓		✓										
	Advanced skills and techniques in producing poultry and games dishes				✓	✓			✓									
	Advanced skills and techniques in producing fish and shellfish dishes				✓	✓				✓								
	The principles of food safety supervision for catering		✓															
	Produce petit fours													✓				
	Produce paste products										✓							
	Produce hot, cold and frozen desserts												✓					
	Produce fermented dough and batter products											✓						
	Produce biscuits, cakes and sponges													✓				
NVQ	Develop productive working relationships with colleagues	✓																
	Maintain the health, hygiene, safety and security of the working environment		✓															
	Maintain food safety when storing, preparing and cooking food		✓															
	Contribute to the control of resources	✓																
	Ensure food safety practices are followed in the preparation and serving of food and drink		✓															

	QUALIFICATIONS	1	2	3	4	5	6	7	8	9	10	11	12	13	14	15	16	17
CHAPTER																		
NVQ	Employment rights and responsibilities in the hospitality, leisure, travel and tourism sector	✓																
	Cook and finish complex vegetable dishes						✓											
	Prepare fish for complex dishes									✓								
	Prepare meat for complex dishes							✓										
	Prepare poultry for complex dishes								✓									
	Cook and finish complex fish dishes									✓								
	Cook and finish complex meat dishes							✓										
	Cook and finish complex poultry dishes								✓									
	Prepare, cook and finish complex hot sauces					✓												
	Prepare, cook and finish dressings and cold sauces					✓												
	Prepare shellfish for complex dishes									✓								
	Cook and finish complex shellfish dishes									✓								
	Prepare game for complex dishes							✓										
	Cook and finish complex game dishes							✓										
	Prepare, cook and finish complex soups					✓												
	Prepare, cook and finish complex pasta dishes				✓													
	Prepare, cook and finish complex bread and dough products											✓						
	Prepare, cook and finish complex cakes, sponges, biscuits and scones													✓				
	Prepare, cook and finish complex pastry products										✓							
	Prepare, process and finish complex chocolate products														✓			
	Prepare, process and finish complex marzipan, pastillage and sugar products															✓		
	Prepare, cook and present complex cold products				✓													
	Prepare, finish and present canapes and cocktail products				✓													
	Prepare, cook and finish complex hot desserts												✓					
	Prepare, cook and finish complex cold desserts												✓					
	Produce sauces, fillings and coatings for complex desserts												✓					
	Produce healthier dishes																	✓
	Contribute to the development of recipes and menus														✓			

About the book

Recipes

COLD LARDER
Balsamic jelly dice
Beetroot and balsamic spaghetti
Carpaccio of beef
Chicken ballotine
Chicken liver pâté
Chicken galantine
Cucumber sheets
Duck liver parfait
Foie gras terrine
Goat's cheese and walnut tartlet
Gravad lax
Pear and calvados caviar
Pear fluid gel
Quail Scotch egg
Smoked duck
Rabbit terrine
Sashimi of tuna
Warm crab cakes
Smoked salmon and prawn terrine
Tian of crab and avocado

COMPLEX FARINACEOUS
Egg pasta dough
Sun-dried tomato pasta dough
Saffron pasta dough
Squid ink pasta dough
Spinach pasta dough
Saffron papardelle with mussels
Tomato linguini
Ricotta and wild sorrel tortellini
Spinach lasagne of lobster
Spaghetti carbonara with ceps
Spinach tagliatelle with sole
Truffled spaghetti with asparagus

Cold larder and farinaceous 4

VRQ
Advanced skills and techniques in producing:
- vegetable and vegetarian dishes
- meat dishes
- producing poultry and games dishes
- fish and shellfish dishes

NVQ
Prepare cook and present complex:
- cold products
- pasta dishes

Mapped to the qualification each chapter addresses a specific unit of the Level 3 Diploma in Professional Cookery qualification.

TASK Reflect on a sports team that you admire and consider the reasons that make them a particularly strong team.

Task boxes provide additional tasks for you to try out.

HEALTH & SAFETY Fire exit doors must be clearly marked, remain unlocked during working hours and be free from obstruction. Fire extinguishers should be available and ready for use in every kitchen.

Health & Safety tip boxes draw your attention to important health and safety information.

SOURCING Growing fresh herbs will not only save money but will give a better flavour.

Sourcing boxes give advice and tips on sourcing ingredients for recipes.

CHEF'S TIP Always try to keep dishes simple when using top-quality fresh ingredients. Using a maximum of five different food components will prevent the dish from becoming too complicated.

Chef's Tip boxes share author's experience in the catering industry, with helpful suggestions for how you can improve your skills.

HEALTHY OPTION To reduce cholesterol, use sunflower oil flavoured with a little sesame seed oil.

Healthy Option boxes indicate where ingredients can be substituted to make a recipe healthier.

WEB LINK For further information on health and safety legislation visit the HSE website at **www.hse.gov.uk**.

Web Link boxes suggest websites to for further research and understanding of a topic.

Learning Objectives at the start of each chapter explain key skills and knowledge you need to understand by the end of the chapter.

LEARNING OBJECTIVES

At the end of this chapter you will be able to:

- **Understand the basic concept of taste.**
- **Explain the physiology of taste.**
- **Explain the influences on eating and drinking cultures.**
- **Understand how science and technology have affected eating and drinking.**
- **Investigate the supply and use of commodities.**
- **Develop new recipe ideas.**
- **Recognize dietary requirements.**
- **Write an informative and balanced menu.**
- **Understand how to market your menu.**
- **Support the implementation of the menu.**

ASSESSMENT OF KNOWLEDGE AND UNDERSTANDING

You have now learned about the use of the different types of pasta and how to produce a variety of them utilizing an array of commodities and cooking techniques.

To test your level of knowledge and understanding, answer the following short questions. These will help to prepare you for your summative (final) assessment. Quality identifications

1 Explain the importance of selecting the correct type, quality and quantity of pasta ingredients and other ingredients used when meeting dish requirements.

2 Give a brief description of durum wheat.

Preparation

1 Explain why colour, texture and flavour are important when creating complex pasta dishes.

2 Explain why semolina is used when rolling out fresh pasta dough.

Cooking

1 Describe how and when fresh pasta should be cooked during service.

Assessment of Knowledge and Understanding
questions are provided at the end of each chapter. You can use questions to test your learning and prepare for assessments.

Step-by-step: Preparing a terrine

1. Lay out prosciutto or Parma ham the width of the terrine mould.

2. Ease the ham into the mould, ensuring the corners are neat and tidy.

3. Combine the raw ingredients carefully.

Step-by-step sequences illustrate each process and provide an easy-to-follow guide.

Spinach lasagne of lobster

Open spinach lasagne of lobster with chervil, tomato and shellfish foam

Ingredients	4 portions	10 portions
Spinach pasta dough	100 g	250 g
Whole cooked lobster	1	2½
Concassé of tomato	2 tbsp	5 tbsp
Chopped chervil	4 tsp	10 tsp
Wild garlic and red pepper vinaigrette	4 tbsp	10 tbsp
Shellfish shells	200 g	500 g
Brandy	30 ml	75 ml
Tomato purée	1 tbsp	2½ tbsp
Fish stock	100 ml	250 ml
Double cream	100 ml	250 ml
Butter	50 g	125 g
Good quality salt and white pepper	to taste	to taste

energy	cal	fat	sat fat	carb	sugar	protein	fibre
3988 kJ	960 kcal	64.4 g	20.9 g	10.1 g	7.8 g	56.6 g	1.5 g

Recipes provide examples of the different cooking processes for you to try out.

Guest Chef

Ginger coated goat's cheese with beetroot cake, pickled baby beetroot and candied beetroot

Chef Michael Evans
Centre Coleg Llandrillo

This brings together the best Welsh goat's cheese with earthy tastes of the beetroot. The mild and creamy taste of the goat's cheese from the Brecon Beacons, blends with the sharpness of the baby beets and the sweetness of the cake.

Ingredients	4 portions
Red beetroot peeled	50 g
Red beetroot finely grated	125 g
Self raising flour	150 g
Eggs	2
Butter	125 g
Caster sugar	125 g
Red wine vinegar	1 tsp
Mixed spice	1 tsp
Apricots dried finely diced	25 g
Pine nuts chopped	25 g
Pantysgawn goat's cheese	100 g
Softened butter	15 g
Baby red beetroot peeled	4
Baby yellow beetroot peeled	4
Baby candied beetroot peeled	1
Beetroot juice	250 ml
Agar agar	2.5 g
Banana shallot rings	25 g
Ginger biscuits crushed	50 g
White wine vinegar	500 ml
Sea salt	2 tbsp
Water	500 ml
Micro herbs	25 g

METHOD OF WORK

1 Pre heat oven 180°C /gas mark 4. Cream sugar and butter, incorporate eggs, then flour and grated beetroot. Pour into a lined tranche tray and bake for 45 minutes.

2 Combine water, white wine vinegar and salt; bring to the boil then separate into two pans. Place red baby beetroot in to one and yellow beetroot into the other, reboil then take off the heat; cover with cling film and leave to cool.

3 Cream goat's cheese in a bowl; add softened butter, chopped apricots and pine nuts. Pipe out onto silicon paper and roll to form a cylinder 2.5 cm in width. Place into freezer to set.

4 On a mandolin slice candid beetroot; lie on a silicon mat and place in to a drying cabinet.

5 Cook remaining beetroot and then puree; adjust consistency with a little cooking liquid and pass through a fine sieve, season. Place into a plastic bottle and keep warm.

6 When cake is cooked cover with silicon paper, then a tray and two 250 g weights to help make sure the cake is even when cut; cool in blast chiller.

7 Bring beetroot juice to the boil then add agar agar. Whisk and bring back to the boil, pour into a tranche tray lined with cling film and leave to set.

8 Cut beetroot cake in to pieces 2.5 cm. Turn out set beetroot juice and cut into pieces 2.5 cm in width.

9 Remove baby beetroots from pickling liquid and drain on to a J cloth, season.

10 Remove goat's cheese from freezer and cut into slices 2.5 cm wide and roll in the ginger biscuits crumbs. Allow to soften at room temperature for 10 minutes.

To finish

11 Squeeze an amount of the beetroot puree onto the plate and drag across the plate. Place beetroot gel onto the plate, place beetroot cake on top. Decorate the top of the cake with pickled beets, slices of candid beetroot, shallot rings and micro herbs. Finally place goat's cheese on to beetroot drag.

Guest Chef Recipes provide examples of the different cooking processes from leading industry figures from colleges throughout the UK.

VIDEO CLIP Canapés: prawn with lemon dressing and pâté en croute

Video Clips if your college adopts Coursemate Professional Chef Level 2, will enable you to view video demonstrations of key processes online.

Introduction

The intention of this book is to guide you to the skills and introduce the knowledge required to become a chef in the hospitality and catering industry.

Cooking, serving and eating food has become a major communication practice across the world. Food is prepared as a gift, as a medicine, to create friendship, to nourish, to celebrate, to generate business and to stimulate happiness. The chef now has the capacity to communicate through their food, initiate fulfilment and joy and conceive relationships.

The basic principles of being a worthy professional chef are to combine good ingredients with sound techniques, skills and basic knowledge of culinary science with attention to detail. Only then will you have the basis to show your culinary artistry and creative talents.

This book will also illustrate some of the top teachers in this country whose talent, dedication and energy have helped them achieve a high standard of excellence in the catering industry today. They share their thoughts, recipes and experience for you to learn from. It will also provide you with an important reference point to attain the professional skills and knowledge for today's classically based modern cuisine.

Enjoy learning and enjoy cooking!

Gary Hunter

Supervisory skills in the hospitality industry

VRQ

Supervisory skills in the hospitality industry

NVQ

Develop productive working relationships with colleagues

Contribute to the control of resources

Maintain the health, hygiene, safety and security of the working environment

Employment rights and responsibilities in the hospitality, leisure, travel and tourism sector

LEARNING OBJECTIVES

At the end of this chapter you will be able to:

- Explain how to apply staff supervisory skills within a small team.

- Apply and monitor good health and safety practices.

- Develop productive working relationships with colleagues.

- Use appropriate behaviours for developing productive working relationships with colleagues.

- Know and understand how to develop productive working relationships with colleagues using general knowledge.

- Know and understand how to develop productive working relationships with colleagues using industry and sector specific knowledge.

- Know and understand how to develop productive working relationships with colleagues using context specific knowledge.

- Be able to contribute to the control of resources.

- Understand how to contribute to the control of resources.

- Be able to maintain the health, hygiene, safety and security of the working environment.

- Understand how to maintain the health, hygiene, safety and security of the working environment.

- Know employer and employee rights and responsibilities and own organizational procedures.

- Know factors that affect your own organization and occupation.

Introduction

The aim of this chapter is to assist you in developing the necessary knowledge and appreciation of how to supervise, lead and train teams and individuals in order to develop sound teamwork in a professional kitchen. We will discuss development and understanding of the range of responsibilities required in a supervisory role, including the functions of supervision and the characteristics of leadership.

We will also detail the contribution of resources within a kitchen and encourage you to develop skills and implement knowledge for controlling resources, including assessment and understanding of the importance of equipment, colleagues and suppliers as resources. This is about ensuring that you, and the staff you are responsible for, use resources effectively and efficiently, without undue waste. It covers obtaining supplies, checking equipment, monitoring the use of resources and keeping records.

Supervision and leadership

Supervisory skills

The definition of supervision is:

- To oversee activity – to watch over an activity or task being carried out by somebody and ensure that it is performed correctly.

- To oversee people – to be in charge of a group of people engaged in an activity or task and keep order or ensure that they perform it correctly.

It is the responsibility of supervisors to directly influence progress and productivity within an organization. Supervision often includes conducting basic management skills (decision making, problem solving, planning, delegation and meeting management), organizing teams, noticing the need for and designing new job roles in the group, training new employees, managing employee performance (including setting goals, observing and giving feedback, addressing performance issues and employee development) and ensuring conformance to personnel policies and other internal regulations.

The scope of supervisory roles and tasks in the professional kitchen

A supervisor will typically undertake the following quality control tasks within a kitchen environment:

1 Forecasting possible and probable outcomes and to plan for them.

2 Plan, organize and supervise the work of the **chefs** within a section.

3 Set and communicate targets stating the quality points that are to be achieved and the time frame considered necessary to establish work schedules.

4 Supervise all food preparation tasks throughout the day and monitor the quality of ingredients, dishes and produce.

5 Ensure that the production of dishes is to customer requirements – including during service – and meets all time constraints and deadlines.

6 Check and order supplies as required by the section or kitchen.

7 Assist in planning menus with the line manager or head chef.

8 Keep quality records in line with health and safety regulations.

9 Make quality reports in line with the organization's requirements.

10 Monitor the behaviour of the team and solve problems that may arise.

11 Contribute to individual and team development, identify training requirements and undertake training sessions in the preparation of dishes and certain everyday tasks.

12 Perform other related duties as assigned by the operational management.

A team leader with his team of trainees

It is generally accepted that a good supervisor is also a strong leader. Supervisors need a wide range of technical, people and conceptual skills in order to carry out their tasks. The diverse nature of the hospitality industry ensures that it is very unlikely that a task is carried out by a single person; there is usually at least one other helping to prepare, serve, clear or manage.

This allows the opportunity for a leader to emerge and help steer the group towards achieving their goal.

Leadership characteristics

When identifying a good leader or assessing your own performance there are several key characteristics worth considering:

Leadership is a skill that requires practice and dedication; motivating a team is a major factor alongside ensuring that the team stays focused on the common goal.

A leader should be:

● Challenging – ensuring that you look for opportunities to improve performance.

● Delegator – the leader empowers others in the team to make decisions and assign responsibility to others.

● Inspirational – motivating individuals and empowering the team at all levels.

● Leading by example – setting guidelines, participating and working in a professional and inspirational way. Making an active contribution to the success of the team.

● Open to discussion – sharing best practice and discussing improvements in a controlled professional manner. The leader shares the decision with the team and therefore is part of the team.

Leadership is often defined in two ways: transactional and transformational leadership. These definitions were developed over years of research and evaluation. A leader meets certain criteria which are then assigned to either category.

A TRANSACTIONAL LEADER

This refers to the way in which a leader achieves their goals by using behaviour, incentives and rewards to motivate their team. The term transaction is the same as in a business transaction where one person receives an exchange or payment for goods or services offered.

Below is an example of how the transactional cycle works:

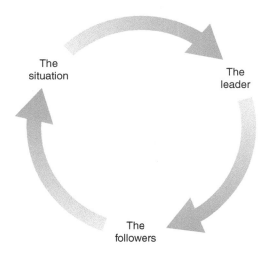

Using the cycle above as a guide we can see how a **sous chef** may offer an incentive, such as additional time off for tighter wastage control of ingredients in a kitchen – this shows the leader offering an incentive to the follower in the situation that requires team improvement.

A TRANSFORMATIONAL LEADER

A transformational leader has the ability to assess, develop and eventually change the behaviour and mindset of the team over a long period of time. This type of leadership is highly sought after as it enables the business to achieve a common goal amongst all team members to exceed their own expectations and deliver a first class service.

A successful leader will work with the team to ensure motivation and encouragement to make individual team members feel respected in their day-to-day work. There are three factors which are essential in becoming a transformational leader:

● Be charismatic.

● Be able to stimulate staff intellectually.

● Have consideration for individuals.

The demands of leadership

A leader has to be able to cope with pressure from all directions and ensure that they always remain composed and self-confident. There are two aspects of a leader's responsibility which they must come to terms with very quickly:

1   Meeting set targets and achieving overall goals.

2   Maintaining and developing positive working relationships.

Unfortunately, the two are not always easy to achieve together as the target may require increasing a person's workload. In the hospitality industry there are many essential and consequential factors that a leader must manage such as:

● the owners' requirements;

● customer needs and expectations;

● employees;

● competitors;

● the head office or directors;

● market fluctuations, e.g. cost, business considerations, costs and the market.

The qualities that are required of a good leader are varied. In order to help meet the increasing demands placed on leadership some qualities, outlined below, are requisite:

● confidence in your own ability and that of your team;

● the ability to demonstrate a logical approach to all tasks;

● forward thinking;

● a good understanding of behaviour concepts;

● a visual awareness and the ability to connect with people;

● a politically correct attitude at all times;

● high motivation;

● an aim to improve the business and the team whenever possible.

Planning for a large dinner function and organizing and co-ordinating staff is an essential leadership skill in the kitchen

Task Consider the qualities you respect the most in a good leader or supervisor.

The purpose of supervision

Supervisors are normally involved in the deployment of resources, most of which directly concerns staffing and equipment and sometimes budget management. The primary role of a supervisor is to ensure that a team of people work cohesively to achieve established objectives and targets set by the nature of the business. The accepted purpose of supervision is determined by a set system of functions that is determined by the employer or establishment. However, generally the hospitality industry addresses the following elements:

Forecasting – before the planning element can take place it is essential to be able to predict and foresee possible outcomes. An example of this is the preparation of the staffing rota and foreseeing busy periods, allowing for potential staff sickness or holiday periods and for balancing the skill set of the team to allow for maximum performance throughout the week. Being able to successfully forecast is the good use of judgement attained from previous knowledge and experiences.

Planning – after the forecasting element comes the planning process. Various questions need to be considered such as how many potential meals need to be prepared for? There are further planning elements that arise from this basic question, for instance; how many staff are required, how much stock do you need to carry, which staff are needed and at what periods, do you need to update equipment and does this need training for the team?

Organization – this involves the supervisor in the production of training programmes, duty rotas, cleaning schedules and food and beverage ordering. If specific functions are to be catered for such as large dinner dances, the organization skills required of the supervisor include precision timing of the service and the capability to work back from this point in order to organize all necessary aspects of the preparation, cooking and service of the food.

A leader of a kitchen has to have good organizational attributes to make sure things run smoothly

Coordination – this skill is needed to ensure all the team work together in a cohesive and timely way. To help achieve this, the supervisor must be able to communicate effectively with all staff and attain a positive relationship with each member of the team and other departments.

Communication – this is probably the most important aspect. To effectively convey orders, information, instruction and operational procedures requires the supervisor to have the correct attitude to the team as a whole. The supervisor needs to have the technical knowledge and ability to direct staff and to carry responsibility to achieve specific objectives.

Controlling – this includes the controlling of processes as well as staff and commodities. This will mean that all health, safety and hygiene processes are stringently adhered to throughout the department. Controlling also involves checking that the finished dish is of the correct standard, quantity, quality and with minimal waste.

Delegation – by giving an element of responsibility to individual team members the supervisor can be more effective in their role of coordinating and controlling. Responsibility should be given to those who have the correct level of ability, potential for development and reliability. A strict list of duties should be set out to the delegated team member so that everyone is totally aware of the requirements and standards to be attained.

Motivation – because not everyone wants or is capable of responsibility, the supervisor still needs to motivate those who are potentially less determined. Most people are prepared to work in order to improve their standard of living, however there is another equal factor in motivational concepts; the need for people to attain satisfaction from the work that they do. The supervisor must acknowledge this theory and judge how different members of the team achieve job satisfaction.

Employee wellbeing – people always work best in good working conditions and these consist of freedom from fear such as discrimination, becoming unemployed and fear of failure in specific tasks or job roles. Employment security and incentives such as opportunities for promotion, pay supplements, profit-sharing and personal and continuous development encourage a superior attitude to work. The supervisor is in a pivotal position to ensure that this all happens.

Leadership styles

Leadership style is the method in which the elements of leadership are carried out and essentially the way a leader or supervisor acts towards the members of the team. You can regard leadership styles in one of two ways:

1   Ask 'what is my leadership style?' This is to focus on what you enjoy, what you may possibly be good at and what strengths and weaknesses you have.

2   Ask 'what leadership style is most suitable for the individual, team or organization that I am leading?' This is to focus on the needs of the business, on the criteria for success and on your approach that will bring about the maximum positive impact.

Modern leadership demands both leadership styles. You need to recognize your own strengths and fully exploit them, but you also need to have an ability to adapt your style to different situations in order to achieve the maximum effectiveness. Rather than completely using their own preferred style, excellent leaders are able to adopt different approaches to suit the various needs of differing circumstances.

The leadership styles listed in the table below are based on Steve Myers' MTR-i (Management Team Role Indicator) model that defines the types of leadership. This model assumes that a modern leader will:

● Develop the flexibility to be able to use any of the styles.

● Recognize the different demands of each situation.

● Adapt appropriately, by using the styles that will give optimal achievement.

The 'Type' column below is based on the MTR-i team role model. It identifies what type or style of contribution is being made to the team. MTR-i team roles change from situation to situation, in accordance with the demands of the modern business environment.

This table of leadership styles can be used to increase the effectiveness of a leader. The key to success is developing an external awareness of what is required, and the internal flexibility to be able to access each style as appropriate in different given situations.

There are other models that explore management and leadership styles in an effective way that may help the supervisor develop their own style to suit the needs of the team or situation. Kurt Lewin (in 1939) led a group of researchers in identifying different styles of leadership. This early study has been very influential and has established three major leadership styles that are widely used in businesses, government and the military today: authoritarian (autocratic), participative (democratic) and delegative (free rein).

AUTHORITARIAN (AUTOCRATIC)

This style is used when leaders inform their employees about what they want done and how they want it accomplished without first obtaining the advice of their team. Two appropriate situations in which to use this style are when you have all the information available to solve the problem, or if you are short on time and your employees are well trained and motivated.

Some chefs or leaders are inclined to think of this style as a vehicle for yelling, using demeaning language and leading by threats or by abusing their power. This is not the authoritarian style; rather it is an abusive, unprofessional style that will lead to a lack of team motivation. It has no place in a leader's repertoire.

The authoritarian style should normally only be used on rare occasions. If you have the time and want to gain more commitment and motivation from your employees, then you should use the participative style.

TYPE	DESCRIPTION	WHEN TO USE	WHEN NOT TO USE
Coach	People-oriented, motivator, builds personal relationships, likeable, interpersonal skills, cares for others	Commitment from others is critical, or in sensitive situations	Decisions need to be forced through, conflict is being avoided
Campaigner	Value-driven, has passion for key issues, focuses on important themes, champions the cause	The group has lost its sense of identity, or it is doing too many unimportant things	There is a problem that needs to be solved with dispassionate objectivity (e.g. technical issues)
Explorer	Tries things that are new, introduces change, looks for unexpected outcomes, creates new opportunities, experiments	The group is 'stuck in a rut', or the status quo needs to be challenged	There are already too many initiatives under way and some stability is needed
Innovator	Develops long-term vision, produces radical ideas, foresees the future, anticipates what is outside current knowledge	Radical change is needed, change is a long-term activity	There are immediate dangers, the group may not survive in the short term
Sculptor	Takes action, produces results, leads from the front, sets an example, does what is asked of others	There is some lethargy, or lack of achievement has destroyed motivation	The group is being too expedient, current success may ebb in the future
Curator	Observes, listens, clarifies goals, establishes realistic expectations, makes aims crystal clear	The direction is vague or expectations have not been articulated	There are already too many goals or too much information
Conductor	Organizes, makes plans, sets measurable goals, coordinates the work of different people, manages resources	There is chaos/lack of organization, or there are no measures of achievement	There are so many processes that creativity has been stifled
Scientist	Analyzes, uses models, produces explanations, compares other situations, engages in intellectual debate	The situation is complex or driven by technical solutions	People's feelings are paramount, or the group goes round in circular arguments

PARTICIPATIVE (DEMOCRATIC)

This style involves the leader including one or more team members in the decision making process (i.e. determining what to do and how to do it). However, the leader maintains the final decision making authority. Using this style is not a sign of weakness; rather it is a sign of strength that your team will respect.

This is normally used when you have part of the information, and your team members have other parts. (Note that a leader is not expected to know everything – this is why you employ knowledgeable and capable team members.) Using this style is of mutual benefit because it allows individuals to become part of the team and allows the leader to make better decisions.

A chef using the 'participative' leadership style

DELEGATIVE (FREE REIN/LAISSEZ-FAIRE)

In this style, the leader allows the team or individuals to make the decisions. However, the leader is still responsible for the decisions that are made. This is used when employees are able to analyze the circumstances and determine what needs to be done and how to do it. A leader must recognize that they cannot do everything. A good leader must set priorities and delegate certain tasks.

This is not a style to use in order that you can blame others when things go wrong; rather this is a style to be used when you fully trust and have confidence in the people in your team. Do not be afraid to use it, however, it must be used astutely. This is also known as 'laissez-faire' style, which means the non-interference in the affairs of others.

A chef using the 'delegative' leadership style

A good leader uses all three styles, depending on what forces are involved between the followers (team members), the leader and the situation. Some examples include:

● Using an authoritarian style on a new employee, such as a trainee chef, who is just learning the skills required. The leader is competent and a good coach. The employee is motivated to learn a new skill. The situation is a new environment for the employee.

● Using a participative style with a team of chefs who know their job. The leader knows the problem, but does not have all the information. The chefs know their jobs and want to become part of the team.

● Using a delegative style with a chef who knows more about the job than you. The chef needs to take ownership of their job. Also, the situation might call for you to be at other places, doing other things.

● Using all three styles – telling your team that a procedure is not working correctly and a new one must be established (authoritarian). Asking for their ideas and input on creating a new procedure (participative). Delegating tasks in order to implement the new procedure (delegative).

Teamwork

How people behave and perform as members of a group or team is as important as their behaviour or performance as individuals. Harmonious working relationships and good teamwork help make for a high level of staff morale and work performance. Successful teamwork is an essential element of management practice such as the use of empowerment. Teamwork is important in any organization but may be especially significant in the hospitality industry where there is a direct impact on customer satisfaction. Effective teamwork will improve organizational competitiveness by:

● improving productivity;

● improving quality and encouraging innovation;

● taking advantage of the opportunities provided by technological advances;

● improving employee motivation and commitment.

The characteristics of a good team

A good team makes all the difference to any business. Team building can at times be a daunting task but it can be achieved with good leadership skills. Setting targets and ensuring the team understands their individual roles and responsibilities will help to build a strong team. Team building activities help a group achieve more and it also helps individuals to bond better. So, what are the characteristics of a good team? Which are the various qualities you should look for in a good team member? Listed below are some of the specific characteristics that are required for a good team:

- Everyone participates actively and positively in meetings and projects.
- Team goals are understood by everyone.
- Individual members have thought hard about creative solutions to the problem.
- Members are carefully listened to and receive thoughtful feedback.
- Everyone takes initiative to get things done.
- Each teammate trusts the judgement of the others.
- The team is willing to take risks.
- Everyone is supportive of the project and of others.
- There is plenty of communication between team members.
- Team decisions are made using organized, logical methods.
- Full team acceptance is expected as decisions are made.
- Dissenting opinions are recorded, and may be revisited if future situations dictate.
- Team goals are given realistic time frames.
- Everyone is focused on the ultimate goal of the project, while also working on the underlying details.

A team of chefs working together during service

Team development

Participating in team development programmes brings the following benefits:

TEAM BENEFITS

- increased confidence within the team;
- improved levels of trust between individual members of staff;
- improved effectiveness of teams, within and beyond their own professional settings;
- enhanced shared leadership skills and effectiveness;
- building capacity for improved team working throughout the organization;
- developing a team vision for improving practice;
- immediate results can be applied to your team.

PERSONAL BENEFITS

- interacting and learning with outside specialists in a range of fields;
- gaining confidence to try things out in your team;
- being challenged and stretched to work collaboratively;
- developing professional relationships;
- developing your problem solving skills;
- building local networks that allow teams to share knowledge together.

Individual team development over a set period with mentoring and support processes in place will be helpful in identifying strengths and gaps in an individual team member's range of skills. The appropriateness of any personal development target being set is crucial to the whole process. Agreeing targets that are too basic indicate that the individual will not be working to their full potential. However, setting targets that are too ambitious may suggest that undue pressure will be put onto the individual.

A simple test as to the appropriateness of a specific development to the team or individual is to review how 'SMART' it is, that is, to check the agreed target against the following criteria:

- Is the target **s**pecific enough – is everyone involved clear about what exactly needs to be achieved?
- Is the target **m**easurable – can you actually demonstrate that a change has taken place?
- Is the target **a**chievable – does the target take into account the existing levels of skill, with some sense of progress that is still possible, given the level of skills at present?

- Is the target **r**elevant – is it an area the individual can actually have a direct impact on?

- Is the target **t**ime-based – does everyone involved know when the target has to be achieved by?

The importance of teamwork

The concept of teamwork is extremely important to the success of any business. Teamwork and unselfishness create the backbone of a great team, without this a team cannot realistically meet their objectives. You can have a group of highly skilled individuals, but if they do not work well as one unit, the likelihood is that they are not going to be as successful as one would hope. The team working as one cohesive unit is going to be the key in their success. This does not mean that the individual is no longer important; however, it does mean that effective and efficient teamwork goes beyond individual accomplishments. The most effective teamwork is produced when all the individuals involved harmonize their contributions and work towards a common goal.

CHEF'S TIP There are no individuals in the kitchen – teamwork is the only way to succeed. Try to contribute to the team rather than make your own mark.

- **Effective teamwork is not automatic –** it takes a great deal of hard work and compromise. There are a number of factors that must be in place to cohere together as a team and work seamlessly.

- **Good leadership –** effective leadership is one of the most important components of good teamwork. The team's leader should possess the skills to create and maintain a positive working environment and motivate and inspire the team members to take a positive approach to work and be highly committed. An effective supervisor will promote a high level of morale and make them feel supported and valued.

- **Clear communication –** this is a vital factor of all interpersonal interaction and especially that of a team. Team members must be able to articulate their feelings, express plans and goals, share ideas and see each other's viewpoints.

- **Establishing roles –** it is absolutely necessary for team members to understand what their role on the team is, what he/she is responsible for. The team leader can enable this by defining the purpose in a clear-cut manner in the beginning of the formation of the team.

- **Conflict resolution –** conflicts will arise no matter how well a team functions together. The best way to counter conflict is to have structured methods of conflict resolution. Team members should be able to voice their concerns without fear of offending others. Instead of

avoiding conflict issues, a hands-on approach that resolves them quickly is much better. It is often advised that the supervisor sit with the conflicting parties and help work out their differences without taking sides and trying to remain objective if possible.

- **Set a good example –** the supervisor must set a good example for strong teamwork to develop. In order to keep team members positive and committed and motivated, the supervisor needs to exhibit these qualities. The team looks to the leader for support and guidance so any negativity on the leader's part can be disastrous.

TASK Reflect on a sports team that you admire and consider the reasons that make them a particularly strong team.

Team diversity

The hospitality industry reflects a great wealth of diversity and this is naturally reflected in the different types of cuisines seen on the average high street in any UK town or city. The kitchen team should reflect this diversity and embrace the positive aspects that this will bring in terms of new skills, techniques and ideas from different cultures.

Diversity recognizes the fact that people are different and this includes cultural, ethnic, gender, disability, sexual orientation, personality, religion, work style, background and age. Developing effective working relationships that recognize and celebrate these differences will harness creativity, innovation, entrepreneurship and a positive working environment. Diversity is about empowering people. It makes an organization effective by capitalizing on all of the strengths of each employee. It is also understanding, valuing, and using the differences in every person.

One of the main failures that prevent a group from becoming a team is the failure to accept others for what they are. It is only when the group members realize that diversity is the key for turning weak areas into strong areas does the group start to grow into a team. Failing to accept the diversity of others keeps the group members from pursuing team goals. Embracing diversity is more than tolerating people who are different. It means actively welcoming and involving them by:

- Developing an atmosphere that is safe for all employees to ask for help. People should not be viewed as weak if they ask for help. This is what helps to build great teams – joining weakness with strengths to get the goal accomplished.

- Actively seeking information from people from a variety of backgrounds and cultures. Also, including everyone in problem solving and decision making process.

- Including people who are different than you in informal gatherings such as lunch, coffee breaks and spur of the moment meetings.

- Creating a team spirit where every member feels a part of the team.

The training requirements of your team

A development plan looks at the personal and professional development of an individual. The main aim is to ensure that an individual is improving their learning and performance through forward planning and setting specific goals which can be appropriately measured.

As a supervisor your role is to support your colleagues by helping them in designing their development plan, and also ensuring that they are aware of the different learning opportunities available to them. It is also important that any learning activity undertaken is constantly reviewed and monitored to check your staff member's progress.

In implementing the individual training needs of the members of your team one key aspect that supervisors and managers need to be aware of is the equal opportunities legislation that applies to training and development. Regardless of the level of knowledge and skill that your employees have, all of them should be treated equally and be given the same opportunities to develop themselves further. Training and personal development can help to:

- Provide recognition or enhanced responsibility for individuals and this can also aid career progression.

- Improve the quality and skills of team members.

- Increase the confidence, commitment and motivation of the team.

- Present a feeling of personal satisfaction and achievement.

There are four main styles of training centred on the reasons that the training should be assigned. These are as follows:

1 Productivity based – designed to help increase output as quickly and efficiently as possible.

2 Performance based – implemented to a stable and large team to help meet team targets, plans and budgeting.

3 Strategic based – training as an integral aspect of the management of teams and individuals.

4 Task based – involving individual team members being placed on short training courses either externally or internally such as hygiene courses or health and safety courses.

Once it has been determined which is the most generally effective and cost effective model, it has then to be decided how to carry out the training itself. There are a variety of different training methods or learning activities that could be used to help employees develop their knowledge, skills and attitude. Some of them are trainer centred, some are learner centred and some can be a mixture of both.

TRAINER CENTRED

This gives the trainer control over the pace and content of the learning. The trainer will decide which exercises to use, structures the session and draws out key learning points, perhaps through a lecture or presentation.

LEARNER CENTRED

This method gives the learner complete control. The learner might use self study texts, questionnaires, learning logs or e-learning.

TRAINER AND LEARNER CENTRED

Coaching is an example of this method. It is a process which will involve both the trainer and the learner. Using strong questioning techniques the trainer will draw out the answers and raise awareness in the learner.

TASK Look at the table 'Training methods chart' on the next page. This lists the most commonly used training methods. Make a note in the last column stating whether you think each is trainer centred, learner centred or if both methods are involved.

Effective and positive working relationships

Hospitality is an industry that revolves around the needs of people. Positive working relationships – between staff and colleagues and between staff and customers (individuals, internal departments and other organizations) – are an essential part of making the business work.

Anything that does not reflect a positive working relationship will inevitably cause staff dissatisfaction, customer dissatisfaction or poor teamwork. These can damage your organization's effectiveness and its vital relationship with the customer. You will be in the front line of this process every day, acting as a crucial link between the business and other people. You will also be the first point of contact for both the customers and management.

TRAINING METHODS CHART

METHOD	DESCRIPTION	USUAL OUTCOME	TRAINER, LEARNER CENTRED OR BOTH
Lectures and presentations	Trainer delivers prepared exposition, preferably using visual aids	Knowledge – fact and opinions	
Briefing groups	Short exposition by trainer, followed by questions and discussion	Knowledge – fact and opinions	
Discussion groups	Participative discussion led by one of the learners on a specified topic	Some knowledge – facts and opinions, attitudes and interpersonal skills	
Plenary discussion	Session following practical or other activity, usually led by the trainer, to pull out key learning points and/or relate theory to practice	Reinforcement and reflection – depending on task under review	
Demonstration	Trainer shows learners how to do a task, e.g. operate a machine	Knowledge – how to, preparation for skills training	
Practical	Learners operate under trainer's supervision and receive feedback	Psychomotor or interpersonal skills	
Role-play	Learners put themselves in someone else's shoes for the purpose of practical exercise	Changing attitudes, interpersonal skills	
Video/DVD	Sound and vision	Knowledge	
Case studies	Write up of an incident or situation with questions for analysis and/or discussion	Analytical and decision making skills	
Business games/ computer simulations	Board or computer games or evolving case studies which allow participants to see the consequences of their decisions	Analytical and decision making skills	
Incident method	Learners are given last item in a sequence of events and asked to reconstruct circumstances through questioning trainer	Analytical and questioning skills	
In-tray exercises	Learners are given a series of memos, and other papers or electronic communications to be prioritized and dealt with	Prioritizing, planning, organizing, delegating and other managerial skills	
Group/individual projects	Investigation and report, usually with recommendations on issues or concern	Knowledge – facts and opinions; investigative, analytical and problem solving skills	
Books, manuals and self study texts	Written descriptions, analyses or instructions, sometimes with checklist and self test questions	Knowledge – facts and opinions	
E-learning	Electronic, internet based media which present learner with information and/or situations and questions and provide feedback on responses	Knowledge – facts and opinions; investigative, analytical and problem solving skills	
Embedded e-learning	Computer 'trains' operator step-by-step as tasks are carried out	Knowledge and skills but varying extent of actual learning	
Learning log	Diary or journal used by learner to reflect on work or learning events and draw out and record learning points	All types	
Team tasks	Practical indoor or outdoor exercises or simulations	Planning, organizing, team and interpersonal skills	
Coaching	Learner takes responsibility for own learning and uses trainer as coach to raise awareness	All types	

To work in this industry, you have to be good with people: the people you work for, the people you work with and the people you provide services for. These skills can be taught, but they require a degree of effort and willingness to succeed. An enthusiastic person with few skills is better than a highly trained one with an uncaring attitude.

Communication is the fundamental building block for an organization's success and growth; without it, business will perish. Chefs have to communicate with other chefs as well as with waiters, managers and customers and each of these relationships is vital.

The main aim is to satisfy, or indeed exceed, the customers' expectations, and this can only be done by the individuals in the organization working as a coherent team. The customers are always at the top of the tree as they pay the bills; they create the cash that will allow the staff to earn a wage and which increases the business's success.

Communication

Good communication is essential for establishing and maintaining effective and positive working relationships. Communication can be verbal, non-verbal (body language) or written.

The basic elements of verbal communication are asking questions and making points; to be effective these take confidence and practice. Questions should be asked in a way that will produce the most informative answer; using inappropriate phrasing or body language may result in an incomplete or unhelpful reply.

During a discussion you should remember the following key points:

- Once a speaker has finished express your appreciation.

- Use a brief summary of the speaker's points to show you have listened and grasped the concept of the discussion.

- Ensure you have your say but in a controlled professional manner. If you need to, write your question down and read it out using a calm, clear voice.

- Always avoid aggression as this will prevent any worthwhile feedback.

Listening skills are of paramount importance in communication and teamwork. They help us to understand what information or support other people need and ensure we can work cohesively as a group.

Non-verbal communication, or body language, is communication without words. Body language can take many forms:

- facial expression – shows emotion and provides feedback;

- touch – shaking hands, greetings, apologies;

- posture – sitting, standing, leaning;

- proximity – the distance between people;

- appearance – dress, clothes, hair;

- eye contact – indicating apathy, interest or boredom;

- hand gestures – disagreement, anger, welcome.

CHEF'S TIP Body language is used by everyone on a daily basis; the skill comes in knowing when you can use body language to your advantage and to create an atmosphere/environment which suits you.

Equal opportunities

It is the right of every person to be able to seek employment regardless of their race, creed, disability, sex or any other distinguishing feature. The law enforces this right to allow people to work and to prevent them from being segregated or victimized.

Everyone comes into the workplace with different skills. It is the job of senior personnel to utilize those skills and help all staff develop into well-rounded employees. Staff should not be chosen because they are black, Asian, white, small or tall, but because they have what it takes to succeed, both individually and for the company.

WHAT ARE EQUAL OPPORTUNITIES?

The policy of equal opportunities aims to effect positive behaviour through legislation so that discrimination is prohibited. It is established on moral and ethical influence and is concerned with promoting the rights of all members in our society.

Equal opportunities focus on assuring the equality of different groups, particularly minorities. It seeks to lessen any disadvantages that can be experienced by being in a minority group. Legislation is supported by practical procedures to assist under-represented groups in the workforce. Programmes are designed to help ensure that training opportunities and funded projects are open to the wider community and those groups who have been traditionally under-represented.

WHAT IS DIVERSITY?

Diversity concentrates on the difference of individuals. Managing diversity is based on an economic case for appreciating and valuing difference, rather than the moral case for treating people equally. Equal treatment offers benefits and advantages to employers to invest in ensuring that everyone in the workplace is valued and given the opportunity to develop their potential, which in turn will develop the potential of the business.

By integrating equal opportunities into your programme structure and embracing diversity you will add value to the work you do and help create a strong team. The employer can demonstrate a commitment to equality in a number of ways, including:

- development of an equal opportunities policy;

- implementation of a policy statement;

- monitor and evaluate the policy with members of staff.

By ensuring these points are understood and made available to all staff, equal opportunities and diversity will be widely acknowledged.

As chefs, we embrace diversity as food has no limitations and the wider the ethnic background of our staff and colleagues, the more information, techniques and products we can source and learn from.

Security, hygiene, health and safety

Each employee must be specifically conscious of the need for good security, hygiene, health and safety practices and it is the supervisor's responsibility to establish and maintain appropriate procedures to meet these needs in their own areas of responsibility.

Health and safety should be discussed with all employees upon appointment and further detailed in their contract of employment. The contract can state full details of procedures, advise of any staff handbook that may be available or give contact details of a relevant manager to communicate with for additional health and safety information. All employees must be fully aware of the need for safety and security and their own legal responsibilities towards themselves, their colleagues, their employers, visiting contractors, suppliers and members of public.

An example of safe practice: using thick oven gloves when removing a hot tray from a deck oven

HEALTH & SAFETY Take time to familiarize yourself with your employer's health and safety procedures. This may seem like a time-consuming process, but it is not only for the benefit the employer, it will also hopefully ensure that you are able to prevent yourself and others from encountering health and safety issues within the workplace.

It is the responsibility of an employer to ensure that all new staff members are fully trained in health and safety. The employer must also maintain ongoing training for existing members of staff so that everyone is up to date with procedures and understands the correct operation and maintenance of equipment and the emergency plan to follow, in line with current legislation.

Given the vulnerability of those who work within a kitchen, there are five main areas that require particular attention when assessing health and safety:

1 The safe and hygienic handling, storage and usage of commodities.

2 The personal hygiene, cleanliness and appearance of employees.

3 The provision of safe and secure premises and the correct training for safe use and storage of all equipment.

4 The correct labelling, notification, training, handling and storage of hazardous substances.

5 That a system of checks makes certain that legislation is complied with.

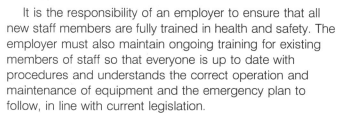

HEALTH & SAFETY It is prudent to regularly check the internet, especially government and local health authority websites, for health and safety updates or amendments, and to make your employer aware if you believe these are not being adhered to. Employees can be liable for negligence as well as employers.

Health and safety inspections

A system of inspections, both spot-checks and frequent inspections at regular intervals, needs to be established and the observations and recommendations resulting from these inspections should be recorded and passed to line managers and supervisors for appropriate action. The inspection record will include details such as the time and date of the inspection, the exact location and a clear description of any health hazard, risk to safety, breach of security or fault of equipment. Inspections are usually carried out by a person specifically responsible for health and safety within the organization, who has the authorization to take appropriate action to resolve faults and discrepancies and instigate improvements.

All equipment needs to be inspected regularly by the supervisor responsible to ensure it is in good working condition and that after use it is restored ready for further use. Security equipment, fire-fighting equipment and first-aid kits must be inspected to check that they are available and ready for use at all times. Security systems and fire-fighting equipment are usually checked by the manufacturers or a maintenance contract company. However, it is still the responsibility of the management team to ensure that this equipment is maintained correctly.

Routine checks need to be carried out to see that standards of hygiene, health and safety are maintained for the benefit of all workers, customers, visitors, suppliers and contractors.

Specific attention needs to be dedicated to exits and entrances, passageways and illumination of work areas (windows and lights). Floors need to be sound, uncluttered and well lit. The disposal of waste and bin areas requires attention regarding hygiene and cleanliness. Toilet areas, staff rest rooms and changing rooms need to be checked regularly and all employees need to adopt stringent hygienic and safe working practices. They should be conscious at all times of the health and safety of the working environment and any discrepancies or damage should be immediately reported.

Health and safety legislation

New health and safety regulations are often introduced and existing legislation is regularly updated to cater for ever-expanding technology, changing working methods and increased numbers of employees within the workplace. You should regularly check government and local authority sources (e.g. websites and official publications) for the latest information and guidance.

> **TASK** Go to **www.hse.gov.uk/catering** to read the Health and Safety Executive's guidance specifically for the catering and hospitality industry.

The main items of legislation that need to be addressed, implemented and adhered to by an employer in a place of work, by law, are laid out in the following sections. In recent years much of Britain's health and safety legislation has originated in Europe. Proposals from the European Commission may be agreed by Member States, who are then responsible for making them part of their domestic law. Modern health and safety law in this country, including much of that from Europe, is based on the principle of risk assessment.

THE HEALTH AND SAFETY AT WORK ACT (1974)

The Health and Safety at Work Act (HASAWA) is in place to cover employees, employers, the self-employed, customers and visitors. It lays down the minimum standards of health, safety and welfare required within each area of the workplace. As with all health and safety provisions, it is an employer's legal responsibility to ensure that the Act is fully complied with and that, as far as reasonably practicable, the health and safety of all those they are responsible for is correctly managed and safeguarded.

The HASAWA requires what good management and common sense should lead employers to do anyway: that is, to look at what the risks are and take sensible measures to tackle them. This law was amended in 1994 to clarify certain aspects.

THE HEALTH AND SAFETY INFORMATION FOR EMPLOYEES REGULATIONS (1989)

Current regulations require that an employer must provide employees with health and safety information in the form of notices, leaflets and posters, all of which are available from the Health and Safety Executive (HSE).

Where an employer has more than five employees, a written health and safety policy must be in place for the establishment. This should be issued to every employee, clearly outlining their personal health and safety responsibilities to the employer, to other staff and to customers, visitors and the public.

THE WORKPLACE (HEALTH, SAFETY AND WELFARE) REGULATIONS (1992)

The key message within these regulations is to ensure that those working in the hospitality and catering industries maintain a safe and healthy working environment. The regulations set out the legal requirements for those in a working environment, such as indoor temperature, lighting, ventilation and staff facilities.

THE FOOD HYGIENE (ENGLAND) REGULATIONS (2006)

These regulations provide the framework for the enforcement of EU legislation in England. There are similar regulations in Wales, Scotland and Northern Ireland. The Food Safety (General Food Hygiene) Regulations (1995) and the Food Safety (Temperature Control) Regulations (1995) no longer apply. Many of the requirements of these regulations are included in new EU legislation, so what businesses need to do from day to day have not changed a great deal. The main requirement is to have 'food safety management procedures' and to keep up-to-date records of these.

THE MANUAL HANDLING OPERATIONS REGULATIONS (1992)

These regulations provide employers and employees with guidelines on how to protect employees from injury when lifting heavy objects. A risk assessment must be carried out for all activities that involve manual lifting and employees must be trained how to correctly handle heavy items and, if applicable, how to use any lifting equipment for this purpose.

THE CONTROL OF SUBSTANCES HAZARDOUS TO HEALTH (COSHH) REGULATIONS (2002)

The COSHH regulations were put in place to ensure the correct storage, handling, use and disposal of hazardous substances and are relevant to everyday working practices. Most hazardous substances are identified through the use of specific symbols, which should be clearly shown and recognizable on items.

Employers are responsible for assessing the risks from hazardous substances and for controlling exposure to them to prevent ill health. Any hazardous substances identified must be formally recorded in writing and given a risk rating. Safety precaution procedures should then be implemented and training given to employees to ensure that the procedures are understood and will be followed correctly.

THE ELECTRICITY AT WORK REGULATIONS (1989)

These regulations are very important in kitchens because frequent heavy use of electrical equipment means that electrical items will be prone to maintenance issues and therefore require regular checking. The regulations state that every item of electrical equipment within the workplace must be tested at least every 12 months by a qualified electrician. In addition, a trained member of staff should regularly check all electrical equipment for safety. It is recommended that this is carried out at least every three months.

THE FIRE PRECAUTIONS ACT (1971)

This Act states that all staff must be aware of and trained in fire and emergency evacuation procedures for their workplace. The emergency exit route must be the easiest route by which all staff, customers and visitors can leave the building safely and quickly. Fire action plans showing the emergency exit route should be prominently displayed throughout the premises.

Where there are more than twenty employees, it is a compulsory requirement of the Act that a fire certificate is obtained. This further applies where there are ten or more employees on different floors at any one time.

THE FIRE PRECAUTIONS (WORKPLACE) REGULATIONS (1997)

These regulations require that every employer must carry out a risk assessment for their premises under the Management of Health and Safety Regulations. The regulations specify that any obstacles that may hinder fire evacuation should be identified as a hazard and dealt with so that all escape route are clearly marked and free from obstruction. Suitable fire detection equipment must be in place and fire alarm systems should be tested on a weekly basis to ensure they are in full operational condition.

HEALTH & SAFETY Fire exit doors must be clearly marked, remain unlocked during working hours and be free from obstruction. Fire extinguishers should be available and ready for use in every kitchen.

THE REPORTING OF INJURIES, DISEASES AND DANGEROUS OCCURRENCES REGULATIONS (RIDDOR) (1995)

The RIDDOR requires all injuries, illnesses and other dangerous incidents occurring in the workplace to be reported to the member of staff responsible for health and safety; this includes injuries involving guests and visitors as well as staff. An accident report book must be completed with basic personal details of the person or persons involved, together with a detailed description of the incident.

An injury may lead to legal consequences; therefore all witnesses must provide a clear and accurate statement of events. Accident report books must comply with the Data Protection Act (2003).

The regulations require you to report any of the following:

- fatal accidents;
- work-related diseases;
- major injuries sustained while at work;
- potentially dangerous event that takes place at work;
- accidents causing more than three days' absence from work.

WEB LINK For further information on health and safety legislation visit the HSE website at **www.hse.gov.uk**.

Maintaining health and safety

Employers should be provided with regular updates on health and safety legislation as and when necessary. However, it is also important to monitor these personally to ensure that there is plenty of time to comply with any changes in legislation.

HSE Inspectors and local authority Environmental Health Officers can carry out spot checks at premises at any time. Strict penalties can be imposed on anyone who does not comply with legal requirements. These officials can issue prohibition notices and improvement notices, and they have the power to prosecute and can seize, render harmless or destroy anything deemed to be of imminent danger.

In addition to ensuring that health and safety law and the legal guidelines are complied with, it must be remembered that if the working duties of staff change or the premises are adapted in any way – whether this be structurally or in terms of business methods – then additional health and safety procedures and risk assessments will have to be considered and implemented.

It is a legal requirement that all health and safety procedures in place must also be clearly set out in report form, in case it should be required by other parties, such as the employer, employee or an enforcement officer. This report will contain a risk assessment, the procedures in place to minimize, reduce or abolish any risks, the procedures for making all persons aware of the policy and the procedures for recording information, such as any accidents that may occur.

The responsibilities of supervisors in the workplace

Although employers have a legal obligation to ensure health, safety and security within the workplace, employees, colleagues and visitors are also responsible for taking these issues in hand.

The supervisor should ensure that they are aware of all health, safety, hygiene and security procedures and regulations that are in place and abide by these as far as possible at all times, being clear as to what applies to a specific area of work. Further, it is important to lead and monitor colleagues within their own particular area of work to ensure continuity and application. The supervisor should also make sure they know who is responsible for health and safety within the company so that they may direct any questions or concerns or report any incidents to them. If you are aware of any member of staff who is not working in accordance with relevant procedures, your employer or line manager should be notified immediately.

As a supervisor, your personal responsibility for health and safety within your area will usually mean that you are responsible for the health and safety of others within this area. As well as monitoring staff to ensure that all procedures are being adhered to, regular checks should be carried out, for example on equipment, to minimize any safety hazards.

Any health, safety, hygiene or security issue, such as a burnt hand or a case of food poisoning, must be reported immediately to the line manager or other designated member of staff. The issue must be recorded appropriately, stating the following:

- date and time of incident;
- name of person(s) involved;
- what happened;
- where it happened;
- who else was present;
- why it is believed to have happened;
- any remedial action that is required.

> **HEALTH & SAFETY** Always ensure that the accident report book is in an accessible place for everyone to use and that everybody is trained in the documentation of accidents. It is important that the report book is monitored for regular occurrences.

Hazard analysis and risk assessment process

The Health and Safety Executive (HSE) is the body appointed in the UK to support and enforce health and safety in the workplace. The HSE has defined the two concepts for hazards and risk:

- A hazard is something with the potential to cause harm.
- A risk is the chance, high or low, that somebody could be harmed by a hazard, together with an indication of how serious the harm could be.

As soon as any hazard is observed, it must be reported to the designated authority or line manager so that the problem can be rectified. Hazards can include:

- obstructions to corridors, stairways and fire exits;
- spillages and breakages;
- faulty electrical machinery.

THE RISK ASSESSMENT PROCESS

A risk assessment is divided into five separate steps:

Step 1 – Identify the hazards.
Initially the supervisor needs to consider how people could be harmed. By working in the same place every day it is easy to overlook some important hazards, so there are some guidelines to help identify the ones that matter:

Walk around the workplace and look at what could reasonably be expected to cause harm. Ask the team or their representatives what they think. They may have noticed things that are not immediately obvious. Visit the HSE website www. hse.gov.uk to check on publications on practical guidance on where hazards occur and how to control them. If you are a member of a trade association, contact them. Many produce very helpful guidance. Check manufacturers' instructions or data sheets for chemicals and equipment as they can be very helpful in spelling out the hazards and putting them in their true perspective. Have a look back at the accident and ill-health records – these often help to identify the less obvious hazards. Remember to think about long-term hazards to health (e.g. high levels of noise or exposure to harmful substances) as well as other safety hazards.

Step 2 – Decide who might be harmed and how.
For each hazard the supervisor must be clear about who might be harmed; it will help to identify the best way of managing the risk. Identify groups of people (e.g. 'people working in the kitchen' or 'customers'). In each case, identify how they might be harmed, i.e. what type of injury or ill health might occur. For example, 'kitchen porters may suffer back injury from repeated lifting of boxes'.

> **HEALTH & SAFETY** Remember some workers have particular requirements, e.g. new and young workers, new or expectant mothers and people with disabilities may be at particular risk. Extra consideration should also be given for those who may not be in the workplace all the time, including cleaners, visitors, contractors, maintenance workers and members of the public.

Step 3 – Evaluate the risks and decide on the precautions.
Having recognized the hazards, the next stage is to decide what to do about them. The law requires that everything

reasonably practicable is undertaken to protect people from harm.

There are many sources of good practice to learn from, for example HSE website as previously mentioned has many concepts of good practice from which to relate. Initially consider what is already in place, such as the current controls and how the work is organized. Then compare this with the good practice to understand if there is anything more that could be done. In asking this, consider:

● Can we get rid of the hazard altogether?

● If not, how can we control the risks so that harm is unlikely?

When controlling risks, apply the principles below, if possible in the following order:

● Seek a less risky option (e.g. switch to using a less hazardous chemical).

● Prevent access to the hazard (e.g. by guarding).

● Organize work to reduce exposure to the hazard (e.g. put barriers between pedestrians and traffic).

● Issue personal protective equipment (e.g. clothing, footwear, goggles, etc.).

● Provide welfare facilities (e.g. first aid and washing facilities for removal of contamination).

Step 4 – Record your findings and implement them.

Placing the results of the risk assessment into practice will make a difference when looking after people and the business. Recording the results of the risk assessment, and sharing them with the team is important. If there are fewer than five employees the business does not have to write anything down, though it is useful so that it can be reviewed at a later date if, for example, something changes. When writing down the results, it is important to keep written statements simple, clear and accurate.

A risk assessment should be suitable and sufficient to relate to each hazard. The assessment needs to be able to demonstrate that:

● A proper check was made.

● It states who might be affected.

● All the significant hazards are dealt with, taking into account the number of people who could be involved.

● The precautions taken are reasonable, and the remaining risk is low.

● All team members or their representatives were involved in the process.

Step 5 – Review the assessment and update if necessary.

Few workplaces remain the same. Sooner or later, new equipment, chemicals, foodstuffs and procedures arrive that could lead to new hazards. It makes sense, therefore, to review the workplace on an ongoing basis. Every year a formal review should be undertaken to ensure the working environment and team are still improving in the health and safety at work.

HEALTH & SAFETY All hazardous substances must be identified when completing the risk assessment. This includes cleaning agents and some preservatives. Where possible, high-risk products should be replaced with lower-risk products. The COSHH assessment should be reviewed on a regular basis and updated with any new products.

Fat overheating in a pan is a very serious hazard with high risk of injury

The hazard and risk assessment table on the next page gives is an example of how to spot and deal with potential risks and hazards and record them proficiently.

TASK Take into account a kitchen in which you have recently worked. List the equipment that you believe to be either low risk or high risk and carry out a risk assessment on these.

Potential hazards and risks can be found in all areas of a kitchen. They will affect every aspect of the kitchen, from the receiving of goods to the preparing of food and from the building itself to the equipment within each area. Therefore, checks have to be made by all staff and at regular intervals. If these are not made then individuals and groups may be responsible, and in turn liable, for injuries or health risks to themselves and others, which can carry fines and heavy penalties. This applies to all staff, regardless of whether they are part-time or full-time.

Signage and information should be readily available for all staff or members within an establishment.

Within catering establishments, extra or special attention is required in four main areas:

1   safe storage of chemicals;

2   safe work and customer areas;

COMPANY NAME				
DATE OF RISK ASSESSMENT				
STEP 1	**STEP 2**	**STEP 3**		**STEP 4**
What are the hazards?	Identify groups of people	What are you already doing?	What action is necessary?	How will the assessment be put into action?
Note: Walking around the workplace; asking the team what they think; visiting the HSE website; checking manufacturers' instructions; contacting your trade association.	Note: Some workers have particular needs; people who may not be in the workplace all the time; members of the public; think about how your work affects others present.	Note: List what is already in place to reduce the likelihood of harm or make any harm less serious.	Note: Ensure that you have reduced risks 'so far as is reasonably practicable'. Compare what you are already doing with good practice. If there is a difference, list what needs to be done.	Note: Remember to prioritize. Deal with those hazards that are high-risk and have serious consequences first.
			Action by whom	Action by when	Done

Step 5 – Review date
If there is a significant change in the workplace, remember to check the risk assessment and where necessary, amend it.

3 safe and hygienic food preparation and service areas;

4 safe customer and staff equipment areas and storage.

Accidents in the workplace

An accident is an unplanned mishap or event which is not expected or designed and which results in an unexpected loss or harm. It can be that an accident is both unplanned and uncontrolled. It may cause injury, damage or loss and it may be an event that could lead to a near miss with no damage, loss or injury.

Accidents arise from a chain of uncontrolled events and some factors which may be responsible are human, occupational, environmental and organizational. Unsafe acts in the kitchen area can include the following:

● carrying saucepans of hot liquid;

● carrying sharp knives or cutting equipment;

● inadequate maintenance of equipment;

● lifting heavy loads in an unsafe manner;

● not wearing the correct protective clothing;

● poor environmental conditions such as extreme temperatures or poor lighting;

● poor working system in practice;

● unclean working environment;

● using damaged equipment;

● using unsafe chemicals without following risk assessment or manufacturers guidelines;

● using unsafe equipment or electric cutting equipment without guards;

● walking on slippery flooring.

Accidents in the workplace can mean that lives may be lost, injury is sustained to employees, money is wasted, reputation of the business is lost and machinery or products can be damaged. Medical costs, loss of earnings and the potential to lose the quality of life in some cases can lead to legal action being taken.

INTERVENTION SYSTEMS

There are specific actions which can be implemented to change the way health and safety is dealt with in an organization. The actions are connected to company policies and procedures and they introduce new ways of working that aim to reduce the number of hazards and the number of risks to health and safety.

Management systems are designed to reduce accidents and illness and these will set the tone and direction for an organization to follow. This will determine the following;

1 commitment to health and safety from the employer;

2 continuous improvement strategies;

3 good monitoring systems;

4 health and safety policy;

5 measures and procedures to the protection of health and safety of people affected by the operation;

6 organizational structure to implement the policy;

7 review process that is timely and rigorous;

8 strong communication systems.

By law all workplaces must take steps to prevent and control accidents, incidents, near misses, personal injury and ill health. When designing and implementing intervention systems it is important to:

- Analyze the causes of accidents.
- Carry out audits of safety plans and fire evacuation procedures.
- Design systems to protect the employee, customers and visitors by reviewing the methods of work used and ensuring the environment is suitable for the type of work being undertaken.
- Identify all preventative measures.
- Implement training and instruction programmes for employees.
- Obtain the commitment of supervisors and managers to work towards high standards of health and safety.
- Raise awareness in the workplace about risks.

The Health and safety Executive (HSE) in partnership with members of the Health and Safety in Hospitality Liaison Forum continues to promote good practice throughout the industry. The Forum comprises representatives from industry trade associations, trade unions and industry stakeholders. Their aim is to improve health and safety in the hospitality industry and to specifically improve the industry performance in key risk areas. HSE and the Forum members will take the following actions:

- Undertake research on the identified key risk areas to determine the accident and near-miss rates and root causes of such incidents.

- The Forum members shall promote training on good practice regarding the key identified risks and raise awareness of any other relevant issues.
- The Forum members shall promote the recording of all health and safety training. The Forum shall assist HSE in populating the hospitality section of the HSE website with good practice information.

Hazard Analysis Critical Control Points

Hazard Analysis Critical Control Points (HACCP) is an internationally recognized and recommended system of food safety management. It focuses on identifying the critical points in a process where food safety problems (or 'hazards') could arise and putting steps in place to prevent things going wrong. This is sometimes referred to as 'controlling hazards'. Keeping records is also an important part of HACCP systems.

HACCP involves the following steps:

- Identify what could go wrong (the hazards).
- Identify the most important points where things can go wrong (the critical control points – CCPs).
- Set critical limits at each CCP (e.g. cooking temperature or time).
- Set up checks at CCPs to prevent problems occurring (monitoring).
- Decide what to do if something goes wrong (corrective action).
- Prove that your HACCP plan is working (verification).
- Keep records of all of the above (documentation).

The HACCP plan must be kept up to date and it will need to be reviewed from time to time, especially whenever something in the operation's working process changes. You may also wish to ask your local Environmental Health Officer for advice. Remember that, even with a HACCP plan in place, you must comply with all of the requirements of current food safety legislation.

Disposal of waste is another HACCP matter, as **bacteria** and other **pathogens** can multiply at an alarming rate in waste disposal areas. In ideal circumstances, the areas for cleaning crockery and pots should be separate from each other and from the food preparation area.

Waste bins in the kitchen should be emptied at regular and short intervals and be kept clean. Food waste can be safely disposed of in a waste disposal unit. Oil can only be disposed of by a specialist oil disposal company and must not be placed in a sink or waste disposal unit.

Manual handling

The improper handling of heavy and bulky loads can cause accidents and injuries, which could result in employees being sick from work for some time. It is important to lift heavy items in the correct way. The safest method to lift items is to bend the knees as opposed to bending your back.

HEALTH & SAFETY Strain and damage can be reduced if two people undertake the lifting rather than one person.

Below is a brief checklist of manual handling best practice:

● Additional care is needed when taking a tray from the oven or **salamander** so that the tray does not burn someone else or spill any hot liquids if tilted.

● In the stores area it is important that heavy items are stacked at the base and that steps are used with care at all times.

● Particular care is required when large pots and pans are moved containing hot liquid. They should not be filled to the brim and should be moved on a trolley if at all possible.

● Warning signs that pot handles and lids are hot should be given. This can also be quickly indicated by a small sprinkle of flour over the hot object.

● When bulky goods are moved on trolleys or any wheeled vehicles, they should be loaded carefully and in a manner that enables the handler to see at all times where they are going.

The Manual Handling Operations Regulations 1992 (as amended) sets no specific requirements such as weight limits. The ergonomic approach shows clearly that such requirements are based on too simple a view of the problem and may lead to incorrect conclusions. Instead, an ergonomic assessment based on a range of relevant factors is used to determine the risk of injury and point the way to remedial action.

The Regulations establish the following clear hierarchy of control measures:

1 Avoid hazardous manual handling operations so far as is reasonably practicable, for example by redesigning the task to avoid moving the load or by automating the process.

2 Make a suitable and sufficient assessment of any hazardous manual handling operations that cannot be avoided.

3 Reduce the risk of injury from those operations so far as is reasonably practicable. Where possible, you should provide mechanical assistance, for example a sack trolley or hoist. Where this is not reasonably practicable, look at ways of changing the task, the load and working environment.

Modern medical and scientific opinion accepts the scale of the problem and stresses the importance of an ergonomic approach to remove or reduce the risk of manual handling injury. Ergonomics is sometimes described as 'fitting the job to the person, rather than the person to the job'. The ergonomic approach looks at manual handling as a whole. It takes into account a range of relevant factors, including the nature of the task, the load, the working environment and individual capability and requires worker participation.

The reporting of maintenance issues

The preparation of food for cookery must take place on surfaces that are hygienic and suitable for use. Work surfaces, walls and floors can become damaged, and they too can be a source of contamination and danger to customers and staff alike. This should be reported to your line manager.

A maintenance reporting system can easily be designed to suit each establishment and each section in that kitchen. Good practice is to carry out a weekly maintenance check and to have a set procedure for repairing or replacing equipment. This can lead to a more economical maintenance programme. It is much cheaper to repair little and often than to wait until equipment is dangerous and perhaps risk injury or litigation. Areas for attention are:

● cracks in walls;

● damage to tables and work benches;

● cooking equipment such as pots, pans and utensils;

● windows, sanitary systems and lights;

● flooring and any other structural issues;

● electrical equipment relating to that particular operation.

EXAMPLE OF A MAINTENANCE REPORT FORM

MAINTENANCE REPORT FORM					DATE:	
AREA	ITEM	PROBLEM	ACTION TAKEN	DATE JOB COMPLETED	SIGNATURE	
Larder	Fridge 1	Seal broken around the door	Reported to line manager on 5/06/13	10/06/13		

Work equipment

Under the terms of the Use of Work Equipment Regulations (PUWER) 1998, work equipment covers all work machinery such as food mixers, slicers, ovens, processors, ice cream makers, vacuum package machines and knives. These regulations place duties on employers to ensure that:

- Adequate information, instruction and training on the use and maintenance of the equipment and any associated hazards are given to employees.

- Equipment is appropriate for its intended use and is maintained in efficient working order and in good repair.

Work equipment that possesses a particular risk must be used only by designated persons who have received the relevant training. The regulations specific requirements cover dangerous machinery parts, protection against certain hazards, such as heat from ovens, the provision of emergency stop controls and isolation from energy sources.

As an example, knives are covered under this Act, so all precautions must be taken as detailed below. This is an example of how to determine, communicate and instruct a team on the use of this specific work equipment but the basis can be used for all work equipment:

WHAT YOU MUST DO

You must ensure that your employees are kept safe from harm so far as is reasonably practicable. This means that the risk from using knives must be controlled to ensure people do not suffer cuts. You must assess the risk of your employees being cut by knives and take reasonable precautions.

WHAT ARE THE RISKS?

- Accidents involving knives are common in the catering industry. They usually involve cuts to the non-knife hand and fingers but can lead to injuries on the upper arm and torso.

- Cleavers are commonly used for chopping and the same controls for knives should be adopted.

WAYS TO MINIMIZE THE RISK

Do:

- Train employees in the safe use of knives and safe working practices when sharpening them.

- Use a knife suitable for the task and for the food you are cutting.

- Keep knives sharp.

- Cut on a stable surface.

- Handle knives carefully when washing up.

- Carry a knife with the blade pointing downwards.

- Store knives securely after use, e.g. in a scabbard or lockable container.

- Use protective equipment as required. For butchery and removing bones from joints and carcasses, it is recommended that a suitable protective glove is worn on the non-knife hand, and a chainmail or similar apron is worn.

Don't:

- Leave knives loose on worktop surfaces where they can be accidentally pushed off.

- Try to catch a falling knife.

- Use a knife as a can opener.

- Carry knives while carrying other objects.

- Engage in horseplay with a knife.

- Carry a knife in your pocket.

Legal responsibilities of employers and employees

Everybody in the place of work has a responsibility for health, safety and security. The Health and Safety at Work Act 1974 makes it plain that employers, managers and workers have a responsibility and obligation. The health and safety law is enforced by the following officers:

- environmental health officers (EHOs) and technical officers from local authorities;

- fire officers from the local fire service;

- health and safety inspectorate from the HSE;

- police officers for security issues.

Every employer has a responsibility to ensure health and safety and welfare at work of all employees in so far as is reasonably practicable. Within the hospitality industry this includes:

- Ensure that storage areas and the transportation of food and other products are safe and that there is an absence of risk to health.

- Information and instruction on training and supervision that is necessary to ensure the health and safety of employees at work is stated and is clearly communicated.

- Maintaining entrances and exits to the workplace and access to work areas that are safe and without risk to health.

- Maintaining the work premises and buildings to ensure that they are safe, secure and pose no threat to health and safety.

- Providing a hygienic and safe environment with good welfare facilities.

- Providing and maintaining kitchens, restaurants, accommodation and systems of work that are safe and without risk to health, safety and injury.

- Where necessary, providing health monitoring and care of all employees.

An administration with a board of directors must formally and publicly accept its collective role in providing health, safety and security leadership in the organization.

Every employee has a duty to take reasonable care of his or her own health and safety and that of other people who may be affected by what he or she does in the course of carrying out their work duties. Employee must cooperate with the employer to enable the employer to comply with the relevant employer's duties.

Enforcement and guidance of legal requirements

Inspectors are appointed by the respective authorities by means of being issued with warrants to inspect workplaces, serve legal notices that require improvements to be made and prohibiting work procedures, processes and the use of work equipment.

If the inspector believes that there is a contravention of health and safety legislation, they can serve an improvement notice on the person responsible, stating the details of the contravention. The notice also requires the person responsible to resolve the contravention. The person responsible can be the director, manager or supervisor in charge at the time of inspection.

The notice must state the following points:

1 Details of the specific point of law contravened.

2 That a contravention exists.

3 That the person responsible must resolve the contravention.

4 The inspectors reasons for the opinion (this may contain photographic evidence).

5 Time given for the improvement to be carried out, by law this is not less than 21 days.

If a person fails to comply with an improvement notice, a criminal offence is deemed to be committed.

The person who is served with an improvement notice can appeal against the notice to an employment tribunal. The grounds of the appeal could be based on the following aspects:

- The inspector interpreted the law incorrectly or exceeded their powers.

- Contravention might be admitted but the appeal would be that the improvement was not reasonably practicable.

- Contravention might be admitted but the appeal is based on the fact that the incident was so insignificant that the notice should be removed.

If an appeal has been made, the improvement notice is suspended until the appeal has been heard.

A contravention of the Health and Safety at Work Act 1974 or any of the regulations made under the Act is a criminal offence. Both an individual and a corporate body can commit an offence and be tried for it in a court of law. It is an offence to:

1 Contravene an improvement notice.

2 Contravene any requirement imposed by an inspector.

3 Contravene any requirement of any health and safety regulations.

4 Fail to carry out a duty placed on employers, self-employed employees, owners of premises, designers, manufacturers, importers and suppliers.

5 Fail to comply with a court order.

6 Intentionally make a false entry in a register, book, notice or other document that is required to be kept.

7 Intentionally or recklessly interfere with anything provided for safety purposes.

8 Intentionally or recklessly make false statements.

9 Pretend to be a health and safety inspector.

10 Prevent or attempt to prevent a person from appearing before an inspector of from answering their questions.

11 Require payment for anything that an employer must by law provide in the interests of health and safety.

If a person is found guilty of a health and safety offence a substantial fine will be imposed.

Fire precautions

The Regulatory Reform (Fire Safety) Order 2005 sets out the law on general fire safety, including means of escape. The CDM Regulations 2007 also impose duties including the requirement to prevent risk from fire. The fire risk from site activities must be assessed and precautions taken to control:

- Combustible material – the quantity of combustible materials on the workplace should be kept to the minimum and all such materials safely stored and used.

- Ignition sources – action is needed to eliminate, reduce and control ignition sources at the workplace.

It places responsibility for the fire safety of the occupants of premises and people who might be affected by fire on a defined person, whom is usually the employer. The responsibilities include:

1 Ensuring that the fire precautions, where reasonably practicable, ensure the safety of all employees and others in the building.

2 Make an assessment of the risk of and from fire in the establishment. Specific consideration must be given to dangerous chemicals or substances and the risks that these set if a fire transpires.

3 Review the preventative and protective measures frequently.

A fire alarm

Many solids, liquids and gases can catch fire and burn. It only takes a source of ignition, which may be a small flame or an electrical spark, together with air. Preventive actions that can be taken include:

- Quantity – fire risk can be reduced by controlling the amount of combustible material in the work area until it is needed.

- Flammability – it may be possible to specify materials that are less combustible.

- Storage – combustible materials should ideally be stored in separate areas; especially volatile materials, e.g. gas canisters for blow torches. Internal storage must be planned and located where it will not put workers at risk.

- Rubbish – good housekeeping and kitchen tidiness are important to prevent fire and to ensure that emergency routes do not become obstructed.

- Volatile flammable materials extra precautions are needed for flammable liquids and gases especially when internally stored.

MEANS OF ESCAPE

Key aspects to providing safe means of escape in the workplace include:

- Routes – your risk assessment should determine the escape routes required, which must be kept available, well signed and unobstructed.

- Alternatives – well separated alternative ways to ground level should be provided where possible.

- Protection – routes can be protected by installing permanent fire doors.

- Assembly – make sure escape routes give access to a safe place where people can assemble and be accounted for.

- Signs – will be needed for people are not familiar with the escape routes. Lighting should be provided for enclosed escape routes and emergency lighting may also be required.

MEANS OF GIVING WARNING

Set up a system to alert people on site. This may be temporary or permanent mains operated fire alarm (tested regularly), a klaxon, an air horn or a whistle, depending on the size and complexity of the workplace. The warning needs to be distinctive, audible above other noise and recognizable by everyone.

MEANS OF FIGHTING FIRE

Fire extinguishers should be located at identified fire points around the workplace. The extinguishers should be appropriate to the nature of the potential fire:

- wood, paper and cloth – water extinguisher;

- flammable liquids – dry powder or foam extinguisher;

- electrical – carbon dioxide (CO_2) extinguisher.

HEALTH & SAFETY Nominated people should be trained in how to use extinguishers.

First aid in the workplace

In the event of injury or sudden illness, failure to provide first aid could result in a casualty's death. The employer should ensure that an employee who is injured or taken ill at work receives immediate attention. The HSE will prosecute in cases where there is a significant risk, a disregard for established standards or persistent poor compliance with the law.

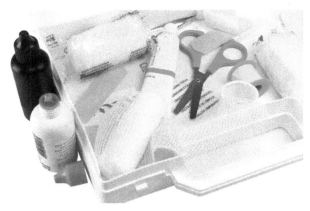

A first aid kit

The Health and Safety (First-Aid) Regulations 1981 require employers to provide adequate and appropriate equipment, facilities and personnel to ensure their employees receive immediate attention if they are injured or taken ill at work. These Regulations apply to all workplaces including those with less than five employees and to the self-employed.

Employers are required to carry out an assessment of first-aid needs. This involves consideration of workplace hazards and risks, the size of the organization and other relevant factors, to determine what first-aid equipment, facilities and personnel should be provided.

WHAT IS A FIRST-AIDER?

A first-aider is someone who has undertaken training and has a qualification that HSE approves. This means that they must hold a valid certificate of competence in either:

- first aid at work, issued by a training organization approved by HSE; or
- emergency first aid at work, issued by a training organization approved by HSE or a recognized Awarding Body of Ofqual/Scottish Qualifications Authority.

Employers can use the findings of their first-aid needs assessment to decide whether first-aiders should be trained in first aid at work or emergency first aid at work.

- Emergency first aid at work (EFAW) training enables a first-aider to give emergency first aid to someone who is injured or becomes ill while at work.
- First aid at work training includes EFAW and also equips the first-aider to apply first aid to a range of specific injuries and illness.

To help keep their basic skills up to date, it is strongly recommended that first-aiders undertake annual refresher training.

WHAT SHOULD A FIRST-AID BOX IN THE WORKPLACE CONTAIN?

There is no mandatory list of contents for first-aid boxes and HSE does not 'approve' or endorse particular products. Deciding what to include should be based on an employer's assessment of first-aid needs. As a guide, where work activities involve low hazards, a minimum stock of first-aid items might be:

- a leaflet giving general guidance on first aid, e.g. HSE's leaflet, 'Basic advice on first aid at work';
- 20 individually wrapped sterile blue plasters (assorted sizes), appropriate to the type of work (you can provide hypoallergenic plasters, if necessary);
- two sterile eye pads;
- four individually wrapped triangular bandages, preferably sterile;
- six safety pins;
- two large, individually wrapped, sterile, unmedicated wound dressings;
- six medium-sized, individually wrapped, sterile, unmedicated wound dressings;
- a pair of disposable gloves;
- tweezers and scissors.

HOW OFTEN SHOULD THE CONTENTS OF FIRST-AID BOXES BE REPLACED?

Although there is no specified review timetable, many items, particularly sterile ones, are marked with expiry dates. They should be replaced by the dates given and expired items disposed of safely. In cases where sterile items have no dates, it would be advisable to check with the manufacturers to find out how long they can be kept. For non-sterile items without dates, it is a matter of judgement, based on whether they are fit for purpose.

HEALTH & SAFETY

- First aid should only be given by a qualified first-aider.
- A first aid certificate is only valid for three years. After this period, it must be renewed with additional first aid training.
- Know what action you can take within your responsibility in the event of an accident occurring.
- An accident report book should be available to record details of any incident that has occurred.

It is good practice to provide your first-aiders and appointed persons with a book in which to record incidents they attend. The information can help you identify accident trends and possible areas for improvement in the control of health and safety risks. It can be used for reference in future first-aid needs assessments. The record book is not the same as the statutory accident book though the two might be combined.

Employers, self-employed people and those in control of premises have a duty to report some accidents and incidents at work under the Reporting of Injuries, Diseases and Dangerous Occurrences Regulations 1995 (RIDDOR).

WHAT INFORMATION SHOULD BE RECORDED?

Useful information to record includes:

● the date, time and place of the incident;

● the name and job of the injured or ill person;

● details of the injury/illness and what first aid was given;

● details about what happened to the person immediately afterwards (e.g. went back to work, went home, went to hospital); and

● the name and signature of the first-aider or person dealing with the incident.

It is usually the first-aider or appointed person who looks after the book. However, employers have overall responsibility.

Security in the workplace

This topic can cover a range of different issues, but in every instance a risk assessment will have to be implemented in order to assess any immediate dangers or threats that are apparent within an establishment. The hotel and catering industry can be an area of high risk due to the many different areas it encompasses, and the risks do not just affect customers but also staff and the establishment itself.

The main security issues within the catering industry are:

● theft;

● fraud;

● assault;

● terrorism;

● vandalism.

A security camera with built in lighting system

THEFT

Theft can cover a range of offences, including such things as the dishonest and unlawful taking of food and drink (by staff as well as by customers), equipment, furniture or furnishings, as well as taking as souvenirs or keepsakes items that are of value.

All items that are unlawfully taken from premises will have to be replaced, either at the company's expense or your own. All property is at risk, regardless of whether it is the customer's, the employee's or the employer's. Theft usually involves the taking of money, which is why many venues have strict measures in place to minimize the amount of money or merchandise on the premises at any one time.

Aggravated theft or robbery, where the use of violent or aggressive behaviour can lead to assault in addition to theft, has to be assessed as a security risk.

FRAUD

This is an ever-increasing security issue due to the way that technology and the electronic world have evolved and continue to change. More and more customers and businesses are using credit cards to pay for goods and items, often via means such as the Internet or card machines. This can make it easy for computer-based fraudsters to access credit card and bank account details.

All employees and employers should be extra vigilant for counterfeit credit cards and currency. Due to modern advances in technology, such items are becoming increasingly harder to spot.

Another growing area of concern is that of false claims for expenses and damages. These can range from dry cleaning bills to personal injury claims. Keeping full and accurate documentation of incidents and occurrences can save companies thousands of pounds a year by preventing fraudulent claims.

ASSAULT

An assault on a staff member or a customer, whether within an establishment or outside, is a very serious security matter. All assaults, physical and verbal, should be dealt with and treated with the utmost importance.

Strict security codes and procedures should be in place to protect everyone at the premises. Staff should be trained on how to correctly manage unexpected situations, both how to deal with an incident and how to recognize and hopefully diffuse any situation before it reaches a critical point – foresight can be a very good deterrent and helpful aid to all.

TERRORISM

This has become a threat that customers and staff are very aware of and should be taken very seriously. All threats of this nature, such as telephone calls and suspect packages, should be dealt with very carefully. Any incidents should be dealt with in the same way as a fire action plan: assess the situation, seek appropriate action or help and then evacuate the area in a calm manner.

VANDALISM

Vandalism, the malicious damage of property by customers, staff or outside influences, can be costly and time-consuming to rectify. It covers a range of security risks, from direct physical damage to property, graffiti and arson, to internal or external damage to the premises. All areas of vandalism need to be considered.

MANAGING SECURITY

Companies, employers and establishments should do all they can to reduce security risks and hazards. In a lot of cases simple procedures, such as taking and logging the contact details of all staff and customers, will not only prove helpful in the event of an incident but can also help to prevent an incident taking place. Deterrents such as signage stating that no valuables or large amounts of money are kept on the premises can deter opportunists or petty criminals from attempting to gain access.

Having effective monitoring procedures for such things as stock rotation and levels and keeping up-to-date records of what has come in and gone out of the premises will help reveal any major discrepancies. If staff and customer records are also held, this should mean that any issues can be thoroughly checked and resolved.

The main areas of premises that require security are the front and back entrances. At the front entrance there should be some sort of reception desk or a person to meet and greet both customers and staff so that information and details can be thoroughly checked. All visitors should sign in and out and be given some form of identification, such as a visitor's pass, to carry when on the premises. Staff should be trained fully, and if at any time they see anyone or anything suspicious or irregular then they should phone or notify the correct person/manager or the police immediately.

At the back door, anyone making a delivery should be expected to have identification. Deliveries should only be accepted from reputable companies that have already been nominated or screened for security. All maintenance personnel should have an appointment or a person or point of contact and be booked in on arrival. If necessary, telephone the visitor's employer to verify their details.

Closed-circuit television (CCTV) can be very useful as a security measure, and signage stating that the premises have CCTV is another good deterrent. Unfortunately CCTV is costly and it can be off-putting to customers and staff. Very discrete camera devices are now available, which can **blend** in with the surroundings very well.

If this type of system is to be used, there should be procedures in place for monitoring and recording the images. The time, date and area should be noted on all recordings so they can be easily listed and checked. This will also help to ensure that the recording media are re-used on a rotation basis. Video monitoring systems for CCTV should be kept in a secured area or office, with limited access by a minimal number of employees, whose names should be recorded.

The amount of cash in an establishment can be of major concern as this can encourage not just petty theft but also organized crime. If it is known that cash is kept on the premises then this can be a serious security risk. Staff should be trained in handling cash and there should be procedures in place so that takings and payments are cashed up at the end of each shift. A safe should be used, or if possible money taken to the bank to avoid large amounts being available.

Businesses can encourage customers to pay by credit or debit cards to help reduce the amount of available cash. This can, however, lead to the risk of credit card fraud, a common scam that is becoming ever more present in all industries. Staff should be trained to check for signatures and name details with all card or cheque transactions. They should also be taught how to check for counterfeit notes and coins.

HEALTH & SAFETY Give all staff a contact list of emergency numbers, or make sure a list is easily accessible, in case of any unexpected situations.

General security measures that are effective are good lighting and clear areas around and close by the premises. These allow customers and staff to see clearly anything suspicious or any potential danger. Leaving lights on or on timers can help to deter potential problems as it can give the impression that someone is present in the building. Doors, windows and access gates must all be locked when leaving a premises after close of business.

Within any establishment, all systems that are in place – whether for food ordering or for security – have to be maintained and managed. Policies or systems have to be introduced to cover the range of potential risks identified in a hazard analysis. Therefore, all staff will have to be trained on all these elements – from security threats to bomb alerts to customer or employee theft. Make sure these policies are strict and are adhered to at all times. Ongoing checks and assessments are needed to monitor present security risks and to identify new ones. Resources should be set aside to cover the cost of security. In the long run this can prove very cost effective. This could be internally by the company or from an external source.

Having an understanding of the relevant legislation means that the establishment and its employees will know their rights and the boundaries of what they are legally required to do. Security and safety go hand in hand. However, they are two separate issues. They need to be managed separately, but coordinated so that a balance between safety and security can be achieved.

Employment Rights and Responsibilities

Upon entry to employment, there are certain rights and responsibilities of both the employer and employee. The employee is protected by legislation from the Government and every employer must follow the guidelines or risk prosecution. From the employer's perspective, they must supply a job description and contract of employment, detailing the following:

- contracted working hours;
- holiday entitlement and notice period;
- detailed description of the job;
- provide a healthy and safe working environment.

From the employee's perspective, they must:

- Work to the conditions as described in their job description and contract of employment.
- Follow organizational policies and standard practices.
- Follow health and safety working practices, including food safety.

An employee is a person who is directly employed by a business under a contract of employment. However, there is also another role known as 'worker' or 'sub-contractor' that has been awarded a contract to deliver services but is not actually an employee of the business awarding the contract. The legislation designed to protect both employees and workers are as follows:

- National Minimum Wage Act 1998;
- Public Interest disclosure Act 1998;
- Part-time Workers (Prevention of Less Favourable Treatment) Regulations 2000;
- Equality Act 2010;
- Working Time Regulations 1998;
- Employment Rights Act 1996;
- Health and safety Legislation;
- Equal Pay Pact 1970;
- Disability Discrimination Act 1995.

When employers seek the recruitment and selection of new members of staff it is important that they are also aware of the following additional legislation:

- Children and Young Persons Act 1933;
- Data Protection Act 1988;
- Licensing Act 1964;
- Human Rights Act 1998;
- Sex Discrimination Act 1975;
- Rehabilitation of Offenders Act 1974;
- Asylum and Immigration Act 1996;
- Race Relations Act 1976.

When advertising for a job it is unlawful to discriminate against job applicants on the grounds of sex, marital status, gender, colour, race, religion, nationality, disability, sexual preference or membership of political movements or trades unions.

Job application forms should always be designed with care and attention to promote inclusion for everyone. Therefore phrases in job descriptions or titles such as 'manageress' should not be used because they indicate an intention to discriminate on the grounds of a person's gender. If sensitive information is needed such as a health record, the reason for this needs to be clearly explained and the information should always remain confidential, in line with the Data Protection Act 1998.

When candidates are informed of the date for their personal interview via a written letter they should also be notified if they need to wear protective clothing whilst on duty and also disclose if the company is likely to carry out any surveillance monitoring.

Sick payments

Employees that take time off from work due to illness might be entitled to sick pay. There are two types of sick pay:

- company sick pay (also called contractual or occupational sick pay);
- Statutory Sick Pay.

If an employer runs their own sick pay scheme it is a 'company sick pay scheme' and an employee should be paid what they are due under that. This will depend on what is included in the employment contract. If an employee is not entitled to anything under a company scheme, the employer should still pay Statutory Sick Pay (SSP), if eligible.

If an employee works for an employer under a contract of service, they are entitled to Statutory Sick Pay (SSP) if the following conditions apply:

- They are sick for at least four days in a row (including weekends and bank holidays and days that you do not normally work).
- They have average weekly earnings of at least £97 a week.

Working time directive

The working time directive applies to all workers and employees within the UK who undertakes work for an employer. The 1998 Regulations are enforced by the employment tribunals and by local authority Environmental Health Officers. The directive covers the worker's statutory right to rest breaks, rest periods and paid annual holiday.

Professional associations

A professional association (also called a professional body, professional institute, professional organization or professional society) is a non-profit organization seeking to further a particular profession, the interests of the individuals engaged in that profession and the overall public interest. Many professional bodies are involved in the development and monitoring of professional educational programs and the updating of skills. This is achieved by directly working alongside colleges, universities and awarding bodies and by hosting competitions.

Some of the associations related to professional cookery:

- Academy of Culinary Arts;
- Academy of Food and Wine;
- Association Culinaire Française;
- British Culinary Federation;
- Craft Guild of Chefs;
- Euro Toques;
- Federation of Chefs Scotland;
- Master Chefs of Great Britain;
- PACE (Professional Association of Catering Education);
- Institute of Hospitality;
- Welsh Culinary Association;
- World Association of Chefs Societies (WACS).

ASSESSMENT OF KNOWLEDGE AND UNDERSTANDING

To test your level of knowledge and understanding, answer the following short questions. These will help to prepare you for your summative (final) assessment.

1 Communication is important when working in a busy environment like a kitchen. State five things you can do to ensure the kitchen operation works smoothly on a daily basis.

2 Give three examples of implications of not conforming to health and safety laws.

3 State who the Health and Safety at Work Act 1974 covers and why it is in place.

4 Explain why it is important to keep yourself up to date with current health and safety legislation.

5 List five points that need to be covered when reporting incidents that occur within the kitchen.

6 Explain why and how customer and employee fraud is a concern for businesses and what measures can be taken to limit it.

7 Design and draw your own kitchen, based on medium-sized premises with approximately 20 kitchen staff. Then, detail a health and safety risk assessment and necessary health and safety action plan to implement.

8 You should ensure that the premises, equipment, food, storage (of equipment and chemicals), room size and space, and number of staff are all taken into consideration.

9 Identify three ways of maintaining good working relationships with other team members.

10 List five Acts relating to equal opportunities.

11 State how diversity within a kitchen can be of benefit.

12 List three examples of effective team work.

13 State the purpose of an appraisal or performance review.

Supervising food safety

2

VRQ

The principles of food safety supervision for catering

NVQ

Maintain food safety when preparing, storing and cooking food

Ensure food safety practices are followed in the preparation and serving of food and drink

LEARNING OBJECTIVES

There are many principal outcomes to this chapter.
At the end of this chapter you will be able to:

- **Ensure compliance with food hygiene legislation.**

- **Apply and monitor good hygiene practice.**

- **Implement food safety management procedures.**

- **Receive and store food safely.**

- **Maintain clean and hygienic work surfaces and equipment.**

- **Check food into the premises and identify specific labels.**

- **Understand the correct use of storage control, the stock rotation system and keeping records.**

- **Understand how to safely defrost food and thoroughly wash foodstuffs.**

- **Fully appreciate the regulations for the safe cooking, the safe holding and the safe reheating of food.**

- **Chill and freeze cooked food that is not for immediate consumption.**

- **Identify food bacteria and other organisms and food hazards in the workplace.**

This chapter introduces the important subject of food safety in catering and the key supervisory responsibilities needed to make sure that food and drinks are suitable, safe and healthy through all correct processes and procedures. The chapter takes account the latest approach to food safety and consumer protection and is set at level three formal training as described in the UK industry guides to good hygiene practice. This will ensure compliance with the Food Safety Act 1990, the Food Hygiene (England, Scotland, Wales and Northern Ireland) Regulations 2005.

The chapter introduces candidates to the importance of food safety in catering and supervisory responsibilities. Food business operators are responsible for identifying the training and instruction needs of food handlers and for determining how these needs are met. The measures put in place should ensure that all food handlers have sufficient knowledge and competence to handle food safely. This training relates to the nature of food handlers' duties, the types of foodstuff handled and associated food hazards and the risks to food safety presented by food operations for which the food handler is responsible.

Food safety procedures must be thoroughly planned, organized and monitored. It involved protecting food from the point of delivery, through its storage, preparation, cooking and serving to avoid the risk of causing illness or harm to all food preparers, servers and customers.

The legality of the information contained within this chapter is current and relevant at the time of printing; however, the acts are routinely and annually analyzed and reformed as appropriate. Care should be taken to ensure that all information is checked against government guidelines. From 1st January 2006, new EU food hygiene legislation has been applied throughout the UK. The legislation has strengthened and introduced the following framework:

- modernized, consolidated and simplified the previous EU food hygiene legislation;

- applies effective and proportionate controls throughout the food chain, from primary production to sale or supply to the final consumer (from 'farm to fork');

- focuses controls on what is necessary for public health protection;

- clarifies that it is the primary responsibility of food business operators to produce food safely.

The three basic EU food hygiene regulations are:

- Regulation (EC) 852/2004 on the hygiene of foodstuffs;

- Regulation (EC) 853/2004 laying down specific hygiene rules for food of animal origin;

- Regulation (EC) 854/2004 laying down specific rules for the organization of official controls on products of animal origin intended for human consumption.

All food businesses are required to be registered with the competent authority; which competent authority will depend on the type of business. Food business operators (except farmers and growers) are also required to put in place, implement and maintain a permanent procedure, or procedures, based on HACCP principles. The legislation is structured to ensure that the appropriate level of public health protection is in place without placing unnecessary burdens on businesses. Food businesses can apply the legislation flexibly and proportionately according to the nature of the business.

The Food Standards Agency was established in 2000 with a role to protect the general public from risks which may arise in connection with the consumption of food and beverages. The agency provides information to public and government agencies on food safety and nutritional matters. A wide variety of information can be found on their website which includes food safety information, nutritional facts alongside information on commodities and products.

WEB LINK Further information about food safety can be sourced from www.food.gov.uk.

Introduction

The chef must be particularly conscious of the need for hygiene: many commodities have to be handled and prepared for the customer without any type of heat treatment. High standards of hygiene are essential to prevent food poisoning, food spoilage, loss of productivity, pest infestation and potential criminal prosecution for malpractice.

Food hygiene implies more than just the sanitation of work areas. It includes all practices, precautions and legal responsibilities involved in the following:

- Protecting food from risk of contamination.

- Preventing organisms from multiplying to an extent which would pose a health risk to customers and employees.

- Destroying any harmful bacteria in food by thorough heat treatment or other techniques.

However, with the recent introduction of legislation it is now also a legal requirement to have a system based on the principles of Hazard Analysis Critical Control Points (HACCP). This system will help to ensure that the identification, assessment and monitoring of critical control points in the storage, kitchen and service areas are maintained alongside corrective actions being put into place. These systems also require to be frequently verified, with accurate documentation made available for inspection at any time with continual review processes in place.

Chef testing the core temperature of roast meat

To help simplify this process for smaller businesses, the Food Standards Agency (FSA) introduced a new system called 'Safer Food Better Business'. All food businesses must now have suitable and up-to-date food safety management based on HACCP and those responsible for the food business must ensure that:

- Where a full HACCP system is established, at least one person who has been trained in the principles of HACCP is included in the design of the whole system.

- The premises (and any delivery vehicles) are registered with the correct local authority.

- The business must be able to provide all records of staff training proportionate to the different job specifications within the business.

- Policies are in place for planning and monitoring all staff training.

- Appropriate levels of supervision are in place.

- They provide adequate provision of materials and equipment for staff, including personal protective equipment (PPE).

- There is sufficient ventilation, water supplies and adequate drainage systems.

- There are separate washing and cleaning facilities for premises, equipment and food handling as well as sufficient hand washing facilities.

- There are records of all suppliers used.

- There are systems for accident and incident reporting.

It is important that all employees recognize their own contribution to food safety and undertake such responsibility, for example:

- Co-operate with their employers and the measures they have put in place to maintain food safety.

- Maintain high standards of personal hygiene.

- Not work in such a way that would endanger or contaminate the food or systems they work with.

- Report any breakages, shortages or defects that could affect food safety.

- Report any illnesses to supervisors or managers before starting work.

- Take part in planned training and instruction.

CHEF'S TIP The HACCP system relies on staff adhering to the food safety regulations. Ensure that all staff are aware of their responsibility at all times.

Food safety legislation

Due diligence is the main legal defence endorsed by the Food Safety Act 2006. It provides the best protection to companies that need to demonstrate that all reasonable precautions have been taken to avoid the sale of unsafe food to customers. For a business to comply with the Act, the food safety management system should always include the following records maintained on a regular and sometimes daily basis:

- essential food business records confirming that reputable suppliers are used with supplier records;

- equipment and premises maintenance records;
- core temperature control and monitoring for foodstuffs, refrigeration and freezing;
- staff sickness records;
- cleaning schedules;
- pest audits;
- training schedules;
- working practices and reports;
- supervision schedules and employee profiles.

Food safety legislation under the 2006 Act is enforced by local authorities through inspections carried out by environmental health officers (EHO) who are empowered to serve enforcement notices through criminal and civil courts. Eventually the Health and Safety Executive (HSE) may also become involved with this process.

Environment health officers

The environment health officer may visit a food premises as part of a scheduled visit, as a follow-up where problems may have been identified or after a complaint from a member of the public. The frequency of visits depends largely on the type of business and the food being handled, possible hazards within the business, the risk rating and if the business has had any previous problems or court actions against them.

Environment health officers can access a food premises at any reasonable time without giving any notice or appointment. The main purpose of these inspections is to identify any possible risks from the business and to assess the business's HACCP system.

In the undertaking of their role the officers can also enforce or provide assistance with the following areas:

- Advise on and deliver food safety training to food business staff.
- Advise on any new food safety legislation or best practice.
- Check food safety law compliance.
- Deal with non-compliance by formal action and the serving of improvement enforcement notices.
- Deal with suspected food poisoning outbreaks.
- Ensure that food offered for selling is fit for consumption.
- Investigate complaints about the food business.
- Monitor food operations within a business and identify possible sources of contamination.
- Monitor the effectiveness of the food safety management system.
- Present professional food safety advice to food businesses on routine visits.

HYGIENE IMPROVEMENT NOTICE

A hygiene improvement notice will be served if an environment health officer believes that a food business does not comply with food safety regulations. The notice is served to the management of the food business in writing and will always state what is not right, why it is wrong and what is required to rectify the problem within a stated timescale. If the work is not completed within the specific time, an offence will be judged to have been committed and further action will be taken.

EMERGENCY PROHIBITION NOTICE

A hygiene emergency prohibition notice is served if the environment health officer considers that there is an impending risk to health from the actual food business. Risks would include such issues as poor drainage, rodent infestation, lack of clean water supply and sewage contamination. By serving this notice, it means that immediate closure of the business for three days will be set. The local authority must then apply to the magistrate courts for an extension to closure. Furthermore public notices will be displayed in a visible place on the food business premises. The owner of the business must apply for a certificate of satisfaction before they can re-open for business.

Magistrate courts can impose large fines, a prison sentence or even both for offences. For serious offences such as knowingly selling contaminated food, this may be taken to a Crown Court where unlimited fines can be imposed and up to two years imprisonment if convicted.

The avoidance of food contamination

The use of food premises which are clean and can be correctly maintained is essential for the preparation, cooking and service of food. **Cross-contamination** risks should be minimized by the provision of separate preparation areas for the various raw and cooked foods. The table on the next page describes the various fittings and fixtures that need to be considered in a kitchen before the main equipment is planned.

Clean food preparation areas play an essential part in the production of safe food. Clean premises, work areas and equipment are essential in the control of the organisms that cause food poisoning. Effective cleaning uses one or more of the following aspects:

- chemicals – detergents, disinfectants and sanitizers;
- mechanical methods – cleaning machines;
- physical – human effort to carry out the task;
- thermal – hot water and **steam**;
- turbulence – rapid movement of liquids.

However, cleaning alone will not be effective in the removal of microorganisms. Disinfection is needed and is often carried out after the cleaning process or during the

FIXTURES AND FITTINGS	RECOMMENDATIONS
Ceilings	White in colour to reflect the light. Smooth-textured, without cracks or peeled paint/plaster. Usually panelled to hide the ventilation system.
Floors	Should have a durable, non-slip and non-permeable material. They can be tiled but polyurethane screeds are now used extensively in food processing areas. This type of screed is fast to install, offers good levels of chemical resistance even to the most aggressive acids and fats and can be installed to withstand steam cleaning. It also has a textured finish, designed to provide a slip-resistant surface.
Lighting	Good lighting is essential to avoid eye strain. Natural light is best but where artificial lighting is used some thought should be given to the type used.
Ventilation	The requirements of a high-performance kitchen ventilation system for the modern kitchen. The extracted air should be free from grease and odours, and be discharged up single or multiple chimney stacks. A canopy system should be built around the existing structure of the kitchen to cover at least all cookery areas. The incorporation of a balancing system to ensure equal extract along the whole cook line is very important. Replacement air is introduced into the kitchen through low-velocity diffusers mounted in the front face of the canopy and spot cooling nozzles can also provide a cooler air temperature in the kitchen. These are a potential source of dirt, grease and dust and should be cleaned on a very regular basis.
Walls	Ceramic wall tiles were considered the best surface for areas where liquids splash a wall surface, potentially overcoming a damp or hygiene problem. Many such areas still exist in industrial and commercial hygiene-sensitive areas. Their durability, long-term appearance and cost of maintenance can be questionable and today there is a viable alternative to consider. Modern alternatives to ceramic wall tiles include PVC wall cladding systems, resin wall coatings and screed mortars. They offer a hygienic finish capable of withstanding heavy-impact use.

cleaning process. Disinfection may be undertaken via the following four activities:

● Chemicals – use specific chemicals for kitchen use only.

● Hot water – kept at a temperature of at least 82°C for a minimum of three seconds.

● **Steam** – used effectively for the disinfection of equipment and work surfaces that are difficult to reach or fully dismantle.

● Combination – a combination of any of the above. This can be found in the use of dishwashers.

Chemicals used in cleaning

The supervisor must help to confirm that all staff are aware of the possible dangers and hazards from cleaning chemicals used on the premises. Recognized COSHH training for staff will increase the knowledge of the risks from chemicals that are regularly used within their area of work. Staff must be made aware through updated training and supervision of the correct use of chemicals, use of PPE and or the correct storage procedures for chemicals. They must be stored well away from food preparation areas and separate and lockable zones. The chemicals must be kept in their original containers so that labels containing COSHH, usage and health and safety information are clearly identifiable.

Some of the chemicals used in cleaning and disinfection include the following:

● Detergent is a chemical used to remove dirt, **grease** and food particles and hold them in suspension in water. It comes in the form of liquid, foam, gel or powder and usually requires hot water to be mixed with them. Detergents do not kill pathogens.

● Disinfectant is a chemical used to reduce the bacteria content to a safe level and is usually applied after cleaning with a detergent.

● Sanitizer is a disinfectant and detergent that has been combined. It usually comes in a spray bottle and is applied to working surfaces and small equipment between preparation tasks. Sanitizers are also used to disinfect hands with the use of an alcohol based spray or foam.

● Sterilizer can be in a chemical form or via extreme heat (steam or **boiling** water) and will kill all living organisms, toxins and spores.

Cleaning with a good use of PPE (personal protective equipment)

The carbon footprint of cleaning

WHAT IS A CARBON FOOTPRINT?

'Carbon footprint' is an often misunderstood expression. When discussing climate change, *footprint* is a metaphor for the total impact that something has, and *carbon* is used as an over-riding term to describe the entire set of different greenhouse gases that contribute to global warming.

Therefore, the term 'carbon footprint' is a term to describe the best estimate that we can obtain of the full climate change impact of something. That something could be anything – an activity, an item, a lifestyle, a company, a country or even the whole world.

Man-made climate change, or global warming, is caused by the release of certain types of gas into the atmosphere. The dominant man-made greenhouse gas is carbon dioxide (CO_2), which is emitted whenever we burn fossil fuels in homes, factories or power stations. But other greenhouse gases are also important. Methane (CH_4), for example, which is emitted mainly by agriculture and landfill sites, is 25 times more potent per kilogram than CO_2. Even more potent but emitted in smaller quantities are nitrous oxide (N_2O), which is about 300 times more potent than carbon dioxide and released mainly from industrial processes and farming, and refrigerant gases, which are typically several thousand times more potent than CO_2.

In the UK, the total impact on the climate breaks down like this: carbon dioxide (86 per cent), methane (7 per cent), nitrous oxide (6 per cent) and refrigerant gases (1 per cent). Given that a single item or activity can cause multiple different greenhouse gases to be emitted, each in different quantities, a carbon footprint if written out in full is confusing. To avoid this, the convention is to express a carbon footprint in terms of carbon dioxide equivalent or CO_2e. This means the total climate change impact of all the greenhouse gases caused by an item or activity rolled into one and expressed in terms of the amount of carbon dioxide that would have the same impact.

DIRECT VERSUS INDIRECT EMISSIONS

Much of the confusion around footprints comes down to the distinction between *direct* and *indirect* emissions. The true carbon footprint of a plastic kitchen spatula, for example, includes not only direct emissions resulting from the manufacturing process and the transportation of the implement to the shop: it also includes a whole host of indirect emissions, such as those caused by the extraction and processing of the oil used to make the plastic in the first place. These are just a few of the processes involved. To consider, tracing back all the points that have to happen to make that spatula leads to an infinite number of pathways, most of which are very small. To make the point clearly, consider following just one of those pathways. The staff in the offices of the plastic factory used paper clips made of steel. Within the footprint of that steel is a small allocation to take account of the maintenance of a digger in the iron mine that the steel originally came from … and so on. The carbon footprint of the plastic spatula includes everything, so working it out accurately is not an easy task.

To give another example, the true carbon footprint of simply driving a supplier's vehicle includes not only the emissions that come out of the exhaust pipe, but also all the emissions that take place when oil is extracted, shipped,

refined into fuel and transported to the petrol station, not to mention the substantial emissions caused by producing and maintaining the vehicle.

CHEF'S TIP For further reading on this subject, evaluate the book *How Bad Are Bananas? The Carbon Footprint of Everything* by Mike Berners-Lee.

DISHWASHER VERSUS HAND WASHING

When it comes to long-standing carbon footprint and usage of water debates, dishwashing by hand versus using a dishwasher is a consideration that all food businesses should pose. Below are some carbon-footprint figures, which hopefully will help the food business understand the energy use differences. As the figures below show, the most careful hot-water hand washing just beats a fully loaded dishwasher. This is partly because most people (in the UK at least) undertake their manual washing up using hot water heated by a gas-fired boiler, whereas dishwashers heat water from cold using electricity. A modern boiler can capture more than 90 per cent of the energy in the gas, whereas most of the energy in the fuel used to generate electricity is wasted in generation and transmission, which gives hand washing an obvious head start.

However, according to evidence few people are really careful with hot water when washing up. If instead you leave the hot tap running – as many people do – then the footprint is *far* higher than using a dishwasher. Even if you do wash up carefully by hand, compared with the dishwasher you still lose out both on hygiene (with nearly 400 times more bacteria left on equipment after washing) and time (taking nearly four times as long as loading and running the dishwasher).

In conclusion it is fair to state that the professional dishwasher is better – assuming that appropriate cycles are used and only run when the machine is full. This is true even if you include the energy used in the production of the dishwasher. As for water consumption and detergent, many dishwasher manufacturers are reducing the need for high levels of water and detergent and therefore greater efficiency.

CHEF'S TIP The carbon footprint of doing the dishes.
540 g CO_2e: by hand, using warm water sparingly
770 g CO_2e: in a dishwasher at 55°C
990 g CO_2e: in a dishwasher at 65°C
8000 g CO_2e: by hand, with the use of plenty of water.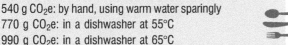

Therefore, to maximize the benefits, you should always choose a model that will last and then ensure that it is correctly maintained. Try to run it fully loaded, using the correct setting.

Glass washing racks for a commercial dishwasher

Basic cleaning and scheduling

It is important to train all staff in the importance of cleaning and working cleanly throughout. The concept of 'clean as you go' means that you should not allow waste to accumulate in the food preparation and cooking area. It is important to understand that it is challenging to keep untidy areas clean and hygienic and therefore help to prevent cross-contamination.

As part of the food safety management system the cleaning of areas and equipment needs to be thoroughly planned and recorded on a cleaning schedule. The schedule needs to include the following information:

- What is to be cleaned.
- Who is tasked to clean it.
- How it is to be cleaned and for approximately how long.
- What is the frequency and when should it take place.
- Which resources, chemicals and PPE should be worn.
- Safety precautions highlighted during the tasks.
- Signatures of cleaner and supervisor checking the work with a time and date.

Cleaning equipment and tasks

Work surfaces and equipment for the preparation, cooking and service of food should be impervious and easy to clean. Equipment should be constructed from materials which are non-toxic, corrosion resistant, smooth and free from cracks. Apparatus such as a **bain-marie** should be able to store hot food for up to two hours at an **ambient temperature** of 63°C and regular temperature checks should be taken to ensure that the correct temperature is maintained. The surfaces should be easy to clean even when hot and should allow the food to be presented in an attractive manner.

WORK SURFACES AND CHOPPING BOARDS

It is very important to keep all work surfaces and chopping boards clean because they touch the food your customers are going to eat. If they are not properly clean, bacteria could spread to food and make your customers ill.

● Always wash work surfaces before you begin preparing food.

● Wipe up any spilt food immediately (remember – *clean as you go*).

● Always wash and sanitize work surfaces thoroughly after they have been touched by raw meat, including poultry, or raw eggs.

● Never put ready-to-eat food, such as tomatoes or fruit, on a worktop or chopping board that has been touched by raw meat, unless you have washed it and sanitized thoroughly first.

If you have a dishwasher, this is a very effective way to clean plastic chopping boards, crockery and knives. Dishwashers wash at high temperatures; the cleaning cycle will usually reach between 50 and 60°C using a detergent with a rinse cycle at 82–88°C, which disinfects the items effectively. By allowing the cleaned items to air dry, means that there is less opportunity for any contamination to directly transfer from drying cloths. Otherwise, wash chopping boards thoroughly by hand with hot water and detergent. Sanitize boards on a regular basis using an appropriate sanitizing substance.

If items need to be washed by hand the suggested way to undertake this task is as follows:

1 Scrape, rinse off any residual food.

2 Wash the items in plenty of hot water (50–60°C) using any PPE such as rubber gloves and detergent.

3 The use of cleaning brushes or scouring pads is recommended.

4 Rinse in plenty of hot water at 82°C for 30 seconds to help the disinfection process.

5 Allow to air dry as opposed to using drying cloths.

Preferably, it is standard practice to have separate chopping boards for raw meat and for other foods. A standardized system of coloured boards, spoons and knife handles which help to minimize cross-contamination are widely available. They should be used as follows (in this book, white and wooden backgrounds may be used for photographic purposes):

● red – raw meat and poultry;

● yellow – cooked meat and poultry;

● blue – raw fish;

● brown – vegetables;

● green – fruit and salads;

● white – dairy and pastry items.

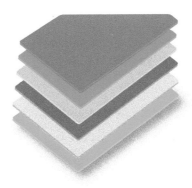

Colour coded chopping boards are used to minimize cross-contamination

These boards must be cleaned between each use, ideally finished with sanitizer. They should be **soaked** overnight in a sterilizing solution on a regular basis. The boards are stored in racks and should not be touching each other. If boards become damaged they should be discarded. Bacteria can multiply in cracks and blemishes, and be the cause of contamination.

A debate of the food safety concerns the use of wood instead of plastic cutting boards. Both materials have their own advantages and disadvantages. Plastic is easier to sanitize and place through commercial dishwasher systems. The colour-coded versions also help chefs to segregate food to avoid cross-contamination. Research suggests however that wood has natural antibacterial activity that helps to disinfect the board surface. Scrubbing the wooden boards with salt as a scouring agent and rinsing with a bleach solution will keep the boards clean and hygienic. This helps to ensure that any deep scratches and scars in the wood are kept clean too.

KITCHEN CLOTHS

Dirty and damp cloths are the perfect breeding ground for bacteria. It is very important to wash kitchen cloths and other cleaning cloths, sponges and abrasive materials regularly and leave them to dry before using them again. Ideally, try to keep different cloths for different jobs. For example, use one cloth to wipe worktops and another to wash dishes. This helps to stop bacteria spreading.

The safest option is the use of disposable kitchen towels to wipe worktops and chopping boards. This is because you throw the kitchen towel away after using it once, so it is less likely to spread bacteria than cloths you use again.

Tea towels can also spread bacteria, so it is important to wash them regularly and be careful how you use them. Remember, if you wipe your hands on a tea towel after you have touched raw meat, this will spread bacteria to the towel. Then, if you use the tea towel to dry a plate, the bacteria will cross-contaminate the plate.

KNIVES, SPOONS AND OTHER UTENSILS

It is important to keep knives, wooden spoons, spatulas, tongs and other utensils scrupulously clean to help stop microorganisms spreading to food. It is especially important to wash them thoroughly after using with raw meat and fish. Once again, a dishwasher is a very effective way to clean knives and other utensils because dishwashers can wash at a very high temperature, which kills bacteria. Otherwise, wash them thoroughly with hot water and detergents finished with a sanitizer.

A growing number of catering companies also use ultraviolet light kits for sterilizing cutting boards, knives and kitchen utensils. These kits use UVC ultraviolet light to kill up to 99.99 per cent of most viruses, bacteria and mould spores by damaging their DNA. Some handheld models sterilize surfaces with as little as ten seconds of exposure. However, UV light cannot kill germs in cracks or shadows, so turn the equipment to expose all surfaces.

Pest control procedures

The presence of pests in food production and preparation areas has always been unacceptable. The risks posed by pests include:

- the spread of disease – pathogens are transferred from the gut or external surface of the pest;
- damage to property;
- contamination of work surfaces and foodstuffs;
- adverse public opinion and loss of reputation;
- prosecution and closure;
- poor staff relations.

According to EC Regulations on the hygiene of food commodities, food business operators are required to put in place procedures, which manage food safety within their establishment. It requires that the procedure or procedures be based upon the HACCP (Hazard Analysis Critical Control Point) principle.

If standards and guidelines for pest control are to achieve the aim of promoting best practice they must be practical and flexible. The standard should be risk-based in order to address the issues raised by the following:

Risk to public health due to activities of pests – pests are known to carry a range of pathogens which can be transmitted to humans either through contaminated food or their presence in the environment.

Risk to food safety – this will be the priority for all staff engaged in the preparation, storage, cooking and service of food. The risks include:

- physical contamination of product by rodent droppings, insect parts or other foreign bodies;
- introduction of microorganisms;
- damage to product or packaging.

PEST MANAGEMENT SYSTEM

The objective of the pest management system is the maintenance of pest-free conditions in all areas of the site. The following systematic approach should be taken to all pest control and pest prevention issues, that being:

- Exclusion – refers to the methods adopted in preventing pest entry into a building. Exclusion is often neglected or ignored with entire reliance being placed on destruction, in many cases after infestation has occurred. The use of pesticides may then fail to achieve the desired result because building structure and conditions within are incompatible.
- Restriction – refers to the methods used in creating unfavourable conditions for pests to harbour and breed.
- Destruction – refers to the physical and chemical methods that are commonly used to control pests.

ROLE OF THE SUPERVISOR

The administration of a reporting system and maintenance of records is essential in pest management. Records must be kept for the following reasons:

1 To highlight any recommendations.
2 To demonstrate compliance with legislation.
3 To monitor pest management processes.
4 As evidence of compliance to third party auditors.

A record should be kept of any pest sightings, including those made by people other than staff involved in pest management. This can be in the form of a book where the following information can be logged:

● name of person making report;

● date and time;

● location;

● pest seen;

● any other relevant information.

In addition to entering the sighting in the book, the sighting must be reported to the appointed manager in charge of pest management who will decide on further action. Other areas of pest management that the supervisor must undertake are the checking and cleaning of refuse areas and that all refuse containers have tight fitting lids and are emptied regularly. Keeping all food preparation areas clean and not leaving any traces of food or liquids out in the open overnight are essential to the prevention of pests. This is alongside the effective stock control and regular cleaning of storage areas. Dry commodities should be kept in sealed containers and off the floor.

HEALTH & SAFETY Check all deliveries for any signs of pest infestation.

Most food premises provide three main attractions for pests:

● Food – most pests actually require very small amounts of food; an adult mouse, for example, can survive on as little as three grams a day. The amount of food material required in order to provide adequate conditions for survival and breeding of insects can generally be met by less than scrupulous cleaning.

● Warmth – a few degrees increase in temperature may be sufficient to encourage infestation, particularly in winter months. Conversely, ultra-low temperatures are no insurance against pests. With most species of pests an increase in temperature generates a corresponding increase in breeding frequency and numbers.

● Shelter – all buildings provide some degree of shelter or harbour for pests. It is commonly assumed that older buildings are more prone to infestation, but new buildings with enclosed roof spaces, suspended ceilings, wall cavities and panelling provide a myriad of shelter areas for pests.

VIDEO CLIIP Control of pests and infestations

PEST CONTAMINATION INFORMATION

PEST	BIOLOGY AND BEHAVIOUR	FOOD CONTAMINATION PROBLEM
Rats, mice, squirrels	Rodents have the ability to adapt themselves to almost any environment.	Rodents can cause damage to food intended for humans, by consumption, contamination with faeces and urine, as well as other physical and microbiological contaminants. Rodents have the capability to spread many human pathogens, such as *Salmonella*, *Listeria*, *Escherichia coli*, *Cryptosporidium parvum*, *Leptospira*, hantaviruses, Bubonic plague and toxoplasmosis.
Cockroaches	Cockroaches are omnivorous. In addition to conventional foodstuffs, they will feed on a wide range of organic matter including other cockroaches. Their activity peaks during hours of darkness.	Cockroaches foul their environment with faeces, regurgitated food and they taint materials with their characteristic smell. Cockroaches also contaminate food directly as they move from filth to food indiscriminately and are therefore implicated in the mechanical transmission of many pathogens, such as those causing food poisoning and wound infections.
Flies	Flies have a complete life cycle, consisting of four main stages – egg, larva, pupa and adult. The duration of each developmental stage is very much dependent on temperature and food/moisture availability.	The fly is a highly mobile pest, able to fly from filth to food carrying with it a wide range of disease-causing organisms on its body. All true flies (adult stage) can only ingest liquid food. Should they land on a solid food source, they produce large quantities of saliva together with regurgitated gut contents.
Ants	Ants live in colonies founded by a single, fertile female or queen. They have a caste system by which nest building, nursing of young and foraging for food is undertaken by workers	Ants find their way into kitchens and production areas and there is a risk that food may become contaminated by ant bodies. Many infectious organisms are present in hospitals and these may be transmitted to patients by ants crawling on infected surfaces and used dressings.

PEST	BIOLOGY AND BEHAVIOUR	FOOD CONTAMINATION PROBLEM
Stored product insects	Stored product insects (SPIs) are significant pests as they spend the majority of their time, including breeding, hidden in their chosen food type. Inspection and early detection can therefore prove difficult. The group known as SPIs in this context includes mites. Commodities attacked include cereals, nuts, dried fruit and pulses.	Due to their close relationship with the product, an infestation of stored product insects can often remain undetected in the initial stages. In order to prevent spread of SPIs the following steps should be taken: ● All incoming raw materials should be sampled for the presence of insects. ● Strict stock rotation must be implemented. ● Thorough cleaning is required to prevent build-up of product within machinery. ● Monitoring procedures should be in place to identify early signs of infestation. ● Staff must be aware of the high-risk areas and products on site.
Birds and other vertebrates	Under the European Wild Birds Directive 1979, all wild birds, including their nests and habitat, are protected. In the UK the relevant legislation is the Wildlife and Countryside Act 1981. However, birds that are recognized as pests can have that protection removed and are listed on the General Licences, issued by Natural England each year. Equivalent licences are issued in Scotland, Wales and Northern Ireland.	The droppings of sparrows and other birds spoil finished products and packages in loading bays, storage areas and warehouses. Nests and droppings block gutters and down pipes. The resulting overflowing water leads to timber decay, broken rendering, ruined decorations and even structural damage. The close association of birds with man gives rise to the possibility of disease transmission. Sparrows, pigeons and gulls may carry bacteria causing *Salmonellosis*. Pigeons carry Ornithosis, a disease similar to viral pneumonia that can be transmitted to man through infected droppings or respiratory droplets.

Standards for food premises

The law requires that the layout, design, construction and size of food premises shall permit adequate cleaning or disinfection. The layout and design should allow access for effective cleaning. Alternatively, equipment must be mobile to enable adequate cleaning and disinfection. Flooring, walls, ceilings and ventilation must be suitable to allow the type of cleaning appropriate to a food production area. Protection against accumulation of dirt, contact with toxic materials, shedding of particles into food and the formation of condensation or mould on surfaces should be maintained at all times.

The layout, design, construction and size of premises must avoid the accumulation of dirt in places inaccessible to cleaning. Coving at wall or floor junctions is recommended to ease cleaning. Construction materials (such as walls, paint, ceilings and flooring) must not include any substance that may add toxic material to food either by direct contact or vapour. The design and construction, especially of high level surfaces, should avoid finishes that may lead to shedding of particles such as flaking paint, plaster or fibres. Any growth of mould within the fabric of the building is undesirable and special attention must be given to areas where steam and humidity are generated in order to avoid the build-up of condensation. This will be linked to the type of ventilation system installed.

Supervise good hygiene practices, including protection against cross-contamination between and during operations, by food, equipment, materials, water, air supply or staff and external sources of contamination such as pests. If high-risk foods are to be stored or handled at the same time as foods which may contaminate them, then there must be enough space to allow high risk food to be stored and prepared on separate work surfaces and equipment.

Provide, where necessary, suitable temperature conditions for the hygienic processing and storage of products. The design and construction of food preparation rooms should avoid the build-up of excessive temperatures and must be capable of keeping food at suitable temperatures.

WASH HAND BASINS

An adequate number of wash hand basins must be available which are suitably located and designated for cleaning hands only. The number of basins will depend on the size of the business and the size and layout of the premises. They must be located close to toilet facilities and at strategic places in the premises, so that workers have convenient access to them.

Wash hand basins must be provided with hot and cold (or appropriately mixed) running water, materials for cleaning hands and for hygienic drying. Antibacterial soap and paper towels are recommended.

Where necessary, the provisions for washing food must be separate from the hand washing facility.

TOILETS

An adequate number of flush lavatories must be available and connected to an effective drainage system. The minimum requirement is one toilet or WC for up to five employees. For more than five employees, additional toilets must be provided on the basis of the Health, Safety and Welfare Regulations 1992.

All sanitary conveniences within food premises must be provided with adequate natural or mechanical ventilation. This is to prevent (as far as possible) aerosols and offensive odours from permeating food rooms. Lavatories must not lead directly into rooms in which food is handled, meaning there must be a lobby between the toilet and any food room, and ideally this lobby will be ventilated.

VENTILATION

There must be suitable and sufficient means of natural or mechanical ventilation. Ventilation must be provided to ensure that heat and/or humidity do not build up to levels that could compromise the safety of food.

A mechanical ventilation system may be necessary and should consist of a suitable canopy and extraction fan to draw air to remove heat, steam, airborne contaminants and grease-laden fumes through an extract point. This may require the incorporation of grease filters which should be removed on a regular basis for cleaning. Mechanical air flow from a contaminated area to a clean area must be avoided.

Ventilation systems must be so constructed as to enable filters and other parts requiring cleaning or replacement to be readily accessible. Before any system is installed you should seek advice from a ventilation engineer. You may also require planning permission for any ventilation stack.

An example of a small industrial kitchen extraction unit situated over a stove unit

LIGHTING

Food premises must have adequate natural and/or artificial lighting. Where fluorescent strip lighting is used over food preparation surfaces these should be protected with a tube shield or diffuser. Lighting must be good enough to allow safe food handling, effective cleaning and the monitoring of cleaning standards.

DRAINAGE

Drainage facilities must be adequate for the purpose intended; they must be designed and constructed to avoid the risk of contamination of foodstuffs.

Drains must have sufficient fall to allow all solid and liquid waste to flow away. All appliances connected to the drainage system must be provided with an effective trap. Inspection points must be available, but they must be adequately sealed.

CHANGING FACILITIES

Adequate changing facilities for staff must be provided where necessary. Provision must be made to allow food handlers to change and to store their street clothes and personal effects away from open foods. It is good practice to have separate changing rooms and to provide secure storage for personal effects.

FLOORING

There are further specific requirements in rooms where food is prepared, treated or processed. Floors must be maintained in a sound condition and must be easy to clean and, where necessary, disinfect. This will require the use of impervious, non-absorbent, washable and non-toxic materials used to construct the floor. Suitable materials are: floor tiles (quarry, vinyl or ceramic) with waterproof grouting, vinyl safety flooring, Terrazzo safety flooring or resin flooring. The edges between the floor and walls should be coved to prevent food debris and dirt collecting in the corners.

Consideration should be given to floor drainage, and the design of the floor should prevent water pooling during normal use. Internal drainage systems should be trapped and inspection covers should be sealed and screwed down to prevent offensive odours entering the food room.

WALLS

Wall surfaces must be maintained in a sound condition and must be easy to clean and, where necessary, disinfect. This will require the use of impervious, non-absorbent, washable and non-toxic materials and require a smooth surface up to a height appropriate for the operations.

Suitable materials are: washable painted plaster, ceramic tiles, stainless steel sheeting, PVC or GRP plastic sheeting, epoxy resin or similar smooth **coating**.

CEILINGS

Ceilings and other overhead fixtures must be designed, constructed and finished to prevent the accumulation of dirt and reduce condensation, the growth of moulds and the shedding of particles.

Suitable materials are similar to those for wall surfaces, (painted plaster etc.). Polystyrene or fibre tiles are not suitable for high humidity locations.

The design of ceilings in food preparation areas often includes suspended ceilings so that all pipe work and electrical wiring can be adequately and safely concealed. Care must be taken to prevent pests from getting into these areas.

WINDOWS

Windows and other openings must be constructed to prevent the accumulation of dirt. Those which can be opened must, where necessary, be fitted with insect-proof screens which can be easily removed for cleaning. Where open windows would result in contamination of foodstuffs, windows must remain closed and fixed during production.

DOORS

Doors must be easy to clean and, where necessary, disinfect. This will require the use of smooth and non-absorbent surfaces, particularly around hand contact areas such as door handles.

SURFACES AND FITTINGS

Surfaces, including surfaces of equipment, that will come into contact with food, must be maintained in a sound

condition and be easy to clean and disinfect. This will require the use of smooth, washable and non-toxic materials.

Suitable materials will include stainless steel, ceramic or food grade plastic. Wood is not appropriate for use with high-risk foods. Joins between work surfaces may allow dirt to become trapped. Continuous surfaces are best, alternatively joins should be sealed with a suitable waterproof sealant, e.g. epoxy grouting or silicon sealant.

Adequate facilities must be provided for the cleaning and disinfecting of work tools and equipment. These facilities, such as sinks and/or dish washing machines with hot rinse cycle, must be constructed of materials resistant to corrosion and must be easy to clean, maintain and have an adequate supply of hot and cold water. Sufficient provision must be made for any necessary washing of food. Every sink or other such facility provided for the washing of food must have an adequate supply of hot and/or cold potable (clean and drinkable) water as required, and be kept clean.

FOOD WASTE

Food waste and other refuse must not be allowed to accumulate in food preparation or service rooms, except so far as is unavoidable during the business operation. It is good practice to remove all waste from the food room at the end of the day.

Food waste and other refuse must be deposited in closable containers. These containers must be of an appropriate construction, kept in sound condition, and where necessary be easy to clean and disinfect. Sufficient provision must be made for the removal and storage of food waste and other refuse. Refuse stores must be designed and managed in such a way as to enable them to be kept clean, and to protect against access by pests, and against contamination of food, drinking water, equipment or premises.

Refuse should be removed frequently and, depending on the size and type of business more than one collection/removal per week may be required.

> **HEALTH & SAFETY** Storage facilities must be kept in a clean condition and the waste protected from rodents or birds.

WATER SUPPLY

An adequate supply of potable water must be provided. Under normal circumstances water provided by national water supplier will meet this requirement. Where water is drawn from a private supply (i.e. well or bore hole) this will have to be of potable quality and meet the standards of the Water Supply Regulations 1991. Further information is available from the Environmental Health Department.

SUITABLE AND SUFFICIENT STORAGE OF FOOD

Refrigeration equipment for chilled, high-risk foods (storage or display) must be capable of maintaining suitable temperatures (e.g. below 8°C) and have sufficient capacity for the amount of food. Foods stores (dry goods, fruit and vegetables) should be ventilated to maintain cool and dry conditions. Ventilation may be provided by either mechanical or natural means. All foods should be stored above floor level to facilitate easy cleaning and pest control.

Frozen storage will depend on the type of business. Equipment must be capable of maintaining suitable temperatures and have sufficient storage capacity.

CHEF'S TIP For more detailed and authoritative advice you should refer to: Catering Guide Industry Guide to Good Hygiene Practice available from the Environmental Health Department.

Food safety and basic microbiology

The many threats to food safety can be linked directly to microorganisms, which are living cells that can only be seen with the aid of a microscope. We refer generically to microorganisms that cause disease as pathogens or pathogenic. Within the broad range of these are several major categories of foodborne pathogens which are the main concern for cooks and chefs. Each class of microbes presents a unique risk and hazard. Cooking and storage methods that deter one kind of pathogen may be useless against another different type. To maintain good culinary hygiene in the kitchen with a working understanding of the differences and similarities among microbes is crucial.

The foodborne pathogens that are known to us vary in size, shape and behaviour. The six groups that pose the greatest concern to chefs are listed below, but each has different risks and play critical roles in causing disease.

Parasitic worms

Tapeworm (Taenia) a common parasite of humans and animals

Parasitic worms are the largest of the foodborne pathogens. They can live for years and grow to dimensions that are clearly visible to the naked eye. They range from microscopic worms to worms that reach nine metres in length at the most extreme level. An associated illness with parasitic worms is *trichinellosis*. Roundworms, such as *Trichinella spiralis* are perhaps the most infamous foodborne worm, because of their ability to burrow into the muscles of pigs and other livestock, infecting people who eat the contaminated meat.

Trichinella worms can survive refrigeration, but sufficient freezing (−21°C for 82 hours) will kill the worms in meat. Safe cooking practices such as meat being cooked to 60°C and held at that temperature for 12 minutes will also kill this parasite. Wild **game** such as venison and boar is also susceptible to parasitic worms and should also be treated in the same way. Cold smoking and drying foods will not kill the parasitic worm.

Protists

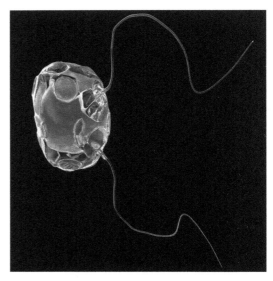

A Protist, single cell micro organism

This diverse group of single celled microorganisms includes varieties that are fungus based, plant based and animal based. Most animal based protists (or protozoa) are harmless but some species such as *Toxoplasma gondii* can be deadly.

Toxoplasma gondii usually infects rodents and the cats that eat them. The primary risk to humans comes by the way of faeces which contain the cysts of the parasite. In principle, we can become infected by eating meat from animals that have consumed oocysts, which then find their way into muscle tissue. However, cysts can also be shed from rodents and cats into water and soil, so vegetables can also become contaminated.

Refrigeration and most freezing will not kill this parasite in either meat or vegetables. However all vegetables need to be washed and peeled or just properly washed to help remove these cysts. Safe cooking of both vegetables and meat must be undertaken to ensure the killing of the parasite.

Bacteria

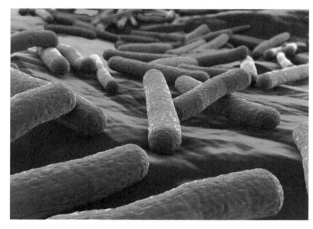

Escherichia coli bacteria is one of the most infamous forms of foodborne micro-organisms

Bacteria are single celled, resilient and highly adaptive microorganisms. They can cause foodborne illnesses in more ways than any other pathogen because they can multiply on food before consumption. Some associated illnesses are salmonellosis, listeriosis and other bacterial infections such as those caused by the *Escherichia coli* and *Campylobacter*.

Under the correct conditions, bacteria can multiply overnight by a factor of one thousand, one million or even one billion. They absorb **nutrients** from their environment and secrete chemicals back into it. Many species are able to travel under their own power too. The conditions required for bacteria to multiply are as follows:

- Time – bacteria can multiply or divide using binary fission every 10–20 minutes.

- Warmth – the optimum temperature for bacteria to multiply is 37°C; however the danger zone of bacterial multiplication is between 5°C and 63°C.

- Nutrients – protein rich foods such as meat, fish and dairy foods support the growth of bacteria. Foods with high concentrations of acid (vinegar), saline (salt) or sucrose (sugar) will limit the growth or prevent the growth of bacteria. This is why these ingredients are widely used as a form of preserving food.

- Moisture – bacteria requires the presence of moisture to support their multiplication. Even small amounts of water activity in foods (such as chocolate) can maintain the life of bacteria.

- Oxygen – some bacteria, known as aerobes need oxygen to multiply. Some bacteria only multiply when oxygen is not present and these are called anaerobes.

- pH – this scale of measurement determines how acid or alkaline a food or liquid may be. Bacterial growth is best sustained near the neutral reading of 7.0 and most bacteria cannot multiply at or below 4.0 because it is highly acidic.

TYPES OF BACTERIA THAT CAN CAUSE FOOD POISONING

Escherichia coli (E. coli)

Most varieties of E. coli bacteria are either beneficial or harmless. They live in the gastrointestinal tracts of humans and animals and are shed through faeces. However, specific strains of E. coli such as E. coli 0157:H7, which has been blamed for multiple foodborne outbreaks linked to contaminated milk, meat and produce such as spinach, will cause potentially life-threatening conditions, especially for young children or elderly adults. Good culinary hygiene practices, which include safe storage and cooking, can minimize the risk of infection.

Clostridium botulinum

This is commonly found in soil and grows best when oxygen and acid levels are low. This bacterium can form spores that survive in a dormant state until conditions improve. Botulism, although quite rare, can be a special concern for sous vide or canning processes that eliminate oxygen. If the procedure is undertaken incorrectly, the spores can germinate within the food. The resulting bacteria quickly multiply and produce a potent toxin that is among the most deadly known.

Clostridium perfringens

This bacterial species normally resides in the stomach of both humans and animals. Problems persist with infected poultry that has been stuffed inside with a traditional stuffing or **farce** that is then roast to the usual temperature guidelines. This means that the poultry will be cooked to a core (internal) temperature of 74°C. The high temperature will kill the bacteria, but it also encourages the germination in the centre of the stuffed poultry of spores, which will develop more toxin-producing bacteria. If the poultry is allowed to sit and rest for too long after the roasting process, bacteria from the germinated spores could produce toxins that will cause food poisoning to people who consume it. This is also true if the poultry is refrigerated whole, because the centre of the poultry could take hours to cool down.

Bacillus cereus

This is a foodborne bacterial pathogen which is anaerobic – it can live with or without oxygen. This microbe is found largely in soil, dust and on dried grains and beans. Although the application of heat kills this bacterium quite easily, the spores of this species are highly resistant to heat and they become even harder to kill in the presence of fats and oils. This pathogen creates two different toxins: the first is a compound that causes diarrhoea and is slow to act and the second is known for causing nausea and vomiting. This pathogen is commonly associated with the batch cooking of rice, cooling it too slowly and then reheating it, causing the spores to activate and develop toxins.

Salmonella

There are over 2000 types of Salmonella; the most common varieties are *Salmonella enteriditis* and *Salmonella typhimurium*. These organisms survive in the intestine and can cause food poisoning by releasing a toxin on the death of the cell. The primary source of salmonella is the intestinal tract of animals and poultry. It will therefore be found in:

- human and animal excreta;
- excreta from rats, mice, flies and cockroaches;
- raw meat and poultry;
- some animal feed.

Staphylococcus aureus

About 40–50 per cent of adults carry this organism in their nose, mouth, throat, ears and hands. If present in food, *Staphylococcus aureus* will produce a toxin which may survive boiling for 30 minutes or more. The majority of outbreaks are caused by poor hygiene practices, which result in direct contamination of the food from sneezing or uncovered septic cuts and abrasions. Frequently, the cooked food has been handled whilst still slightly warm, and these storage conditions have encouraged the organism to produce its toxin.

Campylobacter jejuni

This is found in raw meat and poultry and symptoms include diarrhoea, vomiting, stomach pains and cramps, fever and generally feeling unwell. Mushrooms and shellfish can also be contaminated but this is unusual. Avoid storing raw and cooked foods together and don't use the same work surfaces, or utensils when preparing raw and cooked food. You can also contract campylobacter from infected pets and other animals.

Listeria monocytogenes

Listeriosis, the foodborne illness caused by listeria, is relatively rare but listeria causes more deaths from food poisoning in the UK than other foodborne bugs. Vulnerable groups of the population are at increased risk. It multiplies slowly at low temperatures (below 5°C) and it is linked with chilled products such as unpasteurized cheese, paté and prepared salads.

SPOILAGE BACTERIA

Not all bacteria in food are dangerous. Spoilage bacteria produce liquids and gases that inform us that food has become rotten. Vegetables and fruit may become slimy or mushy,

whereas meat usually begins to smell and feel slimy. With a few exceptions, humans rarely become sick from spoilage bacteria. Food in which spoilage bacteria has been very active, however, is likely to be contaminated with other bacteria that are pathogenic and can render illness very quickly in humans.

> **CHEF'S TIP** Although spoilage and pathogenic bacteria often contaminate food simultaneously, do not assume that the absence of spoilage bacteria means the absence of pathogens.

Some bacteria emit chemicals to prevent their counterparts from sharing their food source. These chemicals are usually acids and alcohol that they can tolerate but their competitors cannot. However, chefs can use this feature to their advantage to prepare fermented foods to which the emitted chemicals provide flavour and texture such as yoghurt, kimchi and sourdough.

Kimchi is a Korean traditional fermented radish, Napa cabbage and vegetable dish that has been fermented in large Kimchi pots

TOXINS AND SPORES

Many bacteria produce harmful toxins. Infectious bacteria secrete those toxins inside your body, where chemicals cause various forms of cellular damage that can make you ill. Toxin production is typical of anaerobic pathogens such as *Clostridium*, but aerobic bacteria can also release poisons. One such pathogen is *Staphylococcus aureus* which also grows on human skin. This bacterium taints food with the toxin that it secretes. The illness that results from this and other foodborne toxins is known as food poisoning.

Because the toxins are already present, food poisoning is characterized by an abrupt onset of symptoms. Commonly, if susceptible food is left at room temperature and long enough for bacteria to multiply and produce toxins, dangerous levels of bacteria and their toxins can accumulate, sometimes even in refrigerated food.

In some instances bacterial toxins can be susceptible to heat and will break down at high temperatures. However, other bacterial toxins tolerate heat very well unless excessive temperatures are used to heat food. Anaerobic bacteria have responded to a fundamental challenge to their survival by evolving the ability to form bacterial spores. The microbe grows a cocoon-like protective covering that encases the dormant bacteria, shielding it from oxygen, dehydration and other potentially lethal environmental conditions. By forming spores, bacteria can hide for a long time until conditions improve.

Bacterial spores are problematic in the kitchen environment because they are much harder to kill than normal bacteria. Because most spoilage bacteria are aerobic, we have developed many methods of preserving food for long periods of time by limiting the food's contact with oxygen. For example, a layer of fat seals oxygen out of a traditional French duck **confit**. An airtight seal is also fundamental to canning food and more recently the concept has been expanded to include cooking sous vide.

However, there can be an unfortunate consequence because these processes improve the growing conditions for anaerobic bacteria, which makes the food more susceptible to contamination by bacterial spores. Because spores can survive heat and other measures that usually kill bacteria, fully cooked food can be full of possible spores. If spore contaminated food is eaten quickly after preparation and cooking, the still dormant spores are unlikely to cause any food poisoning. But if the spores are allowed time to revert into active bacteria, they can quickly reproduce and produce toxins.

BACTERIAL GROWTH

The ability of bacteria to grow if food is improperly handled makes pathogenic bacteria particularly dangerous. One of the principle objectives in food safety is taking measures when food is stored, prepared, cooked and served to prevent this kind of rapid bacterial replication.

Bacterial growth rates depend strongly on temperature and below a critical threshold, bacteria will not reproduce. The same perspective works for bacteria growth above the upper temperature threshold, where most bacteria will be killed. These critical temperatures vary for different species and environmental conditions. Some bacteria will begin to multiply at just above freezing point, although it will be at a slower pace. Bacteria will often begin to grow at temperatures between 3°C and 12°C. As the temperature rises above that range, bacterial reproduction generally accelerates until it reaches its maximum.

Foodborne pathogens typically reach their optimal reproductive rate at between 37°C (the normal body temperature of humans) and 43°C. The pH of food can greatly affect bacterial reproduction. Most bacteria multiply fastest in foods that have a pH near 6.8 (close to the neutral value of 7.0 as previously stated), but they can reproduce in acidic foods with a pH value as low as 4.0 and in alkaline foods with a pH value as high as 8.0.

The concentration of salt, sugar and alcohol also influence bacterial reproduction. Raising the concentrations of these elements lowers the water activity in the food, which can impede bacterial growth. This explains why syrup, molasses and salted meats can be stored with little or no refrigeration. Even though sugar can provide a food source for many bacteria, its concentration in syrup, for example, is so high that they cannot take advantage of it. Very dry foods, because of their low water content are also a poor source for bacterial growth.

> **CHEF'S TIP** Water molecules in a solution are often bound to other molecules that have been dissolved in the water. This makes them unavailable to participate in other chemical reactions or for freezing or drying purposes. Water activity is a measure of the amount of free water, which is not bound to other molecules.

Pathogenic foodborne bacteria stop reproducing below a certain minimum temperature and above a specific maximum temperature. The pH of the food also places limits on bacterial multiplication. The chart opposite shows the tolerances and indicates non-growth for different species of bacteria.

SPECIES	LOWER TEMPERATURE LIMIT	UPPER TEMPERATURE LIMIT	FASTEST GROWTH RANGE	LOWER PH LIMIT	UPPER PH LIMIT
Bacillus cereus	4°C	55°C	28–40°C	4.3	9.3
Campylobacter jejuni	30°C	45°C	37–43°C	4.9	9.5
Clostridium botulinum Type A	10°C	48°C	30–40°C	4.6	9.0
Clostridium perfringens	10°C	52°C	43–47°C	5.0	9.0
Escherichia coli	6°C	50°C	35–40°C	4.0	9.0
Listeria monocytogenes	−1°C	45°C	30–37°C	4.4	9.4
Salmonella	5°C	47°C	35–37°C	3.7	9.5
Staphylococcus aureus	7°C	50°C	35–40°C	4.0	10.0

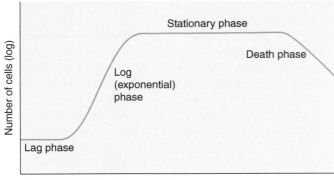

The bacterial growth curve graph

Bacteria display a characteristic four-phase pattern of growth. The initial lag phase is a period of slow growth during which the bacteria are adapting to the conditions in their new environment. This is followed by a log phase during which growth is exponential, doubling every replication cycle. A stationary phase occurs when the nutrients become limiting and the rate of multiplication equals the rate of death. Sometimes there may also be competition between different bacteria for survival. Decline (death) phase occurs when cells die faster than they are replaced. It is noted that this occurs over a much longer period of time that the previous three phases.

DESTROYING BACTERIA

When environmental conditions become lethal, bacteria will begin to die, slowly at first and then with increasing speed as conditions worsen. In the kitchen, high temperatures provide the primary means of killing bacteria. Refrigeration and freezing will slow or stop the reproduction of most bacteria, but it does not kill them.

However, in order to kill bacteria, reaching the critical temperature zone is not enough. Another vital element is time. Time is important because killing bacteria is a gradual process. A technique of sanitizing food through the application of heat was invented by Louis Pasteur. The concept of *pasteurization* was developed initially as a technique for the storage of wine and beer.

Sterilization is another widely used term. This technique is assumed to kill all microorganisms; but it does not always eradicate all bacteria. More often, the heat treatment is designed to kill the most dangerous pathogens, but spare other kinds of bacteria.

The combination of temperature and time required to kill approximately 90 per cent of a bacterial population depends on several factors:

- The type of bacteria present because heat tolerance varies among species.

- The pH and presence of salt or other additives.

- The presence of fats or proteins. Fats can either shield bacteria from the heat or make them more sensitive to increasing temperatures.

Because the rate at which bacteria are killed rises with the increased application of temperature, 15 minutes may be needed to kill 90 per cent of them at a temperature of 54°C, whereas only a few seconds are required to kill them at a temperature of 100°C.

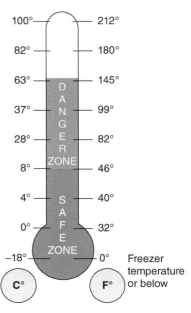

Boiling point for sterilizing equipment/utensils.

Final rinse temperature for dishwashers (82–88°C)

Temperature to keep food warm once cooked.

Do not leave raw or cooked items at room temperature as bacteria and micro organisms rapidly multiply.

Fridges–air temperature at 8°C or below

Freezer temperature or below

The temperature danger zone chart

Viruses

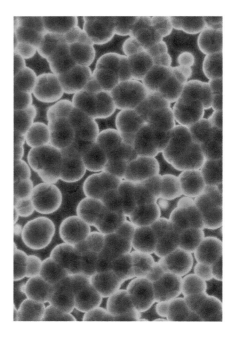

Viruses have genes that are composed of DNA and these microorganisms can evolve in the same way as other life forms. However, they cannot grow or reproduce beyond the confines of the cells that they infect. A single group, the noroviruses, causes a major amount of foodborne illnesses in the western world.

Viruses are extremely small and are only visible with the use of a microscope. They can multiply only within living cells and not on food, although they can be transferred into the stomach via being attached to food. Illness is linked to gastroenteritis and foodborne hepatitis.

Many viruses specialize in infecting human cells. Unlike bacteria, which can sometimes benefit humans, no natural human viruses are known to be beneficial. Nearly all viruses that cause foodborne illness are specialized to live in humans and do not infect plants or animals. Viruses also differ from bacteria by the way they are killed. Because viruses do not live and evolve in the same way as bacteria, we cannot kill them, but deactivate the viral pathogens instead. Refrigeration or freezing does not assist this process but the application of heat can help.

NOROVIRUSES

The highly infectious noroviruses multiply only within the cells of their hosts (i.e. humans). However, they can live in the environment, such as shellfish beds, until consumed. The necessity of good kitchen hygiene and ensuring that sick employees stay at home is the means to keeping this virus away from food contamination, because a large proportion of all outbreaks of the norovirus are due to infected food handlers.

The norovirus can often resist disinfection attempts but the risk can be minimized by carefully washing fruits and vegetables before and after preparation. The correct cooking of shellfish and cleaning potentially infected surfaces with sanitizer or bleach is also important. Hands should always and frequently be carefully washed.

Plasmids

Plasmids are strands of DNA that supplement a microbe's normal set of genes. The DNA strands can often move from one cell to another. The plasmids that reside in bacteria create the power of that bacterium to cause disease, reside in a new environment or resist antibiotics. Associated illnesses can be shigellosis and also infection from *E. coli* 0157:H7.

Prions

Prions are the simplest pathogens known. They are infectious proteins that can change normal bodily proteins into misshapen versions that create disease. These can cause rare foodborne illnesses that eventually prove fatal. Associated illnesses are Creutzfeldt–Jakob disease, bovine spongiform encephalopathy (BSE) or scrapie (a disease found in sheep that is similar to BSE).

BSE (or mad cow disease) is still not officially understood, as to where its origins lay. However, one strong hypothesis is that cattle were given feed that included the ground-up carcasses of sheep that had been infected with scrapie, which fuelled a cycle of animal infections.

High and low risk foods

Some foods support the rapid growth of bacteria better than others and these are often termed as 'high-risk' foods.

High-risk foods

High-risk foods can be defined as 'any ready-to-eat food that will support the growth of pathogenic bacteria easily and do not require any further heat treatment or cooking'. These types of foods are more likely to be implicated as vehicles of food poisoning organisms consumed in food poisoning incidents. Such foods are usually high in protein, require strict temperature control and protection from contamination and include:

- cooked meat and poultry such as beef, pork, ham, lamb, chicken, turkey, duck;

- cooked meat products such as meat pies and pasties, pate, meat **stock** and gravy, cook-chill meals;

- dairy produce such as milk, **cream**, artificial cream, custards, products containing unpasteurized milk, ripened soft and moulded cheeses;

- egg products such as cooked eggs, quiche and products containing uncooked or lightly cooked eggs, for example mayonnaise, mousses and ice cream;

- shellfish and other seafood such as mussels, cockles, cooked prawns, raw oysters;

- farinaceous dishes including cooked rice, pasta, couscous.

Low-risk foods

Low-risk foods are ambient-stable, such as bread, biscuits, cereals, crisps and cakes (not cream cakes). Such foods are unlikely to be implicated in food poisoning and include:

- foods that have been preserved, for example; smoked or salted fish;

- dry goods, those that contain minimal amounts of moisture, such as flour, biscuits;

- acidic foods, for example pickled foods, vinegar, fruit;

- fermented products such as **salami**, pepperoni and Kimchi;

- foods with high sugar/fat content for example jam and chocolate;

- tinned food, whilst unopened.

The preservation of food

Food preservation is the process of treating and handling food to stop or slow down spoilage (loss of quality, edibility or nutritional value) and thus allow for longer storage. The deterioration of food may be caused by exposure to moulds, enzymes, yeasts, bacteria, moisture, oxygen and chemicals. The preservation of food can also retard the oxidation of fats which cause rancidity. Food preservation can also include processes which inhibit visual deterioration that can occur during food preparation; such as the enzymatic browning reaction in apples after they are cut.

Preservation processes include:

- heating to kill or denature microorganisms (e.g. boiling, UHT, sterilization and pasteurization);

- oxidation (e.g. use of sulfur dioxide);

- toxic inhibition (e.g. smoking, use of carbon dioxide, vinegar, alcohol and salt concentrations);

- dehydration (drying);

- osmotic inhibition (e.g. use of syrups);

- low temperature inactivation (e.g. freezing and refrigeration);

- combinations of these methods.

CHEF'S TIP Enzymatic browning is a chemical process, involving polyphenol oxidase, catechol oxidase and other enzymes that create melanins and benzoquinone, resulting in a brown colour. Enzymatic browning generally requires exposure to oxygen. For example the browning that occurs when an apple is cut. Enzymatic browning can be beneficial for:

- developing flavour in tea;

- developing colour and flavour in dried fruit, such as figs and raisins.

Enzymatic browning is often detrimental to fresh, fruit and vegetables, including apples, potatoes and bananas.

Storage of food

The correct storage of food will protect it against contamination, deterioration and damage. In the UK we throw away 8.3 million tonnes of food and drink annually and most of this could have been safely consumed. For food to remain in the best condition and be safe to eat it is important that the correct storage system is utilized and procedures are recognized and followed by the kitchen team. Documentation procedures are required to be completed for all food deliveries in line with food safety management systems. This will help to ensure that food is delivered and stored correctly. Only approved suppliers should be used and they should consistently distribute their food supplies in the best condition, in suitable protective packaging, correctly date coded and always at the correct temperature.

The supervisor should always ensure that the following procedures are carried out when receiving food supplies:

- Create a HACCP food management system to examine the point of food delivery and storage. It should cover the receiving of goods where the core temperatures and condition of the delivery is thoroughly checked.

- Use a calibrated food probe to check the temperature of all food deliveries. Chilled food should be delivered at or below 5°C and frozen foods at −18°C or below.

- Check to see if the supplier will supply a printout of the temperature at which the food was delivered and maintain these for your kitchen records.

- Fresh meat that has been delivered should have a core temperature of a maximum of 8°C.

- All fresh produce should be delivered in unbroken, clean packaging and in clean delivery vehicles that are refrigerated.

- If you suspect a delivery has not met the requirements of your HACCP it should be refused and returned immediately to the supplier. A goods inwards sheet showing the company, invoice number, core temperature, any problems and how they were dealt with allows received goods to be monitored.

After the commodity has been received it needs to be correctly and quickly stored. Raw meat and fish should be stored and covered in separate refrigerators at 4°C. If there is not enough capacity for two separate refrigeration systems, *cooked products must be stored above fresh meat*. Fish should be stored as low in the refrigerator as possible. This is the coldest part of the refrigerator and a layer of crushed ice will help to keep the temperature down. This method eliminates cross-contamination from storage and optimizes quality. All foods should be labelled with the date of delivery/production, a description of the contents and the recommended use by date.

THE USE OF CLING FILM IN THE KITCHEN

It is safe to use cling film as long as it is used correctly. The Food Standards Agency (FSA) has produced advice on using cling film safely. They have also made recommendations to manufacturers on labelling their products to help use them properly. The FSA's advice is that not every type of cling film is suitable for all uses. To protect the quality and taste of food and make sure cling film is used correctly, it is important not to:

- use cling film where it could melt into the food (e.g. in conventional ovens or with pots and pans on cooker hobs);
- allow cling film to touch the food when re-heating or cooking it in a microwave oven;
- use cling film in contact with high fat foods unless the manufacturer's advice says it is suitable for this (e.g. blind baking pastry with cling film).

High fat foods include:

- some types of cheese;
- raw meats with a layer of fat;
- fried meats;
- pastry products;
- cakes with butter **icing** or chocolate coatings.

Plastic food contact materials are regulated by the European Commission Directive 2002/72/EC as amended. The directive controls the substances used in plastic food contact materials and sets out conditions for using them. The directive applies throughout Europe and its rules are included in UK food law. Independent expert committees have examined the plasticizers used in cling film. Where necessary, restrictions have been introduced to protect public health.

When using cling film to protect foods from cross contamination and drying out, it seals in moisture and maintains temperature, and can therefore encourage the growth of moulds and bacteria. Do not leave the cling film wrapped or covered foods in any direct light or heat source.

STORING FOOD IN A REFRIGERATOR

Chilled and high-risk foods need to be kept in a refrigerator to help stop or slow bacterial growth.

- Keep food covered to protect it from cross contamination from raw foods and physical objects.
- Wherever possible, store raw meat and poultry in refrigerators just for meat and poultry storage running at temperatures between 1°C and 4°C. Some butchers refrigerated units will operate between the temperatures of −1°C and 1°C.
- If the raw meat and poultry is not already packaged, place onto clean trays and cover well with plastic film and label correctly.
- If it is necessary to store raw meat and poultry in a multi-use refrigeration unit you should ensure that is covered, labelled and placed below cooked items and salads away from all other items. This will eliminate the risk of contamination from bacteria and blood through spillage.
- Do not store food in open cans because when a can has been opened and the food is open to oxygen, the tin will begin to deteriorate might transfer metal contamination to the can's contents.
- Do not overstock the refrigerator as this will decrease the airflow around the food.
- Do not put hot food into a refrigerator as this will raise the internal temperature of the unit and place other foods at risk from poor temperature control. Always place hot foods in blast chilling cabinets to quickly and effectively reduce the core temperature of the food item.
- A specific fresh fish refrigerator is preferable, running between the temperatures of 1°C and 4°C. Remove all fish from ice containers and place onto clean trays, cover with plastic film and label. If the fish is to be stored in a multi-use refrigerated unit, ensure that it is stored away from other foods and at the bottom of the refrigerator. Odours from fish or other strong smelling ingredients can permeate other food items such as cream, milk and eggs.
- Dairy products such as pasteurized milk, cream and cheese should be stored in their original containers in a refrigerator at between 1°C and 4°C. Eggs should be stored separately from other food items and maintained at refrigeration temperature until required for use. Always ensure that the shells of the egg do not come into contact with other foods.

STORING FOOD IN A FREEZER

You can keep food safely in the freezer as long as it has stayed frozen the whole time; however, the taste and texture of food changes if it has been frozen for too long. Check instructions on food labels or in the freezer's handbook to see how long food should be frozen.

It should be fine to freeze most raw or cooked foods providing you undertake the following procedures:

● Freeze food items before the 'use by' date.

● Follow any freezing or thawing instructions on the label.

● Defrost frozen food required for use in a refrigerator. Ensure that the food has been defrosted completely with no sign of ice crystallization on the food.

● Ensure food is thoroughly defrosted before cooking food. Always allow enough time for the food item to be fully defrosted.

When defrosting frozen meat, poultry and fish, the items may produce excess water. This raw liquid can spread bacteria to other food items, equipment or kitchen surfaces that it touches. Keep the defrosting items in a sealed container at the bottom of the refrigerator, so that it cannot touch or drip onto other foods. Never allow food to be re-frozen once it has been thawed.

STORAGE OF DRY GOODS

Many types of food do not need to be kept in the refrigerator to maintain food safety. For example dry uncooked foods such as rice, pasta and flour, tinned foods, and unopened jars. But it is still important to maintain care whilst in storage.

● Store food in sealed bags or containers. This helps to keep them fresh and stops anything falling into the food.

● Do not store food or beverages near cleaning products or other chemicals.

● Do not use old food containers to store household chemicals, nor store food in containers that have been used for other purposes.

● Do not store food items directly on the floor, because this can encourage mice, ants and other pests.

● Remember that some types of food might need to be kept in a refrigerator once opened – follow any storage instructions on the label.

Ambient stores should be clean and well ventilated, with wire mesh over windows and doors to help with pest control. Doors should be protected with metal kick plates and a plastic curtain to help prevent pests from entering. All foodstuffs must be stored away from the floor, away from direct sunlight from windows and be rotated on a first in and first out basis. Shelving and racking must be produced from non-corrosive, easy cleaning materials and the shelving should be deep enough to store items adequately.

CANNED FOOD

Cans are usually stored in the dry store area and the rotation of stock system should always be used. Canned food will have best before dates shown on the label. Check regularly for 'blown', badly dented, split or rusted cans as these will have been contaminated and should not be used. Once the contents of the can have been opened, any unused food items should be transferred to a clean bowl, covered and labelled and stored in a refrigerator for 48 hours.

● *Use by dates* are found on food that deteriorates quickly, for example, smoked fish, meat products and ready-prepared salads. You should not use any food or beverage after the end of the 'use by' date on the label, even if it looks and smells fine. For the 'use by' date to be a valid guide, you must carefully follow the storage instructions on the packaging or label. 'Use by' does not always mean 'eat by'.

● *Best before dates* are found on a wide range of frozen, dried, tinned and other foods. The 'best before' dates are more concerned with quality as opposed to food safety, except for fresh eggs. When the 'best before' date is exceeded it does not mean that the food will be harmful, but it might begin to lose its quality, flavour and texture. However, you should not consume fresh eggs after the 'best before' date. Remember, the 'best before' date will only be accurate if the food is stored according to the instructions on the label.

HEALTH & SAFETY Check 'use-by' dates on a regular basis and throw out food that has expired using the stock rotation system of 'first in, first out'.

QUICK FOOD STORAGE GUIDE AND TEMPERATURES

● **Raw meat, poultry and game and charcuterie:** 4°C or below. Store away from cooked meat and cooked meat products to avoid any risk of cross-contamination.

● **Cooked meat:** 4°C or below. Keep away from raw meat and meat products.

- **Uncooked fish:** 4°C or below. Keep in separate compartments or in plastic fish trays with lids if possible, and away from other foods which may become tainted.

- **Frozen food:** −18°C or below. Thaw only immediately prior to using the commodity.

- **Fish (smoked or cured):** 8°C or below. Keep in chilled storage away from other foods, which may become tainted.

- **Fruit (fresh and dried):** Store in a cool, dry, well-ventilated area, away from other food, at least 15 cm from the ground. Discard at the first sign of mould growth. Do not overstock.

- **Pasta, rice and cereals:** Store in self-closing tightly lidded containers in dry cool storeroom or cupboard.

- **Eggs:** Refrigerate at 8°C or below. Use strictly in rotation and ensure the shells are clean.

- **Fats, butter, dairy and non-dairy spreads:** 8°C or below. Keep covered and away from highly flavoured food, which may taint.

- **Milk and cream:** 8°C or below. In a separate dairy refrigerator that is used for no other purpose and in strict rotation.

- **Canned and bottled goods:** Cool, dry, well-ventilated storage area. Blown, rusty, heavily dented or split tins must not be used.

- **Root vegetables:** Store in sacks or nets as delivered in cool, well-ventilated area.

- **Leaf and green vegetables:** 8°C. Use on day of delivery if at all possible.

Freezers, whether upright, walk-in or chest freezers, should be maintained at a maximum temperature of −18°C.

HEALTH & SAFETY All food should be covered to prevent freezer burn and labelled with the date of production and a use by date.

The first in – first out (FIFO) system

MONDAY

Item: _____

Date: _____ Time: _____ ☐ AM ☐ PM

Use
By: _____ Time: _____ ☐ AM ☐ PM

Emp: _____ Mgr: _____

Example of a date labelling system

All food items need to be rotated to ensure that the oldest items in storage are used first. The first in – first out (FIFO) method of rotation is used to ensure that all food products are properly rotated in storage.

The FIFO method uses these principles:

1 New items move to the back and on the bottom.

2 Older items move to the front and the left.

3 In any part of the kitchen, the first item used should always be the oldest.

4 Date and mark everything in storage.

Any chef using the FIFO method of food rotation system needs to use food labels. Labelling reduces spoilage and food costs when products are dated correctly and team members become accountable for managing food storage and preparation systems.

Preparing, cooking and holding food safely

Preparation of food

Frozen food should be defrosted in a refrigerator and treated as fresh food with the same use by date. All root vegetables must be washed prior to peeling and then rewashed after peeling. Leaf vegetables such as cabbage and spinach should be washed in several changes of cold, clean water to allow soil and grit to go to the bottom of the sink. Ideally a separate preparation area should be facilitated to help prevent cross-contamination.

Food should not be prepared too far in advance of the cooking process. If food is prepared significantly ahead of the cooking time, various control measure of storage should be applied to ensure that the food remains safe. The food preparation area should ideally be separated from the cooking area.

Using a hygiene strategy for everything in the kitchen including personal hygiene, cooking equipment, food surfaces, cutting boards and knives is important. For many kitchen surfaces and tools, a diluted chlorine (bleach) solution is a good sanitizer used at a ratio of 1:100 dilution with water.

Sometimes crowded conditions in the kitchen prevent you from using separate kitchen areas to carry out delicate food preparation, processing and handling procedures that invite cross contamination. In this case, the supervisor should isolate the procedures in time instead. Do not separate cooked meat into portions next to another chef who might be butchering raw meat, so pick another time during the shift pattern to undertake the cooked food portioning.

Chilling food not for immediate use should ideally be achieved in blast chillers where the core temperature is brought down from 70°C to 4°C in 90 minutes or less. With these temperature ranges both pathogenic and bacterial growth is inhibited although not completely stopped.

> **HEALTH & SAFETY** The correct measurement of temperature should be monitored by the use of an accurate digital food thermometer. The probe is inserted into the centre of meat joints or placed onto the surface of other ingredients to give a temperature reading within a few seconds. Alcohol-based sanitizer wipes should be used to clean the stainless steel probe after every use to prevent cross-contamination.

Cooking of food and temperature measurement

As explained earlier in this chapter, high temperature is one of the best measures to ensure that bacteria in food is destroyed, and a clear recommendation of 75°C as a core temperature to be held for a minimum of two minutes is given by the FSA. However, as the chef strives to produce good food with flavour and texture, this temperature aim may be too high and the preference might be for lower temperatures of cooking to be activated.

The avoidance of undercooked dishes when cooking for groups of people who are the most vulnerable to the effects of food poisoning should be maintained. The use of temperature probes to check core temperatures of food during and after cooking is important. The probe must be regularly calibrated and if a long probe is used, this must be disinfected with each use.

Most digital food probes are rapid response instruments, but they are not instantaneous. It takes any temperature probe a certain amount of time to reach the *equilibrium temperature*. There are two techniques to obtain an equilibrium temperature:

● wait at least ten seconds, then record the reading.

● observe the digital display until a constant temperature reading is obtained.

Supervisors or kitchen staff, who are expected to produce good temperature data must regularly check their instrument for good performance. Digital probes do not ordinarily 'lose' their calibration unless physically damaged or used for extended periods of time in an industrial or commercial setting. Sometimes a probe can begin to break down gradually, so it is impossible to know if you have good readings without undertaking some effort to determine if the readings are correct. You can test a digital thermometer for yourself or send it back to the manufacturer for a traceable and documented calibration. In order to check calibration a simple test can be performed:

Use some distilled water and make ice cubes out of half of the water. Take the cubes out of the freezer and crush them in a blender with the remaining distilled water. Using the tip of the digital probe as a stirring rod, stir the mixture as vigorously as you possibly can. The probe should read *at the extreme* within ± 1.2°C of the true freezing point 32.0°F or 0°C. Please note: this does not mean that the digital probe has this much error in normal use, it is just a practical range to use with a non-laboratory procedure to check the general function of the unit.

If the unit measures outside of these limits (high or low), the digital probe has a calibration problem. It is likely to get worse rather than better so you should not use the probe. If it is inside these limits, it is undoubtedly still sound, so you can proceed and use with confidence.

Low battery power will not affect the accuracy of the digital probe. The first sign you may see is that the display is somewhat weak. If you have a weak display, it is a good idea to replace the battery immediately. Many digital units will give you a battery warning before low battery power affects the accuracy of your reading.

The digital probe will reflect accurate temperatures in the vicinity of the tip for a radius of about five centimetres (two inches) if used for probing meats, dairy products and other high-density commodities. In order to obtain a good reading, therefore, it is important to penetrate the surface of the product by a depth exceeding the radius of measurement. Information from scientific studies has shown that this 5 cm radius is a good rule to follow.

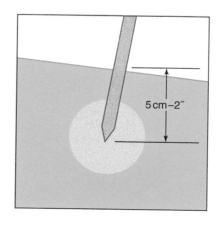

In a refrigerated product in a storage situation, there is very little likelihood that there are substantial variations in core temperature of the stored product, so a single penetration below the 5 cm depth is a good rule to follow for general temperature monitoring.

However, if the product has been in transit, moved from one refrigerated regime to another by a supplier, or is being handled frequently; a single probe measurement may not be adequate. Again, scientific experience determines that we should use the 'rule of three'. Essentially, the rule of three is three specific measurements:

1 Measured at the surface.

2 Measured in the exact middle of the product.

3 Measured approximately one-third of the way into the product.

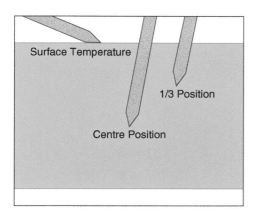

Three measurements of this type will function to answer the question: is this product relatively uniform in temperature? If the difference between any of the three measurements is greater than 1.5°C (3°F), then there is sufficient difference to take notice and not just be satisfied with a single core temperature reading. Anything less than this is probably insignificant and may be due to random variations.

When taking the surface temperature on whole meat, poultry, etc., it is important to apply substantial pressure so that the surface of the product is *compressed in and slightly around* the probe tip. Otherwise, surrounding air temperatures may bias the reading and create an error.

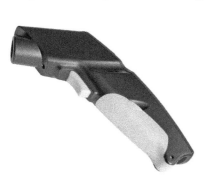

Noncontact infrared (IR) digital thermometer

Noncontact infrared (IR) digital thermometers use infrared technology to quickly and conveniently measure the surface temperature of objects. They provide fast temperature readings without physically touching the object. You simply aim, pull the trigger and read the temperature on the LCD display.

Lightweight and compact, IR thermometers can safely measure hot, hazardous or hard-to-reach surfaces without contaminating or damaging the object. Also, infrared thermometers can provide several readings per second, as compared to contact methods where each measurement can take several minutes. IR thermometers capture the invisible infrared energy naturally emitted from all objects. Infrared radiation is part of the electromagnetic spectrum which includes radio waves, microwaves, visible light, ultraviolet, gamma and X-rays.

The noncontact IR thermometer can be used to check more than just the temperature of food. It can also be used to evaluate the performance of specific kitchen equipment and machinery.

● Detect hot spots or leaks by taking sample spot readings of freezers, walk-in coolers, refrigeration and compressor motors.

● Safely check the temperature and performance of ovens, ranges, rotisseries, deep fryers and dishwashers.

● Check clean dishes immediately after washing to ensure that high enough temperature levels were achieved in the dishwasher for sanitation purposes.

Temperature data loggers automate the process of monitoring temperature. If the temperatures that you need to take and record are of a cold room, freezer room, transit container, refrigerator, cooking vat, chiller bath, sous vide bath or any other type of temperature environment that is supposed to stay at a constant temperature or go through a pre-determined temperature regime temperature data loggers are more consistent to use.

Loggers record the data automatically and store it in an internal memory. This information can be displayed, printed or just simply stored by connecting the logger to an output device, usually a PC computer.

HOLDING FOOD

Food products that are ready to be served or sold and are located in holding or serving areas must be kept out of the temperature danger zone which is 5°C to 63°C.

● Cold holding – with a digital thermometer, quickly verify that the temperature of products held in open-top refrigeration units, such as fresh meat or fish displays, cold **buffets** or preparation units, do not exceed 5°C. Ensure that adequate records are held and check that any food kept above 8°C for four hours on any one occasion is then thrown away after this period of time. This timescale of four hours also includes the preparation time.

● Hot holding – hot cooked, prepared foods that are kept in steam tables, warming ovens and other heated serving and holding areas should be carefully monitored to remain at 63°C or above. The use of a digital thermometer to check the internal temperatures of soups, sauces and other liquid foods by agitating them before reading. Ensure that all equipment used for keeping the food hot (e.g. bain-marie), is clean and pre-heated to the required temperature prior to placing the food in them. Use lids on any open containers to maintain the heat at all times. Hot food kept out of this temperature zone for more than two hours will need to be discarded.

● Cooling – improper cooling is a major cause of foodborne illness. After food has been cooked to be served cold, use a digital thermometer to confirm that food is reduced to an appropriate temperature, from above 63 to 8°C within 90 minutes. A blast-chiller is the most effective equipment to employ when rapidly chilling food. However, if this not available, food in containers can be plunged into iced-water baths or placed onto trays and surrounded with ice or ice packs.

For quick cooling of hot food items, certain methods can be employed to assist this process:

1 Stews, soups, sauces and stocks are to be placed into smaller, shallow containers as the increased surface area and less volume will allow the food to be cooled more quickly.

2 Pour light liquids such as stocks and **consommés** gradually through a large **chinois** or sieve lined with ice bags.

3 Smaller joints of meat should be cooked as these will cool quicker than larger joints.

● Reheating – the last important temperature related checkpoint is reheating. A digital thermometer can confirm that foods are being reheated to at least 75°C to destroy any bacteria caused by improper cooling or storage techniques. Reheated food should also be served quickly and never reheated more than once.

> **HEALTH & SAFETY** The Scottish FSA requires that a temperature of 82°C is reached for reheated food and the USA FDA requires 73.9°C.

HACCP and safe food assurance systems

HACCP is a widely accepted food safety management system, which can easily be adapted to suit all sizes and types of food businesses. The main aim of HACCP is to focus attention on critical points in the operation and to take measures to ensure that problems do not occur.

This section contains general advice only and this guidance is based on the Food Standard Agency's present understanding of the applicable law but it will be for the courts to provide a definitive interpretation of that law. This guidance is not a substitute for the text of relevant legislation which will continue to apply and it will remain the duty of food business proprietors to comply with that legislation.

Process steps

To understand HACCP based procedures, you should consider your catering operation as a sequence of process steps. The first step is the purchase of food, and the last step is serving it to your customers.

The following simplified diagram shows the process steps which may be involved in a typical catering business:

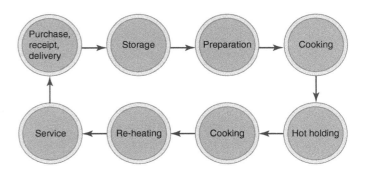

When setting up a new HACCP system it is important to consider the variety of controls and hazards that all require critical control points to be identified:

1 Suppliers should be approved and they should provide written specifications of their own HACCP procedures.

2 Traceability and sourcing – your suppliers should have systems in place to identify the sourcing of all food products and that they can be traceable back to the food producer. Sustainability is also an emerging and increasingly important issue that suppliers should be engaging with.

3 Food premises and equipment – all records should be maintained and an adequate flow diagram needs to be produced to show the process of delivery to service that eliminate any chances of cross-contamination.

4 Storage and stock control – effective stock control, including the rotation of stock and temperature controlled storage systems must be in place and accurately monitored.

5 Staff hygiene – to include toilets, hand-washing facilities, changing areas and protective clothing.

6   Pest control – a pest control policy with a pest management system. Sometimes this is outsourced to contractors.

7   Cleaning and disinfection – a documented system is in place which includes cleaning schedules.

8   Waste management – determining how waste removal will be effectively managed.

9   Staff training – records of all staff training with dates completed.

The seven principles of HACCP

Principle 1 – Conduct a Hazard Analysis
The application of this principle involves listing the steps in the process and identifying where significant hazards are likely to occur. The HACCP team will focus on hazards that can be prevented, eliminated or controlled by the HACCP plan. A justification for including or excluding the hazard is reported and possible control measures are identified.

Principle 2 – Identify the Critical Control Points
A critical control point (CCP) is a point, step or procedure at which control can be applied and a food safety hazard can be prevented, eliminated or reduced to acceptable levels. The HACCP team will use a CCP decision tree to help identify the critical control points in the process. A critical control point may control more that one food safety hazard or in some cases more than one CCP is needed to control a single hazard. The number of CCPs needed depends on the processing steps and the control needed to assure food safety.

Principle 3 – Establish Critical Limits
A critical limit (CL) is the maximum and/or minimum value to which a biological, chemical, or physical parameter must be controlled at a CCP to prevent, eliminate or reduce to an acceptable level the occurrence of a food safety hazard. The critical limit is usually a measure such as time, temperature, water activity (Aw), pH, weight or some other measure that is based on scientific literature and/or regulatory standards.

Principle 4 – Monitor CCP
The HACCP team will describe monitoring procedures for the measurement of the critical limit at each critical control point. Monitoring procedures should describe how the measurement will be taken, when the measurement is taken, who is responsible for the measurement and how frequently the measurement is taken during production.

Principle 5 – Establish Corrective Action
Corrective actions are the procedures that are followed when a variation in a critical limit occurs. The HACCP team will identify the steps that will be taken to prevent potentially hazardous food from entering the food chain and the steps that are needed to correct the process. This usually includes identification of the problems and the steps taken to assure that the problem will not occur again.

Principle 6 – Verification
Those activities, other than monitoring, that determine the validity of the HACCP plan and that the system is operating effectively according to the plan. The HACCP team may identify activities such as auditing of CCP's, record review, prior shipment review, instrument calibration and product testing as part of the verification activities.

Principle 7 – Recordkeeping
A key component of the HACCP plan is recording information that can be used to prove that food was produced safely. The records also need to include information about the HACCP plan. Records should include information on the HACCP Team, menus/recipes, flow diagrams, the hazard analysis, the CCPs identified, Critical Limits, Monitoring System, Corrective Actions, Recordkeeping Procedures and Verification Procedures.

HACCP DOES NOT STAND ALONE

The application of HACCP does not stand alone in a food processing facility. The plan must be built on other food safety programs. Good preparation and cooking routines that are practiced by the kitchen will support HACCP plan and will address food safety and food quality issues that are not critical for the reduction of food safety hazards.

Hazards

A hazard is anything which may cause harm to your customers through eating your food. A HACCP based approach to food safety requires you to identify all of the hazards at each process step in your catering business; this is called hazard analysis. It is at this point that you need to think about what could go wrong in your business or kitchen and then come up with measures that will prevent or control these hazards. There are three types of hazard:

Microbiological hazards include food poisoning bacteria such as *Salmonella*, *E. Coli* and *Bacillus cereus* which are hazardous because they can:

●   Survive inadequate cooking, if already present in food, for example, *Salmonella* in chicken.

●   Multiply to harmful levels in food given the right conditions, for example, poor temperature control during storage, handling or hot holding.

●   Spread from raw foods such as meat, poultry and unwashed vegetables to cooked foods either directly or via food handlers, work surfaces and equipment.

Other microbiological hazards such as certain bacteria, yeasts and moulds may also lead to food spoilage.

Chemical hazards may already be present on certain foods in the form of pesticides or insecticides. Chemical hazards may also arise from incorrect storage and the misuse of chemicals used in food premises such as cleaning chemicals and rodent baits.

Physical hazards include contamination by materials such as glass, plastic, wood, metal, hair and contamination caused by pests.

Control measures

Once you have identified your process steps and the hazards likely to occur, you must locate systems of preventing or controlling these hazards. The measures which you decide upon must make all of the hazards safe – these measures are known as control measures.

Control measures take many forms, for example:

HAZARD	CONTROL MEASURE
Survival of harmful bacteria which may cause food poisoning	Thorough cooking of foods
Spread of harmful bacteria which may cause food poisoning from raw food to cooked food	Careful handling practices such as keeping these foods apart at all times

CRITICAL CONTROL POINTS (CCPS)

A HACCP based approach to food safety helps you to focus attention on the issues which are critical to food safety. CCPs are the stages of your process where the hazards must be controlled for the food to be safe to eat. All hazards at CCPs must be reduced to a safe level or eliminated by a suitable control measure.

HEALTH & SAFETY

Critical control point (CCP) example 1: Cooling rice
If rice is cooled too slowly, it could give your customer food poisoning. In this example, *cooling* is a CCP.

Critical Control Point (CCP) example 2: Cooking a chicken breast from raw

If the chicken breast is undercooked, any harmful bacteria present in the meat will not be destroyed and the surviving bacteria could give your customer food poisoning. In this example, *cooking* is a CCP.

CRITICAL LIMITS

Critical Limits are specified safety limits which you have established and measured against the CCPs.

Some examples are:

● If food is to be kept chilled and you have decided that the temperature of the refrigerator must be no higher than 5°C, then 5°C is the critical limit.

● If one of your methods of preventing cross contamination is the use of different coloured boards and knives bring used for different foods, then your critical limit in this case is for staff to always use the coloured boards and knives

correctly according to food safety guidelines and company policy.

MONITORING

A HACCP based approach to food safety requires that all control measures at CCPs must be monitored.

A monitoring example is the checking of the temperature of a refrigerator to ensure it is within its critical limit. In this instance, the control measure (to prevent bacterial growth) would be temperature control. If the critical limit has been set at 5°C, the purpose of monitoring would be to check that the critical limit of 5°C has been met.

Certain control measures may have critical limits which cannot be easily measured in the way that temperatures can.

The correct use of differently coloured equipment for different purposes is one way of providing the control measure for hazards such as cross contamination. In this case, the most effective monitoring would be as follows: supervision of staff to ensure that they follow the cross contamination prevention kitchen policy.

RECORDS

A requirement of a HACCP based system is that monitoring is recorded at a frequency that reflects the nature and size of the catering business. The supervisor or manager may wish to record the monitoring by designing forms, recording electronically or by the use of a diary. In such cases the supervisor should ensure that the record keeping arrangements are sufficient for the size and nature of your business.

Monitoring which only involves supervision may simply require a supervisor or manager's signature to confirm that the actions have been carried out. HACCP Records must be retained for an appropriate period of time to enable you to demonstrate that your system is working effectively. Your Environment Health Officer can give guidance on this timeframe.

CORRECTIVE ACTION

If you monitor a control measure and find that it has failed to meet its critical limit, you must act to make the food safe or to prevent it being used. This is known as a corrective action. Corrective actions follow on from the monitoring process and must be recorded.

Corrective actions have two functions:

1 To deal with the food in question – either by making it safe or by stopping its use.

2 To prevent the problem happening again – by considering the cause of the failure of the control measure and taking appropriate action.

Corrective action examples:

● If the refrigerator temperature critical limit is 5°C but your monitoring check finds that the refrigerator is running at 12°C, then your corrective action could be to contact the maintenance engineer and consider if the food is safe to use.

● If your cross contamination critical limit is to keep raw and cooked foods separated but your monitoring check finds blood on the board to be used for chopping vegetables, then your corrective action could be to thoroughly clean and disinfect the chopping board, retrain and advise staff and dispose of affected food.

VERIFICATION

Verification involves taking an overview of your HACCP based system to ensure it is working. Verification also involves establishing that your procedures are effective in controlling hazards and checking to see that your procedures are being applied in practice.

Some types of verification examples can be:

● Checking that the control measures at CCPs are being consistently applied.

● Checking that the appropriate corrective actions have been taken.

● Checking that monitoring records are consistent and accurate.

● Checking that your procedures are still relevant and up to date.

DOCUMENTATION

A HACCP based system must have appropriate documentation to demonstrate it is working effectively. Documentation to support your HACCP based procedures must include details of your intentions in all the key areas mentioned throughout this section on HACCP.

Areas where hazards might occur

Receipt of goods	Contaminated high-risk foods Damaged or decomposed goods Incorrect specifications Growth of pathogens between the time of receipt and storage	All deliveries inspected and checked by a staff member Appropriate labelling Prompt and correct storage
Storage	Contamination of high-risk foods Contamination through poor handling Contamination by pests Spoilage of food by decomposition	Correct usage of refrigeration regimes Foods must be suitably stored in the correct packaging or receptacles Materials that are in direct contact with food must be of food-grade quality A contract for a pest control service must be in place Correct stock rotation Out of date and unfit food stuffs must be segregated from other foods and removed from the premises
Preparation	Contamination of high-risk foods Contamination through poor handling Growth of pathogens and toxins	Keep raw and cooked foods separate Use pasteurized eggs for raw and lightly cooked egg dishes All food contact surfaces must be fit for purpose Food handlers must be trained in hygienic food handling techniques Keep the exposure of fresh foods at ambient temperatures to a minimum Label all food that is to be used more than one day in advance of production with its description and use by date
Cooking	Survival of pathogens and spores	Cook all foods to the minimum recommended temperature
Chilling	Growth of pathogens, spores = toxin production Contamination	Cool foods as quickly as possible, to 8°C in 90 minutes Keep food that is chilling loosely covered Use only clean equipment
Hot hold	Growth of pathogens and toxin production Contamination by staff and customers, especially in self-service operations	Maintain food at 63°C and discard after two hours Keep containers covered when not in service Use sneeze screens Supervise self-service
Cold hold	Growth of pathogens and toxin production Contamination by staff and customers especially in self-service operations	Keep food at 5°C and discard after four hours Keep containers covered when not in service Use sneeze screens Supervize self-service

National Food Hygiene Rating scheme

The National Food Hygiene Rating scheme (the 'scores on the doors') is intended to give the public information about the hygiene standards in individual restaurants, pubs, cafes, takeaways, hotels and other places you eat out. Supermarkets and other food shops are also included in the scheme. This is a strategy run in partnership with the Food Standards Agency and local authorities to raise food safety standards and help reduce the incidence of food poisoning. The scheme is run by local authorities in England, Wales and Northern Ireland.

Each business is given a 'hygiene rating' when it is inspected by a food safety officer from the business's local authority. The hygiene rating shows how closely the business is meeting the requirements of food hygiene law.

A food business can be given a rating from 0 to 5. The food safety officer inspecting a business checks how well the business is meeting the law by looking at:

1 how hygienically the food is handled – how it is prepared, cooked, re-heated, cooled and stored;

2 the condition of the structure of the buildings – the cleanliness, layout, lighting, ventilation and other facilities;

3 how the business manages and records what it does to make sure food is safe.

At the end of the inspection, the business is given one of the six ratings. The top rating of '5' means that the business was found to have 'very good' hygiene standards. Any business should be able to reach this top rating.

The food safety officer will explain to the person who owns or manages the business what improvements are needed and how they can achieve the top rating of '5'. The local authority will check that these improvements are made.

Food allergies and intolerances

It is critical to be aware of the issues of food allergies and intolerance when preparing, cooking and serving certain foods.

An *allergy* to food is the hypersensitivity of food constituents. The immune system reacts to a particular food, believing it is not safe to eat. In severe circumstances this can cause a life-threatening reaction and that reaction can occur within a few minutes of exposure to the allergen. Typically the tongue, throat and lips begin to swell and feel itchy, with added vomiting and stomach cramps. In severe reactions, the person may have a lower blood pressure and blocked airways.

It is important to be aware that almost any food or substance can trigger an allergic reaction. There are potential foods such as sesame seeds, peanuts, eggs, dairy products, shellfish and wheat which are fairly common allergy foods.

An *intolerance* to food does not involve the immune system and is generally not life threatening. However, it can still make people ill and it may affect their long-term health.

The following are examples that the chef needs to be aware of:

● Lactose intolerance – a condition in which the body lacks the enzyme lactase and so cannot process lactose. Lactose is present in milk and dairy products.

● Coeliac disease – intolerance to gluten, a protein substance present in wheat, rye, barley and oat products.

● Peanuts and tree nuts – peanuts in particular can cause extreme reactions and even death. It is impossible for the chef to guarantee a nut-free diet to the guest.

● Eggs – intolerance to the proteins in egg whites or yolks, or sometimes both.

● Fish – fish allergies are more common in children than adults; even the smell can bring on a reaction in a sensitive person. Common fish known to cause symptoms are cod, salmon, trout, herring, bass, swordfish, halibut and tuna.

● Shellfish – reactions to the ingestion of shellfish can be severe, even at the level of inhalation of cooking vapours. Great care should be taken to avoid cross-contamination between shellfish products and all other foodstuffs that might be in contact with the diner. Shellfish commonly known to cause allergic reactions include shrimp, crab, crayfish, lobster, oysters, clams, scallops, mussels, squid and snails. People allergic to shrimp often suffer from respiratory allergy. Crab is also a potent allergen. Shrimp, lobster and crawfish contain common major allergens, making cross-reactivity between shrimp and crab, and lobster and crawfish possible.

HEALTH & SAFETY Any produce that may cause an allergic reaction should be stored in a sealed container, away from other foods and only used as required.

Another type of food intolerance is a reaction to certain products that are added to food to enhance taste, add colour or protect against the growth of microbes. Compounds such as **monosodium glutamate** (MSG) and sulfites are tied to reactions that can be confused with food allergy.

MSG is a flavour enhancer. When taken in large amounts, it can cause some of the following:

● flushing;

● sensations of warmth;

- headache;
- chest discomfort.

These passing reactions occur rapidly after eating large amounts of food to which MSG has been added.

Sulfites are found in food for several reasons:

- they have been added to increase crispness or prevent mold growth;
- they occur naturally in the food;
- they have been generated during the winemaking process.

Sulfites can cause breathing problems in people with asthma.

It is important that supervisors train their team in product knowledge and that each chef is fully aware of what ingredients make up each dish on a menu. It is important for the team to be aware of individual customer needs and therefore, should a customer enquire if a food or substance to which they are allergic is included in the recipe ingredients, staff give an accurate and clear answer.

Communicating effective food safety to your team

The effective planning of food safety is essential to ensure that high standards are maintained throughout and that there is strict compliance with the Food Safety Act 2006. The supervisor plays a key role in implementing and managing food safety procedures and is a crucial link between the owners, management and the food service operation. It is also likely that the supervisor will be involved in the planning, setting of standards and management of the day-to-day food safety procedures.

Effective communication of food safety issues to staff is very important and can be achieved through induction processes (for new staff), ongoing staff training that is updated frequently when needed, mentoring, supervising, using media to communicate information such as posters, leaflets, books, films and on-line media. By using regular staff meetings, briefings and handovers to mention and update information on food safety issues, this effective communication must always be clear, consistent and recurring.

Induction of new staff members

Induction of new members of the team plays a very important role in ensuring that food safety standards are fully compliant and that new employees completely understand the requirements of their job role. Supervisors should make certain that induction of all new staff is planned, well

organized and recorded on file. The procedure of inducting new staff should be correlated with mentoring and established staff training followed with regular review meetings to establish that standards are set, understood and adhered to.

Professionally planned and delivered induction training is your new employees' first proper impression of you, your team and your organization. It is also an excellent opportunity to reinforce their decision to come and work for you. Proper induction training is increasingly a legal requirement. Employers have a formal duty to provide new employees with all relevant information and training relating to health and safety particularly.

As a supervisor for new members of your team it is your responsibility to ensure that induction training is properly planned. Even if another 'centre' handles induction training (such as Human Resources) you must make sure it is planned and organized correctly for your new starter. An induction training plan must be issued to each new employee, before the new employee starts, and copied to everyone in the organization who is involved in providing the training, so the new starter and everyone else involved can see what is happening and that everything is included. Creating and issuing a suitable induction plan for each new starter will help them do their job better and quicker, and with less dependence on your time in the future.

Training methods

Food safety training is a legal requirement and is essential in any food business. The person responsible for the business must also be responsible for staff training. The supervisor will frequently deliver, manage and monitor the training and ensure that adequate records of training are kept up to date for possible inspection. Planned training and refresher programmes are essential for all levels of staff in food businesses.

As with other types of training, the learning and development of food safety can be achieved through very many different methods – use as many as you need to and which suit the individuals and the group. Maintain caution – ensure individuals are looked after properly and not left on their own to work things out unless you have a very specific purpose for doing so, or if the position is a senior one.

As with other forms of training, there are alternatives to 'chalk and talk' classroom-style training. Participation and 'GAAFOFY' methods (go away and find out for yourself) can be effective, particularly for groups and roles which require a good level of initiative, such as HACCP training. Here are some examples of training methods which can be used to augment the basics normally covered in a classroom format:

- on the job coaching;
- mentoring;
- delegated tasks and projects;
- reading food safety training packs, such as leaflets, books and online sources;

- presentation of DVDs, interactive quizzes and films;

- attending internal briefings and presentations;

- external delivery of training by the Environmental Health Officer;

- customer and supplier visits;

- attachment to project or other teams or a temporary job-swap;

- shadowing (shadowing another employee to see how they do it and what is involved).

CHEF'S TIP   Charts and posters allow people to absorb information quickly and easily. When displayed in appropriate areas of a kitchen they help to ensure that best practices are used.

Induction training must also include the following elements:

1   General training relating to the organization, including values and philosophy as well as structure and history, etc.

2   Mandatory training relating to health and safety and other essential or legal areas.

3   Job training relating to the role that the new starter will be performing.

4   Training evaluation, entailing confirmation of understanding, and feedback about the quality and response to the training.

Controlling, monitoring and the audit process

It is a requirement to complete monitoring, control and auditing procedures for food safety. The controlling process involves making sure that all agreed and recorded food safety policies are taking place within the day-to-day operations in the kitchen area. This is applied with staff meetings, spot checks, training updates and information sheets.

The monitoring process involves the supervisor and managers checking and recording that controls are being adhered to and are functioning correctly. The majority of the monitoring procedures will be contained within the food safety management system but additional methods of monitoring can include visual inspections and organoleptic checks. Organoleptic tests are sometimes conducted to determine if package materials and components can transfer tastes and odors to the food or products that they are packaged in. Shelf

life studies often use taste, sight and smell (in addition to food chemistry and toxicology tests) to determine whether a food product is suitable for consumption.

HEALTH & SAFETY   Swabbing kits are available from food safety management companies for checking and recording the levels of bacteria on a work surface or a piece of equipment. This may be undertaken at regular intervals and the findings are used to help improve cleaning and disinfection schedules and procedures.

The auditing process is a formal procedure which takes the form of an inspection. This is undertaken by an internal inspector (for example a manager), or an external auditor or consultant may be employed. Auditing is often used to verify that the HACCP system is working effectively. The benefits of an audit programme are as follows:

- Verifiies of the Food Safety and Quality Management System (QMS).

- Ensures constant review of the QMS.

- Provides a due diligence legal defence.

- Meets all legislation requirements.

- Highlights and communicate non-conformances.

- Provides scope for strategies to prevent non-conformances.

- Ensures corrective action plans are formulated.

- Provides documentation of completed corrective actions.

- Ensure company procedures and practices are being followed.

- Formal review of traceability systems.

- Ensure accurate test results from calibrated equipment.

HEALTH & SAFETY   Some food businesses choose to adopt online food safety auditing systems. This system provides instant food safety audit results online so that supervisors, managers and senior staff can be aware of results rapidly. In addition, this allows managers to clear actions on-line, thus completing the audit loop. Some of the checks offered online can include:

- food safety;

- health and safety;

- BRC/SALSA compliance for purchasers and suppliers;

- Scores on the Doors;

- Safer Food Better Business;

- machinery/COSHH safety;

- new process/equipment evaluation.

ASSESSMENT OF KNOWLEDGE AND UNDERSTANDING

To test your level of knowledge and understanding, answer the following short questions. These will help to prepare you for your summative (final) assessment.

1 State what the 'Safer Food Better Business' term refers to.

2 Describe the food safety hazards that wearing jewellery can cause.

3 Describe the food safety hazards that the use of kitchen cloths can cause.

4 Identify who to, and how health hazards are reported in a food business.

5 State why pests are a threat to food safety.

6 Identify the importance of reporting illnesses quickly and state the significance of stomach illnesses.

7 State three reasons why work surfaces and chopping boards should be clean and hygienic.

8 Explain the reason for regular maintenance checks and state how regular these should be.

9 State three major categories of foodborne pathogens.

10 How does the concentration of salt, sugar and alcohol influence bacterial reproduction?

11 Explain the importance of storing food correctly in a kitchen environment.

12 Carry out a HACCP assessment on the following products. Consider the hazard, the critical control point and the action to be taken.

   a fresh raw poultry;

   b fresh fruit and vegetables.

13 Briefly describe the food safety 2006 legislation in relation to your work and how it may affect you as a chef.

14 State why control, monitoring and auditing measures are used within a kitchen environment.

15 Briefly describe due diligence and why it is so important for a professional chef.

16 Using your knowledge of a professional kitchen, whether a school, college, restaurant, hotel, etc., devise a simple HACCP chart. The chart should refer to:

   ● meat;

   ● fish;

   ● dairy products.

   Identify any problems in the existing system and offer possible solutions.

Practical gastronomy

VRQ

Practical gastronomy

NVQ

Contribute to the development of recipes and menus

The aim of this chapter is to enable you to acquire the necessary knowledge and comprehension of the principles of the dining experience. It covers the influences on **gastronomy**, including that of culture, religion, geographical location, the transportation of commodities and science and technology.

You will be able to evaluate the factors that contribute to the dining experience, from a culinary perspective and how customer needs can differ. There are several principal outcomes to this chapter that discuss the importance of understanding issues associated with menu planning, and it includes information on the supply and use of commodities.

An introduction to gastronomy

Gastronomy is the study of the relationship between food and society. There are numerous areas studied in this chapter, including culture, the concept of taste, trends and religion. For many people food and gastronomy are a way of life regardless of whether this relates to a simple family meal or a multi-course tasting menu in a top restaurant. Gastronomy studies the influences and synthesis of eating and drinking, and it expands the relationship between culture and food, art and the science of eating and drinking.

In this modern era full of technological advances geography is no longer a barrier to the consumer or the chef; exotic ingredients and dishes from all over the world are now common. Therefore choosing what to eat can be a complex development process which is learned from childhood and influenced by family, relationships and economics.

Key economic issues such as food sustainability and food sourcing have become an important aspect which many people are striving to improve. Cultural and religious beliefs have also played a large part in the development of gastronomy. A dining experience from India, Asia, Africa, Great Britain or America is readily accessible to all and helps develop a range of exciting styles of cooking and service.

One of the latest and most exciting areas of gastronomy is the use of technology; whether it is the use of an immersion circulator, liquid nitrogen or a vacuum machine, new cooking, serving and entertainment possibilities are changing the way food is considered.

The health issues surrounding diners have played an enormous part in the way food is designed and cooked for consumers. The days of thick gelatinous sauces and high fat meals served regularly have passed on. In their place are light, lower-fat based dishes that form part of a healthy and balanced diet.

Liquid nitrogen used to create a reaction with an amuse appetiser before a dinner

Gastronomy has become a heavily discussed subject with celebrity chefs, food programmes, cooking shows, competitions and kitchen alchemists unlocking the secrets of the professional kitchen and enticing a new breed of gastronome into the mix. The concept of food trends has now become a large factor in menu writing and giving the customer new experiences.

Taste

How do we taste?

We obtain tastes through sensory organs called taste buds which are concentrated on the top of the tongue. There are around 100 000 taste buds that are located on the back and front of the tongue. Others are located on the roof, sides and back of the mouth, and in the throat. The sensation of taste can be categorized into five basic groups:

1 sweet;

2 bitter;

3 sour;

4 salty;

5 umami.

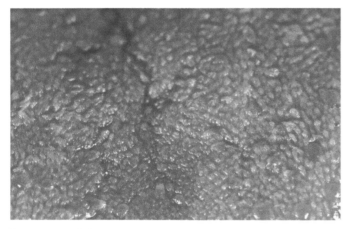

The surface of the tongue with visible taste buds

SWEET

Sweetness, usually regarded as a pleasurable sensation, is produced by the presence of sugars and a few other substances. Sweetness is detected by a variety of G protein coupled receptors found on the taste buds. At least two different variants of the sweetness receptors must be activated for the brain to register sweetness. Taste detection thresholds for sweet substances are rated relative to sucrose, which has an index of one. The average human detection threshold for sucrose is ten millimoles per litre. For lactose it is 30 millimoles per litre, with a sweetness index of 0.3

BITTER

Bitterness is the most sensitive of the tastes, and many perceive it as unpleasant, sharp or distasteful. Common bitter foods and beverages include coffee, unsweetened cocoa, marmalade, beer and many plants from the brassica family. Bitterness is of interest to those who study evolution, as well as various health researchers, since a large number of natural bitter compounds are known to be poisonous. The ability to detect bitter-tasting, toxic compounds at low thresholds is considered to provide an important natural human protective function.

SOUR

Sourness is the taste that detects acidity. Sour taste is detected by a small division of cells that are distributed across all taste buds in the tongue. The most common food group that contains naturally sour foods is fruit, such as lemon, grapefruit, orange, tamarind and lime. Wine also usually has a sour tinge to its flavour, and if not stored correctly, milk can spoil and develop a sour taste.

SALTY

Saltiness is a taste produced primarily by the presence of sodium ions. The further from sodium the less salty the sensation is.

UMAMI

Umami is originally the Japanese word for 'savoury'. Scientists debated whether umami was indeed a basic taste ever since Kikunae Ikeda (1864–1936) proposed its existence in 1908. Umami represents the taste of the amino acid L-glutamate. Glutamate in acid form (glutamic acid) imparts insignificant umami taste; whereas the salts of glutamic acid, known as glutamates, can easily ionize and give the characteristic umami taste. Glutamate has a long history in cooking. Fermented fish sauces, rich in glutamate, were used in ancient Rome. In the late 1800s, Chef Auguste Escoffier, who was the Chef de Cuisine at the Savoy and Ritz Carlton hotels in London, created meals that combined umami with salty, sour, sweet and bitter tastes. However, he did not fully realize the chemical source for this unique quality.

Ripe tomatoes are a strong source of the Umami taste

FACTORS OF FLAVOUR

The tongue is able to distinguish between the different tastes based on different molecules or ions that bind to the taste cell. The basic tastes contribute only partially to the sensation and flavour of food in the mouth. Other factors include smell, detected by the olfactory epithelium of the nose; texture, detected through a variety of mechanoreceptors and muscle nerves, temperature, detected by thermo-receptors; and 'coolness' (such as spearmint or menthol) and 'hotness' (piquancy and spices) – detected through chemesthesis. Chemesthetic sensations arise when chemical compounds activate receptors associated with the mouth.

DRYNESS AS A TASTE SENSATION

Some foods, such as unripe fruits, contain tannins or calcium oxalate that cause an astringent or rough sensation of the mucous membrane of the mouth. Examples include tea, red wine and rhubarb. Less precise terms for the astringent sensation are 'dry', 'rough', 'harsh' (especially for wine), 'tart' (normally referring to sourness) or 'hard'.

When referring to wine, *dry* is the opposite of *sweet,* and does not refer to astringency.

NUMBNESS AND 'HEAT' AS A TASTE SENSATION

Substances such as ethanol and capsaicin cause a burning sensation called chemesthesis, piquancy, spiciness, hotness or prickliness by inducing a nerve reaction together with normal taste reception. The sensation of heat is caused by the food's activating nerves that express two types of receptors found on the tongue. Two main plant-derived compounds that provide this sensation are capsaicin from chili peppers and piperine from black pepper. The piquant (hot or spicy) sensation provided by chili peppers, black pepper and other spices like ginger and horseradish plays an important role in a diverse range of cuisines across the world. This particular sensation, called chemesthesis, is not a taste in the technical sense, because the sensation does not arise from taste buds and a different set of nerve fibres carry it to the brain. Foods like chili peppers activate nerve fibres directly; the sensation interpreted as 'hot' results from the stimulation of somatosensory (pain/temperature) fibres on the tongue.

The sense of smell in determining flavour

Our noses are much more astute than our tongues. We have five-to-ten million olfactory cells sensing smells in our noses. We can detect the smell of some substances when only a few molecules interact with just a small amount of cells. The limitation of smell is that we can only detect air borne molecules. This limits us to smelling small molecules.

When we eat, most of the actual flavour is sensed in the nose. Each time we breathe whilst chewing, some breath is sucked from the back of the mouth into the nasal passage where it is sampled by the olfactory cells. The

resulting sensation is the major part of what we term 'flavour'.

TASK Consider the areas of your tongue which seem to be more receptive to the five tastes of bitter, sour, sweet, salty and umami. Test this by trying different foods with these attributes.

Factors and influences on gastronomy

There are many features that influence our choice of what we eat and these include our own individual preferences alongside our relationships and emotional needs. Other factors such as history, acceptability of food types, food imagery, trends and social influences will also affect our choices.

Social influences

Members of a social group depend on each other, share a common culture, and influence each other's behaviours and values. A person's membership in a particular peer, work or community group impacts food behaviours. For example, a young person at a restaurant may eat certain foods when accompanied by friends and other foods when accompanied by their spouse or family members.

Often the purpose of eating, either within the home or outside, is to provide a social environment to meet people and communicate either on a communal level or within a business setting.

CHEF'S TIP Consider how food plays an important role in an educational setting (either at school, college or university) and how food plays an important role in building relationships.

Religious influences

Different religious beliefs may vary from very relaxed to highly restrictive where gastronomy is concerned. This will affect a follower's food choices and behaviours. For example, in some religions specific foods are prohibited, such as pork among Jewish and Muslim faiths. Alcohol is also banned by some faiths so care must be taken to be prescriptive when producing menus.

Different countries use food to celebrate religious festivals such as the New Year, weddings, funerals, birthdays, Christmas, Hanukkah and Diwali. For example, Shrove

Tuesday is four weeks before Easter. It is celebrated by making pancakes. The idea is to use up all of the rich food – eggs and flour ready for the month-long fast to prepare oneself for the Easter celebration.

Cultural influences

Each culture has speciality foods and differing preparation methods. Britain, France, China, Japan, Mexico, Korea, Italy and India are examples of cultural areas known for their gastronomy. Within each culture there is an etiquette that is followed when eating and drinking. This will vary depending on the country, background and cultural ties of each person.

Knowledge of cultural influences is essential for the hospitality industry because of the rapid increase of tourism which creates a demand for a broader culinary experience. A variety of different restaurant concepts have been developed that represent cultural cuisine that is alien to their locality. Food is used culturally to express a range of emotions, sentiments and festivals.

Media influences

The use of the media to promote gastronomy over the last few years has been immense. Celebrity chefs cooking on television, competitions, back-to-basic cooking programmes and the government campaign encouraging people to eat five portions of fruit and vegetables a day has created intense interest in this area.

In recent years gastronomy blogs have provided an important channel for electronic word-of-mouth to take place and are quickly becoming a popular new source of reading material for blog readers. There are certain factors from gastronomy blogs that play critical roles in predicting readers' intention to taste local food and beverages and visit restaurants. There seem to be three main variables:

1   Inspiring a taste desire (i.e. experiencing appeal and generating empathy for a product or eating destination).

2   Forming taste awareness (i.e. providing images, delivering knowledge and presenting guides).

3   Facilitating interpersonal interaction (i.e. in the form of social influence and cyber community influence).

Excluding the concept of delivering knowledge, all the variables outlined are critical components that significantly influence online readers' intention to taste or visit establishments. This helps hospitality and tourism practitioners to understand the perceptions of potential customers, but also provide evidence of technology's influence on hospitality and gastronomy.

Geolocation is a media concept for turning the anonymous into the known. The common theme is to provide recommendations based on your geographic location (via your smartphone). Users can check in at their current location, find what specials or deals are offered, read helpful tips from other people, check the latest hygiene rating and accumulate points which they might be exchanged for loyalty based special offers. They can also check surrounding competitors and decide which location has the 'best deal'.

Influences from tourism

Gastronomy is becoming an important attribute in the development of niche travel and niche destinations. Although literature supports the view that there is a connection between tourism and gastronomy, little is known about gastronomy tourists. However, it is clear that a destination's gastronomy positively contributes to the tourists' quality of experiences while visiting the destination. There is some evidence to suggest that motivation to travel for gastronomy reasons is a valid theory. Gastronomy plays a major role in the way tourists experience the destination, and indicate that some travellers would return to the same destination to savour its unique gastronomy.

Environmental influences

There are environmental factors that influence the development of gastronomy. There is a close relationship between the advance of gastronomy and the quality of the environment. Therefore it is important to develop and maintain a physical, social, cultural and educational environment that is conducive to culinary creativity and gastronomy.

Eating in a restaurant has accepted social values which can be dependant on setting and ambience

Factors that create a good quality dining experience

When dining out there are numerous factors that can influence our enjoyment of a dining experience. These vary from the delivery and presentation of food to our perception of value for money. On the opposite page is a chart outlining the key areas associated with a perceived good quality dining experience.

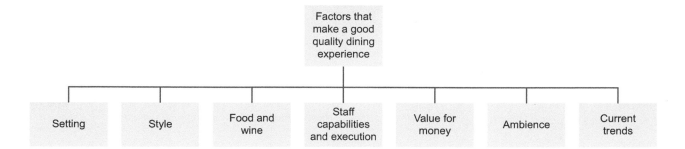

Food businesses must endeavour to deliver not only quality products and service, but also achieve a high level of customer satisfaction, which is very difficult given the many and varied customer demands and competitive business environment. The benefits for achieving customer happiness may encourage return business and a greater market share eventually. However, not all food businesses operate in an identical format. For example, a three-Michelin starred restaurant's standards of service can be significantly higher than those of a self-service canteen operation. The solution to an enjoyable experience is to match or exceed customer expectations within the environment the customer is in. A customer has the right to expect a good level of customer care involving attentiveness, attention to detail, value for money, safe food and beverage consumption and staff friendliness.

SETTING

Not every great restaurant needs an impressive view, but it can certainly help. The location of the restaurant can depend on the occasion or the experience a diner wants to achieve. The decor, appearance and amenities of the restaurant are the tangible elements of the experience. There is a statistically significant effect on the average amount spent by restaurant guests in relation to decor, including items such as outside seating, live entertainment and parking facilities.

STYLE

Various types of restaurant fall into several industry classifications based upon menu style, preparation methods and pricing. Additionally, how the food is served to the customer helps to determine the classification. Different styles can include; fine dining, fast food, casual dining, brasserie, bistro, buffet, café and pubs.

FOOD AND WINE

This is a significant factor and there are many features that contribute to the quality of the food and wine. The first aspect is the flavour and authenticity of the food and wine being offered. This will depend on the brigade of chefs and the service team alongside the commodity sourcing capabilities of the particular business. Other aspects are menu selection and being flexible to cater for specific dietary needs effectively.

Trends in food and drink are for mixing and matching different flavours. The opportunity is here to make a competitive difference from your competitor. Combining authentic multi ethnic, multi sensory dining where flavours clash on purpose and using new flavour concepts alongside organic ingredients is increasingly popular.

STAFF CAPABILITIES AND EXECUTION

An important aspect of building superior performance is having the right people in the right jobs. All levels of staff need formal evaluation on contributions and progress. Besides the daily on-the-job feedback, this requires a periodic sit-down with the supervisor to review staff strengths, areas to improve, development needs and career goals.

VALUE FOR MONEY

Value for money is being redefined in dining out, with consumer expectations enquiring about the product in question: where is it from? Does it fit in with my lifestyle? Is it sustainable? Transparency such as open kitchens, with food safety and hygiene ratings and supplier sourcing, local ingredients alongside food miles (plot to plate or farm to fork), artisan producers, educational values and concepts and above all wellness is taking over from purely financial decision making. Food with meaning is taking choice beyond price, status and materialism. The concept of 'wellness' means an intrinsic health benefit that creates a different attitude on value for money than ever before.

Principally, the impression of what makes the meal a more emotionally memorable experience is the opposite of menu engineering, as the intention is not to reduce value by stealthily playing with portions and prices. The idea is to give value for money by changing the focus away from financial issues and to get customers focused on personal wellbeing.

AMBIENCE

Even some of the best restaurants can be tainted by poor lighting, noisy rooms or a poor choice of music. Defining the correct ambience in a restaurant is a fine balance. Everyone has their own preferences depending on the occasion; however it should be decided what market the restaurant is aimed to entice and anticipate the needs and expectations of that particular client group.

CURRENT TRENDS

The concept of gastronomy is changing as we get more and more used to the feeling of being cosmopolitan. Counter-dining is being popularized across the spectrum from quick-casual dining to Michelin-starred along with huge share tables and distinctive cuisine to match. Sharing and grazing menus has gained pace thanks to a growing number of younger, more affluent diners who eat out numerous times a week and place a strong emphasis on informality. Some of that is a reflection of the informal nature brought by gastropubs which bring the opportunity to eat good food a couple of times a week at lower cost and with little fuss.

However, many people when they finish work do not necessarily want to go to a pub – they want somewhere smart, relaxing and informal where they can drink and maybe eat. Diners are now much happier sharing their experience with other guests and staff and in doing so are satisfying their need for the ethics of community, friendship and gaining a much stronger engagement with the whole dining experience. This is also because customers want more creative engagement with the whole dining process and, in particular, smaller but more dishes in one dining experience goes a long way to achieving that.

THE OVERALL DINING EXPERIENCE

The dining experience will always depend upon the venue selected. This should not, however, detract from the positive feelings a guest should leave with, chief among which are:

- satisfaction;
- value for money;
- attentiveness;
- welcome.

These factors should remain constant and ensure the guest returns.

Lifestyle changes

The modern day climate has seen a move towards ready meals and fast food at one end of the scale with the media and government trying to encourage a more wholesome approach to eating at the other. Factors that affect our lifestyles are also factors that affect consumer's activities and food choices. These can be:

1 activities such as hobbies, work, social events, entertainment, holidays, community, sports, family and shopping;

2 demographics such as age, education, family size, geography, occupation and income;

3 interests such as family, home, profession, recreation, community, achievements, media and fashion/trends;

4 opinions such as social issues, politics, business, economics, education and culture.

Today's population is purchasing and consuming more varied food and beverage products, on more occasions, then ever before. There are a variety of cultural values that govern this concept.

- The introduction of healthy eating initiatives has seen many people return to the kitchen to produce healthy meals for the family and increase their fruit and vegetable consumption. There has been an expansion of **calorie**-reduced pre-prepared meals which include a reduction in salt and fat and an increase in fibre.

- The price of meals offered by many top restaurants has opened the door to many who have begun to find a real appreciation for quality produce, techniques and settings. The interest has led to a huge surge in the market for gastronomy and food in general.

- Casual lifestyles with less formality that simplify meal occasions and offer more individual autonomy over what is eaten. The proposition of multiple and diverse product choices presented at the same meal time alongside less formal meals and mealtimes.

- Increased concern for value-for-money with rising consumer expectations. There is a rise in restaurant-style food available to purchase and take home from supermarkets to create an eating-out experience within the home environment.

- Instant fulfilment in today's modern populace means that there is an increase in luxury items with a more convenient access and availability. This is through a stronger network of food distribution.

- The management and effective use of time leads us to pre-prepared ready meals and packaging that cuts down effort and time in product selection, food preparation, cooking and clearing up.

Meal types

Traditionally common meal types are broken down into the following categories in most western cuisines:

- breakfast;
- elevenses;
- brunch;
- lunch;
- afternoon tea;
- high tea;
- dinner;
- supper.

Breakfast is usually eaten within an hour or two after a person wakes in the morning (literally meaning 'breaking the fast' of the night). Breakfast foods vary widely from place to place, but often include a **carbohydrate** such as grains or cereals, fruit and/or vegetable, a protein food such as eggs, meat or fish and a beverage such as tea, coffee or fruit juice. Nutritional experts have referred to breakfast as the most important meal of the day, citing studies that find that people who skip breakfast are disproportionately likely to have problems with concentration, metabolism and weight control.

Eggs Benedict consists of poached eggs, toasted muffin, cured ham or bacon with Hollandaise sauce

Elevenses, is also called morning tea and usually consists of a drink and a light snack and is taken in the later morning after breakfast and before lunch. It is generally less savoury than brunch, and might consist of some cake or biscuits with a cup of coffee or tea. The name refers to the time of day that it is taken: around 11.00 am.

Brunch is a late-morning meal, usually larger than a breakfast and usually replacing both breakfast and lunch; it is most common on Sundays.

Lunch is eaten around midday, usually between 12.00pm and 2.00pm. Luncheon, commonly abbreviated to lunch, is generally lighter than dinner, which is the main meal of the day whenever dinner is eaten. Since lunch typically falls in the middle of the working day, it can either be eaten on a break from work, or as part of the workday (usually called a working-lunch). In restaurants, lunch meals may take the form of a **table d'hôte**, a set menu with a restricted choice for a set price, a buffet serving hot/cold items or occasionally an **à la** carte menu.

Afternoon tea is a mid-afternoon meal, typically taken between the times of 3.00 pm and 5.00 pm. The custom of afternoon tea originated in England in the 1840s. The custom spread throughout the British Empire and beyond in succeeding decades. Afternoon tea consists of light fare such as small sandwiches, individual cakes and scones with a varying selection of different loose teas.

High tea is a British meal usually eaten in the early evening. Typically eaten between 5.00 pm and 7.00 pm it is now largely followed by a lighter meal later in the evening. High tea typically consists of a hot dish such as shepherd's pie or a pasta dish followed by cakes and bread, butter and jam. Occasionally there would be cold cuts of meat, such as ham salad. Traditionally high tea was eaten by middle to upper class children (whose parents would have a more formal dinner later). The term was first used around 1825 and 'high' is used in the sense of well advanced to signify that it was taken later in the day.

Dinner is a meal eaten in the evening. Depending upon culture, dinner may be the second, third or fourth meal of the day. In some usages, the term *dinner* has continued to refer to the largest meal of the day, even when this meal is eaten at the end of the day and is preceded by other meals. Dinners are often divided into three courses consisting of a starter, main course and a dessert. Traditionally dinner is usually in the form of an **à la carte** menu. Wine is also offered with each course for a supplement.

Supper is a light meal eaten in the late evening or overnight before bed. In the United Kingdom, dinner is used to describe the evening meal in quite formal circumstances. However, 'supper' is used to describe a less formal, simpler meal.

Food science and technology

Food supplies have moved gradually over many centuries from hunter–gatherer and nomad status to the domestication and selection of plants and animals, allowing populations to become more fixed, and to establish permanent villages, towns and eventually cities. Food habits were developed based on the foods available in different parts of the world. The use of fire, fermentation and other food treatments to make many plant and animal derived foods more **palatable** and more easily digested have been introduced.

Local and world population also played an important role in the development of food supplies, trade in food and cuisine. The growth of the world population over the past 100 years, along with improved economies, enhanced information technology, and increased travel between different parts of the world, have had a dramatic effect on agricultural resources, food supplies and on the widening of different cuisines around the world.

As the world population has grown, many people have moved from rural areas to larger towns and cities. Urban growth has also had a dramatic effect on how foods are produced, stored, processed and marketed since most city people are involved in activities other than raising food. Transportation systems for food, wholesale and retail markets, restaurants, canteens for workers and school feeding policies all have had an effect on how food is produced and consumed.

As people moved from one area to another for work purposes, they brought with them the culture, food habits and cuisine from the regions of their origin. Many of these food habits and culinary systems were adopted in other countries, so that at present foods and food service systems in many parts of the world have a very wide choice of different foods and menus available. Different menus and foods from Europe, Africa, the Middle East, Asia and the Americas can be found in many other countries and areas.

All countries produce foods, but practically no country is completely self-sufficient in agriculture so that it can produce all of the food items that are used in local diets, or are used in animal feed for producing cattle, poultry and fish. Most countries have seasonal production of different foods. In many cases sequential surpluses of different food-crops or products during the year will enable trade in surplus foods or food products in domestic markets, or between countries.

With the growth of urban areas and a shift from older systems of local trading, and the lengthening of food supply lines from short, local distances to thousands of miles, preservation or proper storage of foods has become more important. The protection and preserving of the quality and safety of foods has become very important. Local, national, and international standards, laws and rules for foods have been widely developed, along with government and food industry systems to assure compliance with these rules.

Consumers of foods and food products are faced with the challenge of accepting foods that may have a number of quality or safety problems that cannot be detected by visual inspection. Excess water in foods, contamination with pathogenic microorganisms, excessive pesticide residues, mycotoxins and other contaminants cannot usually be detected by consumers, but must be controlled by governments and industry.

Food technologies encompass a very wide spectrum of activities related to foods from basic production techniques, through harvest, transportation, storage, processing, marketing, the production and provision of foods in restaurants and other food service establishments.

Consumer food choices are usually based on taste, texture, convenience, food safety and dietary advice about better nutrition and health protection. These have led to changes in foods and food systems. Some traditional foods such as yogurt, tofu and various herbs and spices have become more popular with a wider range of consumers, and newer technologies such as pasteurization, irradiation,

mechanical refrigeration and simulated ripening have created new products to meet new consumer demands and desires. Other more traditional systems for food preservation such as fermentation and pickling of vegetables and meats, have all been altered to reduce salt content and increase desirable traits such as 'mouth feel' and reduce nitrates in animal products. Usually these changes are accompanied by different systems of food storage such as refrigeration to prevent bacterial growth, and preserve quality and safety.

Various consequences of the development of food science and technology are defined in the following sections.

Food irradiation

This is a processing technique that exposes food to electron beams, X-rays or gamma rays. The process produces a similar effect to pasteurization, cooking or other forms of heat treatment, but with less effect on look and texture. Irradiated food has been exposed to radioactivity but does not become radioactive itself.

Food absorbs energy when it is exposed to ionizing radiation. The amount of energy absorbed is called 'absorbed dose'. The energy absorbed by the food causes the formation of short-lived molecules known as free radicals, which kill bacteria that can cause food poisoning. They can also delay fruit ripening and help stop vegetables, such as potatoes and onions, from sprouting.

This is the Radura logo, used to show a food has been treated with ionizing radiation

Research worldwide has shown that irradiation of food is a safe and effective way to kill bacteria in foods and extend its shelf life. In 2011, the European Food Safety Authority reviewed the evidence and reasserted the opinion that food irradiation is safe. There may be some vitamin loss from irradiated foods however, but this would occur with some other preservation techniques or long-term storage.

The Radura is the international symbol indicating a food product has been irradiated. The Radura is usually green and resembles a plant in circle. The top half of the circle is dashed. Graphical details and colours vary between countries.

Irradiation has not been widely adopted due to an asserted negative public perception, the concerns expressed by some consumer groups and the reluctance of many food producers.

Consumer organizations, environmentalist groups and opponents to food irradiation refer to some studies suggesting that a large part of the public questions the safety of irradiated foods, and will not buy foods that have been irradiated. Concerns and objections include the possibility that food irradiation could have an impact on the following:

● Masks any spoiled food.

● Discourages strict adherence to good food manufacturing practices and processes.

● Preferentially kills 'good' bacteria and encourages the growth of 'bad' bacteria.

● Denatures irradiated food.

● Impairs flavour in irradiated food.

● CauseS chemical changes that are harmful to the consumer.

Food additives

Additives must be assessed for safety before they can be used in food. European Union (EU) legislation requires most additives used in foods to be labelled clearly in the list of ingredients, with their function, followed by either their name or E number. An E number means that it has passed safety tests and has been approved for use here and in the rest of the EU.

Ajinomoto or monosodium glutamate on a spoon. The flavour enhancing chemical is widely used in Asian cuisine and in food processing

Food additives are grouped by what they do and some additives that you are most likely to come across on food labels are:

1 **antioxidants** (prevent food from becoming rancid or changing colour by reducing the chance of fats combining with oxygen);

2 colours;

3 emulsifiers, stabilizers, gelling agents and thickeners (help to mix or thicken ingredients);

4 flavour enhancers (used to bring out the flavour of foods);

5 preservatives (used to keep food safer for longer);

6 sweeteners (intense sweeteners are many times sweeter than sucrose whereas bulk sweeteners have a similar sweetness).

The consumption of mixes of certain artificial food colours and the preservative sodium benzoate could be linked to increased hyperactivity in some children. The artificial colours identified by the FSA are:

● sunset yellow FCF (E110);

● quinoline yellow (E104);

● carmoisine (E122);

● allura red (E129);

● tartrazine (E102);

● ponceau 4R (E124).

As mentioned, all additives in the UK and Europe are controlled by law, and can only be used following stringent tests and approval by an independent committee of scientists and medical experts. However, some scientists have linked additives in general use, particularly tartrazine (E102) to:

● hyperactivity in children;

● allergies;

● asthma;

● migraines;

● cancer.

TASK Reflect on a recipe that you use frequently and consider if there are any additives in the ingredients that you use and the reasons that they are apparent. Can you reduce the additive content without neglecting quality?

Increasing the shelf life of food

The modern food industry has developed because of its ability to deliver a wide variety of high quality food products to consumers on a nationwide and worldwide basis. This achievement has been partly accomplished by building stability into commodities through processing, packaging and additives that enable foods to remain fresh throughout the distribution process.

Consumer demands for convenience have fuelled new innovations in food product development, packaging and chemical industries. The widespread desire for products to use in the microwave-oven has added further impetus to this effort.

As an increasing number of new foods compete for space on supermarket shelves, the words 'speed and innovation' have become the watchwords for food companies seeking to become 'first to market' with successful products. How the consumer perceives the product is the ultimate measure of total quality.

As the mechanisms of food deterioration became known to food scientists, methods of counteracting these losses in quality have been developed. The rate at which these reactions occur are due to the effects of temperature, water and other parameters which have become considered factors contributing to the science of increased shelf-life studies.

The principal factors involved in the deterioration of processed foods are as follows:

1 Microbiological spoilage sometimes accompanied by pathogen development.

2 Chemical and enzymatic activity causing lipid breakdown, colour, odour, flavour and texture changes.

3 Moisture and/or other vapour migration producing changes in texture, water activity and flavour.

Some extension of shelf life methods require the food to be sealed after treatment to prevent recontamination with microbes; others, such as drying, allow food to be stored without any special containment for long periods.

Common methods of applying these processes include drying, spray-drying, freeze-drying, freezing, vacuum-packing, canning and preserving in syrup, sugar crystallization, food irradiation and adding preservatives or inert gases such as carbon dioxide. Other methods that not only help to preserve food, but also add flavour, include pickling, salting, smoking, preserving in syrup or alcohol, sugar crystallization and **curing**.

DRYING

One of the oldest methods of shelf life extension is by drying, which reduces water activity sufficiently to prevent or delay bacterial growth. Drying also reduces weight, making food more convenient. Many fruits can be dried; the process is often applied to apples, pears, bananas, mangoes and apricots. Currants, sultanas and raisins are all forms of dried grapes.

An example of dried fruits

FREEZING

Freezing is also one of the most commonly used processes commercially and domestically for preserving a very wide range of food including prepared food stuffs which would not have required freezing in their unprepared state.

VACUUM-PACKING

Vacuum-packing stores food in a vacuum environment, usually in an airtight bag or bottle. The vacuum environment strips bacteria of oxygen needed for survival, slowing down the spoilage of foodstuffs. Vacuum-packing is commonly used for storing nuts to reduce loss of flavour from oxidation

Vacuum packed fresh salmon in portions

Research considering the safety of chilled vacuum-packed foods concluded that the primary concern with such foods is that of microbiological safety. Concerns with chilled foods include:

- Micro-organisms – in particular, the psychrotrophs that are capable of growing at low temperatures.

- Shelf-life – establishing a safe shelf-life can be complex (particularly for small and medium-sized businesses).

- Pasteurization processes – the trend towards using lower heat treatments to retain product characteristics.

- Temperature control – the requirement for effective temperature control throughout the chill chain.

Although vacuum packing techniques generally increase the shelf-life of chilled foods by removing air, certain bacteria, including *Clostridium botulinum* and *Listeria monocytogenes*, may still be able to develop. *Clostridium botulinum* can produce a very harmful toxin that can cause a fatal form of food poisoning. It is commonly found in the environment as spores and can also be present in food. Removing air from food packaging can allow these spores to grow and produce toxins. Therefore vacuum-packed chilled foods must have controls in place, throughout the shelf-life of the product, to minimize the risk of this bacterium growing and producing toxin.

You should always ensure that separate vacuum packing machines are used for raw foods and cooked foods. General cleaning and disinfection procedures should be employed and monitored and additional disinfection considerations for vacuum packing equipment and machinery need to be in operation.

SUGAR

Sugar is used to preserve fruits either in syrup with fruit such as apples, pears, peaches, apricots and plums or in crystallized form where the preserved material is cooked in sugar to the point of crystallization and the resultant product is then stored dry. This method is used for the **skins** of citrus fruit (candied peel), angelica and ginger. A modification of this process produces **glacé** fruit such as glacé cherries where the fruit is preserved in sugar but is then extracted from the syrup, the preservation being maintained by the sugar content of the fruit and the shallow coating of syrup. The use of sugar is often combined with alcohol for preservation of luxury products such as fruit in brandy or other spirits.

Preserved Apricots in sugar

CANNING AND BOTTLING

Canning involves cooking food, sealing it in sterile cans or jars, and boiling the containers to kill or weaken any remaining bacteria as a form of sterilization. Various foods have varying degrees of natural protection against spoilage and may require that the final step occur in a pressure cooker. High-acid fruits like strawberries require no preservatives to can and only a short cooking cycle, whereas marginal fruits such as tomatoes require longer boiling and addition of other acidic elements. Low acid foods, such as vegetables and meats require pressure canning. Food preserved by canning or bottling is at immediate risk of spoilage once the can or bottle has been opened.

Lack of quality control in the canning process may allow ingress of water or microorganisms. Most such failures are rapidly detected as decomposition within the can causes gas production and the can will swell or burst.

HIGH PRESSURE

High pressure shelf life extension refers to high pressure used for shelf life extension. Food pressed inside a vessel exerting 70 000 pounds per square inch or more, food can be processed so that it retains its fresh appearance, flavour, texture and nutrients while disabling harmful microorganisms and slowing spoilage. This process is being used for products ranging from orange juice to guacamole.

Genetically modified food

Genetically modified foods (GM foods or biotech foods) are foods derived from genetically modified organisms. Genetically modified organisms have had specific changes introduced into their DNA by genetic engineering techniques. Other techniques by which we can modify food organisms include selective breeding of plants and animals. Since genetically modified food has been introduced into the food chain, there has been much controversy as to whether it is actually safe.

Genetically modified foods were first put on the market in 1996. Typically, genetically modified foods are transgenic plant products such as soybean, maize, rapeseed, rice and cotton seed oil. Critics, sometimes referring to genetically modified foods as 'frankenfood', have objected to GM foods on several grounds which include safety issues, ecological and economic concerns.

Within the UK and many other European countries many trial crops are frequently destroyed. The primary concern of the campaigners is contamination of existing crops could destroy existing markets such as organic produce. Scientists take many precautions to minimize the risks as much as possible and point out that the risk of contamination is small. The scientists give several reasons for the need for trials – climate change, a growing global population and reduced use of chemicals. Campaigners draw attention to natural and organic solutions to reduce chemical use and question the usefulness of the trials.

The USA and Canada do not require labelling of genetically modified foods. However in certain other regions, such as the European Union, Japan, Malaysia and Australia, governments have required labelling so consumers can exercise choice between foods that have genetically modified, conventional or organic origins. This requires a labelling system as well as the reliable separation of GM and non-GM organisms at production level and throughout the whole processing chain.

Ripening agents

Ripening agents speed up the ripening process of fruit and vegetables. They allow many fruits to be picked prior to full ripening, which is useful, since ripened fruits do not transport well over long distances. For example, bananas are picked when green and artificially ripened after shipment by being gassed with ethylene.

Calcium carbide is also used for ripening fruit artificially in some countries. Calcium carbide reacts with water to produce acetylene, which acts as an artificial ripening agent. Industrial-grade calcium carbide may contain traces of arsenic and phosphorus which makes it a human health concern. The use of this chemical for this purpose is illegal in most countries.

Catalytic generators are used to produce ethylene gas simply and safely. Climacteric fruits are able to continue ripening after being picked, this is a process accelerated by ethylene gas. Non-climacteric fruits can ripen only on the plant and thus have a short shelf life if harvested when they are ripe.

Use of fertilizers

Fertilizer is any organic or inorganic material of natural or synthetic origin that is added to a soil to supply one or more plant nutrients essential to the growth of plants. A recent assessment found that up to 60 per cent of crop yields are attributable to commercial fertilizer use. They are essential for high-yield harvest: the European fertilizer market is expected to grow to €15.3 billion by 2018.

Fertilizers are broadly divided into organic fertilizers (composed of organic plant or animal matter), or inorganic or commercial fertilizers. Plants can only absorb their required nutrients if they are present in easily dissolved chemical compounds. Both organic and inorganic fertilizers provide the same needed chemical compounds. Organic fertilizers provided other macro and micro plant nutrients and are released as the organic matter decays – this may take months or years to produce. Organic fertilizers nearly always have much lower concentrations of plant nutrients and have the usual problems of economical collection, treatment, transportation and distribution.

Inorganic fertilizers nearly always are readily dissolved and unless added have few other macro and micro plant nutrients.

Organic fertilizers have been known to improve biodiversity and long-term productivity of soil and may prove a large depository for excess carbon dioxide. Organic nutrients increase the abundance of soil organisms by providing organic matter and micronutrients for organisms which aid plants in absorbing nutrients, and can drastically reduce external inputs of pesticides, energy and fertilizer, at the cost of decreased yield.

There are a variety of negative environmental effects of fertilizing crops listed below.

1 *Water quality*
The nitrogen-rich compounds found in fertilizer runoff are the primary cause of serious oxygen depletion in many parts of the ocean, especially in coastal zones. The resulting lack of dissolved oxygen is greatly reducing the ability of these areas to sustain oceanic vegetation.

2 *Atmosphere*
Methane emissions from crop fields are increased by the application of ammonium-based fertilizers; these emissions contribute greatly to global climate change as methane is a potent greenhouse gas.

Through the increasing use of nitrogen fertilizer, nitrous oxide (N_2O) has become the third most important greenhouse gas after carbon dioxide and methane. It has a global warming potential 296 times larger than an equal mass of carbon dioxide and it also contributes to stratospheric ozone depletion.

3 *Soil*
Soil acidification – nitrogen-containing inorganic and organic fertilizers can cause soil acidification when added. This may lead to decreases in nutrient availability in soil which may be offset by a process called liming. This neutralizes soil acidity and increases activity of soil bacteria.

Human and historical influences on gastronomy

The earliest cookbooks on record appear to be primarily lists of recipes for what would now be called *haute cuisine*. These were frequently written mostly to provide a testimony of the author's favourite dishes or to train professional cooks for banquets and upper-class private homes. The earliest collection of recipes that has survived in Europe is *De re coquinaria*, and is written in Latin. An early version was first compiled sometime in the first century and has often been attributed to the Roman **gourmet** Marcus Gavius **Apicius**, though this has been cast in doubt by some recent research.

The earliest cookbooks known in Arabic are those of Ibn Sayyar al-Warraq (10th century) and Muhammad bin Hasan al-Baghdadi (13th century). Huou, Kublai Khan's court chef, composed a collection of recipes called 'The Important Things to Know about Eating and Drinking' in the 13th century; it includes mainly soups as well as general household advice.

The first recipe books to be compiled in Europe started to appear in the late 13th century. The earliest genuinely medieval recipes have been found in a Danish manuscript dating from around 1300, which in turn are copies of older texts that date back to the early 13th century or even at an earlier time. German manuscripts are among the most numerous and among them is *Daz buch von guter spise* (The Book of Good Food) written in 1350 in Würzberg, and *Kuchenmeysterey* (Kitchen Mastery), the first printed German cook book from 1485. Two French collections are probably the most famous: *Le Viandier* (The Provisioner) was compiled in the late 14th century by Guillaume Tirel, master chef for two French kings; and *Le Menagier de Paris* (The Householder of Paris), a household book written by an anonymous middle class Parisian in the 1390s.

Catherine de' Medici (13 April 1519 – 5 January 1589), was the daughter of Lorenzo II de' Medici and of Madeleine de La Tour d'Auvergne, and was a Franco/Italian noblewoman who was the wife of King Henry II of France from 1547 until 1559. Catherine was born in Florence, Italy, as *Caterina Maria Romula di Lorenzo de' Medici*. The Medici family were the effective rulers of Florence; originally bankers, they came to great wealth and power by bankrolling the monarchies of Europe.

Catherine believed in the humanist ideal of the learned Renaissance prince whose authority depended on letters as well as arms. She was inspired by the example of her father-in-law, King Francis I of France, who had hosted the leading artists of Europe at his court, and by her Medici ancestors. In an age of civil war and declining respect for the monarchy, she sought to bolster royal prestige through lavish cultural display.

The tomb of Henri II and Catherine de Medici, from Saint Denis gothic cathedral

She launched a programme of artistic patronage that lasted for three decades. While Catherine de Medici impressed the French court with her sumptuous banquets of unusual dishes, the greatest shock must have been her introduction of the fork. Spoons and knives had been used before, but to dine with a fork was revolutionary. The art of making breads, cakes and pastries, the preparation of fresh vegetables and the serving of fruits and cheeses were also appreciated. Catherine also introduced the French court to iced delicacies and brought with her to the French table a new

dining protocol, such as the separation of savoury and sweet dishes, at a time when sweets were still consumed together with meat and fish in the medieval style all over Europe.

Everyone in France was amazed by the Florentine elegance Catherine introduced, including gracious table settings and dining, embroidery and handkerchiefs, light perfumes, as well as luxurious silverware and glasses.

François Pierre de la Varenne (1615–1678, Dijon), was the author of *Le Cuisinier François* (1651), the founding text of modern French cuisine. La Varenne broke with the Italian traditions that had revolutionized medieval French cookery in the 16th century. La Varenne was the leading member of a group of French chefs, writing for a professional audience, who standardized French cuisine during the age of Louis XIV. La Varenne's work was the first to establish in writing the considerable culinary innovations achieved in France in the 17th century, while measuring food preparation in a systematic method, according to rules and principles of recipes. He introduced the first bisque and Béchamel sauce. He replaced crumbled bread with the first **roux** as the base for sauces, and the use of lard with butter. He also established terms such as **bouquet garni**, fonds de cuisine (stocks) and reductions, alongside the use of egg whites for clarification. His book also contains the earliest recipe in print for mille feuille.

Jean Anthelme Brillat-Savarin (1 April 1755 – 2 February 1826, Paris) was a French lawyer and politician, and gained fame as an epicure and gastronome. His famous work, *Physiologie du goût* (The Physiology of Taste), was published in December 1825, two months before his death. The book has not been out of print since it first appeared, shortly before Brillat-Savarin's death. Its most notable English translation was undertaken by food writer and critic M. F. K. Fisher, who remarked 'I hold myself blessed among translators'. Her translation was first published in 1949. Brillat-Savarin cheese; the Savarin mould, a ring mould with a rounded contour and *gâteau Savarin* are named in his honour. Brillat-Savarin wrote about the pleasures of the table, which he considered a science and coined the famous line, 'Tell me what you eat, and I will tell you what you are'.

Marie Antoine Carême (8 June 1784–12 January 1833) is acknowledged as the 'King of Chefs, and the Chef of Kings'. Carême was an early practitioner and exponent of the elaborate style of cooking known as *haute cuisine*, the high art of French cooking, an extravagant style of cookery favoured by both royalty and by the newly rich of Paris. Carême is often considered as one of the first internationally renowned celebrity chefs. Abandoned by his parents in Paris in 1794 at the height of the French Revolution, he worked as a kitchen boy at a cheap Parisian chophouse in exchange for room and board. In 1798, he was formally apprenticed to Sylvain Bailly, a famous *pâtissier* with a shop near the Palais-Royal.

Carême gained fame in Paris for his *pièces montées*, elaborate constructions used as centrepieces, which Bailly displayed in the **pâtisserie** window. He made these confections, which were sometimes several feet high, entirely out of sugar, marzipan and pastry. He did freelance work creating pieces predominantly for the French diplomat and gourmand Charles Maurice de Talleyrand-Périgord, but also other members of Parisian high society, including Napoleon.

Carême was set a test by Talleyrand: to create a whole year's worth of menus, without repetition and using only seasonal produce. Carême passed the test and completed his training in Talleyrand's kitchens. After the fall of Napoleon, Carême travelled to London and served as *chef de cuisine* to the Prince Regent, later George IV. Returning to the continent he followed the invitation of Tsar Alexander I to work in St. Petersburg, before returning to Paris, where he was chef to banker James Mayer Rothschild.

Georges Auguste Escoffier (28 October 1846–2 February 1935, Villeneuve-Loubet, Alpes-Maritimes) was a French chef, restaurateur and culinary writer who fashioned and updated the traditional French cooking methods. He is a legendary figure among chefs and gourmets, and was one of the most important leaders in the development of modern French cuisine. Alongside the recipes he recorded and invented, another of Escoffier's contributions to cooking was to elevate it to the status of a respected profession by introducing organized discipline to his kitchens. He organized his kitchens by the *brigade de cuisine* system, with each section run by a **chef de partie**.

Escoffier published *Le Guide Culinaire*, which is still used as a major reference work, both in the form of a cookbook and a textbook on cooking. Escoffier's recipes, techniques and approaches to kitchen management remain highly influential today, and have been adopted by chefs and restaurants not only in France, but also throughout the world. Escoffier ran the kitchen of the Hotel National in Lucerne, where he met César Ritz. The two men formed a partnership and in 1890 accepted an invitation from Richard D'Oyly Carte to transfer to his new Savoy Hotel in London, At the Savoy, Escoffier created many famous dishes. In 1893 he invented the *pêche Melba* in honour of the Australian singer Dame Nellie Melba. Other Escoffier creations, famous in their time, were *bombe Néro* (a flaming ice), *fraises à la Sarah Bernhardt* (strawberries with pineapple and Curaçao sorbet), *baisers de Vierge* (meringue with vanilla cream and crystallized white rose and violet petals) and *suprêmes de volailles Jeannette* (jellied chicken breasts with foie gras). He helped to establish the Ritz Hotel Development Company, for which Escoffier set up the kitchens and recruited the chefs, first at the Paris Ritz (1898), and then at the new Carlton Hotel in London (1899), which soon drew much of the high-society clientele away from the Savoy. Escoffier and Ritz also founded the first professional cookery school in the UK in 1910 which was named the Westminster Technical College and now known as Westminster Kingsway College.

The Michelin Guide is a series of annual guidebooks published by Michelin for many countries. The term normally refers to the Michelin Red Guide, the oldest and best-known European hotel and restaurant guide, which awards the Michelin stars. André Michelin published the first edition of the guide in 1900 to help drivers maintain their cars, find decent lodgings and eat well while touring France. It included addresses of filling stations, mechanics and tyre dealers, along with local prices for fuel and auto repairs. The guide was distributed free from 1900 until 1920.

It began recognizing outstanding restaurants in 1926 with a star; two and three stars were added in the early 1930's. In 1933 André Michelin and his brother Édouard Michelin introduced the first countrywide French restaurant listings and introduced the Michelin star system for ranking food, later extended to the rest of the world. The guide awards one to three stars to a small number of restaurants of outstanding quality. One star indicates a 'very good cuisine in its category', a two-star ranking represents 'excellent cuisine, worth a detour', and a rare three stars are awarded to restaurants offering 'exceptional cuisine, worth a special journey'. Michelin reviewers are known to be anonymous and independent; they do not identify themselves and their meals and expenses are paid for by the company founded by the Michelin brothers, never by a restaurant being reviewed.

Fernand Point (1897–1955, Louhans, Saône-et-Loire) was a French restaurateur and is considered to be the father of modern French cuisine. From his restaurant La Pyramide in Vienne, a town situated near the French city of Lyon, he gained three Michelin stars and trained a generation of French master chefs such as: Paul Bocuse, Alain Chapel, Louis Outhier, Georges Perrier and Jean and Pierre Troisgros. He had received his training with Foyot in Paris.

The restaurant was founded shortly after World War I. From its kitchen came the modern light sauces, baby vegetables and other early aspects of *nouvelle cuisine*. During the regime of Vichy France in World War II, Point served refugees fleeing the Nazi invasion of France. When German officers began frequenting his establishment, he stopped serving dinner. When they demanded tables for lunch, he closed his restaurant altogether.

Elizabeth David CBE (born Elizabeth Gwynne, 26 December 1913 – 22 May 1992) was a British cookery writer who, in the mid-20th century, strongly influenced the revitalization of the art of home cookery with articles and books about European cuisines and traditional British dishes.

Born to an upper-class family, Elizabeth rebelled against the social norms of the day. She studied art in Paris, became an actress, and ran off with a married man with whom she sailed in a small boat to Greece. They were nearly trapped by the German invasion of Greece in 1940 but escaped to Egypt where they parted. She then worked for the British government, running a library in Cairo. While there she married, but the marriage was not long lived.

After the war, Elizabeth David returned to England but became disillusioned by the political depression and bad food, so wrote a series of articles about Mediterranean food that caught the public imagination. Books on French and Italian cuisine followed, and within ten years Elizabeth David was a major influence on British cooking. She was a champion of authentic classic dishes and fresh ingredients. She introduced a generation of British cooks to Mediterranean food. David opened a cookery shop selling kitchen equipment in the 1960s. It continued to trade under her name after she left it in 1973, but her reputation rests on her articles and her books, which have been constantly reprinted and provide inspiration to many of today's chefs.

Paul Bocuse (11 February 1926) is a French chef based in Lyon who is famous for the high quality of his restaurants and his innovative approaches to cuisine. He is one of the most prominent chefs associated with the *nouvelle cuisine*, which is less opulent and calorific than the traditional *cuisine classique*, and stresses the importance of fresh ingredients of the highest quality.

Bocuse has made many contributions to French gastronomy both directly and indirectly, because he has had numerous students, many of whom have become famous chefs themselves. Bocuse's main restaurant is the luxury restaurant L'Auberge du Pont de Collonges, near Lyon, which has been serving a traditional menu for many years. It is one of a small number of restaurants in France to receive the coveted three-star rating by the Michelin Guide. He also operates a chain of brasseries in Lyon, named Le Nord, L'Est, Le Sud and L'Ouest, each of which specializes in a different aspect of French cuisine.

Bocuse is considered an ambassador of modern French cuisine. He was honoured in 1961 with the title Meilleur Ouvrier de France. He was an apprentice to Fernand Point and continues to be a major influence on many of today's chefs through his international competition the Bocuse d'Or.

Nouvelle cuisine is an approach to cooking and food presentation. By contrast with cuisine classique, an older form of haute cuisine, nouvelle cuisine is characterized by lighter, more delicate dishes and an increased emphasis on presentation. The term *nouvelle cuisine* has been used many times in the history of French cuisine. In the 1740s for example, the work of Vincent La Chapelle, François Marin and Menon was described as *nouvelle cuisine*.

The modern usage can be attributed to authors André Gayot, Henri Gault and Christian Millau, who used *nouvelle cuisine* to describe the cooking of Paul Bocuse, Alain Chapel, Jean and Pierre Troisgros, Michel Guérard, Roger Vergé and Raymond Oliver, many of whom were once students of Fernand Point. Paul Bocuse claimed that Henri Gault first used the term to describe food prepared by Bocuse and other top chefs for the maiden flight of the Concorde airliner in 1969.

Gault and Millau articulated the formula for nouvelle cuisine in ten characteristics of this new style of cooking. The ten characteristics identified were essentially:

- A rejection of excessive complication in cooking.

- Cooking times for most fish, seafood, game birds, veal, green vegetables and pâtés were greatly reduced in an attempt to preserve the natural flavours. Steaming was an important trend from this characteristic.

- The cuisine was made with the freshest possible ingredients.

- Large menus were abandoned in favour of shorter menus.

- Strong **marinades** for meat and game ceased to be used.

- They stopped using heavy sauces such as *espagnole* and *béchamel* thickened with flour-based roux, in favour of seasoning their dishes with fresh herbs, high quality butter, lemon juice and vinegar.

- They used regional dishes for inspiration instead of *cuisine classique* dishes.

- New techniques were embraced and modern equipment was often used.

- The chefs paid close attention to the dietary needs of their guests through their dishes.

- The chefs were extremely inventive and created new combinations and pairings.

Molecular gastronomy is a discipline of culinary science that seeks to investigate, explain and make practical use of the physical and chemical transformations of ingredients that occur while cooking, as well as the social, artistic and technical components of culinary and gastronomic trends in general. Modernist Cuisine is a contemporary aspect of cooking, which is practised by both food scientists and chefs in many professional kitchens and laboratories and takes advantage of many technical innovations from the scientific disciplines.

The term 'molecular gastronomy' was coined in 1992 by the late Oxford physicist Nicholas Kurti and the French INRA chemist Hervé This. The term molecular gastronomy was originally intended to refer only to the scientific investigation of cooking, though it has been adopted by a number of people and applied to cooking itself or to describe a style of cuisine.

In the late 1990s and early 2000s, the term started to be used to describe a new style of cooking in which some chefs began to explore new possibilities in the kitchen by embracing science, research, technological advances in equipment and various natural gums and hydrocolloids produced by the commercial food processing industry. It has since been used to describe the food and cooking of a number of famous chefs, though many of them do not accept the term as a description of their style of cooking.

Chefs who are often associated with molecular gastronomy because of their embrace of science include Grant Achatz, Ferran Adrià, José Andrés, Sat Bains, Richard Blais, Marcel Vigneron, Heston Blumenthal, Wylie Dufresne, Pierre Gagnaire and Laurent Gras. Frustrated with the commonly misunderstood term of their food and cooking as 'molecular gastronomy', several chefs often associated with the movement (Ferran Adria of El Bulli, Heston Blumenthal of the Fat Duck, Thomas Keller of the French Laundry and Per Se) have since renounced the term, releasing a joint statement in 2006 clarifying their approach to cooking, stating that the term 'molecular gastronomy' was coined in 1992 for a single workshop that did not influence them, and that the term does not describe any style of cooking.

The supply and use of commodities

The effect of geography on food production

Agricultural lands occupy nearly 40 per cent of the Earth's land surface and the majority of raw materials for the food and beverage sector ultimately come from farms. Primary production is closely allied with many core sustainability issues such as water scarcity and climate change.

The term geography, when used within the context of gastronomy, refers to the terrain, lakes, rivers, sea, soil and the climate. Climate change is undoubtedly an area that has seen an important impact on food supply. The rearing of animals or growing of crops is a weather sensitive activity. Too much, or too little water at the wrong time, changes in the pattern of rainfall during the year and other climatic factors will influence the success or failure of strategies to produce food which may have been successful in the past.

Natural geographical resources play a vital role in the development of a society. For instance, the climate and terrain determine the agriculture of a community and thus affect which food products a given culture has available to them. Until the relatively recent development of the extensive import and export of agricultural products, the average resident depended on what agriculture their surroundings could produce. Many communities have a few agricultural products that grow well in their area and become a staple of the diet of the community.

Farming is determined by the geography of the local environment and there are chiefly four types of farming available in the United Kingdom.

Arable farming is the production of crops. Crop growth is affected by light, soil, nutrients, water, air and climate. Crops commonly grown in the United Kingdom include cereals, chiefly wheat, oats and barley; root vegetables such as potatoes and sugar beet; pulse crops such as beans or peas; forage crops such as cabbages, rape and kale; fruit, particularly apples and pears; and hay for animal feed.

An arable farm during harvest time

Pastoral farming is the breeding of livestock for meat, wool, eggs and milk, and historically (in the UK) for labour. Livestock products are the main element of the UK's agricultural output. The most common meat animals in the United Kingdom are cattle, pigs, sheep and poultry. In contrast, mixed farming is the growing of both crops and livestock on the same farm. Pastoral farmers are also known as graziers. Some pastoral farmers grow crops purely as fodder for their livestock; some crop farmers grow fodder and sell it to pastoral farmers.

A small scale pig farm

Organic farming is farming without chemical fertilizers, animal cruelty, most pesticides, genetic modification or the routine use of drugs, antibiotics or wormers. In the United Kingdom it is supported and encouraged by the Soil Association. **Organic farming** is the form of agriculture that relies on techniques such as crop rotation, green manure, compost and biological pest control. Organic farming uses fertilizers and pesticides but excludes or strictly limits the use of manufactured (synthetic) fertilizers, pesticides (which include herbicides, insecticides and fungicides), plant growth regulators such as hormones, livestock antibiotics, food additives, genetically modified organisms, human sewage sludge and nanomaterials.

Biodynamic farming is a method of organic farming that emphasizes the holistic development and interrelationships of the soil, plants and animals as a self-sustaining system. One of the first modern ecological farming systems, it emphasizes a sustainable approach to agriculture. Biodynamics has much in common with other organic approaches: it emphasizes the use of manures, natural minerals and composts and excludes the use of artificial chemicals on soil and plants. Methods unique to the biodynamic approach include the following;

- emphasis on integrating farm animals;
- cultivation of crops;
- care of the land;
- use of fermented herbal and mineral preparations as compost additives and field sprays;
- importance from its beginnings on local production and distribution systems using local breeds and varieties;
- use of a cosmological sowing and planting calendar.

There are independent certification agencies for biodynamic products and most of these agencies are members of the international biodynamic standards group Demeter International.

Local sourcing of fresh produce

Caterers, more than ever before, consider the local sourcing of fresh produce the most important aspect of operating sustainably. By using sustainable local produce not only is there less environmental impact but there is a reduction in air miles, which offsets the carbon footprint and there is the opportunity to encourage growth in the local economy. Many operators now establish an approved list of suppliers and some only use suppliers that have proven sustainability credentials.

Local sourcing offers potential cost benefits. Supply chains are generally shorter with local suppliers, which lead to greater certainty and predictability of delivery times. As such, delivery costs are also normally lower. Local suppliers can also be more reactive during times of high demand when longer international lead times can make it harder to react. Local suppliers can act quickly, increasing speed to market, but also creating flexibility in their service to the customer.

WEB LINK Log onto CourseMate to explore the interactive food map of the United Kingdom.

SUSTAINABLE FOOD SOURCING

Sustainability is about the operation or business managing the financial, social and environmental impact of its own operations. By improving their sustainability, food operations can make a huge difference on issues such as climate change, animal welfare, packaging and food waste.

There is no legal definition of the term sustainable food, although some aspects, such as the terms 'organic' or

'Fairtrade', are clearly defined. As a brief guide sustainable food should be produced, processed and traded in ways that:

- Contribute to thriving local economies and sustainable livelihoods – both in the UK and, in the case of imported products, in producer countries.
- Protect the diversity of both plants and animals (and the welfare of farmed and wild species) and avoid damaging natural resources and contributing to climate change.
- Provide social benefits, such as good quality food, safe and healthy products, and educational opportunities.

SEASONALITY

Some of the food we eat is being transported further than ever, and there is increasing demand for a wide range of ready-prepared and exotic out-of-season produce. These trends are associated with different environmental problems, such as:

- Loss of freshness, natural ripening times, flavour and variety of fruits and vegetables. Long-distance fruit and vegetable varieties are liable to be chosen for their yield and keeping qualities. Many are harvested before they are fully ripe and stored over long periods between production, packing and distribution. Sometimes they are stored with post-harvest chemical treatments such as fungicides to help increase shelf-life. Soft fruits and vegetables deteriorate quickly once harvested – so those that travel long distances have to travel quickly, usually by air, which is the most environmentally damaging form of transport.
- Increasing global warming. Food transport, even if it is not by air, creates greenhouse gas emissions that are contributing to the effects of climate change.
- Loss of food culture. Distinctive varieties of fruit and vegetables and native breeds of meat and fish are integral to our culture and landscape.
- Loss of food knowledge and skills. Many customers have lost connection with the land and seasonal rhythms, and have little or no awareness of when and where various foods are produced.

Environment friendly farming

Farming has an immense impact on our environment. Historically, farming has contributed to the beauty of the British countryside; however, industrialized agriculture has also caused environmental damage such as soil erosion, water pollution and damage to wildlife habitats by using pesticides and other intensive farming techniques.

The best way to support environmentally friendly farming is to ensure the purchase of food accredited to a recognized standard, such as one of the schemes listed below. Many consider organic food to be the most environmentally benign form of farming, with the LEAF (Linking Environment and Farming) scheme assuring some environmental benefits.

Organic and LEAF accreditation is clearly marked on food packaging or on signs at farms and an accredited producer will be able to provide a copy of a valid certificate. Other schemes, such as Assured Food Standards (the 'Red Tractor') guarantee that legal minimum standards have been met. See below for further information on the schemes.

ORGANIC

These standards require farmers to protect the environment, primarily by restricting the use of pesticides, and avoiding the use of artificial chemical fertilizers. Instead, organic farmers rely on developing a healthy, fertile soil and growing a mixture of crops. Studies of organic farming systems show less environmental damage and a greater amount and variety of wildlife than conventional farming systems. Certified organic farmers must also operate to high standards of animal welfare. There is a range of organic inspection and certification bodies of which the Soil Association is the largest. The word organic is defined by law, and all certifying bodies must comply with European Organic Regulations. Some certifying bodies, including the Soil Association, have higher standards than these. Buying seasonal and local organic food brings even greater benefits.

LEAF (LINKING ENVIRONMENT AND FARMING)

This is a scheme in which farmers audit their production systems and examine soil management, fertility, pesticide use and pollution control. It encourages farms to have an 'integrated farm management system' to reduce farming's impact on the environment. Member farmers can use the LEAF logo on their products. This is not a scheme defined in law.

ASSURED FOOD STANDARDS (AFS)

An umbrella body for various different crop and meat assurance schemes. Standards require farmers to comply with UK laws about the environment, food safety and animal welfare. Member farmers can use the Red Tractor logo. AFS standards are not defined in law.

Animal welfare

The majority of consumers already think animal welfare is an important issue and an increasing amount of the population is currently making at least one or two purchase decisions as a result of their attitude to animal welfare standards. Concern for farm animals is mainly focused on factory farming, where farm animals are raised in confinement at high stocking density. Issues revolve around the limiting of natural behaviour in animals and invasive procedures such as de-beaking. Other issues include methods of animal slaughter, especially ritual slaughter.

While the killing of animals need not necessarily involve suffering, the general public considers killing an animal an act that reduces its welfare. This leads to concerns with premature slaughtering, such as chick culling. This applies in a lesser extent to all food animals.

Free range

The description 'free range' is defined in European law, but only for poultry. Free range poultry farming systems must allow poultry to have access to open-air runs that are mainly covered with vegetation, and have rules governing the amount of space that the birds have and the type of shelter provided. Other animals such as pigs are often described as 'free range' or 'outdoor reared', but these terms are not legally defined.

To help offset the carbon-footprint and to help establish animal welfare ethics within your menu purchasing local or British meat produced to high environmental and animal welfare standards will further encourage consumer decision making.

Marine conservation

Over three-quarters of the world's fish stocks are currently either fully or over exploited. The environmental problems associated with fishing include:

● Loss of marine biodiversity, not only from declining fish stocks but also from non-target species such as whales, sharks, dolphins, sea-birds and young fish being accidentally killed by fishing gear.

● Damage to sensitive areas of the sea bed and other marine environments by certain fishing methods, particularly sea bed beam trawling.

Fish farming, or aquaculture, can be part of a solution to many of these problems, and the aquaculture industry has boomed in recent years, with farmed species including salmon, trout, sea bass and prawns. However, aquaculture is often very intensive and is associated with a host of social and environmental problems, such as diseases and parasites such as sea lice, resulting from the high concentration of fish in each pen, which can also spread to wild stocks.

Consumers are already concerned about seafood sustainability and with the current state of fish stocks this concern is likely to grow. To play your part in conserving the marine environment:

● Stop purchasing fish from overfished stocks or badly managed fisheries as listed on the Marine Conservation Society's 'fish to avoid' list.

● Ask your supplier for assurances that the fish they supply has been legally and sustainably caught. Most importantly, ask:

   ● where the fish was caught – as the sustainability of some species varies according to location;

   ● how it was caught – sea bed beam trawling is generally considered to be one of the most environmentally damaging fishing methods. More sustainable methods to look out for include handline (e.g. mackerel), diver caught (e.g. scallops), jigs (e.g. squid) and pots or creels (e.g. lobsters or crabs).

● Support organizations and businesses that promote sustainably caught fish using the Marine Stewardship Council (MSC) logo, which is certified to come from well-managed fisheries and not from endangered stocks.

WEB LINK To find out more about the Marine Stewardship Council see http://www.msc.org

Fair trade

World market prices for commodity crops such as coffee, sugar and rice are highly volatile, often falling below the costs of production. Between 1970 and 2000, prices for some of the main agricultural exports of poorer countries fell by between 30 and 60 per cent. The reasons for this are complex but the world's farmers are faced with falling crop prices, a falling share of the retail price of produce they sell, increased farming costs and competing goods from influential countries flooding markets at subsidized prices.

The consequences can be devastating for both small-scale producers and agricultural labourers, especially in other continents. With few other employment opportunities open to them, and no welfare state to fall back on, many small farmers are unable to afford basic necessities such as food for their families, healthcare, and education for their children.

Buying Fairtrade products is about improving the well-being and livelihoods of agricultural producers and labourers in poorer countries, by improving trading relationships and so ensuring better working conditions, greater access to healthcare and a higher standard of living. Buying Fairtrade products is one way to help people out of the cycle of poverty and illness.

Fairtrade standards are set and monitored by Fairtrade Labelling Organizations International (FLO), and use of the Fairtrade Mark in the UK is licensed by the Fairtrade Foundation. Some products are described as 'fair trade' or 'fairly traded', but only products with the Fairtrade Mark are independently certified to ensure the producers have received the benefits of the internationally agreed Fairtrade system.

FIVE WAYS TO CONTROL SUSTAINABLE PURCHASING	
1	Vet your suppliers and maintain close links with each of them
2	Choose your suppliers on the basis of quality and then sustainability
3	Try to grow some of your own produce and purchase from your own customers if possible
4	Talk to your suppliers to establish their business ethos and build a relationship
5	Be flexible enough to change your menu to suit seasonality

Sustainability is increasingly becoming a strong business strategy. As we have seen, customers respond to the support of elements such as recycled waste management, energy efficiency and sourcing ingredients such as sustainable fish.

Food miles and transportation

'Food miles' refers to the distance food is transported from the time of its production until it reaches the consumer. Food miles are one factor used when assessing the environmental impact of food, including the impact on global warming.

The concept of food miles originated in the early 1990s in the United Kingdom. It was conceived by Professor Tim Lang, at the Sustainable Agriculture Food and Environment (SAFE) Alliance and first appeared in print in a report 'The Food Miles Report: The dangers of long-distance food transport', researched and written by Angela Paxton.

Food distribution lorries contribute heavily to carbon emissions

A range of studies have compared emissions over the entire food cycle, including production, consumption and transport. These include estimates of food-related emissions

of greenhouse gas 'up to the farm gate'. In the UK, for example, agricultural-related emissions may account for approximately 40 per cent of the overall food chain (including retail, packaging, fertilizer manufacture and other factors), whereas greenhouse gases emitted in transport account for around 12 per cent of overall food-chain emissions.

The goal of environmental protection agencies is to make people aware of the environmental impact of food miles and to show the pollution percentage and the energy used to transport food over long distances.

Throughout the world, food is transported over long distances for several reasons:

1 To feed densely populated areas that could not otherwise acquire enough food locally.

2 To provide consumers with greater variety of food.

3 To capitalize on the advantages of specific areas producing specialist foods.

The transportation of food from one location to another is undertaken by air, rail, road and water. Transport is important since it enables trade between different societies, which in turn establishes civilizations.

Transport infrastructure consists of the fixed installations necessary for transport, and may be in the form of roads, railways, airways, waterways and canals. Terminals such as airports, railway stations, bus stations, warehouses, trucking terminals, refueling depots (including fueling docks and fuel stations) and seaports are used and are a major point in regulating transportation. Terminals may be used both for interchange of passengers for tourism, and for cargo including food distribution.

Suppliers

Choosing your supplier

Choosing the right suppliers involves much more than examining price lists. Your choice will depend on a wide range of factors such as value for money, quality, reliability and service. How you weigh up the importance of these different factors will depend on your business priorities and strategy.

Effective purchasing focuses on what your food business needs and what you want to achieve. The right products or services and a good price are not the only factors to consider. For example, if you want to change your menu according to daily availability of high quality, local produce, local suppliers that offer you high quality produce with a quick, reliable delivery will rate higher than those that compete on price alone.

HOW MANY SUPPLIERS?

It is well worth investigating how many suppliers you really need. Procuring from a carefully targeted group could have a number of benefits:

● It will be easier to control your suppliers.

- Your business will become more important to them.
- You may be able to make deals that give you an extra competitive advantage.

However, it is important to have a choice of sources. Purchasing from only one supplier can be precarious – where do you go if they let you down, or even go out of business? Equally, while exclusivity may spur some suppliers to offer you a better service, others may simply become complacent and drop their standards over a matter of time.

THE PARTNERSHIP APPROACH

Focus your efforts on choosing and managing strategic suppliers who provide goods or services that are essential to your business needs and menu development. A strong relationship will benefit both sides. You need your suppliers to make every effort to provide the best service possible. In this aspect you are more likely to create this response by showing your suppliers how important they are to your business.

There are a number of significant characteristics that you should look for when identifying and shortlisting possible suppliers. Good suppliers should be able to demonstrate that they can offer you the following benefits:

1 *Quality and reliability*
The quality of your supplies needs to be consistent – your customers associate poor quality with you and not your suppliers. Equally, if your supplier lets you down with a late delivery or poor quality, you may let your customer down.

2 *Speed and flexibility*
Being able to place frequent and small orders will help to avoid tying up too much working capital in stock. Flexible suppliers will help you to respond quickly to changing menus, customer demands and sudden emergencies.

3 *Value for money*
The lowest price is not always the best value for money. If you require reliability and quality from your suppliers, you will have to decide how much you are willing to reimburse for your supplies and the balance you want to strike between cost, reliability, quality and service.

4 *Strong service and clear communication*
It is essential for suppliers to deliver on time, or to be honest and give plenty of warning if they cannot meet your requirements. The best suppliers will want to talk with you regularly to find out what needs you have and how they can serve you better in the future.

5 *Financial security*
It is always worth making sure the supplier has sufficiently strong cash flow to deliver what you want, when you need

it. A credit check will help reassure that the supplier will not go out of business when you need them most.

WHERE TO FIND POTENTIAL SUPPLIERS

Suppliers can be found through a range of channels. It is best to create a shortlist of potential suppliers through a combination of sources to give a broader base to choose from:

1 *Recommendations*
Ask friends and business contacts for recommendations. You are more liable to receive an honest assessment of a supplier's strengths and weaknesses from someone who has worked with a supplier.

2 *Directories*
If searching for a supplier in a local area, it is worth evaluating directories such as *Yellow Pages* and *Thomson Local* or checking the local newspapers.

3 *Trade associations*
If your needs are specific to a particular trade or industry, there will be a trade or chef associations that can match you with suitable suppliers.

4 *Business advisers*
Business support organizations, such as Chambers of Commerce or Enterprise Agencies can often point you in the direction of potential suppliers.

5 *Exhibitions*
Exhibitions offer an important opportunity to talk with a number of potential suppliers in the same place at the same time. Before you attend an exhibition, check the exhibitors are relevant and suitable for your business.

6 *Trade press*
Trade magazines feature advertisements from potential suppliers. A selection of trade publications and trade press listings should be available at your local business library.

Once you have established a manageable shortlist of suppliers to choose from, the next stage is to approach the potential suppliers. Providing a clear brief, summarizing your requirements and giving an outline of the level of business you hope to place with each supplier is important. Rather than specifying exactly what you want to purchase, you may want to request suppliers provide their own suggestions. For example, you might explain to fish suppliers what you want for your new menu and the specification levels of their produce and ask them to come up with recommendations within your budget.

CHEF'S TIP Communicate your purchasing policy to staff and make sure it is adhered to – but listen to their feedback too.

COMPARE POTENTIAL SUPPLIERS

When you receive the responses, compare the suppliers in terms of what matters most to your business and menu. For example, the quality of their product or service may be most important, while their location may not matter.

Price is important, but it should not be the only reason you choose a supplier. Lower prices may reflect poorer quality goods and services which, in the long run, may not be the most cost-effective option. Be confident that the supplier can make a sufficient margin at the price quoted for the business to be commercially viable.

Wherever possible, meet potential suppliers face to face and see how their businesses operate. It is important to visit the supplier's premises to check their own HACCP management. Checking whether a supplier will be outsourcing any work to subcontractors, or relies on other suppliers for critical commodities is important. If so, you may want to assess these suppliers as well and maybe visit them, especially if they are growers or farmers.

It is essential to also understand that your business reputation may be judged on the labour practices and environmental record of your suppliers. It makes good business sense to consider the ethical and environmental impact of your supply chain.

Managing supplier relationships

Once you have settled on the suppliers that you wish to work with, negotiate terms and conditions and draw up contracts. It is good practice to agree service levels before you start trading so you know what to expect from your supplier – and they know what to expect from you. Make it clear what your priorities are and how they will be judged by you.

A written contract helps avoid uncertainty and minimize the risk of any future disputes. From the outset you should aim to build a good relationship with open communication between yourself and your suppliers. Regular contact allows you to deal with any problems before they escalate and find opportunities to work together more effectively.

Look for opportunities to deepen the relationship with key strategic suppliers, explaining your plans and how they could be involved. For example, your suppliers may be able to help with advice on new commodities and current trends that you could use to improve your service or menu.

Regularly review supplier performance and be prepared to shop around for alternative suppliers if necessary.

REVIEWING YOUR SUPPLIERS' PERFORMANCE

It is a good idea to review your suppliers' performance at regular intervals. If you have a service level agreement (SLA) this will help you to assess the business/supplier relationship in the most objective way possible. If not, even at this stage it may be worth using an SLA to define the terms and level of service you require from your supplier. The review process is particularly important as it will prevent existing suppliers becoming complacent.

Asking the following essential questions will help ensure you are getting the best possible deal:

- Price – Are you getting the best price? Does your supplier offer bulk discounts or other favourable terms?
- Quality – Are you satisfied with the quality of your supplies?
- Innovation – Do your suppliers regularly inform you of new products and services that might help improve your business?
- Delivery – Are your suppliers punctual? Do the supplies arrive in good condition and correct temperatures?
- Account management – Do your suppliers respond quickly to any orders or queries that you place with them?
- Service performance – are your suppliers living up to their side of the agreement?

If, after the review process, you find that your suppliers are underperforming, the SLA will usually provide for compensation, commonly in the form of rebates on monthly service charges. You will also need to review your own performance. For example, failing to pay your suppliers on time will not encourage them to keep their standards high.

Developing recipes and menus

As a chef becomes secure with the pace, balance and structure of an existing menu, it is natural to want to improve or change its content, structure or design in accordance with customer demands. To be able to do this, a thorough understanding of menu planning, engineering and performance is imperative.

When developing new ideas for a menu, clear considerations should be taken into account:

1 seasonality;

2 current trends;

3 kitchen size and staff capabilities;

4 customer relationships;

5 type of menu;

6 dietary needs of the customer;

7 theme of the menu.

SEASONALITY

Most foods are seasonal, such as fruits, vegetables, game, fish and certain meats. Fruit and vegetables can generally be purchased throughout the year; if they are not in season in a home country they can be in season somewhere else globally and able to be transported quickly by air or rail to a destination. However, locally sourced foods are generally cheaper, environmentally friendlier and meet with greater customer expectation in providing a legacy of ethical resourcing.

Another example is that commodities such as fish which are out of season and begin their breeding cycle are usually full of eggs (roe). They will not only have less flavour as a result, but also a lower flesh yield than fish that are in season. This will obviously affect portion control and the overall cost of the dish.

The choice and convenience offered by the all year round availability of a full range of food produce from all over the world has allowed chefs to produce eclectic menus. However, there are many benefits to a return to following the seasonal cycles of nature, and of buying fresh, seasonal produce from local suppliers.

The increasing awareness of health-related issues and concerns about the quality, sources and types of food we consume are increasingly influencing consumers' opinions. The environmental impacts of excessive food miles – the transporting of food produce long distances – and the traceability of food are also key factors that influence consumers' buying behaviour.

Generally, the further food has to travel, the longer it spends in transit. That means that vital vitamin content can be lost and the nutritional value of fresh foods will inevitably decline. Transporting food over long distances will also consume a lot of fuel, whether it travels by road or air. This inevitably increases carbon dioxide emissions and contributes to global warming.

CURRENT TRENDS

Chefs should always be conscious of what their competitors and food trends are doing. Studying the reviews of restaurants and reading the media's commentaries on the attitudes of customers to the new food trends is important research for writing your new menu. Speak to your customers, suppliers and team when creating new dishes, and consider what will both meet the needs of your existing customers and attract new ones.

KITCHEN SIZE AND STAFF CAPABILITIES

Generally, the size of your restaurant will dictate how large your menu is. The bigger the kitchen and brigade of chefs, the more menu items you can offer. If you try to offer a large and complex menu out of a small commercial kitchen you may run into serious problems during busy times. Your restaurant kitchen should be between 15 and 25 per cent of the total space in your restaurant. Any smaller and you run the risk of severely limiting what you can serve during a lunch or dinner service. Any larger and you are wasting precious space that could be used for tables and chairs. Creating a kitchen layout with a good flow will also make it more efficient and easier to work in.

Your team should be able to prepare the items on the menu in a specific time and to an exacting standard. Therefore training and monitoring of quality are the controlling aspects behind writing a menu.

CUSTOMER RELATIONSHIPS

Many food businesses in competing markets will redirect or allocate large amounts of resources or attention towards customer retention. In markets with increasing competition it may cost up to five times more to attract new customers than it would to retain current customers, as direct or 'offensive' marketing requires much more extensive resources to cause defection of customers from one restaurant to another. The practice of relationship marketing has been facilitated by customer relationship management software that allows tracking and analyzing of each customer's preferences, tastes, likes, dislikes and complaints. For example, a restaurant maintaining a database of when and how repeat customers come to their restaurants, the menu dishes they choose and the wine or beverage they consume is in a powerful position to develop one-to-one marketing offers and product benefits.

TYPE OF MENU

À la carte has items on the menu that are individually priced and are cooked or finished to order; this allows the guest to construct their own menu.

Table d'hôte is a set menu, with a set price. Table d'hôte menus usually have only limited choices, such as a meat, fish or vegetarian option, and an option for people with special dietary needs.

Menus can range from a single course to a nine or ten-course 'grazing menu'. The portion sizes should reflect the size of the menu; for a single-course menu the portion size should satisfy the appetite, and with a multi-course menu the entire menu should satisfy the appetite without making guests feel too full or unable to finish their meal.

Banquet and function menus are usually table d'hôte menus, carefully designed with the needs of the customer in mind. Care should be taken not to include dishes that take a long time to assemble or contain food that will deteriorate quickly and so will not hold for service.

Cyclical menus are designed to be repeated at given intervals; usually on a weekly, monthly or seasonal basis. Cyclical menus are usually used in canteens and educational institutions and in facilities that have groups of people for set periods of time, such as training centres. In canteens and staff restaurants, where the customers eat every day, the cycle should be longer and start on different days of the week so that the customers will not feel bored by the repetition of the food on offer. Stock control will be more efficient with cyclical menus: the stock requirements will be known well in advance and therefore stock levels can be kept low. In large operations, long-term agreements or forward purchasing can lead to further discounts with suppliers.

Breakfast is an extremely important part of a hotel's repertoire of food service. Generally, the last impression a guest receives of a hotel's food is the breakfast service. Breakfast menus can be à la carte, buffet style or continental.

DIETARY NEEDS OF THE CUSTOMER

Understanding the various requirements of people who have special dietary needs is a requirement of the modern chef.

Coeliac disease is not a food allergy or intolerance, it is an auto-immune disease. In coeliac disease, eating gluten causes the lining of the small intestine to become damaged. Therefore no gluten is permitted in the diet (e.g. breads, pasta and biscuits; any foods that contain wheat flour). Wheat subspecies such as spelt, semolina and durum, and related species such as barley, rye, triticale and kamut can also induce symptoms of coeliac disease. A small minority of coeliac patients also react to oats. It is most likely that oats produce symptoms due to cross contamination with other grains in the fields or in the distribution channels. Generally, oats are therefore not recommended. However, many companies assure the 'purity' of oats, and are therefore still able to be consumed through these sources. Other cereals such as maize, millet, sorghum, rice, soya flour and wild rice are safe for coeliacs to consume, as well as non-cereals such as amaranth, quinoa or buckwheat. Non-cereal carbohydrate-rich foods such as potatoes and bananas do not contain gluten and do not trigger the symptoms.

Coeliac UK is the leading charity working for people with coeliac disease. Their mission is to improve the lives of people with coeliac disease through support, campaigning and research. Coeliac UK provides ingredient and grain checklists to help people with the disease, but it is also a good source of information for the chef when writing menus.

Even very small amounts of gluten can be damaging to people with coeliac disease. Therefore, taking sensible steps to avoid cross contamination with gluten is important.

CHEF'S TIP Some top tips to avoid cross contamination include:

- Keep cooking utensils separate during food preparation and cooking.
- Avoid frying food in the same oil that has previously been used to cook foods which contain gluten.
- Use a clean grill, separate toaster or toaster bags to make gluten-free toast.
- Use separate breadboards and wash surfaces thoroughly before and after use.
- Use separate condiments such as jam, butter, mustard and mayonnaise for coeliac sufferers.

Diabetes mellitus, or simply diabetes, is a group of metabolic diseases in which a person has high blood sugar, either because the body does not produce enough insulin, or because cells do not respond to the insulin that is produced. Sufferers should avoid foods that contain sugar or **glucose**, and be aware of the sugar content of dishes. Restaurants should consider providing alternative dishes that allow the customer to choose healthy menu items that are high or low on the glycaemic index. The glycaemic index (GI) is a ranking of carbohydrates on a scale from 0 to 100 according to the extent to which they raise blood sugar levels after eating. Foods with a high GI are those which are rapidly digested and absorbed and result in marked fluctuations in blood sugar levels. Low-GI foods, by virtue of their slow digestion and absorption, produce gradual rises in blood sugar and insulin levels, and have proven benefits for health. Low GI diets have been shown to improve both glucose and lipid levels in people with diabetes (type 1 and type 2). They have benefits for weight control because they help control appetite and delay hunger. Low GI diets also reduce insulin levels and insulin resistance.

Because meals including low GI foods allow you to absorb carbohydrates more slowly, they help to maintain even blood glucose levels between meals. The effect of a low GI meal can last into the following meal, which helps keep blood glucose more even during the whole day. Slow acting carbohydrates will also reduce the peaks in blood glucose that often follow a meal, and this may have a role in helping to prevent or reduce the risk of getting type 2 diabetes. Research has shown that people who have an overall low GI diet have a lower incidence of heart disease.

When catering for customers with diabetes your menu should have plenty of starchy carbohydrate foods available. If possible let the person with diabetes help themselves as they will know how much they will need (buffets are often a good way of allowing this). It is helpful to have bread already on the table or offered early as people requiring insulin may have taken their insulin injection and will therefore require some carbohydrate intake within half an hour of their injection. Other key points are identified below:

- Have a variety of dishes from which people can choose.
- People with diabetes need meals that include carbohydrates, such as potatoes, pasta or rice.
- Try to provide low fat and low calorie options, e.g. steamed new potatoes.
- Provide extra vegetables and salad.
- Serve butter, mayonnaise or dressings separately so that people can choose whether to have them or not.
- Provide vegetarian options.
- Serve cream and rich sauces separately so that people can choose whether to add them or not.
- Provide low sugar desserts as an alternative choice to ordinary desserts.
- Water should be available on the table.

Nut allergy, tree nut allergy is a common type of food allergy, affecting millions of people worldwide. It is a hypersensitivity to dietary substances from tree nuts causing an overreaction of the immune system, which may lead to severe physical symptoms. Tree nuts include almonds, Brazil nuts, cashews, chestnuts, hazelnuts, macadamia nuts, coconut, pecans, pine nuts, pistachios and walnuts.

Many different nuts can cause allergic reactions and are often found in foods which you would not expect to contain nuts

Tree nut allergy is distinct from peanut allergy, as peanuts are **legumes**, whereas a tree nut is a hard-shelled fruit of specific plants. People with tree nut allergy are seldom allergic to just one type of nut and are therefore usually advised to avoid all tree nuts, even though an individual may not be allergic to all varieties of tree nuts. The severity of the allergy varies from person to person, and exposure can increase sensitivity. For those with a milder form of the allergy, the raw nut protein usually causes a more severe reaction than the oil, and extra roasting or processing can reduce the allergic reaction. Those diagnosed with anaphylaxis will have a more immediate and severe reaction and be required to avoid all exposure to any allergen-containing products or byproducts, regardless of processing, as they are prone to even greater sensitivity. Menus should indicate clearly whether nut products have been used.

Anaphylaxis is a serious allergic reaction that is rapid in onset and may cause death. It typically results in a number of symptoms including an itchy rash, throat swelling and low blood pressure. Common causes include insect bites/stings, foods and medications.

Seafood allergy is a type of food allergy. It is a hypersensitivity to dietary substances from shellfish, scaly fish or crustaceans, causing an overreaction of the immune system, which may lead to severe physical symptoms. Seafood allergies are usually treated with an exclusion diet and vigilant avoidance of foods that may be contaminated with shellfish or fish ingredients and/or oils. The most severe seafood allergy reaction is called anaphylaxis, which is an emergency, requiring immediate attention. It is treated with epinephrine, which can be administered with an Epi-Pen.

Dairy/milk allergy is a food allergy and an adverse immune reaction to one or more of the constituents of milk from any animal (most commonly alpha S1-casein, a protein in cow's milk). This milk-induced allergic reaction can involve anaphylaxis. It is important to note that a milk allergy is a separate and distinct condition from lactose intolerance.

Different milk products; cheese, cream, yoghurt and milk

Alpha S1-caseins differ between species. This explains why someone with an allergic reaction to sheep's milk cannot drink goat's milk but can drink breast milk without an allergic reaction. Lactose intolerance is non-allergic food sensitivity, and comes from a lack of production of the enzyme lactase, required to digest the predominant sugar in milk. Adverse effects of lactose intolerance generally occur after much higher levels of milk consumption than do adverse effects of milk allergy.

There are many commercially available replacements for milk for children and adults. Rice milk, soy milk, oat milk, coconut milk and almond milk are sometimes used as milk substitutes but are not suitable nutrition for infants. However, special infant formula based on soy, rice, almonds or carob seeds are commercially available. On an avoidance diet, it may be possible to reduce the longer-term risk of calcium deficiency and osteoporosis by incorporating other sources of calcium, although the effect of calcium and vitamin D supplementation on osteoporosis is not always clear.

Vegetarianism includes the practice of following plant-based diets (fruits, vegetables, grains), with or without the inclusion of dairy products or eggs, and with the exclusion of meat (red meat, poultry and seafood). Abstention from byproducts of animal slaughter, such as animal-derived rennet and gelatin, may also be practiced. Vegetarianism can be adopted for different reasons. Many object to eating meat out of respect for conscious life. Other motivations for vegetarianism include health, political, environmental, cultural, aesthetic or economic.

Various packaged or processed foods, including cakes, biscuits, chocolate and sweets often contain unfamiliar animal ingredients which may be a special concern for vegetarians due to the likelihood of such additions. Semi-vegetarian diets consist largely of vegetarian foods, but may include fish or poultry, or sometimes other meats on an infrequent basis. Those with diets containing fish or poultry may define meat as mammalian flesh and may identify with vegetarianism. A pescetarian diet, for example, includes fish but no meat. The common use association between such diets and vegetarianism has led vegetarian groups such as the Vegetarian Society to state that diets containing these ingredients are not vegetarian, due to fish and birds being described as animals.

There are a number of types of vegetarianism, which exclude or include various foods:

- Ovo vegetarianism includes eggs but not dairy products.

- Lacto vegetarianism includes dairy products but not eggs.

- Ovo-lacto vegetarianism (or lacto-ovo vegetarianism) includes animal/dairy products such as eggs, milk and honey.

- Veganism excludes all animal flesh and animal products, including milk, honey and eggs, and may also exclude any products tested on animals or any clothing from animals.

- Raw veganism includes only fresh and uncooked fruit, nuts, seeds and vegetables. Vegetables can only be cooked up to a certain temperature.

- Fruitarianism permits only fruit, nuts, seeds and other plant matter that can be gathered without harming the plant.

- Sentient vegetarianism (also known as yogic diet), a plant based diet which may also include dairy (not eggs) and honey, but excludes anything from the onion or leek family, red lentils, **durian** fruit, mushrooms, blue cheeses, fermented foods or sauces, alcoholic drinks and often also excludes coffee, black or green tea, chocolate, nutmeg or any other type of stimulant such as excess sharp spices.

- Buddhist vegetarianism excludes all animal products as well as vegetables in the allium family (which have the characteristic aroma of onion and garlic): onion, garlic, leeks, scallions or shallots.

- Jain vegetarianism includes dairy but excludes eggs and honey, as well as root vegetables.

- Macrobiotic diets consist mostly of whole grains and beans.

Veganism is the practice of abstaining from the use of animal products. Ethical vegans reject the commodity status of animals and the use of animal products for any purpose, while dietary vegans (or strict vegetarians) eliminate them from their diet only. Another form, environmental veganism, rejects the use of animal products on the premise that the industrial practice is environmentally damaging and unsustainable.

The logo of the British Vegan Society

Well-planned vegan diets have been found to offer protection against many degenerative conditions, including heart disease. They tend to be higher in dietary fibre, magnesium, folic acid, vitamin C, vitamin E, iron and phytochemicals. The diet can also be lower in calories, saturated fat, cholesterol, long-chain omega-3 fatty acids, vitamin D, calcium, zinc and vitamin B12. Because plant foods tend not to contain significant amounts of B12, researchers agree that vegans should eat foods fortified with B12 or take a daily supplement. B12 is a bacterial product that cannot be found reliably in plant foods and is needed for the formation and maturation of red blood cells and for normal nerve function; a deficiency can lead to a number of health problems.

Any plant-based dish may be vegan. Meat analogues, or 'mock meats,' made of soy or gluten – including vegetarian sausage, vegetarian mince and veggie burgers – are widely available. Since, however, some meat-free vegetarian foods, including some vegetarian sausages, may include eggs or dairy products they would be part of an acceptable diet for vegetarians but not for vegans. Cheese analogues made from soy, nuts and tapioca are commonly used.

Clinical nutrition is nutrition of patients in health care. Clinical in this sense refers to the welfare of patients in hospitals. It incorporates mainly the scientific fields of nutrition and dietetics. It aims to keep a healthy energy balance in patients, as well as providing sufficient amounts other nutrients such as protein, vitamins and minerals. Dietitians are health professionals who specialize in human nutrition, meal planning, economics and preparation. They are trained to provide safe, evidence-based dietary advice and management to individuals (in health and disease), as well as to institutions. Clinical nutritionists are health professionals who focus more specifically on the role of nutrition in chronic disease, including possible prevention or remediation by addressing nutritional deficiencies before resorting to drugs.

Any menu in a hospital should be written by both the chef and a dietician. The dietary requirements of the patients are of paramount importance in hospital catering and play a vital role in the recuperation of the patient.

School meals were first introduced in the UK, in the 1870s to combat the high levels of malnutrition amongst children in poor areas. In 1944 it was made compulsory for local authorities to provide school dinners, with legal nutritional requirements. Free school meals were available to children with families on very low incomes. The School Food Trust is a UK Charity and specialist advisor to government on school meals, children's food and related skills. The trust was created in 2005 by the Department for Education and Skills (DfES), following celebrity chef Jamie Oliver's critique of the nutritional quality of school meals in his TV documentary.

School meals must meet the applicable recommendations of the Dietary Guidelines Regulations and establish a standard for school lunches to provide one-third of the Recommended Dietary Allowances of protein, Vitamin A, Vitamin C, iron, calcium and calories. The budgetary constraints placed upon school caterers can be very restrictive in the production of these menus.

College/university menus are similar to schools, the menus on offer should be healthy but substantial to allow for the higher metabolic rates of this group. Menus should reflect a diversity of styles and ethnic cuisines.

People at work require different types of menu, depending on what their occupations are. Soldiers in training and manual workers from a building site, for example, will require a lot of calories, but office workers use fewer calories and may desire a more healthy diet. Chefs working in the financial and corporate business sector may receive requests such as a 'lunch requirement to help secure a big deal'. A substantial contract may be at stake, so the menu should be discussed carefully with the client or principal butler to ascertain the client's requirements.

THEME

A restaurant's menu is an extension of its overall theme. Choose menu colours, layouts and fonts that will complement the theme and decor of the restaurant. Some restaurants are creative and use different items to display a menu such as chalkboards, breadboards or scrolls. The menu should be printed in a font that is easy to read and with a large enough font. Use a background colour that makes the font easy to follow such as white or cream.

MENU ENGINEERING

In general, the term *menu engineering* is used within the hospitality industry (specifically in the context of restaurants), but can also be applied to any industry that displays a list of products or service offerings for consumer choice. Typically the goal with menu engineering is to maximize the profitability by subconsciously encouraging customers to purchase what you want them to buy, and discouraging the purchase of items you do not want them to buy.

Fields of study which contribute most to menu engineering include:

- psychology (perception, attention, emotion/effect);
- managerial accounting (contribution margin and unit cost analysis);

- marketing and strategy (pricing, promotion);
- graphic design (layout, typography).

PSYCHOLOGY

Visual perception is inextricably linked to how customers read a menu. Most menus are presented visually (though many restaurants verbally list daily specials), and the majority of menu engineering recommendations focus on how to increase attention by strategically arranging menu categories within the pages of the menu, and item placement within a menu category.

Customer perception of items offered on a menu can also be affected by subtle textual manipulations. For example, descriptive labelling of item names may produce positive effects, leading to higher customer satisfaction, and higher perceived product value. Similarly, the presence of pound signs or other potential monetary cues may cause guests to spend less.

MANAGERIAL ACCOUNTING

The primary goal of menu engineering is to encourage the purchase of targeted items, presumably the most profitable items, and to discourage purchase of the least profitable items. To that end, food businesses must first calculate the cost of each menu item. This costing exercise should extend to all items listed on the menu and should reflect all costs incurred to produce and serve. Optimally item costs should include: food cost (including product waste calculations and product loss), incremental labour (e.g. costs for in-house butchering, pastry production or general preparation), condiments and packaging.

After an item's cost and price have been determined, evaluation of an item's profitability is based on the contribution margin. The contribution margin is calculated as the menu price minus the cost. Menu engineering then focuses on maximizing the contribution margin of each customer's order. Recipe costing should be updated (at least the ingredient cost portion) whenever the menu is reprinted or whenever items are re-engineered.

MARKETING

By using guest demand (also called the menu mix) and gross profit margins, the relative performance of each menu item is determined and assigned one of the following terms:

- **Stars** are extremely popular and have a high contribution margin. Ideally stars should be your flagship or signature menu items.
- **Work horse** are high in popularity but low in contribution margin. Work horse menu items sell well, but don't significantly increase revenue.
- **Cash cows** are also high in popularity and have a high contribution margin.

MENU ENGINEERING WORKSHEET

Enter Your Restaurant Name Here

Date Prepared: | Jan 13, 2003

Period Covered: | Week Ending Jan 12

A	B	C	D	E	F	G	H	L	P	R	S
Menu Item Name ITEM	Number Sold	Popularity %	Item Food Cost	Item Sell Price	Item Profit (E-D)	Total Cost (D*B)	Total Revenue (E*B)	Total Profit (H-G)	Profit Category	Popularity Category	Menu Item Class
Item # 1	100	10.8%	$1.25	$4.50	$3.25	$125.00	$450.00	$325.00	Low	High	Workhorse
Item # 2	50	5.4%	$1.50	$5.00	$3.50	$75.00	$250.00	$175.00	Low	Low	Dog
Item # 3	60	6.5%	$1.60	$6.00	$4.40	$96.00	$360.00	$264.00	High	Low	Challenge
Item # 4	110	11.9%	$0.95	$5.00	$4.05	$104.50	$550.00	$445.50	Low	High	Workhorse
Item # 5	25	2.7%	$2.00	$4.50	$2.50	$50.00	$112.50	$62.50	Low	Low	Dog
Item # 6	35	3.8%	$1.60	$5.00	$3.40	$56.00	$175.00	$119.00	Low	Low	Dog
Item # 7	75	8.1%	$1.10	$4.00	$2.90	$82.50	$300.00	$217.50	Low	High	Workhorse
Item # 8	90	9.7%	$2.25	$7.00	$4.75	$202.50	$630.00	$427.50	High	High	Star
Item # 9	140	15.1%	$1.95	$6.50	$4.55	$273.00	$910.00	$637.50	High	High	Star
Item # 10	25	2.7%	$1.95	$6.75	$4.80	$48.75	$168.75	$120.50	High	Low	Challenge
Item # 11	120	13.0%	$2.30	$7.50	$5.20	$276.00	$900.00	$624.00	High	High	Star
Item # 12	95	10.3%	$2.00	$6.50	$4.50	$190.00	$617.50	$427.00	High	High	Star

	N						I	J	M
Total	925	100.0%					$1 579.25	$5 423.75	$3 844.50

K = I/J
29.1%
Food Cost %

O = M/N
$4.16
Ave Item Profit

- **Challenges** are generally low in popularity and high in contribution margin. Challenge dishes are difficult to sell but have a high profit margin.

- **Dogs** are low in popularity and low in contribution margin. They are difficult to sell and produce little profit when they do sell.

In general, items within a relevant comparable set should be priced to have similar contribution margins – this way, the restaurant would make the same amount of money, no matter what item the guest chooses to order. Above is a completed menu engineering spreadsheet to demonstrate how the process is performed on the basis of the information needed to run a restaurant.

Writing an informative and balanced menu

Good menus are those which provide appetizing, nutritious meals at prices which are suitable to the target customer and at the same time cover the business operating and service costs.

Many factors must be contemplated when planning menus, including nutritional requirements and communication, availability of food products, seasonality, required stock levels, service and preparation times, customer demographics, religious and cultural beliefs and any special dietary requirements such as vegetarianism.

Menus should be balanced in the food choices that are available, be truthful about the ingredients used, be technically correct and must not create false customer expectations.

It is usual to decide first on the special, meat, fish and main dishes to be served and building the remainder of the menu round these dishes being conscious at all times of the production and likely selling costs of individual dishes. Menus should consist of foods chosen from the five food groups:

- meat and fish;
- milk and milk products;
- fruit and vegetables;
- bread and cereals;
- fats and oils.

Consideration must also be given to the service presentation of dishes including the use of colour, variety of flavour and diversity of textures. When writing a menu the following points should be considered:

Avoid jargon – do not use unnecessary jargon that might intimidate the guest and do not embellish the description of each dish with descriptive words or phrases such as *an assortment of farm fresh*, *home baked* and *oven baked*.

Use local and understandable language – certain words will not translate into English particularly well, words such as *mayonnaise* or *sauerkraut*. These are words that have, over time, become part of the English language and are generally understood by everyone. If foreign language is used, sometimes it is best to state a simple explanation in English underneath or to ensure the front of house service team can translate the menu perfectly for the customer. A mixture of languages on a menu should be avoided if at all possible.

Keep it simple – use menu descriptions that are uncomplicated and easy to understand. Avoid including too many dishes on one menu as the customer may have difficulty in selecting their choice. The way in which a menu is worded can demonstrate culinary flair and professionalism. What is stated about what is served is critical and should include how each dish is prepared, how it is served and any other special features such as specialist or local ingredients. Ensure that menu descriptions are not too lengthy, are written in simple and understandable English and that there are no spelling mistakes.

VIDEO CLIP Menu production, using fridges and storing stock.

The development of the menu

Menus must evolve with the needs of the customer and the business, and for most chefs, change is important because it keeps interest and creativity alive. But changes to menus should be structured to allow for smooth transitions.

Before making any changes, the team should critically evaluate the menu. Check the sales mix of each dish according to your menu engineering spreadsheet and retain those dishes that are perceived as 'signature dishes' and that sell well. Then write recipes that fit in with the structure of the existing menu and complement dishes that you intend to keep. The recipes should be evaluated to establish a cost in production and a selling price should be determined to fit into the business plan and achieve the required profit margins.

VIDEO CLIP Producing a balanced menu.

IMPLEMENTING MENU CHANGES

1 When designing recipes, take into account all previously mentioned factors and ensure that food costs are correct and are closely monitored throughout the menu lifespan.

2 Produce an accurate specification sheet for each dish.

3 Test cook and taste test each dish.

4 Discuss the merits of each dish and make any changes that are deemed necessary.

5 If a dish is approved, present it to the service team to sample and describe the dish to them exactly. It is important that the service team have a full understanding of every dish as their recommendations can lead to the dish being a sales success.

6 Meet with some of the customers who have tried the new menu and obtain their feedback. This has the advantage of making the clientele feel included and builds a rapport with them.

VIDEO CLIP How to cost recipes.

TASK Produce your own specification sheet for a selected dish. This should include recipe, photograph, equipment needed, quality points of the main ingredients, potential food allergies for the dish, method of production and cost of the dish.

The physical menu and how to sell

Menu changes can work in favour of a business if the new menu is well presented. All menu pages should be fully utilized as each page should be viewed as an advertisement for your establishment and vacant pages could be used to sell additional products or services through in-house cross marketing.

ARTWORK AND DESIGN

A smart looking menu is just as important as attractive restaurant décor or fine service. The style or appearance should match the décor and style of your restaurant.

Any menu layout should follow the logical eating and drinking sequence of a meal, and should flow in a consistent layout sequence – top to bottom, left to right and in page sequence.

It is most important that the type size is large enough so that the customer can easily read the menu under the predominant lighting conditions within the restaurant. Care should be given to the font style for presentation and readability, ensuring adequate spacing and no over crowding of words or pictures on the page.

MERCHANDISING

Your menu is a major merchandising tool and can communicate numerous other offerings.

It should include all basic information relating to your operation such as address, phone number and opening times, but can also include other promotional material such as function and outside catering information, or retail items.

MARKETING

Listed items, charges and special features are the whole focal point of the entire food service operation. Menus must be constantly changed to reflect changes in cost structures and the changes in public tastes and expectations.

When devising a marketing strategy, you should consider how best to reach your customers and what you can do to generate interest in your offering:

CREATIVE MENUS GET ATTENTION

Does your menu look different or does it look like every other competitor's menu? An exceptional menu will have unusual design, good use of colour, stimulating paper selection and an unusual shape or fold. Therefore an unusual and creative menu will advertise your operation as different and creative in both cuisine and service.

ASSESSMENT OF KNOWLEDGE AND UNDERSTANDING

To test your level of knowledge and understanding, answer the following short questions. These will help to prepare you for your summative (final) assessment.

1. Discuss the benefits of sourcing local suppliers and interacting with them as a community.

2. List the ten types of establishment that are associated with gastronomy.

3. What are the main factors and influences on gastronomy?

4. Explain how technology and science can both benefit and potentially harm gastronomy in the future.

5. **Research task:**
   Gastronomy has been discussed as a whole within this chapter. Highlight one particular area that is of significant interest to you and research how to develop a dining experience that mirrors these ideas and concepts.

6. State three stages in the development of new recipes.

7. Explain why it is important to give an in-depth briefing to service staff when introducing new menu items.

8. Explain why it is important to consider the customers' needs when developing new recipes.

9. Discuss what the advantages and disadvantages of a cyclical menu are.

10. Explain the terms gross profit and net profit and state how you achieve these.

11. Name two allergies the can bring on anaphylactic shock.

12. **Research task:**
    Using your knowledge of a professional kitchen, devise a simple menu for use in each of the following places (one menu for each):

    ● school;

    ● staff restaurant;

    ● banquet for a wedding at a hotel.

Cold larder and farinaceous

4

VRQ

Advanced skills and techniques in producing:

- vegetable and vegetarian dishes
- meat dishes
- producing poultry and games dishes
- fish and shellfish dishes

NVQ

Prepare cook and present complex:

- cold products
- pasta dishes

Recipes

LEARNING OBJECTIVES

The aim of this chapter is to enable you to develop skills and implement gathered knowledge in the preparation, cookery and presentation principles of different cold starters, salads, **canapés** and farinaceous items. This will also include the appropriate use of materials, ingredients and equipment.

At the end of this chapter you will be able to:

● Identify a range of commodities and their uses in cold larder and farinaceous work.

● Understand the use of relative ingredients, selecting and stating the quality points of various commodities, cold dishes and farinaceous items.

● Prepare, cook and present a range of cold and farinaceous dishes.

● Identify the correct storage procedures and holding temperatures of canapés, salads, cold starters and farinaceous dishes.

● Select the required tools and equipment for preparing and cooking cold and farinaceous dishes.

Introduction to the *chef garde manger*

The *chef garde manger* is a mixed position within the professional kitchen. *Garde manger* is a French term which translates as 'keeping to eat'. Historically, the title was given to a chef whose job was to take charge of raw food and keep it fit to eat. This chef had to be skilled in the science of food preservation and preparation and in the art of food presentation.

The role of the modern chef garde manger, or larder chef, has evolved in response to changes in dining trends and in technology in the kitchen. This chef is still responsible for the production and preservation of cold soups, salads, canapés, charcuterie products, cheeses, condiments and buffets, but now they are also likely to present centrepieces in fat, carved fruits and vegetables and create ornate decorative dishes using poultry, game, fish, shellfish and meat.

VIDEO CLIP Canapés: prawn with lemon dressing and pâté **en croute**

The beginning of a meal

Certain words have been used to describe an element, dish or type of course in the culinary arts. Every once in a while, words used to describe a course or dish can mislead the customer. This can be the case with **amuse bouches**, appetizers and **hors d'oeuvres**. Each term is associated with small, delicate portions of food and so it can easily be assumed that they are all the same type of dish.

● Amuse bouches (sometimes called amuse gueules) – these are little savoury nibbles, to be eaten within two bites and offered just for fun as 'mouth amusements' before the starter course is served. They can be presented hot or cold.

● Appetizers – these are small portions of food that are the first food to be served at the table. They are part of the planned menu, served before the starter or a main course. Some chefs use this small appetizer as something to titillate the appetite. Pre-dessert appetizers are even served in many high-class modern restaurants.

● Hors d'oeuvres – this term, which translates literally as 'outside the works', was borrowed by French chefs to refer to delicate, small portions of food served separately (or apart) from the main meal. Usually served as a starter on its own.

Many different terms are used internationally for starters or hors d'oeuvres, and most countries have some form of starter course or small presentation of food to indulge the appetite. The following are examples of various countries' approaches to small food dishes, either to be served at the beginning of a meal or as the meal itself:

● Antipasti (Italy) – small salads, cooked vegetables, fungi, fish dishes, eggs or cured meats, simply decorated.

● Antojitos (Mexico) – small servings of spiced vegetables and pulses with tortilla bases, such as tacos, quesadillas and enchiladas.

● Chat (India) – small portions of food eaten at all times of the day.

● Dim sum (China) – meaning 'touch the heart', dim sum was originally a Cantonese custom linked to the Chinese tradition of yum cha (drinking tea); served in traditional Chinese tea houses.

● Meze (Greece) – can be as simple as a small bowl of olives, or more complicated, such as stuffed **marinated** vine leaves; served with a pre-dinner drink.

- Tapas (Spain) – the tradition of tapas was to serve a **slice** of ham, cheese or bread over a glass of sherry at roadside inns, and because this custom spurred the sales of alcoholic beverages, tapas became well established; there are many different varieties, with every region having its own speciality tapas.

Hors d'oeuvres

When choosing the menu, the hors d'oeuvres are carefully selected to complement the following courses. The selection of hors d'oeuvres on a menu needs to offer a complete range to cater for all diets (e.g. vegetarian or vegan diets or religious restrictions).

Hors d'oeuvres can be served as a starter or as a main course. An extended selection can be served as a buffet. This is similar to the Russian *zakuskis*, which are usually a collection of small hors d'oeuvres presented on a separate table for guests to help themselves to before the main meal commences.

A single hors d'oeuvre is a simple cold dish with one main ingredient and an accompanying **garnish**. Hors d'oeuvre varies contain a selection of main ingredients; each will contain small quantities of a range of products. The idea for

plated combinations of themed ingredients, or *assiettes*, originated from this.

There are three main types of hors d'oeuvres:

- Hors d'oeuvre **chaud** – hot items, can be vegetable-based, meat, game, fish, egg, dairy, soufflé or tartlet.

- Hors d'oeuvre singulaire – single-food items, served only with certain dressings and in one piece or one portion, for example avocado pears, caviar, stuffed eggs, langoustine, melon, pâté or diverse fruit cocktails.

- Hors d'oeuvre variés – selection of items consisting of multiple ingredients. They can be cut into small dice, strips, cubes or pieces, include pickled, marinated or seasoned ingredients and be served with additional fresh herbs, dressings, vinaigrettes or mayonnaise-based sauces.

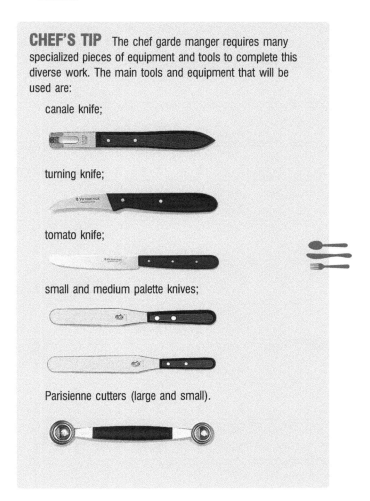

Commodities

Cold red and white meat products

All cuts of meat should be purchased as fresh as possible, and chefs should receive each product and evaluate its quality before using. The chef garde manger should be capable of noting the warning signs when meat is lacking in quality; such as excessive odour, slimy to the touch, incorrect weight, incorrect delivery temperature, dull rather than bright colouring, poor marbling in certain cuts and tough texture.

Storage and hygiene must be thoroughly considered when preparing and cooking meat products. Being high in protein, meats carry a considerable risk of bacterial cross-contamination. Care must be taken to ensure meats are not served undercooked.

The cold state of prepared and cooked meat should be monitored carefully. Red meats have a high fat content, which may begin to solidify and congeal within the presented dish after a period of time.

Pork has a number of uses within the garde manger. Its high fat content makes it a good source of moisture within pâtés, **terrines** and stuffing or farce.

Veal is a very lean meat, similar to beef, and so is lacking in natural fats. Veal tends to be mixed with pork when making terrines, pâtés or raised pies so that the fat from the pork will keep the dish moist.

> **CHEF'S TIP** Other specialist equipment includes:
> - terrine moulds, in a range of sizes;
> - digital thermometer, to gauge internal cooking temperatures;
> - corer or set of specialist knives, to sculpt vegetables;
> - small glazing brush.

> **VIDEO CLIP** Marinated red meat on crispy leaf salad

> **VIDEO CLIP** Marinated white meats with walnut and apple salad

> **HEALTH & SAFETY** Regular checks should be carried out on all items of electrical equipment to ensure that they work properly and conform to all relevant safety regulations.

Cold poultry products

Poultry is the most versatile of all the meats within the garde manger. It is an easy commodity to work with and there is little wastage; all parts of a bird can be used to make items such as **mousses**, **ballotines** and **galantines**. The winglets can be turned into small canapé items, such as chicken cherries. It is an inexpensive commodity and can be very cost effective to serve.

FOIE GRAS

Foie gras is a commodity much prized by chefs throughout the world and is considered a universal delicacy. It is the enlarged liver from a goose or duck that has been force fed and fattened for a period of up to five months. These speciality poultry do not exercise and are overfed, which results in a substantial fatty liver. The following quality checks should be carried out when purchasing foie gras:

- a light yellow to amber colour;
- firm to the touch, but should give slightly under thumb pressure and the mark should remain visible;
- the fewer blemishes apparent, the higher the grade.

Goose foie gras has a very smooth and creamy texture, like silk. Its flavour is very rich, subtle and sophisticated. However, it is more expensive and less available than duck foie gras, which has overtaken in popularity. Approximately 95 per cent of the foie gras produced in France is from ducks, with the remaining 5 per cent coming from geese. The flavour and texture of duck foie gras is more rustic and pronounced than goose foie gras. It also has a stronger aroma.

Although the fattening of geese began in Ancient Egypt 4500 years ago, it is still considered today by some people as a subject for poor animal welfare due to the process of fattening. However, in order to produce the best quality foie gras the wellbeing and comfort of the bird is paramount. The physiological basis of foie gras production is for migratory birds' capacity for weight gain, particularly in the liver, in preparation for their annual migration. Toulouse geese and Mulard ducks are the most commonly used breeds for foie gras. Mulards are a cross breed between a male Muscovy duck and a female Pekin duck.

Geese and ducks are omnivorous, and like many birds, have expansive throats allowing them to store large amounts of food, either whole or pre-digested, in the crop, which is an enlarged portion of the esophagus, while awaiting digestion in the stomach. In the wild this dilation allows them to swallow large foodstuffs, such as a whole fish. The geese or ducks used in foie gras production are usually kept in a building on straw for the first four weeks of their lives, and then maintained as free-range for some weeks, feeding naturally on grasses. The birds are then brought inside for gradually longer periods while introduced to a high starch diet. The next feeding phase, which the French call *gavage* or *finition d'engraissement*, or 'completion of fattening', involves daily ingestion of controlled amounts of feed for 12 to 15 days with ducks and for 15 to 18 days with geese. During this phase ducks are fed daily while geese are fed up to four times daily. In order to facilitate handling of ducks during gavage, these birds are typically housed in group pens during this phase.

Foie gras normally comes in one of four forms:

- Foie gras cru – this is raw foie gras ('cru' means raw). If you are cooking and preparing foie gras yourself, this is what you will need. However, most chefs purchase foie gras pre-cooked.

- Foie gras frais – this is foie gras which has been freshly prepared and cooked ('frais' means fresh). It will keep for approximately one week in the refrigerator (check the best-before date).

- Foie gras mi-cuit – mi-cuit translates as 'semi-cooked' or 'medium-cooked'. In fact, the foie gras has been fully cooked and is ready to eat, but it has been cooked at a moderate temperature (70°C to 80°C) so it will keep only up to three months even though it is bottled or canned (check the best-before date).

- Foie gras en conserve – this is similar to foie gras mi-cuit, except that it has been cooked at a higher temperature (105°C to 115°C). The higher temperature means that it will keep for years, provided the sealed container is not opened.

When preparing foie gras for cold dishes (such as for mousses, terrines, **parfaits** and **forcemeats**) the liver must be cleaned and have all the veins removed before cooking. As little damage as possible should be done to the liver during preparation.

CHEF'S TIP If you do not have a steady hand, squeezable plastic bottles are a good way to apply sauces and dressings to plates.

VIDEO CLIP Deveining a lobe of foie gras

Cold game products

Most game items have a prominent flavour and are relatively simple to use within the garde manger. The flavour and tenderness of game begins to improve as it ages. The technique of aging game is to hang the carcass for between 7 and 14 days (depending on the type of game) at a temperature of 1–3°C. This allows the enzymes in the meat to break down the complex proteins in the carcass.

After the **ageing** process the flavour and tenderness can be further enhanced by marinating. This should, however, never be done to mask or overpower the natural flavours of the meat. The acids contained in a marinade, such as vinegar, citric juices and alcohol, will break down proteins in the meat, making it tenderer. However, the meat should not stay in a marinade for too long. The most common dishes for game products are game pies, terrines and pâtés.

VIDEO CLIP Preparation of duck liver, orange and hazelnut paste

Cured and smoked meats

Curing is the addition of salt, sugar or nitrate to any protein to preserve, flavour and colour the meat. The salt penetrates the flesh and dehydrates the meat by a process called osmosis. This results in a lower moisture content, which inhibits the growth and reproduction of bacteria.

The basic curing methods can be applied to meat products in many different ways:

- Dry curing – the curing ingredients are applied directly onto the meat. This is the slowest method, and is used in curing hams, bacon, salt beef and other small cuts of meat.

- Dry sugar curing – sugar and nitrate are added to salt, which is then directly applied to the surface of the meat. The meat is always cured in a refrigerator. This method can be used for poultry, game and smaller cuts of meat.

- **Brine** curing (pickling) – the meat is cured with a brine made from salt and nitrate, and sometimes sugar. The meat is soaked for a specific time in a refrigerator. Large cuts of meat are cured in this way, such as ham and turkey.

Smoking is another method of preserving meats. It also adds flavour and colour to the meat, and can be used for other commodities such as fish. The process for smoking meats is the same as for curing, followed by washing and smoking.

There are two methods of smoking food:

- Cold smoking – a controlled flow of smoke at about 35°C is blown over the commodity for about five–six hours. This creates a lightly smoked and slightly drier product.

● Hot smoking – the smoking temperature is higher at 70–80°C and the heat of the smoke will cook the product as it is being smoked. This usually produces a stronger, smokier flavour.

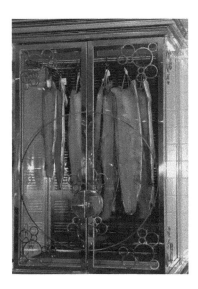

Smoking times will vary for different types of produce, being anything from 20 minutes to several days. The most commonly used woods for smoking are beech, oak and chestnut, with additional flavours such as juniper, sage and rosemary used for aromatic flavourings. Further flavours that can be used include hickory, scented teas (such as jasmine), fir wood and pine needles.

A portable smoking unit

Smoking biscuits/chips

Ingredients used in the smoking process of meats, vegetables and fish

Vegetables and fruit

These are widely used within the garde manger due to the variety of different methods in which they can be cooked and presented.

A wide range of salad greens are available for use in the kitchen and freshness is the key when purchasing. A good salad green is one that has retained its moisture, crispness and colour and is free of bruising.

Good quality bulbs, roots, tubers and young vegetables are easier than ever to source and are increasingly popular for use in **simple salads**. Baby fruits and vegetables are visually appealing food items and require little preparation.

Eggs

The common hen's egg is not the only type of egg to be used in the preparation of salads and cold dishes. Many menus opt for duck or quail eggs, which can transform a simple salad into a diverse culinary experience.

Eggs can be served boiled or poached to accompany salads and cold dishes, and are a valuable source of protein and vital nutrients.

SOURCING When sourcing eggs be sure to pick those with a Red Lion stamp. This means that the farm where the egg was produced has been inspected and the eggs are protected against infection from *Salmonella*.

Farinaceous products

Farinaceous ingredients – starchy products high in carbohydrate, such as polenta, couscous, noodles, bulgur wheat, pearl barley and pastas – are ideal ingredients for salads.

Chefs are rediscovering traditional recipes from around the world, such as tabbouleh and Moroccan couscous.

Fish

Fish is a diverse commodity, and it is generally a light and flavoursome option within a menu. Smoked salmon, fish terrines and *gravad lax* are standard starter dish concepts.

The same health and safety precautions that apply to meat also apply to fish. Fish should not be stored for longer than three days and smoked products and raw products should be kept in separate refrigerators.

VIDEO CLIP Using fish: mixed fish salad with crispy croutons

Dairy-based products

Dairy products, such as fresh milk, different creams, crème fraîche, fromage frais, yoghurt and cheeses, are important commodities in the garde manger. The use of cheese as a course on a menu is increasing in popularity.

When creating a cheese selection for a menu, at least three types of cheese should be offered: a hard cheese, a blue-veined cheese and a soft cheese, either with a downy rind or with a washed rind. (A washed rind cheese is one that has had its rind soaked or rubbed with brine or alcohol,

whereas a downy rind cheese has been left to ripen and develop a white dappled rind.)

To prevent cheeses from drying out they should be wrapped in cheesecloth or waxed paper, depending on the variety, which allow the cheese to 'breath'. All types should be stored in a refrigerator, ideally being removed approximately one hour before serving. By serving cheese at ambient temperature, the customer will be able to fully appreciate the texture, flavour and smell of each cheese.

SOURCING If choosing a selection of cheeses for a board to present to customers, the chef should consider:

– Whether the cheeses are in season, because they will then be at their finest.
– How long they have been matured; the more mature, the stronger and more prominent the taste.
– The use of cheeses produced locally by a farmers or artisan cheese makers.

Fungi

Mushrooms have a broad range of characteristics and different flavours. Although they have high water content, amounts of certain nutritients are greater than in green vegetables, although not as high as root vegetables. There are three main mushroom classifications:

- field or wild mushrooms
- cultivated mushrooms
- exotic mushrooms.

Different types of mushrooms

Fresh hand-picked wild mushrooms are expensive, which will immediately add to the selling price of a dish. Prices for hand-picked mushrooms will also fluctuate due to their availability and seasonality.

One of the most popular ingredients with chefs is the truffle, a type of mushroom that grows underground. Prices for both black and white truffles can be very high, with white truffle prices reaching high into the thousands of pounds per kilogram at certain times of the year. Usually originating in Italy, white truffles are used to flavour oils or are used in cooking a range of dishes, such as risottos.

Rice

Rice is a versatile product to cook and present, and is used as a starchy carbohydrate accompaniment to a number of meat, poultry and fish dishes.

Sushi is essentially cold cooked rice dressed with vinegar, shaped into bite-sized portions, decorated with raw or cooked fish, egg or vegetables and wrapped in seaweed. The vinegar rice used in sushi is slightly harder than plain boiled rice because it is cooked in less water. Quick cooling of the cooked rice while tossing it is the key to producing good, shiny sushi rice.

Pulses

Pulses are beans, lentils and chickpeas, all of which have excellent nutritional benefits and are valuable sources of protein. Pulses are economical ingredients and can be used to make a variety of salads.

Tinned, cooked pulses are liable to be more expensive than dried pulses, but are much easier to use as they do not require soaking. Pulses can be used as a main ingredient for salads.

HEALTHY OPTION Pulses are an excellent source of fibre and cooking pulses in a flavoured or spiced liquid can greatly enhance and complement the flavours of a dish.

Salads

Salads are extremely versatile dishes and can consist of raw, cooked, cold or warm ingredients. Salads will usually be dressed and seasoned (unless requested otherwise by a customer), and can be served as an accompaniment, side dish or main course.

Many different contemporary styles of salad from around the world are used in modern menus.

CHEF'S TIP There are many different salad items, such as lettuce, spinach, herbs, spicy greens, bitter leaves and micro salads. They can be used in different combinations to add a depth of flavour and varying textures.

The main categories of salads are listed below:

- Simple salads – the basis of a simple salad is the use of one main ingredient and an accompanying dressing or garnish. These salads can be either raw or cooked and can be made up of vegetables, fruits, meats, fish or shellfish, but they are always served cold and with a cold dressing such as vinaigrette. An example is a tomato salad.

- **Compound salads** – the aim of a compound salad is to combine multiple contrasting ingredients, differing in texture, flavour and colour, but still utilizing items that are complementary to each other. A classic example is *à la grecque* (meaning cooking in a Greek style), which is cooked and served in a vinegar and oil solution with aromatic spices. Salad components can include meat, fish and vegetables.

- Combination salads – these are made up of several different types of ingredients which have been prepared separately but presented together on one plate. Crucially, the ingredients are not blended together. These are substantial salads and are usually featured on menus as main courses.

- American salads – originating in the USA, these salads are usually served as an accompaniment to a hot dish, such as roast turkey. In North America, salads are traditionally served during a banquet instead of sauces or cooked vegetables. An example is orange and watercress salad with walnut vinaigrette, served to accompany roasted duck.

- Salade tiède – tiède means warm, therefore these salads will typically consist of a hot ingredient accompanied by cold items. Salade tiède is generally served as a starter or a main course.

CHEF'S TIP Ensure that you prepare the cold element of a salade tiède in plenty of time before the hot ingredients are required so that the dish can be served at the correct temperature, giving the right balance of hot and cold temperatures on the plate.

When designing a salad, the chef garde manger must carefully consider the various factors that contribute to a salad's success:

- Appearance – the salad should not only be pleasing and colourful, but also be in keeping with the style of the menu.

- Appropriateness – this is quite a broad issue and often not fully considered. For example, it may not be appropriate to serve certain foods to people of specific religions or ethnic backgrounds or with particular medical conditions. Repeating ingredients used elsewhere in a menu will unbalance the eating experience.

- Flavour – if a food item lacks flavour it should not be considered; salads should always be appealing to the appetite. Salads are frequently used as palette cleansers or as a bridge in a menu between other foods or courses.

- Texture – variety and contrasts in texture add interest and value to most dishes.

- Nutritional value – customers are becoming increasingly concerned about health and nutrition. It is both good business and socially responsible to address this issue by making reasonable changes to ingredients or cooking methods where appropriate.

- Portion size – this is relative to the entire meal. Chefs should consider what an appropriate quantity to serve is. Salad ingredients should not be too large or too small to make a pleasing presentation.

- Cost – it is important to assess and evaluate the cost contribution and margin for profit for all salad and commodity items.

CHEF'S TIP Do not dress a salad with vinaigrette or dressing too early as this will break down the structure and texture of leaves and herbs.

Terrines

These meats, poultry, fish, vegetable or game products are named after the mould in which they are produced. Terrines can be produced in a variety of shapes and sizes, and can be presented as cold mousses, pâtés or parfaits, jellied and layered or by cold **pressing**.

Terrines usually consist of more than one type of food product. The ingredients are used in varying proportions and are prepared in different ways, depending on the effect the chef garde manger wishes to create. The terrine mould will usually be lined with bacon, seaweed, vegetables or fat, which helps to hold the terrine together.

Step-by-step: Preparing a terrine

1. Lay out prosciutto or Parma ham the width of the terrine mould.

2. Ease the ham into the mould, ensuring the corners are neat and tidy.

3. Combine the raw ingredients carefully.

4. Blend the filling to a course or smooth finish as required.

5. Carefully fill the terrine until level with the top.

6. Neatly fold over the ham then cover with cling film, place on the lid and cook in a bain-marie.

VIDEO CLIP Preparation of foie gras, artichoke and herb terrine

Pâtés and parfaits

These products can be made of **offal**, meat, poultry, fish, vegetables or game and are rich in flavour. **Pâtés** can be coarse textured or fine pastes, whereas parfaits have the consistency of whipped cream or butter.

There are two methods for preparing parfaits:

- prepared then cooked
- cooked then prepared.

CHEF'S TIP Use a container of hot water and a clean cloth when slicing products such as terrines and pâtés; a hot, clean knife will slice cleanly and produce neat slices.

The classical prepared then cooked method is to add cooked shallots, **flambéed** with alcohol, to melted **clarified butter**. Egg yolks and blended livers are added to the mixture and butter and cream are slowly mixed in. The mixture is then passed through a sieve, seasoned well and poured into a prepared terrine mould. It is then placed in a bain-marie and cooked in an oven until the core temperature reaches 68°C.

The FSA has issued clear guidance on cooking times and temperatures for livers, as below:

- 65°C for ten minutes
- 70°C for two minutes
- 75°C for 30 seconds
- 80°C for six seconds.

Please make sure you follow these recommendations when preparing and cooking liver.

Step-by-step: Preparation of a chicken liver parfait

1. **Sauté** the shallots, garlic, herbs and **deglaze**.

2. Lightly sauté the chicken livers.

3. Blend the mixture with butter.

4. **Pass** the mixture through a chinois.

5. Set in a lined mould.

6. Finish with whipped butter. Coat three sides, chill until set and then complete the fourth side.

The second method varies in that the ingredients are cooked before preparation. Extra butter is used in this method to counteract the lack of protein structure and to achieve the same effect as the classical parfait. Shallots are cooked in butter with livers to a medium cooked point, alcohol is then added and flambéed. The shallots and livers are left to cool, and then blended together with a small amount of cream until a smooth texture is achieved. The mixture is then passed through a sieve, and softened (but not clarified) butter is folded in. It is then seasoned and poured into the terrine mould and refrigerated until set.

Mousses

Mousses are lighter in texture than pâtés and are not as rich in flavour, which makes them a little more versatile.

A basic raw mousseline recipe for meat, poultry or fish uses 500 g of fresh protein to approximately 900 ml of chilled double cream, four egg yolks and two whole eggs.

The protein needs to be minced twice and passed through a sieve, to break down the protein structure, and then chilled over ice. Using a blender, the protein is combined with the eggs and seasoning, which are added slowly until a smooth texture is achieved. The chilled double cream is incorporated into the mixture slowly to prevent the mousseline from splitting. The mousseline can then be poached, steamed or baked, or used in terrines that are to be cooked.

Cooked mousses differ by using a meat, fish, poultry or vegetable base that has already undergone cooking and **gelatine** or **agar-agar** is used to set the mixture. The base ingredient is blended until smooth while the gelatine or agar-agar is melted. The setting agent is then beaten into the base mixture, which is seasoned as required. Cream, lightly whipped to a soft peak, is gently folded into the mixture to form a light mousse, which can be **piped**, formed into quenelles or layered into a terrine mould, before being allowed to set in a refrigerator.

Step-by-step: Hot water paste pork pies

1. Roll out hot water paste (see page 325).

2. Line small moulds with the hot water paste.

3. Carefully add forcemeat until the moulds are full, cover the top with more hot water paste and **crimp** around the edge.

4. Pierce a small hole (1 cm) in the top and insert an oiled, firm paper funnel to allow steam to escape. Brush the top of the pies with egg wash three times and **bake** for approximately one hour at 190°C.

5. Once cooled, inject a well-flavoured **aspic** jelly into the pie via the hole and chill.

6. The finished pie.

Sushi

Sushi is the most famous Japanese dish outside of Japan, and one of the most popular dishes among the Japanese themselves. In Japan, sushi is usually enjoyed on special occasions, such as a celebration.

During the Edo period, 'sushi' referred to pickled fish preserved in vinegar. Nowadays sushi can be defined as a dish containing rice which has been prepared with sushi vinegar. There are many different types of sushi. Some popular ones are described below:

Nigiri

Small rice balls with fish, shellfish, etc. on top. There are countless varieties of *nigirizushi*; some of the most common are tuna, shrimp, eel, squid, octopus and fried egg.

Gunkan

Small cups made of sushi rice and dried seaweed filled with seafood. There are countless varieties of *gunkanzushi*, some of the most common ones being sea urchin and various kinds of fish eggs.

Norimaki

Sushi rice and seafood rolled in dried seaweed sheets. There are countless varieties of sushi rolls differing in ingredients and thickness. Sushi rolls prepared 'inside out' are very popular outside of Japan, but rarely found in Japan.

Tamaki

Temakizushi (hand rolls) are cones made of **nori** seaweed and filled with sushi rice, seafood and vegetables.

Oshizushi

Oshizushi is pressed sushi, in which the fish is pressed onto the sushi rice in a wooden box.

Inari

Inarizushi is a simple and inexpensive type of sushi, in which sushi rice is filled into *aburaage* (deep fried tofu) bags.

Step-by-step: Sushi techniques

1. With a wet hand, pack the sushi rice onto two-thirds of the nori seaweed, on a bamboo rolling mat.

2. Carefully rub a little wasabi paste across the rice.

3. Arrange cucumber strips, salmon and poppy seeds across the rice.

4. Lightly moisten the edge of the nori seaweed and then use the bamboo mat to roll the seaweed over.

5. Remove the roll from the mat then cut in half using a very sharp knife and slice into neat portions.

6. The finished norimaki sushi.

Recipes

Balsamic jelly dice

Ingredients	4 portions	10 portions
Aged balsamic vinegar	700 ml	1.75 l
Sweet Madeira	300 ml	750 ml
Bronze gelatine leaves	8	20

energy	cal	fat	sat fat	carb	sugar	protein	fibre
690 kJ	166 kcal	0 g	0 g	10.1 g	10.1 g	3.3 g	0.5 g

METHOD OF WORK

1 Soften gelatine leaves in water.
2 Mix vinegar and Madeira together, add gelatine.
3 Heat until gelatine dissolves.
4 Pass through a fine sieve and set in desired shape.
5 Cut into squares if required.

CHEF'S TIP If you want a warm jelly, substitute the gelatine for agar-agar and use 2 per cent to the amount of liquid, bring the mixture to the boil to activate the agar-agar.

Beetroot and balsamic spaghetti

Ingredients	4 portions	10 portions
Cooked beetroot	100 g	250 g
Balsamic vinegar	100 ml	250 ml
Salt	To taste	To taste
Pepper	To taste	To taste
Agar-agar	2 per cent	2 per cent

energy	cal	fat	sat fat	carb	sugar	protein	fibre
74 kJ	18 kcal	0 g	0 g	2.7 g	2.4 g	0.7 g	0.6 g

METHOD OF WORK

1 Puree the cooked beetroot with the vinegar and leave to hang overnight in a muslin cloth.
2 Measure 100 g of juice.
3 Add 2 per cent (2 g) of agar-agar to the juice and allow to dissolve for three minutes.
4 Heat until the mixture boils, remove from the heat and cool slightly.
5 Suck the mixture up with a syringe and inject into some plastic tubing.
6 Detach from the syringe and plunge the tubing into ice water, this will cause the juice to set.
7 Use a clean syringe to force air into one end of the tube, this will cause the 'spaghetti' to come out.

Carpaccio of beef

Carpaccio of beef with rocket and parmesan

Ingredients	4 portions	10 portions
Beef fillet	100 g	250 g
Olive oil	40 ml	100 ml
Sweet corn	2 tbsp	5 tbsp
Lemon juice and zest	½ lemon	1½ lemons
Rocket	60 g	150 g
Shaved Parmesan cheese	40 g	100 g
Reduced sherry vinegar	4 tbsp	10 tbsp
Good-quality salt and ground white pepper	to taste	to taste

energy	cal	fat	sat fat	carb	sugar	protein	fibre
821 kJ	198 kcal	15.2 g	4.3 g	3 g	0.7 g	11.7 g	0.8 g

METHOD OF WORK

1   Heat a frying pan, add a little oil and roll the trimmed beef fillet until **seared** on the outside.

2   Season the fillet and then wrap in cling film.

3   Allow to cool, and then freeze overnight.

4   Remove the beef, unwrap a little, then using a sharp knife or slicing machine shave thin slices and arrange on a plate.

5   Combine the oil, lemon and vinegar, then **drizzle** around as required.

6   Finally, season the beef with salt and pepper and garnish with rocket, sweetcorn and Parmesan cheese.

Chicken ballotine

Ingredients	4 portions	10 portions
Chicken legs	4	10
Pork belly	200 g	500 g
Finely chopped shallots	50 g	125 g
Fresh breadcrumbs	25 g	60 g
Lemon zest	¼ lemon	1 lemon
Finely chopped herbs	2 tbsp	5 tbsp
Egg	1	3
Pigs **caul**		
Good quality salt	To taste	To taste
Pepper	To taste	To taste

energy	cal	fat	sat fat	carb	sugar	protein	fibre
2230 kJ	534 kcal	31.8 g	9.2 g	6.2 g	0.8 g	56.1 g	0.5 g

METHOD OF WORK

1   Pass the pork meat through a fine mincer.

2   **Sweat** the shallots.

3   To make the force meat combine the pork mince with the shallots, breadcrumbs, lemon zest, herbs, and egg and season well.

4   Prepare the chicken legs as shown below.

5   Poach in chicken stock for one and half hours.

6   Chill well (this can be done in or out of the stock).

7   Remove the pig's caul (cloth) and slice as required.

Step-by-step: Preparing chicken ballotine

1. Lay the chicken leg skin side down, with a sharp knife cut around the thigh bone without puncturing the skin.

2. Scrape the exposed bone then continue to remove the other bone (this can also be left in if preferred).

3. Remove any sinew.

4. Lightly bat out the boneless chicken leg using either cling film or a vacuum bag as a shield.

5. Stuff the centre with an appropriate force meat (pork, breadcrumbs, shallots, egg, lemon zest and herbs) then roll into a cylindrical shape (sausage).

6. Lay the chicken leg onto a piece of crepinette (pig's caul) and begin to roll securing tightly.

7. Tie the ballotine neatly to help keep its shape.

8. The neatly tied ballotine ready for poaching or roasting.

9. Cooked ballotine of chicken with baby vegetables.

Chicken liver pâté

Ingredients	4 portions	10 portions
Chicken livers	100 g	250 g
Port wine reduction	25 ml	60 ml
Shallots finely chopped	1	3
Garlic finely chopped	2 cloves	6 cloves
Pork fat finely diced	30 g	75 g
Fresh breadcrumbs	4 tbsp	10 tbsp
Liquid whole egg	20 ml	50 ml
Wild rocket		
Foie gras fine dice	20 g	50 g
Herb oil	2 tbsp	5 tbsp
Ground white pepper	to taste	To taste
Good quality salt	to taste	to taste

energy	cal	fat	sat fat	carb	sugar	protein	fibre
1263 kJ	302 kcal	20.2 g	3.7 g	19.7 g	2.2 g	9.8 g	0.9 g

METHOD OF WORK

1   In a food processor blend the livers, pork fat, egg, reduction, breadcrumbs, shallots and garlic until a course paste is formed.

2   Place into a terrine mould lined with cling film.

3   Cover with foil and steam at 100°C for 25 to 30 minutes, until just set.

4   Remove and chill overnight.

5   When required, use two spoons to form quenelles as shown.

6   Finish with dressed rocket, **diced** foie gras and herb oil.

Chicken galantine

Ingredients	10 portions
Whole chicken (no sinew)	1
Veal	100 g
Belly of pork	100 g
Bread soaked in milk	75 g
Double cream	225 ml
Eggs	1
Blanched and peeled pistachio nuts	15 g
Julienne of cooked ham and tongue	75 g
Good quality salt	To taste
Pepper	To taste

energy	cal	fat	sat fat	carb	sugar	protein	fibre
1769 kJ	425 kcal	27.7 g	10.9 g	4.1 g	0.8 g	39.6 g	0.5 g

METHOD OF WORK

1   Pass the veal and pork through a fine mincer.

2   Combine the meat with the bread, cream, eggs, pistachios and cooked meat and season well.

3   Prepare the chicken as shown below.

4   Poach in chicken stock for one-and-a-half hours.

5   Chill well (this can be done in or out of the stock).

6   Remove the cloth and slice as required.

Step-by-step: Chicken galantine

1. Cut along the backbone then slowly remove the skin and flesh without cutting through the skin.

2. Once the breast bones have been cleaned remove in one piece as shown.

3. Now begin to tunnel bone both legs.

4. This is the boned whole chicken and the two small fillets from the breast.

5. This shows boned chicken with the farce and fillets carefully placed inside.

6. Roll the chicken in muslin tightly.

7. Begin to tie the galantine.

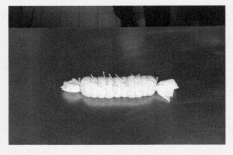

8. The finished tied galantine ready for poaching. *Note*, the colorful ingredients that complement the dish can be used to create a roulade effect.

Cucumber sheets

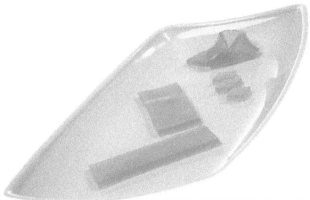

Ingredients	1 l
Cucumber	1 l of juice
Agar-agar	12 g

energy	cal	fat	sat fat	carb	sugar	protein	fibre
4 kJ	1 kcal	0 g	0 g	0.1 g	0.1 g	0.1 g	0.1 g

METHOD OF WORK

1 Mix the cucumber juice and agar-agar powder.

2 Heat the emulsion in a medium saucepan and bring to the boil.

3 As soon as the mixture starts to boil, remove from the heat and pour on to a flat clean tray to the thickness required.

4 Let the sheets set, do not move or cover with clingfilm as any movement at this stage will prevent the sheets from setting.

Duck liver and orange parfait with Melba toast

Ingredients	4 portions	10 portions
Shallots	60 g	150 g
Garlic	1–2 cloves	3–4 cloves
Duck livers (cleaned and trimmed)	200 g	500 g
Olive oil	30 ml	80 ml
Butter	80 g	200 g
Double cream	20 g	50 g
Orange liqueur (such as Grand Marnier)	60 ml	150 ml
Good quality salt and pepper	to taste	to taste
White bread	4 slices	10 slices
Orange segments	12	30
Curly endive		

energy	cal	fat	sat fat	carb	sugar	protein	fibre
2568 kJ	612 kcal	29.5 g	12.6 g	63.3 g	45.9 g	19 g	8.1 g

METHOD OF WORK

1 Finely chop the shallots and garlic. In a frying pan, fry off in the olive oil until *tender and without colour*.

2 Melt the butter in a small saucepan.

3 In a separate hot pan, season and sear the duck livers. When rare, flambé with the orange liquor. Ensure the livers are cooked through to at least 70°C.

4 Place the shallots and duck livers in a blender and blend until a smooth paste is achieved.

5 Slowly add the melted butter and the cream. Season as required.

6 Pour into a terrine mould lined with cling film and leave to set for 24 hours.

7 Slice the parfait with a hot knife and serve with the **Melba toast**, orange segments and lightly dressed curly endive.

Foie gras terrine

Ingredients	4 portions	10 portions
Duck foie gras	400 g	1000 g
Sauternes for terrine	50 ml	125 ml
Coarse sea salt	50 g	125 g
Granulated sugar	50 g	125 g
Good quality pepper	to taste	to taste
Sauternes for jelly	120 ml	280 ml
Bronze gelatine	8 leaves	20 leaves
Brioche loaf	4 thick slices	10 thick slices

energy	cal	fat	sat fat	carb	sugar	protein	fibre
3007 kJ	718 kcal	54.7 g	20.8 g	34.5 g	14.2 g	16.5 g	1.2 g

METHOD OF WORK

1   De-vein the foie gras – see step-by-step below.
2   Flatten foie gras until half-inch thick.
3   Cover with Sauternes, salt and sugar, cover and leave in fridge for two hours.
4   Plunge into iced water to dissolve excess salt and sugar.
5   Leave to soften season with pepper and pack into a terrine mould lined with cling film.
6   Cook in a bain-marie at 120°C until a core temperature of 60°C is reached.
7   Chill quickly, once set remove and scrape any excess fat off.
8   To make the jelly, soften gelatine in cold water, add to the Sauternes and heat until dissolved.
9   Chill until set then chop into pieces around the terrine.

Step by step: Foie gras preparation

1. Separate the foie gras lobes.

2. Use the handle of a spoon to remove the veins.

3. Carefully work your way through the foie gras ensuring all the veins are removed.

4. All the veins have been removed.

5. Place the de-veined foie gras onto a clean piece of cling film.

6. Roll the foie gras in the cling film and secure, as shown, or lay into a mould lined with cling film.

Goat's cheese and walnut tartlet

Ingredients	4 portions	10 portions
Tartlet	4	10
Goat's cheese	100 g	250 g
Walnut	40 g	100 g
Curly endive		
Whole egg	50 ml	125 ml
Double cream	50 ml	125 ml
Good quality salt	to taste	to taste
Pepper	to taste	to taste

energy	cal	fat	sat fat	carb	sugar	protein	fibre
3224 kJ	775 kcal	55.9 g	30.8 g	52.3 g	2 g	16.3 g	2.3 g

METHOD OF WORK

1   Combine the egg, cream and seasoning well.
2   Crumble the cheese and walnuts into **blind baked** tartlet cases, pour over the cream mixture and bake at 160°C until just set.
3   Finish with lightly dressed endive.

VIDEO CLIP   Preparation of gravad lax

Gravad lax

Ingredients	4 portions	10 portions
Salmon fillet (skin on, trimmed and pin boned)	300 g	800 g
Sugar	150 g	425 g
Good-quality salt	180 g	500 g
Orange juice and zest	1 each	3 each
Lemon muslin	4	10
Dill	½ bunch	1½ bunches

energy	cal	fat	sat fat	carb	sugar	protein	fibre
1302 kJ	308 kcal	9 g	1.5 g	42.7 g	41.4 g	16.9 g	0.5 g

METHOD OF WORK

1   Finely chop the dill. Mix the sugar, salt and chopped dill together. Slash the salmon skin and rub the salt mixture on both sides, then leave for at least 24 hours, wrapped in plastic film in a refrigerator.
2   Remove the salmon from the cure and wash off, pat dry and place onto a chopping board.
3   Pack the salmon tightly with chopped dill.
4   Slice the salmon, going from tail to head, into neat pieces.
5   To serve, arrange the salmon neatly on the plate with a lemon muslin and some micro herbs.

Pear and calvados caviar

Ingredients	10 portions
Pear juice	100 ml
Sodium alginate	1.2 g
Sugar	5 g
Pear flavour	1 drop
Calvados	5 ml
Water	100 ml
Calcium chloride	1 g

energy	cal	fat	sat fat	carb	sugar	protein	fibre
98 kJ	23 kcal	0.2 g	0 g	5.5 g	5.5 g	0.1 g	0.9 g

METHOD OF WORK

1 Place pear juice, pear flavour and calvados in the mixer. Using the **whisk** attachment, whisk at the lowest speed.

2 Mix the sodium alginate and the sugar together.

3 Add this mixture slowly to the juice.

4 Try to avoid adding the sodium alginate mixture to the centre of the bowl as it will adhere to the whisk.

5 Continue to whisk slowly for ten minutes.

6 Allow mixture to stand for a further ten minutes, the mixture should be thickened to a syrupy texture and be completely lump free.

7 Place the water into a narrow container, a beaker or measuring jug should be fine add the calcium chloride and stir to dissolve.

8 Draw the pear juice solution into the syringe, hold the syringe approximately six inches above the calcium chloride solution.

9 Push the syringe plunger to create a steady stream of drops.

10 Stir the water lightly to help form cylindrical balls.

11 Leave for about five minutes to allow a skin to form.

12 Pour the caviar balls into a shallow sieve and place in clean cold water.

Pear fluid gel

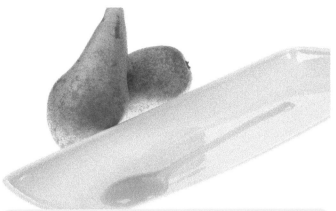

Ingredients	4 portions
Freshly pressed pear juice	1000 ml
Salt	to taste
Gellan gum type F	0.15 g

energy	cal	fat	sat fat	carb	sugar	protein	fibre
2080 kJ	490 kcal	3 g	0 g	120 g	120 g	3 g	22 g

METHOD OF WORK

1 Add the Gellan gum to juice and bring to the boil, whisking constantly.

2 Place in a metal jug and immerse into an iced water bath.

3 Using a hand blender blitz the mixture until cold to ensure that no lumps can form.

4 Pass through a fine sieve.

5 **Season to taste**.

VIDEO CLIP Pear fluid gel

Quail Scotch eggs

Ingredients	4 portions	10 portions
Quail eggs	4	10
Sausage meat	120 g	300 g
Black pudding	80 g	200 g
Shallots	20 g	50 g
Duck fat	100 ml	250 ml
Parsley	1 tsp	2.5 tsp
Tarragon	1 tsp	2.5 tsp
Panko bread crumbs	50 g	500 g
Plain flour	for pane	for pane
Pasteurized whole egg	250 ml	675 ml
Good quality salt	to taste	to taste
Pepper	to taste	to taste

energy	cal	fat	sat fat	carb	sugar	protein	fibre
2157 kJ	516 kcal	42.4 g	14.3 g	19 g	1.5 g	16.5 g	1.2 g

METHOD OF WORK

1 Place quail eggs in **simmering** salted water and cook for two minutes and 30 seconds, **refresh** in iced water, peel and dry.

2 **Brunoise** shallots and confit slowly in the duck fat and drain.

3 Finely dice the black pudding and mix with pork, shallots, herbs and seasoning.

4 Divide the forcemeat into equal parts and wrap carefully around the quail egg, leave to set in fridge.

5 Pane à l'Anglais and **deep fry** at 160°C until golden brown, check for cooking degree and finish in the oven if needed.

VIDEO CLIP Quail scotch egg

Smoked duck

Ingredients	4 portions	10 portions
Smoked duck	200 g	500 g
Quail Scotch eggs	4	10
Sun blushed tomatoes	40 g	100 g
Balsamic vinegar	10 ml	25 ml
Lime juice	1 tsp	2.5 tsp
Good quality salt	to taste	to taste
Pepper	to taste	to taste
Watercress		
Olive oil	2 tsp	5 tsp

energy	cal	fat	sat fat	carb	sugar	protein	fibre
1263 kJ	305 kcal	28.4 g	7.3 g	1.5 g	0.4 g	11 g	0.7 g

METHOD OF WORK

1 Slice the quail Scotch eggs in half.

2 Remove any excess fat from the duck and slice thinly.

3 Arrange the duck on the plate with the sun blushed tomatoes and quail Scotch eggs.

4 Lightly dress the watercress and serve with a split balsamic dressing.

Rabbit terrine

Rabbit terrine with plum chutney and garlic tomatoes

Ingredients	4 portions	10 portions
Flesh from whole rabbit	½	1
Chicken breast	1	2
Pork trimmings	80 g	200 g
Brandy	½ measure	1 Measure
Thyme	4 sprigs	8 sprigs
Bay leaf	½	1
Double cream	100 ml	250 ml
Liver and kidney (from the rabbit)		
Chilled egg whites	1	2
Mace	pinch	pinch
Plum chutney	4 small spoons	10 small spoons
Good quality salt and ground white pepper	to taste	to taste
Cherry tomatoes steeped in garlic oil		
Thyme	2 sprigs	4 sprigs
Bay leaf	½	1

energy	cal	fat	sat fat	carb	sugar	protein	fibre
2366 kJ	565 kcal	24.1 g	13.5 g	5.5 g	4.1 g	73.2 g	0.8 g

METHOD OF WORK

1 Marinate the rabbit, chicken and pork in brandy, thyme and bay leaf overnight.

2 Set aside the rabbit fillets. Mince the rest of the rabbit (including liver and kidneys), chicken and pork, once through a medium mincer and twice through a fine mincer. Then pass through a sieve. Blast chill to get very cold.

3 When the mince is cold, **beat** with the double cream in a Robot-**Coupe**. Season with salt, pepper and mace and quickly add the chilled egg whites.

4 Poach a little to test for holding consistency and taste.

5 Line a small terrine mould with oil and two layers of cling film.

6 Place the rabbit mix in the terrine mould and layer in the slices of rabbit flesh from the fillet. Smooth down and cover with foil.

7 Steam for 25–30 minutes at 100°C in a steamer.

8 Remove and chill until required.

9 To serve, slice the terrine carefully with a warm wet knife and position on the plate with chutney and oil steeped cherry tomatoes.

Sashimi of tuna with wasabi

Ingredients	4 portions	10 portions
Tuna loin	100 g	250 g
Lime juice	½ lime	1½ limes
Olive oil		
Pickled ginger	80 g	200 g
Wasabi paste	20 g	50 g
Shiso leaves		
Sea salt	pinch	pinch
Good quality salt and ground white pepper	to taste	to taste

energy	cal	fat	sat fat	carb	sugar	protein	fibre
541 kJ	129 kcal	3.2 g	0.8 g	16.4 g	0.8 g	9.5 g	2.6 g

METHOD OF WORK

1   Thinly slice the tuna then brush with lime juice and sea salt (this must be served within four minutes).

2   Arrange on the plate with pickled ginger, lightly oiled leaves and wasabi.

Warm crab cakes

Ingredients	4 portions	10 portions
White crab meat	100 g	250 g
Breadcrumbs	100 g	250 g
Mayonnaise	40 ml	100 ml
Finely chopped spring onion	1 tbsp	3 tbsp
Limes	2	4
Finely chopped shallots	1 tbsp	2½ tbsp
Olive oil	3 tbsp	8 tbsp
Sugar	1 tsp	3 tsp
Red wine vinegar	1 tbsp	2½ tbsp
Good quality salt and ground white pepper	to taste	to taste

energy	cal	fat	sat fat	carb	sugar	protein	fibre
1396 kJ	336 kcal	24.5 g	3.5 g	22.1 g	3.5 g	7.8 g	1 g

METHOD OF WORK

1   Sweat the tomato, shallots, sugar and oil until very soft, then add the vinegar, season.

2   Mix the picked crab meat, mayonnaise, spring onion and half the breadcrumbs, tomato mixture season well, then mould into small cakes or balls.

3   Roll the cakes in the remaining breadcrumbs until no crabmeat is showing.

4   Deep fry the crab cakes until a golden brown colour is achieved.

5   Serve with herbs and lime.

Smoked salmon and prawn terrine

Ingredients	4 portions	10 portions
Smoked salmon	400 g	1000 g
Cooked tiger prawns	4	10
Clarified butter	40 g	100 g
Crème fraîche	40 g	100 g
Lime juice	1 tsp	2.5 tsp
Good quality salt	to taste	to taste
Pepper	to taste	to taste
Salmon caviar	2 tsp	5 tsp
Tomato **concassé**	2 tsp	5 tsp

energy	cal	fat	sat fat	carb	sugar	protein	fibre
1153 kJ	277 kcal	17.3 g	8.9 g	0.7 g	0.4 g	29.7 g	0.7 g

METHOD OF WORK

1 Devein the tiger prawns and cut in half lengthways.

2 Line a terrine mould with clingfilm.

3 Start by lining the terrine mould with slices of smoked salmon.

4 Brush with clarified butter and place a layer of prawns into the terrine mould, season well.

5 Place a layer of smoked salmon on top of the prawns ensuring the layers are lying flat.

6 Repeat until the top is reached then lay over the smoked salmon and cling film tightly.

7 Press over night, turn out and slice.

8 Serve with the crème fraîche mixed with the lime juice and the salmon caviar and tomato arranged on the plate.

VIDEO CLIP Smoked salmon terrine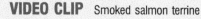

Tian of crab and avocado

Ingredients	4 portions	10 portions
Picked white crab meat	200 g	500 g
Mayonnaise	80 g	200 g
Yuzu juice	5 ml	12 ml
Chopped chives	1 tbsp	2.5 tbsp
Brunoise ginger root	2 g	5 g
Brunoise red chilli	2 g	5 g
Ripe avocado flesh	120 g	300 g
Sun blushed tomatoes	120 g	300 g
Good quality salt	to taste	to taste
Pepper	to taste	to taste

energy	cal	fat	sat fat	carb	sugar	protein	fibre
1692 kJ	410 kcal	39.1 g	5.7 g	2.9 g	1.4 g	11.8 g	3.3 g

METHOD OF WORK

1 Ensure the crab is free of bones and cartilage, mix with the mayonnaise and half the yuzu juice, finish with chives, ginger and chilli and season well.

2 Mash the avocado flesh with the rest of the yuzu juice and season well.

3 Finely chop the sun blushed tomatoes and season.

4 To serve, place the tomato in the bottom of a ring mould, then the crab mixture, finish with the avocado and garnish with micro herbs.

SOURCING When producing this dish try and source the best possible ingredients; a family run business such as Forman's is ideal: http://www.formans.co.uk/

ASSESSMENT OF KNOWLEDGE AND UNDERSTANDING

You have now learned about cold larder work; the range it can cover and the array of commodities and cooking techniques that can be used.

To test your level of knowledge and understanding, answer the following short questions. These will help to prepare you for your summative (final) assessment.

Quality identifications

1   Explain in detail why it is best to use produce that is in season.

2   Name the three main types of hors d'oeuvres and explain the differences between them.

    i

    ii

    iii

Preparation methods

1   Give three examples of different salads and explain what factors should be taken into consideration when preparing them.

    i

    ii

    iii

Cooking methods

1   List five presentation elements that need to be considered when creating salads.

    i

    ii

    iii

    iv

    v

2   Explain the safest way to ensure that terrines or pâtés are cooked through but will still have a pink colour inside.

Health and safety

1   Detail why larder items are at such high risk of cross-contamination.

2   Explain the importance of clear labelling and storage within the larder.

Pasta

Pasta is a generic term used to describe many products made from semolina and/or flour that has been milled from the hardest of all wheat, durum wheat. The name 'durum' comes from the Latin word *durus*, meaning 'hard'.

The key to creating a good pasta dough is to use the strongest flour, which has the highest gluten content. Gluten is essential for creating the elasticity required to form a pliable dough. The amount of water the dough can absorb depends on the quality of the protein and starch. The size of the semolina also plays a key role in this process: too small will result in sticky dough, too large and the dough will be dry, resulting in white spots in the finished product.

Durum wheat's hardness makes it the wheat of choice for producing pasta. When most wheat is milled, the heart of the wheat kernel (endosperm) breaks down into a fine, powdery flour, but the endosperm of durum is hard enough to hold together. The result is the granular product called semolina. Durum wheat kernels are amber-coloured and larger than those of other wheat varieties. Also unique to durum wheat is the fact that its endosperm is not creamy white but yellow, which gives pasta its distinctive colour.

OO flour is now used extensively within the catering trade for making pasta. It is an Italian wheat flour which has a very low extraction rate (this is the amount of whole wheat extracted from the grain during the milling process) and low ash content. Italian flours are classified by ash content, which measures the mineral content of flour.

Wheat kernel

Endosperm makes up 83% of the kernel

Bran makes up 14% of the kernel

Germ makes up 3% of the kernel

Percentages are approximate

Ash

The ash content of flour is determined by burning a given quantity of the flour under prescribed conditions and then measuring the residue. The mineral content varies, depending on many factors such as the variety of wheat, the terrain, the fertilization and the climate. The greater portion of minerals found in a kernel of wheat is contained in the germ and in the **husk** (the bran), and the least amount is in the endosperm. As a consequence, if flour contains a greater number of bran particles, it will have an elevated ash content. The determination of the ash content serves to estimate the degree of the endosperm separation from the bran during milling, i.e. the grade of flour. Generally, flours thought to be of higher quality are more refined and produce less ash. OO flour also has a low protein content.

Making pasta dough

When making pasta dough you should use only the best and freshest ingredients; this will ensure the end product will be of the highest quality in both appearance and flavour.

VIDEO CLIP   Making fresh pasta dough

The traditional way of making pasta dough is to prepare the mixture on a large unvarnished wooden table, which keeps the temperature and humidity constant. The method, still used in classical training, is to create a mound of flour with a well in the centre for the eggs, oil and salt, bring in the flour slowly to form the dough and then **knead**.

The modern method, now widely used, is to place all the ingredients into a food processor and blend for 10–20 seconds until a loose ball is formed.

Whichever method is used, the dough should feel just firm and not sticky. Depending on the size of the eggs used, extra flour may be required to bring the dough together. Knowing the correct feel to the dough will come with experience, and once mastered will allow you to produce perfect paste every time.

The finished dough should be wrapped in cling film and rested for a minimum of 30 minutes (overnight if possible), which will allow the gluten to relax and so prevent shrinkage when the dough is rolled out.

The dough can be rolled out with a rolling pin or using a pasta machine, with the latter allowing large quantities to be rolled out to exact thicknesses and at greater speed.

A–Z of pasta

There are over 500 varieties of pasta, all with different designs and shapes. Here is a selection:

- Angolotti – small, crescent-shaped dumplings, usually stuffed with meat.
- Bucatini – slightly thicker and hollow version of spaghetti.
- Cannelloni – large, short tubes, stuffed with an appropriate filling and baked.
- Capellini – 'angel hair', the thinnest of all pastas, like spaghetti.
- Cappelletti – 'little hats', small peaked-hat shapes stuffed with chicken, pork, mortadella and cheese.
- Conchiglie – small, round shells, either ridged or smooth, the cavity is ideal for stuffing or sauce.
- Farfalle – small bow-tie shapes.
- Fettuccine – like tagliatelle but a bit narrower and thicker.
- Fusilli – spiral-shaped pasta twists.
- Lasagne – the broadest pasta, around 5–8 cm wide, either ridged or smooth.
- Linguini – flat spaghetti.
- Macaroni – short hollow pasta, sometimes with an elbow to form an angle.
- Orecchiette – 'little ears', small ear-shaped pasta.
- Pansotti – triangular ravioli.

Fold over and seal

Finished

- Papardelle – broad egg noodles, sometimes with wavy edges.
- Patina – the term used to describe all the tiny pasta shapes used in soups.
- Penne – tubular pasta, ridged or smooth, about 4–5 cm long, cut on the angle.
- Ravioli – flat stuffed pasta shapes.
- Rigatoni – ridged tubular macaroni, 5 cm long.
- Spaghetti – thin, solid strings of pasta (vermicelli in southern Italy).
- Tagliatelle – long, thin egg noodles, about 6 mm wide.
- Tortelli/tortellini – small, ring-shaped pasta dumplings, stuffed (tortellini are half the size of tortelli).

Cut out squares

VIDEO CLIP Cutting tagliatelle.

VIDEO CLIP Producing various tortellini.

Fill pasta

Recipes

Egg pasta dough

Ingredients	4 portions	10 portions
OO grade flour	110 g	225 g
Eggs	1	2
Egg yolks	1½	3
Olive oil	8 ml	15 ml

energy	cal	fat	sat fat	carb	sugar	protein	fibre
635 kJ	151 kcal	5.6 g	1.3 g	21.4 g	0.4 g	5.1 g	0.9 g

METHOD OF WORK

1 Place flour on to a clean work surface and make a well.
2 In a medium bowl beat the egg yolks and whole eggs together with the olive oil.
3 Slowly add the egg mixture to the flour, stirring in stages, until a paste is formed.
4 Knead the dough until a smooth texture is achieved.
5 Place the dough in a refrigerator to rest for at least 30 minutes before rolling out.

Sun-dried tomato pasta dough

Ingredients	4 portions	10 portions
OO grade flour	110 g	225 g
Eggs	1	2
Egg yolks	1½	3
Olive oil	8 ml	15 ml
Sun-dried tomato paste	15 g	30 g

energy	cal	fat	sat fat	carb	sugar	protein	fibre
648 kJ	154 kcal	5.6 g	1.3 g	21.9 g	0.9 g	5.3 g	0.9 g

METHOD OF WORK

1 In a medium bowl beat the egg yolks and whole eggs together with the olive oil and tomato paste.

CHEF'S TIP When making fresh pasta dough, numerous flavours can be incorporated, such as pesto, tomato or spinach. Care must be taken to adjust the recipe to ensure the same firm consistency is achieved in the finished product.

Saffron pasta dough

Ingredients	4 portions	10 portions
OO grade flour	110 g	225 g
Eggs	1	2
Egg yolks	1½	3
Olive oil	8 ml	15 ml
Saffron strands	2 g	5 g

energy	cal	fat	sat fat	carb	sugar	protein	fibre
636 kJ	151 kcal	5.6 g	1.3 g	21.4 g	0.4 g	5.1 g	0.9 g

METHOD OF WORK

1 Place the flour on to a clean work surface and make a well.

2 Warm the olive oil in a small saucepan and infuse the saffron strands, then leave to cool.

3 In a medium bowl beat the egg yolks and whole eggs together with the saffron-infused oil.

4 Slowly add the mixture to the flour, stirring in stages, until the mixture becomes a paste.

5 Knead the dough until the paste is a smooth texture and yellow in colour. If needed, infuse more oil and saffron then add, introducing more flour to dry the paste.

6 Place the dough in a refrigerator to rest for at least 30 minutes before rolling out.

Squid ink pasta dough

Ingredients	4 portions	10 portions
OO grade flour	110 g	225 g
Eggs	1	2
Egg yolks	1½	3
Olive oil	8 ml	15 ml
Squid ink	2 tbsp	5 tbsp

energy	cal	fat	sat fat	carb	sugar	protein	fibre
635 kJ	151 kcal	5.6 g	1.3 g	21.4 g	0.4 g	5.1 g	0.9 g

METHOD OF WORK

1 Place flour on to a clean work surface and make a well.

2 In a medium bowl beat the egg yolks and whole eggs together with the olive oil.

3 Slowly add the mixture to the flour, stirring in stages, until a paste is formed.

4 Knead the dough with the squid ink (remember to wear gloves for this recipe) until a smooth texture is achieved and it is a subtle black colour.

5 Place the dough in a refrigerator to rest for at least 30 minutes before rolling out.

Spinach pasta dough

Ingredients	4 portions	10 portions
OO grade flour	110 g	225 g
Eggs	1	2
Egg yolks	1½	3
Olive oil	8 ml	15 ml
Spinach	70 g	150 g

energy	cal	fat	sat fat	carb	sugar	protein	fibre
649 kJ	154 kcal	5.7 g	1.3 g	21.5 g	0.6 g	5.5 g	1.2 g

METHOD OF WORK

1 Place the flour on to a clean work surface and make a well.

2 Warm a small saucepan and wilt down the spinach with a small amount of water then allow to cool. Place the spinach into a blender and blend until a smooth paste is achieved.

3 Remove from the blender and spoon into a muslin cloth, then squeeze into a clean saucepan until all the chlorophyll has been extracted.

4 Reduce the liquid until it is a concentrate then chill.

5 In a medium bowl beat the egg yolks and whole eggs together with the chlorophyll.

6 Slowly add the mixture into the flour, stirring in stages, until a dough is achieved.

7 Knead the dough until a smooth texture is achieved and it is a subtle green colour. More flour can be added to the dough if it is too wet.

8 Place the dough in a refrigerator and allow to rest for at least 30 minutes before rolling out.

Saffron papardelle with mussels

Ingredients	4 portions	10 portions
Saffron pasta dough	400 g	1 kg
Mussels	200 g	500 g
Pernod	25 ml	60 ml
Double cream	150 ml	375 ml
Diced onion	75 g	180 g
Baby leeks	50 g	125 g
Assorted wild mushrooms	50 g	125 g
Mussel or fish stock (see recipe p. 156)	75 ml	180 ml
Good quality salt and white pepper	to taste	to taste

energy	cal	fat	sat fat	carb	sugar	protein	fibre
1824 kJ	438 kcal	29.4 g	14.3 g	25.9 g	2.5 g	15 g	2 g

METHOD OF WORK

1   Roll pasta and cut into pappardelle then cook in boiling salted water for two minutes, refresh in ice cold water and drain.

2   In a hot pan, sweat the onion then add the mussels and the Pernod, cover with a lid and cook for one minute.

3   Remove from the heat and pass the liquor.

4   Add the double cream, reduce and season.

5   Cut the leeks into diamonds then sauté with the trimmed wild mushrooms and season well.

6   Mix the sauce through the pasta and mussels and arrange in a bowl.

7   Finish with the leeks and wild mushrooms.

CHEF'S TIP   Once pasta has been blanched, refreshed and drained, mix a little oil through it to ensure the shapes/ strands stay separated.

Tomato linguini

Tomato linguini with black pudding and roasted butternut squash

Ingredients	4 portions	10 portions
Tomato pasta dough	400 g	1 kg
Black pudding	100 g	250 g
Butternut squash	100 g	250 g
Extra virgin olive oil	50 ml	125 ml
Lemon thyme	small sprig	sprig
Chives	small bunch	bunch
Good quality salt and white pepper	to taste	to taste

energy	cal	fat	sat fat	carb	sugar	protein	fibre
1480 kJ	355 kcal	23.6 g	5.1 g	29 g	2.1 g	8.3 g	2.9 g

METHOD OF WORK

1   Roll out the pasta until thin then cut into thin strips.

2   Heat the oil with the lemon thyme and leave to infuse for a minimum of 20 minutes (best overnight).

3   Peel, deseed, dice and roast the squash until caramelized.

4   Cut the black pudding into dice and fry quickly in oil then mix with the butternut squash.

5   **Blanch** the pasta in boiling salted water until **al dente**, then drain and mix with the black pudding mix.

6   Place the pasta into a bowl, drizzle with the remaining oil and garnish with the chives.

CHEF'S TIP   Ensure there is at least double the amount of water to pasta when cooking as this prevents the pasta coagulating.

Ricotta and wild sorrel tortellini

Ricotta and wild sorrel tortellini with a pistachio pesto and garlic foam

Ingredients	4 portions	10 portions
Plain pasta dough	400 g	1 kg
Ricotta cheese	200 g	500 g
Pistachio nuts	50 g	125 g
Parmesan cheese	50 g	125 g
Olive oil	70 ml	175 ml
Basil leaves	¼ bunch	½ bunch
Wild sorrel	70 g	175 g
Garlic	4 cloves	10 cloves
Fresh full fat milk	50 ml	125 ml
Good quality salt and white pepper	to taste	to taste

energy	cal	fat	sat fat	carb	sugar	protein	fibre
2192 kJ	528 kcal	39.7 g	10.8 g	25.6 g	3.3 g	18.5 g	3 g

METHOD OF WORK

1   Mix the ricotta with the chopped blanched sorrel leaves and season well.

2   Roll out the pasta into thin sheets and cut out into circles approximately 5 cm in diameter.

3   Brush the pasta circles with water and spoon the ricotta into the middle.

4   Fold the pasta over and pinch the points together.

5   Make the pesto using half the oil, lightly toasted pistachios, basil and Parmesan by placing all the ingredients in a liquidizer and pulsing until almost smooth (the consistency should be slightly thicker than a sauce).

6   Blanch the garlic in boiling water for two minutes, place the garlic into the milk and bring to the boil; remove the pan from the heat and liquidize.

7   Blanch the pasta in boiling salted water, drain and mix in a bowl with the pesto.

8   Pulse the garlic mixture until a foam appears, spoon over the tortellini and serve.

CHEF'S TIP   When rolling and storing pasta, use semolina and not flour to prevent it sticking together; this will ensure the strands or sheets are separate and prevent the cooking liquid becoming cloudy and thick with gluten.

WEB LINK   The following link is a comprehensive source of cheese, sourcing, equipment and taste tests: http://www.houseofcheese.co.uk/

Spinach lasagne of lobster

Open spinach lasagne of lobster with chervil, tomato and shellfish foam

Ingredients	4 portions	10 portions
Spinach pasta dough	100 g	250 g
Whole cooked lobster	1	2½
Concassé of tomato	2 tbsp	5 tbsp
Chopped chervil	4 tsp	10 tsp
Wild garlic and red pepper vinaigrette	4 tbsp	10 tbsp
Shellfish shells	200 g	500 g
Brandy	30 ml	75 ml
Tomato **purée**	1 tbsp	2½ tbsp
Fish stock	100 ml	250 ml
Double cream	100 ml	250 ml
Butter	50 g	125 g
Good quality salt and white pepper	to taste	to taste

energy	cal	fat	sat fat	carb	sugar	protein	fibre
3569 kJ	860 kcal	64.4 g	20.9 g	10.1 g	1.9 g	56.6 g	1.5 g

METHOD OF WORK

1 Sweat the shells in butter for three minutes.
2 Add the brandy and flambé.
3 Add the tomato purée and cook for two minutes.
4 Add the stock and allow to simmer for 25 minutes, until the liquor has reduced by half.
5 Add the cream and reduce until slightly thickened.
6 Pass, correct the seasoning and keep warm.
7 Roll the pasta dough into lasagne sheets and blanch in boiling salted water until al dente. Drain and pat dry.
8 Add to the shellfish sauce with half the lobster tail meat chopped, tomato concassé and chervil.
9 Arrange the mix into a bowl.
10 Remove a little sauce and blend until a foam is achieved, then spoon over.
11 Finish with the red pepper dressing, remaining lobster tail and claw.

CHEF'S TIP   Always allow a minimum of 30 minutes to rest the made dough in the refrigerator before rolling out. This will allow the gluten in the dough time to relax and prevents shrinkage.

Spaghetti carbonara with ceps

Spaghetti carbonara with a cep mushroom dressing, crispy streaky bacon and a parmesan crisp

Ingredients	4 portions	10 portions
Plain pasta dough	400 g	1 kg
Double cream	100 g	250 g
Fresh eggs	2	5
Parmesan cheese	100 g	250 g
Cep mushrooms (fresh or frozen)	100 g	250 g
Olive oil	50 ml	125 ml
Whole grain mustard	2 tbsp	5 tbsp
White wine vinegar	20 ml	50 ml
Streaky bacon	50 g	125 g
Grated Parmesan cheese	100 g	250 g
Good-quality salt and white pepper	To taste	To taste

energy	cal	fat	sat fat	carb	sugar	protein	fibre
2871 kJ	691 kcal	53.3 g	23 g	23.4 g	2.2 g	30.7 g	1.9 g

CHEF'S TIP Pasta once cooked can be bland and requires careful seasoning; this, however, must be balanced with the addition of sauce and/or garnish.

METHOD OF WORK

1　Roll out the pasta dough thinly and cut into spaghetti.

2　Cook in boiling salted water until al dente then refresh in ice water and drain.

3　Mix the egg, mustard, cream and cheese then slowly heat, stirring constantly until the sauce thickens.

4　Spread the **grated** Parmesan into circles on silicone paper about 7 cm across then bake at 180°C for seven minutes.

5　Once the cheese has slightly coloured, lay over a rolling pin and allow to bend.

6　Sauté the mushrooms in oil and add the vinegar, then season.

7　Mix the pasta with sauce then arrange in a bowl.

8　Finish with mushroom vinaigrette, crispy bacon and Parmesan crisp.

Spinach tagliatelle with sole

Spinach tagliatelle with seared lemon sole and vine-ripened tomato coulis and aged balsamic vinegar

Ingredients	4 portions	10 portions
Spinach pasta dough	400 g	1 kg
Lemon sole	280 g	700 g
Olive oil	50 ml	125 ml
Vine-ripened tomatoes	200 g	500 g
Basil	¼ bunch	½ bunch
Shallots	4	10
Curry powder	pinch	pinch
Good quality salt and white pepper	to taste	to taste

energy	cal	fat	sat fat	carb	sugar	protein	fibre
1453 kJ	348 kcal	19 g	3.2 g	24.7 g	3.3 g	20.7 g	2.5 g

METHOD OF WORK

1 Mix the oil, chopped shallots, basil stalks and chopped tomatoes and place on the heat. Simmer for one hour, remove from the heat and liquidize.

2 Roll out the pasta dough until thin then cut into tagliatelle.

3 Dust the lemon sole with curry powder and sear gently on both sides.

4 Blanch the pasta in boiling salted water then drain, mix with tomato **coulis** and place in a hot bowl.

5 Lay slices of lemon sole over the pasta with tomato coulis and basil.

CHEF'S TIP Do not reboil the tomato coulis once cooked as it will split and unlike other sauces it will not **emulsify** again properly.

Truffled spaghetti with asparagus

Ingredients	4 portions	10 portions
Fresh egg spaghetti	350 g	875 g
Asparagus	1 bunch	2½ bunches
Butter	50 g	125 g
White truffle oil	1 tbsp	2½ tbsp
Grated pecorino cheese	100 g	250 g
Black truffles	10 g	25 g
Rocket	100 g	250 g
Good-quality salt and white pepper	to taste	to taste

energy	cal	fat	sat fat	carb	sugar	protein	fibre
1410 kJ	338 kcal	23.7 g	9.7 g	21.8 g	2.4 g	9.2 g	3.3 g

METHOD OF WORK

1 Place the spaghetti into a large pan of boiling salted water and cook until al dente, refresh in ice water.

2 Peel the asparagus, quarter lengthways and cut into 4 cm strips. Blanch in boiling salted water and refresh in ice water.

3 Reheat the spaghetti and asparagus in the butter then mix together with the rocket.

4 Arrange in a bowl, place the truffles and pecorino onto the pasta. Drizzle some truffle oil over and serve.

CHEF'S TIP Soft poached quail's eggs work very well with this dish; they require a little more effort and practice.

Guest Chef

Ginger coated goat's cheese with beetroot cake, pickled baby beetroot and candied beetroot

Chef *Michael Evans*
Centre *Coleg Llandrillo*

This brings together the best Welsh goat's cheese with earthy tastes of the beetroot. The mild and creamy taste of the goat's cheese from the Brecon Beacons, blends with the sharpness of the baby beets and the sweetness of the cake.

Ingredients	4 portions
Red beetroot peeled	50 g
Red beetroot finely grated	125 g
Self raising flour	150 g
Eggs	2
Butter	125 g
Caster sugar	125 g
White wine vinegar	1 tsp
Mixed spice	1 tsp
Apricots dried finely diced	25 g
Pine nuts chopped	25 g
Pantysgawn goat's cheese	100 g
Softened butter	15 g
Baby red beetroot peeled	4
Baby yellow beetroot peeled	4
Baby candied beetroot peeled	1
Beetroot juice	250 ml
Agar-agar	2.5 g
Banana shallot rings	25 g
Ginger biscuits crushed	50 g
White wine vinegar	500 ml
Sea salt	2 tbsp
Water	500 ml
Micro herbs	25 g

METHOD OF WORK

1   Pre heat oven 180°C /gas mark 4. Cream sugar and butter, incorporate eggs, then flour and grated beetroot. Pour into a lined tranche tray and bake for 45 minutes.

2   Combine water, white wine vinegar, mixed spice and salt; bring to the boil then separate into two pans. Place red baby beetroot in to one and yellow beetroot into the other, reboil then take off the heat; cover with cling film and leave to cool.

3   Cream goat's cheese in a bowl; add softened butter, chopped apricots and pine nuts. Pipe out onto silicon paper and roll to form a cylinder 2.5 cm in width. Place into freezer to set.

4   On a mandolin slice candid beetroot; lie on a silicon mat and place in to a drying cabinet.

5   Cook remaining beetroot and then puree; adjust consistency with a little cooking liquid and pass through a fine sieve; season. Place into a plastic bottle and keep warm.

6   When cake is cooked cover with silicon paper, then a tray and two 250 g weights to help make sure the cake is even when cut; cool in blast chiller.

7   Bring beetroot juice to the boil then add agar-agar. Whisk and bring back to the boil, pour into a tranche tray lined with cling film and allow to set.

8   Cut beetroot cake in to pieces 2.5 cm. Turn out set beetroot juice and cut into pieces 2.5 cm in width.

9   Remove baby beetroots from pickling liquid and drain on to a J cloth, season.

10   Remove goat's cheese from freezer and cut into slices 2.5 cm wide and roll in the ginger biscuits crumbs. Allow to soften at room temperature for ten minutes.

To finish

11   Squeeze an amount of the beetroot puree onto the plate and drag across the plate. Place beetroot gel onto the plate, place beetroot cake on top. Decorate the top of the cake with pickled beets, slices of candid beetroot, shallot rings and micro herbs. Finally place goat's cheese on to beetroot drag.

ASSESSMENT OF KNOWLEDGE AND UNDERSTANDING

You have now learned about the use of the different types of pasta and how to produce a variety of them utilizing an array of commodities and cooking techniques.

To test your level of knowledge and understanding, answer the following short questions. These will help to prepare you for your summative (final) assessment.Quality identifications

1   Explain the importance of selecting the correct type, quality and quantity of pasta ingredients and other ingredients used when meeting dish requirements.

2   Give a brief description of durum wheat.

Materials and storage

1   State the correct temperature for storing fresh pasta.

2   Explain how dried pasta is stored and state what ingredient is usually missing from the dough to make it non-perishable.

Preparation

1   Explain why colour, texture and flavour are important when creating complex pasta dishes.

2   Explain why semolina is used when rolling out fresh pasta dough.

Cooking

1   Describe how and when fresh pasta should be cooked during service.

Health and safety

1   List three possible dangers associated with preparing, cooking and serving fresh pasta dishes.

   i

   ii

   iii

Advanced soups, sauces and dressings

5

VRQ

Advanced skills and techniques in producing vegetable and vegetarian dishes

Advanced skills and techniques in producing meat dishes

Advanced skills and techniques in producing poultry and games dishes

Advanced skills and techniques in producing fish and shellfish dishes

NVQ

Prepare, cook and finish complex hot sauces

Prepare, cook and finish dressings and cold sauces

Prepare, cook and finish complex soups

Recipes

LEARNING OBJECTIVES

The aim of this chapter is to enable you to develop skills and implement knowledge in the preparation and cookery principles of hot and cold sauces, stocks and dressings. This will also include materials, ingredients and equipment.

At the end of this chapter you will be able to:

● **Identify each sauce, stock and dressing variety and finished product.**

● **Understand the use of relative ingredients in stock, sauce and dressing cookery.**

● **State the quality points of various stock, sauce and dressing commodities and end products.**

● **Prepare and cook each type of stock, sauce and dressing variety.**

● **Identify the storage procedures of stocks, sauces and dressings.**

Soup

Historically, soup has been an important part of our nutrition. As time has passed, our nutritional requirements have not changed a great deal, but the sourcing and use of soups have evolved greatly. A soup can provide the main part of a light lunch, or it can be used as a small appetizer at the beginning of a dinner. Soups are used in large modern menus to stimulate the appetite and create a delicate introduction for meat and fish courses. The service has also changed, with soups sometimes being served in small shot glasses, or in demitasse cups with a light foam layered on top to give a frothy cappuccino effect.

Soup should be included on the menu to reflect seasonality. During the autumn and winter, hearty and robust soups accompanied with bread bring a warmth of hospitality that is welcoming on a menu. In the summer months, a chilled soup revives a palette and gives a sense of lightness.

CHEF'S TIP On the contemporary menu, a soup is usually served as a first course, where its purpose is to stimulate the appetite. Soups should have delicate flavour and a natural colour. Thick soups should not be too heavy in consistency.

Special requirements

Consideration should be given to the needs of the diner when preparing soups, for example:

● Patients and the elderly require easily digestible soups that are light and nutritious, such as a chicken broth, and with few complex carbohydrates, such as beans.

● Many medical conditions or dietary restrictions require the use of alternative ingredients:

– *Diabetes* – include as many complex carbohydrates as possible; use foods that are high on the glycaemic index, such as chickpeas, beans and wholemeal flour.

– *Coeliac disease* – use potatoes instead of gluten-rich flour to thicken soups.

– *Dairy intolerance* – use soya milk instead of dairy milk.

– ***Vegetarians*** *and* ***vegans*** – ensure that the base stock is vegetarian and that any fats are vegetable oils and not butter; this seems an obvious point but it can be easily overlooked.

Most guests with specific dietary requirements will make their needs known in advance. However, any prior knowledge of these needs and how to successfully address them will allow the chef to be flexible with the menu and able to accommodate most requirements.

Healthy options

There are always ways to take to make a soup healthier; the addition of yoghurt or single cream instead of double cream and the use of unsaturated oils instead of butter will reduce the fat and cholesterol content. Generally, however, soups are a healthy part of our diet, especially lightly cooked broths, which are nutritious and easily digested.

Soup classification

Soups can be categorized as follows:

● Purée – a soup named after or thickened by its main ingredient, such as mushroom, potato and leek or tomato.

● Cream – a purée soup with the addition of cream, thin béchamel or crème frâiche. Cream of mushroom, cream of potato and leek, cream of tomato and cream of vegetable are all variations. It is essential that these soups have a smooth consistency and have been passed.

● **Velouté** – the quality points of this type of soup are that they should have a delicate flavour and have a velvety, smooth texture. This will be attributed in part to the use of well flavoured stocks, careful simmering and the addition of a **liaison** of egg yolks and cream. Once the liaison is added the soup needs to be reheated very carefully and must never be allowed to reboil.

- Broth – a soup that is composed of a strongly flavoured stock and a named garnish, such as mutton. This type of soup is not passed, and the vegetables are cut in varying shapes according to the recipe's requirement. Examples are mutton broth and Scotch broth. Potages also come under this type of soup.

- Consommé – clear soups that are prepared from stock flavoured with various meats and vegetables. They are clarified and should be clear when finished. **Bouillons** also come under this category, but they are not clarified to the same level. Examples are consommé julienne, consommé celestine and consommé royale.

- Bisque – bisque is a soup made from crustaceans. It is thickened with rice and the shell of the crustacean, and finished with cream. Examples are lobster and prawn bisque.

- Chowder – this is generally a seafood soup, usually based on molluscs but can have added smoked white fish. It is usually associated with New England, and the most popular version is clam chowder. The term may also describe a buttery, hearty soup made with corn and chicken. The term 'chowder' may derive from the French word for a large caldron, *chaudiere*, in which Breton fishermen threw their catch to make a communal fish stew. Examples are clam, cockle or chicken and sweetcorn chowder.

- Foreign – also known as miscellaneous soups, these are all soups of a traditional, modern and national nature that do not fall into any other category. There are many examples, such as the simple Jewish chicken soup; the gumbos made from okra, chicken, seafood or meat in the American south; India has many types of lentil soups; Middle Eastern Muslims break their Ramadan fast with harira, made from lentils, chickpeas and lamb; Japan is famous for soups based on **miso** (fermented soybean paste); Eastern Europe possesses goulash (a beef and paprika stew that started life as soup) and borsch (beetroot and meat soup); Spanish gazpacho is always in vogue; the Greeks have avgolemono, an egg and lemon soup; Italy has numerous bean and pasta soups, such as minestrone; and Scotland is renowned for cullen skink (smoked haddock soup) and Scotch broth (mutton and barley soup).

- Chilled – nearly all soups that are served hot can also be served chilled. However, when chilled the intensity of flavour is reduced. They may therefore need a stronger base or a more intense seasoning.

The skills required to create an outstanding soup are the same as those needed to make a delicate sauce. The modern chef has a wide variety of ingredients at their disposal to meet the requirements of today's more perceptive customers. The balance of flavours, seasoning, consistency, texture and temperature needs to be understood to create a well-flavoured and satisfying soup.

VIDEO CLIP   Preparation of gazpacho.

CHEF'S TIP   It is imperative that unblemished, fresh ingredients are used when making soups. Always check that the ingredients meet with the dish requirements by using correct *mise en place* methods and weighing each ingredient before preparation.

Garnishes and accompaniments

Most soups are accompanied by bread, usually in the form of bread rolls or sliced **baguettes**. However, croûtons, sippets and toasted flutes may also be served at the table. Today, croûtons are often quite rustic is style, with large pieces of bread drizzled with olive oil and baked in the oven until crisp.

- Croûtons – small cubes of white crustless bread (1 cm × 1 cm) that are pan fried in clarified butter. The butter is heated in a pan and the diced bread added; the pan is constantly shaken so that the croûtons colour evenly. The croûtons are spooned out onto kitchen paper and patted dry.

- Sippets – triangles of bread cut from the corners of pan loaves, thinly sliced and toasted in an oven. To add flavour, garlic can be rubbed onto the bread before turning over to toast the other side.

- Croûtes de flûte (toasted flutes) – slices taken from a thin baguette. They can either be toasted on both sides or brushed in melted butter and crisped in the oven.

- Diablotins – thin round slices of toasted bread, topped with grated cheese and browned in the oven. Can be coated with reduced béchamel.

- Melba toast – melba toast is toasted bread that is cut between the toasted surfaces whilst still hot. The uncooked side is rubbed on a service cloth to remove the rough bread and then also toasted.

- Cheese straws – puff pastry strips they have cheese added at the last turn. They are twisted and baked until crisp.

Vegetable garnishes

Used as a light garnish for consommés, broths or purée-based soups. Careful cutting into neat, even and standardized shapes is important to the finished result.

- Brunoise – cut equal amounts of carrot, turnip, leek and celery into 2 mm dice, for consommés and slightly larger for broths

- Julienne – cut equal amountsof carrot, turnip, leek and celery into thin strips up to 35 mm in length

- **Paysanne** – cut equal amounts of turnips, carrots, swede, potato, leek and celery into 1 cm squares.

Serving temperatures and quantities

Hot soups should be served very hot and any accompanying garnishes should be added when serving. The Food Hygiene (England) Regulations 2006 state that hot food needs to be kept at or above 63°C in order to control the growth of pathogenic microorganisms and the formation of toxins. The soup should not be kept for service or on display for sale for a period of more than two hours.

Cold soups should be served chilled at below 8°C and not at room temperature.

When calculating the amount of soup required for a given number of portions, take into account the following points:

- Portion size is dependent on the size and style of the menu and the number of courses that follow.

- The recipe method must be followed correctly.

- Each ingredient must be accurately measured.

- No more than 200–250 ml per portion should be served.

Recipes

Basic velouté

Ingredients	Makes 1 litre
Butter	60 g
Flour	60 g
White stock	1250 ml
Egg yolks	2
Cream	100 ml
Good quality salt and white pepper	to taste

energy	cal	fat	sat fat	carb	sugar	protein	fibre
1552 kJ	375 kcal	34.1 g	18.6 g	14.1 g	2 g	4 g	1.7 g

METHOD OF WORK

1 Prepare a blond roux with the butter and the flour.

2 Mix in the boiling white stock gradually using a wooden spoon. Avoid lumps by adding a little at a time and bring to the boil whilst continuously stirring.

3 Bring back to the boil, **skim** and season and leave to simmer for 45 minutes.

4 Pass through a fine chinois into a clean pan and reboil.

5 Whisk together the egg yolks and cream and add one-third of the soup, whisking quickly. Add to the remaining soup and continuously stir until the liaison is fully combined and has slightly thickened to velouté. Correct the seasoning and add any garnish before serving.

CHEF'S TIP The overriding flavour and colour of bortsch should be beetroot, whether it is a consommé or a more rustic purée.

Bortsch

Ingredients	4 portions	10 portions
Duck stock	1.25 l	3 l
Minced duck meat	100 g	250 g
Minced shin of beef	100 g	250 g
Duck carcass	1	2–3
Egg whites	1	3
Parsley stalks	4	10
Celery	80 g	200 g
Fennel	40 g	100 g
Marjoram	1 tsp	1 tbsp
Grated beetroot	200 g	500 g
Carrot	80 g	200 g
Onion	80 g	200 g
To serve		
Leek	80 g	200 g
Smoked duck	100 g	250 g
Diced rump beef	80 g	200 g
Beetroot	40 g	100 g

energy	cal	fat	sat fat	carb	sugar	protein	fibre
4364 kJ	1049 kcal	74.8 g	38.8 g	56.8 g	10.2 g	37.3 g	4.3 g

METHOD OF WORK

1 Make a consommé (see page 136) using the vegetables, herbs, egg whites, minced beef and duck and duck stock.

2 Cook and purée the beetroot, add to the consommé and pass through a fine sieve.

3 Garnish with a julienne of beef, smoked duck, beetroot and leek.

Chicken consommé

Ingredients	4 portions	10 portions
Minced flesh (e.g. beef, fish, poultry, game)	200 g	1 kg
Carrot	40 g	100 g
Onion	40 g	100 g
Celery	40 g	100 g
Leek	40 g	100 g
Bay leaves	1	2
Thyme	1 sprig	2 sprig
Peppercorns	4	10
Good-quality salt	pinch	5 g
Cold stock (e.g. beef fish, poultry, game)	200 ml	500 ml
Hot stock (e.g. beef fish, poultry, game)	1 l	2.5 l
Egg whites	1	2–3

energy	cal	fat	sat fat	carb	sugar	protein	fibre
435 kJ	103 kcal	2.2 g	0.6 g	4.2 g	2.8 g	16.8 g	1.9 g

METHOD OF WORK

1   Peel and chop all of the vegetables into a **macédoine**.
2   Thoroughly mix all of the minced flesh, vegetables, herbs, seasoning, egg whites and cold stock (this is called the clarification) together and allow to stand for 30 minutes.
3   Mix well with the hot stock and bring to the boil as quickly as possible. Keep the bottom of the pan clear by using a spatula, but avoid disturbing the clarification.
4   Allow to simmer gently for two–three hours.
5   Strain through a dampened muslin cloth and adjust the seasoning with salt only.
6   Serve in a warm consommé cup, plain or with a named garnish.

CHEF'S TIP   Make sure the raft of clarification stays floating. If it starts to sink, raise the temperature. This will help to combat cloudiness.

VIDEO CLIP   Preparation of consommés Celestine.

SOURCING   Growing fresh herbs will not only save money but will give a better flavour.

Chicken velouté with parsley dumplings

Ingredients	4 portions	10 portions
Chicken velouté	1 l	2.5 l
Parsley purée	20 g	50 g
Double cream	20 ml	100 ml
Chicken stock	200 ml	1 l
Fine chicken forcemeat	80 g	200 g
Good-quality salt and pepper	to taste	to taste

energy	cal	fat	sat fat	carb	sugar	protein	fibre
2319 kJ	561 kcal	51.4 g	23.2 g	15 g	2.4 g	10.4 g	2.2 g

METHOD OF WORK

1   Mix the parsley purée and add to the double cream to make a loose purée and season well. Heat carefully in a small saucepan and keep hot for service.

2   Season the forcemeat well. Form **quenelles** using two teaspoons. Place each quenelle in simmering stock and poach until cooked.

3   Heat the velouté and serve with the parsley purée and chicken quenelles.

CHEF'S TIP   This is a visually striking soup, but you can use other purées such as carrot or black bean.

Chicken velouté with tongue and mushrooms *(velouté agnes sorel)*

Ingredients	4 portions	10 portions
Chicken velouté	1 l	2.5 l
Button mushrooms	80 g	200 g
Cooked ox tongue	80 g	200 g
Cooked chicken breast	80 g	200 g

energy	cal	fat	sat fat	carb	sugar	protein	fibre
2046 kJ	494 kcal	42.5 g	19 g	14.2 g	2 g	14.6 g	2.1 g

METHOD OF WORK

1   Cut the chicken, mushrooms and tongue into a fine julienne.

2   Sauté the mushroom and add the tongue and chicken to heat through.

3   Add to the soup just before service.

SOURCING   Use only the freshest mushrooms available as they are not only visible but can be the main flavouring.

Chilled almond and garlic soup

Ingredients	4 portions	10 portions
Crushed garlic	4 cloves	10 cloves
Ground almonds	80 g	200 g
Fresh breadcrumbs	50 g	125 g
Olive oil	80 ml	200 ml
White wine vinegar	20 ml	50 ml
Grape juice	500 ml	1.25 l
Skinned grapes	200 g	500 g
Water	200 ml	500 ml
Sliced toasted almonds	20 g	50 g
Good quality salt and mill pepper	to taste	to taste

energy	cal	fat	sat fat	carb	sugar	protein	fibre
1952 kJ	469 kcal	34.4 g	4 g	34.5 g	24.1 g	7.4 g	3 g

METHOD OF WORK

1 Purée the almonds, garlic and breadcrumbs in a food processor.
2 Add the oil to make a paste.
3 Add the vinegar and then the grape juice and water.
4 Season to taste.
5 Quarter the grapes and mix with the chilled soup.
6 Serve with toasted almonds.

CHEF'S TIP This is a traditional wedding soup of the city of Cordoba in Spain.

Chilled consommé

Ingredients	4 portions	10 portions
Consommé	1 l	2.5 l
Named garnish	200 g	500 g

energy	cal	fat	sat fat	carb	sugar	protein	fibre
1307 kJ	311 kcal	5.8 g	1.8 g	21.6 g	8.7 g	43.6 g	5.8 g

METHOD OF WORK

Chilled consommés are normally placed in the refrigerator one or two hours before service. Their sometimes gelatinous appearance is due to the concentration of protein. The addition of 10 g of leaf gelatine per litre of consommé will set it to the required consistency.

Various flavours can be added to base consommés:

- Consommé Madrilène en Gelée – consommé flavoured with celery, tomato and pimentos, garnished with tomato julienne, shredded fresh sorrel and cooked vermicelli pasta.

- Consommé à l'essence d'estragon en gelée – chicken consommé infused with fresh tarragon leaves after the clarification process.

- Consommé Madeira en gelée – beef consommé flavoured with Madeira.

CHEF'S TIP Instead of using gelatine, an alternative setting gel such as agar-agar can be used.

Clear chicken soup with egg

Ingredients	4 portions	10 portions
Dried shitake mushrooms	4	10
Chicken stock	1 l	2.5 l
Chopped onion	80 g	200 g
Poached eggs	4	10
Fresh chervil	4 pinches	10 pinches
Dark soy sauce	1 tbsp	2 tbsp
Chilli sauce	1 tsp	1 tbsp
Good quality salt and pepper	to taste	to taste

energy	cal	fat	sat fat	carb	sugar	protein	fibre
1017 kJ	243 kcal	6 g	1.6 g	35.6 g	2 g	12.1 g	1.3 g

METHOD OF WORK

1   Boil the mushrooms in water for five minutes. Drain, remove the hard stalks and cut the caps into julienne. Reserve for garnish.

2   Simmer the chopped onions in the stock for 15 minutes, drain and discard the onions.

3   Add the soy sauce, chilli sauce and mushrooms.

4   Bring to the boil, correct the seasoning and strain through muslin cloth. Reboil.

5   Add the whisked eggs in a steady stream to create a long scrambled effect; serve immediately.

CHEF'S TIP The onions are boiled to give a slightly acidic background to the flavours. The mushrooms can be left in to give a more rustic broth.

Consommé with chicken quenelles

Ingredients	4 portions	10 portions
Chicken consommé	1.25 l	3 l
Chicken breast meat	100 g	250 g
Double cream	40 ml	100 ml
Egg whites	1	2
Good quality salt and white pepper	to taste	to taste
Chives	to garnish	to garnish

energy	cal	fat	sat fat	carb	sugar	protein	fibre
1735 kJ	413 kcal	12.9 g	5.3 g	13.5 g	9 g	61.5 g	6 g

METHOD OF WORK

1   Mince the chicken through a fine plate three times, making sure that the flesh is chilled between each mincing.

2   In a metal bowl over ice, beat in the cream to make a fine forcemeat of chicken.

3   Season and test a small piece in simmering stock. Adjust the seasoning if necessary.

4   Make small quenelles of chicken forcemeat and poach in a little of the consommé.

5   Serve the remaining consommé with chicken quenelles and garnish with chopped chives.

CHEF'S TIP Do not return the cooking liquor from the quenelles to the consommé; it will make the consommé cloudy.

VIDEO CLIP Preparation of chicken and herb quenelles.

Consommé with poached quail's eggs *(consommé Colbert)*

Ingredients	4 portions	10 portions
Chicken consommé	1.25 l	3 l
Quail's eggs	12	30
Fine julienne of carrot celery, leek and turnip	160 g	400 g
Butter	20 g	50 g
Chives	to garnish	To garnish

energy	cal	fat	sat fat	carb	sugar	protein	fibre
1719 kJ	409 kcal	14.2 g	5.3 g	14.4 g	9.9 g	56.5 g	6.6 g

METHOD OF WORK

1   Cook the vegetables in the butter in a covered pan until just cooked and drain on dish paper.
2   Poach the eggs in a little of the consommé, taking care to keep the yolks runny. Refresh and keep for service.
3   Place the vegetable garnish and three eggs per portion in the bottom of the consommé cup.
4   Pour the very hot consommé onto the eggs and vegetables.
5   Allow to stand for one minute before service to allow the eggs to heat through.
6   Serve with some chopped chives.

CHEF'S TIP   Hen's eggs are the classical choice for this soup, but the easy availability of quail's eggs means they are now preferable.

Consommé with turned vegetables

Ingredients	4 portions	10 portions
Consommé	1 l	2.5 l
Carrot, turnip, courgette	160 g	400 g
Goose/duck fat	20 g	50 g

energy	cal	fat	sat fat	carb	sugar	protein	fibre
3506 kJ	834 kcal	20.1 g	6.3 g	55.3 g	23.1 g	109.5 g	15 g

METHOD OF WORK

1   Shape the vegetables into small barrel shapes and cook in seasoned boiling water or stock.
2   Serve the soup with the vegetables as a garnish.

CHEF'S TIP   Croûte au pot was originally served from a petit marmite. However, by today's tastes the vegetables would be considered to be overcooked.

Hot and sour soup

Ingredients	4 portions	10 portions
Finely shredded pork or chicken	160 g	400 g
Grated fresh ginger	20 g	50 g
Minced garlic	40 g	100 g
Chopped spring onion	80 g	200 g
Sherry	40 ml	100 ml
Clear chicken bouillon	1 l	2.5 l
Drained straw mushrooms	200 g	500 g
Bamboo shoots	200 g	500 g
Diced firm tofu	200 g	500 g
Cider vinegar	40 ml	100 ml
White pepper	to taste	to taste
Dark soy sauce	to taste	to taste
Red chilli pepper	½	1
Eggs	1	2
Sesame oil	25 ml	50 ml

energy	cal	fat	sat fat	carb	sugar	protein	fibre
1426 kJ	343 kcal	20.1 g	2.7 g	7.5 g	3.8 g	28.9 g	3.2 g

METHOD OF WORK

1 Heat the sesame oil. Add the meat and sauté until cooked. Drain and set aside.

2 Sweat the garlic and ginger, add the sherry and stock.

3 Add the bamboo shoots, mushrooms, onions and tofu and bring to the boil.

4 Flavour soup with the vinegar (which gives the sour taste) and the white pepper (which gives the hot taste).

5 Add enough of the soy sauce to give a brown colour, then season with salt.

6 Cut the chilli pepper into thin slices.

7 Bring the soup back to the boil and add in the sliced chilli pepper. Simmer for three minutes.

8 Slowly and evenly pour in the lightly beaten eggs. Do not stir again until the egg comes to the surface.

9 Add a small amount of the sesame oil for extra flavour and colour.

10 Reheat and serve garnished with chives.

CHEF'S TIP Cayenne or hot chilli powder can also be used to create the hot flavour.

Fish velouté with quenelles and mussels

Ingredients	4 portions	10 portions
Fish velouté	1 l	2.5 l
Mussels	1 kg	2.5 kg
White wine	40 ml	100 ml
Fine fish forcemeat	80 g	200 g

energy	cal	fat	sat fat	carb	sugar	protein	fibre
2442 kJ	584 kcal	32.4 g	16.5 g	19.5 g	0.9 g	52.8 g	0.5 g

METHOD OF WORK

1 Steam the mussels in the wine.

2 Remove the mussel meat and strain the juices into a clean pan.

3 Make small quenelles with the forcemeat and poach in the mussel juices.

4 Add the quenelles and mussels to the soup just before service.

CHEF'S TIP Reduce the mussel juice to enrich the soup, but take care not to over-reduce as the liquor can go from cooked to burnt in an instant. When prepared in smaller quantities there will not be enough mussel juice, so add fish stock and season well.

Iced mussel soup

Ingredients	4 portions	10 portions
Mussels	1 kg	2.5 kg
White wine	80 ml	200 ml
Crushed garlic	1 clove	2–3 cloves
Red pepper	1	2–3
Cucumber (medium sized)	1	2–3
Sliced radish	100 g	250 g
Button mushrooms	200 g	500 g
Peeled broad beans	400 g	1 kg
Peeled tomatoes	300 g	750 g
Lemon juice	½ lemon	1 lemon
Tabasco sauce	to taste	to taste
Good quality salt and mill pepper	to taste	to taste

energy	cal	fat	sat fat	carb	sugar	protein	fibre
1870 kJ	445 kcal	16.2 g	3 g	23 g	9 g	50.1 g	9.9 g

METHOD OF WORK

1 Steam the mussels in the wine and garlic.
2 Remove the flesh and keep the juices.
3 Grill the pepper to loosen the skin and deseed.
4 Peel and chop the cucumber, sprinkle with salt and allow to sit in a colander for ten minutes.
5 Keep some red pepper, mussels and broad beans to one side for garnish.
6 Purée all the ingredients in a food processor, adding water to correct the consistency. Pass through a fine chinois.
7 Chill in the refrigerator for several hours.
8 Serve garnished with a dice of red pepper, mussels, beans and a fresh herb of your choice.

CHEF'S TIP Sauté the mussel garnish in a little green herb oil just before service to give a warm and cold sensation for your guests.

Japanese noodle soup

Ingredients	4 portions	10 portions
Chicken consommé	1 l	2.5 l
Miso	40 ml	100 ml
Soba or egg noodles (cooked)	200 g	500 g
Sake	40 ml	100 ml
Rice vinegar	20 ml	50 ml
Japanese soy sauce	40 ml	100 ml
Sliced asparagus	120 g	300 g
Sliced shitake mushrooms	80 g	200 g
Julienne of carrot	80 g	200 g
Sliced spring onions	40 g	100 g
Chopped chilli	1	2–3
Good quality salt and pepper	To taste	To taste

energy	cal	fat	sat fat	carb	sugar	protein	fibre
1503 kJ	356 kcal	6.8 g	1.6 g	25.5 g	9.8 g	46.6 g	6.9 g

METHOD OF WORK

1 Dissolve the miso in the boiling consommé.
2 Add the soy sauce, vinegar and sake and cook until the alcohol has evaporated.
3 Add the vegetables and simmer for three minutes. Correct the seasoning.
4 Divide the noodles and pour on the soup. Serve immediately.

CHEF'S TIP Miso is made from fermented soya and comes in the form of a paste.

VIDEO CLIP Japanese noodle soup.

Lettuce and asparagus velouté

Ingredients	4 portions	10 portions
Asparagus	200 g	500 g
Iceberg lettuce	200 g	500 g
Onion	50 g	250 g
White of leek	50 g	250 g
Celery	50 g	250 g
Butter	40 g	100 g
Chicken stock	1 l	2.5 l
Flour	40 g	100 g
Bouquet garni	1 small	1 medium
Good quality salt and pepper	to taste	to taste
Double cream	40 ml	100 ml
Egg yolk	1	2–3
Cooked asparagus tips	16	40
Finley sliced lettuce	100 g	250 g

energy	cal	fat	sat fat	carb	sugar	protein	fibre
910 kJ	219 kcal	16.1 g	9.1 g	12.6 g	4.2 g	5.5 g	3.2 g

METHOD OF WORK

1 Sweat the vegetables in the butter.

2 Add the flour to make a roux.

3 Add the stock and bouquet garni. Simmer until all the ingredients are fully cooked.

4 Purée and pass through a fine chinois.

5 Adjust the seasoning and consistency.

6 Whisk the yolks and cream in a bowl until mixed.

7 Add a little of the soup and add the liaison back to the soup.

8 Garnish with the asparagus tips and sliced lettuce.

9 Serve with croutons.

CHEF'S TIP When cooked, iceberg lettuce has a very similar flavour to asparagus.

Petite marmite

Ingredients	4 portions	10 portions
Basic consommé	1.5 l	3.5 l
Diced lean rump beef	80 g	200 g
Chicken wings	4	10
Carrots	80 g	200 g
Leek	80 g	200 g
Turnip	80 g	200 g
Celery	80 g	200 g
Savoy cabbage	50 g	125 g
Bone marrow	8 slices	20 slices
Baguettes	12 slices	30 slices

energy	cal	fat	sat fat	carb	sugar	protein	fibre
1817 kJ	431 kcal	18.3 g	5.1 g	37.4 g	3.9 g	30.3 g	3.7 g

METHOD OF WORK

1 Blanch and refresh the beef, add to the consommé and simmer very gently for one hour.

2 Trim the wings and blanch in boiling water, add to the consommé and simmer for 20 minutes.

3 Turn the carrots and cut the celery into diamonds, add to the consommé.

4 Add the shaped turnips, cut leeks and cabbage and continue to simmer.

5 Dip the slices of bread into the fat from the soup and toast in the oven.

6 **Degrease** the soup and correct the seasoning.

7 Add the sliced marrow to the soup and poach for two–three minutes.

8 Decant into either a single or individual earthenware dishes and serve accompanied by the toasted flutes.

CHEF'S TIP Petite marmite is named after the pot in which it is served: *marmite* = pot, *petite marmite* = small pot.

Prawn bisque

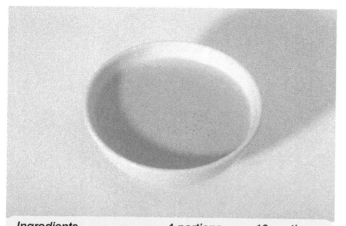

Ingredients	4 portions	10 portions
Named crustacean, shells and flesh	300 g	750 g
Butter	60 g	150 g
Carrots	40 g	100 g
Onion	40 g	100 g
Celery	20 g	50 g
Leek	40 g	100 g
Bouquet garni	1 small	1 medium
Brandy	20 ml	50 ml
Fish stock	800 ml	2 l
Dry white wine	80 ml	200 ml
Tomato purée	20 g	50 g
Cayenne pepper (approx.)	pinch	3 g
Rice flour	60 g	150 g
Unsalted butter	40 g	100 g
Double cream	40 ml	100 ml

energy	cal	fat	sat fat	carb	sugar	protein	fibre
1619 kJ	390 kcal	28.1 g	16.9 g	15 g	2.6 g	12.8 g	1.5 g

METHOD OF WORK

1 Peel, wash, dice and sweat the vegetables in the butter.
2 Add the shells and flesh and cook at a higher temperature for two–three minutes.
3 Raise the heat and add the brandy. Shake the pan and flambé until the flames disappear (this burns off the alcohol).
4 Add the rice flour, tomato purée and cayenne pepper.
5 Add the stock and wine and simmer (skimming when necessary) for 20 minutes.
6 Remove the crustacea and cool slightly.
7 Remove the flesh and pound the shell using a pestle and mortar until smooth. Reserve some of the flesh for garnish.
8 Return the flesh and shell to the bisque and simmer for a further 20 minutes.
9 Purée the soup and pass through a chinois into a clean pan. Adjust the seasoning and consistency.
10 Reboil and add the unsalted butter and cream.
11 Serve with crushed water biscuits, and garnish with the reserved flesh.

CHEF'S TIP For large crustaceans, such as lobster, crawfish and crab, the use of a large mortar and pestle will produce a smoother paste than a food processor.

CHEF'S TIP With lobster and crab, do not use the claws as they can be used as garnish. The broken shells will be collected when passed through a chinois.

VIDEO CLIP Preparation of lobster bisque.

Pumpkin velouté

Ingredients	4 portions	10 portions
Pumpkin flesh	200 g	500 g
Onion	50 g	250 g
White of leek	50 g	250 g
Celery	50 g	250 g
Butter	40 g	100 g
White vegetable stock	1 l	2.5 l
Bouquet garni	small	medium
Double cream	40 ml	100 ml
Egg yolk	1	2–3
Good quality salt and pepper	to taste	to taste

energy	cal	fat	sat fat	carb	sugar	protein	fibre
821 kJ	199 kcal	19.6 g	10.3 g	3.8 g	2.8 g	2.1 g	2.1 g

METHOD OF WORK

1   Peel, de-seed and chop the pumpkin.
2   Sweat the vegetables in the butter with the chopped pumpkin.
3   Add the stock and bouquet garni. Simmer until all the ingredients are fully cooked.
4   Purée and pass through a fine chinois.
5   Adjust the seasoning and consistency.
6   Whisk the yolks and cream in a bowl until mixed.
7   Add a little of the soup and add the liaison back to the soup.
8   Serve with toasted pumpkin seeds.

CHEF'S TIP   This soup can be made from other squashes, such as butternut, but still garnish with roasted pumpkin seeds.

Tomato consommé
(consommé Madrilène)

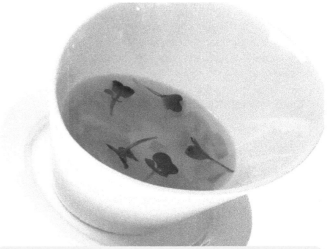

Ingredients	4 portions	10 portions
Basic beef consommé clarification	4 portions	10 portions
Very ripe tomatoes	4	10
Tomato concassé	120 g	300 g
Extra celery	100 g	250 g
Shredded sorrel	1 tbsp	1–3 tbsp

energy	cal	fat	sat fat	carb	sugar	protein	fibre
124 kJ	29 kcal	0.7 g	0.6 g	4.5 g	4.5 g	1.4 g	2.3 g

METHOD OF WORK

1   Squash the tomatoes and squeeze the water into the clarification.
2   Add the tomato flesh and celery to the clarification and proceed as for basic consommé.
3   Serve hot or cold, garnished with the evenly cut tomato concassé and shredded sorrel.

CHEF'S TIP   Tomatoes are over 90 per cent water, therefore it important to squeeze as much out as possible. You can still use the juice in the consommé as long as it is clarified along with the stock.

ASSESSMENT OF KNOWLEDGE AND UNDERSTANDING

You have now learned about the use of the different varieties of soup and how to produce different soups applying an array of commodities and preparation techniques.

To test your level of knowledge and understanding, answer the following short questions.

These will help to prepare you for your summative (final) assessment.

Quality identifications

1   List three examples of velouté.

i

ii

iii

2   List three examples of consommé.

i

ii

iii

3   List the two most important aspects to check before serving every soup.

i

ii

Materials and storage

1   List three pieces of equipment that can be used to pass a soup.

i

ii

iii

2   Give two reasons why the weighing and measuring of ingredients is so important.

i

ii

Preparation

1   Explain the term 'clarification' in relation to consommé.

2   Describe the process of making a royale.

3   List four different accompaniments for soup.

i

ii

iii

iv

Cooking

1   Explain why you should never boil a velouté soup.

2   State three factors in relation to portion control which should be considered when preparing and serving soup.

i

ii

iii

Health and safety

1   List two safety points when passing a hot soup through a chinois.

i

ii

2   State two healthy options when making soups.

i

ii

Sauces

A sauce is most accurately described as a flavoured liquid, which in essence is a base that has been thickened. A stock is generally regarded as the base for many sauces and is an extremely important component.

> **HEALTH & SAFETY**   Many sauces contain dairy produce and so the base ingredients should be kept below 8°C (4°C is best practice) until required.

The thickenings used for sauces vary greatly, depending on the base ingredient. For instance, hollandaise is thickened by adding clarified butter to egg yolks, mayonnaise by adding oil to egg yolks, **beurre blanc** with whisked butter and cream sauces are reduced with double cream.

Modern sauces are lightened by using less fat to take into account society's healthier lifestyles. However, cream, **jus** and butter are still used to complement many dishes.

> **CHEF'S TIP**   Complex sauces used at competition level

A sauce performs an important role in a dish: it complements, enhances and creates an attractive finish to the dish. The sauce's appearance should be glossy and its consistency correct, and it should have a defined flavour but never overpower the flavour of the main ingredient of the dish. The potential of a sauce to highlight a dish is often overlooked, and the seasoning will perform a pivotal role: a bland sauce will ruin a perfectly cooked meal.

There are several basic techniques for making sauces.

Deglazing

This is the process of allowing the caramelized pan or tray juices and sediment to be released into added liquid, which may be water, stock, wine or other liquid-based commodities.

Any excess fat is drained off first, then the liquid is added while stirring rigorously over a hot stove. The liquid is reduced and a good jus or stock added. A small amount of butter can also be added to finish the sauce. The liquid is then passed through muslin cloth and a fine chinois to create a smooth consistency.

Skimming

This process is one of the most important a chef must master. A well skimmed sauce or stock will have clarity and clear flavour, which will be ruined if left unattended. The use of a perforated spoon or small ladle to remove the scum and foam that develops at the surface of a cooking liquid will prevent the stock or sauce from becoming cloudy and bitter.

Any excess traces of fat or oil can be removed by dragging dish papers across the top of the liquid until it is crystal clear. A brown stock can be chilled until it gelatinizes and the fat can then be removed from the surface before using.

Straining and passing

Forcing a liquid or purée through a drum sieve, conical strainer, chinois or muslin cloth will ensure the finished sauce is smooth and emulsified. The use of muslin cloth when passing a jus is essential to remove excess sediment (this process is generally repeated at least twice to ensure a crystal-clear finish).

Reducing

By reducing a liquid over a fierce heat a more intensified flavour is achieved. However, the volume of liquid is reduced, which must be taken into account when preparing a dish and for portion control. Over reducing a liquid can result in the appearance of a bitter flavour.

Whisking and blending

These processes rely on rapid movement to emulsify products such as creams, eggs and purées, giving them a light, smooth and delicate flavour and appearance. This is caused by the increased aeration within the sauce.

Egg-yolk based emulsified sauces, such as hollandaise sauce, require the eggs to be beaten over a bain-marie, which cooks the egg yolks but prevents them from curdling. The vigorous whisking during the cooking process increases the volume of the sauce.

Thickening sauces

ROUX

The best known of all thickening agents in the kitchen, the basic roux is a combination of equal quantities of melted butter and flour mixed together over heat until the mixture comes away from the sides of the pan.

Three types of roux are generally used in professional cookery. A white roux is generally used with the addition of boiled milk to achieve a béchamel sauce. A blond roux is achieved by cooking the mixture for slightly longer until a light sandy colour develops. White stock is then added to create a velouté sauce. The last is a brown roux, which uses flour browned in the oven. Brown stock (estouffade) can then be added to make a brown sauce (espagnole).

BEURRE MANIÉ

Beurre manié is a combination of equal quantities of flour and butter made into a paste. This cold uncooked mix is whisked into hot liquid and cooked out until the desired thickness is achieved.

BREADCRUMBS/RICE

These are used in a raw state and added to a hot sauce. The cooking process makes their starch molecules burst and the starch content will then thicken the liquid.

BUTTER

Whisking or hand blending small cubes of chilled unsalted butter into a hot sauce will give a glossy rich texture. However, the sauce must not be reboiled as the butter within the sauce will split from the water content.

POWDERED STARCH THICKENING AGENTS

These come in numerous forms, such as cornflour, **arrowroot** and fecule. To use these products a little powder should be mixed with cold liquid until a paste is formed, this mix is then whisked into hot liquid which will instantly thicken. The paste must be smooth and gradually added otherwise lumps will form in the sauce.

Arrowroot becomes transparent once added to sauce and is therefore used when thickening hot fruit sauces when clarity is required.

EGG YOLKS AND CREAM (LIAISON)

This mixture is achieved by whisking the egg yolks and cream with a small quantity of a hot sauce. It is then added to the remaining hot sauce. The resultant sauce must not be allowed to boil again as it will **curdle**. This sauce thickening agent is classically used when using velouté sauces; it will enrich the sauce and will only thicken it slightly.

Emulsified sauces

This area of sauce-making requires the most skill. The keys to a good emulsified sauce are the order in which ingredients are added, the temperature and the speed at which the ingredients are blended.

Emulsified sauces are produced by dispersing fats as small droplets in liquids they would not otherwise mix with. Various proteins are used to stabilize the emulsion formed by mixing the two principal ingredients. The most common emulsified sauces are mayonnaise, hollandaise and beurre blanc. However, many other water-based solutions can be emulsified with fats by using egg yolks, powdered lecithin, gelatine or agar-agar as a stabilizer. When egg yolk is used it is the lecithin protein it contains that acts as the stabilizer.

The fat is slowly added to the liquid (e.g. water, vinegar or lemon juice) and this is slowly whisked to form an emulsion. The two liquids will combine with the stabilizer, and if the conditions are right (correct temperature and constant manipulation) they will **coagulate** and form an emulsion.

All emulsified sauces are unstable and will separate if stored for too long or at the wrong temperature. There are methods to rescue a separated emulsification: putting a few drops of hot water in a bowl and whisking the curdled mix into it slowly can sometimes remedy the problem.

Temperature control can be a problem for hollandaise sauce. A mix that has separated due to being too cool can be brought back by whisking it into a little boiling water. A hot mix can be remedied in a similar fashion but instead using iced water.

Butter sauces

Three main types of butter sauce are used in the kitchen:

HOT BUTTER SAUCES

- Beurre fondu – melted butter.
- **Beurre noisette** – nut-brown butter, classically served with fish.
- **Beurre noir** – black butter, classically served with skate wings or veal brains.

Beurre fondu (top), beaurre noisette (middle), beurre noir (bottom)

HEALTH & SAFETY Warm sauces fall into the temperature danger zone and must be carefully controlled to prevent bacterial growth.

WARM BUTTER SAUCES

- Beurre blanc – white butter, classically served with vegetables, fish or white meats.

- Hollandaise – classically served with grilled meats, or made into a derivative such as mousseline or moutarde.

- Béarnaise – similar to hollandaise, but a reduction of shallots, pepper and tarragon is used to create the flavour of the sauce.

VIDEO CLIP Tomato and basil beurre blanc

COLD BUTTER SAUCES

Café de Paris butter – contains a mix of fresh herbs and spices. Other condiments such as marjoram, mustard, dill, rosemary, tarragon, paprika, **capers**, chives, a little curry powder, parsley, shallots, garlic, anchovies and Worcestershire sauce is beaten into unsalted butter. The resulting compound butter is shaped into a cylinder and chilled. When served, a piece is sliced off and allowed to melt on top of, for example, grilled **entrecôte** steaks.

Parsley butter – softened unsalted butter has a little lemon juice and chopped fresh parsley beaten into it. Seasoning and a little cayenne pepper are added and then chilled before use. This butter is sometimes also known as beurre Maître d'Hotel.

Velouté sauces

The velouté sauce is made in the same way as a béchamel sauce except that stock replaces the milk content and no **clouté** is used. A liaison is added to finish the sauce.

Variations of velouté are:

- Aurore – addition of fresh tomato sauce

- Curry – addition of curry paste

- Estragon – addition of tarragon.

Brown sauces (espagnole)

Classically, a brown sauce is made by taking a brown roux and adding brown stock. This can then be mixed with the same quantity of brown stock and reduced by half to create a **demi glace**.

In modern professional cookery, a brown sauce or jus is made by browning meat trimmings and some aromatic vegetables before deglazing with wine and adding brown stock. This is then reduced, passed and seasoned, and the consistency checked before using.

Variations of brown sauce are:

- Bordelaise – addition of red wine and bone marrow.

- Chasseur – addition of mushrooms, white wine, shallots, fresh tarragon and tomato concassé.

- Diable – addition of chopped shallots, vinegar, Worcester sauce, cayenne pepper and peppercorns.

Pureed and blended vegetables sauces

These sauces are the most versatile as they can be used on all types of meat, fish, poultry, game and vegetarian dishes. The sauce base is made by puréeing or blending a cooked main ingredient (e.g. garlic, roasted red peppers) and then a stock, cream or butter is added to obtain a smooth, well flavoured sauce. These sauces can be served hot, warm or cold.

Foams

This type of sauce has recently transformed modern high-class restaurant dishes. The base liquid, which may be cold or hot, is aerated by whisking, blending or by using a gas-charged siphon to create a frothy texture. The foam is then spooned onto the dish; but it should only be added at the last minute to ensure that the air remains in the sauce for the duration of the customer's eating experience. A heavy, well-flavoured sauce can be used to create a light delicate accompaniment that still keeps the taste required. Foams best suit cream, vegetable or fruit sauces as it is difficult to keep denser sauces aerated.

 VIDEO CLIP Producing foams using a bamix and espuma

When aerating a sauce, the size of the container needs to be double the volume of sauce being used. If a blender is used, it should be positioned so that its blades skim the surface of the sauce, which causes the bubbles/froth to develop. A siphon will inject gas directly into the liquid, and will expel the foam directly into the bowl, glass or plate being used to serve the dish.

A gelatinization agent, such as gelatine or agar-agar, is sometimes used to stabilize the foam and create a stronger, foamier texture.

Flavoured oils

The idea of using flavoured oils in sauces is being explored more and more. There are many different oils and flavours available, which makes them extremely versatile. They may be used sparingly to complement sauces and dishes, adding colour and texture, or they may be a main component.

Spices lend themselves exceptionally well to oil flavouring; they are first dry roasted and then added to good quality oil, which is then allowed to simmer for at least an hour. Herbs can be finely chopped or puréed into oil, which allows the natural chlorophyll to turn the oil a green colour.

Oils such as white and black truffle are expensive and very pungent; a few drops added to dishes such as risottos are extremely effective. Flavoured oils can be stored for long periods of time if kept in airtight containers in cool, dry conditions.

Coulis

A coulis is made by very slowly warming through ingredients, such as plum tomatoes, shallots, oil, fresh basil and garlic, and then liquidizing them into a fine sauce. The base ingredients form an emulsion, in which the oil is blended into the sauce. Because of the emulsification, this kind of sauce cannot be served hot and must be carefully monitored.

Fruit coulis are generally puréed fruits that have been combined with sugar in the form of stock syrup to adjust the consistency. A little lemon juice can be added to enhance the natural flavours of the fresh fruits.

Vinaigrettes

Classically, a vinaigrette is an emulsion of three parts oil and one part vinegar, with the addition of a little mustard and various flavourings and seasonings. It is considered to be a typically French dressing, and is used mostly for salads and hors d'oeuvres.

Modern vinaigrettes use the lightest oils, flavoured vinegars and subtle mustards to complement each dish as required. They can be served cold or warm.

SPLIT DRESSINGS

These dressings are technically vinaigrettes as they contain the same ingredients, however due to the fact that emulsification has not taken place they have their own classification.

Mayonnaise

This is an emulsion of egg yolks, oil, mustard, vinegar and lemon juice. The egg yolks form the main structure as the lecithin protein they contain prevents the sauce from splitting. Mayonnaise is the basis of many classical dressings and sauces for the larder section.

> **HEALTH & SAFETY** When making mayonnaise, use only pasteurized egg. This will reduce the risk of salmonella.

Some derivatives of mayonnaise are:

● tartare sauce

● remoulade

● aïoli.

Cream-based sauces

There are two main types of cream-based sauce:

● cooked

● uncooked.

The cooked versions are mentioned earlier; for example fish cream sauce, which is a reduction of fish stock, white wine, shallots and cream, reduced to a coating consistency. Other types of cream sauces can be produced from a basic velouté base by adding cream to the final stages of cooking.

Cold cream sauces can be **whipped**, thickened, flavoured or poured, and can be served as accompaniments with salads, cold meats and starters. Different types of cream base can be used, such as crème fraîche, soured cream, whipping cream and natural yoghurt.

Pesto

This is an Italian sauce that originates from Genoa but is today widely used throughout cuisine. The basic ingredients for pesto are a good quality virgin olive oil, garlic, pine nuts, parmesan cheese and fresh basil. Sun-dried peppers and tomatoes can be added for a twist on this classic sauce.

Pesto and sun-dried tomato pesto

Purée-based sauces

Purée-based sauces are usually cooked recipes containing vegetables or fruits and are blended and passed through a chinois. To produce a coarse purée, the main raw ingredient is blended and not passed.

Salsa

Salsa simply means 'sauce' in Spanish. Salsas can be served either warm or cold and are used either to add spice to a dish or to balance an already heavily spiced dish and 'cool' it down. They can be produced from fruit or vegetables, or a mix of both. Salsas are regarded more as a cross between a salad and a dressing, rather than strictly as a sauce.

Top left – Pickled ginger salsa, top right – Papaya and black bean salsa, bottom left – Mango and lime salsa, bottom right – Tomato, cucumber and shallot salsa

Reduced vinegars

Vinegars such as balsamic, cider or red wine reduce well and form a syrup-like consistency. Reduced vinegars can be presented onto a plate to give a sweet, slightly thick and syrupy appearance. They are used generally to add colour and decoration to a plate, in collaboration with other dressings and sauces.

STORAGE OF COLD SAUCES AND DRESSINGS

Sauces and dressings should be made on a daily basis to get the freshest flavour possible. If they need to be stored, they should be kept chilled and must be correctly labelled and dated during storage.

Some dressings and sauces are, however, better left to mature, such as Cumberland sauce. These should be kept chilled in a covered container.

Dressings that use oil as a main ingredient will begin to solidify when chilled. It will be necessary to allow such dressings to warm up to room temperature before use; this allows the dressing to become fluid again.

An alternative method of storage is to vacuum pack sauces into various sized portions. Some sauces can also be frozen and defrosted as required.

Recipes

Béarnaise sauce

Left – Béarnaise, right – Hollandaise

Ingredients	10 portions
White wine vinegar	2 tbsp
Water	2 tbsp
Fresh tarragon	2 tsp
Crushed peppercorns	1 tsp
Egg yolks	4
Clarified unsalted butter	250 g
Lemon juice	½ lemon
Fresh chopped tarragon	2 tsp
Fresh chopped chervil	2 tsp
Good quality salt and ground white pepper	to taste

energy	cal	fat	sat fat	carb	sugar	protein	fibre
885 kJ	215 kcal	22.7 g	13.6 g	1.2 g	0.2 g	1.6 g	0.3 g

METHOD OF WORK

1 Place the vinegar, water, tarragon and peppercorns in a saucepan and reduce by one-third.
2 Strain the liquid and allow to cool slightly.
3 Mix the egg yolks with the reduced tarragon liquid and whisk over a bain-marie until the ribbon stage is achieved.
4 Slowly pour the warm clarified butter into egg mix, whisking constantly until the sauce is thick and glossy.
5 Add the lemon juice and season.
6 Add the chopped chervil and tarragon to the sauce. Keep warm until required for service.

Beurre blanc

Ingredients	10 portions
Shallots, chopped	2 each
White wine vinegar	3 tbsp
White wine	4 tbsp
Water	2 tbsp
Diced unsalted butter	200 g
Lemon juice	½ lemon
Good quality salt and white pepper	To taste

energy	cal	fat	sat fat	carb	sugar	protein	fibre
647 kJ	157 kcal	16.5 g	10.4 g	0.6 g	0.6 g	0.2 g	0.1 g

METHOD OF WORK

1 Place the shallots, white wine vinegar, white wine and water in a pan and reduce by half.
2 Remove from the heat. Whisk in the diced cold butter until emulsified and the sauce thickens to the correct consistency.
3 Season well and add a little lemon juice.

CHEF'S TIP This sauce works well if fish, chicken or vegetable stock is used instead of water. Ensure the butter is diced small and is cold before whisking in as this helps emulsification.

CHEF'S TIP Keep the béarnaise sauce warm by placing near a heat lamp or hotplate, but ensure the container sits on a cloth and the top is covered to prevent splitting.

Bordelaise sauce

Ingredients	10 portions
Veal jus/demi glace	450 ml
Shallots	4
Vegetable oil	45 ml
Red wine	200 ml
Crushed peppercorns	1 tsp
Bay leaf	1
Bone marrow	60 g
Unsalted butter	40 g
Good quality salt and white pepper	To taste

energy	cal	fat	sat fat	carb	sugar	protein	fibre
688 kJ	166 kcal	15.1 g	3.3 g	1.6 g	1.1 g	2.5 g	0.7 g

METHOD OF WORK

1 Finely chop the shallots. Sweat in the oil with the peppercorns and bay leaf.

2 Add the red wine and reduce by half.

3 Add the jus. Bring to the boil and simmer, skimming occasionally.

4 Soak the beef bone marrow for 20 minutes in cold water, then clean and slice.

5 Add a knob of the butter to the jus and whisk in to give a good **glaze**.

6 Add the marrow to the sauce to warm through and serve.

CHEF'S TIP The marrow can be kept frozen until required and then soaked. This will defrost the marrow and remove any unwanted blood deposits.

Champagne and dill cream foam

Ingredients	10 portions
Shellfish sauce (see recipe)	250 ml
Champagne	100 ml
Fresh chopped dill	3 tsp
Full fat milk	75 ml

energy	cal	fat	sat fat	carb	sugar	protein	fibre
219 kJ	53 kcal	3.4 g	2.2 g	1 g	0.8 g	0.6 g	0.2 g

METHOD OF WORK

1 Bring the sauce to the boil and add the champagne, milk and dill.

2 Place a small amount into a tall jug or container. Using a hand blender, aerate until foam begins to appear.*

3 Spoon the foam over a finished dish at the last minute of service.

*Alternatively, place into a siphon and charge with a gas cartridge. Keep the siphon warm in a bain-marie of hot water at 80°C for service. Shoot the foam through the siphon when required and serve.

CHEF'S TIP Foams are excellent for giving flavour but with a very light taste. The key to a good foam is milk, which allows the sauce to froth and hold volume for long enough to serve.

Court bouillon

Ingredients	10 portions
Leeks	10
Celery	5 sticks
Carrot	5
Onion	5
Shallots	10
Fennel	2½
Garlic	2 cloves
Fresh bay leaf	1 leaf
Fresh parsley	Sprig
Peppercorns	12 each
Juice and zest of lemons	5 lemons
White wine	60 ml

energy	cal	fat	sat fat	carb	sugar	protein	fibre
667 kJ	159 kcal	3.8 g	0.6 g	24.3 g	19.6 g	7.8 g	14.8 g

METHOD OF WORK

1   Chop all vegetables and place in a saucepan with the herbs, cover with cold water and bring to the boil.
2   Add the remaining ingredients and simmer for 30 minutes.
3   Chill and store in a sealed container in a refrigerator until required.

CHEF'S TIP This stock is essential for fish cookery and can be made in advance, but it should not be kept for longer than four days.

Fresh tomato sauce

Ingredients	10 portions
Unsalted butter	100 g
Shallots, finely chopped	4
Fresh chopped thyme	1 tsp
Bay leaf	1
Chopped garlic	4 cloves
Ripe plum tomatoes, chopped	800 g
Tomato purée	25 g
Caster sugar	75 g
Tomato juice	150 ml
Fresh basil stalks	3 tsp
Good quality salt and white pepper	to taste

energy	cal	fat	sat fat	carb	sugar	protein	fibre
541 kJ	130 kcal	8.5 g	6.1 g	12.6 g	12.1 g	1.4 g	2 g

METHOD OF WORK

1   Sweat the shallots, thyme, bay leaf and garlic in butter.
2   Add the chopped plum tomatoes, purée, caster sugar, tomato juice and basil stalks.
3   Simmer for 45 minutes.
4   Blend in a liquidizer until smooth and pass through a chinois.
5   Correct the seasoning and serve.

CHEF'S TIP This sauce is vibrant in colour and flavoursome. As an alternative, the tomatoes can be cut into concassé and the purée omitted. The same cooking procedure applies except do not blend to leave the chunky texture.

Hollandaise sauce

Left – Béarnaise, right – Hollandaise

Ingredients	10 portions
White wine vinegar	2 tbsp
Water	2 tbsp
Crushed peppercorns	1 tsp
Egg yolks	4
Clarified unsalted butter	250 g
Lemon juice	½ lemon
Good quality salt and ground white pepper	to taste

energy	cal	fat	sat fat	carb	sugar	protein	fibre
871 kJ	212 kcal	22.6 g	13.6 g	0.6 g	0.2 g	1.3 g	0.2 g

METHOD OF WORK

1   Place the vinegar, water and peppercorns into a saucepan and place onto a medium heat. Reduce by one-third.
2   Strain the liquid through a fine chinois and allow to cool slightly.
3   Mix the egg yolks with the liquid and whisk over a bain-marie until the ribbon stage is achieved.
4   Slowly trickle the warm clarified butter into the egg mixture, whisking constantly until the sauce has emulsified into a thick and glossy consistency.
5   Add the lemon juice and correct the seasoning. Keep warm until required for service.

CHEF'S TIP   Temperature is very important when making hollandaise sauce: if the liquid is too hot the egg will scramble, and if the butter is too hot or too cold the sauce will split.

Light chicken jus

Ingredients	10 portions
Brown chicken stock	750 ml
Chicken carcasses	400 g
Shallots	5
Mushroom trimmings	10
Garlic	½ bulb
Bay leaf	1
White wine	200 ml
Tomato purée	25 g
Good quality salt and white pepper	to taste

energy	cal	fat	sat fat	carb	sugar	protein	fibre
1501 kJ	365 kcal	35 g	3 g	3.1 g	2.1 g	5.9 g	4.6 g

METHOD OF WORK

1   Chop the chicken carcasses into small pieces. Colour in a hot pan with a little oil until golden brown in colour.
2   Add the chopped shallots, mushroom trimmings, garlic, bay leaf and tomato purée and continue to colour all the ingredients.
3   Add the wine and reduce until only a little liquid is remaining.
4   Add the stock and reduce by half, skimming continuously.
5   Pass through a chinois and muslin cloth, then thicken as required and correct the seasoning.

HEALTHY OPTION   Remove as much fat from the chicken carcasses as possible. This will reduce the amount of fat released into the sauce and will cut down on skimming.

Mussel stock

Ingredients	10 portions
Fresh cleaned mussels	750 g
Water	300 ml
White wine	100 ml
Shallots	50 g
Celery	40 g
Fresh parsley and thyme	sprig of each

energy	cal	fat	sat fat	carb	sugar	protein	fibre
368 kJ	87 kcal	2.1 g	0.4 g	3.2 g	0.5 g	12.7 g	0.2 g

METHOD OF WORK

1 Place the water, white wine, chopped shallots, sliced celery, parsley and thyme into a saucepan and bring to the boil.

2 Add the mussels, cover with a lid and boil for three–four minutes.

3 Remove the mussels and use if required for another dish.

4 Leave the stock to stand for five minutes to let any grit sink to the bottom. Strain through muslin cloth. Use as required.

CHEF'S TIP This is more of a liquor than a stock; however, the flavour that can be produced is excellent and will make a real difference in many dishes.

Reduction sauce

Ingredients	10 portions
Parsley stalks	4 tsp
Shallots, chopped	4 small
Unsalted butter	75 g
White wine	100 ml
White stock	350 ml
Double cream	350 ml
Good quality salt and white pepper	to taste

energy	cal	fat	sat fat	carb	sugar	protein	fibre
1020 kJ	248 kcal	25.6 g	15.8 g	1.8 g	1.7 g	1 g	0.5 g

METHOD OF WORK

1 Sweat off the parsley stalks and shallots in the butter without any colour. Add the white wine and reduce by two-thirds.

2 Add the stock and reduce by a further two-thirds.

3 Add the double cream and simmer until reduced by half and the desired consistency has been achieved.

4 Pass through a fine chinois and correct the seasoning.

SOURCING This sauce relies on the ingredients for its distinctive delicate flavour, so only use good quality wine and stock

Roasted yellow pepper sauce

Ingredients	10 portions
Yellow peppers	400 g
Olive oil	30 ml
Chopped garlic	2 cloves
Chopped onion	80 g
Vegetable stock	250 ml
Double cream	75 ml
Good quality salt and white pepper	To taste

energy	cal	fat	sat fat	carb	sugar	protein	fibre
351 kJ	85 kcal	7.6 g	3.1 g	3.5 g	3.1 g	0.7 g	0.7 g

METHOD OF WORK

1   Pre-heat an oven to 180°C.

2   Deseed and chop the peppers roughly. Place in a bowl with the olive oil, chopped onions, chopped garlic and season well with salt and pepper.

3   Place onto a tray and roast for 20 minutes.

4   Remove the roasted vegetables from the oven and liquidize in a food blender, slowly adding the stock.

5   Pour into a saucepan and bring to the boil, add the cream and cook to the required consistency.

6   Pass through a chinois, correct the seasoning and serve.

CHEF'S TIP   This sauce works with red or green peppers or tomatoes. For a more subtle taste, the vegetables can be blanched in vegetable stock instead of being roasted.

Saffron fish sauce

Ingredients	10 portions
Fish stock	500 ml
White wine	250 ml
Noilly Prat	200 ml
Finely chopped shallots	100 g
Double cream	400 ml
Saffron	1 tsp
Diced unsalted butter	70 g

energy	cal	fat	sat fat	carb	sugar	protein	fibre
1243 kJ	301 kcal	27.7 g	17.1 g	2.4 g	2.4 g	2 g	0.2 g

METHOD OF WORK

1   Bring the stock, white wine, chopped shallots and Noilly Prat to the boil and reduce by half.

2   Add the cream and bring back to the boil. Reduce until the sauce has thickened to the required consistency.

3   Remove from the heat and add the saffron, allowing five minutes to infuse into the sauce.

4   While the sauce is still warm, whisk in the butter a little at a time on the side of the stove.

5   Strain the sauce through a fine chinois. Reheat without boiling and serve as required.

CHEF'S TIP   The sauce can be made without saffron to allow it to be used on other dishes. To add saffron, simply infuse the saffron in a container with some stock and then add to a little sauce as required.

Shellfish sauce

Ingredients	10 portions
Lobster/crab/langoustine shells	450 g
Garlic	3 cloves
Mirepoix of vegetables (carrots, onions, leek and celery)	100 g
Tomato concassé	150 g
Brandy	125 ml
Fish stock	250 ml
Double cream	150 ml
White wine	100 ml
Diced butter	50 g
Fresh dill	2 tsp
Fresh tarragon	1 tsp
Good quality salt and white pepper	to taste

energy	cal	fat	sat fat	carb	sugar	protein	fibre
655 kJ	159 kcal	12.5 g	7.8 g	1.7 g	1.4 g	1.2 g	0.5 g

METHOD OF WORK

1 Roast the seafood shells with the garlic and mirepoix of vegetables until golden brown in colour.

2 Deglaze the pan with brandy and flambé.

3 Add the tomato concassé and fish stock and bring to the boil.

4 Skim constantly and simmer for 40 minutes until reduced by half.

5 Add the double cream and continue to reduce.

6 Pass the sauce through a chinois into a clean saucepan. Bring the sauce to the boil to reduce again and adjust the seasoning.

7 Add the wine. Add the cubes of butter, whisking continuously.

8 Add chopped fresh herbs to finish.

Sweet curry sauce

Ingredients	10 portions
Unsalted butter	30 g
Diced onion	40 g
Diced pineapple	400 g
Diced banana	50 g
Diced apple	50 g
White flour	30 g
Madras curry paste	30 g
Grated coconut	1 tbsp
Chicken stock	500 ml
Bouquet garni	1 small

energy	cal	fat	sat fat	carb	sugar	protein	fibre
362 kJ	86 kcal	4.7 g	2.9 g	10.5 g	7.8 g	1 g	1.1 g

METHOD OF WORK

1 Sweat the onions in the butter, stir in fruit and cook for approximately five minutes.

2 Add in the flour, curry paste and coconut. Cook out for five minutes, stirring continuously to prevent burning. Add the chicken stock and bouquet garni.

3 Bring to the boil and simmer for 45 minutes. Check the seasoning and serve.

CHEF'S TIP If possible, use fresh coconut and add some of the milk to the sauce to give a really authentic taste.

CHEF'S TIP In the shellfish sauce recipe ensure the alcohol is burned away completely or the finished sauce will have a bitter flavour.

Veal jus

Ingredients	10 portions
Brown veal stock	900 ml
Beef trimmings	200 g
Garlic	1 clove
Fresh thyme	3 tsp
Red wine	200 ml
Mirepoix of vegetables (carrots, celery, onion and leek)	100 g
Tomato purée	25 g
Good quality salt and white pepper	To taste

energy	cal	fat	sat fat	carb	sugar	protein	fibre
241 kJ	58 kcal	1.4 g	0.5 g	1.4 g	0.8 g	6.8 g	0.6 g

METHOD OF WORK

1   Brown the beef trimmings with the garlic and thyme in a saucepan or in a roasting tray in the oven at a high temperature.

2   Add the mirepoix of vegetables and tomato purée and brown again.

3   Deglaze the pan with the red wine and remove all sediment from the bottom.

4   Add the stock and reduce by half. Skim continuously to remove the scum.

5   Pass through a chinois, correct the consistency and the seasoning.

CHEF'S TIP   Good flavour and colour are achieved by browning the meat and vegetables: too little and the sauce will be too light, too much and the sauce will taste burnt.

Vegetable nage

Ingredients	10 portions
Onions	80 g
Carrots	80 g
Celery	50 g
Leek	50 g
Garlic	3 cloves
Lemon juice	½ lemon
White peppercorns	¼ tsp
Star anise	1
Water	500 ml
White wine	50 ml
Fresh tarragon, basil, coriander, thyme and parsley	sprig of each

energy	cal	fat	sat fat	carb	sugar	protein	fibre
57 kJ	14 kcal	0.2 g	0 g	2.1 g	0.9 g	0.3 g	0.5 g

METHOD OF WORK

1   Slice all the vegetables and place into a saucepan with the lemon juice, garlic, peppercorns, star anise and water.

2   Bring to the boil and simmer for ten minutes.

3   Remove from heat. Add the wine with all the fresh herbs.

4   Cool and refrigerate for a minimum of 24 hours before using as required.

CHEF'S TIP   This stock really needs 24 hours to sit, to allow the vegetables to infuse the liquor. There is no quick way of making this; but the end product is worth the effort.

Guest Chef

Roulade of chicken and lamb served with a peppercorn sauce

Chef Tom Hall

Centre (college): Carshalton College, Surrey

Romney Marsh Salt Marsh Lamb offers a unique flavour due to the grazing over the natural grasses and samphire of the salt marshes in Essex near the river Colne. These marshes are free from any fertilizers and provide a totally stress-free environment for the sheep to roam. The Meat has a richer and altogether sweeter flavour which is prized by chefs. Label Anglais chickens are a derivative of an old British breed, the Cornish Red. Because of their heritage, Label Anglais are suited to our climate and thrive in their free range pastures. Their breeding also means they are much slower growing than modern chickens, giving the meat longer to develop a good texture and flavour. The feed contains no antibiotics, additives, colourings and is a cereal.

Ingredient	Amount
Roulade of chicken and lamb	
Best end eye fillets of lamb	8
Chicken breast	6
Parsley – finely chopped	2 tablespoon
Cream	350 mls
Shallots – sweated	75 grams
Salt and pepper	To taste
Ice	
Peppercorn sauce	
Dark stock	400 mls
Peppercorns	75 grams
Cream	100 mls
Butter	50grams

METHOD OF WORK

1 Trim and remove any sinew and silver skin from the fillets, lightly season and cut to 9 cm in length.

2 Remove the fillets from the breasts and trim off the any sinew or fat from the chicken. Place into a food blender with the shallots, herbs and blend together.
   Remove from the blender and, pass the mix through a fine tambourine sieve. Place into a bowl and rest the chicken over the ice.

3 Slowly mix in the cream and season the mix, poach off a little of the mix to test adjust the seasoning if needed.

4 Roll out a sheet of cling film 20 x 20 cm. Using a pallet knife spread the mix on to the cling film making a 13 x 13 cm square.

5 Place the lamb fillet to one end of the mix and roll the mix over the fillet.
   Seal the mix in the cling film and tie both ends.

6 Lightly poach or steam the parcels for 12 minutes, remove and allow to rest for two minutes.

Peppercorn sauce

7 Place the stock into a hot pan and reduce by 1/3. Add the peppercorns and cream and allow to simmer for ten minutes; whisk in the butter.

To finish

8 Heat a sauté pan and add a little oil. Remove the cling film from the chicken and place into the pan to quickly colour the chicken. Remove from the pan and cut as required, garnish with the sauce. Serve with fondant

ASSESSMENT OF KNOWLEDGE AND UNDERSTANDING

You have now learned about the use of the different types of dressings and sauces and how to produce a variety of them utilizing an array of commodities and cooking techniques.

To test your level of knowledge and understanding, answer the following short questions. These will help to prepare you for your summative (final) assessment.

Quality identifications

1   Explain the importance of using fresh vegetables when making stocks and sauces.

2   Describe why is it important to use only good quality bones when making stocks.

Materials and storage

1   Explain why sauces should be kept hot in a bain-marie and not on the stove top.

2   State why aluminium pans should be avoided when making a stock.

Preparation

1   Explain how a curdled hollandaise sauce can be corrected.

2   Explain three ways of removing oil from a stock or sauce.

   i

   ii

   iii

Cooking

1   Explain why skimming sauces is important.

2   List four ways to thicken a sauce.

   i

   ii

   iii

   iv

3   Explain what happens if the sabayon overheats when making a hollandaise sauce.

Health and safety

1   Where and how should warm butter sauces be kept for service?

2   Stocks should be chilled as quickly as possible: state how long they should be blast chilled and to what temperature.

Recipes

6 Advanced vegetable and vegetarian dishes

VRQ

Advanced skills and techniques in producing vegetable and vegetarian dishes

NVQ

Cook and finish complex vegetable dishes

VIDEO CLIP   Covent Garden vegetable market

Introduction

The large number of different types and varieties of vegetables enables the chef to give great depth and variety to their menu and to the diet of the customer. A thorough understanding of the various qualities of each group of vegetables and the characteristics of each type within those groups enables the professional chef to create vegetable dishes that exploit those qualities to their own advantage. This understanding gives the diner a true gastronomic journey through a menu.

Brassicas (Brassicaceae)

Brassicas, also known as flower heads, form the mustard and cabbage family. The main edible parts of these plants develop above the ground. Some varieties are grown for their roots (swede, turnip; see Roots).

VEGETABLE	CHARACTERISTICS	QUALITY POINTS	STORAGE	MAIN COOKERY METHODS
Broccoli	Varieties include calabrese (tight green flower heads) and spouting (longer stems and looser head)	Heads should be fresh and aromatic. Avoid wilted or yellowing heads	Refrigerate for two–three days	Boil, steam, **stir fry**
Brussels sprouts	Closely related to cabbage and named after its original place of cultivation. It has a nuttier flavour than cabbage and is most seasonal around the Christmas period	Tight heads with the leaves wrapped around and with no wilting. The cut end should not be overly discoloured	Refrigerate for four–five days	Boil, steam, sauté, stir fry

VEGETABLE	CHARACTERISTICS	QUALITY POINTS	STORAGE	MAIN COOKERY METHODS
Cauliflower	Closely related to broccoli, it is characterized by its tight thick white flower	Look out for frost damage – looks almost black. The plant should feel heavier than it looks. The leaves should be tight to the flower	Keep in a cool place for two–three days	Boil, steam, stir fry, raw, pickle
Cabbage	There are several varieties in use: white, red, green, savoy, spring greens. The younger leaves at the centre of the head are usually used	White and red should be very firm with no obvious discolouration. Loose leaf varieties should have a large heart and no wilting of the outer leaves	White and red: up to 14 days in a refrigerator. Leafier varieties: in a cool place for two–three days	Steam, boil, stir fry, pickle, ferment
Chinese leaves	Also known as Chinese cabbage, it has the same uses as pak choi. It gives a delicate flavour of cabbage	The leaves are pale green with no discolouration and are packed tightly together in a long cylindrical shape	Refrigerate for four–five days	Stir fry, salads
Kale/curly kale	A winter leaf that does not form a head. The leaves grow along a thick stem	Bright green leaves with no discolouration. Should feel firm to the touch and have no limp leaves	Refrigerate for four–five days	Boil, steam
Pak choi/bok choi	A common vegetable used in Chinese cuisine. It has a peppery flavour and lends itself to fast cooking	There should be no blemishes on the stalks and the leaves should be strong dark green colour	Refrigerate for one–two days	Stir fry, white can be **braised**

Bulbs (Alliums)

Bulbs are perennial bulbous plants that have a characteristic pungent flavour and aroma. In culinary terms they are the most important flavour enhancer next to salt and are used in the cuisines of almost every country worldwide. They vary in intensity from variety to variety. The pungency can be tempered with long slow cooking or through an understanding of the qualities of each variety.

VEGETABLE	CHARACTERISTICS	QUALITY POINTS	STORAGE	MAIN COOKERY METHODS
Garlic	Garlic is a bulb that has its own unique flavour which changes if it is crushed or chopped. It benefits from cooking, but can be eaten raw when it has a pungent peppery flavour. The stalk can be eaten early in the season. Usually, the smaller the bulb, the more pungent the flavour	Papery skin, with the cloves tight together. There should be no sprouting and the bulb should feel firm and heavy	In a cool, dry, dark place up to two weeks	Fry, roast
Leeks	The leek does not form a bulbous base. It has a long cylindrical shape with tightly wrapped leaf sheaths. It is used as a flavouring ingredient, and in its own right as a main ingredient. The fibrous and tough green tops are usually used in stocks	The main part of the leek should be white or pale green with little dark green. Bend the leak to check that there is no woody centre (a sure sign that the vegetable had gone to seed, 'bolted'). Avoid buying if the leafy parts have started to yellow. Should feel firm and heavy	One week in a cool dark place, but can be refrigerated	Braise, and as an ingredient in other dishes
Onions	There are many types of onion, almost all have a papery outer skin and a layered moist interior. The main types are red and white, which have a milder and more delicate flavour than the yellow. There is also the small button and pickling onions	Should feel firm and heavy, the skin should be dry and with no mould growing, and there should be no sprouting	Onions can be stored for many months in a dry dark place if they are hung on strings. If in bags store in a cool dark place	Braise, fry
Shallots	A small mildly flavoured onion that has a place of its own in the culinary world. Most commonly available varieties are banana, brown English and the pink shallot. They are mainly used as ingredients in other dishes and impart a mild onion flavour that does not over-power other flavours	Should feel firm and heavy, the skin should be dry and papery and with no mould growing, and there should be no sprouting	Two to three months in a cool dark and dry place. Avoid refrigeration if possible	Ingredient in other dishes
Spring onions	Also known as scallions (Ireland), gibbons (Wales) and cibies (Scotland), these are early-maturing varieties of onion that are harvested before the formation of a bulb. Some varieties do go on to form a small edible bulb	Colour ranging from white at the base to deep green at the top. They should feel firm to the touch, with no wilting or discolouration	Refrigerate for one to two days	Raw, stir fry

Fungi/mushrooms

Historically, fungi have been used as food in a variety of ways. Mushrooms are used in cookery, yeast is used in baking and mycelial fungi are used for making soy sauce and tempeh. Fungi have no green parts and do not need sunshine to grow; they digest their foods externally, absorbing nutrients into their cells.

Mushrooms are the above ground fruiting (spore producing) bodies of a fungus. There are both cultivated and wild varieties of mushroom. If you are buying wild mushrooms be sure that they are from a reputable source as there are many poisonous varieties that take an expert's eye to distinguish. In culinary terms, mushrooms add a huge variety of flavours and textures to any cuisine.

VEGETABLE	CHARACTERISTICS	QUALITY POINTS	STORAGE	MAIN COOKERY METHODS
Ceps	Known as porcini in Italy, ceps are highly prized, with a rich nutty flavour. Small ceps are held in high regard	Should be firm and feel heavy. Avoid slimy textures	Refrigerate in paper bags for one to two days. Can be dried or bottled for extended storage	Sauté
Chestnut mushrooms	Similar to a white mushroom but with a brown cap and a deeper flavour	No blemishes, firm and dry to the touch and feel heavy	Refrigerate in paper bags for one to two days.	Sauté and as an ingredient in other dishes
Chicken of the woods	A large meaty mushroom found on the side of woodland trees (mostly oak). It has a lemony chicken flavour	Use small and immature, or use the tender outer edges of the mushroom	Use within one day, or freeze	Any dish that applies to chicken
Giant puffball	A very large white fungus that has a white firm interior	The exterior should be white and firm. It should sound hollow when tapped and have a meaty aroma	Refrigerate for one day	Can be sliced and fried or used as white mushrooms

VEGETABLE	CHARACTERISTICS	QUALITY POINTS	STORAGE	MAIN COOKERY METHODS
Morels	A highly prize mushroom that appears in the spring. It has a rough exterior with many nooks and crannies and a deep aromatic flavour. They can accompany rich dishes and still be detected.	Check for insects. Morels should be quite spongy with an intense aroma and not slimy	Refrigerate in paper bags for one to two days. Dry very well for extended storage	Stuffed, sauté
Oyster mushrooms	Oyster mushrooms grow on trees but are easily cultivated. They have a pleasant deep flavour. Their texture when cooked is soft but this does not detract from the flavour	The mushroom has a pronounced cap and the gills and stem should be the same colour. Should feel heavy and not slimy	Refrigerate in paper bags for one to two days. Dry very well for extended storage	Stir fry, sauté
Shiitake	Shiitake are delicately textured mushrooms that are harvested from hardwood trees. They come in a range of colours and are quite meaty in flavour and have a slippery texture after cooking	Should not feel too slippery to the touch. Must be correctly delivered in paper-lined boxes with little sign of disturbance and no sign of bruising	Refrigerate for one to two days	Stir fry, sauté
White mushrooms	The most common of the cultivated mushrooms. They are sold as closed-cup and button mushrooms or as flat open mushrooms. Each type has a pleasant and delicate flavour that can carry and enhance the flavours of other ingredients	Button or closed-cup mushrooms should be white with no blemishes, firm to the touch and feel heavy. Flat mushrooms should have dark gills and a pinkish edge. They also should be firm and heavy	Refrigerate in paper bags for one to two days	Sauté, grill, deep and stir fry. Can also be used as a stuffing and as a vegetarian sauté dish, e.g. stroganoff

Tubers

A tuber is a special type of root that acts as the plant's food store and is grown entirely underground. It is generally the only part of the plant used, indeed in the case of potatoes (which is a member of the tomato family) the fruit of the plant is poisonous.

Tubers are the staple food sources of many cultures. Their ease of cultivation, storage properties and versatility make them very important in the diets of these cultures. The potato in particular has many varieties and uses, which are listed in a separate usage chart.

Potatoes are available in many varieties, and most growers produce potatoes that they know will sell and which have distinctive uses.

The main categories of potato are:

- Early or second early – which includes new potatoes. These potatoes are either grown to mature early in the season or are main crop potatoes that are picked before full maturity. These have the advantage of high nutritional values and require simple cookery methods that lend themselves to the delicate flavours. Their disadvantage is a comparatively short storage time.

- Main crop – these potatoes are allowed to come to full maturity and are robust enough for extended storage, which makes them such an important staple food for so many people.

Each type of potato has a unique eating quality, which can be categorized as waxy or floury. This refers to the texture of the cooked potato. As a general rule, waxy potatoes are suitable for salads and boiling whole and floury potatoes are suitable for baking, for chips and for mashing.

VEGETABLE	CHARACTERISTICS	QUALITY POINTS	STORAGE	MAIN COOKERY METHODS
Jerusalem artichokes	Jerusalem artichokes are neither true artichokes nor from Jerusalem. They are the tuberous roots of a plant from the sunflower family	Firm to the touch, moist flesh, not too knobbly	In a dark cool place for eight to ten days	Boil, roast
Potatoes	See potato chart on the following page	See potato chart on the following page	See potato chart on the following page	
Sweet potatoes	Yellow to deep orange in colour (a source of carotene; vitamin A). Historically it was more important than the potato until the popularity of the potato came to the fore. It is the staple food of central America, the Caribbean and the tropical south	Firm flesh, no sign of woodiness and free from blemishes	In a cool dark place for up to three weeks	Fry, boil, roast bake
Yams	All edible yams have to be cooked to destroy dioscorine, a bitter and toxic substance found in raw yams. They are the staple food of western Africa and the Pacific islands. The average size is that of a small marrow	Should have a coarse brown skin, which should be firm and unbroken. The flesh should be moist and creamy	In a cool dark place for up to four weeks	Boil, fry, roast

POTATO VARIETY	WAXY	FLOURY	CHARACTERISTICS	EARLY	MAIN CROP	MAIN COOKERY METHODS
Anna		✓	Uniform shape, white skin and flesh		✓	Bake, boil, mash
Anya	✓		A small variety, nutty flavour, pink skin	✓ 2nd	✓	Boil, salads
Avalanche		✓	White skin, creamy flesh	✓	✓	Bake boil
Cara		✓	White or pink skin, creamy moist flesh		✓	All methods
Carlingford	✓		White skin, oval, good new potato	✓		Bake, boil, mash
Desiree		✓	Pink skin, soft yellow flesh		✓	All methods
Estima		✓	White skin, moist white flesh	✓ 2nd		All methods
Golden Wonder		✓	Brown skin, white flesh, improves with storage	✓		Crisps especially, and all other methods
Jersey Royal	✓		Kidney shaped, pale yellow flesh, excellent new potato	✓	✓	Salads, boil
Kerr Pinks		✓	Pink skin, white flesh	✓	✓	All methods
King Edward		✓	White and pink skin, pale yellow flesh		✓	All methods
Maris Bard	✓		Creamy flesh, white skin	✓		Not suitable for boiling but good for all other methods
Maris Piper		✓	Cream skin and flesh, most popular in fish and chip shops	✓	✓	Chips especially, and all other methods
Pentland Dell	✓	✓	Pale skin and flesh, even sized	✓	✓	Bake, chip, roast
Picasso	✓		Small, pale skin and flesh	✓	✓	Boil, salads
Pink fir apple	✓		Long, knobbly, excellent nutty flavour		✓	Boil, salads. Best cooked in skin and peeled later
Record		✓	White skin, creamy yellow flesh	✓	✓	All methods
Red Rooster		✓	Red skin, creamy yellow flesh	✓	✓	All methods
Vitelotte	✓		Also known as Truffe de Chine, a purple potato with dark knobbly skin	✓		Boil, salads
Wilja		✓	Oval shape, pale skin and flesh	✓ 2nd		All methods

Roots

Edible roots serve the same purpose of any other root in that they take up water and nutrients to nourish the plant. They may or may not be entirely covered with soil. For the chef, they provide flavour, texture, colour and valuable nutrition.

VEGETABLE	CHARACTERISTICS	QUALITY POINTS	STORAGE	MAIN COOKERY METHODS
Beetroot	A deep purple root that has a sweet earthy flavour. It is high in potassium. The leaves can be cooked like spinach	Firm to the touch. Even size and shape. The leaves should be intact and there should be a fresh earthy aroma	In a dark cool place for up to four weeks	Steam, boil, pickle, salad, roast, soups
Carrots	Carrots are the most popular vegetable after potatoes. They can lift a dish with a splash of colour and a sweetness of flavour	Main crop carrots should have no blemishes, cracks or heavy soil deposits. Young carrots should be thin and with fresh foliage	Refrigerate for five to ten days	Buttered, glacé, Vichy, purée, baby, soup
Celeriac	Also known as turnip rooted celery. The plant is grown for its root rather than its stems. It has a faint aroma and taste of celery	Firm, should feel heavy, no blemishes other than the grooves on the skin	In a dark cool place for 10–14 days	Boil, buttered, creamed
Horseradish	Horseradish is a root grown for its powerful flavour and is usually grated to mix with cream for sauces	Should feel heavy. The skin should not be too woody and the flesh should be slightly moist	In a dark cool place for 10–14 days	Grated
Mouli/daikon radish	A long white radish that has a mild flavour and is used extensively in Chinese cuisine	The leaves should be still intact and green, the skin should be smooth and free of blemishes	Refrigerate for 10–12 days	Mainly stir fry
Parsnips	A relation of carrots, parsnips have a very sweet flavour that is evocative of winter and Christmas	Choose medium-sized roots as the fully matured vegetable can be woody, unless it has been subjected to a frost. Should feel firm with no blemishes or shoots	Ten days in a well-ventilated room	Boil, roast, creamed, fry, soups

VEGETABLE	CHARACTERISTICS	QUALITY POINTS	STORAGE	MAIN COOKERY METHODS
Radishes	Radishes are pungent and peppery roots, usually a bright red colour that livens up summer salads	Should be free from blemishes	Refrigerate for two to three days	Grated
Salsify/scorzonera	These roots are closely related; salsify is light in colour and scorzonera is much darker. Both have a white flesh that oxidizes very quickly. They should be stored in acidulated water after peeling	Should be firm to the touch, have their tops intact and snap easily	Refrigerate for seven to ten days	Boil, deep and shallow fry
Swedes	Similar to turnips, the matured roots of a member of the cabbage family. Raw, the flavour is slightly peppery, and cooked a sweet flavour is produced	Not too large, should feel heavy and firm to the touch. Should not be split as this is a symptom of a poor watering regime in the summer months	In a cool dark place for two to three weeks	Boil, buttered, fry, glacé, purée, soups
Turnips	A root of the cabbage family. The flesh is white and the skin is white to purple. A mild peppery flavour. The leaves can be cooked as turnip tops	The leaves should be intact and the flesh should be firm and not spongy	In a cool dry place for up to ten days	Boil, buttered, fry, roast, soups

Leaves

These vegetables, as the name suggests, are mostly leaf and green in colour. Plants grow using photosynthesis, a process that uses water and sunlight to produce natural sugar and oxygen, and this takes place in the leaves. Some varieties of leaves may also belong to other vegetable groups, such as cabbage.

VEGETABLE	CHARACTERISTICS	QUALITY POINTS	STORAGE	MAIN COOKERY METHODS
Chicory	Chicory can be either white or red. Because of its characteristic bitterness it is not always conducive to the northern European palate. If it is sweetened with honey or sugar it can be very pleasant	The leaves should be tight and blemish free. There should be no wilting	Refrigerate for two to three days	Raw for salad, braise
Cress	Delicate leaves with a faint peppery flavour	Fresh vibrant colour and no wilting of the stems	Refrigerate for two days	Salad
Lettuce	There are many types of lettuce. They are usually used in salads to give bulk and freshness. Some have a peppery taste, such as rocket or dandelion, and some have more delicate flavours, such as Iceberg, butterhead and frisee. It is up to the chef to mix varieties and use each type to their best advantage	The leaves should be vibrant, crisp and have no discolouration or wilting	Refrigerate for two days	Salad, braise
Pousse	This is a baby form of spinach. It has a light delicate flavour that is pleasing to the palate	The leaves should be crisp with a small stem	Refrigerate for two to three days	Boil, sauté, creamed, purée, salad
Spinach	A robust leaf that is the mainstay of many dishes. It should have the stem removed before cookery	The leaves should be blemish free, crisp and deep green	Refrigerate for two to three days	Boil, sauté, creamed, purée
Swiss chard	Similar to spinach, this leaf should have the stem removed with a knife	The leaves should be blemish free, crisp and a deep green or mottled red	Refrigerate for two to three days	Sauté, boil
Watercress	A traditional garnish to roast meats in the English style. The peppery properties are an ideal accompaniment	Bright and deep green leaves with no bruising. Delivery should be in iced boxes	24 hours in a cold refrigerator	Garnishes, soups

Stems

These vegetables are rooted and grow out of the ground. They can also have usable leaves but are generally grown for their stems.

VEGETABLE	CHARACTERISTICS	QUALITY POINTS	STORAGE	MAIN COOKERY METHODS
Asparagus	A very luxurious stem that comes in green and white varieties. Should be simply cooked to let its flavour come through	The tips should be compact, the stalks should not be limp or damaged. Avoid any woodiness	Refrigerate for two to three days	Poach, soups
Celery	Celery is at the heart of many dishes because of its distinct flavour and texture	The leaves should be fresh and bright, the stalks should be blemish free and firm	Refrigerate for four to five days	Braise, boil, raw and as ingredient in other dishes
Kohlrabi	A member of the cabbage family, there are two varieties: green and purple. The bulbous stem is eaten rather than the leaves	Look for small young vegetables with no blemishes and firm to the touch	In a cool place for 10–12 days	Boil
Sea kale	A rare vegetable that can be bitter if picked incorrectly. It should be buried with sand to keep the stalks white	Long slender stalks with fresh leaves at the top. Free from blemishes and firm to the touch	Refrigerate for two to three days	Boil, buttered, fry

Vegetable Fruits and Squashes

These vegetables are the fruits of the plants. They usually grow from a stem and have seeds, and can be dry or juicy on the inside.

VEGETABLE	CHARACTERISTICS	QUALITY POINTS	STORAGE	MAIN COOKERY METHODS
Aubergines	An aqueous vegetable that can be a little bitter and sponge-like when cooked. Salting for 30–40 minutes helps to remove this bitterness and reduces the amount of fat that is taken in	It should feel firm and have a fresh aroma and the skin should have a waxy feel	Refrigerate for two to three days	Fry, grill, bake, stuffed
Courgettes	A small variety of the marrow family. Best flavours are obtained from medium-sized courgettes during the summer months	Deep green or yellow in colour, firm to the touch. No wrinkles or blemishes	Refrigerate for four to five days	Fry, stuffed, Provençale
Cucumbers	An aqueous vegetable that is light and delicate in flavour. It refreshes the palate and is very low in calories. The skin and seeds should be removed as they have a tendency to cause indigestion	Should not be too thick or knobbly, but should feel heavy and have a pleasing aroma. The flesh should be firm and very juicy.	Refrigerate for three to five days	Salads
Marrows	A large aqueous vegetable that can be rather bland but has a slightly sweet background flavour	Small vegetables with firm blemish-free skin, should feel heavier than looks	Refrigerate for two to three days	Fry, stuffed, Provençale

VEGETABLE	CHARACTERISTICS	QUALITY POINTS	STORAGE	MAIN COOKERY METHODS
Peppers	Members of the capsicum family, which includes the chilli peppers. The colour can indicate the sweetness: green and black are the sharpest while red, yellow and orange are sweetest	The skin should be shiny, waxy and not wrinkled. The flesh should be crisp	Refrigerate for four to five days	Grill, sauté, stuffed, soups, raw
Tomatoes	A red fleshed fruit that comes in many varieties. Tomatoes are at their best in the summer months. With modern production they are available all year round, but the flavour is best when they are in season. The stronger flavour and characteristic aroma of vine-ripened tomatoes come from the vine and not the tomato	Firm red flesh with no blemishes or cracks in the skin. Break one open to see the flesh, which should be juicy and sweet	Refrigerate for three to five days	Grill, blanch, stuffed

Pods and seeds

These are the seed-bearing pods and seeds of plants, especially those from the pea and bean family (legumes), usually grown as bushes and vines. They epitomize the summer, even though they are now available all year round.

VEGETABLE	CHARACTERISTICS	QUALITY POINTS	STORAGE	MAIN COOKERY METHODS
Broad beans	A large bean that is best eaten when just picked, or peeled and cooked if stored for short period of time	Should be as fresh as possible. The outer pod should feel strong and crisp. The beans should have a skin that is easily peeled	Refrigerate for one to two days after picking, after that frozen broad beans have a superior quality	Boil, stew, soups
Butter beans	A large bean that is best eaten when just picked	Should be as fresh as possible. The outer pod should feel strong and crisp	Refrigerate for one to two days after picking, after that frozen beans have a superior quality	Boil, stew, soups
French/dwarf bean	Long thin pods that are sweet to the taste	Bright green and sweet tasting, not limp	Use on day of purchase	Boil, buttered

VEGETABLE	CHARACTERISTICS	QUALITY POINTS	STORAGE	MAIN COOKERY METHODS
Okra	This pod contains rows of seeds and becomes slimy when cooked. Popular with Cajun and Caribbean cuisines	Should be bright green and not fibrous and have no signs of bruising	Refrigerate for two to three days	Boil, fry, buttered, soups
Peas	Fresh peas are wonderful to eat. Unfortunately it is very difficult to get them fresh as they deteriorate very quickly after picking. Frozen peas are usually the only alternative	Fresh pods should be bright green. If they are shrivelled in any way, insist on a tasting. If they are not tender and sweet, resort to the frozen alternative	Use on the day of purchase. Peas freeze very well when just picked. Use frozen **petit pois**	Boil, buttered
Runner beans	Coarser than green beans, these are only really available in the summer. The pod is the main part that is eaten	Should not be too large and should snap easily	Refrigerate for two to three days. Freeze very well	Boil, buttered
Sugar snaps/ mange tout	Immature peas that are picked for their pods rather than the peas	Bright green and sweet tasting, not limp	Use on day of purchase	Boil, buttered
Sweetcorn	A variety of maize, which has been the staple food of the Americas for many hundreds of years. The plant is very easy to grow and harvest. Sweetcorn is grown chiefly for human consumption, but varieties are grown for animal consumption and flour production	Sweetcorn starts to deteriorate after picking: the sugars begin to turn to starch. Press a kernel: the juice should run clear. The outer leaves should be tight to the cob and the thread-like fronds should be a dark brown	Ideally use on the day of purchase but can be refrigerated for two to three days. Freezes and cans very well	Boil, fry, buttered, soups

Vegetarian diet

A vegetarian is someone living on a diet of grains, pulses, nuts, seeds, vegetables and fruits with or without the use of dairy products and eggs.

A vegetarian does not eat any meat, poultry, game, fish, shellfish or crustacea, or slaughter byproducts.

Types of vegetarian

- Lacto-ovo-vegetarian – eats both dairy products and eggs. This is the most common type of vegetarian diet.

- Lacto-vegetarian – eats dairy products but not eggs.
- Vegan – does not eat dairy products, eggs or any other animal product.

Potential problems for vegetarians

Many foods contain ingredients derived from the slaughter of animals for example:

- Gelatine is made from animal ligaments, tendons, bones, etc., which have been boiled in water. It is often found in confectionery, low fat spreads, desserts and other dairy products.

- The term animal fat refers to carcass fat and may be present in a wide range of foods, including biscuits, cakes and margarines.

- Suet and lard are types of animal fats. Certain food additives (E numbers) may be derived from animal sources.

- Cheese is often made with rennet extracted from the stomach lining of slaughtered calves. (Vegetarian cheese is made with rennet from a microbial source.)

There is an association that supports and promotes vegetarianism. The Vegetarian Society offers guidance not only to its people who have chosen to become a vegetarian but to businesses offering ideas and good working practice ideas.

Many vegetarians that eat eggs will eat only free-range eggs. This is due to moral objections to the battery farming of hens. Many organizations now only endorse products containing eggs if they are certified as free-range.

Practices in catering

Vegetarians dining out will expect work surfaces and chopping boards, utensils and all other kitchen equipment and facilities to be either kept separate from those used for non-vegetarian food preparation, or cleaned thoroughly before vegetarian food preparation.

Caterers should also ensure that fryers, grills and griddles used for preparing non-vegetarian products are thoroughly cleaned. Fryers must be filled with fresh, uncontaminated oil before vegetarian food is cooked.

It is recommended that caterers keep a separate set of utensils for the preparation and serving of vegetarian meals.

Vegetable nutrition

Protein

Vegetarians obtain protein from:

- Nuts – hazels, brazils, almonds, cashews, walnuts, pine kernels, etc.

- Seeds – sesame, pumpkin, sunflower, linseeds.

- Pulses – peas, beans, lentils, peanuts.

- Grains/cereals – wheat (in bread, **flour**, pasta, etc.), barley, rye, oats, millet, maize (sweetcorn), rice.

- Soya products – tofu, tempeh, textured vegetable protein, vegetarian burgers, soya milk.

- Dairy products – milk, cheese, yoghurt (butter and cream are very poor sources of protein).

- Free range eggs.

It is essential to balance the amino acids in a vegetarian diet. Amino acids are the units from which proteins are made and there are 20 different types in all. We can make many of them in our bodies by converting other amino acids, but eight cannot be made, they have to be provided in the diet and so they are called essential amino acids.

Single plant foods do not contain all the essential amino acids we need in the right proportions, but when we mix plant foods together, any deficiency in one is cancelled out by any excess in the other. We mix protein foods all the time, whether we are meat-eaters or vegetarians. It is a normal part of the human way of eating. A few examples are beans on toast, muesli or rice and peas. Adding dairy products or eggs also adds the missing amino acids, for example macaroni cheese, quiche and porridge.

It is now known that the body has a pool of amino acids so that if one meal is deficient, it can be made up from the body's own stores. Therefore, we don't have to worry about complementing amino acids all the time, as long as our diet is generally varied and well-balanced. Even those foods not considered high in protein are adding some amino acids to this pool.

Carbohydrate

Carbohydrate is our main and most important source of energy and most of it is provided by plant foods. There are three main types: simple sugars, complex carbohydrates or starches and dietary fibre.

The sugars or simple carbohydrates can be found in fruit, milk and ordinary table sugar. Refined sources of sugar are best avoided as they provide energy without any associated fibre, vitamins or minerals and they are also the main cause of dental decay.

Complex carbohydrates are found in cereals/grains (bread, rice, pasta, oats, barley, millet, buckwheat, rye) and some root vegetables, such as potatoes and parsnips. A healthy diet should contain plenty of these starchy foods as a high intake of complex carbohydrate is now known to benefit health. The unrefined carbohydrates, like wholemeal bread and brown rice are best of all because they contain essential dietary fibre and B vitamins.

The exact amount of carbohydrate that you need depends upon your appetite and also your level of activity. Contrary to previous belief a slimming diet should not be low in carbohydrates. In fact starchy foods are very filling relative to the number of calories that they contain.

DIETARY FIBRE

Dietary fibre or non-starch polysaccharide, as it is now termed, refers to the indigestible part of a carbohydrate food. Fibre can be found in unrefined or wholegrain cereals, fruit (fresh and dried) and vegetables. A good intake of dietary fibre can prevent many digestive problems and protect against diseases like colon cancer and diverticular disease.

Fats and oils

Too much fat is bad for us, but a little is necessary to keep our tissues in good repair, for the manufacture of hormones and to act as a carrier for some vitamins. Like proteins, fats are made of smaller units, called fatty acids. Two of these fatty acids, linoleic and linolenic acids, are termed essential as they must be provided in the diet. This is no problem as they are widely found in plant foods.

Fats can be either saturated or unsaturated (mono-unsaturated or poly-unsaturated). A high intake of saturated fat can lead to a raised blood cholesterol level and this has been linked to heart disease. Vegetable fats tend to be more unsaturated and this is one of the benefits of a vegetarian diet. Mono-unsaturated fats, such as olive oil or peanut oil, are best used for frying as the poly-unsaturated fats, like sunflower or safflower oil are unstable at high temperatures. Animal fats (including butter and cheese) tend to be more saturated than vegetable fats, with the exception of palm oil and coconut oil.

Vitamins

Vitamin is the name for several unrelated nutrients that the body cannot synthesize either at all, or in sufficient quantities. The one thing they have in common is that only small quantities are needed in the diet. The main vegetarian sources are listed below:

- Vitamin A (or beta carotene) – red, orange or yellow vegetables like carrots and tomatoes, leafy green vegetables and fruits like apricots and peaches. It is added to most margarines.

- Vitamins – this group of vitamins includes B1, B2, B3, B6 and B12. All the B vitamins except B12 occur in yeasts, whole cereals (especially wheat germ), nuts, seeds, pulses and green vegetables.

- Vitamin B12 – this is the only B vitamin that may cause some difficulty as it is not present in plant foods. Only very tiny amounts of B12 are needed and vegetarians usually get this from dairy produce and free-range eggs. It is sensible for vegans and vegetarians who consume few animal foods to incorporate some B12 fortified foods in their diet. Vitamin B12 is added to yeast extracts, soya milks, vegetarian burgers and some breakfast cereals.

- Vitamin C – fresh fruit, salad vegetables, all leafy green vegetables and potatoes.

- Vitamin D – this vitamin is not found in plant foods but humans can make their own when skin is exposed to sunlight. It is also added to most margarines and is present in milk, cheese and butter. These sources are usually adequate for healthy adults. The very young, the very old and anyone confined indoors would be wise to take a vitamin D supplement especially if they consume very few dairy products.

- Vitamin E – vegetable oil, wholegrain cereals and eggs.

- Vitamin K – Fresh vegetables, cereals and bacterial synthesis in the intestine.

Minerals

Minerals perform a variety of jobs in the body. Details of the some of the most important minerals are listed below:

- Calcium – important for healthy bones and teeth. Found in dairy produce, leafy green vegetables, bread, tap water in hard water areas, nuts and seeds (especially sesame seeds), dried fruits and cheese. Vitamin D helps calcium to be absorbed.

- Iron – needed for red blood cells. Found in leafy green vegetables, wholemeal bread, molasses, eggs, dried fruits (especially apricots and figs), lentils and pulses. Vegetable sources of iron are not as easily absorbed as animal sources, but a good intake of vitamin C will enhance absorption.

- Zinc – plays a major role in many enzyme reactions and the immune system. Found in green vegetables, cheese, sesame and pumpkin seeds, lentils and wholegrain cereals.

- Iodine – present in vegetables, but the quantity depends on how rich the soil is in iodine. Dairy products also have plenty of iodine. Sea vegetables are a good source of iodine for vegans.

Recipes
Vegetable recipes

Baby onion tart tatin

Ingredients	4 portions	10 portions
Baby onions	200 g	500 g
Butter	80 g	200 g
Puff pastry	200 g	500 g
Good quality salt and white pepper	to taste	to taste

energy	cal	fat	sat fat	carb	sugar	protein	fibre
1430 kJ	345 kcal	28.3 g	16 g	20.6 g	2.1 g	3.3 g	0.8 g

METHOD OF WORK

1 Cut the onions in half and caramelize in a pan with the butter.
2 Season to taste and allow to cool slightly.
3 Roll the pastry until it is larger than the pan.
4 Place the pastry on top of the onions and fold the edges between the sides of the pan and the onions.
5 Place the pan in a hot oven and bake until the pastry is thoroughly cooked.
6 Place a plate on top of the pan and turn the pan upside down so the tart falls onto the plate. Serve either individually or sliced.

CHEF'S TIP For individual portions use blini pans.

HEALTHY OPTION To reduce cholesterol, use sunflower oil flavoured with a little sesame seed oil.

Braised endive

Ingredients	4 portions	10 portions
White endive	2	5
Orange	½	1–1 ½
Sugar	20 g	50 g
Butter	20 g	50 g
White stock	100 ml	250 ml
Salt and pepper	to taste	to taste

energy	cal	fat	sat fat	carb	sugar	protein	fibre
299 kJ	72 kcal	4.6 g	2.8 g	7.2 g	7 g	0.8 g	1.3 g

METHOD OF WORK

1 Blanch the endives in boiling salted water until half cooked, refresh in iced water and squeeze out excess water.
2 Make a light caramel with the butter and sugar, add the endives and squeeze the orange juice over, bring to the boil and add the stock, season well and cover.
3 Cook in a 160°C oven for 20 minutes until soft.

Confit onions

Ingredients	4 portions	10 portions
Peeled baby onions	200 g	500 g
Duck fat	500 ml	1250 ml
Thyme	2 sprigs	5 sprigs
Bay leaf	1	2–3
Salt and pepper	to taste	to taste

energy	cal	fat	sat fat	carb	sugar	protein	fibre
4660 kJ	1113 kcal	124.9 g	41.5 g	2.4 g	1.3 g	0.4 g	1 g

METHOD OF WORK

1 Melt the duck fat and add the onions and aromatics in a thick-bottomed pan.

2 Cook slowly until onions are tender.

3 Leave onions in fat until needed.

4 Warm through to remove the fat, check seasoning and serve.

Creamed broccoli Pithivier

Ingredients	4 portions	10 portions
Broccoli florets	400 g	1 kg
Vegetable stock	100 ml	250 ml
Butter	50 g	125 g
Double cream	80 ml	200 ml
Puff pastry	200 g	500 g
Good quality salt and white pepper	to taste	to taste
Egg wash		

energy	cal	fat	sat fat	carb	sugar	protein	fibre
1692 kJ	408 kcal	34 g	19.1 g	20.3 g	2.1 g	6.4 g	3.5 g

METHOD OF WORK

1 Blanch and refresh the broccoli, drain well.

2 Boil and reduce the stock by two-thirds, add the cream and reduce to a sauce consistency.

3 Add the butter and shake the pan until the sauce has thickened, adjust the seasoning and allow to cool.

4 Season the broccoli and mix in the now almost set sauce.

5 Roll the pastry and cut into two circles per portion, one slightly bigger than the other.

6 Divide the mixture evenly and place on the smaller of the pastry circles. Brush the pastry edges with water.

7 Place the larger pastry circles on top and crimp the edges. Brush with egg wash. Cut a spiral pattern in the top and bake in a hot oven until the pastry is fully cooked. Serve immediately.

CHEF'S TIP If the Pithivier browns too quickly reduce the oven temperature to 130°C and continue to cook.

CHEF'S TIP Cream sauce is used in this recipe because it has a neutral flavour and so allows the broccoli flavour to come through. However, a béchamel sauce will achieve a similar finish but with less fat.

Fine ratatouille

Ingredients	4 portions	10 portions
Aubergine macédoine	200 g	500 g
Courgette macédoine	200 g	500 g
Onion macédoine	200 g	500 g
Assorted pepper macédoine	200 g	500 g
White wine	50 ml	125 ml
Tomato concassé	200 g	500 g
Chopped onion	50 g	125 g
Crushed garlic	1 clove	2–3 cloves
Olive oil	50 ml	125 ml
Bay leaf	2	5
Thyme	2 sprigs	5 sprigs
Good quality salt and mill pepper	to taste	to taste

energy	cal	fat	sat fat	carb	sugar	protein	fibre
1379 kJ	331 kcal	31.2 g	4.6 g	8.4 g	6.8 g	3 g	3.8 g

METHOD OF WORK

1 Heat the oil in a pan and add the chopped onion and garlic, allow to colour slightly.
2 Sauté the pepper, onion, courgette and aubergine macédoine until just tender.
3 Add the wine and allow to reduce.
4 Add the tomatoes then add the thyme and bay leaf tied together and season.
5 Simmer for 20 minutes, check the seasoning and serve.

CHEF'S TIP Use over-ripe tomatoes to give a deep red colour, or alternatively add a little tomato purée.

CHEF'S TIP Reduce the fat content by simply tossing all the vegetables in half the oil and roasting them together in the oven.

VIDEO CLIP Ratatouille.

Globe artichokes

Ingredients	4 portions	10 portions
Artichokes	4	10
Seasoning	to taste	to taste
Thyme		
Lemon	1	3
Coriander seeds	4	20
Bay leaf		

energy	cal	fat	sat fat	carb	sugar	protein	fibre
119 kJ	28 kcal	0.5 g	0.1 g	4.4 g	1.8 g	4 g	11.8 g

METHOD OF WORK

1 Pour water into a pan and add lemon juice, pinch of salt, coriander seeds, thyme and bay leaf.

2 Remove the stalk from artichoke by breaking it off and removing woody parts. Trim off the base and any rough outer leaves then cut off about the top 3 cm/one-and-a-quarter in of leaves.

3 Using a small knife peel the artichokes removing all the green leaf parts. Rub with half a lemon and place in the pan, adding a little more water to cover if necessary.

4 Bring to the boil then simmer for six to eight minutes. Remove from heat and leave to cool in liquor– you may need to put a small plate on the artichokes to keep them submerged in the liquid.

5 Leave artichokes in the liquor until you are ready to use them so they do not discolour.

6 Serve hot or cold, dishes such as globe artichokes with hollandaise.

Jerusalem artichokes

Ingredients	4 portions	10 portions
Jerusalem artichokes	16	40
Seasoning	To taste	To taste
Water		

energy	cal	fat	sat fat	carb	sugar	protein	fibre
483 kJ	121 kcal	0.2 g	0 g	21.4 g	3.2 g	3.2 g	7.1 g

METHOD OF WORK

1 Wash, peel and rewash the artichokes.

2 Place into a pan of boiling salted water.

3 Cook until tender.

4 Drain and use as required: dishes such as roasted with herb breadcrumbs.

SOURCING Food miles contribute to approximately 2 per cent of the carbon produced in food production, whilst making artificial fertilizer contributes about 30 per cent. Blended fertilizers are better to use but we are running out of the mined ingredients for artificial fertilizer. However, organic and bio-dynamic production use natural methods of soil fertility, which produce better results and are more sustainable.

Mushroom soufflé

Ingredients	4 portions	10 portions
Button mushrooms (fried and puréed)	200 ml	500 ml
Thick béchamel	100 ml	500 ml
Egg yolks	2	5
Egg whites	2	5
Butter	50 g	125 g
Good quality salt and white pepper	to taste	to taste

energy	cal	fat	sat fat	carb	sugar	protein	fibre
1054 kJ	255 kcal	24.1 g	9.9 g	4.4 g	1.7 g	5.4 g	1.1 g

METHOD OF WORK

1   Combine the mushrooms and béchamel and **correct** the seasoning.
2   Mix in the egg yolks.
3   Whisk the whites to form stiff peaks.
4   Add three-quarters of the whites and mix into the mushrooms.
5   **Fold** in the remainder of the whites.
6   Grease the soufflé dishes and fill to two-thirds.
7   Bake at 180°C until well risen and the interior is still soft.
8   Serve immediately.

CHEF'S TIP Dust the interior of the soufflé dish with flour to give a straighter rise.

Onion purée

Ingredients	Approximately 4 portions	Approximately 10 portions
Peeled white onions	100 g	275 g
Butter	50 g	125 g
Double cream	50 ml	125 ml
Bouquet garni	1 small	1 large

energy	cal	fat	sat fat	carb	sugar	protein	fibre
658 kJ	160 kcal	17 g	10.7 g	1.3 g	0.9 g	0.4 g	0.4 g

METHOD OF WORK

1   Slice onions very thinly on a mandolin, cook slowly in the butter with the bouquet garni until very soft and with no colour.
2   Add the cream and warm through.
3   Place into a liquidizer and blend.
4   Pass through a chinois and season to taste.

Petit pois à la Française

Ingredients	4 portions	10 portions
Fresh or frozen peas	400 g	1 kg
Button onions	100 g	500 g
Iceberg lettuce	100 g	500 g
Vegetable stock	1 litre	2.5 litres
Flour	20 g	50 g
Lemon juice	½ lemon	1 lemon
Good quality salt and pepper	to taste	to taste

energy	cal	fat	sat fat	carb	sugar	protein	fibre
592 kJ	141 kcal	5.5 g	1.5 g	16.6 g	4.9 g	7.4 g	7.2 g

METHOD OF WORK

1 Blanch the button onions and **shred** the lettuce.
2 Add the flour and lemon juice to the stock, mix thoroughly and bring to the boil.
3 Add the peas, onions and lettuce. Cook for five minutes.
4 Adjust the seasoning and consistency and serve.

CHEF'S TIP If the sauce is too thin add some beurre manié to thicken.

Royale of carrot

Ingredients	4 portions	10 portions
Carrots	200 g	500 g
Sugar	pinch	pinch
Butter	50 g	125 g
Béchamel	50 ml	125 ml
Double cream	50 ml	125 ml
Egg yolks	4	10
Micro herbs		
Garlic oil	1 tbsp	2½ tbsp
Good quality salt and mill pepper	to taste	to taste

energy	cal	fat	sat fat	carb	sugar	protein	fibre
983 kJ	238 kcal	23.8 g	12.1 g	5.2 g	3.7 g	1.3 g	0.9 g

METHOD OF WORK

1 Cook the carrots in salted water with the butter and sugar.
2 Purée until smooth and combine with the cream, béchamel and egg yolks.
3 Season to taste and pour into buttered moulds.
4 Cook in the oven in a bain-marie until set (approximately 20 minutes).
5 Serve with micro herbs drizzled with the garlic oil.

CHEF'S TIP Other root vegetables can be prepared as royales.

HEALTHY OPTION To reduce the fat content double the béchamel and remove the cream.

Spinach subric

Ingredients	4 portions	10 portions
Spinach	200 g	500 g
Thick béchamel	50 ml	125 ml
Egg yolks	1	2–3
Double cream	1 tsp	1 tbsp
Nutmeg	to taste	to taste
Clarified butter	40 g	80 g
Good quality salt and pepper	to taste	to taste

energy	cal	fat	sat fat	carb	sugar	protein	fibre
540 kJ	131 kcal	12.3 g	7.1 g	2.8 g	1.3 g	2.6 g	1.2 g

METHOD OF WORK

1   Blanch and refresh the spinach.
2   Combine all the ingredients.
3   Allow to cool.
4   Divide into portions, chill the croquettes and then pane.
5   Deep fry until golden brown, ensuring an internal temperature of 75°C.

CHEF'S TIP   Other cooked vegetables can be used for this dish. Just keep the same ratio of ingredients.

HEALTHY OPTION   To reduce fat content use vegetable oil instead of butter.

Tartilflette

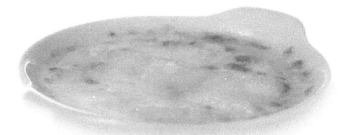

Ingredients	4 portions	10 portions
Peeled, sliced potatoes	200 g	500 g
Finely chopped onions	20 g	50 g
Smoked bacon **lardons**	80 g	200 g
Reblochon cheese	100 g	250 g
Salt and pepper		
Olive oil	2 tbspn	5 tbspn
White wine	50 ml	125 ml

energy	cal	fat	sat fat	carb	sugar	protein	fibre
1168 kJ	282 kcal	21.1 g	7.3 g	10.6 g	1 g	10.7 g	1 g

METHOD OF WORK

1   Preheat an oven to 180°C.
2   Heat the olive oil in a sauté pan.
3   Sauté the onions until softened, add the bacon and cook for a further four minutes.
4   Add the potatoes, white wine, salt, and pepper; bring the mixture to a simmer then cover.
5   Cook gently for ten minutes.
6   Transfer the half of the potatoes to an oven-safe baking dish.
7   Cover the potatoes with half of the Reblochon, and then repeat the layers once, ending with the last of the Reblochon on the top. Bake for 25 minutes, until cooked and lightly coloured.

Celeriac and truffle soup

Celeriac and truffle soup with pan fried ricotta and pine nut ravioli

Ingredients	4 portions	10 portions
Celeriac	400 g	1 kg
Thinly sliced shallots	50 g	125 g
Vegetable stock	400 ml	1 litre
Double cream	160 ml	400 ml
Unsalted butter	40 g	100 g
Egg yolk	2	5
Pasta dough	200 g	500 g
Drained ricotta	200 g	500 g
Pine nuts	20 g	50 g
Chopped chives	1 tbsp	3 tbsp
Chopped truffle	5 g	12 g
Truffle oil	to taste	to taste
Salt and pepper	to taste	to taste

energy	cal	fat	sat fat	carb	sugar	protein	fibre
2173 kJ	525 kcal	46.3 g	24.2 g	16.8 g	4.8 g	11.8 g	5.1 g

METHOD OF WORK

1   Cut the celeriac into small even sized pieces.
2   Sweat the shallots and celeriac in the butter for five minutes, without any colour.
3   Add salt and vegetable stock, simmer gently until the celeriac is very soft.
4   Blitz in a blender until very smooth, pass through a chinois, season well with salt and pepper.
5   Add truffle oil to taste.
6   Mix the ricotta with the pine nuts and chives, season well and make the raviolis.
7   Pan fry the raviolis in a non-stick pan until golden, add some vegetable stock and place a lid on top so the raviolis steam.
8   Reheat the soup and serve with the raviolis and chopped truffle.

Chard and walnut risotto

Crusted chard and walnut risotto with a dark cep sauce

Ingredients	4 portions	10 portions
Plain risotto	400 g	1 kg
Walnuts	50 g	125 g
Walnut oil	5 ml	12 ml
Swiss chard	400 g	1 kg
Egg	to pane	to pane
Plain flour	to pane	to pane
Polenta	to pane	to pane
butter	50 g	125 g
Salt and pepper	to taste	to taste

energy	cal	fat	sat fat	carb	sugar	protein	fibre
2462 kJ	589 kcal	21.9 g	8.1 g	84.5 g	1.2 g	13 g	1.7 g

METHOD OF WORK

1 Mix the walnuts and oil into the cold risotto, split into equal portions and shape into cylinders.
2 Pick down the Swiss chard wash and blanch the leaves in boiling water.
3 Refresh drain and dry the leaves, roll the risotto in some of the leaves and pane.
4 **Chiffonade** the remaining leaves and cook in the butter.
5 Deep fry the risotto until golden brown and hot inside.
6 Serve on top of the chiffonade Swiss chard.

Potato recipes

Anna potatoes *(pommes Anna)*

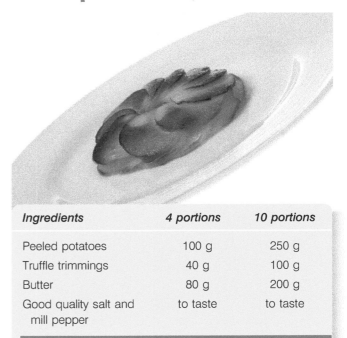

Ingredients	4 portions	10 portions
Peeled potatoes	100 g	250 g
Truffle trimmings	40 g	100 g
Butter	80 g	200 g
Good quality salt and mill pepper	to taste	to taste

energy	cal	fat	sat fat	carb	sugar	protein	fibre
728 kJ	177 kcal	16.5 g	10.4 g	6.7 g	0.3 g	0.7 g	0.7 g

METHOD OF WORK

1 Slice the potatoes on a mandolin set at approximately 2 mm. Do not place the slices in water.
2 Line the base of an Anna mould with silicone paper.
3 Heavily butter the sides of the mould and season the sides and base.
4 Arrange the potatoes in circles, adding a few pieces of truffle and seasoning to each layer, until the mould is full.
5 Cover with another disk of paper and bake at 170°C until the centre is cooked and the edges are golden brown.
6 Half way through the cooking time remove the paper lid.
7 Loosen the edges and turn out onto a dish for service.

CHEF'S TIP This potato dish can be prepared using ramekin dishes for individual portions.

HEALTHY OPTION To reduce the cholesterol content replace the butter with olive oil.

Celeriac and potato croquette

Ingredients	4 portions	10 portions
Celeriac	200 g	500 g
Potatoes	200 g	200 g
Egg yolks	2	5
Grated nutmeg	to taste	to taste
Butter	40 g	75 g
Good quality salt and white pepper	to taste	to taste
Flour, egg wash, fresh breadcrumbs	to pane	to pane

energy	cal	fat	sat fat	carb	sugar	protein	fibre
1027 kJ	247 kcal	16.6 g	7.6 g	18.7 g	3 g	6.6 g	3.1 g

METHOD OF WORK

1   Peel and boil the celeriac until almost tender. Cool and grate on the rough side of the grater.

2   Peel and boil the potatoes. Drain the water and allow residual water to evaporate. Pass the potatoes through a ricer.

3   Add the butter, egg yolk and seasonings.

4   Add the grated celeriac and form into croquettes, 5 cm × 2 cm.

5   Chill the croquettes and then pane.

6   Deep fry until golden brown, ensuring an internal temperature of 75°C.

CHEF'S TIP   Use a dry variety of potato such as Desiree or Maris Piper to get a pleasant finish to the croquettes.

Darfin potatoes

Ingredients	4 portions	10 portions
Peeled potatoes	100 g	250 g
Truffle trimmings (optional)	40 g	100 g
Butter	80 g	200 g
Good quality salt and mill pepper	To taste	To taste

energy	cal	fat	sat fat	carb	sugar	protein	fibre
728 kJ	177 kcal	16.5 g	10.4 g	6.7 g	0.3 g	0.7 g	0.7 g

METHOD OF WORK

1   Julienne the potatoes. Do not place the potato julienne in water.

2   Line the base of an Anna mould with silicone paper.

3   Heavily butter the sides of the mould and season the sides and base.

4   Arrange the potatoes in the mould, adding a few pieces of truffle and seasoning, until the mould is full.

5   Cover with another disk of paper and bake at 170°C until the centre is cooked and the edges are golden brown.

6   Half way through the cooking time remove the paper lid.

HEALTHY OPTION   Reduce or remove the butter content from the celeriac and potato croquette recipe to lower the calories.

Gratin Dauphinoise

Ingredients	4 portions	10 portions
Peeled potatoes	200 g	500 g
Grated gruyere cheese	50 g	125 g
Double cream	200 ml	500 ml
Bouquet garni	1 small	1 large
Garlic cloves	2	5
Salt and pepper	to taste	to taste
Butter	50 g	125 g

energy	cal	fat	sat fat	carb	sugar	protein	fibre
1804 kJ	437 kcal	41.4 g	25.8 g	11.4 g	1.4 g	5.3 g	1 g

METHOD OF WORK

1   Slice the potatoes on a mandolin set at approximately two mm. Do not place the slices in water.

2   Line the base of one inch deep dish with half of the butter.

3   Bring the cream, garlic and bouquet garni to boiling point, remove from the heat and leave to infuse for 30 minutes.

4   Strain through a fine strainer.

5   Place a layer of potatoes on the bottom of the dish and sprinkle with a layer of cheese and season.

6   Continue until just under the rim, pour over the cream, cover and bake in a 160°C oven until cooked through.

CHEF'S TIP This potato dish can be chilled and pressed, cut as required to form neat shapes and then reheated.

Potato blinis

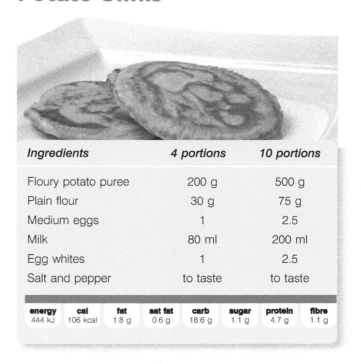

Ingredients	4 portions	10 portions
Floury potato puree	200 g	500 g
Plain flour	30 g	75 g
Medium eggs	1	2.5
Milk	80 ml	200 ml
Egg whites	1	2.5
Salt and pepper	to taste	to taste

energy	cal	fat	sat fat	carb	sugar	protein	fibre
444 kJ	106 kcal	1.8 g	0.6 g	18.6 g	1.1 g	4.7 g	1.1 g

METHOD OF WORK

1   Mix the flour with the potato puree.

2   Add the whole egg.

3   Add the milk and seasoning, whisk the egg whites to soft peaks.

4   Fold a third of the whisked egg white into the potato mixture.

5   Fold in the remaining whisked egg white carefully. Heat a lightly oiled blini pan.

6   Drop in spoonfuls of the potato batter onto the pan and fry until golden brown on both sides and cooked through.

Potato cakes

Ingredients	4 portions	10 portions
Large potatoes	4	10
Egg yolks	2	5
Butter	50 g	125 g
Salt and pepper		

energy	cal	fat	sat fat	carb	sugar	protein	fibre
1834 kJ	440 kcal	13.2 g	7.3 g	74.1 g	3.2 g	7.8 g	6.7 g

METHOD OF WORK

1 Bake the potatoes in the skin until cooked all the way through.
2 Halve and remove the flesh.
3 Mash with the yolks and butter.
4 Season to taste.
5 Mould into 2 cm deep cakes.
6 Lightly flour and fry until golden brown on both sides.

HEALTHY OPTION Wherever possible, cook potatoes in their skins to preserve the minerals and vitamin C which lay under the skin. You could peel after boiling if necessary.

Potato gnocchi

Ingredients	4 portions	10 portions
Floury potatoes	400 g	1 kg
Eggs	1	3
Plain flour	100 g approx	250 g approx
Salt and pepper		

energy	cal	fat	sat fat	carb	sugar	protein	fibre
854 kJ	203 kcal	1.7 g	0.4 g	42.7 g	0.4 g	6 g	2.4 g

METHOD OF WORK

1 Bake the potatoes in the skin until cooked all the way through, pass through a drum sieve.
2 Add the egg, then add the flour until a workable dough is reached do not add too much flour.
3 Season and knead together.
4 Roll into half-inch cylinders, cut into half-inch lengths and shape with a fork.
5 Cook in boiling salted water until they float.
6 Remove immediately.

Potato rösti

Ingredients	4 portions	10 portions
Medium potatoes	4	10
Butter and oil	to fry	to fry
Good quality salt and pepper	to taste	to taste

energy	cal	fat	sat fat	carb	sugar	protein	fibre
861 kJ	206 kcal	2.5 g	0.8 g	43.2 g	1.8 g	3.7 g	3.9 g

METHOD OF WORK

1   Peel the potatoes and boil for ten minutes (the time may vary depending on the size of the potatoes). The potatoes should remain hard; it is important not to boil them for too long.

2   Allow the potatoes to cool slightly then wrap in plastic film and refrigerate for at least one hour. Grate the potatoes (they should be quite sticky), season to taste and divide into individual balls.

3   Form the potatoes into neat patties.

4   Fry in the butter and oil for five to ten minutes on each side or until golden brown.

CHEF'S TIP   Use a floury potato to give a white interior to the rösti.

CHEF'S TIP   For a healthier alternative to frying in butter, brush the röstis with olive oil and bake them in a hot oven.

Saffron potatoes

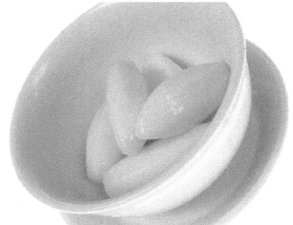

Ingredients	4 portions	10 portions
Maris Piper potatoes	20	50
Saffron	1 g	2–3 g
Double cream	100 ml	250 ml
Vegetable stock	200 ml	500 ml
Butter	40 g	100 g
Good quality salt and white pepper	To taste	To taste

energy	cal	fat	sat fat	carb	sugar	protein	fibre
2656 kJ	639 kcal	23 g	13.9 g	101.1 g	0.7 g	9.6 g	7.1 g

METHOD OF WORK

1   Shape the potatoes with a turning knife until a neat barrel shape is formed (keep the peeled skins).

2   Place half the saffron into salted water. Add the potatoes and bring slowly to the boil, poach the potatoes until just done.

3   Meanwhile, boil and reduce the stock by three-quarters. Add the cream and saffron until a sauce consistency has been achieved. *Monter au beurre* the cream with the butter.

4   Very gently fold the potatoes into the cream and serve.

CHEF'S TIP   Deep fry the skins until crispy and serve with a sour cream dip as a bar snack.

CHEF'S TIP   To lower the fat content use thin béchamel to replace the double cream and butter.

Ingredients	Serves 4
Glamorgan sausages	
Eggs – separated yolks from whites	2
Egg	1
Leek – very finely **diced**	1
Fresh parsley – finely chopped	25 g
Mustard powder	1 tsp
Fresh breadcrumbs	300 g
Caerphilly cheese – grated	190 g
Salt and pepper	To taste
Extra plain flour	For coating
Extra breadcrumbs	For coating
Oil	For deep frying
Plum chutney	
Red plums (stoned and halved)	450 g
Castor sugar	180 g
Cider vinegar	120 ml
Cinnamon stick	12
Star anise	
Saffron oil	
Good quality saffron	2 good pinches
Boiling water	2 tsp
Good olive oil	570 ml
Garnish	
Cherry tomatoes on the vine	4 Vines
Pine kernels	4 tsp

METHOD OF WORK

Glamorgan sausages

1 Mix together the cheese, fresh breadcrumbs, mustard, parsley and leek.

2 Season well.

3 Beat together the two egg yolks and the whole egg and stir into the mix, blending thoroughly then rest the mix for half-an-hour.

4 Form the mix into croquet shapes size to suit your needs.

5 Whip up the two egg whites to meringue consistency.

6 Pass the sausage through the flour.

7 Pass the floured sausage through the whipped egg whites.

8 Pass the egg white coated sausage through the extra breadcrumbs.

9 To cook fry the sausages in a deep fryer until golden brown.

Guest Chef

Glamorgan sausage with plum chutney and a drizzle of saffron olive oil

Chef Paul Palmer

Centre Coleg Morgannwg, Nantgarw, South Wales

Glamorgan sausage (Welsh: *Selsig Morgannwg*) is a traditional Welsh vegetarian sausage for which the main ingredients are cheese (usually Caerphilly but can be any cheese of your choice), leeks and breadcrumbs. The dish most probably dates back to the 11th century. They were originally made with Glamorgan cheese, which is no longer available, but Caerphilly cheese is a direct descendant of the old traditional Glamorgan cheese recipe and lends the same general texture and flavour.

Plum chutney

10 Put all ingredients into a pan and heat gently until the sugar dissolves. Bring to boil and simmer gently for about 20–30 minutes until the plums are tender and liquid is syrup. Cool and keep in fridge.

Saffron oil

11 Crush the saffron with the back of a heavy spoon until you have one teaspoon full.

12 Add the crushed saffron to the two teaspoons of boiling water and infuse for ten minutes.

13 Heat the olive oil in a suitable pan and add to the infused saffron.

14 Cool oil **infusion** enough to pot into a jar tighten lid, shake well and leave for 24 hours before use.

To finish

15 Serve with plum chutney, roast cherry tomatoes on the vine, toasted pine kernels and finish with a drizzle of saffron olive oil.

ASSESSMENT OF KNOWLEDGE AND UNDERSTANDING

You have now learned about the use of the different types of vegetables and how to prepare and cook different vegetable dishes.

To test your level of knowledge and understanding, answer the following short questions. These will help to prepare you for your summative (final) assessment.

Quality identifications

1   List four categories of vegetables.

i)

ii)

iii)

iv)

2   List two examples of each category.

i)

ii)

3   List two quality points you should look for when receiving each type.

i)

ii)

Vegetarians

1   List three types of vegetarians and explain what foods they cannot eat.

i)

ii)

iii)

2   Identify five of the vitamins and minerals naturally occurring in a vegetarian diet to ensure good health is maintained.

i)

ii)

iii)

iv)

v)

Materials and storage

1   Explain the recommended storage method for mushrooms.

2   State three factors in relation to portion control that should be taken into consideration when cooking pommes Anna.

i)

ii)

iii)

Preparation

1   Explain the terms 'blanch' and 'refresh' in relation to cooking green vegetables.

2   Describe the method of preparation for petit pois à la Française.

Cooking

1   Explain what a 'subric' is.

2   Explain the reason for not washing the starch from the potatoes in pommes Anna.

Health and safety

1   State two healthy options when finishing vegetable dishes.

i)

ii)

2   State why it is important to consider using sunflower oil instead of butter when preparing vegetable dishes.

Recipes

BEEF DISHES

Beef Wellington

Braised oxtail with black pudding and turned vegetables

Daube of beef Provençale with garlic mash

Hot smoked fillet of beef with glazed vegetables

Slow cooked fillet of beef, duxelle, light herb and vegetable consommé

Steak and smoked oyster pudding

Tournedos Rossini

VEAL DISHES

Braised cushion of veal with artichokes

Braised veal cheeks with sweetbreads

Osso bucco

Veal kidneys in a Dijon mustard and tarragon sauce

Veal Pojarski with foie gras

LAMB DISHES

Cannon and faggot of lamb

Lamb fillet, mini shepherd's pie and garlic roasted root vegetables

Roast rack of lamb and black olive jus

Rosettes of lamb with gratin potatoes

Roast stuffed saddle of lamb with rosemary jus

Rump of lamb with mushroom sausage

Shoulder of lamb with minted pea puree and fondant potato

PORK DISHES

Roasted rack of pork, black pudding citrus and herb crust, stuffed cabbage with caraway, pomme **cocotte**, beurre noisette hollandaise

Fillet of pork, black pudding tortellini, onion puree

Braised belly of pork, glazed onion, parsnip puree, cider sauce

7 Meat

VRQ

Advanced skills and techniques in producing meat dishes

NVQ

Prepare meat for complex meat dishes

Cook and finish complex meat dishes

LEARNING OBJECTIVES

The aim of this chapter is to enable you to develop skills and implement knowledge in the principles of preparing and cooking complex meat dishes. Generally the most expensive part of a meal is the protein element, whether it is meat, fish or poultry, therefore care should be taken to optimize its potential.

At the end of this chapter you will be able to:

- **Demonstrate a range of skills related to the preparation of meat.**

- **Demonstrate cookery skills using meat as the principal ingredient.**

- **Identify quality points of beef, veal, lamb and pork.**

- **List the health and safety regulations relating to the preparation, cooking and storage of meat and meat dishes.**

- **Identify the different cuts of meat and relate appropriate cookery methods for them.**

- **Identify healthy options with the preparation and cookery of meat dishes.**

Introduction

Meat can be defined as skeletal muscle of an animal reared for the table, the most common meats being beef, pork and lamb. Other types of meat include goat, mutton, veal and venison.

The proteins that make up the muscle are myosin and actin, which are found as long thin molecules in the muscle fibres. These molecules bind together to form complex molecules called acto-myosin. Approximately 15–20 per cent of lean meat is made up of protein, with the remainder of the bulk being 75 per cent water and 5–10 per cent fats and connective tissues. The quality of meat – its colour, texture and flavour – are determined by the arrangement of the muscle fibres, connective tissues and fat.

CHEF'S TIP   Muscle fibres are the part of the muscle that moves. The basic texture of the meat is determined from the mass and thickness of these fibres, which produce the 'grain' of meat.

Connective tissues are those that physically bind all the tissues in the body – they literally connect individual tissues to each other. One of the main types of connective tissue is **collagen**, which breaks down into gelatin when cooked slowly over a long period of time. Muscles that undertake a lot of work (such as leg muscles) have dense fibres and a higher proportion of collagen. Muscles such as the loin have long slender fibres and less collagen. These meats can be cooked much more quickly.

When you cook meat, the protein gradually coagulates (sets) as the core temperature increases. The process of coagulation is complete at 69°C, the protein will then become firmer as continued cooking is applied.

Fat tissue is a form of connective tissue, where some of the cells take on the role of energy storage. Fat is found in three different areas of meat:

- under the skin layer, to help provide insulation to the cold;

- around important organs, such as the kidney, for protection;

- in connective tissues.

CHEF'S TIP Farmed rabbits, chickens and turkeys have predominantly white meat because they do not use their muscles as often as cattle or lamb. Their muscles therefore consist predominantly of white fibres, although their leg muscles are a mixture of half white and half red fibres.

Modern methods of farming tend to produce animals that have little fat. However, the intramuscular fat in meat (marbling) is important for achieving a soft texture. The fat renders (melts) and lubricates the muscle fibres during the cooking process, helping to give flavour and to tenderize the meat.

VIDEO CLIP Smithfield meat market

Meat obtains its colour from two sources:

- Haemoglobin – the red pigment in blood that transports oxygen around the body.

- Myoglobin – a reddish brown protein that stores oxygen in the muscle.

Myoglobin temporarily stores oxygen within the muscle in readiness for action or exercise. Age affects the amount of myoglobin present, which accounts for beef being darker than veal and mutton darker than lamb. Pork is pale because of the early slaughter weight of the animals and their lack of exercise.

When an animal is first slaughtered its blood will be oxygenated (oxymyoglobin) – if the meat is sliced shortly after slaughter the cut surface will be bright red. The blood will then become deoxygenated (metmyoglobin) and change to a burgundy colour. This reaction can take a very short time and it should be noted that it does not mean that the meat is bad. This effect can be prevented by creating a barrier using plastic film or a vacuum pouch.

CHEF'S TIP Well flavoured meat comes from animals that have led a full and active life. However, exercise increases the size and strength of the muscle fibres and so the meat will be tougher.

Organic production

Economics have forced modern suppliers to produce mild, tender meat, which has become the public's usual expectation. However, small producers are now rearing traditional breeds to produce more mature and flavoursome meat for customers who require a high-quality product. The rise of organic farming, with its greater emphasis on animal welfare, has improved distribution and supplies of better quality meat. Generally, organic meat is produced locally and is traceable – the full process it has gone through before it reaches the customer can be tracked. Certain standards must be met before meat can be labelled as organic:

- All meat must be produced to the Soil Association's standards.

- All produce must be sourced either directly from the supplier's farms or from selected local organic producers who adhere to the same Soil Association standards.

- The highest animal welfare standards must be observed at all times.

- All meat must be butchered professionally, on site if possible.

- All produce must be completely traceable.

- There should be minimal transport of live animals, to reduce stress of animals before slaughter.

Organic beef as an example

There can be huge differences in the amounts of time that non-organic cattle spend grazing. The most intensive systems involve keeping bull calves indoors or in yards. Bull calves are used because they grow quickly. They are fed on high levels of concentrated feeds and silage and are fattened up as quickly as possible. The animals are confined in large numbers, which can increase the risk of infectious diseases.

By contrast, less-intensive systems allow the calves – castrated bulls and heifers (female cows) – to remain with their mothers. The whole herd is allowed to graze for one or two summers and may be brought indoors during the winter.

All beef in the UK is either produced from herds that use specific beef breeds, such as Aberdeen Angus, South Devon or Hereford, or from dairy herds where a bull from a beef breed is crossed with the cows. Organic producers are encouraged to choose breeds that suit the conditions on their farms.

Black Aberdeen Angus

An organic beef system allows cows and their calves to graze in pasture for most of their lives. They can be finished in well bedded spacious yards, provided this period does not exceed a fifth of their lifetime. Organic cattle do not have to be housed during the winter, but if they are kept outside, there must be shelter, food and water. At least 60 per cent of the diet must consist of grass, hay or silage. Intestinal worms are a common problem in all cattle. They can be avoided on organic farms by rotating the pastures (moving the cattle between fields) and also by allowing the calves to pick up natural immunity from their mothers.

The beef labelling scheme ensures that any information put onto packs of beef can be verified.

Traceability

Traceability is designed to give the chef and the customer the ultimate guarantee of safety and quality of food. Information can now be communicated through labelling that allows the customer to directly trace a piece of meat back to a particular country of origin, locality/area, farm, breed, abattoir and supplier; effectively giving the history from farm to plate. The label can also include further information, such as the date of slaughter, place of butchery, age and sex of the animal, production method (e.g. organic, grass-fed) and meat maturation time.

Storage and preservation of meat

Bacteria and moulds can multiply and grow very quickly on meat and so it will rot very quickly if it is not carefully stored. There are several methods of preservation that improve the storage life of meat.

- Canning – this was originally done by sealing a square tin can with solder and heating it until the meat was sterilized. Canning continues today but in a much refined form.

- Dehydrating – meat is cut into strips and hung to dry. This method is most popular in countries that have a dry climate.

- Smoking – meat and fish were originally hung in chimneys to dry. As well as having a drying effect, wood smoke contains compounds that have preserving and flavouring qualities.

- Dry curing – until the invention of canning, salting was the most important method of preservation. The meat would be smothered in salt for up to two months. It would then last for many more months.

- Wet curing (pickling) – a heavy salt solution has the same effect as dry curing. The brine can be soaked into the flesh to speed the process and decrease the water content.

- Sealing – meats have been sealed into containers for many hundreds of years. This has the effect of preventing air getting to the meat and so slows the growth of bacteria. Some meats are sealed in fats, such as confit of duck or potted tongue, which can then be cooked in the same fat. Even today, the vacuum pack system relies upon air being excluded. Care should be taken when using this method. Excluding the air affects bacteria that need air to flourish (aerobic) but it does not affect bacteria that do not need air (anaerobic). The smell of decomposing flesh is a safety marker – the smell tells you that the meat is not fit for consumption.

- Refrigeration – meat is kept covered at a temperature range of 1–4°C. This is a method of short-term preservation.

- Freezing – frozen meat is kept at a minimum of –18°C. When meat is frozen quickly the ice crystals that are formed will be much smaller, leading to less cell damage and less water forming during the defrosting process. Care should be taken when storing frozen meat. Freezer burn occurs if the food is not completely covered during the freezing process.

VIDEO CLIP Preparation of beef sirloin

Beef (*Boeuf*)

Beef is the edible meat of domestic cattle. Most beef comes from castrated males killed at 18 months of age. Heifers can also be used for beef if they are not required for breeding.

The carcasses are allowed to cool naturally after slaughter and left to hang for up to 42 days. The **hanging** process (or ageing) creates a slow chemical change during which the meat becomes progressively more flavourful. Enzymes found in the muscle will generate flavour by breaking down other cells, turning large flavourless molecules into smaller well flavoured deposits. Some chefs ask for longer ageing, but no appreciable difference is experienced after 28–30 days.

VIDEO CLIP Preparation of beef fillet

BSE (bovine spongiform encephalitis), also known as mad cow disease, caused the death of millions of cattle. This was brought about by feeding cattle with byproducts derived from sheep that had a brain disease called scrapie. A form of the disease known as variant CJD was also passed to humans. This disease has an extremely long incubation period and so it is not known how long it will take to eradicate. BSE appears to have been eliminated in the UK thanks to the culling of infected herds and changes in feeding practices.

Common breeds used in farming:

- Aberdeen Angus;
- Devon;
- Herefordshire;
- Holstein;
- Cross breed of Limousin and Holstein.

Beef is almost always butchered into quarters and then broken down into primary cuts.

Main beef-producing area

Beef hindquarter

The average hind quarter weight 85–90 kg.

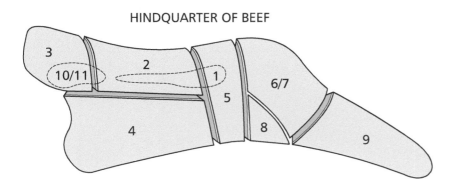

HINDQUARTER OF BEEF

JOINT	FRENCH	USE	AVERAGE WEIGHT
1 Fillet	Le filet	This is the leanest and most tender piece of beef and lends itself to grilling, roasting, frying and pot roasting	3–3.5 kg
2 Sirloin	L'aloyau	A lean piece of meat that is good for frying, roasting and grilling. Care should be taken to remove any sinew from the back prior to roasting and remove any piece of the rump that remains	12–14 kg
3 Wing rib	Les côtes d'aloyau	There are three wing ribs on each side of beef. Can be roasted as a piece or **chined** and cut into **cutlets**	5–6 kg
4 Thin flank	La bavette d'aloyau	Also known as skirt, this is coarse meat with about 50 per cent fat. It is good for sausages or mincing	8–10 kg
5 Rump	Culotte	Frying, roasting, braising. There are several muscles on this joint that give different textural experiences when eating	10 kg
6 Topside	La tranche tendre	Braising, stewing, slow roasting at low temperatures. This piece is used in the sandwich industry and by upmarket delicatessens	9–10 kg
7 Thick flank	Tranche graisse	A large piece of lean meat that lends itself to being braised as a piece as it can disintegrate if used in small pieces in stews	10–11 kg
8 Silverside	Gîte à la noix	Silverside is very coarse and requires long slow cooking. Good for pickling and boiling	12–14 kg
9 Shin	La jambe le jarret	Because of the amount of collagen present, the shin makes excellent consommé	6–7 kg
10 Kidney	Rognon	Pies, puddings	1–2 kg
11 Fat (suet)	Graisse de rognon	Suet pastry, rendering	5–6 kg

Beef forequarter

The average weight of the forequarter is 75–80 kg.

BREAKDOWN ON A FOREQUARTER OF BEEF

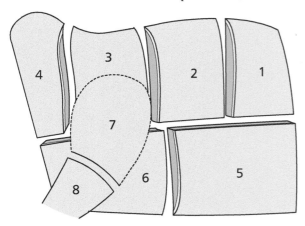

JOINT	FRENCH	USE	AVERAGE WEIGHT
1 Fore rib	Le côte première	The fore rib is the prime roasting joint from the side of beef. It has the best collagen to lean ratio, making it the most succulent. It can also be denuded of fat to give rib-eye steaks, suitable for grilling and frying	6.5 kg
2 Middle rib	Le côte découverte	This is a flavoursome joint that can be used for braising in a single piece or for second-class roasting	8.5 kg
3 Chuck rib	Le côte du collier	The high content of connective tissue in this joint means it benefits from stewing or braising. Be careful to remove all gristle and sinew	13 kg
4 Sticking piece	Le collier-cou	Lean and high in flavour. Ideal for stewing and mincing	7 kg
5 Plate	Le plat de côte	Remove all fat and use for stewing, mincing	8.5 kg
6 Brisket	La poitrine	Brining and boiling brings out the best in brisket, although it can be boiled without brining	16 kg
7 Leg of mutton cut (LMC beef)	L'épaule macreuse	When properly butchered, LMC beef is very lean and makes excellent braising steaks and paupiettes and is good for stewing and mincing	7–9 kg
8 Shank	Jambe de devant	Very lean and high in collagen. Remove any gristle and mince for a consommé clarification mix	5 kg

Recipes

Beef Wellington

Ingredients	4 portions	10 portions
Centre cut fillet of beef	600 g	1.5 kg
Vegetable oil	50 g	100 g
Chestnut mushrooms	300 g	750 g
Finely chopped shallots	50 g	125 g
Dry white wine	20 ml	50 ml
Butter	50 g	125 g
Foie gras pâté	200 g	500 g
Puff pastry	500 g	1 kg
Egg whites	1	2–3
Chopped truffle trimmings	50 g	100 g
Madeira sauce	200 ml	500 ml
Good-quality salt and white pepper	To taste	To taste
Egg wash	1 egg	2 eggs
Herb pancakes		
Fresh eggs	4	8
Soft flour	150 g	300 g
Fresh milk	200 ml	400 ml
Chopped fresh chives and parsley	2 tbsp	4 tbsp
Vegetable oil for frying		
Wilted spinach		

energy	cal	fat	sat fat	carb	sugar	protein	fibre
7311 kJ	1752 kcal	122.9 g	45.4 g	85.9 g	7.7 g	76.8 g	3.8 g

METHOD OF WORK

1   Preheat an oven to 200°C.

2   Tie the fillet of beef to retain its shape, season well and seal in a hot pan with a little fat. Allow to cool completely. Reserve the pan juices. Lightly re-season the beef fillet and reserve in the refrigerator.

3   Finely chop or mince the mushrooms and cook with the shallots in the butter in a saucepan. Add the white wine and continue to cook until the wine has evaporated and the mixture is dry (**duxelle**). Season to taste and allow to cool completely.

4   To make the herb pancakes, beat the eggs and flour in a bowl until smooth. Slowly add the milk to create a thin consistency and then add the chopped herbs and seasoning.

5   Heat a little oil in a pancake pan and cook thin pancakes (one per portion) in the usual way.

6   Remove the beef fillet from the refrigerator and cut into the required portions. Cut away any remaining string.

7   Mix half of the truffles with the pâté and spread over each pancake, then add a layer of the duxelle. Place the sealed beef fillet on top and fold the pancake over to encase the fillet. Trim away any excess pancake. Wrap in plastic film and chill for one hour.

8   Roll out the puff pastry until it is large enough to wrap around the fillet of beef. Leave to rest for 15 minutes.

9   Discard the plastic film and place the pancake-wrapped beef fillet onto the pastry and roll the pastry around the beef, encasing it completely. Seal well to prevent any leakage during cooking.

10   Place on a baking sheet seam-side down and brush with egg wash.

11   Chill thoroughly for at least one hour and egg wash again. **Score** curved lines in the top of the pastry using the tip of a sharp knife.

12   Place in an oven for 20–25 minutes. Reduce the heat to 130°C until the required degree of cooking is achieved.

13   Allow to rest in a warm place for at least five minutes before serving.

14   Heat the pan juices and deglaze with some red wine. Add the Madeira sauce and strain through a fine chinois into a clean pan. Check the consistency and seasoning.

15   Add the remainder of the truffles and heat for two–three minutes.

16   Slice the beef Wellington and serve with wilted spinach and serve with the sauce.

VIDEO CLIP   How to tie knots in butchery.

CHEF'S TIP   Truffles are very expensive. A more economical method is to add a little truffle oil to the duxelle. Another cheaper alternative is to use chicken liver pâté in place of the foie gras. The beef is wrapped in herb pancakes to give extra protection from over-cooking the meat and to retaining the juices produced during the cooking process.

Braised oxtail

Braised oxtail with black pudding and turned vegetables

Ingredients	4 portions	10 portions
Trimmed oxtail	2	5
Black pudding	350 g	900 g
Mirepoix of carrot, onion, celery and leek	200 g	500 g
Chopped tomatoes	200 g	400 g
Fresh thyme	1 sprig	3 sprigs
Fresh bay leaf	1	3
Red wine	400 ml	800 ml
Brown beef stock	600 ml	1.2 l
Beef dripping or oil for frying	50 g	100 g
Good-quality salt and white pepper	to taste	to taste
Garnish		
Turned vegetables	100 g	300 g
Cooked Puy lentils	1 tbsp	3 tbsp

energy	cal	fat	sat fat	carb	sugar	protein	fibre
1918 kJ	461 kcal	31.1 g	8.3 g	19.9 g	5 g	10.1 g	2.5 g

METHOD OF WORK

1   Preheat an oven to 220°C.

2   Using a boning knife, remove excess fat from the tails and bone out the oxtail. Keep the meat whole and retain the bones.

3   Remove the black pudding from the skins and mince it down. Lay it along the centre of the meat. Taper the pudding in the opposite direction to the meat to give an even shape.

4   Roll and carefully tie the tails to give a neat cylindrical shape.

5   Seal the oxtail in a hot pan with the beef dripping and add the mirepoix of vegetables, chopped tomato, thyme and bay leaf. Continue to cook until the mirepoix is golden brown.

6   Brown the bones in the oven and add to the oxtail.

7   Place all the ingredients in a large braising pan or **casserole** with the red wine and the beef stock and cook in the oven for approximately three hours.

8   Remove the oxtails when cooked and strain the sauce through a fine chinois into a clean pan and skim. Reduce the sauce and correct the seasoning and consistency.

9   Add the Puy lentils to warm through.

10 Serve the oxtail sliced with the turned vegetables and Puy lentil sauce.

Daube of beef Provençale

Daube of beef Provençale with a garlic mash

Ingredients	4 portions	10 portions
Daube of beef		
Chuck steak	4 × 150 g	10 × 150 g
White wine	50 ml	125 ml
Cognac	25 ml	70 ml
Crushed garlic	1 clove	2 cloves
Fresh parsley stalks	8	20
White flour	to dust	to dust
Sunflower oil	50 ml	100 ml
Pancetta lardons	100 g	250 g
Black olives	20	50
Carrot	100 g	250 g
Onion	100 g	250 g
Bouquet garni	small	medium
Tomato concassé	100 g	250 g
Sliced chestnut mushrooms	100 g	250 g
Dried orange peel	10 g	25 g
Lemon juice	½ lemon	1 lemon
Good-quality salt and white pepper	to taste	to taste
Garlic mash		
Maris Piper potatoes	400 g	1 kg
Unsalted butter	125 g	250 g
Garlic	2 cloves	4 cloves
Fresh cream	60 ml	120 ml
Good-quality salt and white pepper	to taste	to taste

energy	cal	fat	sat fat	carb	sugar	protein	fibre
4187 kJ	1009 kcal	71.5 g	31.5 g	31 g	3.8 g	56 g	4 g

METHOD OF WORK

1   Trim and slice the beef into neat steaks and marinate for ten hours in the wine, cognac, crushed garlic and parsley stalks.

2   Remove the steaks from the marinade and pat dry with a clean kitchen cloth. Dust the meat with the flour and season with salt and pepper and gently beat it in with the back of a heavy knife. Preheat an oven to 180°C.

3   Season each steak and seal in hot oil, then transfer to a braising pan.

4   Add the cleaned, peeled and chopped vegetables and sauté quickly in the hot fat until golden, then transfer to the braising pot with the beef.

5   Deglaze the pan with the marinade and add to the braising pan.

6   Add the remaining ingredients to the pan. Cover with a tight-fitting lid and place in the oven for two–two-and-a-half hours.

7   When the beef is cooked, remove the beef steaks and cover with plastic film and retain for service. Discard the bouquet garni and orange peel.

8   Reduce the sauce to the required consistency and correct the seasoning.

9   Wash, peel and rewash the potatoes. Cut into a rough dice and cook in boiling salted water until tender. Drain in a colander.

10   Finely chop the garlic and sweat in a little of the butter.

11   Purée the potatoes with the sweated garlic, remaining butter and cream. Season to taste.

12   On a serving plate, pipe the garlic mash and place the **daube** of beef next to it. Spoon the sauce over and garnish as required.

CHEF'S TIP   Daube derives its name from the dish in which it was traditionally cooked (daubière). A paste of flour and water (repère) was used to give a tight seal around the top of a daubière.

HEALTHY OPTION   When you need to fry beef, instead of frying it in oil you could use the natural fat present in the meat. If any excess fat is produced this can be drained off and discarded.

Hot smoked fillet of beef

Hot smoked fillet of beef with glazed vegetables

Ingredients	4 portions	10 portions
The cure	Makes 500 g	Makes 500 g
Salt	250 g	250 g
Dark brown sugar	200 g	200 g
White pepper	10 g	10 g
All spice	10 g	10 g
Ground mace	10 g	10 g
Crushed juniper berries	10 g	10 g
Pink salt	10 g	10 g
The dish		
Centre cut fillet of beef	500 g	1.25 g
Hickory wood chips	75 g	150 g
Horseradish sauce		
Red wine sauce	200 ml	500 ml
Horseradish	5 g	12 g
Double cream	50 ml	125 ml
Garnish		
Turned courgettes	8	20
Turned swedes	8	20
Turned carrots	8	20

energy	cal	fat	sat fat	carb	sugar	protein	fibre
3508 kJ	836 kcal	37.8 g	16.8 g	87.4 g	79.5 g	46.1 g	11.9 g

METHOD OF WORK

1 Combine all the ingredients for the cure and mix together.

2 Trim the beef of all fat and connective tissue.

3 Place a layer of the cure mix on top of a sheet of plastic film, lay the beef on top and cover the beef with a generous layer of cure mix.

4 Roll the beef tightly in several layers of cling film. Place the beef in a tray and lay another tray on top.

5 Place a 1 kg weight on top and leave in the refrigerator for six–eight hours.

6 Remove from the refrigerator, unwrap and wash quickly in cold water. Pat dry with a paper towel and leave to stand in a well-ventilated room (this gives a sticky surface called a pellicle, which allows the smoke particles to adhere to the surface of the meat).

7 Place the beef in a hot smoker set at 90°C for one–two hours until the core temperature of the beef reaches 65°C.

8 Alternatively, preheat an oven to 90°C. Place the wood chips in the bottom of a roasting tray with a grill over the top. Heat the wood chips on a stove until they begin to smoke. Place the beef fillet on top and cover with foil before placing in the oven to cook.

9 Infuse the grated horseradish into the red wine sauce and add the cream, bring to the boil and pass

10 Serve with the sauce and serve with the turned vegetables cooked a la glace.

CHEF'S TIP This method can be used for preparing hot or cold beef. To preserve the beef, cure it for 24 hours and smoke to 70°C.

Slow cooked fillet of beef

Slow cooked fillet of beef, duxelle, light herb and vegetable consommé

Ingredients	4 portions	10 portions
Beef fillet trimmed and cut from centre	1 × 750 g	2 × 900 g
Sunflower oil	50 ml	100 ml
Carrot solferino	80 g	200 g
White radish solferino	80 g	200 g
Swede solferino	80 g	200 g
Chicken consommé	320 ml	800 ml
Tarragon leaves	12	30
Chervil leaves	12	30
Mushroom duxelle	80 g	200 g
Salt and pepper	to taste	to taste

energy	cal	fat	sat fat	carb	sugar	protein	fibre
2752 kJ	659 kcal	39.4 g	14.1 g	7.6 g	4.4 g	69.7 g	3 g

METHOD OF WORK

1 Preheat an oven to 56–59°C.

2 Take the centre-cut fillet of beef and quickly seal in the sunflower oil in a pan until lightly brown all over. Allow to cool.

3 Wrap well in plastic film to help maintain the shape of the beef fillet. Place on a baking tray and place in the oven for a minimum of one-and-a-half hours.

4 To finish the beef, remove from the oven and carefully cut away the plastic film. Heat some sunflower oil in a hot pan and brown for two minutes on all sides.

5 Heat the solferino vegetables in the consommé and pour into bowls.

6 Cut the beef and cover with reheated mushroom duxelle place into the bowl and serve.

CHEF'S TIP It is very important to ensure that the oven temperature is regulated at exactly 56–59°C. This is best done by placing a second oven thermometer directly inside the oven and regulating the heat by leaving the oven door slightly ajar. If the temperature reaches or exceeds 60°C, shrinkage occurs and lots of moisture is lost from the meat due to the collagen cells denaturing (cooking and shrinking).

Steak and smoked oyster pudding

Ingredients	4 portions	10 portions
Suet pastry		
Soft flour	290 g	600 g
Baking powder	10 g	20 g
Beef suet	150 g	310 g
Cold water	75 ml	150 ml
Good-quality salt	to taste	to taste
Filling		
Chuck steak	400 g	800 g
Tinned smoked oysters	125 g	250 g
Thinly sliced onion	70 g	140 g
Fresh thyme	6 sprigs	12 sprigs
Garlic	1 clove	2 cloves
Seasoned soft flour	4 tbsp	8 tbsp
Worcestershire sauce	to taste	to taste
Beaten egg yolk	1	2
Stout gravy		
Finely chopped shallots	100 g	200 g
Garlic	1 clove	2 cloves
Fresh thyme	1 sprig	2 sprigs
Bay leaf	½ leaf	1 leaf
Crushed black peppercorns	5	10
Stout beer	600 ml	1.2 litres
Red wine	400 ml	800 ml
Beef stock	2 litres	4 litres
Good-quality salt and white pepper	to taste	to taste

Broccoli and baby onions		
Good quality salt and white pepper	to taste	to taste

energy	cal	fat	sat fat	carb	sugar	protein	fibre
5059 kJ	1212 kcal	63.3 g	34.8 g	86.4 g	10.7 g	50.4 g	8.6 g

METHOD OF WORK

1   To make the suet pastry, sieve the flour, salt and the baking powder together. Add the beef suet and mix in the cold water a little at a time. This pastry should not be too sticky, so there may be a little water left over depending on the quality of flour used. Knead until a smooth and elastic pastry is formed. Wrap in plastic film and refrigerate until required.

2   Cut the chuck steak into small (1.5 cm) cubes and reserve any meat trimmings for the sauce. Mix the cubed beef in a bowl with the drained smoked oysters, onion, thyme, garlic and flour.

3   Line **dariole** moulds with plastic film, overhanging by a few centimetres. Pin out the suet paste and cut one 18 cm disc and one 6 cm disc per portion. Leave to rest in a refrigerator, covered, for five minutes.

4   Line each mould with the larger disc of pastry, pushing well into the base of the mould. Leave a 1 cm overhang of pastry around the edge.

5   Divide the filling between the moulds and pour in some cold water, to come three-quarters of the way up the mould. Sprinkle with a few drops of the Worcestershire sauce.

6   Brush inside each pastry mould with the beaten egg yolk and place the smaller disc on top. Fold over the overhanging pastry and pinch inwards to seal the top. Wrap each mould tightly with plastic film twice.

7   Place the puddings into the steamer and steam for two hours.

8   To make the stout gravy, place the shallots, garlic, herbs, peppercorns and salt in a pan with the left over meat trimmings and carefully sweat for ten minutes. Remove the lid and increase the heat to begin to **caramelise** the ingredients.

9   Add the red wine and reduce by three-quarters. Add the stout and reduce in the same way. Add the stock and reduce to the required consistency. Pass through a fine chinois and correct the seasoning.

10 To serve, unwrap the puddings and turn out onto serving plates. Warm the broccoli and baby onions in butter until hot, seasoning to taste. Serve the stout sauce around the pudding and drizzle a small amount over the pudding also. Using a dessert spoon.

Tournedos Rossini

Ingredients	4 portions	10 portions
Centre cut fillet of beef	600 g	1.5 kg
Foie gras	160 g	400 g
Thin slice of truffle (soaked in brandy)	4 slices	10 slices
Madeira sauce	200 ml	500 ml
Butter	40 g	100 g
Madeira wine	35 ml	75 ml
Anna potatoes	4 discs	10 discs
Good-quality salt and white pepper	to taste	to taste

energy	cal	fat	sat fat	carb	sugar	protein	fibre
4434 kJ	1061 kcal	52.1 g	23.4 g	86 g	4.9 g	58.6 g	7.8 g

METHOD OF WORK

1   Completely remove any fat or connective tissue from the fillet and wrap tightly in plastic film. Place into a refrigerator and chill for a minimum of three hours. This allows the meat to set into a round shape.

2   Remove from the refrigerator and slice into the required tournedos steaks at approximately 150 g per portion.

3   Remove the foie gras from the refrigerator for five minutes before slicing and cut into the required number of **collops**. Return to the refrigerator until required.

4   Heat the butter in a shallow pan until it starts to foam. Place the fillets into the pan and cook on both sides to the required core temperature.

5   Season the fillets, remove from the pan and keep warm.

6   Add the Madeira wine to the pan and deglaze with the cooked juices from the meat. Add the Madeira sauce and bring to the boil. Simmer for up to four minutes.

7   Strain the sauce into a clean pan, reheat and check the seasoning and consistency.

8   Sear the foie gras in a hot dry shallow pan until the collops are golden brown on each side. Place one on top of each fillet and keep warm.

9   Place the Anna potatoes into a hot oven to warm through.

10   To serve, arrange the Anna potato in the centre of each plate. Place the tournedos with the foie gras and sliced truffle on top with a **cordon** of Madeira sauce around it.

> **CHEF'S TIP**   Tournedos are cut from the centre of the beef fillet and are usually sautéed in butter with a named garnish or sauce.

GARNISHES FOR ALTERNATIVE TOURNEDOS DISHES

NAME	GARNISH
Alsacienne	Toss lardons in hot fat with sauerkraut. Dress on a fried croûton with the garnish
Béarnaise	Serve with watercress and Béarnaise sauce
Choron	Serve with sauce choron (tomato flavoured sauce Béarnaise), garnished with artichoke bottoms filled with peas and noisette potatoes
Duroc	Coat with chasseur sauce and serve with tomato concassé and noisette potatoes
Forestière	Serve on a croûton with sautéed wild mushrooms and lardons accompanied by Parmentier potatoes. Can be served with a red wine sauce
Helder	Serve with sauce Béarnaise, piped on top with cooked tomato concassé in the centre with a **jus lie** and Parisienne potatoes
Rivoli	Set on Anna potatoes with truffle sauce

Veal (*Veau*)

Veal is the meat from beef calves, usually male calves from dairy herds. It has generally not been an important part of British cuisine, but it is very popular in Italy, Spain, France, Austria and Germany. There are moral arguments about the way that veal is reared.

Veal calves should be fed exclusively on milk – there should be a milky aroma from the kidneys and fat. The calves are slaughtered at between two-and-a-half and four months. Because veal is very young it is low in myoglobin, which accounts for its pale colour.

The fat content is also minimal, and therefore the use of ingredients such as cream adds to the eating experience. Care should be taken not to over-cook veal, especially the parts that are grilled and roasted, as they can become dry and tough – they should be just cooked (**à point**) or slightly under-cooked.

VIDEO CLIP Preparation of veal cushion.

Side of veal

BREAKDOWN ON A SIDE OF VEAL

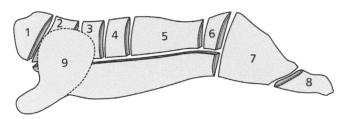

JOINT	FRENCH	USE	AVERAGE WEIGHT
1 Scrag	Le cou	This joint that makes excellent stock. Can also be used for mince to make Pojarski or for blanquettes	1.25 kg
2 Neck	Collet	The neck can be prepared for stews or **fricassée**. If **minced** it can be used for fine forcemeats	3 kg
3 Neck end	Côte découverte	Used for stewing. Bone and remove sinew before cutting into 2.5 cm cubes	2 kg
4 Best end	Le carré	The best end is a prime cut that is suitable for roasting, pot roasting, cutlets and frying	2–3 kg
5 Loin	La longe	This is a lean joint, good for roasting. It can be cut into chops or steaks, but its lack of marbling precludes successful grilling. Braising is a good option	4 kg
6 Rump	Le quasi or cul de veau	Used for **escalope** of veal or for sauté dishes. The rump can be roasted or braised as steaks. The trimmings can be used for stewing	2 kg
7 Leg	Cuisseau	The leg can be cut into the following joints: cushion (noix); under-cushion (sous-noix); thick flank (noix pâtissière). Each can be used for pot roasting, frying or grilling. The cushion is the main joint from which escalopes are taken	6–8 kg
8 Knuckle/shank	Le jarret	Mince, stews, first-class stocks and osso bucco ('bone with a hole', an Italian dish of braised shank)	2 kg
9 Shoulder	L'épaule	The shoulder can be stuffed and roasted or used for braised dishes	3–5 kg
10 Breast	La poitrine	The breast can be removed and braised or stewed, but care should be taken not to over-cook the joint. Using a fatty stuffing or **barding** the joint helps to prevent it drying out when roasting	2–3 kg

Step-by-step: Larding a cushion of veal

1. Insert a strip of fat onto the larding knife.

2. Carefully insert the knife into the tied cushion.

3. Ensure the knife and fat are completely through the veal.

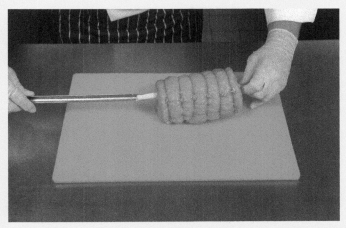

4. Take hold of the fat at one end and gentle remove the knife, leaving the fat in place.

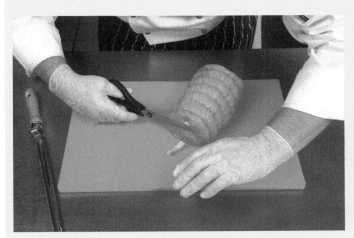

5. Trim any excess fat away, repeat the process until a suitable amount of fat has been deposited.

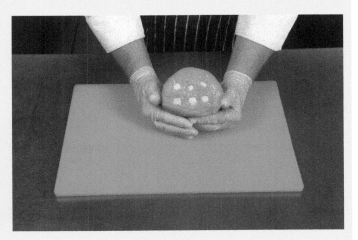

6. The completed cushion of veal.

Recipes

Braised cushion of veal

Braised cushion of veal with artichokes (*Fricandeau de veau*)

Ingredients	4 portions	10 portions
Cushion of veal	500 g	1.5 kg
Italian lardo	200 g	500 g
Carrots	200 g	500 g
Onions	200 g	500 g
Celery	200 g	500 g
White of leek	200 g	500 g
Bouquet garni	1 small	1 medium
Veal stock	1 l	2.5 l
Cooked Jerusalem artichoke	4	10
Cooked asparagus spears	8	20
Cooked morel mushrooms	8	20
Salt and pepper	to taste	to taste

energy	cal	fat	sat fat	carb	sugar	protein	fibre
3196 kJ	768 kcal	64.7 g	12 g	13 g	7.1 g	32.4 g	8.3 g

METHOD OF WORK

1 Preheat an oven to 170°C.

2 Lard the veal with the lardo by inserting strips of fat into the joint using a larding needle. Trim and tie the joint with string.

3 Wash, peel and cut the vegetables into equal sizes and lightly fry in some fat. Transfer into the bottom of a heavy braising pan.

4 Place the joint into the hot fat to seal on all sides before placing on top of the bed of vegetables.

5 Add the veal stock and bouquet garni and season well.

6 Bring to the boil, skim, cover with a tight-fitting lid and place in the oven. **Baste** every ten minutes until the veal is cooked through, approximately one hour.

7 Remove the lid from the braising pot and continue cooking for a further 30 minutes so that the liquid begins to reduce. Baste frequently so that the stock forms a glaze and coats the veal.

8 Remove the veal from the braising pot and leave to rest for five minutes. Pass the sauce through a fine sieve. Correct the seasoning and consistency of the sauce.

9 Serve with the artichokes, morels, asparagus and sauce.

CHEF'S TIP The veal should be constantly basted to prevent it from drying out during cooking.

WEB LINK All animals for the professional culinary market, including veal calves, should have a good standard of living and welfare. Use this web link to research what is meant by animal welfare: http://www.meateat.co.uk/why-british-veal-more-ethical-choice.html

Braised veal cheeks with sweetbreads

Ingredients	4 portions	10 portions
Veal cheeks		
Trimmed veal cheeks	4	10
Diced carrot	100 g	200 g
Diced onion	200 g	400 g
Chopped garlic	4 cloves	8 cloves
Chopped celery	80 g	160 g
Bay leaves	3	6
Fresh thyme	4 sprigs	10 sprigs
Veal stock	1 l	2.5 l
Black peppercorns	8	20
Good-quality salt	to taste	to taste
Veal sweetbreads		
Veal sweetbreads (trimmed, blanched and pressed)	400 g	1 kg
Vegetable oil	50 ml	125 ml
Chopped onion	50 g	100 g
Diced carrot	50 g	100 g
Veal stock	200 ml	550 ml
Good-quality salt and white pepper	to taste	to taste
Baby carrots		
Baby carrots	6	15
Butter	75 g	150 g
Light chicken stock	75 ml	150 ml
Good-quality salt and white pepper	to taste	to taste

energy	cal	fat	sat fat	carb	sugar	protein	fibre
2209 kJ	532 kcal	40.3 g	15.7 g	14.8 g	10.7 g	29.1 g	6 g

METHOD OF WORK

1   Preheat an oven to 180°C.

2   Trim, roll and tie the veal cheeks. Place all the ingredients into a pan with the veal cheeks. Slowly bring to the boil and cover with a lid. Pull to one side of the stove and slowly braise until the cheeks have cooked (approximately three hours).

3   For the veal sweetbreads, heat some of the oil in a shallow pan. Season the sweetbreads and quickly seal on both sides. Remove from the pan and add the carrots and onion to sweat for two minutes. Place the sweetbreads on top of the vegetables and add the veal stock. Cover with a buttered cartouche of silicone paper and place in the oven for approximately 40 minutes, basting occasionally with the cooking liquor.

4   Wash and trim the carrots. Add the butter to a saucepan to melt before adding the carrots and the stock. Continue to slowly cook on the stove until the stock has reduced.

5   Remove the veal cheeks and strain the cooking liquor into a saucepan. Reduce the liquid to a coating consistency, correct the seasoning and reserve. Remove the string.

6   Arrange the dish as shown.

CHEF'S TIP   The veal cheeks can be braised the day before and simply reheated in veal stock to serve. This gives the cheeks time to set and so they will be easier to cut or carve.

Osso bucco

METHOD OF WORK

1 Preheat an oven to 180°C.
2 Dust the osso bucco veal slices with the flour and season well. Heat the olive oil in a shallow pan and add the veal slices, colouring on both sides.
3 Add the chopped onion, carrots, celery and garlic and continue to cook, with a lid placed firmly on the pan, for three minutes.
4 Drain any excess fat and add the white wine to deglaze the pan. Add the veal stock and the lemon and orange skin plus the tomato purée and bring to the boil.
5 Place the lid on the pan and place into the oven for one-and-a-half hours to cook.
6 Add the tomato concassé and correct the seasoning. Return to the oven for a further 15 minutes.
7 Make the gremolata by combining all the ingredients together.
8 Correct the seasoning and consistency of the osso bucco and serve with creamed potatoes or risotto and drizzled with the gremolata dressing.

> **CHEF'S TIP** Osso bucco is a classic dish from Milan that is served with risotto but it can also be served with plain boiled rice or a crisp green salad. It has many regional variations. The name 'osso bucco' means a bone with a hole, describing the veal marrow bone with the meat on the outside.

Ingredients	4 portions	10 portions
Slices of veal knuckle (shank) on the bone	4 × 300 g	10 × 300 g
Olive oil	40 ml	100 ml
Flour for **dusting**	30 g	70 g
Diced onion	100 g	250 g
Diced celery	75 g	150 g
Diced carrot	75 g	150 g
Chopped garlic	2 cloves	5 cloves
Tomato concassé	500 g	1250 g
Tomato purée	100 g	250 g
Dry white wine	400 ml	1 l
Veal stock	400 ml	1 l
Dried lemon skin	25 g	60 g
Dried orange skin	25 g	60 g
Good-quality salt and white pepper	To taste	To taste
Gremolata		
Chopped flat leaf parsley	1 tbsp	2 tbsp
Grated lemon zest	1 lemon	2 lemons
Lemon juice	½ lemon	1 lemon
Olive oil	25 ml	70 ml
Crushed garlic	1 clove	2 cloves
Good-quality salt and white pepper	to taste	to taste

energy	cal	fat	sat fat	carb	sugar	protein	fibre
3538 kJ	848 kcal	30.1 g	7.2 g	22.8 g	13.5 g	100.7 g	5.8 g

Veal kidneys in a Dijon mustard and tarragon sauce

Ingredients	4 portions	10 portions
Veal kidneys (skinned, trimmed and sliced in half)	400 g	1 kg
Vegetable oil for frying		
Chopped shallots	80 g	200 g
Butter	50 g	130 g
Brandy	30 ml	80 ml
Dry white wine	50 ml	125 ml
Double cream	250 ml	700 ml
Dijon mustard	3 tbsp	8 tbsp
Fresh chopped tarragon	4 tsp	10 tsp
Good quality salt and white pepper	to taste	to taste

energy	cal	fat	sat fat	carb	sugar	protein	fibre
2460 kJ	595 kcal	48.8 g	28.7 g	5.1 g	3.3 g	26.3 g	0.7 g

METHOD OF WORK

1. Heat the oil in a shallow pan. Season the kidneys lightly and sauté for three–four minutes. The kidneys should be slightly coloured on the outside but still pink inside.
2. Tip the kidneys into a colander to drain.
3. Add the butter and the shallots and sweat for a few minutes without colour. Add the dry white wine and reduce by half. Add the brandy and reduce by half again.
4. Pour in the cream, bring back to the boil and reduce to a sauce consistency. Remove from the heat and stir in the mustard and fresh tarragon and season to taste.
5. Add the kidneys and carefully reheat the sauce without boiling.
6. Serve with braised rice.

Veal Pojarski

Veal Pojarski with foie gras and Smitaine sauce

Ingredients	4 portions	10 portions
Minced lean veal	400 g	1 kg
Fresh milk	200 ml	600 ml
Unsalted butter	60 g	125 g
Double cream	100 ml	250 ml
White breadcrumbs	100 g	250 g
Grated nutmeg	to taste	to taste
Good-quality salt and white pepper	to taste	to taste
Smitaine sauce		
Finely chopped onion	50 g	125 g
Butter	25 g	70 g
Dry white wine	80 ml	200 ml
Lemon juice	¼ lemon	½ lemon
Soured cream	300 ml	700 ml
Garnish		
Foie gras	100 g	250 g
Baby spinach, washed and picked	400 g	1 kg
Tomato concassé		

energy	cal	fat	sat fat	carb	sugar	protein	fibre
3768 kJ	906 kcal	70.2 g	37.8 g	28.7 g	8.8 g	38.5 g	2.9 g

METHOD OF WORK

1. Ensure that the minced veal has been passed through the mincer twice to break the protein down.

2. Soak the breadcrumbs in the milk for a few minutes and then squeeze out any surplus milk.

3. Add the breadcrumbs to the veal and mix well. Season with salt, pepper and nutmeg. Work in the cold double cream, a little at a time, using a spoon. Mix thoroughly and beat well.

4. Divide the mixture into equal portion sizes and mould into round discs about 3.5 cm thick. Use some flour to help mould the shapes.

5. Heat the butter in a shallow pan and carefully place the Pojarskis to shallow fry. Fry until golden brown on both sides and thoroughly cooked (up to 15 minutes approximately). To check, press the Pojarskis gently – the juices should run out clear and with no sign of blood, indicating they are cooked through. Retain in a warm place for service.

6. To make the Smitaine sauce, place the chopped onion in a saucepan with the butter and sweat without colour. Drain off the excess fat and add the white wine, reduce by two-thirds.

7. Add the lemon juice and then the soured cream. Continue to reduce the sauce to a coating consistency. Season well and pass through a fine sieve. Keep hot.

8. In a separate shallow pan quickly seal and cook the foie gras on both sides, season and retain for service. Place the washed spinach in the same pan. Season well and cover with a lid, place on the side of the stove until the spinach is wilted. Drain any excess moisture in a colander.

9. To serve, spoon the spinach into a stainless steel ring placed in the centre of a serving plate. Remove the ring, position the pojarski on the spinach and place a slice of foie gras on top. Spoon over the Smitaine sauce. Garnish with the tomato concassé.

CHEF'S TIP   The bread and milk mixture is called 'bread panade' and is used as a binding agent in meat-based **galettes**.

Lamb and mutton (*Agneau* and *Mouton*)

Lamb is the meat from young sheep and has a characteristic and delicate flavour. The flavour develops, becoming much deeper, as the lamb develops. Mutton is the meat from the adult sheep.

- Spring lamb – lamb in its first six months, but usually slaughtered at three–four months.

- Lamb – lamb up to one-year-old or when the lamb grows its first pair of permanent teeth.

- Hoggett – one–two years old; without the developed flavour of mutton.

- Mutton – over two-years-old, and with a strong and well-developed flavour.

In the UK, the sheep industry is located so that particular breeds occupy specific environments to which they are adapted. The sheep of these environments are connected by the movement of lambs and older animals from higher to lower ground.

VIDEO CLIP Preparation of lamb best end.

The hills – hardy hill and mountain sheep are largely kept as pure breeds. Lambs not required to maintain flock numbers are transferred to the lowlands as store lambs to be fattened.

The uplands – in upland areas there are again specific breeds. These and older draft mountain ewes are crossed with the longwool breeds.

The lowlands – in the lowlands, the sheep are crossed with lowland sires to produce lambs that can be fattened on summer grass. These are slower growing lambs join those that have arrived from the hills and upland areas to be fattened on root crops over the autumn and winter months.

VIDEO CLIP Preparation of lamb shoulder.

It is important to keep lamb and mutton cold when cutting the meat as the fat becomes greasy and knife handles become slippery to use.

The main lowland sheep areas of Great Britain

Side of lamb/mutton

The average weight of a side of lamb or mutton is 18–21 kg.

BREAKDOWN OF A SIDE OF LAMB/MUTTON

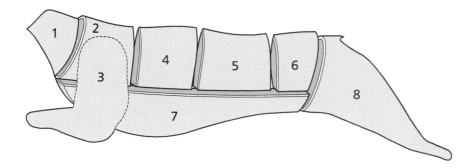

JOINT	FRENCH	USES	AVERAGE WEIGHT
1 Scrag	Le cou	Stewing and for broths This is the toughest part of the lamb and is traditionally cooked on the bone in Irish stew	1 kg
2 Middle neck	Côte découverte	Stewing when the neck fillet is removed or grilling as uncovered cutlets. Be sure to remove all traces of **elastin**	2 kg
3 Shoulder	L'épaule	Roasting, stuff with forcemeat and roast slowly. Can also be served as a half shoulder braised in a rich sauce, or diced for stewing	2 × 2.5 kg
4 Best end	Le carré	The best end can be prepared into racks for roasting, or into cutlets, noisettes or rosettes for grilling and frying	2 kg
5 Saddle	La selle	The saddle can be roasted on the bone or boned and stuffed. The loins can be removed and cut into rosettes and noisettes for frying and grilling. Fillet mignon also comes from the saddle, as do the cannons	3.5 kg
6 Rump/chump	Le quasi	A rump of lamb will yield four pieces for braising or roasting	2 kg
7 Breast	La poitrine	The breast can be boned and rolled for slow roasting, or steamed and pressed to make epigrams	2 kg
8 Leg	Le gigot	The leg can be used for roasting and the shank can be used for braising. The leg can also be broken down into its various muscle groups for frying and grilling. Mutton leg can also be used for boiling	2 × 2.5 kg

Step-by-step: The preparation of lamb into cutlets

1. Prepare the lamb by removing the bark with a sharp knife.

2. Clean away the flesh and sinew from the bones.

3. Lift the bones away from the flesh.

4. Turn the lamb over and scrape each bone and then push the flesh from each bone from the side.

5. Cut along the bones to leave a clean finish.

6. Turn the lamb over and cut through in between the bones, or cut through every second bone to create a double cutlet.

7. Cut away the second bone to produce a double cutlet.

8. Cut through the bone with the heel of the knife.

9. The single and double cutlet.

Step-by-step: Preparation of a saddle of lamb

1. Score the saddle of lamb down the centre, not cutting too deep.

2. Carefully cut back the bark to expose the clean fat layer.

3. Turn the saddle over and remove the excess fat.

4. Carefully remove the two fillets as shown.

5. Remove any sinew and fat to leave two clean fillets.

6. Cut under the exposed bones as shown, taking care not to damage the cannons beneath.

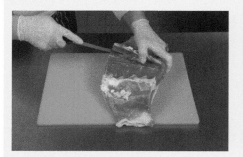

7. Carefully cut both sides, removing as little flesh as possible.

8. Remove the central bone structure as shown.

9. Lay the saddle flat and slowly remove the layers of excess fat.

10. Continue until a thin layer is achieved, this can then be made thinner using a meat bat.

11. Return the fillets as shown and also place a layer of force meat in the centre.

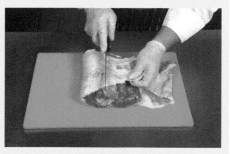

12. Flap over the sides and trim any excess off.

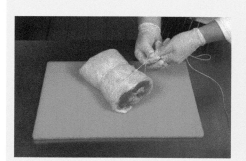

13. Roll into a neat shape and tie.

14. The finished saddle.

Recipes

Cannon and faggot of lamb

Ingredients	4 portions	10 portions
Saddle of lamb	1 saddle	2 ½ saddles
Fresh rosemary	2 sprigs	5 sprigs
Sunflower oil	40 ml	100 ml
Lamb jus	300 ml	850 ml
Fresh thyme	2 sprigs	5 sprigs
Dry white wine	40 ml	100 ml
Lamb faggot		
Lamb liver	200 g	600 g
Lamb breast	100 g	300 g
Finely chopped onion	60 g	180 g
Butter	40 g	80 g
Fresh chopped parsley	2 tbsp	6 tbsp
Fresh chopped thyme	2 tbsp	6 tbsp
Garlic	1 clove	3 cloves
Whole egg	1 small egg	2 eggs
Wholemeal bread crumbs	75 g	225 g
Pigs caul	4 sheets	10 sheets
Strong lamb stock	1 l	2.5 l
Salt and pepper	to taste	to taste

energy	cal	fat	sat fat	carb	sugar	protein	fibre
2652 kJ	637 kcal	47.6 g	18.2 g	13.8 g	2.8 g	37.6 g	4.4 g

METHOD OF WORK

1. For the lamb faggots, preheat an oven to 180°C. Finely chop the liver and breast of lamb and place in a saucepan with the chopped onion, garlic and the butter. Stew slowly for about 30 minutes with the lid on, do not colour the ingredients at this stage.

2. Strain off the fat and put the mixture into a bowl with the herbs and season well. Add the egg and combine all ingredients well.

3. Add enough breadcrumbs to make a mixture that will just hold together. Divide the faggot mixture into 60 g pieces and wrap each in as little caul as possible to hold together.

4. Shape into balls and put into an earthenware dish. Pour the lamb stock over, enough to come half way up the faggots.

5. Bake in the preheated oven for approximately 45 minutes until the faggots have a brown colour. Reserve until required.

6. Remove the cannons from the saddle by cutting at the chine bone and following the bone with the knife until each cannon is released.

7. Carefully trim any silver membrane and fat. Remove the fillets and trim off any fat.

8. Season and seal the cannons in hot oil in a shallow pan until browned on all sides. Place the cannons into the preheated oven for six minutes until the lamb is just pink inside, continually baste the cannon during the cooking process.

9. Remove from the oven and allow the lamb to rest for two–three minutes.

10. Deglaze the shallow pan with the white wine and add the chopped fresh rosemary and thyme.

11. Reduce by two-thirds and add the lamb jus. Bring back to the boil and adjust the consistency and seasoning, then pass through a fine chinois.

12. Place a lamb faggot next the potato. Carve the cannons and place around the faggots. Serve with the rosemary jus.

Lamb fillet and a mini shepherd's pie

Lamb fillet, mini shepherd's pie and garlic roasted root vegetables

Ingredients	4 portions	10 portions
Prepared lamb fillets	2 × 400 g	5 × 400 g
Olive oil	40 ml	100 ml
Black olives	200 g	500 g
Anchovy fillets	50 g	125 g
Garlic	2 cloves	5 cloves
Pig's caul	4 sheets	10 sheets
Mini shepherd's pie		
Finely chopped onion	75 g	225 g
Finely diced carrot	50 g	150 g
Olive oil	40 ml	100 ml
Minced lamb	200 g	600 g
Lamb stock	100 ml	350 ml
Peas	50 g	150 g
Mashed potato		
Butter	25 g	100 g
Fresh thyme	4 sprigs	10 sprigs
Garlic roasted root vegetables		
Baby carrot	1 large	3 large
Baby turnip	1 medium	2 medium
Button onions	16	40
Garlic	8 cloves	20 cloves
Olive oil	50 ml	145 ml
Rosemary and redcurrant jus		
Strong lamb stock	400 ml	1 l
Port	75 ml	200 ml
Chopped shallots	50 g	145 g
Redcurrants	40 g	120 g
Fresh chopped rosemary	1 tbsp	2 tbsp
Good quality salt and white pepper	to taste	to taste

energy	cal	fat	sat fat	carb	sugar	protein	fibre
4534 kJ	1090 kcal	77.4 g	23.4 g	42.4 g	14.3 g	53.6 g	10.9 g

METHOD OF WORK

1 Bone the fillets and trim from fat and sinew. Preheat an oven to 180°C.

2 For the tapenade, put all the black olives and garlic in a pan with a little olive oil and sweat for two minutes. Place in a blender with the anchovy fillet and blend together with the seasoning to make a thick paste. Take it out and keep until required.

3 To prepare the lamb, lay the caul on a clean working surface and spread the tapenade evenly on the caul according to the width of the lamb fillets. Lay the lamb fillets on the caul and roll the caul around each fillet so that the tapenade is all around the lamb. Wrap the fillets in cling film as tightly as possible and put into a refrigerator for about 15 minutes.

4 Cook the fillets in a preheated steamer for approximately 12 minutes.

5 For the shepherd's pies, sweat the onion and carrot in a little olive oil. Add the minced lamb and season well. Add the lamb stock and peas and simmer for five minutes.

6 Spoon the potato out of their jackets and mash with the butter, chopped fresh thyme, salt and pepper. Fill china dishes (one per portion) and half fill with the minced lamb. Pipe the mashed potato on top and place into the oven for 15 minutes.

7 For the garlic roasted root vegetables. Blanch each vegetable separately in boiling salted water. Place the olive oil in a sauteuse and heat on the stove, adding the blanched vegetables, garlic cloves and seasoning. Toss the vegetables for a few minutes before placing in the oven to roast for 15 minutes.

8 To make the sauce, reduce the lamb stock by half with the rosemary and in a separate pan reduce the port, redcurrants (washed and stalks removed) and chopped shallots by half. Add the rosemary stock and reduce until the correct consistency has been obtained. Pass through a fine chinois and correct the seasoning.

9 To serve, place the shepherd's pie at the top of the service plate and arrange a selection of the roasted vegetables in the middle. Slice each lamb fillet and place onto the bottom of the plate. Pour the sauce around the plate and serve.

CHEF'S TIP Dried rosemary can be used for this dish, but the weight should be quartered to allow for the intensity of flavour of the dried herb.

Roast rack of lamb and black olive jus

Ingredients	4 portions	10 portions
Best ends of lamb (prepared into racks)	2	3
Garlic	8 cloves	20 cloves
Fresh thyme	8 sprigs	20 cloves
Chopped shallots	200 g	500 g
Brown lamb stock	2 l	4.5 l
Black olives	100 g	250 g
Fresh chervil	4 sprigs	10 sprigs
Good-quality salt and white pepper	to taste	to taste

energy	cal	fat	sat fat	carb	sugar	protein	fibre
1478 kJ	353 kcal	27.2 g	10.2 g	7.4 g	2.7 g	19.8 g	3.4 g

METHOD OF WORK

1 Preheat an oven to 200°C.

2 Place the prepared racks of lamb into a pan and brush with olive oil. Chop half of the fresh thyme and sprinkle on the lamb, season well.

3 Place in the oven to roast for about 16–20 minutes until pink.

4 For the black olive jus, reduce the lamb stock with the remaining cloves of crushed garlic. Correct the consistency and seasoning and reserve for service.

5 Add the olives to warm through.

6 Slice the lamb into two pieces and sit upright, garnish with the fresh chervil. Finish with the black olive jus.

CHEF'S TIP In the rosettes of lamb recipe, if required, remove the fat from the lamb rosette before grilling and slightly reduce the cooking time.

Rosettes of lamb with gratin potatoes

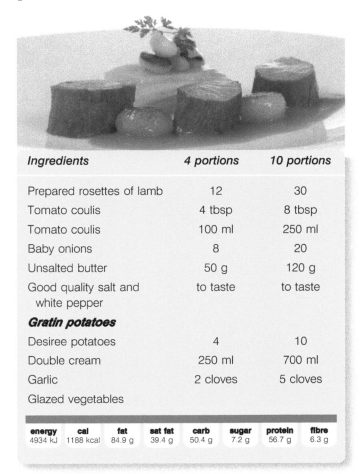

Ingredients	4 portions	10 portions
Prepared rosettes of lamb	12	30
Tomato coulis	4 tbsp	8 tbsp
Tomato coulis	100 ml	250 ml
Baby onions	8	20
Unsalted butter	50 g	120 g
Good quality salt and white pepper	to taste	to taste
Gratin potatoes		
Desiree potatoes	4	10
Double cream	250 ml	700 ml
Garlic	2 cloves	5 cloves
Glazed vegetables		

energy	cal	fat	sat fat	carb	sugar	protein	fibre
4934 kJ	1188 kcal	84.9 g	39.4 g	50.4 g	7.2 g	56.7 g	6.3 g

METHOD OF WORK

1 Brush each rosette with oil and season well.

2 Wash, peel and rewash the potatoes. Slice each potato into three even slices. Using a plain pastry cutter, cut out circles of potato the same size as the rosettes.

3 Put the cream and crushed garlic into a pan. Bring to the boil and season. Place the potato discs into the cream and gently cook until soft.

4 Carefully remove the potatoes from the cream and place onto a baking tray, spoon a little of the cream over each potato and reserve.

5 Grill the rosettes until golden brown on the both sides and slightly pink in the centre.

6 Place the gratin potatoes in a preheated oven at 180°C while the lamb is cooking. Cook for approximately six minutes until lightly golden.

7 Sauté the onions in butter until cooked and caramelized

8 To serve, place the gratin and three pieces of lamb on a plate, with the onions, tomato coulis and glazed vegetables

Roast stuffed saddle of lamb with rosemary jus

Ingredients	4 portions	10 portions
Saddle of lamb (boned)	1	2
Minced chicken	150 g	300 g
Chopped fresh tarragon	2 tbsp	4 tbsp
Egg whites	1	2
Double cream	75 ml	150 ml
Lamb or pig caul (crepinette)	1 sheet	2 sheets
Carrots	100 g	250 g
Onion	100 g	250 g
Celery	100 g	250 g
Leek	100 g	250 g
Brown lamb stock	1 l	2.5 l
Rosemary leaves	3 tbsp	8 tbsp
Balsamic vinegar	3 tsp	7 tsp
Red wine	80 ml	200 ml
Sauté wild mushrooms		
Good quality salt and white pepper	to taste	to taste

energy	cal	fat	sat fat	carb	sugar	protein	fibre
1507 kJ	361 kcal	25.1 g	12.1 g	7.9 g	3.4 g	22.8 g	4 g

METHOD OF WORK

1 Season the lamb well.

2 Mix the chopped tarragon with the minced chicken and place into a food blender. Add the egg whites while blending the ingredients then slowly add the cold double cream. Season well.

3 Place some of this stuffing in the centre of the two attached cannons in the saddle. Lay one of the detached fillets on top of the stuffing and cover the fillet with some more of the stuffing. Repeat with the second fillet and cover with the remaining stuffing.

4 Lift up one of the belly flaps and fold it over so that the cannons sandwich the fillets and stuffing in the middle. Repeat with the other side. Season well.

5 Rinse half the caul in cold water and then carefully lay on a board. Lay the saddle on the centre of the caul and bring the sides up to enclose it. Rinse the rest of the caul and lay it flat on the board. Position the saddle on the nearest edge of the caul and roll it up. Tuck in the flaps at each end. The saddle can be tied or roasted as it is.

6 Preheat an oven to 220°C.

7 Wash, peel and rewash the vegetables, chop and place into the bottom of a roasting pan.

8 Place the saddle to sear in a pan with some hot oil. Transfer to the roasting tray and roast in the oven for 30 minutes.

9 Remove the roasted saddle of lamb and allow to rest on a wire rack in a warm place.

10 Place the roasting pan on a hot stove and brown the vegetables further.

11 Add the vinegar, wine and the fresh rosemary to deglaze. Continue to cook on the stove for a further three–four minutes.

12 Add the stock to the roasting pan and deglaze.

13 Strain into a saucepan and reduce to the required consistency. Correct the seasoning.

14 Carve the lamb in thick slices and serve with the rosemary jus and the wild mushrooms.

Rump of lamb with a wild mushroom sausage and Madeira jus

Ingredients	4 portions	10 portions
Rump of lamb boned	1	2
Minced chicken	150 g	300 g
Wild mushrooms (Sautéed)	200 g	500 g
Egg whites	1	2
Double cream	75 ml	150 ml
Brown lamb stock	1 l	2.5 l
Rosemary leaves	3 tbsp	7 tbsp
Balsamic vinegar	3 tsp	7 tsp
Red wine	80 ml	200 ml
Salt and pepper	To taste	To taste
Deep fried basil leaves		
Tomato chutney		

energy	cal	fat	sat fat	carb	sugar	protein	fibre
2047 kJ	492 kcal	35.5 g	13.6 g	8.1 g	3.5 g	31.7 g	4.9 g

METHOD OF WORK

1   Season the lamb well.

2   Place the minced chicken into a food blender. Add the egg whites while blending the ingredients then slowly add the cold double cream. Season well. Fold in the mushrooms.

3   Lay a sheet of cling film out and pipe on the wild mushroom mixture, roll into a sausage and secure at either end.

4   Preheat an oven to 220°C.

5   Sear the lamb rumps in a pan with some hot oil. Transfer to the roasting tray and roast in the oven for until pink in the centre.

6   Remove the lamb and allow to rest on a wire rack in a warm place. Place the roasting pan on a hot stove and add the vinegar, wine and the fresh rosemary to deglaze.

7   Continue to cook on the stove for a further three–four minutes. Add the stock to the roasting pan and deglaze.

8   Steam the sausage until a core temperature of 65°C has been achieved, remove from the steamer, take off the cling film and slice.

9   Strain into a saucepan and reduce to the required consistency. Correct the seasoning.

10   Carve the lamb in thick slices and serve with the sausage, tomato chutney quenelle and basil leaf as shown.

Shoulder of lamb with minted pea puree

Shoulder of lamb with minted pea puree and fondant potato

Ingredients	4 portions	10 portions
Boned shoulder of lamb	1 × 2 kg	2 × 2 kg
Olive oil	4 tbsp	8 tbsp
Fresh rosemary	8 sprigs	16 sprigs
Garlic	4 cloves	8 cloves
Chopped shallots	100 g	200 g
Chestnut mushrooms	140 g	280 g
Chopped flat leaf parsley	50 g	100 g
Brioche crumbs	100 g	200 g
Butter	50 g	100 g
Salt and pepper	to taste	to taste
Minted pea puree		
Finely chopped shallots	50 g	125 g
Fresh mint	4 stalks	10 stalks
Double cream	75 ml	200 ml
Garden peas	400 g	1 kg
Salt and pepper		
Pomme fondant	4	10
Glazed baby carrots	4	10

energy	cal	fat	sat fat	carb	sugar	protein	fibre
7293 kJ	1751 kcal	116 g	47.9 g	26.2 g	11.7 g	152.3 g	11.3 g

METHOD OF WORK

1 Preheat an oven to 200°C.

2 Trim the shoulder of lamb and process the trimmings in a blender until smooth. Gently fold in the chopped parsley. Season well.

3 Sweat the shallots with the chopped chestnut mushrooms and, when cooled, add to the parsley mixture.

4 Mix together the brioche crumbs, the softened butter and the parsley and mushroom mixture. Stuff the shoulder with the mixture and tie up. Rub with a little salt, pepper and olive oil.

5 Make eight incisions in the shoulder, cut each clove of garlic in half and insert half a clove and a sprig of rosemary into each incision.

6 Heat a large roasting tray on the stove with a little of the oil and seal the prepared joint until brown on all sides. Remove from the pan and set aside.

7 Position the shoulder of lamb on top of a wire rack Place in the oven for 30 minutes and then reduce the oven temperature to 150°C.

8 Baste every 15 minutes. The lamb should be cooked after another one hour and 20 minutes. Remove the lamb and allow the joint to rest.

9 For the pea purée, cook the peas with the mint stalks in a little boiling water until tender, and refresh quickly to retain the colour.

10 Sweat the finely chopped shallots, adding the cream and seasoning.

11 Remove the mint stalks. When cooled slightly add the chopped mint and purée until smooth. Pass the mixture and reserve warm for service.

12 To serve, spoon the pea purée next to the lamb and serve with the fondant potato, cooking liquor and baby carrots.

Pork (*Porc*)

Pork is the fresh meat of the domestic pig. Pigs are easy to breed and make slaughter weight in usually six months. Pork is widely used across the world, except within the Jewish and Muslim communities.

 VIDEO CLIP Preparation of pork loin for roasting.

In the past it was recommended that pork should always be over-cooked to eliminate trichinosis (caused by the larvae of a worm that can be passed to humans from under-cooked pork). However, with modern rearing, storage and preparation techniques, trichinosis has been practically eradicated, although care should be taken to cook the meat to 70–75°C. Pork is usually supplied butchered into sides.

 VIDEO CLIP Preparation of pork belly.

New breeds of pig developed for the table have a high yield of flesh and a low proportion of fat, examples are Landrace and Duroc. Traditional breeds such as the Tamworth and Gloucester Old Spot have a greater covering of fat and much more tender flesh because they are generally reared free-range and are allowed to forage for food, especially acorns and apples.

WEBLINK Use the following web link for guidance: http://eatseasonably.co.uk

Main pig production areas

Side of pork

Excluding the head, the average weight of a side of pork is
16–18 kg.

BREAKDOWN OF A SIDE OF PORK

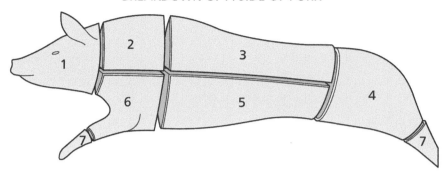

JOINT	FRENCH	USES	AVERAGE WEIGHT
1 Head	La tête	The head can be boned and stuffed, or it can be boiled and the flesh pressed for brawn. The cheeks can be braised. The head can also be boiled and presented with chaud-froid as a centrepiece for a buffet	4 kg
2 Spare rib	L'échine	With the gristle removed, used for sausages, pork pies, slow roasting	2 kg
3 Loin	La longe	Chops and cutlets are obtained from the loin, as is the fillet. All are suitable for frying and grilling. The loin can also be boned and rolled for roasting	5 kg
4 Leg	Le cuissot	On or off the bone, pork leg is suitable for roasting. The legs can be dissected into individual muscles for cutting into steaks or stir frying. The leg can also be cured for ham, either a wet or dry cure can be used	4 kg
5 Belly	La poitrine	Braised belly of pork is very popular. When boned and chopped it makes good emulsion sausages	3 kg
6 Shoulder	L'épaule	With fat and gristle removed, the shoulder can be used to make sausages and forcemeats and can be diced for stews	3 kg
7 Trotters	Le pied	The trotters should be blanched and then refreshed. They can be used to make gelatinous stock, stuffed and braised, or the meat can be picked off and added to brawn	0.5 kg

Step-by-step: The preparation of pig's trotters

1. Score along the underside of the trotter.

2. Slowly cut away the bones from the flesh, removing all the bones and sinew.

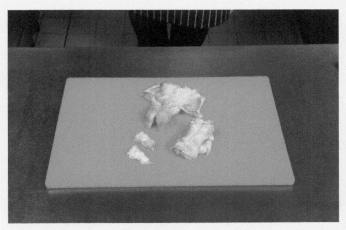

3. This is the **deboned** trotter.

4. Stuff the trotter with a suitable forcemeat and flap over the excess skin.

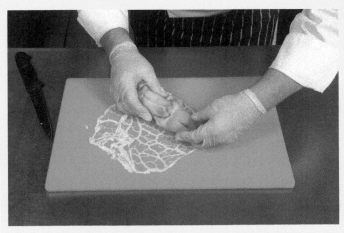

5. Secure the trotter within pigs caul (crepinette).

6. Roll into a neat shape, removing any excess pigs caul.

Pork recipes

Roasted rack of pork

Roasted rack of pork, black pudding citrus and herb crust, stuffed cabbage with caraway, pomme cocotte, beurre noisette hollandaise

Ingredients	Makes approximately 4 portions	Makes approximately 10 portions
4 bone rack of pork French trimmed	1	3
Mirepoix	100 g	250 g
White wine	50 ml	125 ml
Brown stock	500 ml	1.2 l
Dijon mustard	20 g	50 g
Black pudding	100 g	250 g
Fresh bread crumbs	60 g	150 g
Lemon zest	1	3
Lime zest	of ½ lime	of 1½ limes
Whole egg	1	2–3
Unsalted butter	50 g	125 g
Chopped sage	1 tbsp	2–3 tbsp
Chopped parsley	1 tbsp	2–3 tbsp
Stuffed cabbage		
Savoy cabbage	1	2–3
Caraway seeds	1 tsp	2–3 tsp
Rendered pork fat	For sautéing	For sautéing
Sliced shallot	20 g	50 g
Crushed garlic	½ clove	1½ cloves
White wine	20 ml	50 ml
Pomme cocotte		
Maris Piper potatoes	4 large	10 large
Vegetable oil	50 ml	125 ml
Salted butter	75 g	180 g
Beurre noisette hollandaise		
Egg yolks	3	6
White wine vinegar	50 ml	125 ml
White wine	50 ml	125 ml
Sliced shallots	20 g	50 g
Thyme	1 sprig	2–3 sprigs
Bay leaf	½	1 large
Peppercorns	3	8
Beurre noisette	200 ml	500 ml
Salt and pepper		

METHOD OF WORK

1   Tie the rack of pork and season well, caramelize in hot oil remove and caramelize mirepoix.

2   Place pork on top of mirepoix and add 100 ml water, roast in a preheated oven at 200°C until centre reaches 70°C, leave to rest for 20 minutes, reserve roasting tray.

3   To make the crust, mix all ingredients together in a food processor until smooth, season well, spread evenly 0.5 cm thick, cover and refrigerate.

4   For the cabbage, discard the outer tough leaves, take the required number of tender large leaves and blanch in well salted boiling water until tender, refresh immediately, dry and flatten with a rolling pin.

5   Chiffonade the remaining cabbage, removing stalk.

6   Wash well and dry, sauté in the pork fat with the shallots until lightly golden, add the toasted caraway seeds, garlic and wine, reduce wine until evaporated.

7   Chill immediately.

8   Once chilled, place the leaf on oiled and seasoned cling film, divide the chiffonade mixture and place into the centre of the leaf, roll into a neat ball and tie.

9   Reheat in a steamer for five minutes until hot.

10   For the pomme cocotte, wash and peel the potatoes, turn five cocotte potatoes per portion and leave in cold water for 20 minutes, do not chill.

11   Drain and dry the cocottes, lightly colour in hot oil, add the butter and place into a 200°C oven turning occasionally until evenly browned and crispy, drain and season.

12   For the hollandaise, place the white wine, vinegar, aromatics, shallots and pepper corns in a saucepan and reduce by half, pass the reduction through a fine chinois.

13   Place the reduction in a concave metal bowl and set over a bain marie; add the egg yolks and whisk with a balloon whisk until the ribbon stage sabayon is achieved.

14   Add the warm but not hot beurre noisette which has been passed through muslin cloth slowly until emulsified, season well and hold between 50 and 55°C.

15   Cut the crust to desired size leave to soften, brush pork with Dijon mustard mixed with a little water, place softened crust carefully on top.

16   Place back into a 220°C oven until crust starts to colour, remove and leave for five minutes.

17   Degrease the pan with the mirepoix and roasting juices then place on top of the stove, deglaze with wine and add the stock, simmer for five minutes then pass into a saucepan.

18   Reduce gently skimming constantly until a gravy consistency is reached, pass through muslin and keep hot.

19   To serve, carve the pork between the bones and season well, reheat the cabbage and cocottes, serve the hollandaise on the side.

Fillet of pork, black pudding tortellini, onion purée

Ingredients	4 portions	10 portions
Butter	75 g	150 g
Trimmed pork fillet	2 × 300 g	5 × 300 g
Black pudding tortellini		
Pasta dough	200 g	500 g
Black pudding	200 g	500 g
Onion puree		
Thinly sliced white onions	100 g	250 g
Butter	50 g	125 g
Bouquet garni	1 × small	1 × large
White chicken stock	50 ml	125 ml
Double cream	40 ml	100 ml
Salt and pepper	To taste	To taste

energy	cal	fat	sat fat	carb	sugar	protein	fibre
3226 kJ	775 kcal	53.1 g	26.1 g	19.7 g	1.4 g	55.8 g	0.9 g

METHOD OF WORK

1   Preheat an oven to 180°C. Heat butter in a shallow pan, season the fillet and quickly brown on both sides.

2   Place the pan into the oven to finish cooking for 15 minutes, basting the fillet continuously. Remove from the oven and rest for five minutes before finishing for service.

3   To make the tortellinis, roll out the pasta and fill with 50 g of black pudding, seal and cook in boiling salted water.

4   For the onion purée, sweat the onion and bouquet garni in the butter without colouring until soft, add the stock and simmer for 20 minutes.

5   Remove the bouquet garni and blitz then pass through a chinois and finish with the cream and seasoning.

Braised belly of pork with cider sauce

Braised belly of pork with glazed onion, parsnip puree, cider sauce

Ingredients	4 portions	10 portions
Pork belly	600 g	1.5 kg
Cider	320 ml	800 ml
Brown stock	160 ml	400 ml
Diced cooking apples	240 g	600 g
Demerara sugar	40 g	100 g
Diced onion	100 g	250 g
Mirepoix	200 g	500 g
Parsnip puree		
Thinly sliced parsnips	100 g	250 g
Butter	50 g	125 g
Milk	200 ml	500 ml
Double cream	50 ml	125 ml
Glazed onions		
Peeled button onions	8	20
Butter	5 g	12 g
Sugar	2 g	5 g
Salt and pepper		

energy	cal	fat	sat fat	carb	sugar	protein	fibre
3200 kJ	767 kcal	51.7 g	23.1 g	31.1 g	27.9 g	41.4 g	3.4 g

METHOD OF WORK

1. Remove the bone from the belly and singe any hairs with a flame.
2. Neatly trim the edges of the pork and then roll up the joint. Do not roll too tightly.
3. Starting in the centre, tie string around the joint. Repeat at 2.5 cm intervals.
4. Preheat an oven to 180°C.
5. Season and sprinkle the belly of pork with the sugar. Heat a little oil in a hot pan (large enough to take the whole belly of pork) and place the belly of pork in the pan. Colour on each side until golden brown.
6. Remove and set aside. Sweat the mirepoix and diced onion in the butter for four minutes without colour.
7. Place the mirepoix, diced cooking apples, pork, cider and stock in a covered pan and bring to the boil.
8. Place in the oven and braise for one-and-a-half hours. Check occasionally and add more stock or water as required.
9. Remove the lid and continue to cook for a further one hour, basting frequently. Remove the pork and liquidize the cooking liquor. Pass through a fine chinois into a clean pan and correct the seasoning and consistency.
10. For the parsnip puree, sweat the parsnips in the butter for five minutes without colouring, add the milk and salt, simmer until tender, strain.
11. Blitz the parsnips with a little of the milk, then pass through a chinois, add the cream and season well.
12. Cook the onions with the sugar and butter – *glacé à brun*.

Braised pork cheek with parsnip and ginger

Ingredients	4 portions	10 portions
Pork cheeks	4	10
Curing salts	10 g	30 g
water	1 l	3 l
Vegetable oil	50 ml	125 ml
Brown stock	1.5 l	4 l
White wine	80 ml	200 ml
Mirepoix	200 g	500 g
Bouquet garni	1 small	1 large
Parsnips	200 g	500 g
Unsalted butter	50 g	125 g
White chicken stock	300 ml	700 ml
Double cream	40 ml	100 ml
Caramelized baby onions	8	20
Salt and pepper	to taste	to taste

energy	cal	fat	sat fat	carb	sugar	protein	fibre
1440 kJ	348 kcal	29.4 g	10.9 g	15.2 g	9.8 g	3.2 g	5.4 g

METHOD OF WORK

1 Mix the curing salts with the water and whisk until dissolved.
2 Add the pork cheeks and cure for two hours.
3 Remove from the brine and soak for one hour to remove excess salt.
4 Colour the cheeks in the oil, remove.
5 Add the mirepoix and brown add the wine and cook for two minutes.
6 Add the stock, cheeks and bouquet garni cover with baking paper and foil.
7 Braise in 160°C oven until tender, around one-and-a-half hours.
8 Leave to cool in the braising liquor then vac pac with a little of the liquor.
9 Reduce the braising liquor to coating consistency and strain through muslin.
10 Peel the parsnips and remove core save some thin slices and deep fry until golden and crispy, drain and season.
11 Slice the remaining parsnips very thinly and toss in butter for five minutes without colour.
12 Add the white chicken stock and salt, simmer until very tender and strain.
13 Puree in a blender with a little of the cooking stock.
14 Pass through a chinois and add the cream, season well.
15 Reheat the cheeks in boiling water.
16 Serve with the onions, puree and crisps with a little of the sauce.

Fillet of pork with pea purée

Fillet of pork with pea purée, herb noodles and sherry jus

Ingredients	4 portions	10 portions
Butter	75 g	150 g
Trimmed pork fillet	2 × 300 g	5 × 300 g
Pea purée		
Finely chopped shallots	50 g	150 g
Fresh thyme	1 sprig	2 sprigs
Double cream	75 ml	300 ml
Garden peas (fresh or frozen)	400 g	1 kg
Good quality salt and white pepper	to taste	to taste
Herb noodles		
Fresh noodle paste	350 g	700 g
Butter	50 g	100 g
Fresh chopped herbs (parsley, tarragon, chives and basil)	2 tbsp	5 tbsp
Sherry jus		
Olive oil	40 ml	80 ml
Finely chopped shallots	75 g	150 g
Chestnut mushrooms	75 g	130 g
Dry sherry	75 ml	150 ml
Madeira	50 ml	100 ml
Chicken stock	200 ml	400 ml
Veal jus	100 ml	200 ml

energy	cal	fat	sat fat	carb	sugar	protein	fibre
4818 kJ	1156 kcal	69.8 g	29.4 g	59.6 g	6.1 g	66.8 g	8.9 g

METHOD OF WORK

1 Preheat an oven to 180°C.

2 Heat butter in a shallow pan, season the fillet and quickly brown on both sides. Place the pan into the oven to finish cooking for 15 minutes, basting the fillet continuously. Remove from the oven and rest for five minutes before finishing for service.

3 For the pea purée, cook the peas with thyme stalks in a little boiling water until tender. Refresh quickly to retain the colour.

4 Sweat the finely chopped shallots and add the cream and seasoning.

5 Purée the peas until smooth. Pass the mixture and reserve warm.

6 For the noodles, roll out the paste to a very thin rectangle using a pasta roller. Cut into five mm wide strips and spread out onto a lightly floured tray and leave to dry for at least 30 minutes.

7 Place the noodles in a pan of boiling salted water and allow to simmer for eight minutes. Drain in a colander. Melt the butter in a sauteuse, add the noodles and the herbs. Season well and toss until the herbs have fully mixed into the noodles. Reserve warm for service.

8 For the sherry jus, heat the oil in a saucepan and add the shallots and chestnut mushrooms and cook with a little colour. Add the sherry and Madeira and reduce by half. Add the chicken stock and veal jus and reduce by half again.

9 Pass through a fine chinois and correct the seasoning.

10 Arrange on the plate as shown.

Pork and rabbit tourte with vegetable cream sauce

Ingredients	4 portions	10 portions
Diced shoulder of pork	175 g	350 g
Skinned and boned rabbit	75 g	150 g
Smoked streaky bacon (rind removed)	25 g	50 g
Black pudding	50 g	100 g
Shredded suet	10 g	20 g
Brandy	50 ml	100 ml
Sherry	50 ml	100 ml
Fresh chopped thyme	½ tbsp	1 tbsp
Fresh chopped parsley	1 tbsp	2 tbsp
Fresh chopped sage	1 tsp	2 tsp
Puff pastry	250 g	500 g
Egg yolks (beaten for glaze with a drop of water)	1	2
Good-quality salt and white pepper	to taste	to taste
Vegetable cream sauce		
Carrot, leek, celery, red pepper cut into julienne	180 g	350 g
Fresh chopped chives	1 tbsp	2 tbsp
Dry white wine	50 ml	100 ml
Vegetable stock	125 ml	250 ml
Double cream	125 ml	250 ml
Good quality salt and white pepper	to taste	to taste

energy	cal	fat	sat fat	carb	sugar	protein	fibre
3857 kJ	924 kcal	51.6 g	26.3 g	29.6 g	3.9 g	74.6 g	1.6 g

METHOD OF WORK

1   Cut the pork, rabbit, bacon and black pudding into small dice. Mix together in a plastic bowl with the suet. Add the brandy, sherry, herbs and seasoning. Cover with plastic film and leave to marinate in a refrigerator for 24 hours.

2   Drain off the marinade and place the ingredients into a blender. Blend into a farce or a finer texture. Test cook a small piece of the mixture in a frying pan to taste for seasoning.

3   Cut the puff pastry in half and pin out both pieces to approximately 3 mm thick. Cut out 12 cm discs (two per portion) and chill in a refrigerator for one hour.

4   Take approximately 100 g of the meat mixture and roll to form a ball. Place in the centre of one puff pastry disc and brush around the edges with the beaten egg yolk. Cover with another disc of pastry and press the pastry discs together to form a seal. Trim the tourte with a 4 cm plain cutter. Brush with the egg yolk mixture and chill in a refrigerator for 30 minutes. Brush once again with the egg glaze.

5   With the tip of a sharp knife, create curved shallow lines on the surface of the pastry. Preheat an oven to 180°C and bake the tourtes for 20–25 minutes, until the pastry is golden and well risen.

6   For the sauce, place the vegetable julienne into a saucepan with the white wine and slowly poach for a few minutes. Gradually reduce the wine before adding the stock. Reduce by half and add the cream. Bring to the boil and check the consistency and seasoning of the sauce. Add the chopped chives just before service.

7   Place a tourte into the centre of a service plate with the sauce spooned around.

Roast loin of pork and mustard cream sauce

Roast loin of pork, sautéed cabbage, gratin potatoes, mustard cream sauce

Ingredients	4 portions	10 portions
Loin of pork joint	600 g	1.5k g
Chiffonade of Savoy cabbage	200 g	500 g
Smoked pancetta lardons	50 g	125 g
Gratin potatoes	300 g	750 g
Dijon mustard	20 g	50 g
Double cream	50 ml	125 ml
Reduced brown stock	300 ml	750 ml
Salt and pepper		

energy	cal	fat	sat fat	carb	sugar	protein	fibre
2416 kJ	581 kcal	37.5 g	15.4 g	17.4 g	2.8 g	43.9 g	3.7 g

METHOD OF WORK

1   Preheat an oven to 220°C.

2   Dry the pork skin with kitchen paper and leave to dry out for 20 minutes. Brush the skin lightly with the oil and season well with the salt and pepper.

3   Place into the preheated oven for 30 minutes and then reduce the temperature to 170°C.

4   Occasionally baste the joint lightly. Allow 25 minutes per 500 g of pork plus an extra 15 minutes cooking time.

5   When the pork is cooked, remove from the oven. Cover loosely with foil and rest for 20 minutes.

6   Allow the cooking juices and sediment from the pork to settle in the roasting tin, then drain off the fat without disturbing the sediment. Add the brown stock, bring to the boil and allow to simmer. Reduce to the correct consistency and season with a little salt if required. Pass through a fine chinois and skim off any remaining fat.

7   Add the mustard and cream to the stock to finish the sauce.

8   Using a sharp **carving** knife, remove the crackling from the loin of pork and cut the crackling into pieces.

9   Sauté the bacon lardons in some of the pork fat and add the Savoy cabbage; cook until soft; season with pepper.

10 Slice the pork and serve with the potatoes and cabbage and bacon.

CHEF'S TIP To achieve a successful crackling, ensure that there is a good layer of fat beneath the skin and that the skin has been evenly scored and well dried before roasting.

Stuffed pig's trotter

Stuffed pig's trotter with ceps, girolles, onion purée and pomme pailles

Ingredients	4 portions	10 portions
Long pigs' trotters	2	5
Chicken mousse	200 g	500 g
Ceps	50 g	125 g
Diced shallots	20 g	50 g
Chopped chervil	1 tbsp	3 tbsp
Brown stock	2 l	5 l
Madeira	200 ml	500 ml
Mirepoix	80 g	200 g
Bouquet garni	1 small	1 large
Girolles mushrooms	8	20
Unsalted butter	10 g	25 g
Pomme pailles	80 g	200 g
Onion purée	80 g	200 g
Salt and pepper	to taste	to taste

energy	cal	fat	sat fat	carb	sugar	protein	fibre
1814 kJ	435 kcal	22.9 g	10.6 g	15.6 g	5.3 g	29.7 g	2.8 g

METHOD OF WORK

1 Soak the trotters in cold sated water for 24 hours.
2 Shave the bristles off and bone to the knuckle from the bottom of the trotter.
3 Clean the inside and remove veins and excess tissue.
4 Sauté the mirepoix and deglaze with the Madeira, reduce by half and add the brown stock and trotters.
5 Cover with baking paper and a lid, place in to a 150°C oven and braise slowly until soft, about three hours.
6 Leave in the liquid to cool slightly but not cold.
7 Dice the ceps and sauté with the shallots; add the chicken mousse with the chervil, season and test.
8 Place into a piping bag.
9 Remove the trotters from the braising liquor, pass the liquor through a chinois and reduce to coating consistency.
10 Place the trotter upside down onto tin foil while warm and pipe in the mousse.
11 Roll tightly in the foil and poach for eight minutes or until the core temperature reaches 70°C.
12 Remove and leave to rest for five minutes.
13 Sauté the girolles in butter.
14 Remove the foil and brush with some of the reduced braising liquor.
15 Serve with the pome paille, onion puree and some of the braising liquor.

Bacon

Bacon is the cured side of a baconer pig (a pig that is allowed to grow bigger than a porker pig, usually a hybrid of Landrace and Tamworth). The meat is cured by either the wet cure or dry cure method. Dry cure is superior as it causes less shrinkage; the sides are strewn with salt and cured for 14 days. The pinkness comes from the addition of nitrate and the reaction of salt-tolerant bacteria. The cured bacon, referred to as green bacon, can be smoked or sold unsmoked.

Bacon has been a staple of British society for many hundreds of years and was originally used as a way to store meat. Although the invention of refrigeration has made meat storage much easier, bacon continues to be produced because of its flavour. Bacon is still produced for the British market in many other parts of the world, the biggest producer being Denmark.

Side of bacon

The average weight of a side of bacon is 28–30 kg.

JOINT	USES	AVERAGE WEIGHT
1 Gammon	Boiled gammon is usually served cold, but it can be glazed, baked and served hot. Can also be sliced to make gammon steaks and grilled or fried	7–8 kg
2 Back	**Rashers** of bacon and bacon steaks for grilling and frying	9–10 kg
3 Collar	The collar can be tied for boiling or diced for pies and fricassées	4–5 kg
4 Hock	The hock should always be boiled, but can also be roasted afterwards and served with mustard	4–5 kg
5 Belly	Streaky bacon is taken from the belly and can be grilled or fried	4–5 kg

BREAKDOWN OF A SIDE OF BACON

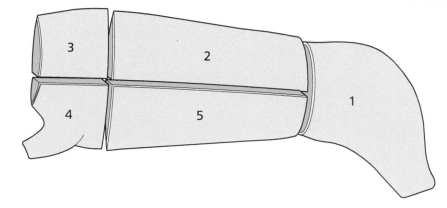

Guest Chef

Hertfordshire roast belly pork with sour cherry chutney, a warm carrot and spinach mousse and pork jus

Chef Barry Bridgen
Centre Hertfordshire Regional College

This uses locally bred pork from our regional farms. Cut the pork into rectangles pour boiling water over the scored belly of pork, dry and roast. This will give you crisp crackling to accompany the dish. This dish is suitable for any occasion but is ideal for dinner parties.

Ingredient	4 portions
Roast pork	
Pork belly	1000 g
Sea salt	
Vegetable oil	
Chutney	
Vegetable oil	80 ml
Onions	100 g
Black cherries	350 g
Star anise	2 g
Balsamic vinegar	50 ml
Spinach and carrot mousse	
Carrots	400 g
Unsalted butter	80 g
Salt and pepper	to taste
Eggs medium	4
Double cream	100 ml
Baby spinach	500 g

METHOD OF WORK

Pork

1 Pour boiling water over the pork and dry thoroughly. Rub sea salt into the skin and place into roasting tray on a trivet, lightly cover with oil and place into the oven 200°C gas mark 8, 400°F for 15 minutes. Turn the oven down to 170°C Gas 5, 300°F until the pork is cooked. Probe accordingly.

Chutney

2 Heat the oil in a saucepan and soften the onion over a low heat for approximately 15 minutes. Add the cherries and the syrup from the cherries, star anise and Balsamic Vinegar. Simmer until syrup is reduced for approximately 30 minutes.

Spinach and carrot mousse

3 Cook the carrots in salted water until tender, drain and dry thoroughly on top of the stove. Place in a food processor with butter and seasoning and process until smooth. Pass through a sieve and add one or two egg yolks and a little cream depending on the consistency of the puree. Wash and cook the spinach until wilted, squeeze out the excess moisture, blend in a food processor, pass through a sieve add one or two egg yolks with a little cream depending on the consistency of the puree.

Divide the carrot mixture into buttered ramequins with the spinach on top. Build up in layers until both the mixtures have been used up. Smooth and cover each ramequin with foil or silicone paper.

4 Place into a bain-marie and half cover the ramequins with water.

5 Bake in the oven 170°C gas mark 5 350°F for approximately 20 minutes or until firm to the touch.

To serve

6 Cut the pork into squares, or into three thick slices and serve with the warmed chutney, carrot and spinach mousse and pork jus.

ASSESSMENT OF KNOWLEDGE AND UNDERSTANDING

You have now learned about the use of the different varieties of meat and how to prepare and cook different meat dishes.

To test your level of knowledge and understanding, answer the following short questions. These will help to prepare you for your summative (final) assessment.

Quality identifications

1   List three quality points you should check when receiving a veal delivery.

i)

ii)

iii)

2   State how marbling occurs in red meat and why it is important.

3   State why it is important to consider the traceability of meat products purchased from suppliers.

4   List four criteria for organic products.

i)

ii)

iii)

iv)

Materials and storage

1   Explain the main benefit of hanging meat.

Preparation

1   Describe the method of preparation for a stuffed shoulder of lamb.

Cooking

1   Explain the reason for resting roasted meats prior to carving and serving.

2   Explain why meat should be browned or caramelized before being put into a stew.

Health and safety

1   List two safety points to observe when removing a heavy joint of meat from a hot roasting tray.

i)

ii)

2   Describe two safety procedures required when preparing a boned and rolled shoulder of pork.

i)

ii)

Poultry and game

VRQ

Advanced skills and techniques in producing poultry and games dishes

NVQ

Prepare poultry for complex dishes

Cook and finish complex poultry dishes

Prepare game for complex dishes

Cook and finish complex game dishes

Recipes

POULTRY DISHES

Spatchcock poussin Lyonnaise

Royale of chicken purée with truffle, cucumber and baby onion

Guinea fowl, creamed peas, lardons, white wine jus

Stuffed chicken with peppers, sauté potatoes, tomato butter sauce

Glazed duck breasts with sesame tuille and baby turnips

Suprême of duck en croûte with spinach

Confit duck leg, fondant potato, five spice jus

Breast of duck, duck faggot with jasmine sauce

Roast goose with semolina dumplings

Seared chicken livers with a Madeira jus, saffron risotto and Parmesan crisp

Supreme of turkey wrapped in bacon with turkey ballotine

GAME DISHES

Pot roasted snipe with dumplings

Stuffed pheasant legs

Crown of partridge with turned vegetables

Loin of rabbit wrapped in pancetta

Quail and black pudding sausages

Saddle of rabbit stuffed with black pudding

Loin of venison with baba ganoush

Confit of pigeon with spinach and beetroot salad

Sous vide venison and pithivier

LEARNING OBJECTIVES

This chapter describes how to prepare a variety of poultry dishes using some technically advanced skills and presentation expertise. The aim of this chapter is to enable you to develop skills and implement knowledge in the preparation and cookery principles of complex poultry.

At the end of this chapter you will be able to:

● **Identify each variety of both feathered and furred game as well as poultry and their finished dish.**

● **Understand the use of relative ingredients in poultry and game preparation and cookery.**

● **State the quality points of various poultry and game items and dishes.**

● **Prepare and cook each type of poultry and game variety.**

● **Identify the storage procedures of all types of poultry and game, both raw and cooked.**

● **Be competent at preparing and cooking a range of basic poultry game-based dishes.**

Poultry

When we refer to poultry we describe birds specifically reared for the table. This includes chicken, guinea fowl, turkey, goose and duck.

Chicken (*poulet*)

Chickens are members of the pheasant family and originate from northern India and southern China.

In the UK, more than 90 per cent of chickens are battery reared. Because of intensive husbandry, the birds achieve slaughter weight at six weeks. The birds grow very quickly and live relatively short lives, and the meat is bland and can have a grainy texture.

Free range and especially organic chickens are allowed to forage in the open and have space to develop muscle and a stronger bone structure. The term 'free range' only means that the birds have access to an outdoor pen. There are several labelling systems in use for these birds, such as the Soil Association scheme. One British company has developed a system of labelling and rearing chickens similar to the French *Label Rouge*. 'Label Anglaise' shows that the chicken has been produced by farmers who use older breeds, such as Cornish Red and White Rock, and free range/organic methods of rearing:

● The diet consists of 70 per cent cereals, including maize.

● No antibiotics, hormones or growth stimulators are used.

● Slaughter is after 81 days.

The label is featured on menus and assures the customer that the chicken has been well reared and is flavoursome.

Corn-fed chickens are fed on a diet of maize or containing a proportion of maize. This does not guarantee any kind of quality assurance. The distinctive yellow colouring of the skin is often gained by the introduction of a yellow dye into the feed and not by the natural colour of the maize itself.

QUALITY POINTS

When buying chickens we should be able to identify the quality points associated with them:

Clear skin with no blemishes and unbroken; the colour varies from breed to breed, but the most common battery-reared breeds – the hybrids, Ross and Cobb – have a pale creamy colour

Flesh should be firm and pliable

Not too much fat; check the abdominal cavity for excess

No bruising, blood clots, ammonia sores on the legs or cuts

The breastbone should be pliable (this is for younger birds that are destined to be grilled, roasted or sautéed).

PURCHASE SPECIFICATIONS

In general, older and larger birds will have a more pronounced flavour. Organic poultry will ultimately have the best flavour, but it will be more expensive to purchase.

TYPE	AGE	AVERAGE WEIGHT
Poussin	Up to six weeks	250–400 g
Spring chicken	six–eight weeks	1–1.25 kg
Chicken	12–20 weeks	1–2 kg
French Label Rouge	11.5 weeks	1–1.6 kg
Capon (castrated male)	Up to 32 weeks	2–4 kg
Boiling fowl	Up to 40 weeks	2–4 kg

Turkey (*dinde*)

Turkeys are members of the pheasant family and were first domesticated by the Aztecs and Mexicans. They were introduced to Europe by the Spanish in the sixteenth century via Asia and became popular because of the delicate flavour of their meat. The term 'turkey' is thought to reflect the belief that they were imported from Turkey, at that time part of the vast Ottoman Empire.

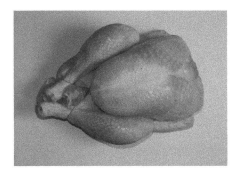

The huge modern turkeys are mainly battery farmed. This practice originated in the late 1920s in British Columbia, when a breeder developed an 18 kg bird with oversized leg muscles. This stock was used to perfect the more common broad-breasted Bronze.

Once again, it is well worth spending time sourcing organic and free range birds, should budgets permit.

QUALITY POINTS
Cock birds have a tendency to be drier and tougher than hens.
Bronze birds can have residual dark feather stubs; these can be removed with duck tweezers.
The flesh should be dry to the touch and without excess blemishes.
If the windpipe is still intact, it should be pliable and not rigid.
The breast should be plump in intensively reared birds and slightly leaner in the rarer organic varieties.

Turkey is available in many weights, ranging from 4–15 kg. The broad-breasted White turkey is the most common in today's marketplace and has a white, smooth and generally unblemished skin. Bronze turkeys are so called because of their distinctive plumage. Both Norfolk Black and Cambridge Bronze turkeys are worth looking out for as most of these birds are raised using traditional non-intensive farming methods. This means they take longer to mature, which contributes to a better overall flavour.

Duck (*canard*)

Duck is a web-footed water fowl, originally domesticated by the Chinese about 2000 years ago. It is highly appreciated for its rich moist meat. The common duck is the wild mallard, which is native to the northern hemisphere. The Barbary duck is a descendant of the Muscovy duck of Central and South America.

The type and breed of duck should be taken into account when purchasing. Barbary duck yields excellent suprême portions while Aylesbury is ideal for roasting. Gressingham duck has a good flavour due mainly to the fact that the birds are slaughtered at an older age. It is also smaller than the other ducks. Nantais duck is a traditional French breed that is becoming fewer in number.

Ducks are usually slaughtered from 6 to 16 weeks. Strictly speaking, the term 'duck' is applied to birds that are more than two months old; the younger birds are called 'ducklings'.

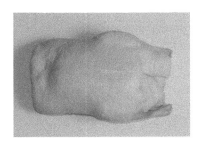

QUALITY POINTS
General
Pale skinned and undamaged (except with wild varieties)
Feet and bills should be brightly coloured
Fresh pleasant smell
Moist but not sticky
Free from bruises, feathers and blemishes
Breeds
Aylesbury – a small bird with white feathers and delicate flesh
Gressingham – a cross between a domesticated duck and a mallard, a highly prized breed with a low fat content and rich flesh
Norfolk – from the county of Norfolk, a domesticated fowl with similar attributes to Aylesbury
Lincolnshire – as Norfolk, a common duck with similar attributes to Aylesbury
Barbary – firm lean flesh with a strong flavour
Nantais – small and slightly fatty with delicate flesh
Rouennais – a larger duck than the Nantais, similar to the Aylesbury

Guinea fowl (*pintade*)

This is an excellent alternative to battery-farmed chicken in that the flesh is comparable to organic free-range chicken. It can have a tendency to be dry so care must be taken when cooking. All recipes that apply to chicken also apply to guinea fowl. The meat has a more pronounced flavour and the birds are usually aged between 10 and 15 weeks before they are slaughtered.

Goose (*oie*)

Goose has a rich dark flesh with a copious covering of fat which means that it will very rarely dry out during cooking. They can weigh anything from 2.5 to 12 kg, depending on whether or not they were used for the production of foie gras. Goose should have the same quality points as duck. When not in season it can be purchased frozen. Geese are usually aged between 24 and 28 weeks at slaughter.

Poultry offal (giblets)

The giblets of poultry have many uses and can be essential in the preparation of many dishes. Although most poultry is purchased without giblets, they are still available from good suppliers. With correct storage and when used as fresh as possible they will enhance your repertoire of poultry dishes.

POULTRY OFFAL	USES
Livers	Garnishes, pâtés, terrines, stuffings, sautés; foie gras is the liver of specially fed ducks and geese
Cockscombs and kidneys	Classic garnishes such as favourite, Chevalière and Tivoli
Hearts	Stocks, consommés and salade Périgourdine

POULTRY OFFAL	USES
Necks	Stocks and consommés
Gizzards	Stocks, stews and pies
Winglets	Garnishes, boned and stuffed for braising

White meat and dark meat

The differences between white and dark meat are due to the work performed by the various muscles. Leg muscles contain more fat than breast meat, and even in intensive rearing they get used and exercised. The result is that they are more grainy and tougher in texture. The leg muscles use oxygen to burn fat to generate energy, and myoglobin – a reddish brown protein – stores the oxygen in the muscles. The extra myoglobin and fat in the legs accounts for the slightly stronger flavour and darker colour of the meat.

White meat from the breast and in battery-reared poultry is muscle that is seldom used. These muscles use glycogen – a form of sugar – as a source of energy. Glycogen does not need oxygen or fat, and therefore there is a lack of myoglobin and very little fat in the breast meat.

The storage of poultry

Poultry is a highly perishable commodity and so requires careful storage control. Fresh and chilled birds should be placed on clean trays in single layers, not stacked on top each other. The optimum storage temperature range is 1–5°C. Poultry should be used as quickly as possible, but at least within three days. Refrigeration leaves the poultry relatively unchanged from its fresh condition; both bacteria and meat enzymes become less active at lower temperatures thus slowing down spoilage.

The modern practice of vacuum packing butchered poultry and meat has the economic advantages of reduced storage space and a longer shelf life. It stores well because the raw protein does not have prolonged exposure to oxygen and therefore the fatty elements do not break down as quickly. Oxygen in the air and direct light will cause the flesh to become a dull colour and will slowly change the flavour.

The freezing of poultry greatly extends storage life because all biological processes are halted. Frozen poultry must be kept in a deep freeze until required and must be completely thawed before being cooked. Freezing immobilizes the liquid/water content and therefore the meat will continue to be preserved so long as a temperature of –18°C is maintained. It is advised that 24 hours is allowed when defrosting poultry in a refrigerator. Wrapped poultry can be quickly defrosted in an iced water bath, which keeps the surface of the flesh safely cold.

Health and safety

Salmonella and *E. coli* are always a cause for concern when dealing with poultry. All safety procedures must be adhered to, from the receiving of deliveries to the service of finished dishes.

Salmonella causes more serious food-borne diseases in Europe than any other microbe. It often has no effect on the animal carriers, but in humans it can be the cause of chronic infection and sickness. A particular strain of *E. coli*, named 0157:H7, can cause kidney failure, especially in children and the elderly.

To help prevent bacterial infection from poultry, it should always be assumed that all meat and poultry is infected with at least some bacteria. Measures must be taken to prevent cross-contamination; all hands, knives, chopping boards and workbenches used in preparation must be cleaned thoroughly with hot soapy water. *E. coli* is killed at 68°C. At this temperature the protein content in poultry and meat will denature and coagulate, any connective tissue will begin to dissolve and the flow of protein bound water (meat juices) will stop.

Preparation techniques

It should be noted that the structures of the different types of poultry birds are very similar and therefore the various preparation techniques can be transferred between the different varieties.

PREPARATION OF SPATCHCOCK AND CRAPAUDINE

Spatchcock and crapaudine can be prepared from a single poussin, double poussin or a spring chicken. The cooking method used is grilling, which dictates the tenderness of the bird.

Step-by-step: Preparation of crapaudine

1. Start by removing the wishbone of a poussin.

2. Lift the breast and cut beneath just above the legs.

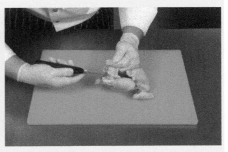
3. Lifting the breast slightly cut either side to separate the connection.

4. Open the poussin so the carcass is touching the board, and then exert pressure to flatten the bird.

5. Take a soaked skewer and pass it through the bird as shown; making sure the skewer passes through the wings.

6. Repeat the process; this time skewering the thighs. The poussin is ready for use.

VIDEO CLIP Removing the breast from guinea fowl

VIDEO CLIP Removing legs from a guinea fowl

VIDEO CLIP Guinea fowl ballotine

VIDEO CLIP Galantine of chicken

Poultry recipes

Spatchcock poussin Lyonnaise

Ingredients	4 portions	10 portions
Poussin	4 × 300 g	10 × 300 g
Pommery grain mustard	150 g	375 g
Fresh breadcrumbs	400 g	1 kg
Unsalted butter	100 g	250 g
White chicken stock	100 ml	250 ml
Double cream	200 ml	500 ml
Tarragon	¼ bunch	½ bunch
Tomato concassé	50 g	125 g
Red onion	50 g	125 g
Good-quality salt and pepper	to taste	to taste

energy	cal	fat	sat fat	carb	sugar	protein	fibre
4279 kJ	1025 kcal	65.6 g	35.8 g	82.6 g	8.3 g	31.2 g	4.9 g

METHOD OF WORK

1 Check that the poussin meets with quality standards. Spatchcock each poussin by splitting, flattening and securing with two skewers.

2 Season and seal in a hot pan.

3 Coat the poussin with half the mustard, leave for 30 minutes.

4 Melt the butter. Roll the poussin in breadcrumbs, sprinkle with the melted butter and grill until cooked.

5 Add the tarragon stalks to the stock and reduce by half. Add the double cream and remaining grain mustard then reduce by half again.

6 Pass through a chinois. Add chopped tarragon and correct the seasoning.

7 Mix the concassé with the finely chopped red onion, olive oil and seasoning and place on the chicken.

8 Serve sauce separately.

CHEF'S TIP Care should be taken when grilling with breadcrumbs. Always ensure that the breadcrumbs are well soaked with butter to keep them moist. The majority of the butter will leave the breadcrumbs as they crisp up.

Royale of chicken purée with truffle

Royale of chicken purée with truffle, cucumber and baby onion

Ingredients	4 portions	10 portions
White chicken meat	100 g	250 g
Béchamel sauce	50 ml	125 ml
Double cream	200 ml	500 ml
Egg yolks	6	15
Confit baby onions	12	30
Turned cucumber	12	30
Black truffle	4 g	10 g
Chicken velouté	120 ml	300 ml
Salt and pepper	to taste	to taste

energy	cal	fat	sat fat	carb	sugar	protein	fibre
2365 kJ	575 kcal	42.1 g	22.3 g	26.2 g	20.7 g	22.7 g	8.8 g

METHOD OF WORK

1   Poach the white chicken meat then purée in a food processor.

2   Add the béchamel and half the double cream then pass through a drum sieve.

3   Bind with the yolks and season well. Place the mixture into buttered dariole moulds.

4   Place into a bain-marie so the water comes half way up the sides of the dariole moulds and cook in the oven at 200°C for 15–20 minutes.

5   Cook the cucumber in boiling salted water, brown the confit onions and place into a bowl with the mousse in the centre.

6   Garnish with the truffle and chicken velouté.

CHEF'S TIP   Line the bottom of the mould with a circle of silicone paper to prevent sticking.

Guinea fowl, creamed peas, lardons, white wine jus

Ingredients	4 portions	10 portions
Whole guinea fowl	2	5
Mire poix	200 g	500 g
Fresh peas shelled	200 g	500 g
Double cream	200 ml	500 ml
Thyme	2 sprigs	5 sprigs
Garlic crushed	1 clove	2–3 cloves
Bouquet garni	1 × small	1 × large
Lardons	200 g	500 g
Reduced brown guinea fowl or chicken stock	500 ml	1.2 l
White wine	100 ml	250 ml
Unsalted butter	40 g	100 g

energy	cal	fat	sat fat	carb	sugar	protein	fibre
3632 kJ	875 kcal	54.6 g	28.2 g	9.2 g	4 g	79 g	4 g

METHOD OF WORK

1   Prepare the guinea fowl for roasting.

2   Season and seal in a hot pan and colour, remove fowls and soften the mirepoix in the pan.

3   Place the fowl on top of the mirepoix and roast in a 200°C oven for 35–40 minutes.

4   Remove the fowls and leave to rest, drain off the fat and place the pan back on the stove.

5   Add the white wine and reduce by half, add the stock and simmer gently for 20 minutes.

6   Strain off, mount with butter and reserve.

7   Reduce the cream with the garlic and bouquet garni until thickened, add the blanched peas and season well.

8   Caramelize the lardons and add the fat to the peas.

9   Portion the guinea fowls, cut the breasts in two and separate the drumstick and thigh.

10   Serve with the peas, lardons and peas.

CHEF'S TIP   Using a treacle cured piece of bacon adds extra flavour to the dish.

Stuffed chicken with peppers

Stuffed chicken with peppers, sauté potatoes, tomato butter sauce

Ingredients	4 portions	10 portions
Chicken suprêmes	4 × 170 g	10 × 170 g
Sautéed mixed pepper strips	200 g	500 g
Large floury potatoes	4	10
Duck fat	200 g	500 g
Ripe tomatoes	200 g	500 g
Fine mirepoix	100 g	250 g
Smoked bacon	40 g	100 g
White chicken stock	400 ml	1000 ml
Unsalted butter	80 g	200 g
Salt and pepper	to taste	to taste

energy	cal	fat	sat fat	carb	sugar	protein	fibre
5566 kJ	1331 kcal	79.3 g	32 g	89.9 g	3.3 g	68.5 g	7.8 g

5. For the sauce, sweat the mirepoix with the bacon until lightly coloured, add the tomatoes roughly chopped and cook for five minutes.
6. Add the stock and simmer slowly for 30 minutes.
7. Push through a fine sieve and reduce; finish with the butter.
8. Cook the chicken in a saucepan of water for approximately ten minutes.
9. Remove from the cling film and fry in butter until golden.
10. Slice the stuffed chicken and arrange overlapping. Finish with the potatoes and sauce.

CHEF'S TIP Add a little chicken forcemeat to the farce to bind it and make carving easier.

METHOD OF WORK

1. Place the peppers under the skin of the chicken suprêmes.
2. Season the chicken and wrap in cling film to form cylindrical shapes then chill.
3. Par boil the potatoes until half cooked, peel and slice into half-inch slices.
4. Cut out with a ring cutter and fry in the duck fat until golden brown and crispy.

Glazed duck breasts

Glazed duck breasts with sesame tuille and baby turnips

Ingredients	4 portions	10 portions
Duck breasts	4 × 170 g	10 ×170 g
Honey	20 ml	50 ml
Soy sauce	4 tbsp	10 tbsp
Sesame oil	2 tbsp	5 tbsp
Sesame seeds	1 tbsp	3 tbsp
Filo pastry	3 sheets	9 sheets
Baby turnips	12	30
Bok choy	400 g	1 kg
Salt and pepper		

energy	cal	fat	sat fat	carb	sugar	protein	fibre
3998 kJ	966 kcal	83.9 g	23 g	11.7 g	9.9 g	41.2 g	5 g

METHOD OF WORK

1   Trim and **score** the duck breasts, **sear** skin-side down in a dry pan until coloured and the majority of fat has rendered down.

2   Pour the fat into a small saucepan, turn the duck over and drizzle with honey, place into a hot oven 180°C for seven minutes, remove and rest.

3   Cook the baby turnips in the duck fat until tender remove and keep warm.

4   Cut the bok choy into quarters and cook in sesame oil.

5   Brush one sheet of filo with some sesame oil and sprinkle with sesame seeds, repeat twice.

6   Cut into triangles and bake between two trays until golden.

7   Arrange the bok choy and turnips on the plate and pour the liquid over.

8   Cut the duck in slices and lay on top, overlapping slightly.

9   Finish with the sesame crisp.

Suprême of duck en croûte with spinach

Ingredients	4 portions	10 portions
Duck breasts	4 × 170 g	10 × 170 g
Puff pastry 10 × 10 cm	5 sheets	13 sheets
Butter	100 g	250 g
Baby spinach	200 g	500 g
Fresh cranberries	50 g	125 g
Duck jus	200 ml	500 ml
Caster sugar	10 g	25 g
Red wine	50 ml	125 ml
Oranges	1	3
eggs	1	3
Salt and pepper	to taste	to taste

energy	cal	fat	sat fat	carb	sugar	protein	fibre
4653 kJ	1124 kcal	98.3 g	37.4 g	7.7 g	7 g	46 g	2.5 g

METHOD OF WORK

1   Trim the duck breasts and remove the fat, then seal in a hot pan all over. Chill and season.

2   Take three-quarters of the rolled out puff pastry and wrap thinly around the duck. Brush with beaten egg.

3   With the remainder of the puff pastry, form a trellis and wrap around the outside, brush again with beaten egg.

4   Chill for 30 minutes.

5   Bake the duck at 170°C for 25 minutes. Remove from the oven and rest for five minutes.

6   Heat the cranberries and add the zest of the oranges then add the sugar. Deglaze with red wine and orange juice, reduce then add the jus.

7   Wilt the spinach in butter and season.

8   Place the spinach on the plate, duck on top and cranberry jus around.

Confit duck leg, fondant potato, carrot puree, five spice jus

METHOD OF WORK

1   Remove the thighbone from the duck legs and score the skin. Singe or pluck any remaining feathers and chop off the knuckle. Marinate for 24 hours in salt, crushed cinnamon sticks, chopped garlic and orange zest and juice.

2   Wash duck legs and place in duck fat.

3   Heat in a pan then cover and place in the oven 150°C for two to three hours until very tender. Remove from the fat and drain over a wire rack.

4   For the carrot purée, sweat the carrots in the butter until they start to lightly caramelize, add the stock and simmer until very tender, blitz and pass.

5   For the jus, caramelize the bones and degrease the pan, add the mirepoix and soften, add the five spice and cook for two minutes.

6   Add the port and reduce by two-thirds. Add the stock and simmer for 20 minutes.

7   Pass through muslin and reduce to consistency.

8   Colour the duck in the oven and glaze with some of the sauce.

9   Serve with puree, potato and jus.

Ingredients	4 portions	10 portions
Duck legs	4	10
Sea salt	100 g	250 g
Cinnamon	1	2
oranges	1	2
Garlic	20 g	50 g
duck fat	500 g	1.25 kg
Fondant potato	4	10
Carrot purée		
Finely sliced carrots	200 g	500 g
Butter	80 g	200 g
White stock	200 ml	500 ml
Five spice jus		
Reduced duck stock	400 ml	1000 ml
Duck bones finely chopped	200 g	500 g
Five spice	1 tsp	1 tbsp
Mirepoix	80 g	200 g
port	200 ml	500 ml
Salt and pepper	to taste	to taste

energy	cal	fat	sat fat	carb	sugar	protein	fibre
3109 kJ	751 kcal	61.1 g	23.9 g	15.8 g	12.7 g	21.9 g	2.7 g

Breast of duck, duck faggot with jasmine sauce

Ingredients	4 portions	10 portions
Butter	50 g	125 g
Small ducklings (1 kg)	2	5
Clear honey	2 tbsp	5 tbsp
Finely diced onion	100 g	250 g
Veal jus	125 ml	300 ml
Garlic, finely chopped	1 clove	2 cloves
Pearl barley	20 g	50 g
Fresh thyme	1 sprig	3 sprigs
Fresh parsley	1 small bunch	2 small bunches
Bay leaf	1	2
Duck livers	2	5
Duck hearts	2	5
Pig's caul	4 good pieces	10 good pieces
Veal stock	1000 ml	2500 ml
Finely diced carrots	50 g	125 g
Chopped shallots	50 g	125 g
Diced leeks	50 g	125 g
Red wine	100 ml	250 ml
Lime juice	¼ lime	½ lime
Sea salt and black pepper	to taste	to taste
Red onion marmalade	40 g	100 g

energy	cal	fat	sat fat	carb	sugar	protein	fibre
3936 kJ	942 kcal	84.5 g	32.4 g	14.7 g	12.1 g	25.3 g	2.7 g

METHOD OF WORK

1   Cook the pearl barley by bringing to the boil in salted water and cooking for one hour. Refresh immediately. Sweat the onions and garlic in some vegetable oil. Add the veal jus to cover the onions and garlic. Allow to reduce. Remove from the heat and allow to cool.

2   Mince the livers, hearts and thigh meat from the duck legs. Add to the reduction and incorporate the chopped fresh herbs. Season well. Fold in the cooked pearl barley. Wrap in pig's **caul**, creating one faggot per portion. Allow the faggots to rest in a refrigerator for at least 30 minutes before cooking. Colour the faggots in fat taken from the duck and then **braise** in the veal stock until just cooked.

3   Remove the duck breasts from the carcasses and score the skin.

4   Fry the vegetables and the broken down duck carcasses. Drain off any excess fat. Place in a pan and cover with cold water. Add thyme, bay leaf and parsley stalks. Allow to simmer for two hours, strain, and bring back to the boil. Incorporate the braised faggot cooking liquor. Add the red wine.

5   Add the lime juice and bring back to boil. Adjust the consistency and the seasoning.

6   Season the duck breasts and fry with the skin side down until rendered and coloured. Brush warmed honey on the skin side and turn over to finish, cooking until golden brown and the breasts are still pink. Leave to rest in a warm place.

7   Carve each rested duck breast into thin slices and allow any juices to drain. Arrange on a plate with the red onion marmalade and faggot.

8   Check the seasoning and consistency of the sauce before serving.

Roast goose with semolina dumplings

Ingredients	4 portions	10 portions
Young oven-ready goose	1 × 2.5 kg	3 × 2.5 kg
Medium-sized dessert apple	1	3
Onion	1	3
Fresh tarragon	1 sprig	3 sprigs
Water	250 ml	750 ml
Brown chicken stock	400 ml	1200 ml
Butter	150 g	450 g
Eggs	4	12
Semolina	250 g	750 g
White bread	200 g	600 g
Soured cream	125 ml	375 ml
King Edward potatoes	450 g	1350 g
Sea salt	to taste	to taste
Turned apple	8	20
Good-quality salt and pepper	to taste	to taste

energy	cal	fat	sat fat	carb	sugar	protein	fibre
5492 kJ	1313 kcal	65.9 g	31.7 g	137.8 g	45.6 g	49.2 g	12.7 g

METHOD OF WORK

1 Rinse the goose, pat dry, cut off the fat by the vent and season inside with salt. Peel, halve and core the apple, stuff into the goose together with the whole onion and tarragon sprigs. Pour the water into a large roasting pan. Bring to the boil on top of the stove, then lower in the goose.

2 Roast for approximately one-and-a-half–two hours in a preheated oven at 220°C. Baste frequently with the cooking juices. After an hour, remove the stuffing from the goose and place in the roasting pan. Return to the oven.

3 Beat the butter until light and creamy in texture. Add the eggs a little at a time, beating well between each addition. Then add the semolina. Leave the egg and semolina mixture to stand for one hour in a refrigerator.

4 **Steep** the diced bread in the soured cream to soften. Steam the potatoes until quite soft then peel, chop coarsely and lay out on a baking sheet. Place into the oven and lower the temperature to 200°C and dry out the potatoes for approximately five minutes. Push through a coarse sieve and season with salt and nutmeg, mixing thoroughly. Work this potato into the semolina dough.

5 Remove the goose from the roasting pan and keep warm. Add the stock to the pan, bring to the boil and pass through a fine sieve lined with muslin cloth. Skim off any excess fat and adjust the seasoning and consistency of the jus.

6 Form the dough into small dumplings and drop gently into boiling salted water. Cook for approximately 15 minutes.

7 Carve the goose into thin slices and allow any residual juices to drain. Arrange on a plate. Check the seasoning and consistency of the sauce and spoon some over the goose. Serve with two semolina dumplings per portion and turned apple. Serve the rest of the sauce separately.

Seared chicken livers with a Madeira jus

Seared chicken livers with a Madeira jus, saffron risotto and parmesan crisp

Ingredients	4 portions	10 portions
Chicken livers	12	30
Madeira	35 ml	70 ml
Brown chicken jus	50 ml	145 ml
Finely diced onion	40 g	100 g
Chopped flat leaf parsley	4 tbsp	10 tbsp
Butter	100 g	250 g
Arborio rice	100 g	250 g
Saffron white chicken stock	400 ml	1 l
Grated Parmesan cheese	100 g	250 g
Fresh chervil	¼ bunch	1 bunch
Good-quality salt and pepper	to taste	to taste

energy	cal	fat	sat fat	carb	sugar	protein	fibre
1963 kJ	473 kcal	31.9 g	18.9 g	24.2 g	1.8 g	20.2 g	2.1 g

METHOD OF WORK

1 Take half the parmesan cheese and place onto a non-stick mat or silicone paper in a circular shape.

2 Bake in the oven at 180°C until bubbling and very slightly golden.

3 Remove from the oven and reserve.

4 Sweat the onions in a little butter and oil, then add the rice and cook for a further two minutes. Add the hot stock and continue to cook the risotto until al dente. Finish with butter, parmesan and flat leaf parsley.

5 Quickly fry the chicken livers in a hot pan until pink, then deglaze with Madeira and add the brown chicken jus.

6 Place the risotto into a bowl, top with the livers and drizzle the sauce around, garnish with the crisp.

Supreme of turkey with turkey ballotine

Supreme of turkey wrapped in bacon with turkey ballotine

Ingredients	4 portions	10 portions
Turkey supreme	1 × 600 g	1 × 1.5 kg
Streaky bacon	10 rashers	20 rashers
Turkey leg	1 small	1 large
Cumberland sausage meat	200 g	500 g
Dried cranberries	50 g	125 g
Fresh cranberries	80 g	200 g
Sugar	as required	as required
Turkey jus	125 ml	300 ml
Roasted baby onions	12	30
Chestnuts	12	30
Deep fried sage leaves	4	10
Salt and pepper		

energy	cal	fat	sat fat	carb	sugar	protein	fibre
3883 kJ	924 kcal	37.1 g	12.2 g	20.7 g	15.3 g	128.4 g	3.9 g

METHOD OF WORK

1 Lay the bacon **rashers** onto cling film. Season the turkey suprême with pepper and roll tightly.

2 Remove all bone, skin and sinew from the turkey leg. Mix the dried cranberries with the sausage meat and spread on top.

3 Roll the leg and tie at 2 cm intervals. Wrap in cling film and then in foil.

4 Steam or poach the suprême for 40 minutes, remove to a roasting pan and remove the cling film. Roast for a further 40 minutes or until a core temperature of 70°C has been reached for five minutes.

5 Place the ballotine in an oven and bake for one hour.

6 Place the fresh cranberries in a pan with the sugar and heat for two–three minutes until the cranberries start to release their juices.

7 Add the jus and bring to the boil, simmer for two–three minutes.

8 Carve the suprême and ballotine and serve with the onions, chestnuts and sage leaves.

CHEF'S TIP This is the ideal dish for Christmas banqueting as it lends itself to dining-room carving. The shape and lack of bones allow efficient slices to be carved.

ASSESSMENT OF KNOWLEDGE AND UNDERSTANDING

You have now learned about the use of different types of poultry and how to prepare and cook a variety of poultry dishes using different commodities and preparation techniques.

To test your level of knowledge and understanding, answer the following short questions. These will help to prepare you for your summative (final) assessment.

Quality identifications

1 List three types of chicken.

i)

ii)

iii)

2 List three quality points you should look for when receiving poultry.

i)

ii)

iii)

3 Explain why free range and organic methods of rearing are so important when considering the quality of poultry.

Materials and storage

1 Explain why a heavy-bottomed sauté pan should be used when making sauté chicken dishes that have the sauce finished in the same pan.

Preparation

1 Explain the term 'sauté' in relation to cooking chicken.

2 Explain the difference between white and dark meat in poultry.

3 Describe the method of preparation for spatchcock.

Cooking

1 Explain the reason for resting poultry before carving.

Health and safety

1 State two healthy options when finishing poultry dishes.

i)

ii)

Game

The term 'game' encompasses all wild birds and animals that are hunted for sport and human consumption. Hunting is an age-old and worldwide tradition and is still a prominent part of life in many countries.

With domestic meat and poultry being comparatively predictable in flavour, this is where game comes into its own. The different grazing and eating habits of various types of game result in subtly different flavours, which can vary from region to region – such as wild rabbit from Provence in France where the diet consists chiefly of rosemary and thyme. The varying eating habits of game therefore create individual and delicately flavoured meats, before a chef adds further ingredients to a dish.

Game is a versatile product to prepare and to cook with as it is extremely flavoursome and of good texture in its natural cooked state. Is also very lean and low in cholesterol, which instantly makes it a healthier meat option.

There are two main classes of game:

- feathered game – any wild bird;
- furred game – any wild ground animal.

Furred game is also split into two sub-categories:

- small furred game;
- large furred game.

Game is seasonal, and the quality and flavour of meat is much better when the bird or animal is in season and at its prime. The only exceptions to this are rabbit and hare, which due to their breeding habits are readily available all year round.

Feathered game

WOOD PIGEON

This bird inhabits woods, fields and gardens, feeding on grain crops and a variety of vegetable shoots. It is now viewed more as a common pest and is available all year round, although it is considered to be at its best from April to October.

WOOD PIGEON PURCHASE CHART

Feet	Red to orange in colour, medium in length, scaled effect
Feathers	Grey in colour with a white belly but can also be brown and cream in colour
Wings	Large wings the same colour as the body with dark flecks to tips of wings
Beak	Short and orange or grey in colour
Size/weight	Both: 600 g Medium-sized birds
Cuts	two legs, two wings, two breasts
Best used for:	Roasting (whole or crown), sautéing, grilling, braising/stewing, poaching, pot roasting

PHEASANT

The pheasant inhabits woodland, hedgerows and open farmland, feeding on various types of vegetation and insects. It can be farm reared and then released into the wild. Considered to be at its best from October to early February.

PHEASANT PURCHASE CHART

Feet	Long, thick legs with chicken-like spurs on cocks, grey in colour
Feathers	Cocks: Rich chestnut or golden-brown with long tail, green head and red wattling on face Hens: Mottled pale brown and black
Wings	Both: Large and rounded Cocks: Same colour as body with some light blue depending on sub-species Hens: Same colour as body
Beak	Both: Large and pointed, off-white in colour

PHEASANT PURCHASE CHART

Size/weight	Cocks: 1.5 kg Hens: 1.2 kg Large birds
Cuts	two legs, two wings, two breasts
Best used for:	Roasting (whole or crown), confit, braising/stewing, grilling sautéing, pot roasting

WOODCOCK

Inhabiting marshy inland areas and woodland areas, it is inclined to be nocturnal and feeds on surface insects and earthworms. Considered to be at its best in November and December.

WOODCOCK PURCHASE CHART

Feet	Short thin legs, yellow in colour
Feathers	Both: Mottled brown with flecks of black and beige, tiger stripe effect to the back of the head
Wings	Both: Same colour as body, short in size and slightly rounded in shape
Beak	Both: Medium pointed, off-white in colour
Size/weight	Cocks: 400 g Hens: 325 g Small birds
Cuts	Tends to be cooked whole due to small size but can get two legs, two wings, two breasts
Best used for:	Roasting (whole only due to small size), pot roasting, spatchcock, grilling, braising/stewing

SNIPE

Like woodcock, snipe inhabits marshy inland areas, but is not found in woodland areas. It feeds on small invertebrates, worms and inset larvae. Considered to be at its best in December and January.

SNIPE PURCHASE CHART	
Feet	Very thin long legs, long toes, dark grey in colour
Feathers	Both: Dull brown and cream striped head, body speckled all over
Wings	Both: Same in colour as body, small and slightly pointed
Beak	Both: Long (only game bird other than woodcock that can be **trussed** using its own beak), creamy brown in colour
Size/weight	Cock: 125 g Hen: 100 g Very small birds
Cuts	Tends to be cooked whole due to small size but can get two legs, two wings, two breasts
Best used for:	Roasting (whole only due to small size), pot roasting, spatchcock, grilling, braising/stewing

TEAL

This small duck inhabits coastal and marshy areas, feeding on seeds and small invertebrates. Considered to be at its best in October and November.

TEAL PURCHASE CHART	
Feet	Webbed feet, the same as for mallard or other duck varieties
Feathers	Drake: Head tends to be red and green in colour, body is grey/silver with an off-white tail Ducks: Brown and grey
Wings	Drakes: Same as body generally, some light green flecks depending on sub-species Ducks: Same as body Both: Large wings
Beak	Both: Short and pointed, off-white to grey in colour
Size/weight	Drakes: 500 g Ducks: 400 g Large birds
Cuts	two legs, two wings, two breasts
Best used for:	Roasting (whole or crown), confit, braising/stewing, grilling, sautéing, poaching

RED-LEGGED PARTRIDGE

This bird inhabits dry, open countryside, feeding on crops and vegetable matter. Considered to be at its best in October and November.

Red-legged (below) and grey-legged (top) partridges

RED-LEGGED PARTRIDGE PURCHASE CHART	
Feet	Short and thin red legs with very small spurs on cocks
Feathers	Both: Grey with white throats, black, brown and grey flecks to body
Wings	Both: Grey in colour, small and rounded
Beak	Both: Small and pointed, red in colour
Size/weight	Cocks: 500 g
	Hens: 400 g
	Small birds
Cuts	two legs, two wings, two breasts
Best used for:	Roasting (whole or crown), sautéing, grilling, braising/stewing, poaching, pot roasting

GREY-LEGGED PARTRIDGE

Similar to the red-legged partridge, it inhabits dry, open countryside and also feeds on crops and vegetable matter. Considered to be at its best in October and November.

GREY-LEGGED PARTRIDGE PURCHASE CHART	
Feet	Short and thin legs, grey in colour
Feathers	Both: Orange/red head, red/brown heart shape to the middle of a grey breast
Wings	Both: Red/brown in colour with a mottled effect, small rounded wings
Beak	Both: Short, grey in colour
Size/weight	Cocks: 400 g
	Hens: 350 g
	Small birds
Cuts	two legs, two wings, two breasts
Best used for:	Roasting (whole or crown), sautéing, grilling, braising/stewing, poaching, pot roasting

SQUAB

Squab is a young domesticated pigeon and therefore tends to inhabit built up areas. It is usually slaughtered when four weeks old and as its wings have not fully developed it is very tender. It will be fed regurgitated insects and domesticated food by its parent. Domesticated pigeon is considered a pest. It is available all year round, but is considered to be at its best during the summer months.

SQUAB PURCHASE CHART

Feet	Medium length and of scaled effect, red/orange in colour
Feathers	Both: Grey with white belly but can also be brown and cream
Wings	Both: Same as body in colour with dark flecks to tips, large
Beak	Short, orange or grey in colour
Size/weight	Both: 600 g
	Medium-sized birds
Cuts	two legs, two wings, two breasts
Best used for:	Roasting (whole or crown), sautéing, grilling, braising/stewing, poaching, pot roasting

QUAIL

Quail inhabit open grassland and cereal fields, feeding on grain crops and insects. They are available and at their best all year round.

QUAIL PURCHASE CHART

Feet	Short and thin, grey in colour
Feathers	Both: Mottled brown in colour, grey/off-white underneath
Wings	Both: Same as body in colour, small and rounded, short in wingspan so do not fly
Beak	Both: Short and stumpy, grey in colour
Size/weight	Cocks: 170 g
	Hens: 150 g
	Very small birds
Cuts	two legs, two wings, two breasts
Best used for:	Roasting (whole or crown), sautéing, grilling, braising/stewing, poaching, pot roasting, confit

RED GROUSE

Inhabiting moorland, the red grouse is largely dependent for feeding on wild heather but will eat insects during the summer months. Red grouse is considered to be at its best from August to October.

RED GROUSE PURCHASE CHART

Feet	Short and thick legs, covered in feathers
Feathers	Cocks: Reddish brown, two scarlet combs above eyes
	Hens: Duller in colour with no combs above eyes
Wings	Both: Wings same as body in colour, large and rounded, very powerful
Beak	Both: Small and pointed, black in colour
Size/weight	Cocks: 750 g
	Hens: 650 g
	Medium-sized birds
Cuts	two legs, two wings, two breasts
Best used for:	Roasting (whole or crown), sautéing, grilling, braising/stewing, poaching, pot roasting

AGE

It is not easy to determine the age of any wild animal, but there are three main indicators that can give a good indication of an approximate age:

● Spurs – with cock (male) birds, the spurs get longer as the birds become older.

- Beaks – the younger a bird, the more pliable the beak will be.
- Feet – in younger birds with webbed feet, the webbing will tear more easily.

HANGING AND PREPARATION

When preparing game birds to be hung or for cooking, the following points should be taken into consideration and the bird thoroughly checked:

- Tears or breaks to the skin and broken limbs.
- Bruising or shot damage.
- Skin should not be slimy to the touch, smell pungent or have darkened patches.
- Prominent breast and shape.
- Not too dark meat, which could mean excess blood in the meat due to not being properly hung or being bruised.
- Size of the bird.

Small furred game

WILD RABBIT

Rabbit inhabits farmland and woodland, feeding off pasture land and crops. Regarded as a pest, it is available all year round, but it is considered to be at its best between September and November. Domesticated rabbit differs greatly in flavour and texture as it does not benefit from the same varied diet as wild rabbit, nor will it have the same amount of exercise and therefore it will use its muscle tissues less.

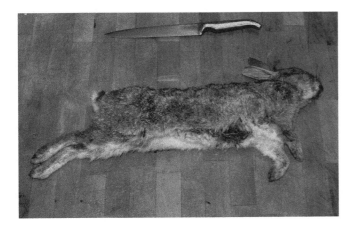

WILD RABBIT PURCHASE CHART	
Appearance	Grey/brown in colour, long ears, short front legs, grey and white tail
Meat	Rosy pink in colour, quite strong in flavour compared with 'hutch' rabbit, which is lighter in colour and has a flavour similar to poultry
Joints	two legs, one saddle*, two shoulders, one ribcage, one liver
Size/weight	1.5 kg
Best used for:	Stewing/braising, grilling, poaching, confit, roasting, pot roasting, sautéing

*Saddle is cut as one joint for roasting but can be cut into two separate joints for other dishes.

BROWN HARE

The hare inhabits exposed grassland and more open woodland areas, feeding on pasture land and crops. Baby hares, known as leverets, are much more tender than the fully grown hare. Brown hare is considered to be at its best between October and January.

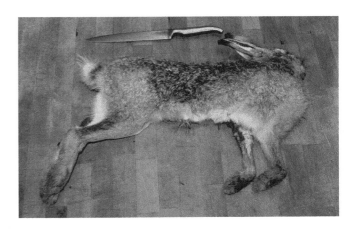

BROWN HARE PURCHASE CHART	
Appearance	Coat colour can vary depending on age, either being light ginger/grey or a deep reddish brown. Long black ears, very long hind legs and a black and white tail
Meat	Dark red in colour, very strong in flavour
Joints	two legs, one saddle, two shoulders, one ribcage, two liver, blood
Size/weight	Adult: 3 kg Leveret: 2 kg
Best used for:	Braising/stewing, roasting, pot roasting, confit

AGE

The best indicators of the age of small furred game animals are:

● Teeth – in young rabbits and hares the two front teeth will be quite white, clean and not protrude from the mouth.

● Feet – in both rabbits and hares, the longer the claws, the older the animal.

● Ears – the ears on young rabbits and hares will tear more easily.

HANGING AND PREPARATION

When preparing small furred game to be hung or for cooking, the following points should be taken into consideration and the animal thoroughly checked:

● excess blood on fur;

● tears or breaks to the skin and broken limbs;

● shot damage and bruising;

● pale pink meat with no dark spots;

● fresh smell and not be tacky to the touch;

● size of the animal.

Large furred game

RED DEER

The red deer typically thrives on open moorland and eats grasses and tree bark. Considered to be at its best in July and August for stags and December to February for hinds.

RED DEER PURCHASE CHART

Appearance	Both: Dark reddish brown to grey in colour
Meat	Rich red in colour, very strong, very little fat
Joints	two haunches or legs, two flanks, one saddle, one best end, two shoulders, one neck, two small fillets
Size/weight	Stags: 90–190 kg
	Hinds: 63–120 kg
	Large deer
Best used for:	Sautéing, grilling, stewing/braising, grilling, roasting, pot roasting

FALLOW DEER

Tending to be more prominent on open pasture land, the fallow deer again will feed off pasture land and tree bark. Considered to be at its best in October and November for bucks and from December to February for does.

FALLOW DEER PURCHASE CHART

Appearance	Both: Light to darker brown in colour with white spots in the summer months
Meat	Rich red in colour, strong, very little fat
Joints	two haunches or legs, two flanks, one saddle, one best end, two shoulders, one neck, two small fillets
Size/weight	Bucks: 46–94 kg
	Does: 35–56 kg
	Medium deer
Best used for:	Sautéing, grilling, stewing/braising, grilling, roasting, pot roasting, confit

PURCHASING AND PREPARING

Two important factors should be taken into consideration when considering the purchase of large furred game:

● Time of year – bucks or stags (male deer) are at their best just before the breeding season commences. This is because they have built up fat reserves to give them strength at this particular time of year. The same applies for does or hinds (female deer) as food will have been rich at this time of year which will have allowed them to prepare for the winter. This small amount of fat adds to the quality and flavour of the meat.

● Antlers – It is advisable to steer clear of 'trophy animals', such as large adult deer with large antlers (bucks or stags in most species), as these will be older animals, and even though they would have a high meat yield it will be tough and if taken at the wrong time of year can be tainted by a strong musk flavour.

When preparing large furred game to be hung or for cooking, the following points should be taken into consideration and the animal thoroughly checked:

● shot damage, which tends to be more prominent in large game;

● deep-red coloured meat, strong in smell but not too pungent;

● excess fat and/or marbling.

Hanging of game

It is usual to hang game once it has been killed. Before hanging, the meat is often quite mild in flavour and is unrefined in taste and texture. Older animals will also tend to be quite tough after cooking if they have not been hung.

Hanging game for a few days in a cool place allows enzymes within the carcass to initiate a chemical reaction. This changes the tenderness of the meat by allowing the muscle to relax and helps to define some flavour compounds.

Terms used in the hanging of game are:

● Hanging – the hanging of a game carcass in order to improve the flavour and/or texture of meat.

● De-furring/feathering – the removal of fur or feathers from the carcass.

● Drawing/gutting – the removal of the internal organs of the carcass.

● Bleeding – the draining of blood from the carcass.

Feathered game is hung to mature the flavour of the bird; the flavour will not be at its best if the bird is eaten straight after being killed. Birds to be hung should be bled but left feathered and undrawn. A bird can be hung for between one and seven days, the exact length of time being dependent on the weather

conditions, type of bird and taste preference. The modern tastes of the general public seem to prefer a shorter hanging time so that the full gaminess of the flavour does not develop.

Pheasant and woodcock should be hung for five to seven days; snipe should be hung for up to five days; grouse achieves its best potential when hung for three to four days; while wild duck should be hung for only two to three days. Farmed quail does not benefit from being hung and should therefore be frozen or cooked immediately after being killed.

Furred game is hung not only to improve and develop its flavour but also to tenderize the meat. Hare and wild rabbit should be hung and bled, but not skinned or drawn until the hanging time is complete. Venison is usually bled and gutted but not skinned before being hung.

CHEF'S TIP Ensure that all factors are taken into consideration when deciding how long to hang game: you do not want to waste produce by under or over 'ripening'.

Wild rabbit and hare only needs to be hung for one day to mature the meat fully, while venison is usually at its best after five days of hanging. Domesticated rabbit, if used, does not benefit from being hung, and like farmed quail should be frozen or cooked immediately after being killed.

To be suitable for hanging game, a room must be:

● cool and dry;

● well ventilated;

● inaccessible to insects, vermin or other wild animals.

In hot weather the meat will need to be stored in a refrigerated room at between 0°C and 5°C.

A carcass should be hung so that the air can circulate freely all around it. Feathered game should be hung by the neck and furred game by the hind legs. With both types, it should be ensured that the carcasses are hung separately and do not touch one another otherwise the meat will bruise and putrefy, rendering it inedible.

CHEF'S TIP Older game can be further tenderized by marinating for 24 hours.

Preparation of feathered game

All birds are plucked and drawn using the same method. It is a tiresome process but one that requires attention at all times, especially when drawing. If it is not done properly it will not provide good results, and it will become messy and take longer to do.

Step-by-step: Plucking

1. Always pluck in a draught-free area and ensure that a bag or box is close to hand into which feathers and down can be placed. Feathers should only be plucked a few at a time. It is easiest to start by plucking the breast of the bird and work around it, followed by the wings.

2. Lay the bird on its back and start plucking from the base of the breast. To pull the feathers away, hold the skin taught at the base of the feathers and pull firmly in a downwards motion. Once the breast has been plucked, complete the sides, back and legs.

3. To remove the wing feathers, with the bird still on its back, extend the wing fully by pulling away from the carcass in order to spread the feathers as far as possible. Pluck out the feathers, remembering to only go as far as the wing tip joints as the wing tips will be cut off. Repeat the process to the back of the wings.

4. Finally, remove the neck and tail feathers.

Once a bird has been fully plucked, it will need to have its innards removed. The only exceptions to this are snipe and woodcock, which after having the gizzard removed can be cooked whole. In addition to being drawn, ducks should have the oil glands at the base of their tails removed as if left these can give the meat a musky flavour.

Step-by-step: Drawing

1. Lay the plucked bird on its back. Cut off the hind and front toes and the wing tips. Singe any downy feathers that may still be on the bird.

2. Cut off the bird's head from the top of the neck, then using a sharp knife slit through the skin at the back of the neck, down to the shoulders. Peel back the flap of skin (leaving it intact) and sever the neck where it joins the body.

3. Feel into the neck cavity for the windpipe, gullet and crop and gently pull free. To remove the intestines and innards, make an incision by pinching the skin at the base of the breastbone, cutting away from the bird so as to not pierce the intestines. Create an opening from left to right just large enough to insert a finger.

5. To remove the two oil glands, use a sharp knife to cut out the tail section of the bird that contains the glands.

6. To remove the gizzard, use a sharp knife to make a slit in the abdomen, slightly right of the centre. Insert a trussing needle to locate the hard lump of the gizzard. Pull out gizzard and sever it from the remaining innards.

4. Put a finger inside the bird and gently loosen the membranes that attach the innards to the muscle. Carefully remove the innards from the bird, using your forefinger and thumb. They should come out in one whole piece. Ensure the bird is checked thoroughly and all innards are removed.

The wishbone can be removed once a bird has been plucked and drawn. This should be carried out before any type of portioning, preparation or carving.

Step-by-step: Removing the wishbone

 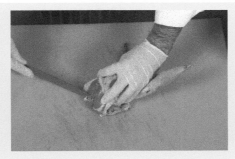 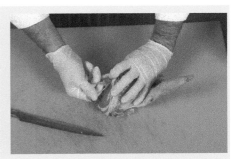

1. Expose the wishbone. It is attached to the wing bones at both sides of the bird, runs either side of the cavity left by the crop and meets at the tip of the breastbone.

2. Slip a sharp knife behind the bone and cut in a downwards motion to release at the wing. Repeat the other side.

3. When the wishbone has been fully detached from the wings, carefully twist it three to four times until it is released from the tip of the breastbone.

Most game birds have very tough and sinewy legs, which if used in a dish will require a long cooking time to tenderize them. Their strong taste makes them ideal in stocks. The breast, however, can be cooked quickly and will only have one piece of sinew running along the inner fillet.

Step-by-step: *Removing legs and breasts*

1. Pulling the leg away from the body, cut into the thigh muscle and around the oyster.

2. When removing the breast, cut along one side of the breastbone, starting at the neck and moving down to the vent. At the wing, cut through the second joint, leaving the bone on the breast. Repeat the process on the other side of the bird. The only bones in the cut breasts will be those from the wings.

3. Trim and remove any excess skin from the breasts. The bone and skin may be removed depending on how the breast is to be prepared.

4. The wing bones should be cleaned by scraping down the flesh and removing the ends.

Cooking a game bird whole results in very even cooking and gives good moisture retention. It also creates a visually appealing and uniform dish.

The wishbone should be removed before trussing.

Step-by-step: Trussing whole birds for roasting

1. Thread a trussing needle with butcher's twine.

2. Assuming the wing is intact, push the needle between the bones in the wing, just after the first joint from the tip, then through the fleshy part of the wing bone. Push the needle through the carcass, under the breast meat and out the other side, piercing the wing bone on the other side.

3. Pull the twine through, ensuring that enough extra line is left on the other side to tie-off.

4. Pull the legs back and place the needle under the bone at the first joint. Push the needle through the carcass and out the other side, making sure to hold the legs back. Pull the twine through and remove the needle.

5. Tie the twine in a butcher's slipknot, pull tight.

6. Tie a further knot to help hold the twine in place.

Splitting and flattening is best used with small game birds that are to be grilled, barbecued or sautéed. Remove the wishbone before you start.

Step-by-step: Splitting and flattening

1. Using poultry scissors, split the bird lengthways by cutting down the backbone from the crop to the vent. Repeat to the other side and remove the backbone.

2. Turn the bird over. Use the palm of your hand to flatten the breast, pulling the legs around to either side of the breast.

3. Push a skewer under the leg bone at the first joint, go through the breast and out the other side. Repeat for the other leg. By doing this it will hold the legs and breast together and allow the bird to cook evenly.

VIDEO CLIP Preparation of the breast of a small game bird for frying

Basic preparation of small furred game

After hanging, small furred game animals need to be skinned and drawn, with the same techniques generally applying to both rabbits and hares. The animals should be skinned before being drawn. Ensure a container is at hand to dispose of the fur and innards. During the hanging process, the blood will collect in the chest cavity and can be retained for use in certain dishes.

Step-by-step: Skinning, drawing and jointing

1. Remove the head as shown

2. Laying on its back make an incision as shown.

3. Carefully open the cavity and inspect the area.

4. Remove all of the intestines within the cavity as shown.

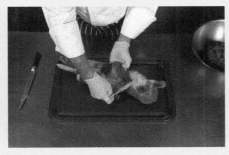

5. Peel back the fur as shown and work your hands between the flesh all around.

6. Firmly hold the skin which has been split along the middle, pull in a smooth motion until it reaches the neck at one end and the tail at the other.

7. Ensure the skin is pulled completely over as shown.

8. Using a chopping knife, remove all four feet.

9. Laying the rabbit on its back carefully cut around the anus, taking care not to slice inside.

10. Remove the anal tract in one movement and discard.

11. Cut around the legs, between the ball and socket joint and remove.

12. Cut around the shoulders and remove.

13. Cut the top portion off as shown.

14. Trim any excess skin away, then cut the bottom portion away.

15. Laying the saddle down trim around the edge and remove any sinew.

16. This shows the jointed rabbit, the saddle has been cut in half, this can be trimmed further into loins as required – removing all the bones.

VIDEO CLIP Dissecting a hare

VIDEO CLIP Preparation of a saddle of hare for roasting

Basic preparation of large furred game: venison

The skinning and gutting of large furred game is carried out in much the same way as it is for small furred game, but it will produce extra joints and obviously will be much larger in size. Large furred game will /provide the following joints:

- haunch or leg (including rump);
- loin;
- shoulder;
- breast;

- middle neck;
- best end;
- saddle with fillets.

VIDEO CLIP   Preparation of a loin of venison

VIDEO CLIP   Boning, barding and tying a haunch of venison

Step-by-step: Removing and preparing the best end

1. Cutting through the best end to create two racks

2. Pulling back the fat from the rack

3. Removing the fat and sinew from the bones cleanly

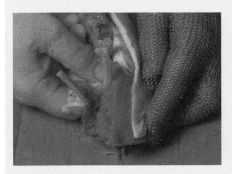

4. Exposing the bones from the rack

5. Trimming away the sinew from the best end

6. Preparing venison cutlets

Removing and preparing the best end

1 The best end should be cut with seven bones, one of which will be removed to produce a six-bone best end. Cut close to the last bone on the best end, all the way through to the backbone. Repeat on the other side, joining the cuts at the backbone.

2 Being careful not to damage the eye of meat on each loin, gently saw through the backbone to detach the saddle from the best end and middle neck.

3 From the bottom of the best end, count seven bones. Cut across to and through the backbone.

4 Keeping as close as possible to the bone, cut lengthways along the backbone to loosen the meat and down to the top of the rib bones. Repeat this on the other side.

5 Pull the eye meat away from the backbone and use a meat cleaver to cut through the base of the rib bones.

6 Remove any meat between the bones then scrape the rib bones clean with a small knife.

7 Clean the base of the eye meat and remove any unwanted sinew.

8 Remove the sinew from the outer side of the best end and cut out the last bone closest to the end, which will give a six-bone best end.

9 This can now be cut into cutlets or two three-bone portions for roasting whole.

Step-by-step: Preparing the saddle

The saddle can be left on the bone, with just the sinew removed, and roasted whole. The loins are removed in much the same way as the best end is removed, except there are no ribs and the meat is cut away from the bone.

1. The fillets, which are usually quite small, should be removed.

2. Cutting either side of the backbone remove the two loins as shown.

3. Cut the flesh away taking care to leave as little flesh on the bones as possible.

4. Separate the loin from the sinew as shown.

5. With the loin, remove all sinew using a sharp knife, use long strokes with the blade to give a smooth finish.

6. Trim the fillets in the same way as the loin.

7. Cut the loin into even pieces, then roll in cling film tightly to create a uniform shape When preparing steaks, the loin can be wrapped in plastic film and chilled in a refrigerator for an hour or overnight to firm up to give a cleaner cut when portioning.

8. Cut the loins neatly into medallions as shown. The loins can be left whole or cut into cannons, medallions or steaks.

Storage of game

It is most convenient for kitchens to receive prepared game as the whole process of preparing game – hanging, bleeding, drawing and jointing – is very time consuming.

Once game has been hung for the correct amount of time it is quite safe to freeze the meat. All game that is to be frozen should be sealed in an airtight and water-impervious material, such as polythene bags. It must then be clearly labelled, stating the type of meat, the date of freezing and the date it should be used by. Feathered game can be safely frozen for six to nine months and furred game for up to six months. Once the meat is defrosted, it should be cooked immediately.

When refrigerating game, it should preferably be stored in a separate refrigerator to all other foods to minimize any possible risk of cross-contamination. As with other meats, game stored within the refrigerator should placed so that cooked items are at the top and raw items are at the bottom. Any raw or defrosting items should regularly be drained of excess blood or juices to ensure that the meat is not tainted. All items stored should be tightly wrapped and clearly labelled.

Game recipes

Pot-roasted snipe in stout

Pot-roasted snipe in stout with onion and rosemary dumplings

Ingredients	4 portions	10 portions
Snipe (whole)	4	10
Stout	250 ml	750 ml
Game stock	250 ml	750 ml
Plain flour	50 g	125 g
Butter	50 g	125 g
Carrot, celery, turnip, swede into macédoine	100 g of each	220 g of each
Soft flour	95 g	230 g
Baking powder	5 g	20 g
Water	100 ml	250 ml
Beef suet	50 g	125 g
Olive oil	1 tbsp	2 tbsp
Onion (finely chopped)	1	2
Fresh rosemary (finely chopped)	1 tbsp	2 tbsp
Good-quality salt and pepper	to taste	to taste
Turned Carrots (blanched)	12	30

energy	cal	fat	sat fat	carb	sugar	protein	fibre
3319 kJ	792 kcal	33.2 g	15.2 g	60.3 g	28.4 g	63 g	11.9 g

METHOD OF WORK

1   Preheat an oven to 180°C.

2   Season and flour each whole snipe. Melt the butter in a large ovenproof casserole dish. Place the snipe into the dish and lightly colour on all sides.

3   Remove the snipe and leave to one side. In the same dish, brown the macédoine of vegetables, season well and add the stout and game stock and bring to the boil. Return the snipe to the casserole dish, cover with a lid and cook in the preheated oven for 45 minutes.

4   In a small saucepan season and sweat down the onions with the olive oil and rosemary until tender. Remove from the heat and cool.

5   Once cooled, stir in the suet and sieve in the soft flour and baking powder. Slowly add the water until a dough is formed. Shape into medium size round balls, allowing one per portion.

6   In a pan of boiling salted water cook the dumplings until they float. Remove from the water and leave to cool slightly.

7   Once the snipe is cooked, remove from the sauce and leave to one side to rest. Pass the sauce through a strainer or chinois into a clean pan. Correct the seasoning and consistency.

8   Now return the snipe and dumplings to the sauce, with the blanched carrots. Place back in the oven at 180°C and cook for a further 15 minutes.

9   For service, allow one snipe and dumpling per portion with a serving of vegetables and sauce.

CHEF'S TIP   Always remove excess flour from products before frying to stop the starch from burning and leaving a bitter taste in the final dish. This will also prevent lumps of raw flour appearing in a sauce.

Stuffed pheasant legs

Stuffed pheasant legs with baby vegetables and cep foam

Ingredients	4 portions	10 portions
Pheasant legs	4	10
Pheasant breast	2	5
Duck livers	250 g	625 g
Juniper berries (soaked in the gin below)	100 g	250 g
Gin	30 ml	75 ml
Double cream	300 ml	750 ml
Onion	1	2
Garlic	1 clove	2–3 cloves
Thyme	a few sprigs	a few sprigs
Butter	50 g	125 g
Brown chicken stock	150 ml	400 ml
Dried cep mushrooms	20 g	50 g
Baby leeks and turnips	4	10
Fresh herbs	10 g	25 g
Good-quality salt and pepper	to taste	to taste

energy	cal	fat	sat fat	carb	sugar	protein	fibre
3648 kJ	880 kcal	70.5 g	37 g	12.7 g	3.6 g	44.9 g	2.1 g

METHOD OF WORK

1   Tunnel bone each pheasant leg to remove the thighbone. Neatly trim the drumstick flesh.

2   Season the duck livers. Over a high heat, quickly pan fry the livers and the soaked juniper berries in a shallow pan. Flambé with the gin. Remove from the heat and allow to cool.

3   In a food processor blend the pheasant breast and duck liver. Pass the mix through the back of a sieve to remove any sinew or large pieces.

4   Semi-whip half the cream, ensuring the bowl used is freezing cold before use, then fold in the passed pheasant breast. Season, cover, place in a fridge and chill.

5   Once chilled, place the mixture into a piping bag with a plain tube and pipe into the legs. Carefully wrap the filled legs in the pig's caul before wrapping in plastic film and chilling further in the refrigerator.

6   Preheat an oven to 180°C.

7   Soak the cep mushrooms in a small pan of boiling water for ten minutes. Remove the ceps and drain any excess water.

8   In a sauté pan gently sweat the garlic, onion and thyme in a little butter. Add the ceps, stock and a small amount of the water the ceps were soaked in and reduce by half. Add the remaining cream. Continue to cook for a further five–ten minutes to infuse flavour into the sauce.

9   Using a hand blender or a food processor, blend the sauce ingredients together to maximize the cep flavour. Pass through a chinois.

10 Place into a tall container and use a hand blender to create a foam – if required add a little lecithin to this to aid the foaming process.

11 Season the stuffed legs. In a medium-hot pan with a small amount of oil seal the legs to give colour. Then place into a hot oven to cook for about 25 minutes. Remove from the oven and allow to rest.

12 To serve, warm the baby vegetables in butter arrange on the plate with slices of stuffed leg and spoon a little foam around as shown.

CHEF'S TIP   Dried wild mushrooms can be an economic commodity. As they are dried their flavour is much stronger. They are as good as fresh mushrooms for flavouring stocks, but only half the amount is required.

Crown of partridge with turned vegetables

Ingredients	4 portions	10 portions
Crown of partridge	2	5
Mirepoix	150 g	400 g
Unsalted butter	125 g	250 g
Blanched turned vegetables	1	2
Game stock	200 ml	500 ml
Redcurrant jelly	50 g	125 g
Good quality salt and pepper	to taste	to taste

energy	cal	fat	sat fat	carb	sugar	protein	fibre
2039 kJ	490 kcal	33.4 g	18.2 g	10.5 g	10 g	37.5 g	1.3 g

METHOD OF WORK

1 Preheat the oven to 180°C.

2 Soften 100/200 g of the butter. Season the crown of partridge and coat the breasts with the butter. Place the crown on a tray with the mirepoix on the base. Roast in the oven for 15–20 minutes until golden brown and cooked all the way through. Use a digital thermometer to measure the temperature of the partridge inside. Remove from the oven, place on a cooling rack and rest.

3 Drain off any excess fat from the tray and then place on a stove and heat through. Add the game stock and deglaze the pan. Simmer for a few minutes then pass through a fine chinois into a clean pan. Warm the sauce. Add the redcurrant jelly and melt into the sauce. Correct the seasoning and consistency.

4 To serve, arrange the partridge on the plate with turned vegetables and the sauce.

CHEF'S TIP Roasting certain game birds on the bone can help to keep the meat moist and improve flavour. Coating with butter before roasting can also greatly improve the succulence of the meat.

Loin of rabbit wrapped in Pancetta

Ingredients	4 portions	10 portions
Rabbit loins	4	10
Chicken mousse	200 g	500 g
Medjool dates	50 g	125 g
Diced shallots	10 g	25 g
Madeira	40 ml	100 ml
Pancetta slices	16	40
Round shallots	8	20
Brussel sprouts	8	20
Madeira sauce	200 ml	500 ml
Vegetable oil	for cooking	for cooking
Salt and pepper	to taste	to taste

energy	cal	fat	sat fat	carb	sugar	protein	fibre
7235 kJ	1728 kcal	78.2 g	38.5 g	12.6 g	9.8 g	239.1 g	3.4 g

METHOD OF WORK

1 Sauté the shallots in butter until soft with no colour; deglaze with Madeira and reduce until syrupy; chill.

2 Stone and dice the dates mix with the shallots and chicken mousse.

3 Seal the rabbit loins in a hot pan, chill well.

4 Wrap the loins in the mousse and pancetta, then a sheet of oiled tin foil roll to create a sausage shape and chill.

5 Roast the round shallots in the oven until very soft, keep warm.

6 Cook the sprouts in boiling water until tender.

7 Heat a little oil in a frying pan and seal the rabbit evenly, roast in a 180°C oven until the core temperature reaches 70°C.

8 Remove the foil and slice, serve with the sprouts, shallots and Madeira sauce.

Quail and black pudding sausages

Ingredients	4 portions	10 portions
Quail meat (leg and breast removed from the bone)	600 g	1.5 kg
Black pudding	200 g	500 g
Breadcrumbs	150 g	375 g
Double cream	100 ml	250 ml
Onions diced	50 g	125 g
Egg	1	3
Apple Juice	100 g	250 g
Agar-agar	2 g	5 g
Red chicory and watercress	garnish	garnish
Partridge or chicken stock (brown)	200 ml	500 ml
Cider	100 ml	250 ml
Unsalted butter	100 g	250 g
Tomato coulis	50 ml	125 ml
Good-quality salt and pepper	to taste	to taste

energy	cal	fat	sat fat	carb	sugar	protein	fibre
4109 kJ	985 kcal	68.3 g	31.7 g	42.2 g	6.8 g	48.6 g	1.7 g

METHOD OF WORK

1 Remove the quail breasts and flatten in between cling film.

2 Finely chop the black pudding and the quail leg meat and pass through a mincing machine. Soak the breadcrumbs in the smaller quantity of cream.

3 Preheat an oven to 180°C.

4 Fry the onions in a small amount of the butter in a frying pan until transparent but no colour. Allow to cool.

5 Mix the minced meat, egg and onions together to form a paste. Fold in the breadcrumbs and beat to a paste. Season well.

6 Fill a piping bag fitted with a plain tube with the sausage mix. Pipe the mixture onto the breasts and then form a sausage in cling film.

7 Place on a tray in a refrigerator to set.

8 Combine the apple juice and cider with the agar-agar and allow dissolving, heating until the liquid boils, removing from the heat and pouring into a square container ½ cm thick.

9 Allow to cool then cut into suitable squares for garnish.

10 In a frying pan seal the sausages. Then place in a preheated oven at 200°C for 15–20 minutes until cooked all the way through and golden brown.

11 To serve, slice the quail, place between the red chicory and finish with apple and cider gel, tomato coulis and watercress.

CHEF'S TIP   Making sausages can be a good and cost-effective way of utilizing leftover meats.

Rabbit stuffed with black pudding

Saddle of rabbit stuffed with black pudding, braised endive and rosemary jus

Ingredients	makes 4 portions	makes 10 portions
Rabbit saddles, boned whole	2	5
Mirepoix for roasting	300 g	500 g
Black pudding	200 g	500 g
Caul fat	100 g	250 g
Braised endive	2	5
Fondant potato	4	10
Rabbit bones from saddle	2 carcasses	5 carcasses
Mirepoix for jus	100 g	250 g
Rosemary	2 sprigs	5 sprigs
Brown stock	200 ml	500 ml
White wine	40 ml	100 ml
Unsalted butter	40 g	100 g
Salt and pepper	To taste	To taste

energy	cal	fat	sat fat	carb	sugar	protein	fibre
2141 kJ	513 kcal	38.7 g	16.8 g	11.2 g	2.7 g	28.8 g	1.5 g

4   For the jus, cut the bones into small pieces and brown in a hot saucepan.

5   Add the mirepoix and lightly colour, add the wine and reduce by half.

6   Add the stock and simmer for 30 minutes.

7   Strain through muslin and add half the rosemary, reduce to coating consistency, strain again and infuse with the rest of the rosemary.

8   Brown the rabbit in a roasting pan then remove, add the mirepoix and soften.

9   Place the rabbit on the mirepoix and roast in a 200°C oven for 20–25 minutes.

10   Leave to rest for ten minutes.

11   Carve and serve with the endive, fondant potato and jus.

CHEF'S TIP   Try using different dried fruit with game dishes as the sweetness helps bring out the rich game flavour of the meat. Cranberries can give a nice sweet and sour effect.

METHOD OF WORK

1   Place the rabbit saddles top side down on a red chopping board.

2   Fill the cavity with the black pudding, roll together.

3   Cover with caul fat and tie with string, chill.

Loin of venison with baba ganoush

Loin of venison with baba ganoush, beetroot and balsamic purée, chestnuts and game jus

Ingredients	makes *4 portions*	makes *10 portions*
Loin of venison	500 g	1.2 kg
Sumac spice	100 g	250 g
Aubergine	4	10
Tahini paste	1 tsp	2.5 tsp
Garlic	1 clove	3 cloves
Lemon juice and zest	1 lemon	3 lemons
Olive oil	100 ml	250 ml
Cooked beetroot	200 g	500 g
Balsamic vinegar	40 ml	100 ml
Caster sugar	20 g	50 g
Chestnuts	8	20
Game jus	200 ml	500 ml
Salt and pepper	to taste	to taste

energy	cal	fat	sat fat	carb	sugar	protein	fibre
2710 kJ	649 kcal	37.1 g	8.6 g	29.2 g	15.2 g	49.1 g	2 g

METHOD OF WORK

1   Preheat an oven to 180°C.

2   Split the aubergine and roast in the preheated oven in a little olive oil. Cool until the outside is golden and crisp and the centre is soft and cooked through.

3   Cool the aubergine and remove the flesh. Pass through a fine sieve. Purée the garlic and add to the aubergine along with the sumac, tahini, lemon juice and zest and the olive oil, season to taste.

4   Cook the venison loins in a water bath at 56°C for 20 minutes or until the centre reaches 56°C.

5   Blitz the beetroot to a smooth paste, make a gastric with the vinegar and sugar and add to the beetroot.

6   Heat the chestnuts in the game jus.

7   Remove the loins from the water bath and dry; seal in a very hot pan to colour lightly.

8   Carve the venison and serve with the baba ganoush, beetroot, chestnuts and game jus.

CHEF'S TIP   For venison, the longer the resting period, the more tender the meat becomes.

Confit of pigeon

Confit of pigeon with spinach and beetroot salad

Ingredients	4 portions	10 portions
Pigeon legs	8	20
Duck fat	1 l	2.5 l
Rock salt	50 g	125 g
Granulated sugar	50 g	125 g
Orange/lemon zest	½ each	1 each
Star anise	1	2–3
Cinnamon stick	½ inch piece	1 inch piece
Baby spinach	100 g	250 g
Cooked beetroot	200 g	500 g
Balsamic vinegar	50 ml	125 ml
Caster sugar	10 g	25 g
Beetroot leaves	to garnish	
Mizuna	to garnish	
Bacon lardons	200 g	500 g
Salt and pepper	to taste	to taste

energy	cal	fat	sat fat	carb	sugar	protein	fibre
1712 kJ	409 kcal	25.1 g	8.5 g	23.5 g	20.5 g	22.8 g	1.8 g

METHOD OF WORK

1   Mix the sugar, salt cinnamon, star anise and citrus together and blitz in a food processor.

2   Sprinkle over the flesh side of the pigeon legs, marinate covered in the fridge for two hours.

3   Wash off marinade and dry, place into duck fat and cook slowly on top of the stove until tender.

4   Thinly slice the beetroot and dry, boil the balsamic and sugar together to make a gastric, mix the beetroot with the gastric and season well.

5   Fry the lardons in some of the duck fat and drain, Crisp up the legs in hot duck fat.

6   Place some spinach leaves on the plate, next the legs and mizuna.

7   Scatter over the lardons and dress with the lardon fat, season well.

Sous vide venison and pithivier

Ingredients	4 portions	10 portions
Venison loin	4 × 120 g	10 × 120 g
Olive oil	100 ml	250 ml
Thyme	4 sprigs	10 sprigs
Bay leaf	4 halves	10 halves
Diced venison shoulder	400 g	1 kg
Mirepoix	100 g	250 g
Red wine	50 ml	125 ml
Port	50 ml	125 ml
Bouquet garni	1 medium	1 large
Juniper berries	2	5
Game stock	1 l	2.5 l
Puff pastry	400 g	1 kg
Egg wash	as needed	as needed
Butternut squash	400 g	1 kg
Unsalted butter	50 g	125 g
Crones (Japanese artichokes)	160 g	400 g
Cavolo nero	200 g	500 g
Salt and pepper	to taste	to taste

energy	cal	fat	sat fat	carb	sugar	protein	fibre
4170 kJ	1001 kcal	66.6 g	23 g	53.9 g	9.8 g	51.5 g	2.9 g

METHOD OF WORK

1   Place the loins in individual sous vide bags with one sprig of thyme and half a bay leaf, olive oil salt and pepper, seal tightly.

2   Caramelize the shoulder with the mirepoix, deglaze with the alcohol, add the stock and bouquet garni, braise for two hours or until tender.

3   Drain off the meat remove the vegetables and reserve the cooking liquor, **flake** into pieces, cut the mirepoix into **brunoise** and add to the meat, reduce 25 per cent of the cooking liquor down and bind into the meat, season well, roll into balls in cling film and chill.

4   Once cold make the pithiviers, roll out the puff pastry and cut out discs, and brush with a little water, place the shoulder meat on top and then cover with another disc of puff pastry.

5   Seal the edges, egg wash and chill.

6   Once chilled score with a knife.

7   Sweat the diced squash slowly in butter until very tender, blitz and pass.

8   Prepare the crones.

9   Cook the loins in a water bath at 62°C until the centre reaches 60°C.

10 Bake the pithiviers until golden.

11 Pass the remaining cooking liquor through muslin and reduce to sauce consistency.

12 Sauté crones in butter until tender with the cavolo nero.

13 To plate, remove loins from bag and seal in a very hot pan to colour; serve with the squash puree, pithivier, crones, cavolo nero and sauce.

SOURCING Game to eat is an industry leader promoting game within the UK, sourcing sustainable, local quality produce; use the following link to broaden your knowledge: http://www.gametoeat.co.uk

Guest Chef

Roasted Silver Hill duck breast, confit duck pie, duck parfait, barley, nettle and hazelnut pilaff, celeriac purée, liquorish jus

Chef John Crowe
Centre (college): North West Regional College, Northern Ireland

Silver Hill duck is produced in the village of Emyvale, Co Monaghan. It is a duck that is full of flavour, succulent, tender and consistent in its quality. Chef Heston Blumenthal showcased the Silver Hill duck in his programme *In search of perfection*. The award winning Broighter Gold rapeseed oil is grown and processed in Limavady, near Derry. It has half the saturated fat of olive oil, ten times more omega 3 and also vitamin E.

Ingredients	2 portions
1 Silver Hill Duck	1 approx. 1.6 kg
Duck confit	
Leg and thigh	
Broighter Gold rapeseed oil	Sufficient to cover
Rock salt,	10 g
Garlic	2 cloves
Peppercorns	5 g
Bayleaf	1
Star anise	1
Thyme	1 sprig
Rosemary	1 sprig
Cep mushrooms	50 g
Spinach	50 g
Shallot	50 g
Jus	to bind
Pie pastry	
Plain flour	200 g
Soft butter	100 g
Water	75 ml
Salt	2 g
Duck parfait	
Duck livers	200
Double cream	100 ml
egg	1
Brandy, port, madeira,	10 ml
Garlic	½ clove
Clarified butter	200 ml
Fleur de sel, milled pepper	to taste
Barley pilaff	
Barley	50 g
Shallot, nettle leaves, hazelnuts	1, 20, 4
Chicken stock	100 ml
Butter	25 g
Cream cheese	50 g
Whipped cream	25 ml
Salt, pepper	to taste
Liquorish jus	50 ml
Celeriac puree	
Celeriac	100 g
Milk	35 ml
Cream,	35 ml
Salt, pepper	to taste

METHOD OF WORK

Duck

1 Remove the duck breasts, trim, score and reserve for cooking later. Next remove duck leg and thigh, remove sinew, coat in rock salt and refrigerate for 24 hours. Wash off salt, pat dry, dry fry to develop colour on the skin and place in a casserole dish with aromatics and cook in the oven for one-and-a-half hours at 150°C. Once cooked remove, and allow to cool in the oil. Then strip meat from the bone and use in step 3.

Parfait

2 Blend duck livers, add whole egg, alcohol, cream, fleur de sel and milled pepper. Next add clarified butter (room temperature), then pass through fine chinois into terrine and cook in a bain-marie at 130°C for 40 minutes.

Pie

3 Mix confit meat with fried shallot, ceps and spinach, add a little jus to bind, season and fill pre-prepared pie moulds. Brush with egg yolk and cream and bake for 15 minutes at 180°C.

Barley pilaff

4 Pre-soak barley, wash nettles three times (remember to use gloves) and blanch and reserve. Dry roast hazelnut, skin and slice thinly on mandolin, reserve. Sweat shallot in butter, add drained barley, gradually add chicken stock until just cooked, then incorporate nettles, hazelnuts, cream cheese and whipped cream, check seasoning.

Celariac puree

5 Place celeriac in milk and cream and cook until tender, purée and pass through fine sieve, season to taste.

Duck breast

6 Heat small frying pan without oil, add duck breasts, seal fat side down to develop, add star anise to pan and baste, turn and seal other side. Roast for eight minutes at 180°C, remove and allow to rest.

To finish

7 Place the components of the dish on the plate and drizzle with liquorish jus and Broighter Gold rapeseed oil. Serve with fondant potatoes and glazed vegetable, stacked to one side.

ASSESSMENT OF KNOWLEDGE AND UNDERSTANDING

You have now learned about the different types of furred and feathered game. You will have gained an understanding of how to identify the different types of game and an awareness of their quality points. This will enable you to effectively recognize, assess and implement the knowledge gained in order to choose quality game products.

To test your level of knowledge and understanding, answer the following short questions. These will help to prepare you for your summative (final) assessment.

Quality points and types of game

1 Name four types of feathered game and a suitable dish for each.

i)

ii)

iii)

iv)

2 Name two types of small furred game and a suitable dish for each.

i)

ii)

Preparation techniques

1 List and detail the procedure to fully joint a wild rabbit.

2 Describe the process of trussing a whole game bird and give examples of two dishes suitable for a trussed bird.

Storage of game

1 Explain why it is best to drain raw or defrosting game regularly of excess blood and juices.

2 Discuss why it is best to store game in a separate refrigerator to other food items.

Recipes

FISH DISHES

Char grilled tuna Niçoise with saffron potatoes and vine ripened tomato coulis

Deep fried ray, nut brown butter, capers and gnocchi Parisienne

Grilled gravadlax with asparagus and grain mustard mayonnaise

Grilled swordfish with borlotti beans, lime and peppadews

Hot smoked Halibut, clam chowder and crab beignet

Miso glazed black cod, salmon mousse with razor clams and pollock brandade

Monkfish and tiger prawn skewers with pickled vegetable julienne and chilli

Pan fried pollack with shellfish bisque and oyster beignet

Pan fried fillet of red mullet with lemon and thyme noodles and fine ratatouille

Pan fried Herring coated in rolled oats, roasted Beets, Aioli and pickled cucumber

Poached cornish pollack with Caerphilly mash, crispy leek, langoustine beurre blanc

Roasted pavé of wild salmon, swiss chard ravioli, parmesan foam and dried tomato skin

Seared sea bass with curry oil, yoghurt, onion bhaji and spiced plum chutney

Smoked haddock brandade, soft poached egg, wilted spinach and chive cream sauce

Trio of Alaskan salmon

9 Fish and shellfish

VRQ

Advanced skills and techniques in producing fish and shellfish dishes

NVQ

Prepare fish for complex dishes

Cook and finish complex fish dishes

Prepare shellfish for complex dishes

Cook and finish complex shellfish dishes

LEARNING OBJECTIVES

The aim of this chapter is to enable you to develop skills and apply knowledge in the preparation and cookery principles of fish and shellfish. This will also include references to materials, ingredients and resources.

At the end of this chapter you will be able to:

● **Identify fish varieties and the use of each variety.**

● **Indicate the quality points of fish and shellfish.**

● **Prepare and cook a range of fish and shellfish.**

● **Identify the storage procedures for fish and shellfish.**

● **Illustrate an understanding of the fishing methods used and how to purchase fish and shellfish efficiently.**

● **Understand the importance of careful menu planning with regard to sustainable fish stocks and introducing variety.**

SHELLFISH DISHES

Crab and grain mustard beignets with an iced gazpacho

Crayfish mousse with a shellfish bisque

Fried medallions of lobster with coral pasta and a bisque foam

Langoustines cooked in a sweet curry sauce with coconut rice

Mussels cooked with garlic cream sauce, sun-dried tomato bread

Scampi fritters with a baby herb salad and vine tomato coulis

Deep fried oysters with a Thai salad

Seared scallops with a sweet caper dressing and cauliflower purée

Tiger prawn and lemongrass cakes with coriander mayonnaise

Fish

For the professional chef, fish has possibly become the most important ingredient on the menu. It is one of the most fulfilling foods to prepare and cook and there is a wide variety of fish and shellfish available to choose from, but the chef must reflect on the health aspects of fish, select carefully from the wide variety available and ensure that the menu choice helps to contribute positively to the issues of fish sustainability. When selecting fish for a menu, the chef should consider the quality, freshness, availability – due to weather conditions or seasonality – and suitability for different cooking techniques.

Fish types

Fish can be divided into two distinctive types:

● Pelagic – fish that swim relatively close to the surface of the sea or in the water column.

● Demersal – fish that are found on or near the seabed.

Demersal fish can also be further divided into subcategories:

● flat;

● round;

● oily;

● non-bony.

CHEF'S TIP   If there have been several days of bad weather, the choice of fresh seafood will be limited. Be guided by your fish supplier, and remember that there are fish that can be substituted, such as megrim instead of lemon sole and pollack or gurnard instead of cod.

CATEGORIES OF FISH

PELAGIC FISH	DEMERSAL FISH			
	FLAT FISH	**ROUND FISH**	**OILY FISH**	**NON-BONY FISH**
Herring	Brill	Cod	Salmon	Monkfish
Mackerel	Dover sole	Conger eel	Trout	Ray (skate)
Sardine	Lemon sole	Grey mullet	Tuna	Shark
Sprat	Megrim sole	Hake		
	Turbot	Pollack		

CHEF'S TIP Stocks of skate have been depleted in certain regions, and in Cornwall almost all the fish landed and sold as skate are in fact ray. The two names tend to be interchangeable, which is quite confusing for chefs and customers. The species of ray landed include blonde rays, owl rays, star rays and thornback rays.

The sea contains a wide variety of flat fish and round fish. The colour and pattern of their skin is used as camouflage to protect them from potential predators. Most fish have darker shades of skin on the top of the body, which makes them blend into the sea floor when viewed from above. When viewed from below, the pale undersides blend in with the light from above.

The percentage of weight loss should be taken into account when considering fish dishes for a menu. It is unusual to have more than 60 per cent of usable flesh when preparing filleted fish. If preparing round fish for grilling whole, there will be an approximate 5 per cent weight loss from the discarding of the trimmed fins and the gutting, with a further 10 per cent loss if the head is removed.

To estimate the weight loss of fish, the calculation below should be applied:

$$\frac{Total\ waste\ weight}{Total\ original\ fish\ weight} \times 100 = \%\ wastage$$

A John Dory fish at market

Fish sustainability

The figures in the table below illustrate the quantities of fish landed by UK vessels into the UK in 2005, for the five most popular species of fish.

COMMERCIAL FISHING

SPECIES	TONNES LANDED
Mackerel	120 600
Herring	76 400
Haddock	47 600
Blue whiting	28 800
Cod	13 800

Source: UK Sea Fisheries Statistics, DEFRA

The decline of the North Sea cod stocks is a serious problem for the UK. The pressures on fish stocks have made the UK seafood industry adapt, so that fish stocks are better managed in order to meet present needs without compromising the needs of the future. Consumers can, however, still eat fish, a fact that is recognized by leading environmental fisheries campaigners at the WWF (the global conservation organization) and the Marine Conservation Society.

Chefs and consumers must be more inquisitive and taste a wider range of seafood in order to reduce the pressure on more traditional species – such as cod and skate. There are 21 000 species of fish and shellfish in the world, and at least 100 different varieties available in the UK.

Cod landed in the UK is caught within strict management regimes. The control measures already in place at a European level to help preserve stocks include, for example, the closure of certain fisheries during the spawning seasons, catch quotas and restrictions on the type of fishing gear that can be used. The quota system sets safe limits for catches agreed by fishermen, scientists and government. Cod is caught within these agreed limits so consumers can eat it without concern.

CHEF'S TIP When selecting fish for menus try to use alternative under-utilized local varieties, such as pollack, coley or dab. All have great flavours and are not in short supply.

Fish is also traded on an international market. The UK's buyers, processors and retailers source imported supplies from sustainable sources to compensate for reduced landings from their own fleets while work is undertaken to recover stocks in the North Sea. Obviously, purchasing fish from further distances increases the carbon footprint of the ingredient, and it may also lead to concerns over quality and freshness. Currently almost 90 per cent of the cod eaten in the UK comes from waters outside the UK, such as Icelandic and Norwegian waters.

OVER-FISHING

Many once-common fish, such as cod and skate, are now quite rare, with cod close to commercial collapse. Due to over-fishing, the productivity of our seas and rivers is becoming exhausted. The UN Food and Agriculture Organization reports that nearly 70 per cent of the world's fish stocks are now fully fished, over-fished or depleted. If a responsible attitude to fishing is not adopted and the public does not embrace changes to eating habits, the consequences on the world's fisheries will become disastrous. Consumers can contribute to the responsible management of fish stocks by demanding that the fish they eat is from sustainable, managed stocks and that the way in which it is caught or farmed causes minimum damage to the marine environment.

A small fish boat in Cornwall used for hand-line fishing.

Fishing methods

Fishermen use a variety of methods to catch fish, but each is based on one of four basic techniques:

- Pulling an open net through a shoal of fish, either above the seabed or on the seabed itself; this captures the fish in the path of the net and is known as trawling or **dredging**.

- Enclosing an area with a net and then advancing inward, trapping the fish within the encircled area; this is sometimes known as purse-seining or seining.

- Snaring passing fish in set nets.

- Attracting fish to either bait or bright lures, such as in lining or potting.

VIDEO CLIP Sea fishing

TRAWLING

There are three types of trawler:

- beam;
- mid-water;
- bottom.

A beam trawler has two nets (one on either side of the boat), each suspended from a metal beam. The nets have chains in the front edge, which will generally dig 3–8 cm into the seabed to help gather the demersal fish – such as cod, monkfish and sole – into the net.

This type of fishing has attracted many critics because of the potential for damage to the seabed and because the nets pick up everything that gets in their way (including urchins and starfish, which are not used). Most skippers of these trawlers use technology such as sonar, echo sounders and computerized 3D maps to find the softer, sandy ground that is suited to this type of trawling. It would be counterproductive to trawl on rocky ground or over wrecks as this would damage the nets. Recent research has shown that 95 per cent of beam trawlers now use wheels on their beams to help increase fuel efficiency and reduce contact with the seabed.

A fisherman repairing a trawler net.

NETTING

Static nets are fixed on the seabed (known as tangle nets), around wrecks or at sea (known as gill nets), and are left for several hours before being hauled in. This method tends to capture a broad range of species, such as monkfish, pollack, turbot, hake and spider crabs, although this will always depend on locality and location. Mesh sizes are controlled to avoid catching small and immature fish.

HANDLINING

This method is used by inshore and day boats, where baited hooks on lines are dropped into the sea. The number of hooks used per line depends on the species being caught. Handlining is used mostly for mackerel, sea bass, pollack and cod.

Handlining for Mackerel on a small inshore boat.

This is a preferred method because each fish can be marked and traced and is generally in very good condition. Small fish are rarely caught, but if caught they are returned alive immediately. Line fishing also has no unwanted by-catch. Chefs and customers will pay a higher price for fish caught by handlining.

CARING FOR THE CATCH AND INSPECTION AT THE MARKET

Catching fewer fish but ensuring that they are effectively cared for can result in increased freshness, quality and value in the fish caught. Seafish Quality Advisors, working mainly in Scotland, Northern Ireland, Cornwall and the Humber, provide free independent and unbiased assessment on catch quality for fishermen and their crews.

Fish are inspected at the market for standards of grading, size, gutting, washing, icing and presentation, and the quality advisors can advise on how to improve quality of preservation and presentation, thus increasing the value of the catch. A scored analysis report shows the quality of the fish compared with the average for a particular port.

Skippers on pelagic vessels are encouraged to track times of hauls and record the temperature of tanks and details of the frequency and type of cleaning carried out aboard. This information is forwarded to processors and customers.

Quality advisors have also been working with skippers to show that if they weigh fish boxes at sea, and not over-fill them, the quality of the catch is improved. By restricting boxes to a stated weight, and labelling when and where caught, fish can achieve an increased value at market.

Line-caught Mackerel stored in a seawater slush to help maintain the quality of the fish before market.

Small handline boats use large plastic tubs filled with a slush of ice and seawater (usually held at a temperature of 0°C). The fresh catch is put into the slush straight from the line to maintain its freshness and quality.

Seafood Cornwall and Seafood Scotland have employed former skippers as Seafood Quality Advisors. This is another significant quality control step to help ensure that fish suppliers and chefs receive the best possible standard of fish.

> **CHEF'S TIP** The first hour after the fish has been caught is the most crucial for maintaining its quality and freshness. Therefore, the correct storage and rapid chilling of fish as soon as it is caught significantly improves shelf life, appearance and keeping qualities.

TAGGING: THE MARK OF QUALITY

In 2001 the South West Handline Fishermen's Association (SWHFA) was among the first UK fisheries to gain accreditation from the Marine Stewardship Council (MSC), for its handline mackerel scheme. Mackerel carrying the MSC mark is guaranteed to have been caught in south-west waters using the traditional method of handline fishing. Recently, the SWHFA has introduced tagging schemes for handline caught sea bass and pollack, clearly identifying these fish as being caught in Cornish waters. Customers who purchase these species with tags can match the tag numbers with the fisherman and boat on a website (www.linecaught.org.uk).

Tagged sustainable line-caught Sea Bass.

This method has developed a new market, where small numbers of dedicated boats can sell directly to suppliers using this tag as a sign of quality and sustainability. The volume of fish caught is very small compared with what a trawler will catch in one day, but the fish is arguably better quality and there is no 'unwanted catch'. The fish will also have a smaller carbon footprint because the boats used are smaller and do not travel so far out to sea. Because sustainability of fish supplies is the major factor, the emphasis is on the quality rather than the quantity.

The fish market

After fish has been landed, some is sold at the fish market in the port of landing and some is sent to other markets around the UK, such as Billingsgate in London. The quality of product and food safety issues are of utmost importance throughout this process. UK seafood markets are constantly taking steps to ensure that only the best quality product reaches the customer. There is constant investment in innovative procedures, such as temperature controlled fish halls and electronic auctions and/or remote bidding. Also, major new investments have been made in building new markets at some ports, such as Hull and Peterhead.

A fish market in Newlyn, Cornwall.

WHAT TO LOOK OUT FOR WHEN PURCHASING FISH

- Fresh whole fish will have eyes that are bright and not sunken and the skin will have a shiny, moist and firm appearance. There will be a pleasant sea-fresh aroma if the fish is really fresh.

- When buying fillets, look out for neat, trim fillets and a white translucent appearance.

- Smoked fish should always appear glossy and have a fresh smoked aroma.

- When purchasing frozen seafood, check that the fish is frozen solid with no signs of partial thawing. Ensure that the packaging is undamaged and there is no sign of freezer burn to the fish.

VIDEO CLIP   Billingsgate fish market

Fish farming

Aquaculture is an important industry in the UK, made up of an established shellfish sector and a rapidly developing fish sector. Many of the sheltered bays, estuaries and lochs around the UK coastline are suitable for farming a wide range of species. With the development of new equipment that can withstand more extreme weather conditions, opportunities to move to sites further offshore are likely to arise. The shellfish species that are currently produced in UK waters include:

- mussels;
- oysters;
- clams;
- scallops.

The main fish species being farmed at the moment are:

- salmon;
- halibut;
- turbot.

The farming of haddock and Dover sole is still at the research or semi-commercial level. Farmed sea bass is also now starting to appear in UK supermarkets.

How fish are farmed

In most cases, young fish are produced in land-based hatcheries and then transferred to sea cages for growing on to market size. This is taking place in Scotland, where the infrastructure for producing salmon is well established, and some of the producers are diversifying into other species. Norway is another country where this is happening. Recirculation systems are gaining interest, especially in areas where there are no sheltered sites for the mooring of cages.

The selection of a suitable site is crucial to the success of any aquaculture business. Growth and survival of the stock, whether fish or shellfish, are influenced by a range of physical and biological factors, including seawater temperature, exposure of the site to the elements, dissolved oxygen and pollutants. Sites near large urban and industrial developments are generally unsuitable for cultivation because of potential pollutants in the water. More specifically for shellfish, growth and survival are also affected by water flow rates, food (phytoplankton) in the water, predators and fouling organisms. Starfish and crabs, abundant in estuaries and coastal waters, are probably the most damaging of all the shellfish predators.

Fish preparation

Step-by-step: Filleting and pin boning a mackerel

1. Cut around the gills and insert the knife along the backbone, work the knife towards the tail.

2. Carefully remove the fillet using long knife strokes.

3. Turn the fish over and repeat the process.

4. Remove the second fillet.

5. Trim the fillets to remove any excess fat or bone.

6. Laying the fillets skin side down make a 'V' shaped incision either side of the central bones – taking care not to cut through the skin.

7. Squeeze the central bones as shown and pull towards the tail, they will come away cleanly.

8. This shows the completed trimmed mackerel fillets.

Step-by-step: Preparation of a skate wing

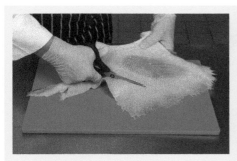

1. Following the natural shape of the skate wing cut away the thin excess as shown.

2. This shows the trimmed skate wing and the excess.

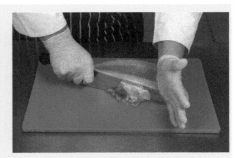

3. Cut through the connecting bone as shown to leave a smooth finish.

4. Cut along the top and then work the knife under the flesh and along the bones.

5. The skate flesh is cut away as shown.

6. Using long knife strokes remove the flesh, and then repeat on the other side.

7. Follow the natural shape of the skate wing and trim as shown.

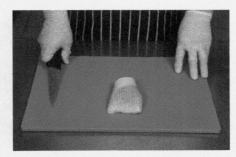

8. Roll the skate wing as shown; this can now be cut to shape and cooked as required.

VIDEO CLIP   Preparing a délice and paupiette

Recipes

Char grilled tuna Niçoise

Char grilled tuna Niçoise with saffron potatoes and vine ripened tomato coulis

Ingredients	4 portions	10 portions
Tuna	4 × 160 g	10 × 160 g
Fine green beans	100 g	250 g
Plum tomatoes (blanched, deseeded and cut into quarters)	4	10
Black olives (halved)	2 tbsp	5 tbsp
Turned New potatoes (cooked in saffron liquid)	12	30
Lemon juice and zest	1 lemon	2½ lemons
Grain mustard	2 tbsp	5 tbsp
Egg yolks	1	3
Olive oil	100 ml	250 ml
Sherry vinegar	100 ml	250 ml
Good-quality salt and white pepper	pinch	pinch
Boiled quail eggs	8	20
Vine ripened tomato coulis		

energy	cal	fat	sat fat	carb	sugar	protein	fibre
3993 kJ	958 kcal	46.7 g	10 g	46.2 g	6.6 g	83.6 g	7.2 g

METHOD OF WORK

1 Cut the green beans into 6 cm lengths, blanch in boiling water and refresh in iced water. Split each bean lengthways.

2 Cut each tomato quarter in half on an angle and mix with the green beans, black olives and saffron potatoes. Season the salad well.

3 To create the emulsion, blend the egg yolk, grain mustard, lemon juice and zest and slowly add the olive oil in a blender. Season with salt and white pepper.

4 Use the emulsification to dress the salad.

5 Bar mark the seasoned fresh tuna to a quadrillage style on a grill and cook until pink in the centre.

6 Arrange the salad on the service plate, place the tuna on top and brush with a little oil, drizzle the coulis around.

CHEF'S TIP Use only the freshest tuna possible, and when cooking aim to serve it pink in the centre. The tuna can be marinated in lime, garlic and chilli then seared quickly.

CHEF'S TIP When grilling fish, always brush the grill bars with oil to prevent the fish from sticking.

Deep fried ray, nut brown butter

Deep fried ray, nut brown butter, capers and gnocchi Parisienne

Ingredients	4 portions	10 portions
Ray wing boned and cut into 4 x 4 cm pieces	20 pieces	50 pieces
Seasoned flour	for dusting	for dusting
Salted butter	200 g	500 g
capers	40 g	100 g
Lemon	1	2–3
Chopped parsley	2 tbsp	5 tbsp
Gnocchi parisienne	20 pieces	50 pieces
Salt and pepper	to taste	to taste
Vegetable oil	for frying	for frying

energy	cal	fat	sat fat	carb	sugar	protein	fibre
2181 kJ	526 kcal	44.3 g	26.9 g	3.1 g	0.9 g	29.8 g	0.9 g

METHOD OF WORK

1   Dust the wings with the flour and deep fry at 190°C until golden; drain and keep warm.

2   Cook the butter until nutty and brown, add juice from the lemon and the capers and parsley.

3   Heat the gnocchi gently in the butter mixture and serve with the wings.

Grilled gravadlax

Grilled gravadlax with asparagus and grain mustard mayonnaise

Ingredients	4 portions	10 portions
Pavé of gravadlax	4 × 100 g	10 × 100 g
Tomato concasse	400 g	1 kg
Asparagus, blanched	100 g	250 g
Grain mustard mayonnaise	200 g	500 g
Fresh dill	50 g	125 g
Vinaigrette		
Good-quality salt and white pepper	to taste	to taste

energy	cal	fat	sat fat	carb	sugar	protein	fibre
680 kJ	164 kcal	12 g	2.7 g	10.4 g	8.9 g	4.4 g	3.3 g

METHOD OF WORK

1   Thoroughly wash the gravadlax and dry well. Grill the gravadlax maintaining a slightly pink centre. Retain warm for service.

2   Warm the asparagus and tomato in a pan with a little vinaigrette and season.

3   Serve the salmon as shown with piped grain mustard mayonnaise.

4   Finish with the remaining sprigs of fresh dill.

SOURCING Asparagus is not seasonably available all year. Selecting seasonable vegetables to complement these dishes will give an enhanced flavour and maintain cost effectiveness.

Grilled swordfish

Grilled swordfish with borlotti beans, lime and peppadews

Ingredients	4 portions	10 portions
Swordfish	4 × 160 g	10 × 160 g
Borlotti beans	350 g	875 g
Lime	1	3
Peppadews	4 tbsp	10 tbsp
Olive oil	50 ml	125 ml
Fresh coriander	8 tsp	20 tsp
Good quality salt and white pepper	to taste	to taste
Micro herbs		

energy	cal	fat	sat fat	carb	sugar	protein	fibre
2156 kJ	516 kcal	23.7 g	4.4 g	21.5 g	5.8 g	51.1 g	9.8 g

METHOD OF WORK

1 Wash and drain the beans.
2 Mix the beans with the lime, peppadews, oil and chopped coriander.
3 Warm the mixture on the stove and reserve.
4 Grill the swordfish until pink in the centre and marked with a quadrillage.
5 Place the warmed bean mixture on the service plate and arrange the swordfish on top.
6 Finish with micro herbs.

CHEF'S TIP If the swordfish is hard, has a rubbery texture and breaks easily it has been over cooked. It will have lost its moisture content and nutritional value.

Hot smoked halibut

Hot smoked halibut, clam chowder and crab beignet

Ingredients	4 portions	10 portions
Hot smoked halibut	4 × 160 g	10 × 160 g
Palourdes (clams)	400 g	1 kg
Mirepoix	100 g	250 g
Macédoine of potato	100 g	250 g
Tomato concasse	40 g	100 g
Diced onion	80 g	200 g
Milk	200 ml	500 ml
Double cream	100 ml	250 ml
Chopped dill	1 tbsp	2–3 tbsp
Unsalted butter	50 g	125 g
Crab beignet		
Choux paste	200 g	500 g
Picked white crab meat	160 g	400 g
Diced shallot	40 g	100 g
Salt and pepper	to taste	to taste

energy	cal	fat	sat fat	carb	sugar	protein	fibre
4628 kJ	1110 kcal	53.6 g	26.1 g	34 g	6.6 g	118.1 g	3.3 g

METHOD OF WORK

1 To make the chowder, cook the clams with the mirepoix until just opened, drain save juice and chill.
2 Once chilled pick the meat and discard shells.
3 Sweat the onion in the butter until soft, no colour, add potato and sweat for one minute.
4 Add milk and simmer until potatoes are just cooked, add the cream, tomato and clams, finish with salt, pepper and chopped dill.
5 For the crab beignet, mix all ingredients together, shape into quenelles and deep fry at 160°C for six minutes or until golden brown and cooked through.

Miso glazed black cod

Miso glazed black cod, salmon mousse with razor clams and pollack brandade

Ingredients	4 portions	10 portions
Miso cod		
Black cod	4 × 50 g	10 × 50 g
White miso paste	100 g	250 g
Caster sugar	100 g	250 g
Mirin	100 ml	250 ml
Julienne leeks	40 g	100 g
Julienne of carrots	40 g	100 g
Julienne of white radish	40 g	100 g
Sesame oil	50 ml	120 ml
Vegetable oil	50 ml	120 ml
Salmon mousse		
Salmon fillet	200 g	500 g
Razor clams	2	5
Double cream	150 ml	150 ml
Egg white	1	2–3
Baby spinach	100 g	250 g
Pollack brandade		
Pollack tails	200 g	500 g
Rock salt	50 g	120 g
potato	100 g	250 g
Milk	500 ml	1200 ml
Crushed garlic	2 cloves	5 cloves
Bouquet garni	1 × small	1 × large
Olive oil	80 ml	200 ml
Flour	for pane	for pane
Eggs	for pane	for pane
Bread crumbs	for pane	for pane

energy	cal	fat	sat fat	carb	sugar	protein	fibre
4770 kJ	1146 kcal	77.2 g	21 g	67.1 g	34.2 g	47.3 g	1.5 g

METHOD OF WORK

1 For the cod, mix all ingredients apart from cod and reduce slowly on stove until thickened; leave to cool.

2 Once cool marinate the cod in the mixture and refrigerate for 24 hours.

3 Sauté the julienne of vegetables in the two oils and cool.

4 For the salmon, make a mousse with the salmon, cream and egg white, season and test.

5 Steam the razor clams and remove the meat, roll the mousse into cylinders with the clam in the centre, steam until middle reaches 60°C, chill if not needed immediately.

6 For the brandade, cure the pollack in the salt for 30 minutes, wash and dry.

7 Cook in the milk with the garlic thinly sliced potato and bouquet garni until cooked through.

8 Remove the bouquet garni and blitz the remaining ingredients in a food processor and emulsify the oil into the mixture.

9 Shape into small balls and blast chill until set, pane a l'Anglaise and deep fry at 160°C until golden.

10 Serve the cod on the julienne, salmon on the wilted spinach and the brandade on a little reduced cream.

Monkfish and tiger prawn skewers

Ingredients	4 portions	10 portions
Monkfish	320 g	800 g
Peeled tiger prawns	320 g	800 g
Spaghetti of vegetables	400 g	1 kg
White wine vinegar	50 ml	125 ml
Olive oil	30 ml	100 ml
Chilli flakes	2 tbsp	5 tbsp
Mustard seeds	2 tsp	5 tsp
Coriander	1 punnet	2½ punnets
Good-quality salt and white pepper	to taste	to taste

energy	cal	fat	sat fat	carb	sugar	protein	fibre
1720 kJ	410 kcal	16.3 g	2 g	23.3 g	7.1 g	42.5 g	16.5 g

METHOD OF WORK

1   Soak the bamboo skewers in water for one hour. Put the prawns and diced monkfish alternately onto the skewers (one portion should equal a total weight of 160 g).

2   Marinate the skewers with chilli, oil, mustard seeds and seasoning for at least 20 minutes.

3   Steep the vegetables in the remaining vinegar and oil and season well, reserve until required.

4   Shallow fry the fish skewers and finish in the oven if required.

5   Arrange the vegetable son the plate and finish with the skewers and coriander.

CHEF'S TIP   To test if fish is correctly cooked, the flesh should feel tender to the touch and offer little resistance.

Pan fried pollack with shellfish bisque and oyster beignet

Ingredients	4 portions	10 portions
Pollack	4 × 120 g	10 × 120 g
Vegetable oil	for frying	for frying
Unsalted butter	20 g	50 g
Lemon juice	to taste	to taste
Peeled celeriac	200 g	500 g
Peeled carrots	100 g	250 g
Unsalted butter	50 g	120 g
Shellfish bisque	200 ml	500 ml
Oysters shucked	4	10
Light tempura batter		
Salt and pepper	to taste	to taste
Micro herbs	garnish	garnish

energy	cal	fat	sat fat	carb	sugar	protein	fibre
2734 kJ	659 kcal	39.7 g	20.9 g	14 g	3.6 g	52.7 g	2.8 g

METHOD OF WORK

1   Cut the celeriac and carrot into 1 cm pieces and sweat slowly in the butter until soft, crush with a fork and season well, reserve.

2   Pan fry the pollack in vegetable oil and finish with butter and lemon juice.

3   Serve the pollack on top of the crushed carrot and celeriac.

4   Dust the oysters with seasoned flour, then coat in the tempura batter, deep fry at 180°C until just cooked.

5   Spoon hot bisque around, garnish with micro herbs and oyster beignet.

Pan fried fillet of red mullet with lemon thyme noodles

Pan fried fillet of red mullet with lemon thyme noodles, fine ratatouille sauce and crispy spring onion

Ingredients	4 portions	10 portions
Red mullet fillets	4 × red mullet fillets	10 × red mullet fillets
Linguini noodles (cooked with cream and chopped thyme and lemon juice)	400 g	1 kg
Courgette	40 g	100 g
Aubergine	40 g	100 g
White onion	40 g	100 g
Mixed peppers	40 g	100 g
Tomato Coulis	8 tbsp	20 tbsp
Spring onions	1 bunch	2½ bunches
Butter	50 g	125 g
Olive oil	50 ml	125 ml
Black olives	2 tbsp	5 tbsp
Good quality salt and white pepper	to taste	to taste

energy	cal	fat	sat fat	carb	sugar	protein	fibre
2409 kJ	575 kcal	35.6 g	11 g	37.1 g	4.2 g	28.4 g	4.7 g

METHOD OF WORK

1 Prepare the fillets by cutting into a **butterfly**. In a frying pan heat a little oil until it just begins to smoke.

2 Season and lay the fish into the pan, skin-side down, and shallow fry until the skin just begins to crisp without burning.

3 Turn the fish over and allow to cook for a further 30 seconds.

4 Neatly dice the courgettes, aubergines, peppers and onions. Sweat in a little butter in a heavy-based saucepan until just cooked and season well. Reserve to one side.

5 Using a pestle and mortar, grind the black olives and remaining olive oil into a paste.

6 Slice the spring onions finely into julienne and dry them of any excess water. Place into hot oil (180°C) and deep fry until they are crisp. Reserve under hot lamps for service.

7 Ensure the linguini noodles are cooked and well seasoned then arrange in the centre of the plate. Lay the cooked fish on top.

8 Arrange the fine ratatouille vegetables around the edge and spoon the warmed tomato coulis around the plate, finish with drops of black olive purée and the crispy spring onion.

CHEF'S TIP The mullet should only be gently cooked to retain as much of its flavour and nutrients as possible. However, the dish requires a crispy skin so ensure the fish is skin-side down for at least 80 per cent of the cooking time.

Pan fried herring coated in rolled oats

Pan fried herring coated in rolled oats, roasted beets, aioli and pickled cucumber

Ingredients	4 portions	10 portions
herring	4 × fillets pin boned	10 × fillets pin boned
Plain flour	for dusting	for dusting
Milk	for coating	for coating
Rolled oats	100 g	250 g
Red beetroot	200 g	200 g
Golden beetroot	200 g	200 g
Vegetable oil	for frying	for frying
Olive oil	50 ml	120 ml
Honey	20 g	50 g
Thyme	2 sprigs	5 sprigs
Bay leaf	1	2–3
Garlic crushed	2 cloves	5 cloves
Salt and pepper	to taste	to taste
Cucumber	½	1 ½
Rice wine vinegar	200 ml	500 ml
Caster sugar	50 g	120 g
aioli	100 ml	250 ml

energy	cal	fat	sat fat	carb	sugar	protein	fibre
3184 kJ	766 kcal	52.9 g	8.9 g	44.6 g	25.5 g	27.8 g	3.6 g

METHOD OF WORK

1   Season the herring fillets and dust in flour, dip in milk and coat with oats, reserve in fridge.

2   Peel and cut the beetroots into one cm dice, sauté in a pan with the oil and garlic for two minutes.

3   Season well and add the honey, thyme and bay leaf, cover and roast in a hot oven until tender.

4   Remove the garlic, thyme and bay leaf, reserve.

5   Peel the cucumber and cut using a spaghetti cutter, squeeze out excess water.

6   Dissolve the sugar in the vinegar and pour over the cucumber, leave for five minutes, then strain.

7   Pan fry the herrings in the oil and serve with the beetroot, aioli and cucumber shaped with a carving fork.

Poached cornish pollack with Caerphilly mash

Poached cornish pollack with Caerphilly mash, crispy leek, langoustine beurre blanc

Ingredients	4 portions	10 portions
Pollack fillets	4 × 160 g	10 × 160 g
Mashed potato	400 g	1 kg
Caerphilly cheese	40 g	100 g
Leeks, chiffonade	12	30
Butter	50 g	125 g
Langoustines	12	30
Beurre blanc sauce	200 ml	500 ml
Fish stock	300 ml	750 ml
Fresh dill	4 tsp	10 tsp
Good-quality salt and white pepper	pinch	pinch

energy	cal	fat	sat fat	carb	sugar	protein	fibre
4125 kJ	994 kcal	61.5 g	36.7 g	28.9 g	6.8 g	71.4 g	6.7 g

METHOD OF WORK

1   Prepare and wash the langoustines. Poach in the fish stock, remove and allow to cool. Save the claws for decoration and carefully remove the flesh from each tail.

2   Put the langoustine tail shells into a little of the fish stock and slowly reduce to a glaze, extracting as much flavour from the shells as possible.

3   Pass the langoustine glaze and carefully whisk into the beurre blanc.

4   Poach the pollack in the fish stock until the flesh is creamy and just set. A lightly buttered cartouche may be required to help with the cooking process.

5   Deep fry the leeks until crispy, season well and reserve for service.

6   Heat the mashed potato in a heavy-based saucepan with a little butter and add the grated Caerphilly cheese. Check the seasoning, and while still hot pipe onto a warmed service plate. Top with the poached fish.

7   Finish with the crispy leeks, langoustine beurre blanc.

8   Serve with the beurre blanc and the fresh dill.

CHEF'S TIP Ensure the langoustines are fresh, and alive where possible, before preparation; this will help to achieve a higher quality end product.

Roast pavé of wild salmon, Swiss chard ravioli

Roasted pavé of wild salmon, swiss chard ravioli, parmesan foam and dried tomato skin

Ingredients	4 portions	10 portions
Wild salmon pavés	4 × 120 g	10 × 120 g
Vegetable oil	for frying	for frying
Unsalted butter	50 g	120 g
Cooked Swiss chard leaves	200 g	500 g
Lemon juice	to taste	to taste
Melted unsalted butter	20 g	50 g
Pasta dough	200 g	500 g
Grated parmesan	50 g	120 g
Milk	150 ml	360 ml
Lecithin	1.5 g	3.6 g
Tomato skin	4 pieces	10 pieces
Salt and pepper	to taste	to taste
Micro cress	garnish	garnish

energy	cal	fat	sat fat	carb	sugar	protein	fibre
2230 kJ	535 kcal	37.6 g	15.1 g	14.5 g	2.5 g	35.8 g	0.6 g

METHOD OF WORK

1 Place the tomato skin under hot lights and dry until crisp.

2 Chop the Swiss chard leaves very finely and push through a drum sieve and fold in the melted butter, season with lemon juice, salt and pepper.

3 Make the raviolis.

4 Place the parmesan in the milk and heat to 80°C, leave to infuse for 30 minutes.

5 Pass through a chinois and add the lecithin.

6 Roast the salmon until slightly pink in the centre and cook the raviolis.

7 Serve the salmon on top of the ravioli, foam the parmesan stock and spoon over the fish finish with micro cress and tomato.

CHEF'S TIP To make a tomato fondue, sweat some finely chopped shallots in butter in a small saucepan then add chopped ripe tomatoes and cook over a moderate heat for several minutes until the juices have evaporated and the tomato pulp has thickened enough to hold its shape lightly in a spoon. Season carefully to taste.

CHEF'S TIP When roasting fish, always constantly baste with olive oil or butter to help maintain the moisture and prevent it from burning in a dry heat.

Seared sea bass with curry oil

Seared sea bass with curry oil, yoghurt, onion bhaji and spiced plum chutney

Ingredients	4 portions	10 portions
Sea bass	4 × 150 g	10 × 150 g
Diced potatoes	400 g	1 kg
Turmeric	2 tsp	5 tsp
Fresh baby spinach	200 g	500 g
Mustard seeds	1 tsp	3 tsp
Curry powder	2 tbsp	5 tbsp
Olive oil	200 ml	450 ml
Greek yoghurt	50 ml	125 ml
White onions sliced	2	5
Flour	100 g	250 g
Garam masala	2 tbsp	5 tbsp
Plums (stoned and chopped)	500 g	1250 g
Red chillies chopped	2	5
Brown sugar	6 tbsp	15 tbsp
Cinnamon stick	1	3
Red wine vinegar	50 ml	125 ml
Red onion chopped	2	5
Good quality salt and white pepper	to taste	to taste

energy	cal	fat	sat fat	carb	sugar	protein	fibre
4614 kJ	1105 kcal	59.5 g	9.3 g	98.2 g	49.5 g	47 g	13 g

METHOD OF WORK

1   Mix the plums, red chillis, sugar, cinnamon, red wine vinegar and chopped red onion together. Simmer for four hours until totally broken down and thickened, chill and store in an airtight container.

2   Mix the curry powder with a little olive oil to form a paste, then gradually add the remaining oil. Simmer for one hour until the spices are cooked through and the oil is brightly coloured and flavoured.

3   Thin the yoghurt with a little water or fresh milk until it resembles a sauce consistency.

4   Bring the washed potatoes to the boil with the turmeric, a little water to cover and the mustard seeds. When cooked, pour off any excess water and add the spinach over the heat, allow the mix to break down a little.

5   Mix the sliced onions with the garam masala, a little water and the flour and leave the paste aside for one hour.

6   Form small flat bhajis and deep fry until golden in colour.

7   Sear the seasoned sea bass in a shallow pan of oil, skin-side first, and finish cooking in a hot oven until just cooked.

8   Spoon the yoghurt on the plate and drizzle on the curry oil.

9   Position the potato mixture, with the sea bass on top, the plum chutney and then the onion bhaji to serve.

CHEF'S TIP There is very little connective tissue in fish, making it very fragile during cooking. All fish should be cooked as little as possible to maintain its shape and moisture content.

Smoked haddock brandade, soft poached egg, wilted spinach and chive cream sauce

Ingredients	4 portions	10 portions
Home-smoked haddock	400 g	1 kg
Fresh milk	500 ml	1250 ml
Dry mashed potato (with chopped parsley)	400 g	1 kg
Lemon juice and zest	1 lemon	3 lemons
Free range eggs	4	10
Fresh baby spinach	100 g	250 g
Butter	50 g	125 g
Fish cream sauce	200 ml	500 ml
Chopped chives	6 tsp	14 tsp
Good-quality salt and white pepper	pinch	pinch

energy	cal	fat	sat fat	carb	sugar	protein	fibre
2951 kJ	710 kcal	51.3 g	30.1 g	30.3 g	10.5 g	33.5 g	3 g

METHOD OF WORK

1   Heat the milk in a large heavy-based saucepan and add the smoked haddock. Slowly poach until the flakes of the fish can easily be separated from the fillet.

2   Drain the fish and carefully flake the flesh. Mix the fish gently into the warmed mashed potato with the lemon juice and zest. Season well. Retain the mixture warm for service.

3   Wilt the washed and drained baby spinach in a little butter for a few seconds and place into the base of a bowl plate.

4   Top with the haddock brandade, shaped in a stainless steel moulding ring.

5   Poach the eggs until soft then arrange on top of the haddock.

6   Mix the chopped chives with the fish cream sauce and delicately **nape** over the poached egg.

CHEF'S TIP The eggs can be poached in advance and reheated to order; this will help to guarantee uniformity of shape and size and improve speed of service.

VIDEO CLIP Smoked haddock brandade.

Trio of Alaskan salmon

Ingredients	4 portions	10 portions
Salmon rillette		
Salmon belly skin on	200 g	500 g
Rock salt	20 g	50 g
Olive oil	500 ml	1200 ml
Lemon peel	1 small piece	1 large piece
Garlic clove crushed	2	5
Green pepper corns	4 g	10 g
Bouquet garni	1 small	1 large
Crème fraiche	50 g	120 g
Salt and pepper	to taste	to taste
Hot smoked salmon pavé	4 × 50 g	10 × 50 g
Slow cooked salmon		
Salmon pavé	4 × 50 g	10 × 50 g
Oil from rillette	for sous vide	for sous vide
Celeriac and horseradish puree		
Diced celeriac	100 g	250 g
Vegetable stock	200 ml	500 ml
Double cream	50 ml	120 ml
Unsalted butter	20 g	50 g
Horseradish grated	5 g	12 g
Salt and pepper	to taste	to taste
Micro herbs	garnish	garnish
Melba toast	4 slices	10 slices

energy	cal	fat	sat fat	carb	sugar	protein	fibre
6518 kJ	1579 kcal	154.8 g	30.7 g	20.8 g	2.3 g	27.2 g	1.7 g

METHOD OF WORK

1   For the rillette, cure the belly with the salt for 20 minutes, wash and dry.

2   Place the oil, peppercorns, lemon peel, bouquet garni in a pan with the salmon and heat to 65°C, cook for 20 minutes.

3   Remove belly and strain oil then cool, remove the bouquet garni, lemon peel and garlic, put the green peppercorns onto the salmon and flake, leave to cool.

4   Add the crème fraîche and season well, reserve.

5   Vac pac the salmon pavés with the rillette oil and cook in a water bath at 48°C for 25 minutes; probe to check temperature.

6   For the celeriac puree, place the horseradish in the cream and bring to boil, remove and cover, leave to the side.

7   Sweat the celeriac in butter then add stock and simmer until very tender, strain and blitz, pass through a chinois.

8   Strain off the horseradish from the cream and mix the cream with the celeriac puree.

9   Serve the three types of salmon with the puree, garnish with micro herbs.

HHEALTHY OPTION Oily fish contain a large amount of polyunsaturated fatty acids which may help to fight against heart disease.

Shellfish

Shellfish is a collective term for crustacean, mollusc and cephalopod seafood. Using shellfish can be a rewarding experience, both in preparation and cooking. Each group of shellfish includes a range of species, each with its own method of preparation.

Molluscs can have a single shell, univalves; a pair of shells, bivalves; or no shell and tentacles, cephalopods. Crustaceans have an external skeleton.

CLASSIFICATION OF SHELLFISH

UNIVALVE	BIVALVE	CEPHALOPOD	CRUSTACEAN
Limpets	Cockles	Octopus	Lobsters
Whelks	Mussels	Cuttlefish	Crabs
Winkles	Razor shell clams	Squid	Crayfish
Tower shells	Scallops		Prawns
Tusk shells	Oysters		Shrimps
	Carpet shells		Langoustine
	Paddocks		
	Clams		

Shellfish generally live in, on or near the seabed, on the continental shelf, shelf slope and in very deep water. They can be obtained in two ways: by farming or by harvesting from the wild. There are good and bad points for each method.

Larger crustaceans, such as lobsters, crabs and crayfish, are often caught by small inshore fisheries, and prawns, shrimps and langoustine may be targeted by trawlers. Langoustine is fished extensively in the North Sea.

Univalve and bivalve molluscs, including scallops, oysters, mussels, clams, cockles, whelks and snails, can all be gathered by hand, trapped or dredged. Cephalopods (squid, cuttlefish and octopus) can be harvested using nets or hook and line.

The most common way to gather scallops is to dredge the seabed with a net. This method can result in bycatch of undersized individuals or other species and can damage the shells. An alternative method is diving, where by divers collect the scallops by hand from the seabed. This method is more selective, and dived scallops will sell at a higher price.

Sustainability

The Sea Fish Industry Authority (Seafish) works across all sectors of the UK seafood industry to promote good-quality, sustainable seafood. Its research and projects are aimed at raising standards, improving efficiency and ensuring that the fishing industry develops in a practical and sustainable way. Established in 1981, it is the UK's only cross-industry seafood body working with fishermen, processors, wholesalers, seafood farmers, chefs, caterers, retailers and the import/export trade.

Seafish is helping the industry to become more sustainable through a variety of activities:

- The Seafish Sustainable Fisheries Advisory Committee brings together fishermen and environmentalists from across all sectors of the seafood industry to consider the need for conservation and stability and to advise Seafish.

- Seafish marine technologists work with fishermen to develop and test trawling gear designs that are more selective and less damaging to the seabed.

- Guidelines have been produced for the use of square-mesh panels in prawn trawls, which reduce the by-catch of juvenile fish such as haddock and cod.

- An international research project on scallop dredge design to reduce environmental damage is coordinated by Seafish.

- A new trawl design with an escape hatch for dolphins is being developed.

Forthcoming projects include:

- Developing a UK training course in responsible fishing.

- Coordinating a pilot project to develop a high-quality, low-volume sustainable pelagic fishery in Cornwall, and eventually a model which can be developed throughout the UK.

- Investigating new ways to use the waste products left over from the UK's processing industry.

- Leading an international project called Tracefish, developing a Europe-wide scheme which traces seafood from net to plate. This will help the seafood industry to deliver consistent, clear labelling for seafood so that consumers can make informed choices about what to purchase.

Shellfish and their preparation

Bivalve molluscs

SCALLOPS

Scallops are highly regarded and are expensive to purchase. The rounded, fan-shaped shells vary in size, from the smaller queen scallops about 7 cm across to the larger ones up to 18 cm across. The edible parts are the round white muscle and the orange and white roe (coral). The frilly gills and mantle can be used for soup and stocks.

Scallops can be opened by separating the shells with a knife. This can be done relatively easily once the basic techniques have been mastered. Discard the skirt or save for making a stock. Separate the white from the coral and gently wash both and store until required. If the scallops are fresh, well prepared and in excellent condition, they can be used raw, simply marinated with an acidic dressing to gently denaturize the flesh.

CLAMS

Clams are well known for the classic dish clam chowder, which is mainly associated with the east coast of the United States.

RAZOR SHELL CLAMS

Razor shells clams are shaped like cutthroat razors. They are caught by tipping salt onto the sand: the shells pop out of the ground and are carefully harvested.

OYSTERS

Many species and varieties of oyster are found around the world and so oysters come in a many shapes and sizes. The best British oysters are the 'native' or 'flat' oysters. Other British oysters include 'rock' oysters. Natives are available from September to April, though they are at their best from late October to late February when the sea is colder. Pacific oysters are available all year.

Oyster shells must be scrubbed well before opening and an oyster knife should always be used to open the shells.

It is important to use an oyster knife because a normal kitchen knife could break. An oyster knife also has a small guard near the handle to help prevent the hand from slipping and cutting against the sharp shell.

Any oysters that have an unusual smell should be discarded. Native oysters are best eaten raw, and as soon as possible after capture. Raw oysters are traditionally eaten with lemon and a little cayenne pepper. Cooked rock oysters are used to produce chowders and fish stews.

MUSSELS

These molluscs, which have a distinctive oval blue-black shell, are often seen attached to rocks and wooden structures around coastlines worldwide. The vibrant orange-coloured meat inside is sweet and salty. Mussels should only be harvested from unpolluted waters between September and March; they should be left alone during the summer months. Cultivated mussels are also available.

Purchase smaller or medium-sized mussels, and always buy more than you need because there will always be some dead ones that will need to be discarded.

Univalve molluscs

WHELKS

Whelks resemble pointed snails when fresh, and are usually sold ready-cooked. Only retain the good whelks and discard any that are damaged or smell strongly.

WINKLES

Winkles, known as 'black sea snails', are served as appetizers. They are usually sold pre-cooked, and can be seasoned with fresh tarragon or parsley and a little white wine. They are quickly and easily removed from their shells using a pin when cooked.

Cephalopod molluscs

SQUID

Squid varies in size, from small ones of about 7 cm to larger ones of about 25 cm. Squid is available most of the year, either fresh or frozen. It freezes very well, and preparing squid is relatively straightforward. If the ink sac can be recovered intact from inside the squid, it can be used to colour and flavour risottos, pastas and sauces. There is a transparent flexible cartilage within the squid, which must be removed. Cooking must be either very quick or very slow, otherwise the flesh will be tough to eat.

Crustaceans

LOBSTER

Lobsters are more expensive than their close relatives the crabs because of the superior flavour and texture of their meat. When alive, lobsters' shells are mottled with dark green, blue and brick red colours, but they turn to their distinctive bright red on cooking.

Lobsters can grow to 4.5 kg, but are best eaten at about 500 g to 1.4 kg. The smaller lobsters are more tender. Cold-water lobsters from the northern seas are considered the finest: the males have denser, meatier flesh and the females have a more subtle flavour and an orange roe, the 'coral', which can be used to colour sauces.

Most of the lobster is edible, except the transparent bag-like stomach and the dark intestines. These should be removed with a sharp knife point. Do not remove the creamy green-grey liver, known as the 'tomalley', which has an excellent flavour. It can also be used to flavour sauces and soups.

Purchase lobsters that feel heavy for their size, with both claws intact, and preferably buy them while they are still alive and cook them yourself. A 1.4 kg lobster should be enough for two portions.

Step-by-step: Method of preparing a live lobster

1. Place a large cook's knife into the small indentation of the head, using a firm downward force pierce the shell and continue down to the chopping board.

2. Split the head in half as shown.

3. Turn the lobster around, follow the previously cut line through the tail.

4. Carefully remove the lobster flesh and reserve.

5. Remove the waste sack.

6. Remove the spinal cord as shown.

7. Holding firmly onto the claw cut into the top and twist the knife to separate the shell.

8. Once the claws are split into two remove the flesh carefully as shown.

VIDEO CLIP Deep poaching lobsters in court bouillon

Lobster is best cooked simply – boiled, steamed or grilled – and can be served either hot or cold. Serve with melted butter, lemon juice or mayonnaise. Crack the claws with a hammer or back of a large knife to extract the meat. The shells can be used for fish soup, the base for bisque or a lobster sauce.

The reason for cooking lobsters alive is that once killed their flesh starts to deteriorate very quickly. Fishmongers and wholesalers will only buy live lobsters to sell, and in turn chefs and cooks, when cooking fresh lobster, will always choose live specimens for freshness. Lobsters sold in supermarkets in this country are generally sold already cooked as the demand for live lobsters is not as great as it is abroad.

The main methods of killing and cooking lobster are as follows:

- The standard way of cooking is to place the live lobster head first into a pan of boiling water – the lobster dies very quickly.

- Another method is to freeze the live lobster for approximately 30 minutes to desensitize it and then cook it in boiling water.

- A third method it to kill the lobster before cooking: in one sharp blow, pierce the live lobster between the eyes, which kills it instantly, then cook it in the usual way.

Step-by-step: Method of preparing a cooked lobster

1. Twist the tail away from the head of the lobster.

2. Using a sharp pair of scissors cut either side of the tail as shown.

3. Once both sides have been cut, carefully remove the tail meat.

4. Twist both legs away from the body of the lobster as shown.

5. Firmly take hold of the smaller pincer and pull upwards,; this will separate the shell from the flesh.

6. Using a large knife cut though the top of the claw carefully and twist; this will separate the shell and expose the flesh inside.

7. Separate the shell and carefully remove the flesh inside.

8. Using the tip of a knife, ease the remaining flesh from the shell.

VIDEO CLIP Lobster Thermidor

CRAB

There are many varieties of crab and many regions throughout the world where crabs are abundant:

Brown Crab

- Europe – the brown crab and the spider crab.
- Eastern USA – the blue crab.
- Pacific coast of the USA – the Dungeness crab.

The soft brown flesh under the hard upper shell is strong and full-flavoured, this contrasts well with the sweet, delicate white flesh found in the claws and body. Male crabs often have larger claws and so more white flesh than females.

Purchase crabs that feel heavy for their size and smell fresh and sweet, whether alive or cooked. If there is a smell of ammonia, do not buy. Crabs are best bought alive and cooked fresh. You will need approximately 115 g of meat per portion – about 450 g of whole crab (with shell intact).

VIDEO CLIP Dressed crab

The brown crab from Europe is available all year. It reaches 20–25 cm across and has heavy front claws with almost-black pincers. Its shell is rusty-red or brown, and its legs are hairy and red but mottled with white.

The velvet crab, sometimes known as the swimming crab, grows to 10–15 cm. Its body is coated with short hairs, giving it a velvet-like appearance. It is one of the major crab species in UK waters, and is found in rocky areas near the shoreline and down to a depth of approximately 65 m. Velvet crab fetches the highest price, especially abroad, such as in Spain, Portugal and France, where it is seen as a luxury food item.

The popularity of spider crab is increasing, and as the waters around the south-west coast of the UK begin to warm up the population of these crabs is increasing. Tangle nets are the main fishing method used to capture spider crabs. Netting is less sustainable than potting; with potting there is no bycatch and undersized crabs can be returned to the sea alive. Avoid using immature crabs (the legal minimum landing size is 120 mm maximum body width), egg-bearing crabs and fresh (not previously frozen) crabs caught during the spawning season (April to July).

Velvet Crab

Spider Crab

LANGOUSTINE

Also known as Dublin Bay prawns, Norway lobster and scampi, these orange-pink shellfish from the north-east Atlantic and Mediterranean resemble small, slim lobsters. They are an expensive choice with little meat, but are delicious if freshly caught and cooked.

The best specimens can be bought from late spring to late autumn and are cooked in the same way as lobster. Because of their smaller size, they need less cooking. Usually only the tail is sold. In their shells, 200 g should be enough per portion, but removed from their shells, half this quantity will be enough. They are available frozen all year round.

PRAWNS

There are many prawn species and they vary in size from 5 to 18 cm long. King prawns grow even larger at up to 23 cm. They also come in many colours, from the familiar common pink prawns to the brown-blue tiger prawns.

Prawns are available all year round, though usually frozen in the UK. Fresh raw prawns are the tastiest. They should be firm and springy with bright shells. If they are limp, soft or have an ammonia smell then discard them. Ensure frozen prawns are properly defrosted before heating.

Prawns can be prepared in the same way as langoustine but do not require scissors to cut and peel as the shells are much softer.

CRAYFISH

Crayfish are freshwater crustaceans resembling small lobsters, to which they are related. They breathe through feather-like gills and are found in fresh water that does not freeze to the bottom; they are also mostly found in rivers and streams where there is fresh water running, and which have shelter against predators.

Step-by-step: Method of preparing crayfish

1. Holding the crayfish flat against the board lift the central tail flap towards the head.

2. Pull the spinal cord out in one clean motion as shown.

3. Crayfish can be cooked in a number of ways such as steamed, in a court bouillon or fried in butter.

Transportation and storage

The best transportation and storage for live shellfish is to use a seawater or freshwater tank. For shellfish to be transported in these conditions the following points should be observed:

- controlled water temperature within the tanks.
- good aeration of the water.
- suitable water quality depending on the type of crustacean or mollusc.
- species should be separated into independent tanks.

However, this method is costly and only catering establishments that specialize in serving shellfish will have this facility. Fish and shellfish suppliers will also have this facility on their own premises, but generally when being delivered crustaceans such as lobster, crabs and crayfish will be packed in cases (usually polystyrene), covered with wet cloths and kept in a refrigerated environment.

Follow these guidelines when storing fresh shellfish:

1 Keep the shellfish at a temperature of between 2°C and 8°C.

2 Keep shellfish in its packaging until preparation, this is to prevent moisture loss.

3 Ensure that all shellfish remain moist.

4 Molluscs should be kept in a container embedded in ice. The round side of the shell should face downwards to help collect and retain the natural juices.

5 Check regularly to make sure that they are still alive. Reject any dead or dying specimens.

Shellfish allergy

Allergy to shellfish is quite common and people who are sensitive can react to a number of different types of shellfish, such as shrimps, prawns, lobsters and oysters. People who are allergic to one type of shellfish often react to others. Shellfish allergy can often cause severe reactions, and even the vapours from shellfish being cooked may be enough to trigger a reaction in some people.

Since November 2005, prepacked food sold in Europe must show clearly on the label if it contains crustaceans, including lobster, crab, prawns and langoustines. However, other groups of shellfish, such as molluscs (including mussels, scallops, oysters, whelks, squid and octopus) do not need to be labelled individually.

Shellfish is, however, recognized as being a healthy food which is low in cholesterol. It is important to support the UK's territorial fisherman and to utilize their skills in catching only what is required. This will help to increase the stock levels and generate a healthier UK economy.

Shellfish Recipes

Crab and grain mustard beignets

Crab and grain mustard beignets with an iced gazpacho

Ingredients	4 portions	10 portions
White crab meat	200 g	500 g
Grain mustard	2 tbsp	5 tbsp
Choux paste	100 g	250 g
Pink peppercorns	1 tsp	2½ tsp
Fresh chopped parsley	2 tbsp	5 tbsp
Tomato juice	100 ml	250 ml
Cucumber brunoise	1 tbsp	2½ tbsp
Red wine vinegar	50 ml	125 ml
Olive oil	2 tbsp	5 tbsp
Finely chopped garlic	1 tsp	2½ tsp
Fresh basil	4 leaves	10 leaves
Shallot brunoise	1 tbsp	2½ tbsp
Salt and white pepper	to taste	to taste

energy	cal	fat	sat fat	carb	sugar	protein	fibre
2027 kJ	495 kcal	24.1 g	6.4 g	40.2 g	28.8 g	28.2 g	13.8 g

METHOD OF WORK

1 Combine the prepared tomato, cucumber, shallot, garlic, vinegar and oil together. Season well and place in the freezer until required for service (it is essential that it is not allowed to freeze completely).

2 Mix the choux pastry with the crab, ground peppercorns, fresh chopped parsley and grain mustard and season well.

3 Quenelle the choux mixture neatly, one quenelle per portion, and deep fry in groundnut oil at 190°C until golden in colour and completely cooked through.

4 Spoon the chilled gazpacho into a cold serving bowl and drizzle a little olive oil around.

5 Set the crab beignet on top and dress with the chiffonade of fresh basil.

Crayfish mousse with a shellfish bisque

Ingredients	4 portions	10 portions
Crayfish (prepared, cooked in fish stock and peeled)	15	40
Egg yolks	2	5
White wine	50 ml	125 ml
Onion macédoine	1 tbsp	3 tbsp
Leek macédoine	1 tbsp	3 tbsp
Celery macédoine	1 tbsp	3 tbsp
Butter	100 g	250 g
Fresh lemon sole (minced)	200 g	500 g
Egg whites	2	5
Double cream	200 ml	500 ml
Bisque	100 ml	250 ml
Fresh full fat milk	50 ml	125 ml
Saffron	pinch	pinch
Fresh chervil	sprigs	sprigs
Salt and white pepper	to taste	to taste

energy	cal	fat	sat fat	carb	sugar	protein	fibre
4147 kJ	1001 kcal	80 g	47.8 g	17.8 g	4.9 g	44.2 g	1.8 g

METHOD OF WORK

1 Sweat the vegetables in butter for three minutes without colour. Add the crayfish and wine, cover with a lid and cook for three minutes. (Reserve some tails for garnish).

2 Mince the crayfish with the lemon sole and chill over ice for ten minutes.

3 Add the egg yolks and cream very slowly while continuously beating over the ice, season well.

4 Whisk the egg whites to firm peaks then fold into the crayfish mixture.

5 Quenelle the mixture into stock and simmer gently until cooked.

6 Heat the bisque.

7 Serve the quenelles with sauce and reserved langoustine tails.

Fried medallions of lobster with coral pasta

Fried medallions of lobster with coral pasta and a bisque foam

Ingredients	4 portions	10 portions
Fresh lobster (hen)	1	3
Fresh egg pasta dough	200 g	500 g
Shellfish bisque	100 ml	250 ml
Fresh full fat milk	50 ml	125 ml
Double cream	50 ml	125 ml
Lemon thyme	sprig	sprig
Butter	100 g	250 g
Salt and white pepper	to taste	to taste

energy	cal	fat	sat fat	carb	sugar	protein	fibre
4251 kJ	1023 kcal	69.1 g	38.4 g	18.8 g	3.8 g	71.4 g	1.7 g

METHOD OF WORK

1 Remove the coral from the hen lobster and add to the pasta dough when initially mixing the ingredients.

2 Kill the lobster by plunging a knife through the cavity in the centre of its head.

3 Steam the lobster for six minutes and cool quickly.

4 Remove the tail meat and claws then reserve.

5 Heat the bisque and separate into two, add double cream to one half and allow to reduce to form a sauce and season well.

6 Blanch the pasta in boiling salted water, drain and add to the sauce.

7 Slice the tail meat (two slices per portion) and quickly fry in butter with the claws until golden and season.

8 Add the milk to the remaining bisque and blend using a handheld blender until a foam appears.

9 Lay the pasta neatly into a bowl, top with the lobster, spoon over the foam and finish with the lemon thyme.

CHEF'S TIP European lobsters take five years to reach a size of just over 500 g. They cast their complete shell to grow and can live to 15 years or more. Retain any leftover lobster or prawn shells for making bisques, sauces and shellfish stocks.

Langoustines cooked in a sweet curry sauce

Langoustines cooked in a sweet curry sauce with coconut rice

Ingredients	4 portions	10 portions
Langoustines	20	50
Unsalted butter	100 g	250 g
Finely chopped onion	4 tbsp	10 tbsp
Long grain rice	200 g	500 g
Fish stock	400 ml	1 l
Fresh coconut	¼	1 whole
Flat leaf parsley	4 sprigs	10 sprigs
Sweet curry sauce	200 ml	500 ml
Lemon juice and zest	½ lemon	1 lemon
Finely chopped garlic	2 tsp	5 tsp
Finely chopped red chilli	1 tsp	2 tsp
Good quality salt and white pepper	to taste	to taste

energy	cal	fat	sat fat	carb	sugar	protein	fibre
2756 kJ	663 kcal	43.2 g	29.3 g	22.5 g	5.6 g	45.9 g	1.8 g

METHOD OF WORK

1 Preheat an oven to 180°C.
2 Take half of the unsalted butter and melt in a heavy-based saucepan, add the chopped onion and sweat until translucent.
3 Add the rice and cook for a further two minutes allowing the grains to become coated in butter and completely mixed with the onion.
4 Add the hot fish stock and bring to the boil, cover with a buttered cartouche and braise in the preheated oven for ten minutes or until the rice has just cooked.
5 Remove from the oven, fluff the rice over with a fork and fold in the coconut, seasoning and chopped parsley.
6 Marinate the peeled langoustine tails in garlic and lemon for five minutes before quickly frying in the remaining butter.
7 Carefully place the langoustines into the sauce and cook for one minute.
8 Arrange the rice neatly in a bowl, add the langoustines and garnish with red chilli.

Mussels sun-dried tomato bread

Mussels cooked with garlic cream sauce, sun-dried tomato bread

Ingredients	4 portions	10 portions
Fresh mussels	400 g	1 kg
Garlic	1 clove	3 cloves
Dry white wine	50 ml	125 ml
Shallot brunoise	2 tbsp	5 tbsp
Double cream	150 ml	375 ml
Sun-dried tomato bread	4 rolls	10 rolls
Baby herbs	75 g	180 g
Lemon oil	2 tbsp	5 tbsp
Fish stock	100 ml	250 ml
Fresh coriander	4 sprigs	10 sprigs
Good-quality salt and white pepper	to taste	to taste

energy	cal	fat	sat fat	carb	sugar	protein	fibre
5344 kJ	1283 kcal	60.9 g	25.8 g	128 g	9.9 g	48.3 g	10.2 g

METHOD OF WORK

1   Place the mussels, shallots, chopped garlic and white wine in a hot saucepan. Cover with a tight-fitting lid and cook for two minutes. The mussels should have all opened (discard any that remain closed).

2   Remove the mussels and keep warm, add the fish stock to the saucepan and reduce by half over a medium heat.

3   Add the double cream and reduce until the sauce thickens to the correct consistency.

4   Return the mussels to the sauce and warm through gently, check the seasoning.

5   Slice open the rolls and warm through the oven.

6   Add the mussels and the sauce.

7   Dress the baby herbs with lemon oil and arrange neatly to the side of the bowl and serve with the coriander.

CHEF'S TIP   Before cooking mussels always ensure that they are washed well under plenty of cold running water. Remove all beards and barnacles. Any mussels that are still open at this point should be discarded.

Scampi fritters

Scampi fritters with a baby herb salad and vine tomato coulis

Ingredients	4 portions	10 portions
Shelled cooked scampi	20	50
Olive oil	100 ml	250 ml
Lemon zest and juice	1 lemon	3 lemons
Cayenne pepper	pinch	pinch
Self raising flour	100 g	250 g
Finely chopped parsley	1 tbsp	3 tbsp
Baby herbs (tarragon and dill)	100 g	250 g
White wine vinegar	50 ml	125 ml
Dijon mustard	1 tbsp	3 tbsp
Vine tomato coulis	4 tbsp	10 tbsp
Good quality salt and white pepper	to taste	to taste

energy	cal	fat	sat fat	carb	sugar	protein	fibre
1852 kJ	444 kcal	28.3 g	4.1 g	29.7 g	2.4 g	21 g	3.7 g

METHOD OF WORK

1　Marinate the scampi in lemon, cayenne and a little olive oil.

2　Mix the flour and parsley and enough water to form a light batter, season well (reserve a little flour to coat the scampi).

3　Dust the scampi with flour, dip into the batter and deep fry at 180°C until golden brown.

4　Produce a vinaigrette with the mustard, vinegar and olive oil then dress the baby herbs.

5　Arrange the herbs on a plate, add the scampi and spoon over the tomato coulis.

Deep fried oysters with a Thai salad

Ingredients	4 portions	10 portions
Fresh oysters	12	30
White breadcrumbs	200 g	500 g
Lime juice and zest	1 lime	2 limes
Flour	100 g	250 g
Whole egg pasteurized	100 ml	250 ml
Chinese leaf lettuce (cut into chiffonade)	¼ lettuce	¾ lettuce
Assorted peppers (cut into julienne)	½ of each colour	1 of each colour
Red onion finely sliced	50 g	125 g
Baby gem lettuce (cut into chiffonade)	1	2
Julienne of carrot	80 g	200 g
Thai dressing	200 ml	500 ml
Salt and white pepper	to taste	to taste

energy	cal	fat	sat fat	carb	sugar	protein	fibre
5789 kJ	1390 kcal	84.2 g	14.3 g	103 g	8.9 g	56 g	5.8 g

METHOD OF WORK

1　Carefully remove the fresh oysters from their shells and wash to remove any grit.

2　Marinate the oysters in the lime juice for five minutes.

3　Pané the oysters through the flour, then the beaten egg and finally the breadcrumbs with the finely grated lime zest mixed through.

4　Prepare the vegetables as required and dress with the Thai dressing.

5　Season well and arrange on a serving plate.

6　Quickly deep-fry the oysters at 180°C until golden and serve on top of the salad.

Scallops with cauliflower purée

Seared scallops with a sweet caper dressing and cauliflower purée

Ingredients	4 portions	10 portions
Fresh scallops	12	30
Curry powder	5 g	10 g
Capers	80 g	200 g
Caster sugar	2 tbsp	5 tbsp
White wine vinegar	40 ml	100 ml
Vegetable stock	100 ml	250 ml
Cauliflower	¼	¾
Béchamel sauce	50 ml	125 ml
Olive oil	2 tbsp	5 tbsp
Fresh dill	4 sprigs	10 sprigs
Salt and white pepper	to taste	to taste

energy	cal	fat	sat fat	carb	sugar	protein	fibre
990 kJ	237 kcal	13.4 g	2.9 g	16.7 g	12.4 g	13.4 g	2.4 g

METHOD OF WORK

1 Carefully remove the scallops from the shells and remove the corals.

2 Trim the scallops, wash, dry and dust lightly with the curry powder.

3 Drain and wash the capers, then blend with the vinegar, oil and sugar to form the dressing.

4 Cut the cauliflower into small florets and cook in the vegetable stock until tender. Drain and blend the cauliflower with the béchamel until smooth, pass through a sieve. Season to taste.

5 Quickly sear the scallops in a hot pan with a little oil for one minute on each side.

6 Spoon the purée and dressing onto a serving plate, arrange the scallops on top and finish with a sprig of fresh dill.

CHEF'S TIP Oyster and scallop shells can be washed and used for decoration. The rings on a scallop's shell can be used to age it; some scallops live for ten years or more.

Tiger prawn and lemongrass cakes

Tiger prawn and lemongrass cakes with coriander mayonnaise

Ingredients	4 portions	10 portions
Minced tiger prawns, saving two for garnish	16	40
Lemon grass brunoise	1 tbsp	2.5 tbsp
Red chilli brunoise	2 tbsp	5 tbsp
Shallot brunoise	1 tbsp	2.5 tbsp
Garlic puree	1 tsp	2.5 tsp
Ginger puree	1 tsp	2.5 tsp
Corn flour	50 g	125 g
Soy sauce	2 tbsp	5 tbsp
Mayonnaise	200 g	500 g
Chopped coriander	2 tbsp	5 tbsp

energy	cal	fat	sat fat	carb	sugar	protein	fibre
2124 kJ	512 kcal	40.8 g	6 g	20.8 g	3.1 g	16.3 g	4.8 g

METHOD OF WORK

1 Preheat oven to 180°C.

2 Mix the minced prawn meat with the lemongrass, garlic, ginger, corn flour, soy sauce and seasoning. Leave for 20 minutes.

3 Divide the prawn paste into equal pieces, one per portion. Dust with a little corn flour and form into round shapes.

4 Fry until golden in a little heated oil, remove from the pan and bake in the preheated oven for two minutes.

5 Add the whole tails at the last minute to the pan and flash fry until just cooked.

6 Mix the mayonnaise and coriander together and serve with the cakes and tails.

Guest Chef

Poached fillet of sea bass filled with chancre crab and lobster, crushed Jersey Royals

Chef *Dominic Farrell*
Adrian Goldsborough
Eileen Buicke-Kelly

Centre *Academy of Culinary Arts, Highlands College, Jersey*

The Jersey Royal season begins in November with planting under glass or plastic. However, many farmers still use seaweed harvested from Jersey beaches as a natural fertilizer (known locally as Vraic). The main outdoor crop is planted from January to April and harvesting usually begins in April through to the end of June. The peak of the season is May, when up to 1500 tonnes of Royals can be exported daily.

Ingredients	4 portions
Jersey Royals	450 g
Chives	25 g
Bok choy	125 g
Lemon juice	½
Sea bass fillets, skin on scaled and pin boned	4 × 100 g
White and brown crab meat	80 g
Cooked lobster claw	200 g (4)
Cooked sliced lobster tail	250 g (12 slices)
Sunflower oil	6 tbpsn
Pea foam, pea puree, shelled peas and pea shoots	

METHOD OF WORK

1   Portion the fillets to 100 g each, place skin side down on the board and create a pocket in the flesh without scoring the skin.

2   Pick the white crab meat and bind with the brown meat, season with salt, pepper and lemon juice.

3   Place the sea bass skin side down onto a sheet of cling film and fill the pocket with the crab mixture. Secure the fish tightly with cling film and set aside in the fridge.

4   Gently wash the Jersey Royals and place into boiling salted water until cooked.

5   Secure a metal spoon to the underside of the lobster tail and fasten with string. Place head first into boiling water (six minutes per lb) and refresh in ice water.

6   Once cold, remove the tail and claws and remove all the meat from the claws and tail, ensuring that the meat remains whole for presentation purposes. Place in the fridge until ready to use.

7   Cook the bok choy in boiling salted water for 30 seconds, refresh.

8   Crush the hot Jersey Royals and season with salt, pepper, lemon juice and finely chopped chives.

9   Place wrapped bass fillet into poaching water for eight minutes (cooking time may vary according to the size of the fillet).

10   Slice the lobster tail into slices and place on a lightly oiled grilling tray allowing three slices per portion and one claw per portion. Lightly season and grill until hot.

To Finish

11   Place the reheated bok choy and the grilled lobster claw on top of the potatoes.
Sit the sea bass on the top and finish with the three grilled slices of lobster. Serve with pea foam, pea puree, shelled peas and pea shoots.

ASSESSMENT OF KNOWLEDGE AND UNDERSTANDING

You have now learned about the use of the different types of fish and shellfish and how to produce a variety of fish and shellfish dishes utilizing an array of commodities and cooking techniques.

To test your level of knowledge and understanding, answer the following short questions. These will help to prepare you for your summative (final) assessment.

Fish preparation

1   Explain why the removal of fins is important during preparation of exotic fish.

2   Describe how the skinning of Dover sole is different from the skinning of other flat fish and explain the process.

Shellfish quality identifications

1   Explain when oysters should be bought and in what condition.

2   Explain the difference between crustaceans, molluscs and cephalopods.

Shellfish preparation

1   Describe the method for opening oysters.

2   Explain how langoustines should be prepared before cooking.

3   Identify which parts of lobsters and crabs should be discarded and why.

Materials and storage

1   Describe how shellfish should be transported.

Cooking

1   Describe the cooking of crab.

Health and safety

1   List the months during which raw oysters should not be eaten.

Producing pastry and pâtisserie items

10

VRQ

Produce paste products

NVQ

Prepare, cook and finish complex pastry products

LEARNING OBJECTIVES

The aim of this chapter is to enable the reader to develop the necessary advanced techniques, knowledge and understanding of the principles in preparing and cooking classical and modern pastries and *pâtisserie*.

The emphasis in this chapter is on developing precision and control in existing skills and perfecting refined, contemporary and advanced techniques. Also included in this chapter is further information on culinary materials, ingredients and equipment.

At the end of this chapter you will be able to:

- **Understand the concepts and techniques of baking.**

- **Understand the principles common to pastry making.**

- **Clearly identify each variety of paste.**

- **Recognize the quality points of ingredients and various baking products.**

- **Comprehend the concept for convenience pastes.**

- **Identify important storage techniques within hygiene regulations.**

- **Prepare and produce different pastes for advanced pâtisserie products.**

- **Be able to present a range of advanced pastry and pâtisserie products.**

Introduction

The origins of the art of pastry making can be attributed to the Egyptians, who were the first to make basic yeast cakes. The ancient Greeks and Romans produced a variety of confections, primarily from seeds, honey, almonds and flour. The introduction of sugar to Europe via Asia gave impetus to the first European pastry cooks, who in France were then called *oubloyers* after a type of waffle (oublies). Great innovations in pastry making were later introduced in other countries, most notably Italy, Switzerland and Spain. However, the greatest innovator was working at the beginning of the 19th century and his name was

Marie-Antoine Carême (1784–1833). He took pâtisserie to new heights through his introduction of ornate sugar designs, by perfecting the recipe for puff pastry and creating some principal techniques in pastry work still used to this day.

VIDEO CLIP French pâtisserie

New techniques are being developed constantly as the modern pastry kitchen has become well equipped with innovative machinery and small equipment such as Combi-ovens, chocolate tempering machines and the pastry-break. These also help the chef to produce high-quality, standardized products that are well presented and economical.

An electric pastry break used for rolling out pastry mechanically

Identifying the correct tools and equipment for each job is as important as reading recipes carefully. As mundane as this might sound, the careful identification of the correct ingredients, tools, equipment and production method is the first stage to creating success in a pastry team. In this modern era full of technological advances geography is no longer a barrier to the pastry chef; exotic ingredients from all over the world are now common.

There are several different varieties of pastry, each with a different texture and structure. These depend on two key elements: the way fat is incorporated into the paste and the development of gluten in the flour. The incorporation of fat is very specific and crucial to a good pastry. Pastry chefs work in fat so that it isolates very small flour particles from each other, isolates larger masses or even whole layers of paste from each other. It is also essential to control gluten development to avoid making a paste that is difficult to shape and a pastry that is tough and chewy instead of tender and delicate.

The difference between tender and flaky pastes

One of the primary steps in pastry making is the understanding of the difference between tender (crumbly) and flaky (paper thin) pastes. Certain fats are referred to as shortenings because tenderness results when the fat shortens the strands of gluten, preventing them from joining together and producing a tough pastry crust.

Flakiness results when fine layers of fat act as leaves between fine layers of paste and melt when baked leaving spaces of air. The air pockets expand and any moisture present turns to steam, pushing apart each fine layer. This expansion separates each layer to produce flakiness as shown in the diagram 'Tender paste versus flaky pastes'.

⬤ Fat   ▬▬ Paste

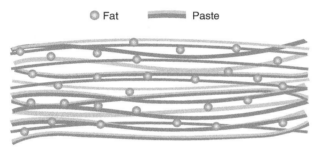

Tender paste with the fat more evenly distributed in smaller, finer pieces. The fat melts into the pastry paste creating tenderness by coating gluten strands but producing little flakiness.

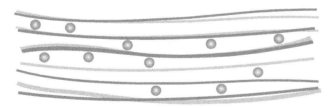

Flaky paste with fat in pea-sized pieces unevenly distributed in the pastry paste. The fat melts into the pastry paste creating spaces during baking which separates the layers producing flakiness.

Tender paste versus flaky pastes

The technique and fundamentals of baking

To understand the concept of baking and how to achieve consistent results there is a requirement to appreciate the most important factor in baking: humidity. As the oven transfers heat to food, moisture from the food evaporates into the air as water vapour. Eventually the water vapour disappears out of the oven vent, but before withdrawing it lowers the effective temperature inside the oven. This is the primary cause of erratic baking results.

Water vapour is important because it determines the actual baking temperature inside the oven as opposed to what the oven temperature dial is set at. Humidity inside a conventional bakery oven is largely under the control of the food placed in the oven and the temperature will invariably change, sometimes dramatically, during the process of baking.

> **CHEF'S TIP** Pre-heating the oven is important, hot oven walls will help to maintain a steady baking temperature. This is one of the reasons wood-fired ovens are so good for baking because they have thick brick and masonry walls to hold the heat effectively.

Pre-heating the oven

Pre-heating is important because it gives the oven a large and somewhat well-controlled pool of heat energy to draw on as it reacts to the flood of cold air that occurs when the oven door is opened and the food is placed inside. It is this important step that will help to create the consistent baking of food products.

In all bakery recipes it is important to set the temperature of the oven first because it takes a long time for the oven to meet the correct temperature. This is because most of the hot air is wasted. Although the actual energy required to heat an oven element is relatively small, it is the walls of the oven that require pre-heating, not the air. The heat must pass through the air to get to the oven walls and air is a poor conductor of heat. Air also expands when heated (because it is effectively a gas) and will find ways of escaping the oven chamber.

The inside of a wood-fired brick oven. The hot oven walls will radiate the intense heat stored within them after the pre-heating process has been completed

Skipping the pre-heating step is not an option. If you place food inside the oven as soon as the air inside is hot, but before the oven walls achieve the target temperature, the cold food will warm only slightly before the air drops most of its heat. Exacerbating this situation, the warming food will emit water vapour as a cool and dense gas. The water vapour will drop to the base of the oven which forces warmer air to the top of the oven and usually out of the oven vent. The oven will now have to work harder to heat up the water vapour and the baking of the food will slow down. If the oven door is opened to adjust or check on the food, the hot air and vapour will escape to be replaced by cooler air. The temperature in the oven will plummet and the oven will recover slowly.

Pre-heating the oven walls will help to prevent such drops in temperature. The walls can store large quantities of heat energy and can release it quickly when needed to rapidly restore the oven temperature.

Using a forced-air convection oven

When baking food, heat moves via convection to the surface of the food item to produce a crust. This allows heat to move into the food via a combination of conduction of the food heating up and convection of the water vapour created from inside the food.

Forced-air convection baking is faster than a conventional oven system although forced convection does not actually make baking more even, as many people seem to suggest. The fan in the oven blows water vapour near the surface of the food and mixes it with drier surrounding air. When the food is exposed to a steady supply of dry air, the water evaporation zone recedes deeper into the food which helps to drive heat conduction to the core.

The problem of uneven baking still exists in forced-air convection because the convection air is not the only

source of heating. Radiant heat is also apparent. The hot oven walls will radiate infrared energy and the hotter the oven temperature, the more intense the infrared radiation will be. Unfortunately, oven walls will radiate heat unevenly due to the walls being thicker in some spots than in others and some parts of the wall are closer to the burners or heating elements than others. Many oven doors contain a window which radiates a lot less heat than the walls do.

> **CHEF'S TIP**   The oven walls of a typical oven will have hot-spots and cold-spots that make it difficult to bake food evenly. Any food or grease stains on the walls will burn to carbon and become hot-spots because dark surfaces are more efficient in emitting heat. The lesson here is to keep your oven clean.
>
>

Strategies for consistent baking results

In understanding the factors that influence baking we can begin to create baking strategies to help achieve consistent results. Below are a few suggestions:

1   Calibrate the oven thermostat. The use of a reliable thermometer to check the air temperature of the oven in the centre is important. By adding another oven thermometer and placing it into the centre of the oven will help give more accurate oven temperature readings.

2   Know the real baking temperature of the oven. Constantly monitor the baking process by probing a thermometer just beneath the surface of the food if possible. Pay close attention to the water vapour in the oven and slightly open the oven door to lower the humidity if required.

3   Bake in consistent batch sizes. A batch size has a dramatic effect on baking times. After 20 minutes of baking at 180°C in a fully loaded oven the core oven temperature will be approximately 80°C lower. In moderately or lightly loaded ovens the drop in temperature is much more (sometimes up to 100°C). Therefore a fully loaded oven often bakes food faster.

4   Pay attention to the Maillard reaction and move the food around as often as necessary to keep hot-spots of radiant heat from scorching the food. Generally the front of the oven (nearest to the door) is the coolest area and the hottest part of the oven interior is generally towards the back, near the corners.

Types of pastry

Les pâtes friables – short pastes

This family of short pastes comprises several different varieties, each one having its own method of preparation and use. All of the pastes are easy to prepare, but they do require careful handling, thoughtful techniques and an understanding of their individual characteristics. The art of making short pastry is to ensure that the paste remains in a controllable form, whilst as far as possible preventing gluten formation.

HYDRATION AND FORMING GLUTEN STRUCTURES

Gluten is formed only when wheat flour is deformed in the presence of moisture, such as water or milk. The moisture will partially dissolve or swell the flour proteins. The process of swelling the protein molecules with water is often referred to as 'hydration'. This is the first stage in forming a gluten structure. Once the protein molecules have been hydrated, they must be denatured by mechanical manipulation (mixing or kneading) where they are able to reform into new structures where several proteins bind together.

There are two distinct components in gluten:

1 Gliadin is a sticky and partially fluid protein that is soluble.

2 Glutenin is not soluble and has a fibrous and elastic texture.

Gluten is formed when lots of links are created between many different gliadin and glutenin proteins. This can only take place once the proteins are well hydrated; sometimes double the water by the protein weight is needed for this process to begin. This requirement of a large amount of water to hydrate the proteins provides a key to the control of gluten formation. By controlling the rate at which water or milk is added and the extent to which the water can reach all the starch granules in the flour, the overall degree of hydration of the proteins can also be controlled. For example, **rubbing in** fats to coat the surface of individual grains of flour will be liable to resist water from the surface and thus decrease the rate at which hydration can be achieved. The use of this technique in pastry making helps to control the amount of gluten formation.

With further manipulation these proteins begin to strengthen their bonds and the stretching process starts to develop gluten. If the paste is allowed to relax before the gluten is fully formed it will be much easier to work with, shape and bake. This is why many pastry recipes mention resting periods between rolling and making and states the importance of avoiding over working each short paste.

THE PRINCIPLES OF ELASTICITY AND PLASTICITY

One of the most important considerations when making pastry is to control the elasticity of the paste. If a paste is too elastic it will snap back to its original shape when rolled out. However, if the paste is too plastic it will flow easily and not be able to hold its own shape after moulding.

When pastes are formed and rolled out they will partially recover their original shapes at the end of this process. This is called elastic whereas a paste that holds its shape after rolling out is known as plastic.

The elasticity of paste is determined largely by the moisture content and the level of gluten formation. Drier pastes will generally be stiffer and a little more plastic, while those with high gluten content will be very elastic (such as puff pastry). To maintain the correct texture of a paste the chef needs to be able to keep the gluten content and the water content under control.

Resting the paste is important to prevent shrinkage during manipulation and baking

Essentially, when producing short pastes there are three exceptional techniques that need to be addressed to ensure the correct amount of elasticity and plasticity:

● Add the correct amount of moisture (water, milk or raw egg content) to control the hydration process and control the gluten formation. Consider the technique of rubbing in the fat and flour before adding the moisture.

● Reduce the degree to which water penetrates into the starch granules and swells the surface proteins. Keeping the flour and the moisture as cold as possible will reduce the hydration of the starch granules and will assist in control of the gluten content.

● Once the pastry has been made allow it to relax for up to 20 minutes. After rolling out, once again let the paste relax and before placing it into a mould and into the oven to bake let the paste relax again. If this process is not followed the paste will contract during the baking process and will change shape.

VARIETIES OF SHORT PASTE

There are six different short pastes identified in this chapter which come under the collective heading of *les pâtes friables*, all of them being short, crisp and friable (crumbly):

- shortcrust pastry – *la pâte brisée;*
- lining paste – *la pâte à foncer;*
- pie paste – *la pâte à pâté;*
- sweet paste – *la pâte sucrée;*
- shortbread/sable paste – *la pâte sablée;*
- linzer paste – *la pâte à linzer.*

The objective with these types of pastes is to make a fine, friable textured final product that crumbles in the mouth, so it is very important to prevent as far as possible any gluten being created as the flour is rolled and formed. Two main methods are used to obtain the characteristic of these pastes:

- Sablage (rubbing in) – the aim of this method is to coat the particles of flour with a layer of fat to protect them from the liquid ingredients. This helps to prevent the gluten from becoming activated, which would result in a paste that is too elastic.

- Creaming – in this method the liquid ingredients are first combined with the butter and worked to a smooth cream. This method is generally used for recipes that contain a high proportion of fat. The flour is added at the last stage and is not manipulated for as long as in the 'rubbing in' method and therefore the fat and moisture tends not to penetrate the flour particles.

PREPARATION DETAILS FOR SHORT PASTES

It is important to be aware of the roles of the different ingredients. For instance, any increase in the fat content will shorten the paste by reacting with the proteins in the flour. It will also enhance the flavour and colour the paste if the correct type of fat is used, such as a good butter. The following points are identified to help assist in the preparation of short pastes.

- **La pâte à foncer, la pâte brisée and la pâte à pâté**
  These pastes are always prepared using the sablage technique. The use of water as the binding agent produces an elastic paste that must be rested for approximately 30 minutes before use. The pastes must be rested again after manipulation into moulds before baking. Baking temperature: 230°C.

- **La pâte sucrée**
  This paste may be prepared using either the sablage or the creaming technique. The paste is soft and fragile; therefore it must be handled very carefully. Flour should be used when rolling out the paste, but too much flour during this process will produce a heavier texture to the finished item. Baking temperature should be 200°C.

- **La pâte sablée and la pâte à linzer**
  It is extremely short and difficult to use. This is due to the high fat and egg content. This should be used in small quantities and kept refrigerated at all times. Finished products should be kept in an airtight container otherwise they will quickly become soft; this is due to the hygroscopic properties of the ingredients such as sugar which is used in high proportions.

Problems with the making of short pastes can arise and the general rule is to discard the paste and start over again after identifying the problem. However, there are some solutions to offer when problems are encountered. The table below will help with this concept.

PROBLEM	CAUSE	SOLUTION
Paste is very dry and breaks when rolled out	Insufficient water has been added to the recipe	Chill the paste until very cold and carefully break up the paste with a sharp knife and add a little more water and remix
Paste is damp and sticky	Too much water has been used to make the paste	Usually this is not salvageable, however carefully cut the chilled paste into small pieces and sprinkle with flour before moulding back into a ball, avoiding the stretching of the paste
Cooked pastry is tough	Too much gluten was formed during the mixing and rolling processes	More care is needed to avoid stretching and overworking the paste
Pastry blisters during baking	Water pockets have developed in the pastry causing blisters of steam during baking	More care is needed to ensure the water is uniformly distributed through the paste
Pastry shrinks during baking	The rolled out paste was not rested long enough or the shaped paste was further stretched before baking	More relaxing time of the paste is required and avoid stretching the paste before baking

CHEF'S TIP You can use a food processor to make a short pastry. Place the flour and salt in the processor bowl fitted with a cutting blade and add the fat cut into small cubes. Process at a medium speed and the fat will be better rubbed into the flour. The advantage of this method is that you can reduce the fat content of your recipe by 10 per cent. Do not be tempted to add the water using the food processor as the action of the blade will knead the paste and gluten will be developed.

Pâte à feuilletée – puff paste

Puff paste is fundamentally a set of thin sheets of high-gluten content paste which are separated by layers of fat. When baked steam is generated from the fat layers, which separates the leaves of the paste so that a multi-layered and fine textured crisp product is produced.

This specific structure, consisting of numerous alternating layers of **détrempe** (the basic paste) and *beurrage* (the butter or fat used) is obtained by repeatedly folding and rolling the paste; this is known as giving the paste a 'turn'.

The puff paste itself should always have a somewhat firm consistency and should be completely chilled to at least 5°C while laminating. The détrempe must not become too elastic during the processing technique. It is therefore important not to overwork the ingredients while preparing the paste.

Uses of puff pastry

The following are examples of items made with puff pastry:

- vol-au-vents;
- allumettes;
- bande aux fruits;
- Eccles cakes and Banbury buns;
- beef Wellington;
- **fleurons** and various savoury decorations;
- tart shells for assorted large and individual tarts;
- palmiers;
- chaussons aux pommes;
- gateau pithivier;
- gateau mille-feuille.

CHEF'S TIP A variety of puff pastry made with oil can be traced back to the ancient Greeks. In France, records show a type of puff pastry being made in the 13th century, and a charter written by Bishop Robert of Amiens in 1311 mentions desserts using puff pastry. The creation of talmouses (puff pastry wrapped around a savoury farce) popularized this pastry in the early 15th century. Carême, in his book Le Pâtissier Royal, honoured Feuillet by describing his pastries as beautiful and inspiring.

Five different methods for making puff paste

- **French method**
  It is essential to work on a cool marble work surface, using the 'envelope' method to position the fat inside the paste. Fold and give three 'book' turns.

- **English method**
  Roll the détrempe out to an oblong shape and place the beurrage over one-third of the détrempe. Give six single turns.

- **Scottish method**
  The beurrage is incorporated to the détrempe in small pieces. This is a fast method and can be processed carefully on a mixing machine.

- **Reversed method (inverted method)**
  This method reverses the positions of the two principal elements. The détrempe is assembled in the same manner as in a basic puff paste. The butter is softened, and then mixed with a little flour. A simple blending of the two ingredients is sufficient before rolling out the chilled butter and placing the détrempe on top. This produces a crumblier but denser finish to the baked pastry.

● **Viennois**

This method is primarily the same as the French method but with a subtle difference. Enriching ingredients are added to the détrempe to give richer flavour and colour to the finished article, for example the addition of egg yolks can be added alongside a small amount of sugar.

Key aspects on the production of puff pastry

1 Flour – use strong flour to increase the gluten content. Most white flour milled in the UK is no longer bleached and contains grey particles which look like ash. This may give a slightly dull look to the paste but will not affect the structure or flavour of the paste itself. Ensure the gluten content of the flour is high.

2 Salt – any type of salt that is easily soluble can be used, but a good quality sea salt is preferable.

3 Water – cold tap water is adequate. The quantity of water required will vary according to the flour used and its absorption rate.

4 Acid – if lemon juice or vinegar is added to the paste, it will gain elasticity and aids the relaxation of gluten.

5 Fat – unsalted butter has higher moisture content than pastry margarine so it is best to use a hard unsalted butter specifically produced for pastry production. It is helpful to prepare it in a flat, plastic square about 20 mm thick. Butter makes puff pastry more appetizing and colourful, but pastry margarine is easier to work with. A little malt extract added to the paste can compensate for lack of colour. The more butter a puff pastry contains, the lighter, softer and higher quality it will be. However, a ratio of 1:1 butter to flour content should not be exceeded.

6 Temperature – it is possible to make puff paste in a warm kitchen, up to 22–25°C, but working with butter will become progressively more difficult. It is important to maintain the ingredients, work surface and the paste as cool as possible.

7 Rolling – always place the puff paste in the refrigerator, covered in baking parchment, to rest before turns are made. Sometimes wrapping in plastic film for a long storage in a refrigerator will create condensation on the paste surface. This produces oxidation and creates a grey colouration to the paste. Keep the paste a uniform thickness during rolling and maintain straight sides and corners when rolling so that it will fold up into a neat rectangular shape after each turn. Puff paste is rolled in the opposite direction to how it is folded. This counters the direction of the roll and helps to ensure even layering.

8 Resting – The puff paste needs to rest for approximately 30 minutes between each turn.

9 Work surface – cool marble is the best surface to use because it remains cooler for longer periods than stainless steel surfaces. It is also slightly porous, which makes rolling easier. Keep it cleaned at all times and use an ice-bag to place on top of the surface if the kitchen is warm in between turns.

10 Single turn – involves folding the rolled sheet of puff paste into three.

11 Double turn – also called a 'book turn', involves folding the paste sheet into four. The two sides are folded into the middle and then closed up like a book.

12 Rotating – after each turn it is important to rotate the folded paste through 90° before rolling it out again. Always roll out evenly, treating the paste with care.

13 Baking – bake at 210°C to ensure the pastry cooks thoroughly before it colours too much. Once the puff pastry is baked, move directly to a wire rack to allow cooling and prevent the softening of the pastry from condensation.

Problems with the making of puff paste can arise and the general rule is to discard the paste and start over again after identifying the problem. However, there are some solutions to offer when problems are encountered. The table below will help with this concept.

PROBLEM	CAUSE		SOLUTION
Pastry fails to rise during baking	i	The fat has become mixed in with the paste layers and not formed separate layers of fat and paste.	Next time work the paste more to create a stronger gluten formation before rolling and placing the fat into layers.
	ii	The paste did not contain enough gluten so it could not facilitate the rising process during baking.	Ensure that the fat is chilled before rolling (approximately 5°C).
	iii	The puff paste was not rested and chilled between turns for long enough	Ensure enough time is given between turns to relax the paste. Approximately 20 minutes.
	iv	Too many turns have been given to the puff paste.	Do not roll out the pastry less than 2 cm thick otherwise there is a risk that the layers will become too thin and break.
The puff paste rises unevenly	The fat layers have broken down during the rolling process. The paste rises where there is fat between the layers.		When making the paste, be careful to roll the pastry evenly and do not allow the fat to become too cold.

Pâte à choux – choux paste

Choux paste is used for the production of a variety of classical and contemporary pastries, both sweet and savoury. It is made by melting fat in hot water and then quickly adding flour. This fast addition of the flour is important since the hot water is very quickly absorbed by the flour and it is important to ensure that the uptake of water is uniform throughout the paste.

Essential techniques for making choux paste

During the first part of the production of choux paste it is important to dry out the mix of water, fat, flour, sugar and salt. This will denature and change the structure of the starch found in flour, resulting in a thick paste. Note that the flour needs to be added quickly at this point to the hot water and melted fat.

The second phase is the re-moisturizing of the paste through the addition of eggs in order to obtain a paste of piping consistency. This paste therefore contains a lot of moisture (that remaining from the first part of the process and that from the addition of the egg). During the baking process the moisture will create steam, which acts as the raising agent for the paste.

> **CHEF'S TIP**   The origin of choux paste dates back to the 16th century. Its invention is attributed to an Italian pastry chef named Popelini, who created a gâteau called Le Popolin. The gâteau was made from a paste dried out on the stove and which resembled a type of raw pasta dough. This paste was also known *as la pâte à chaud.*

THE ROLE OF THE INGREDIENTS IN CHOUX PASTE

- **Water**
  The water can be half or totally replaced with milk. The resulting paste will be finer, more enriched and slightly softer in texture, but it may be a little heavier.

- **Fat**
  The choice (butter or margarine) and quantity of fat will depend on the role required of the finished paste. The proportion can vary between 400 g and 500 g per litre of liquid. Salted butter is the preferred fat due to its colour and flavour-enhancing properties.

- **Salt**
  This helps to improve the flavour. Use a fine salt, and ensure it is correctly weighed so as not to produce an over-salted taste.

- **Sugar**
  The role of sugar is to produce a good colour during baking. Use a fine-grained sugar (caster). The quantity of sugar may be varied according to the temperature of the oven: for a higher oven temperature, a smaller quantity of sugar should be used.

- **Eggs**
  The eggs should never be added to the **panada** when it has first been cooked out as the temperature of the initial paste (approximately 82–88°C) will cook the egg protein. This will make the paste less elastic and less able to retain steam and so will limit its ability to rise. The eggs should always be added when the paste is warm to the touch as this will aid the general incorporation and mixing process. The protein value of eggs helps to give colour to the paste. Eggs also help to produce the blown texture of choux paste.

- **Flour**
  Strong flour should be used. The quantity of flour may vary between 500 g and 800 g per litre of liquid according to the recipe.

During the baking process, the heat from the oven will turn the moisture in the paste to steam. At the same time, the eggs and the starch from the flour begin to coagulate, forming a layer on the outside of the paste which retains the steam. The steam inflates the paste, which continues to coagulate and becomes solid as it has cooked. The result is the choux pastry's distinctive blown appearance.

Problems with the making of choux paste can arise and the general rule is to discard the paste and start over again after identifying the problem. However, there are some solutions to offer when problems are encountered. The table below will help with this concept.

PROBLEM	CAUSE	SOLUTION
Choux paste fails to rise	The egg protein coagulated and cooked before the choux paste was baked in the oven	Ensure the panada has cooled well below 55°C before adding the eggs and ensure that plenty of air has been beaten into the paste at this point too
Choux paste does not crisp during baking	The paste preparation was too moist, the baking time was too short or the oven was not hot enough	If the choux pastry has browned on the outside, the most likely cause it a mixture that is too moist – reduce the liquid intake. If the choux pastry has not browned it is likely that the oven temperature is too low or too short baking time has transpired – increase the oven temperature or baking time.
When split after the baking process there are no holes inside to fill	Mixture is too stiff or insufficient air incorporated into the mixture	Beat in plenty of air during the addition of the eggs and make sure it is still soft but holds its own shape before piping

Strüdel paste

The strüdel paste consists of flour, water, salt, eggs and oil. It is important to give as much elasticity to the paste as possible. To help create this elasticity, use a fine graded strong flour that is high in protein. Once the paste has been made it is brushed with oil and allowed to rest for about 60 minutes.

An apricot strudel

The paste is then worked by hand, using fingertips which have been dipped in oil. It is gradually stretched from underneath until it is paper thin. This process should be carried out on a large, flour-dusted linen cloth.

CHEF'S TIP The word 'strüdel' is a derivative of the old German word streden, which means to boil or bubble. This is an apt description of the finished pastry as it often appears very wrinkly and bubbly on the surface. The actual pastry is thought to have originated from Bavaria in southern Germany or in Austria, and was the creation of a Hungarian pâtissier. It has also been suggested that strüdel is a relative of baklava, the Turkish sweet which comprises very thin layers of paste sandwiched together with a filling of chopped nuts and honey-based syrup. Strudel is most often associated with Austrian cuisine but is also a traditional pastry in the whole area formerly belonging to the Austro-Hungarian Empire. The oldest strudel recipe (a Millirahmstrudel) is from 1696, a handwritten recipe at the Viennese City Library, Wiener Stadtbibliothek.

Strüdel filling

The ingredients for strüdel filling vary from recipe to recipe. This may be due to regional preferences and traditions, or to individual chefs changing the components of a recipe at their own discretion. However, certain rules should always be followed in the make-up of a strüdel filling. The main one is that the recipe should have an equal balance of wet and dry ingredients: if the filling is too wet the strüdel may collapse, and if it is too dry it will not be pleasing to the palette.

The best-known kinds of strudel are Apfelstrudel and Topfenstrudel (with sweet soft quark cheese, in German Topfen cheese), followed by the Millirahmstrudel (Milk-cream strudel, Milchrahmstrudel). In Slovenia, cottage cheese is used instead of quark. Other strudel types include sour cherry

PROBLEM	CAUSE	SOLUTION
Holes appear when stretching the paste	The paste might be slightly dry and has been exposed to air for too long. Too much flour has been used when rolling out the paste	Brush the rested paste with a little olive oil over its surface. Reduce the amount of flour being used when rolling out the paste
The paste does not stretch and keeps shrinking	Insufficient resting period for the paste	Leave the paste to relax for a little longer at room temperature
The strudel collapses during baking	Filling for the strudel is too wet or the oven is not hot enough	Add more dry ingredients such as breadcrumbs to the filling and monitor the oven temperature closely

(*Weichselstrudel*), sweet cherry, nut filled (*Nussstrudel*), apricot strudel, plum strudel and poppy seed strudel (*Mohnstrudel*). There are also savoury strudels incorporating spinach, cabbage, pumpkin and sauerkraut alongside versions containing meat fillings.

VIDEO CLIP Strüdel paste

Problems with the making of strudel paste can arise and the general rule is to discard the paste and start over again after identifying the problem. However, there are some solutions to offer when problems are encountered. The table above will help with this concept.

Hot water paste (raised pie pastry)

Hot water paste may be a sweet or savoury based paste. Savoury hot water paste is used for pork pies, veal and ham pies, game pies and a variety of terrines. The paste must be used while it is warm; if it is too hot it will be difficult to handle and if it is too cold it is liable to crack during handling.

VIDEO CLIP Hot water paste

The basic difference between hot water pastry and short crust is the requirement to make the hot water pastry strong enough that it will not collapse under the weight of the filling as it bakes. This requirement means that the starch granules in the flour need to be swollen before baking starts. The use of hot water quickly swells the starch granules and will also make the formation of gluten much more likely,

therefore the pie crust will have a tougher and harder texture than short crust pastry.

Pork pies

To shape a pork pie case successfully, a block of approximately 10 cm in diameter is required. Special wooden blocks are available for this purpose, but if one is not available a suitable alternative – such as a tin can or individual mousse ring mould – can be used.

Pork, black truffle and pistachio pie

The heel of the hand is used to form a cup shape, with the paste around the mould. The block is then rotated while pressing firmly to raise the paste up the side. The paste is then allowed to set and is removed from the block.

The meat filling is made into a ball and dropped into the case and then carefully pressed to remove any air spaces. The lid is made from the same pastry, which is rolled to a thickness of 3 mm and cut with a plain cutter a little larger than the diameter of the pie. A hole is cut in the top of the lid to act as a steam vent. The top inside edge of the lid is washed with egg or water and the lid is then placed on the case. It is pressed firmly into the sides and pinched with fingers or crimpers to seal. The sides and top are washed with egg and decoration applied to the top, such as diamonds of paste or leaf shapes. It is essential that the meat is thoroughly cooked to help prevent the build up of food-poisoning bacteria.

Key points to consider in the production of hot water paste

1 Ensure the pastry case is well sealed and there are no holes in the sides.

2 Allow the pastry case to cool and hardened before removing it from a mould (if using).

3 Cut a small hole in the top of the pie to allow steam to escape and to add some jellied stock after the pie has cooked.

Problems with the making of hot water paste can arise and the general rule is to discard the paste and start over again after identifying the problem. However, there are some solutions to offer when problems are encountered. The table below will help with this concept.

Key ingredients of pastry

Fats

Fats are used in pastry making to add flavour and texture. Certain fats are referred to as 'shortenings' because they give a tender, crumbly texture to pastes by shortening the strands of gluten, preventing them from coming together and preventing a tough finish to the pastry.

Flakiness in a pastry is produced by creating layers of fat between layers of paste. When placed into an oven to bake, the fat melts and pockets of hot air expand from where the fat was present. This expansion separates the layers of paste which, after the baking process is complete, will produce a flaky pastry. This is the basis of puff pastry.

Butter used for pastry production

PROBLEM	CAUSE	SOLUTION
The pie case collapses under its own weight	Either the paste was prepared with too much liquid or it was used whilst still too warm or not kneaded enough before use	Next time use a little less liquid in the paste.
Paste is too brittle to mould	Either too little liquid was added to the paste, or it was allowed to cool too much before handling	Try to gently warm the paste in a covered basin in the oven to soften it enough to make it pliable
Cracks appear in the case during cooking	The paste was not correctly moulded, so that in places where there were joins in the paste it has not properly sealed to itself	Prepare a little additional hot water paste and after coating the cracks with some beaten egg wash, fill with the new paste to prevent leakages. This repair should be made whilst the pie is still baking and should allow at least another 20 minutes for the added paste to bake

An important difference between butter and lard or shortening is that butter is approximately 15 per cent water by weight and therefore can be quite soft. Hence why pastry chefs prefer to use **'dry' butter** with reduced water content.

There are two basic types of fats: unsaturated and saturated. The chart below shows the main differences.

UNSATURATED FATS	SATURATED FATS
Usually of vegetable origin.	Usually of animal origin.
Are soft or liquid at room temperature.	Are solid at room temperature.
Monounsaturated fatty acids have double-bonded carbon atoms with one hydrogen atom attached. Usually soft at room temperature but solidifies at 4°C or below.	Highly evident in butter, lard, coconut oil, hard margarine, egg yolks, hard cheeses, cream and cocoa butter.
These can be found in both animal and vegetable fats and especially in olive oil which has oleic acid.	Filled to capacity with hydrogen atoms; each carbon atom is bonded to two hydrogen atoms.
Polyunsaturated fatty acids have more than one double bond. These fats are liquid at room temperature and will not solidify at temperatures of 4°C. Good sources are walnut, soya bean, corn and sunflower oils	Raises low-density lipoprotein (LDL or 'bad') cholesterol that increases the risk of coronary heart disease

HEALTHY OPTION Positive health effects of oleic acid have been documented and it may be responsible for the hypertensive (blood pressure) reducing effects of olive oil. Oleic acid also keeps cell membranes soft and fluid, allowing helpful anti-inflammatory substances like omega-3 fatty acid to penetrate the cell membrane more easily and preventing the negative effects of bad cholesterol. Adverse effects also have been documented, however, since both oleic and monounsaturated fatty acid levels in the membranes of red blood cells have been associated with increased risk of breast cancer.

UNDERSTANDING THE ROLE OF FATTY ACIDS

In biochemistry, a fatty acid is known as a carboxylic acid with a long chain, which is either saturated or unsaturated. Most naturally occurring fatty acids have a chain of an even number of carbon atoms, from 4 to 28. Fatty acids are usually derived from triglycerides or phospholipids. When they are not attached to other molecules, they are known as 'free' fatty acids.

Fatty acids are important sources of fuel because, when metabolized, they yield large quantities of adenosine triphosphate (ATP). ATP transports chemical energy within cells for metabolism. Many cell types can use either glucose or fatty acids for this purpose. In particular, heart and skeletal muscle prefer fatty acids. The brain cannot use fatty acids as a source of fuel; it predominantly relies on glucose. Fatty acids that have double bonds are known as unsaturated. Fatty acids without double bonds are known as saturated. Fatty acids that are required by the human body but cannot be made in sufficient quantity and therefore must be obtained from food are called essential fatty acids.

Some common examples of fatty acids are:

1 butyric acid with four carbon atoms (contained in butter);

2 lauric acid with 12 carbon atoms (contained in coconut oil, palm kernel oil, and breast milk);

3 myristic acid with 14 carbon atoms (contained in cow's milk and dairy products);

4 palmitic acid with 16 carbon atoms (contained in palm oil and meat);

5 stearic acid with 18 carbon atoms (also contained in meat and cocoa butter).

It has been commonly believed that consumption of foods containing high amounts of saturated fatty acids (including meat fats, milk fat, butter, lard, coconut oil, palm oil and palm kernel oil) is potentially less healthy than consuming fats with a lower proportion of saturated fatty acids.

HYDROGENATED FATS

Since the turn of the 20th century, manufacturers have been making hydrogenated fats – solid pastry shortenings and margarines – from liquid seed-based oils. Hydrogenated fats are essentially unsaturated fatty acids that have been saturated with hydrogen. This gives the fat the desired texture for baking and also extends its shelf life. Most of these compound fats have no flavour and are free of salt.

Changing the degree of saturation of a fat changes some important physical properties such as the melting range, which is why liquid oils become semi-solid. Solid or semi-solid fats are preferred for baking because the way the fat mixes with flour produces a more desirable texture in the baked product. Because partially hydrogenated vegetable oils are cheaper than animal source fats, are available in a wide range of consistencies and have other desirable characteristics (e.g. increased shelf life), they are the predominant fats used as shortening in most commercially baked goods. Hydrogenated fats have excellent shortening capabilities and can be used in the production of convenience pastes, especially puff paste.

HIGH-RATIO FAT

When used with high-ratio flour for making cakes, high-ratio fat has the ability to absorb higher amounts of liquid and sugar than usual. If an increase of sugar or liquids is introduced to a conventional cake formula the finished product will have a fault. This is because the formula will not be in balance, for example too much liquid results in a cake with a closed texture and poor volume.

By using a high-ratio fat, which is hydrogenated edible oil with a refined emulsification agent such as glycerol monostearate, this will help to absorb increased sugar and liquid. Commercial bakers make these types of cakes because they are easier to produce, cheaper to produce because water can replace egg and milk content and they have a longer shelf life because of the additional liquid and sugar content.

These fats are usually stored in coloured plastic wrapping otherwise light may destabilize the colour. They must be kept covered in a refrigerator. Do not store next to produce with strong odours, such as cheese.

MARGARINE

This product was developed in France in the 19th century as an inexpensive fat to supplement inadequate supplies of butter. Modern margarine is made from hydrogenated liquid vegetable oils and has a minimum of 80 per cent fat and a maximum of 16 per cent water. The water content is usually derived from a skimmed milk product, which helps to deliver flavour and colour. Salt may also be added; this type of margarine is sometimes known as 'stick' or 'table' margarine.

Pastry margarine is formulated to produce a higher melting point and has a good plasticity to aid the production of certain pastes. Margarine is best stored covered in a refrigerator at 1–4°C.

VEGETABLE SHORTENING

Manufacturers of vegetable shortenings control the consistency of their product by hydrogenation of the base oil used. Standard shortening has between 15–20 per cent solids over a temperature range triple that of butter (12–30°C). It is therefore easier to make puff pastry with shortening than with butter and there are specialist puff pastry shortenings available on the market for this. Some puff pastry shortenings work at up to 46°C. However, a high melting point has a disadvantage in that fat remains solid at mouth temperature. Shortenings can leave a waxy residue in the mouth and have no true flavour value.

BUTTER

This is the most widely used fat in the production of pastes. It is composed of milk fat, lactose, water and casein and can have salt added to improve flavour and shelf life. Unsalted butter is sometimes specified in recipes due to its intense creaminess. Because it is a saturated fat, butter is stable and is slower to become rancid than unsaturated fats. However, the storage criteria for butter are the same as for margarine.

At any given temperature solid fats will have different consistencies that depend on what fraction of their molecules is in a solid crystal form, and fraction is in a liquid form. Above 25 per cent solids, fat will be too hard and brittle to roll into an even layer. Below 15 per cent solids and the fat will be too soft. Butter has the right consistency for making pastry in a relatively narrow temperature range of 15–20°C. This is why pastry chefs often pre-chill their ingredients and utensils and work on cold marble surfaces that keep the ingredients cool during mixing and rolling out.

It is also important to understand that the melting point of butter to a thin liquid consistency is at 32–35°C. Butter, because of its superior flavour, is a common choice for the fat in most pastry recipes, but it can be more difficult to work with than shortening because of its low melting point.

LARD

This is a rendered fat derived from pork. It has no colour but it does have a distinct flavour. In paste recipes, such as pâte brisée, lard is usually combined with butter or margarine to create a shorter textured finish. Like butter, lard has between 15–25 per cent solid fat crystals at kitchen temperature, which make them both ideal for pastry making. However lard works best at temperatures up to 25°C. Storage is the same as for margarine.

SUET

Commercial suet can be either beef fat obtained from around the kidneys or a vegetable fat such as palm oil that has been hydrogenated and mixed with a little wheat or rice flour to prevent the fat pieces sticking together. Suet is a hard fat and does not have creaming properties. Traditionally it is used for the production of suet paste and puddings. It should be stored in a refrigerator in an airtight container.

Eggs

Fresh eggs will keep for up to four weeks in a refrigerator. To determine the freshness of an egg, crack it onto a plate and check that the white is holding the yolk firmly in the centre and that the yolk is standing high rather than flat. Eggs keep best when stored away from foods with strong odours, such as cheese, onions or garlic, because the eggshell is porous and will allow air and moisture to enter the egg.

PASTEURIZED EGGS

Eggs can be purchased frozen and pasteurized and also dried. Chefs will often use pasteurized eggs in the professional pastry kitchen because of their ease of use and also to help reduce the risk of salmonella. Pasteurized eggs are eggs that have been heat-treated in order to reduce the possibility of food-borne illness in dishes that are not cooked or lightly cooked. They may be sold as liquid egg products or pasteurized in the shell.

The processing of egg products includes breaking eggs, filtering, mixing, stabilizing, blending, pasteurizing, cooling, freezing or drying and packaging. Egg products include whole eggs, whites, yolks and various blends with or without non-egg ingredients, such as egg custard, that are processed and pasteurized and may be available in liquid, frozen and dried forms. This is achieved by heating the products to a specified temperature for a specified period. It is important to note that the Food Standards Agency recommends that pasteurized egg should be used in any dish in which the egg will not be completely cooked.

Always read the label on the packaging because other ingredients may also be present in liquid pasteurized egg, products such as salt to aid shelf life and beta-carotene to simulate the colour of egg yolk can be added to certain egg products.

SALMONELLOSIS

A health issue associated with eggs is contamination by pathogenic bacteria, such as *Salmonella enteriditis*. Contamination of eggs exiting a female bird via the cloacae may also occur with other members of the *Salmonella* genus, so care must be taken to prevent the egg shell from becoming contaminated with fecal matter.

In commercial practice, eggs are quickly washed with a sanitizing solution within minutes of being laid. The risk of infection from raw or undercooked eggs is dependent in part upon the sanitary conditions under which the hens are kept. Egg shells act as hermetic seals that guard against bacteria entering, but this seal can be broken through improper handling or if laid by unhealthy chickens. Most forms of contamination enter through such weaknesses in the shell.

In the UK, the British Egg Industry Council established the Lion Quality Code of Practice in 1998 and included compulsory vaccination against *Salmonella enteriditis* of all chickens destined for Lion egg-producing laying flocks. They also included independent auditing, full traceability of hens, eggs and feed and a 'best-before' date stamped on the shell and pack, as well as on-farm stamping of eggs and packing station hygiene controls.

USING EGGS IN PASTRY

Eggs serve many functions in pastry. They add flavour and colour, contribute to product structure, incorporate air when beaten, provide liquid and moisture, add quantities of fat and protein and emulsify fat with liquid ingredients. Reducing or omitting egg yolks can result in less tenderness. When a recipe calls for an egg, the best size to use is approximately 60 g. This means that the yolk weighs approximately 20 g, the white 30 g and the shell is about 10 g. Eggs are available in four different weight grades:

1 small – 48 g;

2 medium – 58 g;

3 large – 68 g;

4 very large – 76 g.

The use of convenience pastes

Being able to purchase ready-made and ready-to-use pastes has been both a revelation and a concern for many chefs in the industry. The issues of ease of production, use of human resources, cost and standardization of the product suggest that the purchase of convenience commodities is inevitable in many high-turnover restaurants. In contrast, the issues of quality, freshness and flavour can discourage the purchase of such products, especially in the case of artisan pâtisseries and restaurants.

Example of convenience pastry

The popularity of filo paste is largely attributed to its success as an easy to use, convenient paste – it is no longer necessary to spend the time needed to make it from fresh. Other pastes that require skilled labour and are potentially time inefficient can also now be presented on a menu with relative ease, such as puff paste and strüdel paste.

Most pastes can be purchased as a convenience product in either a frozen or fresh variety. If using frozen paste it is important that the paste is correctly defrosted in a refrigerator and in the packaging in which it was first purchased (provided that it is hygienic and intact). The paste should then be stored as for fresh paste: wrapped in plastic film or baking parchment, refrigerated and accurately labelled.

The word 'convenience' simply refers to something that is easy to use. Another convenient way of using pastes is to prepare large batches of different pastes using your own recipes and techniques, thus ensuring quality, and then to freeze them individually for use at a later date.

Recipes

Shortcrust paste *(Pâte brisée)*

Ingredients	makes approximately 400 g
Soft flour	250 g
Butter (chilled)	160 g
Whole egg (lightly beaten)	1
Good-quality salt	5 g
Cold fresh milk or water as required	1 tbsp

energy	cal	fat	sat fat	carb	sugar	protein	fibre
1104 kJ	265 kcal	17.5 g	10.7 g	23 g	0.6 g	3.9 g	0.9 g

METHOD OF WORK

1. **Sift** the flour onto a clean work surface or into a stainless steel bowl.
2. Cut the chilled butter into small pieces and rub into the flour with the salt.
3. When the butter has been rubbed into the flour, incorporate the cold liquid and the whole egg.
4. Gently amalgamate the ingredients, forming a light paste. Do not overwork this paste because the gluten will begin to develop.
5. Wrap well in polythene or silicone paper and place in a refrigerator for 30 minutes to relax before using.

CHEF'S TIP If using a forced-air convection oven to bake pastry it is often necessary to use a lower temperature than stated in the recipe. Follow the manufacturer's recommendations at all times and reference the section in this chapter about baking and pre-heating the oven.

Lining paste *(Pâte à foncer)*

Ingredients	makes approximately 500 g
Soft flour	250 g
Butter	125 g
Caster sugar (optional)	20 g
Whole egg	60 g
Cold water	40 ml
Good-quality salt	5 g

energy	cal	fat	sat fat	carb	sugar	protein	fibre
845 kJ	202 kcal	11 g	6.6 g	23 g	2.5 g	3.2 g	0.8 g

METHOD OF WORK

1 Sift the flour onto a clean work surface or into a stainless steel bowl.

2 Cut the chilled butter into small pieces and rub into the flour with the sugar (if required) and the salt.

3 When the butter has been successfully rubbed into the flour, incorporate the cold water and the whole egg.

4 Gently amalgamate the ingredients, forming a light paste. Do not overwork this paste.

5 Wrap well in polythene or silicone paper and place in a refrigerator to relax for 45 minutes before using.

CHEF'S TIP If the oven has too much bottom heat it will cause the underside of pastries to colour too quickly. Use two baking sheets, one on top of the other, to help insulate the paste on the bottom and prevent over colouring.

Shortbread paste *(Pâte sable)*

Ingredients	makes approximately 500 g
Soft flour	250 g
Ground almonds	30 g
Unsalted butter	140 g
Icing sugar	100 g
Whole egg (beaten)	60 g
Good-quality salt	5 g
Vanilla extract or zest of 1 lemon	optional

energy	cal	fat	sat fat	carb	sugar	protein	fibre
1102 kJ	263 kcal	13.9 g	7.5 g	31.6 g	10.9 g	3.8 g	1 g

METHOD OF WORK

1 Sift together the flour and ground almonds onto a clean work surface or into a stainless steel bowl.

2 Cut the butter into small pieces and place into the centre of the flour well with the sieved icing sugar.

3 Cream together the butter and sugar with the salt and then slowly incorporate the whole egg. Mix well and add any additional flavours (such as the vanilla or lemon zest) at this point.

4 Gently incorporate the flour and almonds with the other ingredients, forming a light paste. Do not overwork this paste as the development of the gluten does not require to be activated.

5 Wrap well in polythene or silicone paper and place in a refrigerator to relax for a minimum of two hours before using.

Note: the use of ground almonds can be replaced with rice flour or soft flour if required for dietary purposes.

CHEF'S TIP If at any point during the rolling the paste gets too soft or too warm, slip it onto a baking sheet lined with silicone, cover with plastic wrap and refrigerate until firm. Alternatively, you can continue to roll out the paste on the silicone-lined baking sheet and then cut it to the desired shape without having to move it again.

Sweet paste *(Pâte sucrée)*

Ingredients	makes approximately 500 g
Soft flour	250 g
Butter	120 g
Caster sugar	70 g
Whole egg (beaten)	80 g
Good-quality salt	5 g
Vanilla pod or extract or a little grated lemon zest	optional

energy	cal	fat	sat fat	carb	sugar	protein	fibre
937 kJ	224 kcal	10.7 g	6.3 g	29.1 g	7.8 g	3.4 g	0.8 g

METHOD OF WORK

Creaming method

1 Place the flour onto a clean work surface or into a stainless steel bowl. Make a well in the centre.
2 Cut the butter into small pieces and place in the centre of the well with the salt and sugar.
3 Work the butter and sugar with your finger tips until completely creamed together and pale in colour.
4 Slowly incorporate the whole egg, mixing well until the mixture is completely smooth and creamy. At this stage you can add a few drops of vanilla extract or lemon zest to help flavour the paste.
5 Gradually draw the flour into the creamed butter and when all ingredients are thoroughly mixed, lightly work the paste to a smooth texture. Do not overwork the paste at this point.
6 Wrap well in polythene or silicone paper and place in a refrigerator to relax for 60 minutes before using.

Alternative method of work (sablage method)

1 Sieve the flour and the salt together. Lightly rub in the fat to achieve a sandy texture.
2 Mix the sugar and the beaten egg separately.
3 Create a well in the centre and add the sugar and the beaten egg.
4 Gradually incorporate the rubbed in flour and fat and carefully mix to a light paste.
5 Allow to rest in polythene or silicone paper and place in a refrigerator to relax for 60 minutes before using.

CHEF'S TIP When rolling out this paste into a thin sheet, rotate it frequently to prevent sticking and lift it off the work surface several times to check the elasticity. If the paste is too elastic, allow it to rest for a few minutes on the work surface and then resume rolling.

Three-quarter puff pastry with pastry margarine
(Pâte feuilletée)

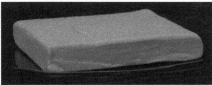

Ingredients	makes approximately 2.5 kg
Strong flour	1 kg
Butter	150 g
Pastry margarine	600 g
Lemon juice	1 tbsp
Salt	30 g
Cold water	500 ml (approx)

energy	cal	fat	sat fat	carb	sugar	protein	fibre
637 kJ	151 kcal	20.9 g	2.7 g	25.1 g	0.5 g	3.9 g	2.1 g

METHOD OF WORK

1 Sift the flour separately into a bowl.
2 Dissolve the salt, lemon juice and water into another bowl.
3 Rub the butter into the flour.
4 Mix in the liquid with the rubbed in flour and butter to form a firm but elastic paste (détrempe). Cover a rest in a refrigerator for 20 minutes.
5 Temper the pastry margarine (beurrage) by forming it into the desired shape, size and thickness for incorporating into the détrempe.
6 On a lightly floured marble top roll out the détrempe to form a rectangle twice as long as broad and about 20 mm thick. Brush any residual flour off the surface.
7 Take the square of pastry margarine (just slightly under 20 mm thick) which will fit neatly on to one end and covering two-thirds of the rolled out détrempe.
8 Fold the détrempe over half of the beurrage, and the remaining beurrage over the détrempe to enclose it so that you have two layers of fat and three layers of paste. Seal the edges well.
9 Roll out the paste to 15–20 mm thick; it must be four times as long as it is broad and at a precise rectangle.
10 Give one single turn and brush off any excess flour. Wrap in silicone paper and rest in a refrigerator for 20 minutes.
11 Repeat this process including the resting periods five more times. It is then ready to use.

Puff pastry with butter
(Pâte feuilletée)

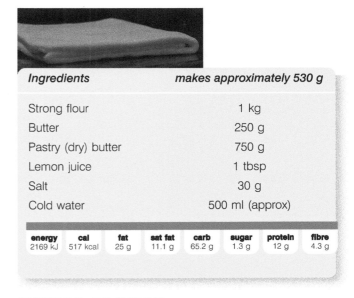

Ingredients	makes approximately 530 g
Strong flour	1 kg
Butter	250 g
Pastry (dry) butter	750 g
Lemon juice	1 tbsp
Salt	30 g
Cold water	500 ml (approx)

energy	cal	fat	sat fat	carb	sugar	protein	fibre
2169 kJ	517 kcal	25 g	11.1 g	65.2 g	1.3 g	12 g	4.3 g

METHOD OF WORK

1 Sift the flour into a bowl.
2 Dissolve the salt, lemon juice and water in a separate bowl.
3 Rub the first quantity of butter into the sieved flour.
4 Mix in the salt liquid to the flour and butter to form a firm but elastic paste. Wrap in silicone paper and rest in a refrigerator for approximately 20 minutes.
5 Prepare the dry pastry butter by tempering it onto a marble slab and forming it into the desired size, shape and thickness for the paste.
6 On a lightly floured marble top, roll out the paste to form a square with the centre slightly raised to create a large envelope; to use the French method.
7 Take the tempered dry pastry butter (in a square) which will fit neatly onto the centre of the envelope of paste.
8 Fold the 'ears' of the paste envelope over the fat to enclose it. Seal the edges well and ensure a square shape is maintained.
9 Roll out the paste to 15–20 mm thick. It must be four times as long as it is broad and a precise rectangle.
10 Give one book turn (double turn). Wrap the paste with silicone paper and rest in a refrigerator for 20 minutes.
11 Repeat this process three more times including the resting period between each turn. It is then ready to use.

CHEF'S TIP To create a reversed puff paste, use this method but reverse the butter and paste so that the paste is placed onto the butter envelope and continue with the book turns. It is crucial to master a chilled temperature control for this method to prevent the butter from becoming too soft. The results of this method produce a crispy and superior pastry in colour and flavour.

Choux paste *(Pâte à choux)*

Ingredients	20 éclairs or 40 profiteroles
Water	150 ml
Butter (cut into small cubes)	60 g
Strong white flour (sieved)	90 g
Caster Sugar	5 g
Salt	5 g
Whole eggs (beaten)	3

energy	cal	fat	sat fat	carb	sugar	protein	fibre
205 kJ	49 kcal	3.3 g	1.8 g	3.7 g	0.3 g	1.5 g	0.3 g

METHOD OF WORK

1   Place the water and butter into a saucepan and bring to the boil ensuring that the butter has completely melted.
2   Take off the heat and quickly stir in the sieved flour, salt and sugar.
3   Return to the heat and cook out, continuously stirring until it leaves the sides of the pan clean to create a panada.
4   Allow this mixture to partly cool.
5   Beat in the eggs a little at a time, making sure that they are well incorporated into the mixture to produce a 'dropping' consistency.

CHEF'S TIP   When drying out the panada, do so only until it leaves the side of the pan clean. Do not overcook the panada otherwise the fat content will separate and imbalance the recipe. The eggs should be beaten first and added gradually when the panada has cooled to below 55°C. This will aid the mixing process and ensure the eggs are totally integrated into the panada and some aeration can take place.

Strüdel paste

Ingredients	enough for 2 large strudels
Strong graded flour (sieved)	700 g
Olive or vegetable oil	110 g
Warm water (at 37°C)	180 g
Whole eggs (lightly beaten)	3
Vinegar	3 tsp
Salt	5 g
Caster sugar	5 g

energy	cal	fat	sat fat	carb	sugar	protein	fibre
760 kJ	181 kcal	6.8 g	1.1 g	26.6 g	0.8 g	4.9 g	2.2 g

METHOD OF WORK

1   Place the flour, salt and caster sugar in a bowl and make a well in the centre.
2   Add the oil, eggs, water and vinegar. Using an electric mixer and a dough hook, mix until the paste is soft and comes away from the sides of the bowl. The paste should be elastic to the touch.
3   Transfer the paste to a lightly floured surface and knead well for approximately 15 minutes or until it is soft and pliable.
4   Depending on the number of strudels to make, divide the paste into two or three pieces. Using a pastry brush, lightly brush the pieces of paste with oil, cover with plastic film and leave to rest for a minimum of 60 minutes on the side of a table (not in a refrigerator) before using.

CHEF'S TIP   *Make the strüdel paste the day before you need to use it. This will allow the paste to rest even longer, improving its flexibility. Ensure that it is covered and refrigerated.*

Hot water paste

	makes approximately 900 g
Ingredients	
Lard	150 g
Good quality salt	10 g
Soft white flour	500 g
Water	250 ml

energy	cal	fat	sat fat	carb	sugar	protein	fibre
847 kJ	202 kcal	10.3 g	4.1 g	24.3 g	0.4 g	3.1 g	1 g

METHOD OF WORK

1   Sift the flour and the salt together into a stainless steel bowl.

2   Boil the water and the lard together, ensuring that the lard has completely melted.

3   Pour the boiled liquid into the flour and begin to mix carefully with a spoon.

4   Gently amalgamate the ingredients. When you are able to touch the paste by hand, begin to knead.

5   Use immediately. Keep the paste warm by placing an upturned stainless steel bowl over it on a wooden chopping board or work surface to keep in the heat and moisture.

Suet paste

	makes approximately 500 g
Ingredients	
Soft flour	250 g
Baking powder	5 g
Beef or vegetable suet	150 g
Good-quality salt	3 g
Cold water	125 ml
Caster sugar (optional)	25 g

energy	cal	fat	sat fat	carb	sugar	protein	fibre
916 kJ	220 kcal	13.3 g	7.5 g	22.9 g	3 g	2.4 g	0.8 g

METHOD OF WORK

1   Sift together the flour, baking powder and salt into a stainless steel bowl. Add the suet and lightly mix in with a spoon.

2   If using sugar as part of the recipe, add to the water to dissolve. Make a well in the centre of the flour mixture and add the water or sugar solution.

3   Mix together to form a firm paste. Rest for five minutes in the bowl covered with plastic film before using.

CHEF'S TIP   Suet is a hard fat that surrounds beef kidneys (to protect them) and is grated and lightly floured for commercial use. It is creamy white in colour, should be dry to the touch and can be stored in a refrigerator for two to four weeks in a sealed container. Ensure suet does not come into close proximity to strongly flavoured ingredients as it easily absorbs aromas. Vegetable suet can be used to replace the beef suet if vegetarian products are required.

Scottish oat biscuits

METHOD OF WORK

1   Pre-heat an oven to 180°C.
2   Mix together the oatmeal, **bicarbonate of soda** and salt in a large stainless steel bowl.
3   Place the cream, water and milk together in a separate bowl and then add to the dry ingredients. Stir to form a thick paste that will stiffen as it rests.
4   Cover and leave for 15 minutes to firm up. If it hardens a little too much add a little more water to it.
5   Lightly dust the work surface with a little more oatmeal. Roll out the paste carefully until it is 5 mm thick. Prevent the paste from sticking to the surface by keeping it on the move and sliding a palette knife underneath from time to time.
6   Using an 8 cm plain pastry cutter, cut the discs from the paste. Transfer onto a baking tray with a non-stick baking mat.
7   Sprinkle with a little extra oatmeal if desired and bake for 15–20 minutes, or until the oat biscuits are dry and light brown in colour. Remove them onto a wire rack to cool and store in an airtight container for service when cool.

Ingredients	Makes approximately 12–15 biscuits
Fine oatmeal plus extra for rolling and sprinkling	200 g
Bicarbonate of soda	4 g
Double cream	30 g
Good quality sea salt	4 g
Milk	50 g
Water	50 g

energy	cal	fat	sat fat	carb	sugar	protein	fibre
356 kJ	84 kcal	2.9 g	0.9 g	13 g	0.2 g	2.4 g	0 g

Derivatives of pastry cream

From left to right: crème mousseline, crème diplomat and crème St Honoré

CRÈME MOUSSELINE

Ingredients	makes 900 g	makes 1.8 kg
Fresh milk	500 ml	1 l
Egg yolks	6	12
Caster sugar	100 g	200 g
Flour	70 g	140 g
Vanilla flavour or pod	1 pod	2 pods
Unsalted butter	250 g	500 g

energy	cal	fat	sat fat	carb	sugar	protein	fibre
510 kJ	123 kcal	9.9 g	5.8 g	7.4 g	5.2 g	1.7 g	0.1 g

METHOD OF WORK

1   If using a vanilla pod, split it in half and remove the seeds. Add the pod and seeds separately to the milk and bring to the boil.

2   Mix together the egg yolks, caster sugar and the flour. Add the boiled milk and return to the pan to cook out the mixture.

3   Strain through a fine chinois.

4   Cut the butter into small pieces. Add one-third to the mixture while beating with a whisk and continue beating until it clears.

5   Cool the crème to 20°C. Place the remaining butter in a mixing bowl and using a mixing machine beat until softened. On a medium speed add the pastry cream a little at a time. Ensure all the pastry cream is incorporated.

6   Beat a few minutes to produce a light and creamy finish. Use as required.

CHEF'S TIP   Crème mousseline will keep in a covered plastic container in refrigerated conditions for up to four days. The crème can be flavoured with fruit purées, alcohol, chocolate or praline.

CRÈME DIPLOMAT

Ingredients	makes 600 g	makes 1.2 kg
Fresh milk	250 g	500 g
Egg yolks	40 g	80 g
Caster sugar	70 g	140 g
Custard powder	20 g	40 g
Gelatine leaves	10 leaves	20 leaves
Kirsch	to taste	to taste
Whipped cream	310 g	620 g

energy	cal	fat	sat fat	carb	sugar	protein	fibre
497 kJ	119 kcal	9.2 g	5.5 g	7.6 g	6.3 g	2 g	0 g

METHOD OF WORK

1   Bring the milk to the boil.

2   Mix together the egg yolks, caster sugar and custard powder. Add the boiled milk and return to the pan to cook out the mixture.

3   Pass the crème through a fine chinois. Soften the leaves of gelatine in cold water.

4   Strain the gelatine sheets from any excess water and add to the hot, cooked crème. Stir until the gelatine has melted and fully incorporated into the crème.

5   Cool the crème to 20°C and add the Kirsch. Carefully fold in the whipped cream without losing any air from the whipped cream. Use as required.

CHEF'S TIP   Crème diplomat is a derivative of crème pâtissière and can be flavoured according to the requirements of the recipe by using a particular alcohol or flavouring such as vanilla. Crème diplomat is also used as a filling in pastries, tarts, cakes, gateaux and various desserts.

CRÈME ST. HONORÉ

Ingredients	approximately 800 g	approximately 1.5 kg
Fresh full fat milk	350 ml	700 ml
Vanilla flavour or pod	½ pod split	1 pod split
Egg yolks	6	12
Caster sugar	70 g	120 g
Custard powder	20 g	40 g
Cornflour	10 g	20 g
Granulated sugar	300 g	500 g
Water	80 ml	150 ml
Glucose	25 g	45 g
Egg whites	6	12

energy	cal	fat	sat fat	carb	sugar	protein	fibre
484 kJ	114 kcal	2.3 g	0.9 g	22.7 g	20.7 g	2.2 g	0 g

METHOD OF WORK

1 Bring to the boil the milk and vanilla flavour or pod.
2 Whisk together the egg yolks, caster sugar, custard powder and cornflour.
3 Combine the ingredients and cook out, stirring constantly, to make a basic crème pâtissière.
4 Reserve to one side, adding a little melted butter to the surface of the crème to prevent a skin forming.
5 To create an Italian meringue, carefully boil the granulated sugar, water and glucose to 121°C. Meanwhile, whisk the egg whites to soft peaks. Gently pour in the hot sugar solution in a thin stream while still whisking. Continue to beat at a low speed until the mixture is completely cold.
6 While the crème pâtissière is still slightly warm, using a whisk stir in one-third of the meringue. Next, using a spatula, fold in the remaining meringue until completely incorporated. Do not over mix at this stage or the crème will collapse.
7 Use the crème St Honoré as required but the cream will need at least 30 minutes to set in a refrigerator after using.

CHEF'S TIP The use of glucose in the Italian meringue is essential as it helps sugar crystals to form in the meringue. To create a firm meringue, more sugar per egg white (70 g per egg white) is required; this should help the crème St Honoré retain its stability. You can also add one-and-a-half sheets of gelatine to the crème pâtissière base to help set the cream. This will make it easier to serve. You can also enhance the flavour of this crème by adding finely grated orange zest to the boiling milk and some Grand Marnier at the final stage.

CHEF'S TIP This recipe provides a good base to receive additional flavours such as Kirsch, Cointreau, grated orange zest or coffee. It can be used as the base for other derivatives of this cream, fruit tarts and soufflés.

Pastry cream (French version) *Crème pâtissière*

Ingredients	makes approximately 1 litre
Milk	1 l
Caster sugar	190 g
French custard powder (crème poudre)	95 g
Whole eggs	200 g
Unsalted butter	25–50 g
Vanilla (optional)	

energy	cal	fat	sat fat	carb	sugar	protein	fibre
397 kJ	94 kcal	2.4 g	1.2 g	16.8 g	9.9 g	2.5 g	0 g

METHOD OF WORK

1 Carefully bring the milk and the vanilla to the boil in a heavy based saucepan.
2 Meanwhile mix together the French custard powder, eggs and caster sugar.
3 Slowly pour the boiled milk onto the egg mixture and stir well until all the ingredients are thoroughly incorporated.
4 Return the contents to a heavy based stainless steel saucepan and begin to cook out the mixture, stirring constantly to prevent the pastry cream from burning.
5 As it reaches boiling point the pastry cream should have thickened. Remove from the heat and beat for five minutes with a wire whisk and pour into a cold stainless steel bowl. Beat the unsalted butter cubes into the warm pastry cream.
6 Cover with a cartouche of baking parchment to cool down before placing into a refrigerator for later use.

CHEF'S TIP Another name for Crème St Honoré is Crème Chiboust. Crème Chiboust can be flavoured with praline, lemon zest and different liqueurs. If it is bound with prepared fresh fruit, it becomes known as a different classical cream called crème plombières.

Frangipane and crème d'amande

From left to right: frangipane and crème d'amande

FRANGIPANE

Ingredients	approximately 400 g
Butter or margarine	100 g
Caster sugar	100 g
Whole egg	100 g
Ground almonds	75 g
Cake crumbs	30 g
Soft flour	20 g
Lemon zest	½ lemon

energy	cal	fat	sat fat	carb	sugar	protein	fibre
844 kJ	203 kcal	13.4 g	5.7 g	18.3 g	11.8 g	3.3 g	0.8 g

METHOD OF WORK

1   Cream together the fat and the caster sugar until a pale cream colour has been achieved.

2   Gradually incorporate the eggs, and ensure that they are completely mixed in to the creamed fat and sugar.

3   Add the ground almonds, cake crumbs, flour and the finely grated lemon zest. Mix well and set aside in a covered container, at 5°C or below until ready for use.

CRÈME D'AMANDE

Ingredients	approximately 400 g
Unsalted butter	100 g
Tant-pour-tant	225 g
Eggs	2
Soft white flour	30 g
Almond flavour or dark rum	30 g

energy	cal	fat	sat fat	carb	sugar	protein	fibre
941 kJ	226 kcal	16.5 g	6.1 g	16 g	13.1 g	4.3 g	1.2 g

METHOD OF WORK

1   Cream together the tant-pour-tant and the unsalted butter until the ingredients have completely amalgamated.

2   Slowly beat in the eggs, one at a time.

3   Add the flour and almond flavour or dark rum.

4   Hold in a covered container at 5°C or below until required for use.

CHEF'S TIP   Tant-pour-tant is equal quantities of ground almonds and icing sugar that has been sieved together three times before using.

CHEF'S TIP   Frangipane is a filling made or flavoured from almonds. This filling can be used in a variety of confections including cakes, tarts and other pastries. An alternative French spelling from a 1674 cookbook is 'franchipane' with the earliest modern spelling coming from a 1732 confectioners' dictionary. Originally designated as a custard tart flavoured by almonds or pistachios it came later to designate a filling that could be used in a variety of confections and baked goods. In some anecdotes this is a kind of sweet a noblewoman Jacopa da Settesoli brought to St. Francis of Assisi, when he was dying in 1226.

English pork pie

Ingredients	makes approximately 8–10 small pies
Hot water paste	1 quantity
Filling	
Shoulder of pork (boned)	350 g
Fresh chopped thyme	10 g
Fresh chopped sage	10 g
Fresh chopped parsley	10 g
Good quality salt	10 g
Finely chopped white onion, sweated off	75 g
Finely chopped leek, sweated off	50 g
White veal or chicken stock	25 ml
Powdered white pepper	5 g
Powdered nutmeg	pinch
Gelatinous meat stock	as required
Gelatine	as required

energy	cal	fat	sat fat	carb	sugar	protein	fibre
1596 kJ	381 kcal	18.4 g	7.2 g	37.7 g	1 g	16.4 g	2 g

METHOD OF WORK

1 Mince the pork shoulder coarsely and then combine with the rest of the filling ingredients, mixing well in a stainless steel bowl. Check the seasoning and consistency before moving to the next stage.

2 Prepare the paste as per the recipe in this chapter.

3 Keep the paste warm by placing an upturned stainless steel bowl over it on the work surface to keep in the heat and moisture.

4 Keeping a quarter of the paste warm, roll out the rest and carefully line some well-greased individual raised pie or stainless steel ring moulds. Ensure that all cracks and holes have been plugged with additional hot water paste if required.

5 Add the filling to the top of each mould and press down firmly. Roll the remaining hot water paste out to create individual pastry lids.

6 Egg-wash the tops of the edges of each pie and seal the edges when placing the lid on top, trimming off any surplus paste. Cut a 5 mm-diameter hole in the centre of the pie lid. Decorate the lid as appropriate.

7 Egg wash and place into a preheated oven at 220°C for 20 minutes, then reduce the oven temperature to approximately 160°C and bake for a further 40 minutes or until the pastry and the meat centre have fully cooked.

8 Remove from the oven and leave to cool for a minimum of 30 minutes. Using the small hole created in the top of the pie lid, fill with a hot gelatinous meat stock containing dissolved gelatine to create aspic inside the pie (approximately 400 ml stock to five leaves of gelatine).

9 Cool and leave the aspic to fully set in a refrigerator. Serve as desired.

CHEF'S TIP If the pies colour too quickly during baking, cover with either silicone paper or foil and continue baking. An oiled silicone paper funnel can be inserted into the hole in the lid to keep the hole open, allowing steam to escape during cooking.

Apple strudel *(Apfel Strüdel)*

Ingredients	makes approximately 1 large strudel
Strudel paste	
Apple filling	
Bramley apples	1.5 kg
Lightly roasted ground almonds	150 g
Brioche crumbs	200 g
Clarified butter	75 g
Cinnamon sugar	125 g
Finely grated zest of lemon	1 lemon
Sultanas **macerated** in dark rum for three days	200 g
Melted butter	200 g

energy	cal	fat	sat fat	carb	sugar	protein	fibre
1975 kJ	473 kcal	30.8 g	15 g	47.8 g	41.2 g	5.2 g	4.9 g

VIDEO CLIP Making apple strudel

METHOD OF WORK

1 Make the strudel paste and set aside to rest.

2 Prepare all of the filling components ready to assemble the strudel.

3 Meanwhile, peel and slice the Bramley apples thinly and mix with a little additional cinnamon if desired. In this recipe we can encourage the oxidization of the apple as it adds colour to the finished presentation.

4 Fry the brioche crumbs in a little clarified butter until they turn a very light golden colour.

To prepare the strüdel

1 Spread a clean linen cloth, dusted with flour, over a table and initially pin out the paste as thinly as possible.

2 Very carefully begin to stretch the paste using your fingertips dipped in a little oil from underneath the paste. The paste should eventually be stretched paper thin and you should be able to read the writing of this recipe through the paste without any holes appearing. The paste should have covered the circumference of the whole table or linen cloth.

3 After stretching, trim the edges and brush the paste with the melted butter.

4 Carefully build up layers of filling with each ingredient, apples first and then the remaining ingredients. Leave a margin of approximately 5 cm on each side and at the bottom of 8 cm. These margins should be brushed again with melted butter.

5 Fold in the margins of the paste and, using the cloth, roll it carefully towards you to resemble a Swiss roll. Wrap it as tightly as possible without breaking the paste layer. Transfer onto a double baking sheet and brush again with melted butter.

6 Place into a pre-heated oven at 225°C and bake for approximately 35–45 minutes.

7 Two-thirds of the way through the baking process remove the strüdel from the oven and dredge with icing sugar. Replace to continue baking.

8 Serve warm with whipped cream, crème Anglaise and dusted with icing sugar.

CHEF'S TIP You can replace the apples and add your own fruit of choice to create an alternative variety of strüdel, but you must always balance the water content of the fruit against the dry ingredients in the filling to prevent the strüdel from collapsing during baking.

Leek, truffle and goat's cheese tart (Tart aux poireau, truffle et fromage de chèvre)

Ingredients	4 × 90 mm × 15 mm tartlet tins	1 × quiche tin loose base 24 cm × 2.5 cm
Shortcrust paste (pâte brisée)	200 g	500 g
Full-fat goat's cheese	130 g	260 g
Chopped fresh mixed herbs (basil, chives, parsley)	2 tbsp	5 tbsp
Leeks	100 g	200 g
Black truffle (fresh or preserved)	1	2
Eggs	2	4
Single cream	250 ml	450 ml
Truffle oil	a few drops	a few drops
Ground black pepper, paprika and good-quality salt	to taste	to taste

energy	cal	fat	sat fat	carb	sugar	protein	fibre
2253 kJ	542 kcal	41 g	25.1 g	26.6 g	3.3 g	17.1 g	2.3 g

METHOD OF WORK

1 Prepare the tartlet or tart tins by ensuring that they are clean, dry and lightly greased.

2 Roll out the paste thinly (about 3–4 mm thick) on a cold work surface. Carefully line the tartlet or tart tins and chill for 15 minutes in a refrigerator.

3 Preheat an oven to 200°C. Bake the cases blind, using baking parchment and baking beans, for approximately ten minutes. Remove from the oven and reduce the oven temperature to 190°C.

4 Wash, slice, wash again and dry the leeks. Quickly sweat them off in a little butter or olive oil to begin the cooking process. Put aside to cool.

5 Slice the Goats cheese, and place them onto a tray sprinkled with the freshly chopped herbs, thinly sliced truffles and a few drops of truffle oil.

6 Mix the leeks in a bowl with the beaten egg, cream, salt, paprika and pepper and mix again. Add some extra drops of truffle oil if required.

7 Divide the Goats cheese and the leek mixture evenly into the pastry cases and return to the oven for 10–15 minutes, until the filling has just set.

8 Serve warm or cold.

CHEF'S TIP Chilling or freezing the lined tins before blind baking allows the fat to harden and relaxes the paste. Substitute mushrooms for truffles to reduce the cost of this recipe.

Lemon tart *(Tarte au citron)*

Ingredients	8 portions 1 × tart tin loose base 28 cm × 2.5 cm	16 portions 2 × tart tin loose base 28 cm × 2.5 cm
Sweet paste (pâte sucrée)	250 g	500 g
Lemons	4	8
Eggs	9	18
Caster sugar	380 g	700 g
Double cream	300 ml	600 ml
Icing sugar	50 g	100 g

energy	cal	fat	sat fat	carb	sugar	protein	fibre
2590 kJ	618 kcal	32.6 g	18.1 g	75.5 g	62.1 g	9.6 g	0.7 g

METHOD OF WORK

1   Preheat an oven to 200°C.

2   Lightly grease a flan ring and carefully line with the sweet paste. Leave to rest for 15 minutes in a refrigerator.

3   Blind bake in the preheated oven for approximately 20 minutes. Remove from the oven and rest.

4   Lower the oven temperature 150°C.

5   Wash and dry the lemons and finely grate the zests. Extract the juice and mix together.

6   Break the eggs into a separate bowl and lightly beat in the caster sugar. Add the cream and lemon and mix. Remove any froth from the top. Place in a refrigerator for 15 minutes to settle before using.

7   Carefully pour the lemon preparation into the blind baked pastry case and bake for approximately 30 minutes or until the lemon filling has only just set.

8   Remove from the oven and set aside on a wire rack to cool. When cooled, carefully remove the flan ring.

9   Leave to cool at room temperature for at least one hour.

10   Portion the tart if required, or leave whole for service and dust the top with icing sugar before serving. The tart can be caramelized using a blowtorch or under a salamander.

CHEF'S TIP   On no account put the tart in the refrigerator: keep at room temperature otherwise the pastry will soften. This tart should be made just prior to service to give the best fresh lemon flavour.

HEALTH AND SAFETY   How to use a blow torch. Some chefs consider that using a blow torch is the same as using a salamander or grill. However salamanders and grills use radiant heat to work whereas a blow torch relies on convective heat transfer from fast-moving and very hot gases. A mechanical effect from blowing aspect of a blow torch is that it will accelerate heating further. The fast moving ignited gases blows away moisture evaporating from the surface of the food being torched. Together this makes blow torches an effective way of searing and caramelizing quickly.

However, sometimes foods that have been blow torched can taste like fuel. The chef should always point the end of the blow torch flame at the food only when the flame is lit and then turns blue. Unburned fuel often squirts from the tip of the blow torch at the moment of ignition; a yellow flame is a telltale sign that the fuel is not being completely burned. Always ensure that the blow torch flame is warmed up and adjusted before bringing the flame to the food.

Always keep flammable products such as paper, plastic film and other fuels away from the flame and always ensure that clothing and hands are completely out of the way when attempting to blow torch food.

Chocolate and banana tart

Ingredients	4 × tartlet tins 100 mm × 18 mm	10 × tartlet tins 100 mm × 18 mm or 1 × quiche/tart tin loose base 20 cm × 2.5 cm fluted
Dark **couverture** chocolate (70% cocoa solids minimum)	80 g	220 g
Unsalted butter	50 g	110 g
Whole egg	55 g	150 g
Egg yolk	1	3
Caster sugar	30 g	75 g
Icing sugar	60 g	120 g
Banana (to slice and caramelize)	1	2
Sable paste (pâte sable)	250 g	550 g

energy	cal	fat	sat fat	carb	sugar	protein	fibre
2944 kJ	704 kcal	38.9 g	16.3 g	82.2 g	43.5 g	9.5 g	1.6 g

METHOD OF WORK

1 Melt the dark chocolate couverture and butter together in a microwave oven or over a bain-marie of hot water, taking care not to burn the chocolate.

2 Whisk the eggs and sugar until thick in a mixing machine using a whisk attachment, fold together with the melted dark couverture and cool.

3 Line individual tartlet cases with the sable paste and bake blind in a preheated oven at 200°C. Remove from the oven and leave to cool. Reduce the oven temperature to 150°C.

4 Slice the banana into small slices and sprinkle over with a little icing sugar. Quickly caramelize using a blowtorch or a hot salamander. Add three or four slices to the bottom of the blind-baked tartlet cases. Retain some of the caramelized banana slices for decoration.

5 Pour the dark couverture mixture equally into each tartlet case and bake at 150°C for six to ten minutes. Leave to one side to keep warm and let the residual heat finish cooking the filling.

6 Serve the chocolate and banana tarts either warm or at room temperature dusted with some cocoa powder, a quenelle of crème Chantilly, chocolate decoration and the caramelized banana slices.

CHEF'S TIP Using a good-quality high cocoa content dark chocolate for this recipe will obtain a depth of flavour and consistency in this recipe. As an alternative to the basic sable paste, substitute 25 g of flour from the recipe with 25 g of cocoa powder.

Red berry streusel tart
(Tarte streusel aux fruits rouges)

Ingredients	1 × 20 cm × 2.5 cm tart	3 × 20 cm × 2.5 cm tarts
Lining paste (pâte à foncer, see recipe page 331)	175 g	550 g
Pistachio crème		
Melted butter	50 g	125 g
Icing sugar	50 g	125 g
Ground almonds	50 g	125 g
Whole eggs	40 g	100 g
Cornflour	5 g	20 g
Crème pâtissière	50 g	100 g
Pistachio paste	10 g	40 g
Kirsch	5 g	20 g
Cinnamon streusel		
Ground almonds	40 g	100 g
Butter	40 g	100 g
Soft flour	40 g	100 g
Caster sugar	40 g	100 g
Powdered cinnamon	1 g	2 g
Red berry garnish		
Cherries steeped in kirsch	30 g	100 g
Raspberries	30 g	100 g
Strawberries	30 g	100 g
Redcurrants	30 g	100 g

energy	cal	fat	sat fat	carb	sugar	protein	fibre
1432 kJ	343 kcal	21.8 g	9.5 g	32.3 g	16.1 g	5.6 g	1.9 g

METHOD OF WORK

1   Prepare a tart ring and lightly grease it. Line the ring with the lining paste, **dock** the base and leave to rest in a refrigerator until required. Pre-heat an oven to 170°C.

2   To make the pistachio crème, mix together the melted butter, ground almonds, icing sugar, eggs and cornflour to a smooth paste.

3   Fold in the crème pâtissière and the pistachio paste. Mix well and finally add the Kirsch.

4   Pipe this preparation into the base of the lined tart to about two-thirds of the way up.

5   Ensure all the fresh berries are well washed and prepared. If the strawberries are too large, cut them so that all the berries are similar in size.

6   Mix the berries together with some of the juice/kirsch from the cherries. Place a layer of this fruit gently on top of the pistachio crème.

7   Bake in the preheated oven for approximately 20–25 minutes.

8   To make the streusel, rub the ground almonds, butter, sugar and cinnamon into the flour, until a large crumb has been produced. Place this in a ring on top of the tart and place back into the oven for a further ten minutes.

9   Remove from the oven when completed cooked through and the streusel has a golden brown tinge. Decorate the centre with some fresh berries and serve.

> **CHEF'S TIP** Use fresh fruit that is in season. Source fruits from a supplier as local as possible to help ensure they are fresh, sustainably grown and in top condition. This also reduces food-miles. Orchard fruits such as pears, peaches and nectarines work well with this recipe too.

Gâteau Basque

Ingredients	8 × 7 cm × 7 cm stainless steel rings or 1 × 20 cm × 2.5 cm pastry ring	16 × 7 cm × 7 cm stainless steel rings or 2 × 20 cm × 2.5 cm pastry ring
Butter	125 g	250 g
Hazelnut tant-pour-tant(equal quantities of ground hazelnuts and icing sugar)	50 g	100 g
Caster sugar	125 g	250 g
Good-quality salt	3 g	5 g
Finely grated lemon zest	½ lemon	1 lemon
Egg yolks	2	4
Whole egg	½ egg	1 egg
Soft flour	250 g	500 g
Baking powder	5 g	10 g
Almond filling	*makes approx 500 g of filling*	*makes approx 1 kg of filling*
Full fat milk	175 ml	350 ml
Vanilla pod	½ pod split	1 pod split
Egg yolks	3	6
Caster sugar	40 g	70 g
Custard powder	10 g	20 g
Cornflour	5 g	10 g
Ground almonds (baked until golden brown)	100 g	200 g
Dark rum	5 ml	10 ml
Fresh apricots poached in syrup or tinned, cut into quarters	250 g	500 g
Flaked almonds	50 g	100 g

energy	cal	fat	sat fat	carb	sugar	protein	fibre
2233 kJ	533 kcal	29.3 g	10.7 g	59.7 g	33.1 g	10.8 g	3.4 g

METHOD OF WORK

1 To make the pâte à Basque, cream together the butter with the hazelnut tant-pour-tant, caster sugar, salt and lemon zest in a stainless steel bowl.

2 Gradually incorporate the egg yolks and whole egg to the creamed mixture.

3 Sift the flour and baking powder together twice. Add the sifted flour mixture and begin to knead the ingredients into a light paste. Take care not to overwork the paste. Place in a refrigerator wrapped in plastic film or baking parchment to rest for at least one hour.

4 Preheat an oven to 177°C.

5 To make the almond cream, bring to the boil the milk and vanilla pod.

6 Whisk together the egg yolks, caster sugar, custard powder and cornflour.

7 Combine the ingredients together and cook out, stirring constantly, to make a basic crème pâtissière. Reserve to one side, adding a little melted butter to the surface of the crème to prevent a skin forming.

8 When the almond cream has cooled, incorporate the dark rum and ground almonds and reserve to one side.

9 To assemble the gateau, line individual flan rings or tart ring with the pâte à Basque and pipe the base with the almond pastry cream.

10 Place the quartered apricots on top of the pastry cream and place a disc of the pâte à Basque on top of the flan. Glaze with egg wash. Place in a fridge to rest for 30 minutes. Mark the top with a sharp knife.

11 Bake in the preheated oven at 177°C for approximately 30 minutes. Halfway through baking sprinkle a few flaked almonds and icing sugar on top.

12 De-mould and serve warm with a hot apricot sauce and an appropriate accompaniment such as vanilla ice cream or crème Chantilly.

CHEF'S TIP When using the tant pour tant, ensure that you pass both the icing sugar and the ground nut content through a sieve at least twice. This will help to aerate the composition of ingredients and aid creaming with the butter. Gâteau Basque is a traditional dessert from the Basque region of France. Typically Gâteau Basque is constructed from layers of an almond flour based cake with a filling of pastry cream, apricots or preserved cherries.

Lemon meringue pie

Ingredients	1 × 20 cm × 2.5 cm pie	2 × 20 cm × 2.5 cm pies
Lining paste (pâte à foncer)	200 g	400 g
Lemon filling		
Butter	125 g	250 g
Caster sugar	125 g	250 g
Eggs	4	8
Lemon zest and juice	2 lemons	4 lemons
Swiss meringue		
Egg white	250 g	375 g
Caster sugar	125 g	180 g
Icing sugar	125 g	180 g

energy	cal	fat	sat fat	carb	sugar	protein	fibre
1889 kJ	450 kcal	20.9 g	12.2 g	61.3 g	50.6 g	7.6 g	0.7 g

METHOD OF WORK

1 Pre-heat an oven to 200°C.

2 Line a 20 cm × 2.5 cm tart ring with the lining paste and bake blind with minimal colour using baking parchment and baking beans. Remove from the oven and leave to cool.

3 To prepare the lemon filling, combine the finely grated lemon zest and juice in a saucepan with the caster sugar and butter.

4 Bring the ingredients to the boil, ensuring that the butter has completely melted and that the sugar has dissolved.

5 Gradually add the beaten eggs, constantly stirring vigorously with a whisk until all of the egg content is successfully incorporated and the mixture has cooked out to a thick and creamy consistency.

6 Pour this lemon cream into the blind-baked tart case and leave to cool and set.

7 To prepare the Swiss meringue, whisk all the ingredients together in a stainless steel bowl using a balloon whisk and place into a bain-marie over simmering water. Add a pinch of salt to the meringue mixture.

8 Whisking continuously to aerate the egg whites, heat the mixture to 60°C. Use a thermometer or digital probe to accurately gauge the temperature and do not go above this other the egg whites will coagulate too much.

9 Immediately transfer the egg white mixture into a mixing machine with a whisk attachment and beat until cold. The meringue will now begin to completely aerate as it cools down.

10 Transfer the Swiss meringue to a piping bag with a plain tube and pipe onto the set lemon cream in a decorative manner.

11 Lightly dust the meringue with icing sugar and place into a hot oven at 180°C to colour the meringue. Serve either at room temperature or slightly warm as desired.

CHEF'S TIP To help to stabilize the Swiss meringue further, a pinch of cream of tartar can be added during the cooking stage. With constant whisking and the protective effects of sugar and the cream of tartar, you can heat this meringue mixture up to 75°C and still maintain successful, although dense, foam stabilization.

Linzer torte

Ingredients	1 × 20 cm × 2.5 cm torte	2 × 20 cm × 2.5 cm torte
Soft white flour	180 g	360 g
Ground hazelnuts	75 g	150 g
Icing sugar	60 g	120 g
Finely grated lemon zest	1 lemon	2 lemons
Grated nutmeg	pinch	pinch
Powdered cinnamon	5 g	10 g
Butter	125 g	250 g
Egg yolks	2	4
Raspberry or redcur-rant jam	200 g	380 g
Lemon juice	¼ lemon	½ lemon
Apricot glaze	75 g	140 g

energy	cal	fat	sat fat	carb	sugar	protein	fibre
1601 kJ	382 kcal	19.7 g	9 g	47.9 g	31.1 g	5.1 g	2.2 g

METHOD OF WORK

1   Preheat an oven to 175°C.
2   Sift together the flour, ground hazelnuts, icing sugar, cinnamon and nutmeg. Repeat this process to consolidate the aeration and mixing of the ingredients.
3   Dice the butter and rub into the flour and hazelnut mix with the lemon zest until the mixture reaches a crumbly texture. Add the egg yolk and carefully form into a light Linzer paste.
4   Cut the paste into three equal pieces and wrap each paste in plastic film or baking parchment and rest in a refrigerator for 30 minutes.

5   Prepare the flan ring and lightly grease it, placing onto a double baking sheet with a disc of baking parchment on the base or a baking sil-pat mat.
6   Using the first piece of the rested Linzer paste. Roll out and use it to line the flan ring. Ensure a good lining technique to ensure an evenly lined pastry case.
7   Mix the raspberry or redcurrant jam with the lemon juice and bring to the boil, spoon half of it into the lined case.
8   Roll out the second Linzer paste that was set aside and cut a disc that fits neatly on top of the jam on the base of the linzer tart.
9   Finally take the third piece of the Linzer paste, pin it out and cut into strips. Spread the remaining jam on top and lay the strips over to create a lattice pattern.
10 Seal the edges well and place in the oven to bake for approximately 30 minutes.
11 To finish, brush with the apricot glaze and fill the centres of the squares with more jam if required. Serve warm or chilled with crème Chantilly.

CHEF'S TIP   This is a traditional torte that takes its name from the Austrian town of Linz, where it is served in coffee houses as an afternoon pastry. For a long time a recipe from 1696 in the Vienna Stadt und Landesbibliothek was the oldest version known. In 2005, however, Waltraud Faißner, the library director of the Upper Austrian Landesmuseum and author of the book Wie mann die Linzer Dortten macht ('How to make the Linzer Torte') found an even older Veronese recipe from 1653 in the archive of Admont Abbey.

The invention of the Linzer torte is subject of numerous legends, describing a Viennese confectioner named Linzer (as given by Alfred Polgar) or a baker named Johann Konrad Vogel (1796–1883), who in 1823 at Linz started the mass production of this torte that made it famous around the world. Linzer torte is a holiday classic in the Austrian, Hungarian, Swiss, German and Tirolean traditions, often eaten at Christmas.

It can be stored in a refrigerator for up to a day after production. Do not store next to strongly flavoured products such as cheese as the classic Linzer paste is light enough to absorb other strong flavours.

Pear Bourdaloue tart

Poire flan Bourdaloue

Ingredients	1 × 20 cm × 2.5 cm tart (8 portions)	2 × 20 cm × 2.5 cm tarts (16 portions)
Sweet paste (la pâte sucrée)	175 g	350 g
Crème pâtissière	75 g	150 g
Unsalted butter	100 g	225 g
Tant pour tant	225 g	450 g
Eggs	2	4
Soft white flour	30 g	60 g
Almond flavour or dark rum	30 g	60 g
Poached pear halves		
Fresh pears	3–4	7–8
Vanilla pod, split lengthwise and scrapped	1	1
Stick of cinnamon	1	2
Star anise	1	2
Clove	1	2
Caster sugar	60 g	120 g
Water	to cover	to cover
1 tsp orange blossom water (optional)	to taste	to taste
Sieved apricot jam	50 g	100 g
Stock syrup	25 g	50 g
Chopped pistachio nuts or flaked almonds (optional)	25 g	50 g

energy	cal	fat	sat fat	carb	sugar	protein	fibre
1994 kJ	477 kcal	27.8 g	10.8 g	51.3 g	36.3 g	8.1 g	2.3 g

METHOD OF WORK

1   For the poached pears; place the water and sugar into a saucepan and bring to the boil to prepare a sugar syrup.

2   Add the peeled and halved pears, scrapped vanilla pod and remaining spices. Maintain the pears upright if possible to ensure even cooking and place a cartouche over them. When the water returns to a boil, lower the heat and let it simmer for about 15 minutes.

3   Remove from the heat and allow the syrup to cool down before transferring to an airtight container. Allow the pears to steep in the cooking liquids overnight in the in a refrigerator to allow the flavours to intensify.

4   Preheat an oven to 180°C.

5   To make the crème d'amande; cream together the tant pour tant and the unsalted butter.

6   Slowly beat in the eggs, flour and almond flavour or dark rum.

7   Mix the crème pâtissière into the almond preparation and set aside in a refrigerator. For a traditional Bourdaloue filling, create a mix using two parts crème d'amande to one part crème pâtissière.

8   Prepare a flan ring and lightly grease it. Line the ring with the sweet paste and trim the edges.

9   Pipe the Bourdaloue cream into the bottom of the lined tart ring to two-thirds full.

10   Slice each poached pear half thinly and arrange on top of the filling, slightly fanned out but maintaining the shape of the pear.

11   Place in the centre of the oven and bake for approximately 40 minutes or until completely baked. Check that it is baked by inserting a small knife into the Bourdaloue cream and see if it is clean when removed. The tart should also be golden brown in colour.

12   Carefully remove from the oven and cool on a wire rack. In a small saucepan, bring the sieved apricot jam and stock syrup to the boil, stirring constantly to produce an apricot glaze. Apply the hot apricot glaze carefully with a pastry brush and decorate with the chopped pistachio nuts or flaked almonds if required.

13   Serve warm or chilled.

CHEF'S TIP You can vary the type of fruit used, but it is best to use fruits such as apples, quinces and plums due to the baking time of the tart. Tarte Bourdaloue is thought to have been named after the street 'Rue Bourdaloue' which, in turn, had been named for a 17th-century priest, Louis Bourdaloue. Reflecting religious beliefs, the pears are sometimes arranged into a cross, however, you can arrange them as you like, such as in a radial pattern or a flower shape.

Engadiner nusstorte

Ingredients	1 × 20 cm torte	2 × 20 cm tortes
Shortbread paste (pâte à sucrée)	200 g	500 g
Glucose	50 g	100 g
Granulated sugar	150 g	300 g
Double cream	300 g	600 g
Clear honey	115 g	230 g
Caster sugar	225 g	450 g
Walnuts – chopped	275 g	550 g
Candied orange peel (optional)	50 g	100 g
Icing sugar for dusting	50 g	100 g

energy	cal	fat	sat fat	carb	sugar	protein	fibre
3507 kJ	839 kcal	50.7 g	18.8 g	93.3 g	79.9 g	7.6 g	2.1 g

METHOD OF WORK

1 Preheat an oven to 180°C. Prepare a flan ring and lightly grease it.

2 Roll out half of the pâte sucrée to about 3 mm thick and line the flan ring. Place in a refrigerator to relax.

3 Cook the glucose and granulated sugar in a heavy based saucepan to a light caramel.

4 In a separate saucepan place the cream, honey and sugar and carefully boil together to the soft ball stage (118°C). Meanwhile warm the walnuts in the oven for a few minutes.

5 Add the boiled honey to the caramel and then the walnuts bringing the mixture back to the boil and stir well before cooling down. Add the candied orange peel at this stage if you require this in the recipe.

6 Place the walnut mixture into the tart case and roll out the remaining paste to cover and encase the filling.

7 Place in the oven to bake for approximately 30 minutes or until the pastry is golden brown. Remove from the oven and place onto a wire rack to cool and dust with icing sugar before serving either slightly warm or cold.

CHEF'S TIP The Engadiner Nusstorte is also known as the Bündner Nusstorte and is a traditional sweet, caramelized nut (generally walnut) filled pastry from canton Graubünden in Switzerland. The modern filled nusstorte was first widely available in the 1960s though it was invented in the 1920s. While the nusstorte is associated with Graubünden, the nuts are always imported because Graubünden's climate will not support nut trees.

Baked sultana and vanilla cheesecake

Ingredients	1 × tin cake springform non-stick 20 cm × 7 cm deep 6 portions	2 × tin cake springform non-stick 20 cm × 7 cm deep 12 portions
Digestive biscuits	180 g	360 g
Unsalted butter (melted)	60 g	120 g
Full fat cream cheese	380 g	760 g
Caster sugar	150 g	300 g
Whole eggs	240 g	480 g
Vanilla pods	2	3
Lemon zest and juice	1	2
Soured cream	380 ml	760 ml
Sultanas steeped in dark rum	100 g	200 g
Apricot glaze	50 g	100 g
Preserved vanilla pod for decoration	1	2

energy	cal	fat	sat fat	carb	sugar	protein	fibre
2791 kJ	670 kcal	44.9 g	26 g	62 g	36.7 g	8.5 g	0.3 g

METHOD OF WORK

1   Pre-heat an oven to 160°C.

2   Place the digestive biscuits into a food processor and blend until they have broken down to a crumb. Stir in the melted butter and then press the biscuit preparation into a lightly greased baking tin as specified in the recipe.

3   Blend together the cream cheese, caster sugar, eggs, scrapped out vanilla pod seeds, lemon zest and juice. Stir with a spatula until the mixture is smooth and free of any lumps.

4   Blend in half of the sultanas that have been drained of their dark rum syrup.

5   Place the remaining half of sultanas on to the biscuit base and then pour on the cream cheese mixture. Place the cheesecake into a bain-marie ensuring that the baking tin is fully sealed.

6   Place into the oven and bake for approximately 30 minutes.

7   Remove the cheesecake from the oven and leave to cool slightly for about ten minutes.

8   Spread the soured cream over the top and return to the oven for another ten minutes.

9   Remove from the oven and allow to cool and set. Remove from the baking tin and place in a refrigerator to chill until required.

10   To serve carefully brush or spray with warm apricot glaze and decorate with the preserved vanilla.

CHEF'S TIP   By baking this cheesecake in a bain-marie in the oven will help to keep the top of the cheesecake from cracking and splitting. The water in the bain-marie will create an even temperature around the cheesecake and maintain moisture in the oven chamber.

Gâteau Saint Honoré

Ingredients	14 portion gateau	2 × 14 portion gateaux
Base of the Gateau		
Basic choux paste	150 g	300 g
Basic puff paste trimmings	250 g	500 g
Egg wash (whole egg beaten with a pinch of salt)	1 egg	1 egg
Crème St Honoré	**approx 800 g of crème**	**approx 1.5 kg of crème**
Fresh full fat milk	350 ml	700 ml
Vanilla pod	½ pod split	1 pod split
Egg yolks	6	12
Caster sugar	70 g	120 g
Custard powder	20 g	40 g
Cornflour	10 g	20 g
Granulated sugar	300 g	500 g
Water	80 ml	150 ml
Glucose	25 g	45 g
Egg whites	6	12

energy	cal	fat	sat fat	carb	sugar	protein	fibre
2068 kJ	492 kcal	20.6 g	9.1 g	69.6 g	30.9 g	11.4 g	2.5 g

METHOD OF WORK

1 Pre-heat an oven to 220°C.

2 On a floured surface, roll out the puff paste into a 25 cm disc. (Use puff paste trimmings rather than virgin paste to reduce the rise in this pastry.) Prick with a fork or pastry dock to reduce the opportunity for the puff paste to rise too much.

3 Using a piping bag with a 1.2 cm plain nozzle, pipe the choux paste around the edge of the puff paste disc, leaving a gap of approximately 1 cm from the edge.

4 Egg-wash the puff paste and the choux paste. Leave to rest in a refrigerator for 30 minutes before baking.

5 Pipe small choux buns, about 1.5 cm in diameter, onto a separate baking sheet. Brush with egg wash and press lightly with the back of a fork.

6 Bake at 220°C for about ten minutes with the vents of the oven open (if you have this facility). Lower the temperature to 200°C and bake the small choux buns for a further ten minutes and the base for a further 20 minutes. Remove and cool on a wire rack when cooked.

7 To make the crème St Honoré, bring to the boil the milk and vanilla pod.

8 Whisk together the egg yolks, caster sugar, custard powder and cornflour. Combine the ingredients and cook out, stirring constantly, to make a basic crème pâtissière.

9 Reserve to one side, adding a little melted butter to the surface of the crème to prevent a skin forming.

10 To create an Italian meringue, carefully boil the granulated sugar, water and glucose to 121°C. Meanwhile, whisk the egg whites to soft peaks. Gently pour in the hot sugar solution in a thin stream while still whisking. Continue to beat at a low speed until the mixture is completely cold.

11 While the crème pâtissière is still slightly warm, using a whisk stir in one-third of the meringue. Next, using a spatula, fold in the remaining meringue until completed incorporated. Do not over mix or the crème will collapse.

12 To assemble the gâteau, cut a small hole in the base of each profiterole with the point of a knife or a cream horn mould. Dip the tops into some caramelized sugar and place onto a baking sheet to cool. Decorate each alternate choux buns with a small crystallized violet petal whilst the caramel is still soft.

13 When cool and the caramel is set, fill the profiteroles with some of the crème St Honoré.

14 Pipe the remaining crème St Honoré using a St Honoré piping tube decoratively in the centre of the baked choux/puff pastry base.

15 Position the profiteroles along the edge of the gateau on top of the choux ring, using a little of the caramelized sugar to help adhere if you wish.

16 Leave the Saint Honoré in a refrigerator for approximately two hours before serving.

Epiphany cake *(Galette des Rois)*

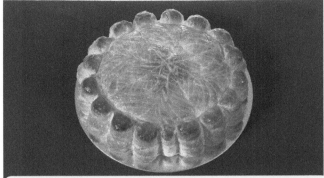

Ingredients	8 portions	16 portions
Butter puff paste	500 g	1000 g
Frangipane	400 g	800 g
Sieved apricot jam	50 g	100 g
Egg yolk lightly beaten with a little milk for egg-wash	1	2
Icing sugar for glazing	45 g	80 g

energy	cal	fat	sat fat	carb	sugar	protein	fibre
5089 kJ	1215 kcal	61.6 g	26.9 g	148.4 g	27.3 g	25.8 g	8.6 g

METHOD OF WORK

1 Preheat an oven to 240°C.

2 Prepare the frangipane and set aside for later use.

3 Cut the puff paste into two pieces, one slightly larger than the other.

4 Roll out the smaller piece of paste until you have a disc of approximately 28 cm in diameter.

5 Place onto a baking sheet lined with silicone paper and use the larger piece of puff paste to roll out for the top. Pin it out slightly larger and about 2 mm thicker.

6 Spread the apricot jam on the base of the puff paste but maintain 3 cm of the edge clear. Pipe the frangipane onto the jam.

7 Glaze the exposed puff paste edge with the egg-wash.

8 Place the second disc on top and press the edges of the two discs firmly together so that they are well sealed. Chill for 30 minutes to relax.

9 Remove from the refrigerator and press down a 24 cm flan ring over the puff paste and with a sharp knife trim the edges neatly before then cutting a scalloped border around the puff paste. Glaze the top with egg-wash and chill again for 20 minutes.

10 As shown in the picture below, brush once again with egg-wash and then using a sharp knife create a decorative scoring on the puff paste.

11 Bake the galette for ten minutes and then lower the temperature to 220°C. Bake for a further 25 minutes.

12 Dust the galette with the icing sugar and bake for a final five minutes to give a sugar glaze.

13 Serve warm with crème Chantilly.

CHEF'S TIP The Epiphany cake is also known as the King's cake and is a type of cake associated with the festival of Epiphany in the Christmas season in a number of countries. It is a popular food item during the Christmas season (Christmas Eve to Epiphany) in France and Belgium. The cake has a small trinket (often a small plastic baby, said to represent baby Jesus) inside, and the person who gets the piece of cake with the trinket has various privileges and obligations. La galette des Rois (literally 'the flat pastry cake of the Kings') is traditionally sold and consumed a few days before and after the 5th January. In France, the cakes can be found in most bakeries during the month of January. A paper crown is included with the cake to crown the 'king' who finds the trinket in their piece of cake. Formerly, the cake was divided in as many portions as guests, plus one additional portion. The latter, called 'the share of God', 'share of the Virgin Mary' or 'share of the poor' was intended for the first poor person to arrive at the home.

Profiteroles with pistachio ice cream *(Profiteroles aux glace de pistache)*

Ingredients	20 portions	40 portions
Profiteroles		
Basic choux paste	150 g	300 g
Chopped blanched pistachios	45 g	70 g
Nibbed sugar	25 g	50 g
Pistachio ice cream		
Fresh full fat milk	225 ml	550 ml
Skimmed milk powder	20 g	40 g
Double cream	35 ml	70 ml
Egg yolks	25 g	50 g
Caster sugar	50 g	100 g
Glucose syrup	15 g	25 g
Pistachio paste	35 g	70 g
Ice cream stabiliser	3 g	5 g
Kirsch	5 g	10 g

energy	cal	fat	sat fat	carb	sugar	protein	fibre
426 kJ	102 kcal	6.2 g	2.6 g	9.1 g	5.8 g	2.9 g	0.6 g

METHOD OF WORK

1 Fold two-thirds of the chopped pistachio nuts into the choux paste.

2 Using a piping bag with a large star nozzle pipe individual profiteroles onto a baking sheet.

3 Sprinkle the top with the remaining chopped pistachio nuts and the nibbed sugar crystals. Lightly dust with icing sugar. Bake in a pre-heated oven at 190°C for about 20 minutes with the vents of the oven open (if the oven has this facility). Remove when cooked and cool on a wire rack.

4 To make the pistachio ice cream, bring to the boil the milk, cream, stabilizer, pistachio paste and glucose syrup.

5 Whisk together the egg yolks, caster sugar and milk powder.

6 Combine the ingredients and reheat to 85°C stirring constantly.

7 Reserve to one side. Add the kirsch and cool down to a minimum of 4°C within one hour.

8 Freeze in an ice cream machine and reserve in a freezer in piping bags with star tubes for use.

9 To serve, cut the profiteroles in half lengthways.

10 Pipe the pistachio ice cream into the bottom half of the profiteroles.

11 Place the tops back on and dust with a little icing sugar.

12 Serve approximately three profiteroles per portion and present with an appropriate garnish and a raspberry coulis and foam or gels for a contemporary presentation.

CHEF'S TIP Alternative ice cream or sorbet preparations can be used in this recipe. However, in order to help accentuate the flavour of the ice cream and also to settle the fat content in the mixture it is advisable to leave the cooked mixture to mature for 24 hours in a refrigerator at 0–3°C.

Salambos

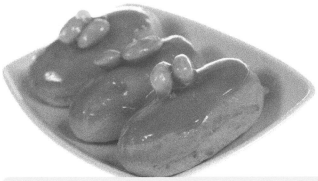

Ingredients	1 × 10 portions	2 ×10 portions
Basic choux paste	400 g	700 g
Whole almonds	50 g	90 g
Crème pâtissière	500 g	900 g
Caster sugar	250 g	400 g
Glucose	20 g	40 g
Water	100 g	170 g
Crushed praline	100 g	200 g

energy	cal	fat	sat fat	carb	sugar	protein	fibre
1999 kJ	476 kcal	21.9 g	9 g	63.8 g	46.3 g	10.4 g	2.3 g

METHOD OF WORK

1 Fill a piping bag fitted with a 1 cm plain nozzle with choux paste. Pipe out three salambos per portion. Each salambo should be 4 cm in length on a lightly greased baking sheet. Each salambo should be a kidney shape.

2 Egg-wash the tops. Bake at 220°C in a pre-heated oven for about 20 minutes. Cool on a wire rack.

3 To make the praline cream, mix together the crème pâtissière with the crushed praline.

4 Fill the salambos from underneath with the praline cream.

5 Bring the sugar and the water to the boil in a heavy based saucepan and then add the glucose. Cook to a light caramel colour.

6 Dip the tops of the salambos into the caramel, set aside and then dip the whole almonds into the caramel and place two almonds on each pastry.

7 Serve as an afternoon pastry.

Warm cherry samosas

Ingredients	4 portions	8 portions
Melted butter	60 g	120 g
Filo paste sheets	4	8
Griottines soaked in Kirsch	125 g	200 g
Cornflour	5 g	10 g
Icing sugar	60 g	120 g

energy	cal	fat	sat fat	carb	sugar	protein	fibre
1929 kJ	458 kcal	15.2 g	8.1 g	73 g	24.2 g	7.7 g	2.1 g

METHOD OF WORK

1 Gently heat the griottines in a heavy based saucepan. Mix the cornflour with a little cold water.

2 Add the diluted cornflour and cook until the griottines and Kirsch mixture has thickened.

3 Take two sheets of the filo paste, brush one with the melted butter and place the other on top. Cut into strips and place the cooled griottines mixture in the centre.

4 Fold into a samosa shape. Repeat this process for the required number of samosas.

5 Brush the samosas with the melted butter and dust well with the icing sugar.

6 Bake on a lined baking sheet in a pre-heated oven at 200°C until golden brown in colour.

CHEF'S TIP The samosas can be deep fried instead of baked. This will help to achieve an all round golden colour, but it will also increase the fat levels to the palette when eating.

Chocolate and coffee petit gateaux religieuse

Ingredients	8 portions	16 portions
Basic choux paste	500 g	700 g
Crème pâtissière	400 g	800 g
Coffee diluted to an espresso	50 ml	70 ml
Dark chocolate, melted	60 g	120 g
Fondant	300 g	600 g
Chocolate buttercream	100 g	200 g
Coffee buttercream	100 g	200 g

energy	cal	fat	sat fat	carb	sugar	protein	fibre
3000 kJ	715 kcal	37.8 g	17.5 g	85 g	58.8 g	13.7 g	2.1 g

METHOD OF WORK

1. Fill a piping bag fitted with a 12 mm plain nozzle with choux paste. Pipe two rows of large choux approximately 5 cm across and two rows of small choux approximately 2.5 cm in diameter on a lightly greased baking sheet.

2. Brush the choux with egg-wash and then dip a fork in egg-wash and lightly press down to even their shape.

3. Bake at 210°C in a pre-heated oven for about 20 minutes, rotating the baking sheet as they begin to colour. Cool on a wire rack. Use a small knife and pierce a hole in the bottoms of the choux.

4. Beat the pastry cream until its texture loosens and then split into two equal portions. Flavour one with chocolate and the other with coffee. Transfer to two separate piping bags fitted with 6 mm plain tubes.

5. Fill half of the choux with chocolate flavoured pastry cream and the other with the coffee flavoured crème pâtissière, piping it through the holes made underneath the choux.

6. For the fondant; stir gently with a spatula and warm gently in a bain-marie. Add some coffee and if the fondant remains thick when warmed to blood temperature add a few drops of stock syrup and stir it in. Continue to stir the fondant until it coats the back of spoon in a thick, shiny layer. The ideal temperature for using is 37°C.

7. Repeat the same steps to prepare the chocolate fondant.

8. To ice the choux; dip the tops in the fondant corresponding to their filling. Ensure that any drips are cleaned off with your clean fingers. When all the choux has been iced, place the appropriate flavoured buttercream in two separate piping bags fitted with a small star tube and pipe a small rosette on top of each large choux.

9. Add the small choux on top of the larger one and pipe a collar around each little choux and finish with a small rosette on to with a light chocolate decoration if required.

10. Serve as an afternoon pastry.

CHEF'S TIP La religieuse was created in Frascati, a 19th century Paris restaurant that was closed down for illegal gambling. La religieuse translates as 'the nun' and the pastry itself is modelled after the habit worn by nuns.

Guest Chef

Raspberry and pistachio mille feuille with bitter chocolate mousse

Chef Dominic Farrell
      Adrian Goldsborough
      Eileen Buicke-Kelly

Centre Academy of Culinary Arts,

Highlands College, Jersey

The versatility of this dish is the key to its success. Much of the preparation of this dish can be done in advance. It can be served to large numbers or at à la carte dinners. Also the fruit that on the dish can vary according to the season, which in turn supports your local growers and reduces the carbon footprint of the food. The secret to this pastry dish is the accuracy in weighing, and ability to follow the recipe.

Ingredients	Amount
Fresh raspberries	2 punnets
Whipping cream	250 ml
Pistachio compound	1 Tbsp
Sable biscuits	
Plain/soft flour	250 g
Butter	200 g
Yolk	1 individual
Castor sugar	100 g
Chocolate mousse	
125 ml stock syrup at 30 **Baumé**	125 ml
Pasteurized egg yolks	80 ml
Bitter chocolate couverture	250 g
leaf gelatine	2 leaves (silver)
Whipping cream, whipped	200 ml
Garnish	
Bitter chocolate	200 g
Icing sugar	enough to dust
Vanilla bean Anglaise	200 ml
Raspberry coulis	200 ml

METHOD OF WORK

1 Soak the two leaves of gelatine in cold water.

2 Boil the syrup to 30 Baumé, meanwhile whisk the egg yolks and pour in the stock syrup and continue to whisk until pale and creamy.

3 Drain the gelatine, melt it and fold it into the sabayon mixture.
Add all the couverture at once, and fold it in quickly.
Add all the whipped cream at once and fold it in carefully.

4 Place the mixture into moulds and refrigerate or chill straight away. The gelatine in this recipe allows for the mousse to be turned out or quenelle. If you are setting the mousse in a mould and serving it in the mould then omit the gelatine.

5 For the sable biscuits mix the flour, butter and the sugar using a paddle until it resembles fine bread crumbs and then add the egg yolk.

6 Please do not over mix the paste as this will over develop the gluten. Cling film into discs and place in the fridge or freezer.

7 Pin out the rested pastry as thin as possible and cut out to the required size. (For sable biscuits to be at their best, you should be able to see your fingers through the biscuits when they are held up against the light.)

8 Cook at 160°C for the appropriate time. This will depend on the thickness of the pastry and the type of oven being used.

9 To assemble the dish, firstly make a pipette, melt the chocolate and pipe out the required design on the plates. Next, lay out three biscuits and dust the presentation one with icing sugar. Heat a metal skewer up over a naked flame, and quickly score the top of the presentation biscuit with the icing sugar. (Be sure not to keep the skewer in contact with the biscuit for too long as it will burn through the biscuit.)

10 Whip the cream and the pistachio compound, and place in a piping bag with a plain nozzle.

11 Pipe the cream into the middle of the two unscored biscuits, and surround them very neatly with the fresh raspberries. Place the presentation biscuit on top and using a palette knife or a fish slice place it very gently in the middle of the dressed plate.

12 Using a hot tablespoon, Rochelle the chocolate mousse on top and in the middle of the presentation biscuit.

13 Fill the chocolate design on the plate with alternate sauces, Anglaise and coulis.

14 Finally garnish with a nougatine crisp or mint as you desire.

ASSESSMENT OF KNOWLEDGE AND UNDERSTANDING

To test your level of knowledge and understanding, answer the following short questions. These will help to prepare you for your summative (final) assessment.

1 Name four types of fat used in the production of pastes and state two uses of two of the fats mentioned.

2 Explain the quality points to look for when producing puff paste.

3 Describe two causes of lack of volume in puff pastry products.

4 Explain the importance for pre-heating an oven before baking.

5 Explain why when producing strüdel paste is it necessary to use a linen cloth during the stretching of the paste and finishing of the strüdel.

6 Describe the effect that the development of gluten has on sweet paste.

7 Explain why it is important to shape hot water paste while it is still warm to the touch.

8 Describe how the fat and flour are incorporated into choux paste and why this technique is crucial to the overall success of the paste.

9 Describe how you would test a choux bun to see if it is correctly baked.

10 Explain the process of lamination and why it is crucial to the success of puff paste.

11 Suggest what changes the chef can make to the recipe for a pear Bourdaloue tart to create a healthier option.

Producing dough and fermented products

11

VRQ

Produce fermented dough and batter products

NVQ

Prepare, cook and finish complex bread and dough products

LEARNING OBJECTIVES

The aim of this chapter is to enable the reader to develop the necessary advanced techniques, knowledge and understanding of the principles in preparing and producing a range of complex breads, dough and fermented products.

The emphasis of this chapter is on developing knowledge attained in the previous Professional Chef Level 2 book and perfecting refined, contemporary and advanced bread making techniques. Also included in this chapter is further information on bakery materials, formulas, ingredients and equipment.

At the end of this chapter you will be able to:

- Identify the main methods of production for advanced fermented dough products including formula writing for recipes.

- Understand the elements of bread production.

- Understand the development of flavour in bread and dough.

- Understand the preparation of natural ferments.

- Identify each type of complex fermented dough and finished bread product at this advanced level.

- Comprehend the function of enriching ingredients in bakery.

- Understand the quality points of various complex dough products.

- Prepare, bake and present each type of complex dough product.

- Distinguish the storage procedures of fermented dough products.

- Identify the correct tools and equipment used in the production of fermented dough products.

Introduction

To make good bread and fermented dough products it is important to understand the functions and behaviours of the basic components such as flour, salt, water and yeast, and how they can be controlled using appropriate methods of making dough for different types of products.

VIDEO CLIP A professional bakery at work

Bread is a fundamental part of our diet: 99 per cent of UK households purchase bread. Unfortunately, most of the bread sold in the UK is made using methods that arguably have little regard for its nutritional qualities or the environmental and social impact of its production and distribution.

Bread is made with simple, natural and often organic ingredients that are a beneficial part of the human diet. The majority of the bread that is produced in the UK is from factories using a variety of additives and often larger amounts of salt and fat. High speed mixing, high levels of yeast and sometimes the use of enzymes are engaged to drive the dough to rise quickly, as opposed to allowing the dough to ferment and ripen and develop complex flavours in its own time. These products can have other additives such as calcium propionate added to prevent the growth of mould and lengthen shelf life.

The real bread campaign and bread additives

Part of the charity Sustain, which is an organization for better food and farming, the Real Bread Campaign is a membership that brings together bakers, independent millers, cereal growers, researchers, activists and teachers who care about the heritage of real bread.

The production of real bread does not involve the use of any processing aids, artificial additives (which includes most flour 'improvers', dough conditioners and preservatives) and chemical leavening (e.g. baking powder). It is considered that real bread contains the four important ingredients of flour, water, yeast and salt only.

Many of the industrial breads and fermented products that are widely available in supermarkets and some bakeries will use a variety of different additives such as:

- E481 (sodium stearoyl lactate) used as an emulsifier and stabilizer.

- E472e (diacetyltartaric acid esters of monoglycerides and diglycerides) used as an emulsifier and stabilizer.

- E920 (L-cysteine) used as a bread enhancer to stabilize the structure of leavened bread.

- E282 (calcium propionate) is used as a preservative, mainly against fungal growth on the finished product.

- E220 (sulphur dioxide) prevents enzymatic and bacterial spoilage of dough products. It also acts as an oxidizing agent, with bleaching effects and is used as a bleaching agent in flour.

- E300 (**ascorbic acid**) is vitamin C. However, it cannot be added as a vitamin supplement when labelled E300. When added to foods it functions as an anti-oxidant and bread enhancer.

- E260 (**acetic acid**) is used as a preservative against bacteria and fungi and it is also used as an aroma component.

During the production process other substances including phospholipase, fungal alpha amylase, transglutaminase, xylanase, maltogenic amylase, hemicellulase, oxidase, peptidase and protease are added, but if the manufacturer deems them to be a 'processing aid', it is unnecessary by law to declare them on the label. This could apply to a wrapped/sliced factory loaf or one from a supermarket in-store bakery.

The Real Bread Campaign is campaigning to find ways to make bread better for consumption, better for communities and better for the planet. Some areas which are detailed include:

- Bulk fermentation of at least four hours, preferably in the presence of sourdough bacteria/yeast.

- Production of bread that uses not only roller-milled white flour but uses stone-ground or all flour that is over 80 per cent extraction rate.

- Made in one continuous process, i.e. no part-baking or freezing of the dough.

- Made using at least 20 per cent (by weight) locally milled flour in accordance with FARMA guidelines. A definition of 30 miles is ideal, up to 50 miles is acceptable for larger cities and coastal or remote towns and villages.

- Has a salt content in line with FSA guidance – 1 per cent or less of final product weight.

- Product is certified organic.

Formulas in dough making

Two main formulas are used in bread making to accurately determine the percentage of ingredients used in a recipe and for creating the correct water temperature for making the fermented dough. Bakers and pastry chefs use the percentage formula because it is more accurate when scaling up a recipe to produce a higher yield of product.

The percentage (bakers) formula

The proportion of water to flour is the most important measurement in a bread recipe, as it affects texture and crumb the most. Professional bakers use a system of percentages known as baker's percentage in their recipe formulations. They measure ingredients by weight instead of by volume, because measurement by weight is much more accurate and consistent than measurement by volume, especially for the dry ingredients.

> **CHEF'S TIP** The term crumb is used to identify the texture of the soft, inner part of the bread.
>

Using the percentage formula below, the amount of flour is always stated as 100 per cent, and the amounts of the remaining ingredients are expressed as a percent of that amount by weight.

$$(\textit{Ingredient}) = 100\% \times \frac{\textit{ingredient mass}}{\textit{flour mass}}$$

For example, if a recipe calls for 1000 g of flour and 620 g of water, the corresponding bakers' percentages will be

100 per cent and 62 per cent. Because of the way these percentages are stated, as a percent of flour mass rather than of all ingredients, the total will always exceed 100 per cent. Using this, the bread formula could be expressed as shown in the table below.

FLOUR	100%
Water	62%
Yeast	4%
Salt	1.2%

To derive the actual individual ingredient weights when any weight of flour is chosen the following formula is used:

$$Ingredient\ weight = \frac{flour\ weight \times baker's\ percent\ (ingredient)}{100\%}$$

INGREDIENT	%	WEIGHTS	ACTUAL WEIGHT
Flour	100	× 1.00	1000 g
Water	62	× 0.62	620 g
Yeast	4	× 0.04	40 g
Salt	1.2	× 0.012	12 g

Determining the water temperature for fermented dough

Certain fermented dough recipes specify a particular working temperature for the dough to ferment correctly and by a specific time. This represents the temperature the dough should be before fermentation begins. If the dough is too cold, fermentation will be slower. The following method is recommended for determining the temperature of the water for the dough:

1 Measure the temperature of the flour to be used.

2 Subtract that value from twice the required dough temperature.

3 The result will be the required water temperature.

The equation to determine the correct water temperature for hand made dough is below.

$$\frac{Water}{Temperature} = \frac{(Required\ Dough \times 2)}{Temperature} - \frac{Flour}{Temperature}$$

Small quantities of dough up to 5 kg can be successfully kneaded by hand. This is a good method to use to be able to control the dough during production, create aeration of

the dough and to develop the gluten structure. However, this takes time and many chefs may prefer to use an electric mixer with a dough hook attachment. The act of electronic mixing will produce energy, which is transferred to the dough as heat and will increase the dough temperature. Bakers call this friction and this should be taken into consideration when calculating the required water temperature.

Friction can be measured by taking the temperature of the dough before mixing and then directly after mixing. The difference in the two numbers is the temperature increase due to friction. This is known as the friction factor and it can be calculated by the following formula:

$$Friction\ factor = (actual\ dough\ temp \times 3)$$
$$- (room\ temperature + flour\ temperature$$
$$+ water\ temperature)$$

A mixer with a dough hook can be used for producing large quantities of dough but caution should be taken due to increased temperature of the dough due to the production of additional heat from friction energy

Equipment used in dough production

A proving cabinet (prover) is a standard piece of equipment in patisseries and bakeries. Some cabinets have steam injection. The first **prove** should be between 21°C and 28°C. The second prove must be warmer depending on the dough and formula used, but never hotter than 40°C. If you do not have a proving cabinet, wrap the bowl containing the dough in a plastic bag and leave it in an appropriately warm place.

Proving baskets

Wicker proving baskets are lined with heavy canvas or a linen cloth and are used for holding large loaves such as a sourdough as they prove. The wicker allows the air to circulate around the dough with sticking. Although not all proving baskets are made from wicker, some are plastic, wood or handmade reed baskets.

Baker's couche

This is a heavy canvas cloth made from untreated natural fibre which is used for laying shaped loaves and baguettes on whilst they prove. The cloth is stiff enough to be folded into pleats to keep the loaves and baguettes separate. Sometimes special baking trays are used with pre-moulded inserts or a normal baking sheet with a baking cloth can be used instead. The couche should be brushed and dried after each baking session.

Soft brush

A natural fibre hand brush is required to be used exclusively for baking to brush away any excess flour from the work surface. Keeping the work surface clean from debris using a brush and kitchen scraper is essential for hygiene and quality dough production.

Laying loaves onto a Baker's couche in a bakery to prove

Cooling rack

The use of a wire rack to cool down the bread or dough products is important to let the cool air circulate around the baked product and prevent moisture from forming underneath during the cooling process.

Baking tins

Non-stick loaf tins are best for producing a rich brioche loaf because of the high fat content within the recipe. Small tins (400–600 g loaf size) and large tins (800–1000 g loaf size) are generally used.

Wooden baker's peel

This is used for transferring proved loaves onto a hot baking stone or tray in the oven and pulling them out again to check that they are baked. Some peels have long handles for deeper ovens and have different shaped paddles according to the type of loaf that is being produced. Wooden peels are perfect for sliding the loaves in and out of the oven quickly so that minimum heat is lost when the oven door is opened.

A wooden baker's peel being used to remove baked loaves from an oven

Thermometers

These are used to check ingredient, water and room temperature in the calculation of formulas. As second oven thermometer is important to regulate the temperature inside the oven during the baking process.

Lame

This is a specialist baker's tool which is essentially a small handle with a razor blade fitted into it. A small sharp knife, modelling knife or scalpel can be used instead. The purpose is for slashing the tops of the bread before they are baked.

Oven

Provided that the dough has been properly handled, you will not need a steam-injected oven. Preheating the oven to a temperature ranging from 180°C to 250°C is crucial to producing a high quality bread or dough product. Any oven can be used to bake fermented products but the addition of a baker's stone is to try to recreate a traditional baker's oven where the bread is usually baked directly onto a hot brick or stone floor. Using a rough slab of granite stone on each shelf is enough to create this environment and once again the pre-heating of an oven is crucial to the success of the quality of the baked product.

Developing flavour in bread and fermented dough

There are many factors that contribute to the development of flavour in bread and fermented dough products. The fermentation process provides a starting point to the development of flavour and one of the reasons for this is the enzymes found in flour and yeast releasing simple sugars from the starch molecules in flour. These enzymes start the fermentation process by breaking down the starch molecules in flour into the simple sugars that yeast is able to feed on. It is this important process which begins fermentation. Other factors also help develop flavour.

Temperature

The temperature at which dough is formed affects the flavour as fermentation speeds up at higher temperatures of 32°C and above. These higher temperatures can cause negative flavours to develop while different acids are produced at the increased rate of fermentation and the yeast multiplies more quickly. This eventually causes the yeast to run out of the simple sugars used as food because they have consumed most of them within the flour.

Fermentation set a too low a temperature also has an affect on flavour as dough that is fermented at a temperature below 21°C will develop little flavour because the yeast is not active enough to produce the acid by products of fermentation.

Time

The amount of time allowed for fermentation plays a large part in introducing flavour. The longer the fermentation time, the more flavour is imparted to the dough because the enzymes have more time to break down starch molecules. Longer fermentation times also allow for more flavour to be produced from the acids during this process. Hence sourdough is a particularly flavoursome dough because it is given a lot of time to slowly develop its flavour during fermentation.

However, if fermentation is too prolonged the yeast will run out of food and begin to die. This produces dough with little flavour and poor volume. There will also be few simple sugars left within the dough to help enhance the crust colour and browning during baking. Browning the crust provides a source of great flavour due to the Maillard reaction.

Ingredients

The ingredients in dough will produce flavour and some experimentation should be taken with different types or combinations of flours such as spelt, kamut and rye flours. Enriching ingredients will also add flavour to dough to create variation in the menu offer.

Enriching ingredients

Bread and fermented goods are sometimes enriched with a variety of additional ingredients. These are included to help increase the food value, add to the flavour, produce a softer crumb and retard staling. Fermentation will be slower in enriched dough.

SUGAR

This is an ingredient that requires careful usage in the presence of yeast. It should be used sparingly and should never come into direct contact with yeast because the yeast will be chemically broken down and become inactive. Sugar will help to increase the water retention of the dough, which will in turn enhance the softness of the crumb. However, sugar is used in fermented products to produce a sweet flavour, to give colour to the crust or to create a decorative effect on certain finished products (such as fondant and nibbed sugar).

MILK

As with water, milk will contribute to the moisture content of the product. Its fat content will also help to ensure that the dough will have a softer crumb. It also plays a role in helping to colour the crust and crumb during baking. Because of its natural sugar content, milk will have an important influence on the flavour of the fermented product. Generally, milk powder is usually used in the production of bread.

EGG

An average fresh egg will weigh approximately 50 g, of which nearly 60 per cent is egg white. The white has a high water concentration and contains minute traces of fat. The protein found within the white, albumin, has the ability to create a foam. Egg yolk has a high fat content and contains little water. It also contains the protein lecithin, which has the ability to emulsify fat-based and water-based ingredients. Egg yolk can be used in fermented goods to provide colour, additional liquid and fat content. It can also help to increase the shelf life of the product.

BUTTER

The high fat content of butter means it is used primarily to create a softer texture to the baked dough. It will also add some colour and flavour to the overall finish. Butter contains approximately 16 per cent water, and in the case of fermented goods such as brioche it will considerably change the texture, colour and flavour of the finished product. Salt may have to be reduced when using salted butter or margarine (which contains approximately 2 per cent salt).

SPICES, HERBS, FRUITS, VEGETABLES AND FLAVOURINGS

These are all added to enhance the flavour and texture of the finished product. Because of their varying fat or sugar contents they will have an effect on the fermentation process and may slow it down considerably. During fermentation the chef or baker should always observe the physical reactions taking place in the dough to gauge the consequence of the added enriching agents.

Flour

Flour contains a high proportion of starches, which are a subset of complex carbohydrates also known as polysaccharides. The kinds of flour used in baking include strong flour, soft flour and medium flour. The higher the protein content the harder and stronger the flour and this will produce crusty and leavened breads. The lower the protein the softer the flour is and will be used for cakes, shortbreads, biscuits and short pastries.

The milling of flour is accomplished by grinding grain between stones or steel wheels. Stone-ground usually means that the grain has been ground in a mill in which a revolving stone wheel turns over a stationary stone wheel, vertically or horizontally with the grain in between. Modern mills typically use electricity or fossil fuels to spin heavy steel, or cast iron, serrated and flat rollers to separate the bran and germ from the endosperm. The endosperm is ground to create white flour, which may be recombined with the bran and germ to create whole grain or whole wheat flour.

Picture of an old stone grinding wheel. Note the grooves made in the stone to let the flour escape when ground

The different milling techniques produce visibly different results, but can be made to produce nutritionally and functionally equivalent output. Stone-ground flour is, however, preferred by many bakers and chefs because of its texture, nutty flavour and the belief that it is nutritionally superior and has a better baking quality than steel-roller-milled flour. It is claimed that, as the stones grind relatively slowly, the wheat germ is not exposed to the sort of excessive temperatures that could cause the fat from the germ to oxidize and become rancid, which would destroy some of the vitamin content. Stone-milled flour has been found to be relatively high in thiamin, compared to roller-milled flour, especially when milled from hard wheat.

In some countries, the different flour varieties are labelled according to the ash mass (mineral content) that remains after a sample is incinerated in a laboratory oven (typically at 550 to 900°C). This is an easily verified indicator for the fraction of the whole grain remaining in the flour, because the mineral content of the starchy endosperm is much lower than that of the outer parts of the grain. Flour made from all parts of the grain (extraction rate: 100 per cent) leaves about 2 g ash or more per 100 g dry flour. Plain white flour (extraction rate: 50–60 per cent) leaves only about 0.4 g.

Some of the types of flour used by chefs and bakers in fermented dough and bread production are as follows.

Spelt

Spelt is a species of wheat and was an important staple in parts of Europe from the Bronze Age to medieval times. It now survives as a relict crop in the UK and Europe and has found a new market as a health food. Spelt flour is becoming more easily available, being sold in some supermarkets; it has a slightly sweet and nutty flavour. Although spelt flour contains gluten, it is less strong and therefore may need to be combined with other stronger flours to make bread.

Grains of ripe spelt

Strong white

Strong flour is always made from hard red winter or spring wheat. It has very high protein content, between 10 per cent and 13 per cent, making it excellent for bread baking. Naturally strong, organic bread flour will create dough with more gluten being formed which in turn creates elastic dough more capable of rising and resulting in a light and airy structured loaf. Traditional stone-ground flour will not have been bleached, unlike many commercial flours, so they tend to have a slightly ivory colour.

Wholemeal

Sometimes referred to as whole-wheat flour it is derived by grinding the whole grain of wheat. The term 'whole' refers to the fact that all of the grain (bran, germ and endosperm) is used and nothing is lost in the process of making the flour. This is in contrast to white, refined flours, which contain only the endosperm. Because the whole flour contains the remains of all of the grain, it has a textured, brown coloured appearance. Wholemeal flour is robust, full flavoured and more nutritious than refined white flour. It is a good source of calcium, iron, fibre and other minerals. Wholemeal flour has a shorter shelf life than white flour, as the higher fat content leads to rancidity if not stored properly, such as in dry and cool areas.

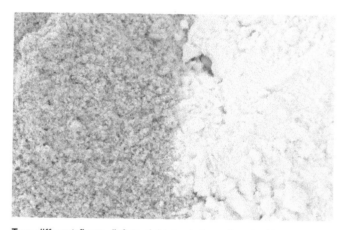

Two different flours (left to right – wholemeal and white strong)

Khorasan or Kamut

Khorasan wheat is an ancient grain type. This grain is two times larger than modern-day wheat and is known for its rich nutty and slightly earthy flavour. The grain itself is very high in protein content. It also contains a high mineral concentration especially in selenium, zinc and magnesium. Because of its low oxidation levels it loses little nutritional content when being ground and processed. Again, to create good flavoured and well-risen bread this flour needs to blended with high gluten white flour.

Rye

Rye is a grass grown extensively as a grain and as a forage crop. It is closely related to barley and wheat. Rye flour is high in gliadin but low in glutenin. It therefore has lower

gluten content than wheat flour. It also contains a higher proportion of soluble fibre. Rye flour is used to bake the traditional sourdough breads of Germany, Austria, Switzerland, Czech Republic, Poland and Scandinavia. Most rye breads use a mix of rye and wheat flours because rye does not produce sufficient gluten and the bread is quite dense in structure. Pumpernickel bread is usually made exclusively of rye, and contains a mixture of rye flour and rye meal. There are three different types of rye flour: light, medium and dark.

How gluten traps carbon dioxide gas

To understand how fermented dough rises, it is important to appreciate the role of gluten. Glutenin is produced from the proteins in flour and gives strength, elasticity and structure to baked goods. Although there are many different types of flour used in baking, wheat flours contain two main proteins called gliadin and glutenin. Gluten develops when water is mixed into the flour and the more gluten-producing proteins contained in flour, the more water it will be able to absorb.

As gluten develops inside the dough, it begins to create a web-like structure. This structure allows carbon dioxide to become entrapped as the yeast feeds on the simple sugars from the flour and releases the gas, ethyl alcohol and acid. As fermentation continues, more carbon dioxide is produced causing the gluten fibres to stretch and hold more gases.

The figure shown below demonstrates how this is achieved and eventually the dough is ready to be baked. These gases, alongside the ethyl alcohol vapours expand in the dough while any moisture turns to steam. This combination of gases and steam expanding inside the dough causes the network of gluten to stretch even further forcing it to rise and increase in volume.

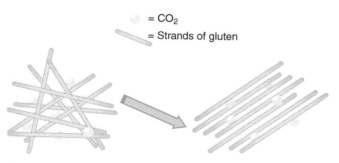

= CO_2

= Strands of gluten

Carbon dioxide gets trapped inside strands of gluten.

After kneading, gluten strands line up like soliders, making the gluten stronger.

Diagram showing the result of carbon dioxide caught into gluten before and after kneading

The techniques and methods of producing fermented dough

There are four basic methods of producing fermented dough; each method has its own characteristic and application:

1 bulk fermented dough;

2 'no-time' dough (ADD);

3 ferment and dough;

4 sponge and dough.

Bulk fermented dough method (straight dough)

This is the main process bakers and chefs use to make bread. It is a simple and effective method that is used in many recipes. Flour and salt are blended together with water and yeast. These are mixed and worked into a smooth, clear dough that is ready for fermentation. The dough is then covered with a plastic sheet or clean kitchen cloth to prevent it drying out and forming a skin ('skinning'). It is given a 'bulk fermentation time' (BFT), allowing fermentation to occur over a set period of time to give the yeast a resting period to ferment and for the flavours and gases to develop.

The next stage is the folding of the dough. This careful technique is used between each resting or fermentation period to reinforce and develop the dough structure. This sequence is usually termed '**knocking back**' in text books (or de-gassing) although this term is associated with heavy kneading of the dough after the BFT which is wrong as it will tighten the dough and knock all the gases out of the dough. Gentle folding should be encouraged to continue yeast activity, develop the gluten in the flour and ensure an even dough temperature.

The dough is rested for a few minutes, covered as before, and then scaled off for shaping into the various products required by the baker or chef. The shaped dough products are then allowed to prove for a second time before baking. The total BFT can vary from 1 to 12 hours, depending on the recipe and the quantities of the ingredients, so it is important to always follow the recipe given.

CHEF'S TIP The fermentation process starts the development of flavour in the dough. Enzymes in the flour and yeast release simple sugars from the starch molecules in the flour.

'No-time' dough method (activated dough development)

This method speeds up the fermentation through the addition of an improver. The improver contains chemicals and minerals that speed up the process of fermentation. This process is used by large-scale producers of packaged breads, such as factories, supermarkets and large bakeries.

Flour, salt, yeast, water and the improver are blended and mixed to a soft dough. An electric mixing machine is required as the mixing time is approximately double the normal time. The mixing speed is also higher to help develop the gluten quickly and to use the friction energy to increase the temperature of the dough. Fermentation progresses quickly due to the effects of the improver on the other ingredients, thus cutting down the time required to produce large quantities of fermented dough products. When this stage is complete the dough is ready for scaling off, moulding into the required shape and proving before baking.

Extra yeast is required in some recipes that use improvers as the normal growth rate of the yeast cannot keep up with the speed of the fermentation. As this process does not allow time for the gluten to develop, about 4 per cent extra water is usually added to the dough. No-time dough is used for production systems with limited time, facilities and space. With the use of improvers in this method giving a certain stability to the product; the dough will be temperature stable which can facilitate the retardation of dough during the production process.

CHEF'S TIP Retarding fermented dough means to slow down the fermentation process by placing the dough into refrigerated storage (1–4°C). This suppresses the activity of the yeast. Dough can therefore be produced the day before it is required and 'retarded' overnight before finishing and baking the next day.

Ferment and dough method

This process is intended for heavily enriched dough to allow the yeast to become accustomed to the high levels of fat and sugar in a recipe, which slow yeast activity considerably.

The first stage is to produce a ferment; the yeast is blended to a thin batter and fermented with about 20 per cent of the recipe's flour and all of the water. Fermentation time depends on the yeast content, but it is ready when the ferment begins to drop back (the ferment rises so much that it cannot support its own bulk and starts to drop back). It is best fermented in a proving cabinet as it needs to be sufficiently warm after dropping back to maintain the correct dough temperature.

The ferment is then blended with the remaining flour, salt, fat and other enrichening ingredients to form a dough. The dough is then bulk fermented for approximately the same time as the ferment and then scaled off. This method is sometimes known as a 'flying ferment'.

Sponge and dough method

This method is used by many artisan bakeries and chefs who wish to create natural, full-flavoured and textured breads such as sourdough. The 'sponge' is a thick batter which ferments slowly, helping to maximize the amount of flavour in the finished bread. It is made by combining equal amounts of liquid, flour and yeast and may contain some salt. It is then left to ferment for between 6 and 24 hours, depending on the recipe and the amount of yeast used. This is sometimes referred to as a 'poolish'. Sometimes natural ferments are produced from fruit such as grapes, raisins or apples which imparts different flavour properties.

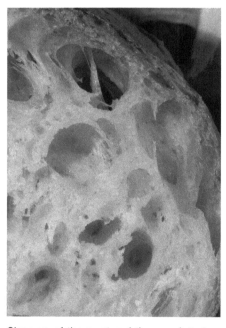

Close up of the crust and the crumb texture of sourdough bread

It is then made into dough with the addition of more liquid and flour. The dough can be used almost immediately as the yeast is fully activated. This method will sometimes create a sourdough that is packed full of the natural flavours of the acids developed during the slow fermentation process.

Making a natural ferment

Using a ferment will help to produce breads and yeast-based products with more flavour, improved crust colour and better crumb texture. It will also allow the chef and baker to reduce the yeast content and can increase the shelf life of the products.

Many artisan bakeries and kitchens maintain ferments from day to day for many months, ranging from basic recipes to natural starter-based recipes that contain little or no yeast at all. There are various methods of producing a ferment.

Method 1 – Retain a 200 g piece of dough from the first batch of bread you make. This can be kept in the refrigerator or a cool room. Add this to the next batch of dough to enhance it. Retain another 200 g from the new batch of dough to use the following day.

Method 2 – An extension of the above method is to retain 200 g of dough and leave it for two days at a temperature of 12–18°C in an airtight plastic container. Add the same amount of water (200 g) and double its weight in flour (400 g). Mix well until a dough is formed. This process is known as 'refreshing'. The dough will need to be refreshed every five days, or when some of the ferment is used to create bread dough.

Method 3 – The third method is to produce a natural starter using good-quality stone-ground organic flour with high gluten content. A simple organic flour and water culture can create a ferment over a few days. However another typical recipe for this method is as follows:

Raisins, apples, grapes or sultanas	250 g
Sugar or organic honey	15 g
Water (at 20°C)	250 g
Fresh yeast (optional)	4 g

Place the fruit in a clean plastic container. Cover the fruit with the water (a natural mineral water if possible) and add the sugar and the yeast if required. Leave for approximately four to five days, until the fruit can be seen to be fermenting. Press the fruit mixture through a sieve and measure the following ingredients:

Fermented fruit juice	250 g
Strong organic stone-ground flour	350 g

Knead for five minutes at a low speed to create a firm dough and leave to rest in a warm place, covered for a minimum of four hours. Refresh this ferment with the following ingredients:

Water	250 g
Strong organic stone-ground flour	375 g

Knead for five minutes at a low speed. Leave to rest in a cool place or in a refrigerator and begin to use after 24 hours. The starter dough can now be produced from this ferment by using the base recipe below. Alternatively, keep refreshing the ferment every day; for every 200 g used, refresh with 100 g flour and 100 g water.

CHEF'S TIP   Many ferments can be slowly fermented in a refrigerator. The longer, cooler fermentation process allows more flavour to develop. This is also known as 'retarding'; the yeast activity slows down but still continues.

CHEF'S TIP   Two varieties of bacteria are present in sourdough: Acetobacter and Lactobacillus. These impart acetic and lactic acids during fermentation, which help to expose the strong flavours required.

Making a starter (poolish)

To make a starter you will require the following ingredients:

Water	300 g
Ferment	100 g
Strong organic stone-ground flour	540 g

Carefully place the ferment into the water and slowly add the flour. Combine the ingredients together to create a soft-textured dough. Sprinkle some flour into the bottom of a bowl and place the starter into it. Set in a proving cabinet and leave to ferment for up to five hours (or until it has doubled in size). The fermentation time can vary. This starter can now be used for the country bread recipe in this chapter.

Brioche

Brioche is a type of rich bread containing butter and eggs in different quantities. There are four basic grades of brioche, describing the levels of richness:

- surfine;
- fine;
- ordinaire;
- commune.

The grades correspond to the different amounts of butter and egg used in the brioche and therefore how rich it is in taste, colour and texture. Commune contains the least amounts of egg and butter and so is the least rich.

Brioche is at its best within the first couple of hours of baking, once it has cooled, and should be eaten within a day. Brioche can be frozen, but it will lose its fine texture and will generally not be as pleasant as freshly baked. There are two basic processes of making pâte à brioche. The first is a straight dough method, where all the ingredients are mixed together. The second uses a **levain** (a yeast sponge), which is added to the dough.

Types of brioche

Brioche comes in many shapes and sizes:

Mousseline	A round brioche in shape. It can be baked in a cylindrical tin, buttered and lined with greaseproof paper. The dough is moulded into a ball, placed into the tin and proved until above the sides.
À tête	This well-known shape has a small head placed on top of a bun. Small brioches can weigh from 50 g, large ones up to 1 kg. They should always be baked in fluted moulds.

Nanterre or Nantaise	Made in a straight-sided loaf tin, either in one piece or by laying balls of dough next to each other.
Couronne or Pompe	A large ring, snipped at intervals with scissors to produce a decorative effect. The ring is made by moulding a ball, making a hole in the centre and forming into a ring by gradually increasing the size of the hole.
La tresse	A plaited loaf that resembles the shapes of Jewish Cholla breads.

CHEF'S TIP Brioche can be stored in a refrigerator, but it must be wrapped in plastic film and stored away from strong smelling foods such as cheese.

Goods made from brioche

A range of goods are produced from brioche and it has a number of uses in the kitchen.

Croûtes

- Aux fruits – slices of brioche sprinkled with icing sugar, glazed, covered with a fruit compote mask with a kirsch-flavoured apricot sauce.

- **Lyonnaise** – slices of brioche spread with a chestnut purée, coated with apricot glaze and sprinkled with roasted flaked almonds. Served dressed as a crown with the centre filled with marrons glacés.

- Madère – slices of brioche formed into a crown with the centre filled with a macédoine of fruits, sultanas, currants and raisins and coated with Madeira-flavoured apricot sauce.

- Bostock – stale Nantaise is cut into slices, imbibed with stock syrup, spread with crème d'amande, dusted with icing sugar and glazed in a hot oven.

- Goubaud – produced by lining a flan ring with brioche paste. Another piece of paste is rolled into a rectangle, sprinkled all over with pieces of glacé fruit macerated in kirsch, rolled up and cut into 2 cm slices. The slices are placed into the prepared ring, egg glazed, proved and baked. After cooling on a wire cooling rack it is finished with apricot glaze and a kirsch water icing.

Kitchen uses for brioche

- coulibiac.

- foie gras en croûte.

- loaves for sandwiches, rolls and fingers.

- crumbs (**chapelure**) for coating suprême of chicken and similar dishes.

Savarin

Gâteau Savarin is a classic French fermented sponge cake, which was invented by the renowned Parisian pâtissier Auguste Julien in 1845. It is basically a rum baba baked in a circular (ring) mould.

The cake is named in honour of Jean-Anthelme Brillat-Savarin (1755–1826), the French politician, lawyer and gastronome, who also has a cheese named after him. A Savarin is a yeast dough soaked in rum flavoured syrup with the centre hole decorated with crème Chantilly and fresh fruit. The dessert is a close relative of the Eastern European baba, which includes dried fruit in the dough.

Baba

Babas are small cakes made from yeast dough containing raisins or currants. They are baked in cylindrical moulds and soaked with sugar syrup usually flavoured with rum (originally they were soaked in a sweet fortified wine).

After these cakes were soaked in the wine sauce for a day, the dried fruits would fall out of them. It is believed to be a version of a Kugelhopf, which was invented in Lemberg in the 1600s. The baba was brought to France by King Stanislas Leszczynska, the deposed King of Poland and the father-in-law of King Louis XV (1710–1774) of France when he was exiled to Lorraine. According to legend, he found the local French Kouglhopf too dry for his liking and dipped the bread in rum. He was so delighted that he named the cake after one of the heroes of his favourite book, Ali Baba from A Thousand and One Nights. Later, his chef refined the cake by using a type of brioche dough and adding raisins to the recipe.

Recipes

Almond croissants

Ingredients for the almond filling	makes approximately 1500 g
Unsalted butter	400 g
Tant-pour-tant (equal quantities of icing sugar and ground almonds)	800 g
French custard powder (poudre à crème)	10 g
Whole egg	240 g
Dark rum	80 g

energy	cal	fat	sat fat	carb	sugar	protein	fibre
1826 kJ	437 kcal	26.2 g	9.9 g	42.5 g	19.8 g	8.8 g	2.7 g

METHOD OF WORK

Almond filling

1 Beat the butter with the sugar and almond mix and add the French custard powder.
2 Add the egg, a little at a time. Continue to beat the mixture.
3 Add the rum and set aside.
4 For an option, you can add 50 per cent of crème pâtissière to this recipe to make it lighter.

To finish the almond croissants

5 Pipe the almond filling inside the croissant triangle and carefully roll up into the croissant shape without pressing out any of the almond filling.
6 Prove and egg wash as for plain croissants.
7 Sprinkle the tops of the croissants with flaked almonds and bake in a pre-heated oven at 220°C.
8 Make a glaze to brush on top of the croissants as they are removed from the oven; equal parts fresh milk and caster sugar brought to the boil in a heavy based saucepan. Continue to stir until the liquid begins to reduce a little and slightly thicken.
9 Remove the almond croissants from the oven when they have baked to a golden brown colour and lay them out onto a wire rack.
10 Immediately brush with the milk and sugar glaze and let the croissants cool before serving.

Brioche

Brioche (using the straight dough method)

Ingredients	25 brioche à tête or 2 loaves	45 brioche à tête or 4 loaves
Strong flour	500 g	1 kg
Fresh yeast	25 g	50 g
Fresh milk	75 ml	150 ml
Good-quality salt	15 g	30 g
Caster sugar	50 g	100 g
Type of brioche to be created		
Commune		
Eggs	4	8
Butter	125 g	250 g
Ordinaire		
Eggs	6	12
Butter	200 g	400 g
Fine		
Eggs	6	12
Butter	350 g	700 g
Surfine		
Eggs	8	16
Butter	500 g	1 kg

energy	cal	fat	sat fat	carb	sugar	protein	fibre
332 kJ	78 kcal	0.3 g	0.1 g	17.3 g	2.5 g	2.5 g	1.4 g

METHOD OF WORK

1   Preheat an oven to 220°C.
2   Warm the milk to 30°C. Dissolve the yeast and sugar in the milk.
3   Sieve the flour and salt together. Add to the milk-yeast mixture and mix to a clear paste. Add the eggs to form a smooth and elastic dough. It is easiest to use an electric mixer if available.
4   Carefully cut in the soft butter into small cubes and mix into the dough well so that no traces of butter are found. Place into a refrigerator to rest for at least one hour.
5   To create brioche à tête, scale the dough at 50 g each and mould into boules.
6   Create the 'heads' (têtes) by rolling the side of the hand, one-third of the way up each boule to nearly separate a piece of dough for the head.
7   Place each boule into a prepared individual fluted tin and press the head firmly in the centre of the body, on top. Glaze with an egg wash.
8   Bake in the preheated oven. The baking time will vary according to the size of the brioche so take care and inspect the brioches every five minutes during baking. It is baked when a golden brown colour has been created on the crust and if a tapping sound on the base of each brioche sounds hollow.
9   Turn out of the baking tins onto wire racks to cool.

Step-by-step: How to make brioche a tête

1. Scale the dough to 50 g per piece. Ensure accuracy for portion control.

2. Mould into round boules with your hands in a circular motion and with as little flour as possible on the work surface.

3. Create the head with a gentle sawing action of the side of the hand, creating a head one-third the size of the body.

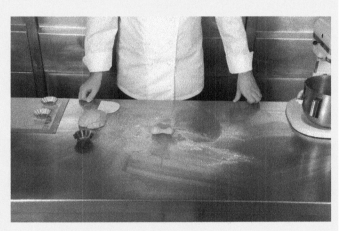

4. Do not detach the head from the body.

5. Carefully place the brioche into a prepared, fluted brioche mould ensuring the head remains in the centre and on top.

6. Dip the end of a small doweling or wooden pastry brush into flour and push into the head halfway through into the brioche body to help pin the head in place.

Brioche

Brioche (using the levain method)

Ingredients	1 Nanterre loaf or18 rolls	2 Nanterre loaves or 40 rolls
Levain		
Fresh milk	130 ml	260 ml
Slower acting fresh yeast (French Hirondelle; if using British yeast then use only 20 g and 40 g)	25 g	50 g
Strong flour	250 g	500 g
Dough		
Strong flour	750 g	1.5 kg
Good-quality salt	20 g	40 g
Caster sugar	25 g	50 g
Size 4 fresh eggs	10	20
Unsalted butter (keep at a temperature which leaves it plastic and manageable; not cold and hard or too warm and soft)	700 g	1.4 kg
Egg wash glaze		
Whole egg	125 g	200 g
Caster sugar	15 g	20 g
Good-quality salt	pinch	pinch

energy	cal	fat	sat fat	carb	sugar	protein	fibre
2292 kJ	550 kcal	36.2 g	21.3 g	47.7 g	3.7 g	11.3 g	3.7 g

METHOD OF WORK

1 Preheat an oven to 220°C.

2 To make the levain, warm the milk to approximately 30°C. Dissolve the yeast in the milk. Combine the flour with the yeast-milk and mix to obtain a stretchy and elastic dough. This will take ten minutes by hand, less in a machine using a dough hook at medium speed.

3 Shape the dough mixture into a ball and stand in a bowl of tepid water (20–25°C). Leave the levain to ferment and develop. When it is ready it will look like a large swollen sponge floating on the surface of the warm water.

4 When the levain is nearly ready make the second part of the dough. Combine the strong flour, salt and sugar. Make a well in the centre of the flour and pour in the lightly beaten eggs.

5 Work the eggs into the flour. Knead by hand for about 15 minutes.

6 Temper the butter by flattening it with your hand or a rolling pin. Take about a quarter of the dough and work it into the butter. Combine the butter with the rest of the dough and mix until smooth, either by hand or using a machine.

7 Incorporating the levain is a very delicate process. It is easiest to use an electric mixer and a dough hook. However, if you are working by hand lay the soft levain onto the slightly flattened dough and gently knead the two ingredients together.

8 Cover with a clean kitchen cloth and prove the dough until it is well risen or doubled in size.

9 Knead the brioche gently on the work surface by folding it back into three, as though you were preparing puff pastry. Flatten it and again fold into three. Wrap the dough in plastic and chill for two hours.

10 To finish the brioche, lightly grease a bread tin. Unwrap the brioche dough and scale each brioche piece at 50 g, gently moulding into a boule and placing side by side into a prepared bread tin to produce a brioche Nanterre. If making individual brioche buns, scale into the required 50 g weight and mould into boules.

11 Prove the brioche at 30°C. It should slowly double in size. To test whether it is ready, lightly press the surface with a finger; the depression should spring back.

12 Brush the top of the brioche with the egg glaze, made by mixing the egg, sugar and salt together and passing through a chinois.

13 Bake in the preheated oven. The baking time will vary according to the size of the brioche, from a few minutes to 45 minutes. Remove when golden brown and cooked through. Check for a hollow sound to the finished brioche to tell if it is completely baked.

14 Remove from the oven and immediately turn out of their baking tins onto wire racks to cool down.

Blinis

Ingredients	15 individual	30 individual
Strong flour	110 g	220 g
Buckwheat flour	110 g	220 g
Fresh yeast	10 g	20 g
Warm milk (30°C)	280 g	560 g
Separated eggs	2	4
Good-quality salt	to taste	to taste
Finish		
Clarified butter	200 g	400 g

energy	cal	fat	sat fat	carb	sugar	protein	fibre
694 kJ	167 kcal	12.3 g	7.4 g	11.7 g	1.3 g	3.4 g	1.3 g

METHOD OF WORK

1   Sieve the two flours together and mix the fresh yeast with the warm milk.

2   Add the sieved flour to the yeast-milk and carefully mix to create a delicate dough.

3   Cover the bowl with plastic film and leave to ferment for up to one hour.

4   Add the egg yolks and beat in well. Rest the mixture for a further 30 minutes.

5   Aerate the egg whites to soft peaks with a little salt added to help stabilize the foam. Carefully fold the aerated egg whites into the fermented batter with a spatula, a little at a time.

6   Place small non-stick blinis pans onto a stove to heat and pour a small amount of the clarified butter into each one.

7   Ladle some of the blinis mixture into each pan and fry to cook on both sides until each side is golden brown; the blinis should be springy to the touch but thoroughly cooked inside. Serve as quickly as possible.

CHEF'S TIP   Blinis can be used for canapés and hors d'oeuvre and are traditionally served with ice-cold caviar, smoked salmon and soured cream. They are sometimes used as an accompaniment to other types of smoked and cured fish.

Stöllen (Christstöllen)

Ingredients	3 loaves	6 loaves
Ferment ingredients		
Warm water	150 ml	300 ml
Milk powder	15 g	30 g
Whole egg	100 g	200 g
Caster sugar	30 g	60 g
Fresh yeast	60 g	120 g
Strong flour	80 g	160 g
Dough ingredients		
Strong flour	600 g	1.3 kg
Good-quality salt	5 g	10 g
Caster sugar	80 g	160 g
Mixed spice	3 g	5 g
Unsalted butter	125 g	250 g
Fruit		
Currants	60 g	120 g
Sultanas or raisins	60 g	120 g
Mixed peel	100 g	200 g
Glacé cherries	50 g	100 g
Juice and finely grated lemon zest	½ lemon	1 lemon
Dark rum	25 ml	50 ml
Flaked almonds	50 g	100 g
Rope of marzipan	3 × 75 g	6 × 75 g

energy	cal	fat	sat fat	carb	sugar	protein	fibre
1390 kJ	330 kcal	10 g	4 g	54.6 g	25.9 g	7.3 g	3.6 g

METHOD OF WORK

1 Preheat an oven to 200°C.

2 Wash the currants and sultanas/raisins and drain well. Place them into a stainless steel bowl with the mixed peel, cherries, flaked almonds and juice and zest of lemon and then add the dark rum. Leave to macerate for at least one hour but preferably overnight.

3 To make the ferment, blend the yeast with the milk powder, egg, sugar, water and flour. Set the ferment at 26°C for 30 minutes. When it is ready it will begin to drop back.

4 Mix the dough ingredients together and incorporate the butter by rubbing in.

5 Blend the ferment with the flour mixture to form a soft dough. Blend in the fruit ingredients carefully; avoid breaking or bruising the fruit.

6 Bulk ferment the dough for one hour.

7 Carefully knock back to release only some of the fermentation gasses. Scale off each loaf at 450 g.

8 For each loaf, knead the dough into a rectangle slightly longer than the marzipan rope. Fold in the sides to prevent the marzipan from leaking.

9 Place the marzipan in the centre and then roll up. Set the stöllen onto a baking sheet lined with a silicone mat and prove for a further 45 minutes.

10 Bake in the preheated oven for approximately 40 minutes. Remove from the oven and while still hot brush well with melted butter. Leave to cool for fifteen minutes and brush once more with melted butter then completely coat with sieved icing sugar.

11 Leave to cool on a wire cooling rack.

12 Wrap well in plastic film and store in a cool, dry area. To serve, simply slice and warm under a salamander with a little unsalted butter to spread.

> **CHEF'S TIP** The Christstöllen, or just stöllen, is a formed cake filled with dried fruits and nuts and covered in powdered sugar. It is available only during Advent and Christmas time. Its shape is supposed to resemble the Christ Child wrapped in a blanket.
>
> The dough of the stöllen is traditionally heavy and thick. Additional ingredients can be used. These then determine the type of stöllen the cake becomes.
>
> **Almond stöllen (**Mandelstöllen)
> This is a Stöllen in which the dough contains a minimum of 20 g of almonds for every 100 g of flour. Sometimes almond paste is added, but this is not traditional.
>
> **Butterstöllen**
> This stöllen contains at least 40 g of butter for every 100 g of flour. It must also contain dried fruits, candied orange and lemon peel.
>
> **Poppy seed stöllen (**Mohnstollen)
> This stöllen contains a minimum of 20 g of poppy seeds for every 100 g of flour. Usually this is added as a filling and not simply mixed throughout the dough. Dried fruits and candied orange and lemon peel can be added to the dough.
>
> **Nut-stöllen (**Nuss-Stöllen)
> This is a stöllen in which the dough contains a minimum of 20 g of finely chopped nuts for every 100 g of flour.
>
> **Schittchen**
> This is the name for a stöllen in the German state of Thüringen. It is considered a specialty of the city of Erfurt. The Schitten is recognizable by the slit length-wise across the top of it. The ingredients of the Schittchen include vanilla sugar, candied lemon and orange peel, raisins, chopped and ground almonds, almond flavour, rum or brandy.

Step-by-step: How to mould, prepare and add the marzipan to the stöllen

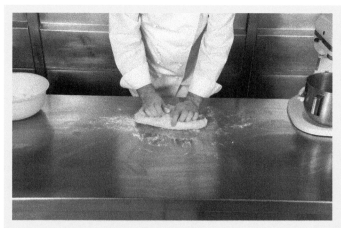

1. Carefully knead the macerated fruits into the dough without bruising the fruits.

2. Dust with a little extra flour if required and knead the dough into a rectangle as shown.

3. Place the rope of marzipan into the centre of the dough.

4. Fold the ends of the rectangle over the marzipan to envelope it and prevent the marzipan from leaking out.

5. Roll up the dough to ensure the marzipan remains central to the finished dough.

6. This is the finished shape of the stöllen before proving and baking.

Croissants and pain au chocolat

Ingredients for croissants	15 individual	30 individual
Strong flour	500 g	1 kg
Good quality fine salt	10 g	20 g
Fresh yeast	25 g	40 g
Caster sugar	30 g	60 g
Fresh milk (at 20°C)	300 ml	600 ml
Dry pastry butter	250 g	500 g
Finish		
Egg wash	100 g	150 g

energy	cal	fat	sat fat	carb	sugar	protein	fibre
861 kJ	204 kcal	5.7 g	1.5 g	33.5 g	4 g	6.9 g	2.3 g

VIDEO CLIP Croissants

METHOD OF WORK

1 Sieve the flour, salt and sugar together. Mix the fresh yeast in with the milk.

2 Add the flour to the milk to create a soft dough.

3 Place in the proving cabinet to ferment at 28°C for approximately 25 minutes.

4 Gently knock back the dough. Roll out the dough into a rectangle to a thickness of 8 mm.

5 Temper the butter by forming it to two-thirds the size of the dough with a rolling pin. Place the butter over two-thirds of the surface of the dough. Fold the dough in three, turn a quarter of the way around and roll out again to 5 mm thick.

6 Fold the dough into three again and wrap in plastic film and refrigerate for one hour. Repeat the rolling and folding process one more time and rest in the refrigerator for a further hour.

7 Roll out the dough to 3 mm thick and cut into rectangular strips approximately 30 cm in depth. Cut out triangles from the strips and roll up into a croissant shape.

8 Alternatively, cut into smaller rectangles, place a stick of chocolate in the centre of each and roll up.

9 Preheat an oven to 220°C.

10 Place all the croissants onto a baking tray set with silicone paper or a silicone baking mat. Lightly egg wash each croissant and prove at no warmer than 27°C with high humidity for up to two hours or until they have doubled in size.

11 Place into the oven and bake for approximately 15 minutes. Cool on a wire cooling rack before serving slightly warm.

Step-by-step: How to prepare and shape croissants

1. Pin out the layered croissant dough to 3 mm thick.

2. Trim the croissant dough.

3. Mark the cutting points for each croissant to ensure portion control.

4. Cut the croissants into the required shape and size.

5. Cut a small 2 cm dash along the base of the croissant to aid rolling.

6. Roll up the croissant by gently stretching and holding the tail of each croissant to help create the shape.

PAIN AU CHOCOLAT

Prepare the croissant dough and roll it out to 2.5 mm thickness. Cut the dough into rectangles, place chocolate strips in the centre and roll up. Glaze with egg wash before baking.

Three different types of croissant; clockwise from top – plain, almond and pain au chocolat

Step-by-step: How to prepare, shape and finish pain au chocolat

1. Cut the croissant dough into 14 cm rectangles which has been pinned out to 2.5 mm thick.

2. Place one or two chocolate sticks across the rectangle of croissant dough.

3. Roll up each croissant to encase the chocolate inside. Prove at 27°C for one-and-a-half hours and bake at 180°C for approximately 15 minutes.

Danish pastries

Ingredients	15 individual	30 individual
Strong flour	450 g	900 g
Good-quality salt	5 g	10 g
Butter	25 g	50 g
Fresh yeast	15 g	30 g
Caster sugar	30 g	60 g
Fresh milk (at 20°C)	250 ml	500 ml
Whole egg	1	2
Butter	200 g	400 g

Finish

As required

energy	cal	fat	sat fat	carb	sugar	protein	fibre
982 kJ	235 kcal	13.4 g	8.2 g	25.6 g	3.4 g	4.6 g	2 g

CHEF'S TIP It is preferable to make the Danish paste a day before you need to use it to let it rest so it is easier to use and manipulate into the required shapes and designs.

VIDEO CLIP Technique for Danish pastries

METHOD OF WORK

1 Preheat an oven to 220°C if baking the Danish pastries on the same day of production.

2 Sieve the flour into a warm stainless steel basin and rub the smaller quantity of butter into the flour.

3 Make a well in the centre of the flour.

4 Mix half the milk with the yeast and the remainder of the milk with the salt, sugar and eggs.

5 Pour each of the solutions into the prepared well and mix thoroughly. Begin to knead the dough until it is an elastic consistency and free of any lumps.

6 Cover with plastic film or a clean kitchen cloth and leave to rest for at least 20 minutes at room temperature. Carefully knock back the dough with a gentle manipulation.

7 Roll out the dough to an 8 mm thick rectangle, as for the croissant recipe.

8 Temper the butter and spread over two-thirds of the surface of the dough. Fold the dough into three, turn a quarter of the way around and roll out again to 5 mm thick in a rectangle.

9 Fold the dough into three once more, wrap in plastic film and refrigerate for one hour. Repeat the rolling and folding process one more time and rest the dough in the refrigerator for a further hour.

10 Roll out and cut and shape as required and add any fillings. Place onto silicone baking mats on baking sheets and prove at 27°C for up to two hours or until they have doubled in size.

11 Bake in the oven for approximately 15 minutes or when the Danish Pastries are golden brown.

12 Remove from the oven and immediately place onto a wire rack to cool down.

VARIATIONS FOR FINISHING DANISH PASTRIES

Moulins à vent

Cut the rolled dough into equal squares (approximately 9 cm × 9 cm). Glaze the sides with egg wash. Pipe a small rosette of almond cream or frangipane in the centre using a piping bag with a plain tube. Fold the four corners into the centre. Place a small disc of paste on top in the centre. Prove and bake. Glaze the pastries with a hot apricot glaze as soon as they are removed from the oven.

Tortillons

Roll out the dough sheet to 3 mm thick. Cut out 6 cm × 12 cm rectangles and glaze with egg wash and sprinkle with granulated sugar. Then cut a slit in the centre and intertwine: pull one end through the cut slit and pull through to the other side. These can then be filled with almond cream if desired, and are baked and finished as above.

Apricot Danish pastry

Roll out the dough to 2 mm thick. Cut out discs 10 cm in diameter and place into the bottom of 8 cm diameter moulds. Fill with crème pâtissière and place an apricot half on top. Roll out a top sheet for the pastries, preferably using a marking device such as a perspex template to create a design. Garnish and leave to prove for 45 minutes at 27°C. Bake at 180°C for 15 minutes. Glaze with a hot apricot glaze and cool.

Pistachio and chocolate roulade

Roll out the dough to 2 mm thick. Mix the crème pâtissière with the pistachio paste and spread onto the dough. Add a few chocolate drops and roll up to form a roulade. Cut the roulade into slices of approximately 2 cm thick (about 60 g). Place the end of the roll underneath to prevent it from unfurling. Leave to prove for about 45 minutes and bake at 180°C for 15 minutes. Glaze with apricot glaze and sprinkle with chopped pistachio nuts.

Cockscombs

Cut the Danish paste into two large rectangle strips (approximately 50 cm × 20 cm). Pipe frangipane or crème pâtissière down the centre of each strip and place a desired fruit or nut of your choice on top if required. Brush egg wash along the edges of each strip and then fold over the strip to encase the filling and gently seal with the fingertips. Make a series of 1.5 cm cuts along the sealed edge and then cut into 8 cm long pastries. Brush with egg wash and decorate with chopped or flaked nuts before proving at 27°C and then baking at 180°C.

Cinnamon fan roulade

Roll out the dough to 2 mm thick. Mix the crème pâtissière with some cinnamon and spread onto the dough. Roll up the dough to form a roulade and cut 3 cm slices. Place three additional cuts through each individual roulade without cutting all the way through. Fan out each leaf to form a roulade fan. Leave to prove for about 45 minutes and bake at 180°C for 15 minutes. Glaze with apricot glaze.

Panettone

Ingredients	1 cake	2 cakes
Strong flour	400 g	800 g
Good-quality salt	3 g	6 g
Fresh yeast	15 g	30 g
Fresh milk (at 30°C)	120 g	240 g
Whole egg, lightly beaten	2	4
Egg yolk	40 g	80 g
Caster sugar	75 g	150 g
Butter, softened	150 g	300 g
Mixed peel	120 g	240 g
Sultanas or raisins	70 g	140 g
Dark rum or Marsala	75 g	150 g
Egg wash to glaze		

energy	cal	fat	sat fat	carb	sugar	protein	fibre
1974 kJ	470 kcal	9 g	10.9 g	63.3 g	26.3 g	9.2 g	4.3 g

METHOD OF WORK

1   Preheat an oven to 190°C.
2   Macerate the dried fruit and mixed peel in the alcohol and set aside.
3   Prepare a round cake tin, 18 cm in diameter by lining it with a double layer of silicone paper. Ensure that the paper rises 8 cm above the level of the cake tin.

4   Sieve the flour and salt together into a warm stainless steel basin and make a well in the centre.
5   Mix together the yeast and warmed milk. Pour into the centre of the flour well and add the whole eggs.
6   Mix together to begin to form a smooth dough before adding the egg yolks and sugar. Continue mixing.
7   Gradually begin to work in the softened butter until no trace of butter can be seen in the dough. Place the dough into a clean bowl, cover with a clean kitchen cloth and place in a proving cabinet set at 36°C for approximately one hour.
8   Drain the macerated fruit and mix in the peel and sultanas or raisins by placing them into the centre of the dough and continually folding the dough on itself to distribute the fruit.
9   Place the dough into the prepared tin, brush with egg wash. Place in the proving cabinet and allow to double in size.
10   Place into the preheated oven for 20 minutes before reducing the temperature to 170°C for a further 30 minutes.
11   Allow to cool in the tin for ten minutes when removed from the oven and then turn out onto a wire rack to continue cooling.

> **CHEF'S TIP**   In Italy and France, the panettone is associated with an often varied history, but one that invariably states that its birthplace is Milan. The word panettone derives from the Italian word *panetto*, meaning 'small loaf of bread'. The origins of this cake appear to be ancient, dating back to the Roman Empire, when Romans sweetened a type of leavened bread with honey. The first recorded association of panettone with Christmas can be found in the writings of 18th century illuminist Pietro Verri. He refers to it as *Pane di Tono* (luxury bread).

Savarin

Ingredients	12 individual savarin rings	24 individual savarin rings
Savarin		
Strong flour	200 g	400 g
Good quality salt	5 g	10 g
Caster sugar	15 g	30 g
Fresh yeast	10 g	20 g
Eggs, lightly beaten	2	4
Water (at 35°C)	100 ml	200 ml
Soft butter	50 g	100 g
Additional Ingredients		
Crème Chantilly	400 ml	800 ml
Mixed fresh fruits	500 g	1 kg
Sugar decoration	12	24
Preserved vanilla stick	12	24

energy	cal	fat	sat fat	carb	sugar	protein	fibre
1132 kJ	271 kcal	18.2 g	10.7 g	23.9 g	11.1 g	4.3 g	1.9 g

Baba and savarin dough are prepared using the same method as for brioche. Always use a good quality, high-gluten flour and simply cream or soften the butter at room temperature. Baba and savarin dough are softer than a brioche dough because the weight of the liquid ingredients is equal to that of the flour.

CHEF'S TIP For babas, prepare the raisins, checking them for stones, then rinse and drain them. The raisins are added to the dough at the last minute, just before moulding. Normally, raisins make up about 20–25 per cent of the overall weight of the dough.

METHOD OF WORK

1 Preheat an oven to 200°C.

2 Dissolve the yeast and sugar in the water.

3 Sift the flour and salt together. Add to the water-yeast with the eggs to form a smooth and elastic dough. It is easier to do this task using an electric mixing machine.

4 Carefully blend in the softened butter and mix in well. Place in a refrigerator to rest for at least one hour.

5 Take care when preparing the savarin moulds. Wipe the moulds with a lightly oiled and clean kitchen towel. Do not butter heavily unless you have previously experienced problems with baked savarins sticking to the moulds. Too much butter on the moulds can pit the surface of the savarin, giving an unattractive appearance and rendering them less able to absorb syrup.

6 Pipe the savarin mixture into the prepared non-stick individual savarin moulds. Place in the proving cabinet set at 36°C until they have doubled in size.

7 Place into the preheated oven to bake for approximately 20 minutes or when they have turned golden brown and have thoroughly baked. Remove from the oven and leave to cool on a wire cooling rack.

8 To present, bring to the boil a large pan of stock syrup flavoured with dark rum, lemon zest, orange zest, cardamom seeds, vanilla pods and cinnamon sticks. Set on a very low heat and add the savarins to soak up the syrup. The hotter the syrup, the quicker the savarins will absorb it.

9 Remove the savarins from the syrup and leave to drain and cool on a wire rack.

10 Decorate as required with prepared fresh fruit and crème Chantilly.

CHEF'S TIP The rising times for babas and savarins are minimal. The temperature does not need to be so precisely controlled as with bread. Even though baba and savarin dough are much softer than brioche dough, it is still important that the gluten is activated and that the dough has enough elasticity.

ADDITIONAL NOTES

Warm water is used in this recipe for two main reasons:

1 It will penetrate the flour and reach the gluten more quickly than cold water, giving the dough maximum body and elasticity. This method can be used because the dough requires practically no rising time; ten minutes maximum. Letting the dough rise too long can negatively affect the gluten in the dough; the heat and acidity generated by rapid fermentation cause the gluten to break down.

2 Warm water helps activate yeast. This is important because the rising time for babas and savarins is so short.

Babas and savarins should be baked in a moderate oven, 180–200°C, for individual sized cakes and a slightly slower oven, 170–180°C, for larger cakes. The cakes should be placed in the oven without being glazed. If oven vents are available, they should be left open during baking to enhance the drying and colouring of the dough. To check that they have been baked, the cakes should slip out of the moulds quite easily. They should be pale brown on the bottom and very dry.

The pâte à savarin can be used to make a range of products:

● Pomponette – piped into tartlette moulds.

● Marignan – piped into **barquette** moulds.

● Baba – piped into baba moulds or dariole moulds.

● Savarin – piped into savarin moulds.

Pain de mie

Ingredients	2 loaves	4 loaves
Strong white flour	500 g	1000 g
Fresh yeast	20 g	35 g
Water (at 30°C)	300 g	600 g
Full fat milk	50 g	100 g
Good-quality salt	10 g	18 g
Some butter for greasing		

energy	cal	fat	sat fat	carb	sugar	protein	fibre
930 kJ	219 kcal	1.1 g	0.3 g	47.4 g	1.2 g	7.7 g	4.2 g

METHOD OF WORK

1 Preheat an oven to 250°C.

2 Grease 500 g loaf tins with a little butter.

3 To make the dough, rub the yeast into the flour using your fingertips. Add the salt, milk and water. Work the dough for two to three minutes until a dough starts to form.

4 Lightly flour a work surface, place the dough on the flour and form the dough into a ball by folding each edge in turn into the centre. Place the dough into a stainless steel bowl and cover with a clean kitchen cloth. Rest for at least one hour.

5 Turn the dough out onto a floured work surface and divide the dough into equal pieces. Mould each piece tightly into a loaf shape.

6 Once the dough are in the tins, leave to prove for up to one hour. When the dough level is to the top of the tin, cover with a lid of a heavy tray weighed down, so that the dough cannot rise any further.

7 Place the tins into a pre-heated oven, turn down the heat to 220°C and bake the loaves for 25 minutes, covered and then a further five minutes uncovered, until light and golden brown. Remove the loaves from the tins and cool on a wire rack.

Crumpets

METHOD OF WORK

1   Combine the flour, sugar, yeast, salt, water and milk in a warm stainless steel bowl and gradually beat together to a smooth batter.

2   Leave in a warm area for up to 45 minutes covered with a clean kitchen cloth at least until the batter has started to ferment and bubble.

3   Lightly grease a large heavy based frying pan or griddle. Also lightly grease 10 cm diameter metal ring moulds. Place the moulds onto the pan or griddle and heat on an open flame. When both the pan or griddle and the rings are hot, reduce the heat immediately to a low flame and leave for two minutes.

4   Stir the dissolved bicarbonate of soda into the batter and then pour a little of the batter into each ring mould to a depth of approximately 1 cm.

5   Leave the batter to cook for three minutes or until the surface has holes and the batter is almost set.

6   Turn the crumpets over and cook on the other side until lightly coloured.

7   Remove from the pan or griddle and the rings and place each crumpet onto a wire rack to cool down and serve as required.

Ingredients	10 individual crumpets	20 individual crumpets
Strong white flour	125 g	250 g
Good-quality salt	3 g	6 g
Caster sugar	15 g	30 g
Fresh yeast	7 g	14 g
Fresh milk (at 32°C)	2	4
Water (at 32°C)	100 ml	200 ml
Bicarbonate of soda, dissolved in boiling water	5 g to 1 tsp of water	8 g to 2 tsp of water

energy	cal	fat	sat fat	carb	sugar	protein	fibre
209 kJ	49 kcal	0.2 g	0 g	11 g	1.8 g	1.5 g	0.9 g

CHEF'S TIP   A regional variation of the crumpet is the pikelet, whose name derives from the Welsh *bara piglydd*. The word spread initially to the West Midlands, where it became anglicized as pikelet and subsequently to Cheshire, Lancashire and other areas of the north and west. The main distinguishing feature of the Welsh or West Midlands pikelet is that it was traditionally cooked without a ring mould, with an end result slightly flatter or thinner than a crumpet.

Sour dough bread

Ingredients	3 loaves	6 loaves
Water	500 g	1 kg
Good-quality salt	20 g	40 g
Wheatgerm	10 g	20 g
Ferment starter	350 g	700 g
Strong white flour	700 g	1.4 kg
Dark rye flour	80 g	160 g
Finish		
Flour for dusting	as required	as required

energy	cal	fat	sat fat	carb	sugar	protein	fibre
966 kJ	227 kcal	1 g	0.2 g	50 g	1 g	7.6 g	4.7 g

METHOD OF WORK

1   Preheat an oven to 230°C.

2   Place the starter in the water with the salt, wheatgerm, white flour and the rye flour. Knead in a mixing machine at a low speed for ten minutes or mix and knead by hand for approximately 15 minutes or until you have a smooth, soft, dough that is elastic and not sticky or dry.

3   Place into a bowl and cover with a clean kitchen cloth and leave to rest for one hour.

4   Turn the dough out onto a lightly floured work surface and shape the dough into a ball. Place back into the bowl, cover and leave to rest for 30 minutes.

5   Turn the dough out onto a lightly floured work surface and scale off the dough at 500 g per loaf. Shape each piece into a ball. Rest the dough for ten minutes under a sheet of plastic or a clean kitchen cloth.

6   Shape each ball into fat batons and place onto dusted linen cloths or wicker baskets. Prove again for a minimum of two hours at 20°C, or until they have nearly doubled in volume.

7   Place the loaves carefully onto a wooden peel or a flat edged baking tray, seam side down. Dust with flour and cut a decorative marking on each bread with a lame or a sharp knife.

8   Mist the inside of the pre-heated oven with a water spray and quickly slide the loaves onto the base of the oven (preferably a baking stone base) and bake for five minutes.

9   Reduce the oven temperature to 220°C and bake for a further 35 minutes until they are dark brown. The loaves should sound hollow if tapped on the base with your finger.

10   Remove from the oven and cool on a wire rack.

CHEF'S TIP Instead of using a ferment starter you can use the same quantity of rye dough left in a bowl to ferment for four to six hours, or overnight in a refrigerator and then slowly brought back to room temperature.

Focaccia (olive and herb)

Ingredients	1 flat loaf	2 flat loaves
Ferment ingredients		
Strong flour	150 g	300 g
Fresh yeast	7 g	15 g
Water (at 20°C)	200 g	400 g
Dough ingredients		
Strong Italian flour	375 g	725 g
Good quality salt	10 g	20 g
Water (at 20°C)	150 g	300 g
Extra virgin olive oil	20 g	40 g
Finish		
Fine sea-salt crystals	20 g	45 g
Fresh rosemary leaves	20 leaves	50 leaves
Black or green olives	75 g	140 g
Extra virgin olive oil	40 ml	90 ml

energy	cal	fat	sat fat	carb	sugar	protein	fibre
2580 kJ	611 kcal	19.1 g	2.8 g	101.1 g	1.8 g	15.6 g	9.9 g

METHOD OF WORK

1   Mix the ingredients for the ferment together to form a smooth and soft dough. Place in a clean bowl and cover with plastic film or a clean kitchen cloth and leave in a closed cupboard at room temperature for up to two hours to slowly ferment.

2   Preheat an oven to 230°C.

3   To make the dough, mix the water and extra virgin olive oil together and add the ferment. Combine the flour and salt, and knead well until soft.

4   Place in a clean bowl and leave to rest for 15 minutes covered with a clean kitchen cloth.

5   Turn the dough out onto a lightly oiled surface and fold and gently knead the dough for a few minutes. Fold and stretch the dough gently to incorporate air to the dough. Leave to rest for ten minutes and then repeat the process.

6   Lightly flatten the dough onto a baking tray rubbed with extra virgin olive oil. Stretch the dough out until it reaches the corners of the tray, but ensures that it is at least 2 cm thick.

7   Cover with a clean kitchen cloth and leave to prove for 25 minutes. Remove from the proving cabinet and press holes into the dough using your fingers. Brush with some more oil on top.

8   Leave to rest covered with a clean kitchen cloth for approximately 20–30 minutes.

9   Sprinkle a little water, extra virgin olive oil, sea salt, rosemary leaves and olives on top. Press down lightly onto the dough with your finger tips to create a dimpled effect.

10 Bake in the oven for 15 minutes then reduce the temperature to 180°C for a further 15 minutes. Remove from the oven and leave to cool on a wire cooling rack.

CHEF'S TIP When working with a soft dough such as focaccia, it is important to keep the work surface and your hands clean and oiled with a little olive oil.

Tomato, garlic and basil bread

Ingredients	2 loaves	4 loaves
Strong white flour	500 g	1000 g
Fresh yeast	20 g	35 g
Water (at 30°C)	300 g	600 g
Fresh basil	a few leaves	a few leaves
Concassé of plum tomatoes	120 g	240 g
Sun dried Tomatoes	50 g	100 g
Garlic	4 cloves	8 cloves
Good-quality salt	10 g	18 g
Some butter for greasing		

energy	cal	fat	sat fat	carb	sugar	protein	fibre
1058 kJ	250 kcal	4.2 g	0.7 g	48.2 g	1.6 g	7.9 g	4.9 g

METHOD OF WORK

1. Preheat an oven to 250°C.

2. Grease 500 g loaf tins with a little butter.

3. To make the dough, rub the yeast into the flour using your fingertips. Add the salt and water. Work the dough for two to three minutes until a dough starts to form.

4. Lightly flour a work surface, place the dough on the flour and form the dough into a ball by folding each edge in turn into the centre. Place the dough into a stainless steel bowl and cover with a clean kitchen cloth. Rest for at least one hour.

5. Meanwhile chop the sun dried tomatoes and finely chop the garlic. Sweat the two ingredients together for two minutes without colour and add the concassé. Remove from the heat and set aside. Chop the basil leaves and mix into the tomato mixture.

6. Turn the dough out onto a floured work surface and divide the dough into equal pieces. Add a little of the tomato and basil mixture to each piece of dough and gently knead in. Mould each piece tightly into a loaf shape.

7. Once the dough are in the tins, leave to prove for up to one hour. When the dough level is to the top of the tin equally spread the remaining tomato and basil mix on top of each loaf.

8. Place the tins into a pre-heated oven, turn down the heat to 220°C and bake the loaves for 25 minutes, covered and then a further five minutes uncovered, until light and golden brown. Remove the loaves from the tins and cool on a wire rack.

Pancetta bread rolls

Ingredients	25 rolls	50 rolls
Strong flour	500 g	1000 g
Fresh yeast	10 g	20 g
Water (at 20°C)	350 g	700 g
Good-quality salt	10 g	20 g
Finish		
Fine sea-salt crystals	10 g	15 g
Pancetta	20 slices	40 slices

energy	cal	fat	sat fat	carb	sugar	protein	fibre
306 kJ	72 kcal	0.6 g	0.2 g	15.1 g	0.3 g	2.5 g	1.3 g

METHOD OF WORK

1 Preheat an oven to 250°C.

2 Rub the yeast into the flour using your fingertips and then add the salt and water.

3 Work the dough with one hand for two to three minutes until the dough begins to form.

4 Lightly flour a work surface and place the dough on the flour and form the dough into a ball by folding each edge in turn into the centre.

5 Place the dough into a mixing bowl and cover with a clean kitchen cloth. Rest for 25 minutes in a warm place.

6 Take a third of the pancetta and chop into small pieces. The remaining pancetta should be cut into 5 cm strips.

7 Turn out the dough onto a well floured work surface and be careful not to deflate it too much. Carefully fold the chopped pancetta into the dough.

8 Scale off the dough into rolls weighed at 50 g each. Rest on a lightly floured work surface under a clean kitchen cloth for ten minutes.

9 Mould each roll into the required shape and place onto a lightly greased baking sheet.

10 Place the pancetta slices on top and place the rolls in a proving cabinet to almost double in volume.

11 Bake in the pre-heated oven for approximately 20 minutes.

12 Remove from the oven and place quickly on a wire rack to cool down.

Bacon and thyme bread

Ingredients	25 rolls	50 rolls
Strong flour	500 g	1000 g
Fresh yeast	10 g	20 g
Water (at 20°C)	350 g	700 g
Good-quality salt	10 g	20 g
Finish		
Fresh thyme	8 sprigs	16 sprigs
Streaky bacon	10 slices	20 slices

energy	cal	fat	sat fat	carb	sugar	protein	fibre
299 kJ	70 kcal	0.4 g	0.1 g	15.2 g	0.3 g	2.5 g	1.4 g

METHOD OF WORK

1 Preheat an oven to 250°C.

2 Rub the yeast into the flour using your fingertips and then add the salt and water.

3 Work the dough with one hand for two to three minutes until the dough begins to form.

4 Lightly flour a work surface and place the dough on the flour and form the dough into a ball by folding each edge in turn into the centre.

5 Place the dough into a mixing bowl and cover with a clean kitchen cloth. Rest for 25 minutes in a warm place.

6 Take the streaky bacon and chop into small pieces. The fresh thyme should be removed from the stalks and mixed in with the bacon and then quickly sautéed in a little olive oil. Leave to one side to cool.

7 Turn out the dough onto a well floured work surface and be careful not to deflate it too much. Carefully fold the bacon and thyme into the dough.

8 Scale off the dough into rolls weighed at 50 g each. Rest on a work surface lightly dusted with fine semolina, under a clean kitchen cloth for ten minutes.

9 Mould each roll into the required shape and place onto a lightly greased baking sheet.

10 Bake in the pre-heated oven for approximately 20 minutes.

11 Remove from the oven and place quickly on a wire rack to cool down.

Olive and parmesan bread sticks

Ingredients	35 sticks	70 sticks
Strong flour	500 g	1000 g
Coarse semolina	20 g	40 g
Fresh yeast	10 g	20 g
Water (at 20°C)	320 g	640 g
Good-quality salt	10 g	20 g
Extra virgin olive oil	50 g	100 g
Finish		
Fresh thyme	6 sprigs	12 sprigs
Chopped olives	50 g	100 g
Grated Parmesan cheese	75 g	150 g

energy	cal	fat	sat fat	carb	sugar	protein	fibre
315 kJ	75 kcal	2.4 g	0.7 g	11.4 g	0.2 g	2.5 g	1.1 g

5 Place the dough back into a mixing bowl and cover with a clean kitchen cloth. Rest for 20 minutes in a warm place.

6 While the dough is resting prepare the additional ingredients of the Parmesan cheese, olives and thyme.

7 Using semolina as a dusting agent, roll out the dough into a rectangle.

8 Sprinkle the olives, Parmesan and thyme over the dough.

9 Fold the dough into thirds and gently roll out.

10 Cut into strips approximately 1.5 cm wide, twist and place onto a baking tray.

11 Rest for 15 minutes and then place in the oven to bake for ten minutes, or until golden brown.

12 Brush with olive oil when removed from the oven and leave to cool on a wire rack.

METHOD OF WORK

1 Preheat an oven to 250°C.

2 Rub the yeast into the flour using your fingertips and then add the semolina, salt, olive oil and water.

3 Work the dough with one hand for two to three minutes until the dough starts to form.

4 Lightly flour a work surface (or use semolina), place the dough on the flour and form the dough into a ball by folding each edge in turn into the centre. Keep working the dough until it comes cleanly away from the work surface.

Guest Chef

Stuffed focaccia

Chef *Karen Rivers*

Centre *Petroc Tiverton Campus*

A simple tasty focaccia stuffed with two local cheeses, local grown herbs and vine tomatoes to eat on its own or to accompany a light lunch. Cut up and serve with cool crisp Italian wine or with a local wine from Yearlstone vineyard, which is only four miles from our college. The filling of cheese and herbs can be varied to your taste or changed to match other menu items. I used a blue cheese from Totnes called Beenleigh Blue and blissful buffalo mozzarella from Holsworthy. The herbs are all home grown or grown locally. The tomatoes are from Halberton farm shop four miles away.

Ingredients	Amount
Focaccia	
Dried yeast	*2 tsp*
Water	350 ml
Strong white flour	500 g
Olive oil	3 tbsp
Salt	1.5 tsp
For filling	
Blue cheese (Beenleigh Blue from Totnes)	200 g
Mozzarella	200 g
Olive oil	4 bsp
Fresh vine tomatoes	100 g
Rocket leaves	handful
Basil leaves	handful
Rosemary sprigs	
coarse salt	0.5 tsp

METHOD OF WORK

1 Sprinkle yeast into water, stir and leave for five minutes. Place flour and salt into a bowl make a well in the centre; pour in yeasted water and oil.

2 Mix in the flour and knead until smooth and elastic about ten minutes. Place in oiled bowl and leave covered to rest for at least one hour.

3 Knock back the dough and cut into two pieces. Knead for another five minutes. Roll each half into a round or square approximately 24 cm (nine-and-a-half inches). Place one half on oiled baking sheet.

4 Place the filling on top; rip leaves, slice tomatoes thickly, and rip cheese. Make layers with the filling. Place the rest of the bread on top. Seal edges gently. Cover and leave to rest for 30 minutes or until double in size.

5 Use your finger tips to press dimples into the bread and sprinkle with coarse sea salt and olive oil. Finish by inserting rosemary in some of the dimples.

6 Bake in pre-heated oven 200°C/400°F/gas mark 6 for 30–45 minutes.

ASSESSMENT OF KNOWLEDGE AND UNDERSTANDING

To test your level of knowledge and understanding, answer the following short questions. These will help to prepare you for your summative (final) assessment.

1   Explain the importance of selecting the correct type, quality and quantity of ingredients when producing a natural starter.

2   State two advantages of using a proving cabinet, and what you would need to use if there is not one available.

3   Briefly describe how to retard dough.

4   Describe how you would laminate croissant dough and explain the need to rest the dough in a refrigerator.

5   If the required dough temperature is 38°C, and the flour temperature is 17°C, state what the water temperature should be.

6   Explain the difference between a commune and surfine brioche.

7   Identify the critical quality points for the following baked products: brioche, focaccia, Danish pastry and croissants.

8   State three factors that contribute to the development of flavour in bread and fermented dough products.

9   What is a 'No-time' dough and what does ADD stand for

10   Explain why it is necessary to have a formula for measuring friction when making fermented products if using a mixing machine.

Hot, cold and frozen desserts

12

VRQ

Produce hot, cold and frozen desserts

NVQ

Prepare, cook and finish complex hot desserts

Prepare, cook and finish complex cold desserts

Produce sauces, fillings and coatings for complex desserts

Recipes

Yogurt and mascarpone Ice Cream
Sous vide vanilla ice cream
Honeycomb ice cream
Olive oil ice cream (using a Pacojet)
Praline iced soufflé (*soufflé glacé au praline*)
Fromage frais sorbet
Apple and basil sorbet
Chocolate sorbet
Strawberry sorbet
Chocolate sauce
Fruit coulis
Muscat wine sabayon
Coconut foam
Chocolate foam
Raspberry foam
Caramel foam
Chocolate jelly
Sous vide poached Victoria plums

LEARNING OBJECTIVES

The aim of this chapter is to enable the reader to develop the necessary advanced techniques, knowledge and understanding of the principles in preparing and producing a range of complex hot, cold and iced desserts with a variety of accompanying sauces and decorative products.

The important emphasis of this chapter is placed on developing knowledge attained in the previous Professional Chef Level 2 book and perfecting distinguished, contemporary and advanced dessert production techniques. Also included in this chapter is further information on materials, ingredients and equipment.

At the end of this chapter you will be able to:

● Identify the main methods of production for advanced hot, cold and iced desserts.

● Identify each type of accompaniment, sauce and cream that can be served with a range of desserts.

● Understand the use of the main ingredients in the development of complex desserts.

● Understand the factors for stabilizers and gelatinization in desserts.

● State the quality points and critical control points of a variety of desserts and accompaniments.

● Prepare, cook and present each type of complex hot, cold and iced desserts.

● Distinguish the storage procedures of finished hot, cold and iced desserts.

● Identify the correct tools and equipment used in the production of complex desserts.

Introduction

The first desserts have consistently been attributed to the ancient Egyptians, who began harvesting honey from bees in around 5500 BC. A variety of fruits, nuts and cereals were also important ingredients, from which confections were created to show off great wealth during banquets and for use as gifts during religious festivals. Many of these ingredients (especially honey) were also used medicinally.

The European discovery of sugar in Asia in the twelfth century played a significant role in the development of more complex desserts. In the 15th century, the recently opened trade routes with Africa, Asia, East Asia and the Americas allowed spices and cocoa to be used as flavourings for desserts as well as for medicinal purposes, previously the main use of such extravagant commodities.

Eventually, these new ingredients became widely available and Europe was recognized as the focus of the development of more sophisticated recipes. The most famous chef of the early nineteenth century was Marie-Antoine Carême (1784–1833). His spectacular architectural constructions of sugar, meringue, pastries and desserts earned him great fame as the 'king of chefs and chef to kings'. Most of his career was spent in the service of nobility and royalty, such as the Prince Regent, Tsar Alexander I and Napoleon I. Throughout his career he dedicated his skills to the art of the pâtissière and generally changed the way menus were created and food was served. By the time of Carême, desserts were large, elaborate set pieces, often fashioned in great detail and presented on large buffet tables.

In the 20th century, advances in technology such as refrigeration, sophisticated ovens and air transportation contributed immensely to the production of both simply designed and more complex desserts, and their popularity continues to grow. With the advent of a more diet-conscious public, desserts have had to adapt by using less sugar and fat commodities, but they retain their sense of decadence, art and flavour.

The skill of the pastry chef is to be able to create a dessert that is appealing to the eye, stimulates the palette through flavour, aroma, temperature and texture, and maintains a lightness that will not leave the customer feeling overindulged.

The use of spices in desserts and patisserie

Spices offer the chef a wide range of rich flavours for use throughout the menu. Influences from China, India, Thailand and other countries can be used to create different fusions of cuisines and exciting new dishes.

Spices are the dried fruits, flowers, buds, seeds, roots or bark of plants. Sometimes more than one part of a plant is used, and the same plants, such as coriander, may also present a herb. All spices are best used as fresh as possible because the oils which give the aroma and flavour will deteriorate with age. Both ground spices and whole spices must be stored in airtight, lightproof plastic containers to maintain the aroma and flavour as much as possible.

Spices are used in dessert and pastry production to create added flavour, aroma, texture and colour to a finished product. Some of the commonly used spices are detailed below.

Star anise

Commonly known as star anise, star aniseed or Chinese star anise, it is a spice that closely resembles anise in flavour, obtained from the star-shaped pericarp of *Illicium verum*, a medium-sized native evergreen tree of northeast Vietnam and southwest China. The star shaped fruits are harvested just before ripening.

It is widely used in Chinese cuisine, in Indian cuisine where it is a major component of garam masala and in Malay and Indonesian cuisine. It is widely grown for commercial use in China, India and most other countries in Asia. Star anise is an ingredient of the traditional five-spice powder of Chinese cooking.

Star anise

The distinctive aniseed flavour comes from the oils found within the seed. These oils are also found in unrelated plants, such as fennel, tarragon and liquorice. This spice is used to flavour drinks, breads and pastries, but is also used as flavouring in crèmes and mousses.

Cardamom

Cardamom is best purchased as green pods, which contain the brown seeds packed full of flavour, although another variety is black cardamom. Cardamom has a strong, unique taste, with an intensely aromatic, resinous fragrance. Black cardamom has a distinctly smokiness aroma, with a coolness some consider similar to mint.

Green cardamom is one of the most expensive spices by weight, but little is needed to impart the flavour. It is best stored in pod form because once the seeds are exposed or ground into powder, they quickly lose their flavour and aroma. However, high-quality ground cardamom seed is often more readily, and cheaply available and is an acceptable substitute. Grinding the pods and seeds together lowers both the quality and the price.

Guatemala is the biggest producer and exporter of Cardamom in the world, followed by India. Some other countries such as Sri Lanka have also begun to cultivate this commodity too. It is the world's third most expensive spice by weight, outstripped in market value only by saffron and vanilla. Cardamom is used in baking for pastries and in crèmes, sweet sauces and **Bavarois**.

Cardamom powder and green pods

Cinnamon

This spice is obtained from the inner bark of several trees from the genus *Cinnamomum* that is used in both sweet and savoury foods. While native only to the island of Sri Lanka, cinnamon trees are now naturalized in South East Asia. A number of species are often sold as cinnamon:

- *Cinnamomum verum* ('true cinnamon', Sri Lanka cinnamon or Ceylon cinnamon);
- *C. burmannii* (Korintje, Padang Cassia or Indonesian cinnamon);
- *C. loureiroi* (Saigon cinnamon, Vietnamese cassia or Vietnamese cinnamon);
- *C. cassia* (Cassia or Chinese cinnamon).

It can be broken down into small pieces or ground to a powder. Cinnamon is used to flavour creams, syrups, apple tarts and sauces. It is one of the most commonly used spices in the pastry kitchen.

Cinnamon powder and stick

Cloves

Cloves are native to the Maluku islands in Indonesia and used as a spice in cuisines all over the world. Cloves are harvested primarily in Indonesia, India, Madagascar, Zanzibar, Pakistan and Sri Lanka. They have a numbing effect on the mouth.

Cloves are often used in Asian, African and Middle Eastern cooking. They are also used to create sweet dishes and are especially well paired with fruits such as apples, pears or rhubarb. Cloves are considered a very strong spice due to the eugenol chemical that makes up most of the clove's taste, the quantity of clove used in recipes is therefore usually small. It also pairs well with cinnamon, allspice, vanilla and red wine. Cloves are the dried buds from a tropical tree and are usually purchased whole, and are used in British cuisine as additional flavouring for steamed puddings, apple pies and mincemeat.

Cloves

Ginger

Ginger is one of the most widely used spices across the world. It is the root of a plant usually found in East Asia. Ginger produces clusters of white and pink flower buds that bloom into yellow flowers. Because of its aesthetic appeal and the adaptation of the plant to warm climates, ginger is often used as landscaping around subtropical homes. It is a perennial reed-like plant with annual leafy stems, about a meter tall.

Traditionally, the rhizome is gathered when the stalk withers; it is immediately **scalded**, or washed and scraped, to kill it and prevent sprouting. Fresh ginger can be substituted for ground ginger at a ratio of six to one, although the flavours of fresh and dried ginger are somewhat different. Powdered dry ginger root is typically used as a flavoring for recipes such as **gingerbread**, biscuits, creams and cakes.

Ginger has a strong flavour and can be used fresh, dried, powdered, pickled or candied. Ginger can also be used with a combination of other spices to create alternative flavourings, such as 'mixed spice' and 'Chinese five-spice'.

Candied ginger

Root and powdered Ginger

Nutmeg and mace

This is the nut of an evergreen Indonesian tree. The nutmeg tree is important for two spices derived from the fruit: nutmeg and mace.

The first harvest of nutmeg trees takes place seven–nine years after planting, and the trees reach full production after 20 years. Nutmeg and mace have similar sensory qualities, with nutmeg having a slightly sweeter and mace a more delicate flavour. Mace is often preferred in light dishes for the bright orange colour it imparts. Nutmeg is used for flavouring many dishes, usually in ground or grated form, and is best grated fresh in a nutmeg grater. Ground nutmeg will lose its flavour if kept for too long.

Mace is the dried 'cage' that separates the nutmeg from the outer fruit. It is more expensive than nutmeg and has a more delicate flavour. It is used grated or powdered to flavour cakes and various desserts and sauces.

Ground and whole nutmeg

Mace

Saffron

Crocus flower with saffron stigmas

Saffron is the most expensive spice in the world. It is the orange-red stigmas of a purple flowering crocus. Each saffron crocus grows to 20–30 cm and bears up to four flowers, each with three vivid crimson stigmas. Together with the stalks that connect the stigmas to their host plant, the dried stigmas are used mainly in various cuisines as a seasoning and colouring agent.

Saffron's aroma is often described as reminiscent of metallic honey with grassy or hay-like flavour notes, while its taste has also been noted as hay-like and sweet. Saffron also contributes a luminous yellow-orange colouring to foods. Saffron is widely used in Indian, Persian and European cuisines. Sometimes saffron is also used in Arab and Turkish cuisines. To produce 500 g of saffron, up to a quarter of a million flowers are harvested by hand. It is produced in Spain, India, Asia and North Africa. It has also been cultivated in England, near the town of Saffron Walden in Essex. It is used to flavour crèmes, sauces, cakes and breads.

Saffron

Vanilla

Vanilla is a flavour derived from orchids and there are approximately 75 different varieties of vanilla growing in the world's tropical regions. Initially discovered by the Aztecs and used to flavour cocoa-based drinks, vanilla is now produced predominantly in Madagascar, Indonesia, Réunion, Martinique, Tahiti and Guadalupe.

Vanilla pods offer the best flavour and aroma for all desserts, crèmes, cakes and sauces. They should be split and infused in a liquid to impart as much flavour as possible. The pods can be reused two or three times. Dried pods can be stored in an airtight container with caster sugar so that the flavour of the vanilla permeates the sugar, creating vanilla sugar.

Vanilla pods with the seeds

Genuine vanilla extract is an alternative to using pods. However, the labelling is not always clear and care must be taken to ensure that vanilla flavour is not substituted; this is a chemical-based vanilla flavouring that bears no resemblance to the aroma and flavour of real vanilla.

There are different types of vanilla that have different flavour strengths and complexities.

- Bourbon vanilla or Bourbon-Madagascar vanilla is produced from *V. planifolia* plants introduced from the Americas. It is the term used for vanilla from Indian Ocean islands such as Madagascar, the Comoros and Réunion, which is formerly known as the *Île Bourbon*. It is also used to describe the distinctive vanilla flavour derived from *V. planifolia* grown successfully in tropical countries such as India.

- Mexican vanilla, made from the native *V. planifolia*, is produced in much less quantity and marketed as the vanilla from the land of its origin. Vanilla sold in markets around Mexico is sometimes not actual vanilla extract, but is mixed with an extract of the Tonka bean, which contains coumarin. Tonka bean extract smells and tastes similar to vanilla, but coumarin has been shown to cause liver damage in laboratory tests and is banned in food in the USA.

- Tahitian vanilla is the name for vanilla from French Polynesia, made with the *V. tahitiensis* strain. Genetic analysis shows this species is possibly a hybrid-cross of *V. planifolia* and *V. odorata*. The species was introduced by French Admiral François Alphonse Hamelin to French Polynesia from the Philippines, where it was introduced from Guatemala by the Manila Galleon trade.

- West Indian vanilla is made from the *V. pompona* strain grown in the Caribbean and Central and South America.

Tonka beans

Dipteryx odorata is a species of flowering tree in the pea family, Fabaceae. It is native to the Orinoco region of northern South America. Its seeds are known as Tonka beans. They are black and wrinkled and have a smooth, brown interior. Their fragrance is reminiscent of vanilla, almonds, cinnamon and cloves. The Tonka seed contains coumarin; this is a chemical responsible for the pleasant fragrance of the seeds and is used in the perfume industry. Coumarin is bitter to the taste, however and, in large oral doses, can cause liver damage. It is therefore controlled as a food additive by many governments. Tonka beans had been used as a vanilla substitute, as a perfume, and in tobacco before being banned in some countries. They are used in some French cuisine dishes, particularly in desserts and stews. Today, the main producers of the seeds are Venezuela and Nigeria.

Tonka beans

CHEF'S TIP Keep all spices, whole or ground, in containers that are airtight and lightproof. Maintain them in a dry and cool storage area. Only purchase spices in small quantities to establish a regular stock rotation and so ensure freshness and maximum flavour properties.

The use of salt in cookery

Salt (sodium chloride) is one of the most important ingredients in any recipe. It is a necessary part of the human diet and is present in many different types of natural food. All of the recipes mentioned in this book state that 'good-quality salt' is used. This is because the salt composition of human tissue is similar to that of seawater and sea salt (such as large flake salt) provides one of the simplest ways of meeting our nutritional requirements.

Sea salt crystals

Good-quality sea salt retains the valuable natural trace elements which are often removed during the processing of some table salts. The distinctive flavour of a good-quality salt means that less is required for flavouring and cooking. This is an advantage for those wishing to reduce salt intake in their diet. The production of sea salt relies on favourable dry weather conditions. Seawater for processing is taken after a period of dry weather, when the salt content is at its maximum. The water is transferred to large holding tanks where it is allowed to pass through a filtration system and settle. After further filtering it is drawn off as required and used to fill saltpans, where the water is evaporated off.

The large stainless steel saltpans are mounted on a brick heating system designed to give the specific heating pattern required to evaporate the water. During the evaporation of the water, salt crystals begin to form on the surface. These crystals are known as *fleur de sel* and can be removed and used as a special high-quality salt. However, as the crystals become heavier they sink to the bottom of the saltpan. The pans are allowed to cool slowly and the salt is then harvested. The salt is put into shallow drainage bins before finally being transferred to the salt store for drying and packaging.

Salt is available in many different forms, such as table salt, iodized salt, flake salt, kosher salt, unrefined sea salt, fleur de sel and flavoured salts, such as celery or garlic salt.

Salt can be used as a preservative because it discourages the growth of bacteria in food. It also allows harmless flavour-producing bacteria to grow and thus improves the flavour of the food while preserving it at the same time.

The addition of salt will enhance flavour in many recipes, whether sweet or savoury. Salt is now combined with alternative flavouring commodities to provide contrast in flavour and texture, such as caramel and sea salt combined to create an interesting filling for chocolate.

In the UK, the Food Standards Agency defines the level of salt in foods as high levels being more than 1.5 g salt per 100 g (or 0.6 g sodium). Low is 0.3 g salt or less per 100 g (or 0.1 g sodium). If the amount of salt per 100 g is in between these figures, then that is a medium level of salt. The FSA also recommends no more than 6 g of salt intake per day.

Stabilizers and gelatinization

Various stabilizers, starches and emulsifiers are used throughout the kitchen to thicken or bind ingredients to create durable textures, different appearances and thickened liquids. In some instances they are used to retain water to make a gel. For example; ice cream can have gelatine added to the mixture to help prevent water crystal formation.

Starch

Starches are generally used to thicken sauces and creams and some fillings for gâteaux and tarts. Starch granules are made up of two types of molecule: *amylose*, which has a long, straight chemical chain of glucose sugars, and *amylopectin,* which has a branched chemical structure. These structures determine the different thickening properties. The amylose molecules require more liquid, higher temperature and longer cooking before the starch molecules are broken down; they then re-form on cooling.

Gelatinization is the process that starch molecules undergo to thicken a liquid. There are three stages of gelatinization using starch:

THE THREE STAGES OF GELATINIZATION	
1	Heating the starch – the starch is heated with the liquid to be thickened
2	Absorbing the liquid – as the temperature rises, the bonds within the molecules of starch begin to break down, which allows them to take on board and trap liquid, causing the molecules to expand
3	Thickening the liquid – once the starch molecules have absorbed the liquid they become soft and have a gel-like texture, and as more heat is applied the liquid becomes thicker

FACTORS THAT AFFECT GELATINIZATION

There are several factors that can affect the gelatinization of liquids:

● The amount of liquid used – there must be an adequate balance of liquid to starch molecules to activate thickening.

● Temperature – different starches require different temperatures to thicken. Some starches, such as tapioca and potato starches, can be overheated, which can reverse the effects of gelatinization and result in a thinner product.

● Stirring – over-stirring can cause thinning of a mixture. The starch molecules are broken down and release any liquid that was absorbed.

● Acids – can break down starches, preventing them from swelling and thickening. If possible, acids should be added after gelatinization has taken place. Alternatively, modified starches which are resistant to acid conditions can be used.

● Raw egg yolks – contain an enzyme called alpha-amylase, which causes starches to break down. Pastry creams containing egg yolks should be brought to boiling point to destroy the alpha-amylase and so prevent it from breaking down the starch. Pastry creams that contain starch mixed with the egg yolk will not curdle when boiled due to the starch molecules protecting the yolks.

● Sugar – an excess of sugar can prevent gelatinization by blocking the absorption of the liquid. When baking pastry, gelatinization of starch is required to set the pastry. Pastry recipes with high sugar content (such as pâte sablée) will therefore have a softer texture when cooked than recipes with lower sugar content. This is the basic principle for how sugars tenderize baked goods.

● Time – starches that have been stored for a long period of time may lose their ability to gelatinize and therefore a greater quantity of starch will be required to thicken a liquid.

Arrowroot

Arrowroot

Arrowroot makes clear gels and prevents ice crystals from forming in ice cream. It can also be used as a thickener for acidic foods. It is extremely valuable in cooking when you wish to have a clear, thickened sauce, for example, a fruit sauce. It will not make the sauce go cloudy, like cornstarch, flour or other starchy thickening agents would. The lack of gluten in arrowroot makes it useful as a replacement for wheat flour in baking. Like other pure starches, however, arrowroot is almost pure carbohydrate and devoid of protein, thus it does not provide a complete substitute for wheat flour.

Arrowroot thickens at a lower temperature than flour or cornstarch, is not weakened by acidic ingredients and is not affected by freezing. It is recommended to mix arrowroot with a cool liquid before adding to a hot fluid. The mixture should be heated only until the mixture thickens and removed immediately to prevent the mixture from thinning. Overheating tends to break down arrowroot's thickening property.

Gelatine

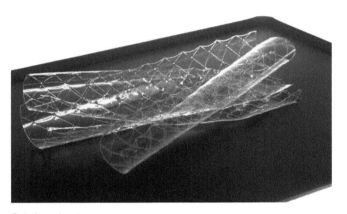

Gelatine sheets

Gelatine is a protein that is produced from the skin, connective tissue and bones of animals (primarily pork, veal and beef). These are soaked in an acid to break down the collagen and the gelatine molecules are then carefully extracted at low temperatures. Because the gelatine molecules are long and flexible, when they are warmed they disperse in liquids and will set the liquid into a gel. Gelatine will thicken and stabilize the consistency and texture of foods that cannot be further heated, such as ice cream.

Gelatine can be purchased in 2 g sheets or in a granulated form. Gelatine sheets, which are also known as 'leaves', should be washed and bloomed in cold clean water to help remove any impurities and to soften the gelatine ready for the next stage of use. The liquid that is to be thickened must be heated to at least 40°C, and the carefully drained gelatine sheets are then melted in the hot liquid.

When using granulated gelatine, the liquid to be thickened should be added cold to the required quantity of granules. The granules are then dissolved before the liquid is warmed over a bain-marie. The granules will sometimes stick together, but constant warming and stirring will disperse

them. The standard proportion advised by gelatine manufacturers is 7 g granulated gelatine to 250 ml liquid.

To set a dessert or ingredient after gelatine has been added it must be chilled in a refrigerator. The mixture can sometimes be set over an iced water bath while constantly stirring – this is a quicker method of setting.

FACTORS THAT AFFECT GELATINE SETTING

There are several factors that can affect gelatine:

- The amount of gelatine used – if too little gelatine is added to the liquid ingredients, insufficient gelling will occur. The amount required will vary between recipes, depending on the final texture desired, but a general rule is that six leaves of gelatine will set 480 ml of liquid.

- The amount of sugar added – mixtures that contain a lot of sugar will take longer to gel, or may not even gel at all. More gelatine is added to compensate for this effect.

- The amount of acid present – acid can weaken the structure of gelatine and therefore more gelatine may be required to produce a set liquid.

- Enzymes in fresh fruits – the protease enzyme found in some fresh fruits, such as pineapple, kiwi fruit, melon, papaya and ginger, completely prevents gelatine from setting. This enzyme is inactivated or destroyed at 85°C, so canned or cooked fruit will not be affected.

- The addition of salt – salt reduces the strength of gelatine and so additional quantities may have to be added.

Lecithin

Powdered lecithin

The non-toxicity of lecithin leads to its use with food, as an additive or in food preparation. It is used in foods requiring a natural emulsifier or lubricant. For use in confectionery, lecithin reduces viscosity, controls sugar crystallization and the flow properties of chocolate. It also helps in the homogeneous mixing of ingredients, improves shelf life for some products and can be used as a coating.

Lecithin stabilizes emulsions and improves flavour release. In dough and bakery, it reduces fat and egg requirements, helps even distribution of ingredients in dough, stabilizes fermentation, increases volume, protects yeast cells in dough when frozen, and acts as a releasing agent to prevent sticking and simplify cleaning. It can be used as a component of cooking sprays to prevent sticking and as a releasing agent.

Other stabilizers

There are several other substances that work in a similar way to gelatine but which are derived from plants. Collectively referred to as 'gums', they are long chains of glucose sugars that are capable of absorbing large quantities of water:

AGAR-AGAR

Derived from red algae, this has greater gelatinization properties than gelatine so less is required for a recipe. It can be purchased in whole or powdered form and is suitable for vegetarian diets. White and semi-translucent, it is sold in packages as washed and dried strips or in powdered form. It can be used to make jellies, puddings and custards.

CARRAGEEN

A similar substance to agar-agar and also a type of seaweed. Food manufacturers use this to thicken foods containing dairy products, such as cottage cheese and ice cream. There are several varieties of carrageen used in cooking and baking. Kappa-carrageen is used mostly in breads and batters due to its gelling nature. Lambda carrageen is a non-gelling variety that assists in binding, retaining moisture and in contributing to viscosity in sweet dough. Iota carrageen is used primarily in fruit applications and requires calcium to develop a heat-reversible and flexible gel.

GUM ARABIC

Also known as acacia gum is derived from the hardened sap of the acacia tree this has been used to stabilize icing, frostings, glazes and some fillings and creams.

CAROB GUM

Also derived from a tree (the carob tree), the seeds are used to make a gum that is used to stabilize ice creams and sorbets. An added benefit is that this substance will also improve a mixture's resistance to heat.

PECTIN

Many fruits naturally contain **pectin**, but fruits that are particularly high in pectin are apples, plums, cranberries and citrus fruits. Pectin is used to thicken glazes, jams, jellies and preserves. Pectin needs to be used with sugar to create a gel.

Soufflés

Soufflé is a French word derived from the verb *souffler*, which means to puff or to blow up. The soufflé was originally made in a croustade, which was a straight-sided pastry case into which the soufflé mixture was poured (but the croustade was never eaten). Modern practice it to use an ovenproof ramekin dish.

There are four main types of soufflé:

- Hot soufflé – this is a very fragile and delicate blend of eggs, flour, butter and egg whites and can be sweet or savoury. Hot soufflés must be served the moment they are released from the oven.

- Pudding soufflé – these are baked in a bain-marie in a metal mould (dariole). They are turned out and always served with a sauce. Pudding soufflés are not as light in texture as a hot soufflé and are normally served for luncheon.

- Cold soufflé – a soft mixture of meringue, cream, egg yolks and sugar together with gelatine. The soufflés are set in prepared soufflé dishes or ramekins and served cold.

- Iced soufflé – this is prepared in a similar way to the cold soufflé but without the gelatine and is frozen like a parfait. A derivative of this type of soufflé is the omelette soufflé, which is produced directly onto a silver flat with a base of Génoise sponge; ice cream and fresh fruit, then decoratively covered with meringue and flash cooked under a grill or in a hot oven.

Ordinary hot sweet soufflés are served at the table in the dish that they were baked in. They are traditionally served without a sauce, but it is now commonplace to have a sorbet, ice cream or hot sauce as an accompaniment.

Soufflés are delicate and can be difficult to make. They are generally made using a base of crème pâtissière combined with flavouring and aerated egg whites. The air trapped in the egg whites expands at cooking temperatures and the egg protein, along with the starch molecules found in the crème pâtissière base, will set the hot dessert. However, as the soufflé cools down the trapped air will escape and the soufflé will sink.

The basic principles of soufflé making

1 It is important to place the soufflés into a hot oven so that they begin baking immediately. The aerated egg whites when added to the soufflé preparation will begin to collapse, so the sooner it begins to cook, the better.

2 The oven needs to be at the correct temperature, if the temperature is too high then the soufflé may burn on the exterior before the interior is cooked. Baking at too low a temperature however, can mean that the soufflé does not

rise very well, as the egg proteins cook and stiffen the foam before enough steam is generated to make the soufflé rise.

3   Greasing the moulds is essential to allow the soufflé to rise correctly. Any hard fat, such as butter, is suitable. Hard fats are preferable to soft ones as they are less likely to flow away during the baking process. Egg proteins react with the glaze in the moulds and greasing will help to create a barrier between them.

4   Cleaning away any excess mixture from the rims of the dishes is essential as this mixture would bake first and may adhere to the rims of the moulds so preventing the soufflé from rising.

5   A soufflé mould or dish should have smooth vertical sides so that the soufflé does not change its shape as it rises.

6   Cleanly separating the egg yolks from the whites is important when creating really stiff foams with the egg whites. The bowl and the whisk must be free from any dust, dirt or grease. When aerating, the smaller the bubbles in the foam, the better because they will provide a uniform and smooth texture to the soufflé. Essentially, the more the egg white is beaten, the smaller the bubbles will be.

7   When choosing the ingredients to flavour the soufflé, avoid using fats as far as possible. This is important because fats will break down the egg white foam.

8   Prepare the base preparation as a firm paste and fold in the aerated egg whites. This provides the strength for the baked soufflé and enables it to support its own weight.

Ice cream

VIDEO CLIP Ice cream

Ice cream is made by freezing a liquid mixture containing carefully balanced ingredients after it has been subjected to heat treatment. The conditions of the heat treatment are carefully governed by legal standards, and the process is subjected to regular scrutiny by local health officials.

Scrupulous cleanliness must be observed in every stage of ice cream making. The materials used can easily become contaminated and give rise to food poisoning bacteria. A special area should be reserved for the production of ice cream, appropriately equipped and kept solely for this purpose. Moreover, the equipment should be used solely for the making of ice cream. An abundant supply of hot and cold water for washing purposes is also essential.

Pasteurization

The process of pasteurization is essential to the production of ice cream. In 1864, while studying the fermentation of wines, vinegar, beers and milk, Louis Pasteur discovered that fermentation was caused by micro-organisms and realized that many infectious diseases derived from specific microbes. Pasteur ascertained that by boiling milk to over 100°C, all dangerous microbes could be destroyed. However, this heating also reduced the nutritional value of the milk itself. By carrying on his experimentation, Pasteur found out that heating milk to 65°C, keeping it at this temperature for 30 minutes, and then cooling it to 4°C destroyed all pathogenic microbes while leaving the main nutritional and structural characteristics of the milk unchanged.

It is important that all ingredients in the ice cream mix are subjected to heat treatment for the correct time periods and are then cooled down quickly. The treated ingredients must be kept covered to prevent any new contamination.

Homogenization

This process is not usually associated with ice cream production for a small restaurant or hotel business. The base mix is **homogenized**, which forms a fat emulsion by breaking down or reducing the size of the fat globules found in milk or cream. Homogenization provides the following functions in ice cream production:

● Reduces size of fat globules to create a better texture.

● Increases surface area of fats to increase aeration.

By helping to form the fat structure, it also has the following indirect effects:

● makes a smoother ice cream;

● gives a greater apparent richness and palatability;

● better air stability;

● increases resistance to melting.

Homogenization of the mix should take place at the pasteurizing temperature. The high temperature produces more efficient breaking up of the fat globules at pressure. No one pressure can be recommended that will give satisfactory results under all conditions. The higher the fat and total solids in the mix, the lower the pressure should be.

Ageing

The mix is aged for at least four hours and usually overnight. This allows time for the fat to cool down and crystallize, and for the proteins and polysaccharides to fully hydrate. Aging improves the aeration qualities of the base mix and body and texture of the finished ice cream. There are also flavour improvements providing fresh flavourings are used and not synthetic flavourings. It does so by:

- Providing time for fat crystallization, so the fat can partially combine.

- Allowing time for full protein and stabilizer hydration and a resulting slight viscosity increase in the mix.

Ageing is performed in insulated containers in the refrigerator. The base temperature should be maintained as low as possible without freezing, at or below 5°C.

Freezing and hardening

Following the preparation of the base mix, it then enters the freezing process which both freezes a fraction of the water and whips air into the frozen mix at the same time.

Ice cream contains a considerable quantity of air. This gives the product its characteristic lightness. Without air, ice cream would be similar to a frozen ice cube. The air content is termed as *overrun*.

Before starting to freeze the ice cream, ensure all parts of the internal freezer of the ice cream machine coming in contact with the ice cream mix are clean and have been scalded. Turn on the machine to let the inside cool before pouring in the mix. This should not be filled over two-thirds full to allow sufficient room for air incorporation.

Freezing with liquid nitrogen

Using liquid nitrogen to freeze ice cream is a method that has been used for many years to harden ice cream. The use of liquid nitrogen in the primary freezing of ice cream, and effect the transition from the liquid to the frozen state without the use of a conventional ice cream freezer, has only recently started to see commercial viability. The preparation results in a column of white, condensed water vapor cloud. The ice cream, dangerous to eat while still 'steaming', is allowed to rest until the liquid nitrogen is completely vaporized. Sometimes ice cream is frozen to the sides of the container, and must be allowed to thaw. Making ice cream with liquid nitrogen has advantages over conventional freezing. Due to the rapid freezing, the crystal grains are smaller, giving the ice cream a creamier texture, and allowing the chef to obtain the same texture by using less milk-fat.

HEALTH & SAFETY   The Dairy Products (Hygiene) Regulations 1995 state:

1   Pasteurized ice-cream shall be obtained by the mixture being heated:

   a.   to a temperature of not less than 65.6°C and retained at that temperature for not less than 30 minutes.

   b.   to a temperature of not less than 71.1°C and retained at that temperature for not less than ten minutes.

   c.   to a temperature of not less than 79.4°C and retained at that temperature for not less than 15 seconds, and then reduced to a temperature of not more than 7.2°C within one-and-a-half hours and kept at such temperature until the freezing process is begun.

2   If the temperature of ice-cream has risen above minus 2.2°C at any time since it was frozen it should not be sold or offered for sale unless:

   a.   it has again been subjected to the heat-treatment to which as a mixture it was required to be subjected under paragraph 1 above, plus

   b.   after having again been frozen, it has been kept at a temperature not exceeding minus 2.2°C.

It is also essential that all hygiene regulations are followed, including those that relate to:

- daily cleaning routines;

- preparation of the mixture and the close monitoring of temperature control;

- the selling and dispensing of ice cream;

- customer hygiene measures;

- hygiene of specialist equipment, such as self-pasteurizing machines;

- storage of ice cream.

Storage of ice cream

Ice cream is delicate and can be damaged by factors such as mechanical force and shock, pressure, external odours, exposure to air, high storage temperature and thermal changes.

Ice cream should be stored at the lowest temperature possible, but in any event not higher than –20°C. However, at this temperature the ice cream is very hard and unsuitable for service. It should be brought out of storage prior to service and stored at a temperature of between –6°C and –12°C, according to the type of ice cream used and the consistency required for service.

Stabilizers in ice cream

To improve the texture, mouth feel and storage of ice creams and sorbets it is recommended to use a stabilizer. In addition to texture the stabilizers will enable you to maintain sorbet and ice cream structure at room temperature for longer periods.

Stabilizers are a group of compounds, usually polysaccharide food gums, which are responsible for adding viscosity to the base ice cream mix and the unfrozen phase of the ice cream. This will result in many benefits, such as release of flavour and also extends the shelf life by limiting ice re-crystallization during storage. Without the stabilizers, the ice cream would become coarse and icy very quickly due to the migration of free water and the growth of existing ice crystals.

TYPES OF ICES	
Sorbet	Made from fruit purée or pulp and stock syrup
Water ice	Made from fruit juice and stock syrup
Spoom	A sorbet mixture with Italian meringue
Granite	Crystallized flavoured syrup or fruit purée
Pâte à bombe	A special preparation of ice cream
Pâte à biscuit glacées	As a pâte à bombe mixture but in a biscuit mould, sometimes lightened with meringue
Soufflé glacé	Iced soufflé
Ice cream	Contains egg, cream and usually milk
Omelette soufflé	Ice cream encased in a meringue preparation on a base of Génoise and fruit
Marquise	Granite with crème Chantilly folded in before service
Gelato	Italian ice cream with a slightly softer texture

Sorbets

Sorbet is a frozen dessert made from sweetened water flavoured with fruit (typically juice or purée), wine or liqueur. Sorbet is variously explained as either a Roman or Persian invention. Whereas ice cream is based on dairy products with air whipped in, sorbet has neither, which makes for a dense and extremely flavourful product. Sorbet is served as a non-fat or low-fat alternative to ice cream.

It is essential that the highest quality ingredients are used to make sorbets and that any fruit used is perfectly ripe. The amount of fruit used per recipe depends on the acidity and type of fruit required. Therefore the amount of sugar solution will depend on the type of fruit being used.

As with ice cream, the base sorbet mix should be aged for between 4 and 24 hours in a refrigerator and then the stabilizer added just before freezing and always according to the manufacturer's recommendations.

Dessert sauces and presentation

Dessert sauces can be defined as a thickened liquid that is used to accompany and decorate specific dessert component. These are used to elevate the finished dish and create an additional aspect of elegance at the end of a meal.

They serve many purposes and are used in combination to brighten the colour value of a dessert. There are four main reasons to use dessert sauces:

1   To add moisture and texture to the presented dessert.

2   To add richness to desserts.

3   To add complementary flavours to desserts.

4   To enhance presentation.

It is important to work with sauces that are approximately the same thickness or viscosity and if using foams, they are stable enough to hold their shape next to other sauces. Making test plates of the intended design before plating the actual dessert so that the chef can determine whether the sauces need to be warmed or thinned out. Often refrigerated sauces become thicker after a few hours of storage, especially if they have been thickened with starch.

Decorating a plated dessert

Decorating a plate with sauces adds depth and elegance to a dessert. One last component of the dessert that should not be overlooked is an additional element or garnish, which is edible and balances the overall dessert.

Garnishes and decorations add height, texture, colour, flavour and will potentially lift the dessert to another level.

Considerations for balancing and scaling ingredients in recipes

All dessert and pastry recipes, and bakery formulas, produce a specific number of servings of a given product. This meets the needs of the business in several ways; for example in portion control and cost control. But, if the chef requires more or less food to be produced and the recipe does not fit the amount of food required how do you alter the recipe to fit your needs?

Scaling a recipe means increasing or decreasing the amount of food a recipe produces. Though no strict guidelines govern how to scale a recipe, there are some practical considerations to help you adjust your recipes with greater success.

Changing a recipe's yield: points to consider

A recipe's yield could be, for example, ten portions of chocolate mousse. A recipe specifies the ingredients and the measurements required for a set amount. If the yield is either more or less than what you want to produce, you may need to scale the recipe.

Though some recipes, such as casseroles, stews and other main dishes, usually lend themselves to a simple increasing or decreasing of the amount of ingredients, others do not. For example, baked goods requiring leavening agents such as baking powder, baking soda or yeast, which may not work very well doubled or quadrupled.

Here are several factors to consider before increasing or decreasing the number of servings of a given recipe:

1   Equipment – when you scale a recipe, match your equipment to the volume of the food. Larger batches need bigger bowls and larger or extra baking pans. Likewise, smaller batches require smaller bowls and baking pans.

2   Cooking times – cooking times may stay the same. For instance, when preparing soufflés, it does not matter whether you bake six or 26 soufflés; the cooking time remains the same. Some recipes may, however, require a longer cooking time. Conversely, heavy sponge cake that serves eight portions will need a much shorter baking time than one that serves 20 portions.

3   Cooking temperature – in most cases, you do not have to change the cooking temperature when you scale a recipe. The exception is when you have multiple items in the oven and may therefore require a slightly higher baking temperature.

4   Seasonings – spices and other seasonings, including salt, do not always need to be increased or decreased in the same proportion as the other ingredients. Instead, add seasoning and flavourings to taste until you obtain the result you want.

5   Alcohol – in recipes, alcohol such as white wine or rum can quickly overpower the flavour of the food if too much is used. Do not therefore increase the alcohol content as you would other ingredients. Consider also the effect that alcohol as an ingredient may have in certain recipes such as ice cream where additional alcohol will lower the freezing point of the ice cream mixture.

Best practice for scaling a recipe

In order to obtain the best results you should be familiar with your original recipe, experiment with your adjustments and make separate batches, if necessary.

●   Make the original recipe first. Identify how the recipe should look and taste before you make any adjustments. The original is then a benchmark for comparing the success of the adjusted recipe. Plus, the original may yield fewer or more servings than expected and the recipe may not need to be adjusted after all.

●   Test first, and then serve. You may not find success when scaling a recipe for the first time. So test your scaled dishes first, before serving them. Experiment with what works and what does not work. Ingredients interact with each other differently, and cooking methods, temperatures or times may need to be adjusted accordingly. Also, it is important to recognize the importance of using good quality ingredients and the detrimental effect that poor quality ingredients can have on the final result.

●   Make food in batches. If you increase a recipe and lack the time to experiment, produce several individual batches. This way you end up with the amount you need based on the original recipe.

No specific rules dictate how to scale a recipe due to the diverse nature of the ingredients that we use. However, certain scientific formulas can explain how to produce the best soufflé, mousse or ice cream, based on the amount and type of fat, liquid and solids used.

Recipes

Lemon cream

Ingredients	makes 1 kg	makes 2 kg
Whole eggs	10	20
Caster sugar	360 g	720 g
Finely grated zest of lemon	5 lemons	10 lemons
Lemon juice	480 g	960 g
Caster sugar	300 g	600 g
Gelatine	5 leaves	10 leaves

energy	cal	fat	sat fat	carb	sugar	protein	fibre
570 kJ	134 kcal	2.1 g	0.6 g	28.2 g	27.9 g	2.7 g	0.3 g

METHOD OF WORK

1   Bring to the boil the lemon juice, zest and the smaller quantity of caster sugar, stirring continuously. Meanwhile, soak the leaves of gelatine in cold water to soften and bloom.

2   Mix together the whole eggs and the larger quantity of caster sugar.

3   Add this mixture to the boiled lemon mixture and place back onto the stove.

4   Cook out the lemon cream to 85°C, stirring constantly.

5   The lemon cream will thicken as it cooks out. Remove from the stove and add the softened gelatine (which has been squeezed to remove the excess water).

6   Strain through a fine chinois, cool and chill in a refrigerator.

7   Use as required.

CHEF'S TIP This recipe can be used as an alternative to lemon curd and as a preserve, flavouring for creams or a dessert accompaniment.

Pâte à bombe

Ingredients	makes 180 ml	makes 360 ml
Granulated sugar	40 g	80 g
Water	75 g	150 g
Egg yolks	3	5

energy	cal	fat	sat fat	carb	sugar	protein	fibre
231 kJ	55 kcal	2.6 g	0.7 g	7 g	7 g	1.4 g	0 g

METHOD OF WORK

1   Place the water into a heavy-based saucepan and add the sugar. Heat slowly until the sugar dissolves.

2   Increase the heat, and using a sugar thermometer to measure the temperature of the solution, boil the sugar solution to 121°C (hard ball stage).

3   Meanwhile, whisk the egg yolks in an electric mixing machine (or by hand using a balloon whisk) until they have reached a pale yellow colour.

4   Whilst still whisking the egg yolks, very carefully pour the hot sugar solution in a thin but steady stream onto the egg yolks. Continue this until all of the hot sugar has been added.

5   Continue whisking to increase the volume of the mixture and to cool it down. The mixture should stand to a peak when cold and fully aerated.

6   The pâte à bombe mixture should be kept covered in a refrigerator for up to two days.

CHEF'S TIP This classical preparation is an important base for other recipes, such as mousses, parfaits and iced soufflés. It provides the stabilized foam of egg yolks and sugar to be flavoured accordingly and sustain the addition of whipped cream or aerated egg whites.

Swiss meringue

Ingredients	400 g mix	800 g mix
Egg whites	4	8
Caster sugar	150 g	300 g
Icing sugar	150 g	300 g
Cream of tartar	Small pinch	Small pinch
Vanilla flavour	A few drops	A few drops

energy	cal	fat	sat fat	carb	sugar	protein	fibre
437 kJ	102 kcal	0 g	0 g	26.3 g	26.1 g	0.9 g	0 g

METHOD OF WORK

1 Bring a saucepan of water to a simmer and set on a low heat.

2 Using a balloon whisk, mix the egg whites with the caster sugar and the cream of tartar in a stainless steel mixing bowl.

3 Place the bowl over the saucepan of water to create a bain-marie and begin to aerate the egg whites and icing sugar.

4 Continue aerating on the bain-marie until the meringue mixture reaches 60°C. Use a digital thermometer to assess the temperature of the meringue and maintain the whisking to prevent the heat from the bain-marie building up at the base of the stainless steel bowl and thus overcooking the eggs.

5 Add the icing sugar and vanilla, continuing to beat until the icing sugar is completely incorporated and remove from the bain-marie.

6 Place the meringue onto a machine to further beat and aerate using a whisk attachment until the meringue is completely cold and reaches stiff peaks.

7 The meringue is now ready to use for a variety of different options such as lemon meringue pie or piped into shapes on a baking sheet lined with silicone paper.

8 The oven should be preheated to 110°C and the meringues should take approximately one-and-a-half hours to dry out.

9 The meringues are ready when both the top and bottom are dry.

CHEF'S TIP When egg whites are beaten, some of the hydrogen bonds in the proteins break, causing the proteins to unfold (denature). This change in structure leads to the stiff consistency required for meringues. The addition of cream of tartar is required to additionally denature the proteins to create the firm peaks; otherwise the whites will not be firm. Plastic bowls, wet or greasy bowls will likely result in the meringue mix being prevented from becoming peaked. Wiping the bowl with a wedge of lemon to remove any traces of grease can often help the process.

When beating egg whites, they are classified in three stages according to the peaks they form when the beater is lifted: soft, firm and stiff peaks.

Step-by-step: Swiss meringue

1. Create a bain-marie with a saucepan and water on the stove and ensure that your equipment is clean and free from grease. The egg whites should be free of shell and yolk.

2. Begin beating the egg whites and incorporating the cream of tartar and the caster sugar whilst set over the bain-marie.

3. Continue aerating the meringue mixture and bring the temperature of the meringue to 60°C.

4. Now add the vanilla and the icing sugar one the temperature of 60°C has been reached.

5. Transfer the meringue to a clean stainless steel bowl to continue beating until the meringue is cold.

6. Beat until stiff peaks have formed.

French meringue

Ingredients	6 portions	14 portions
Egg whites	4	10
Caster sugar	200 g	400 g
Vanilla flavour	A few drops	A few drops
Crushed Pistachio nuts (optional)	50 g	100 g

energy	cal	fat	sat fat	carb	sugar	protein	fibre
801 kJ	190 kcal	4.4 g	0.5 g	35.9 g	35.6 g	3.7 g	0.9 g

METHOD OF WORK

1 Using a balloon whisk, aerate the egg whites to a soft peak.

2 Gradually sprinkle in the sugar and the vanilla and mix in to the egg whites.

3 Place the meringue into a piping bag and pipe the required shapes onto a Sil-pat baking mat or silicone baking paper onto a baking sheet. Sprinkle the chopped pistachio nuts on top if desired.

4 Place into a preheated oven set at 110°C to dry out the meringues without colour.

CHEF'S TIP This recipe can use pasteurized egg whites in order to reduce the possibility of food-borne illness.

Italian meringue

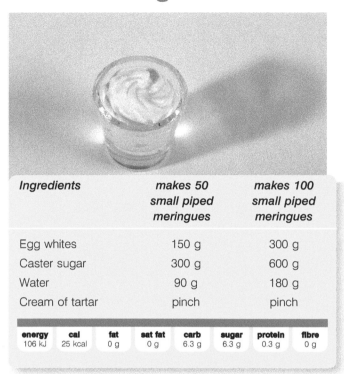

Ingredients	makes 50 small piped meringues	makes 100 small piped meringues
Egg whites	150 g	300 g
Caster sugar	300 g	600 g
Water	90 g	180 g
Cream of tartar	pinch	pinch

energy	cal	fat	sat fat	carb	sugar	protein	fibre
106 kJ	25 kcal	0 g	0 g	6.3 g	6.3 g	0.3 g	0 g

METHOD OF WORK

1 Place the water into a heavy-based saucepan and add the sugar and cream of tartar. Heat slowly until the sugar dissolves.

2 Increase the heat, and using a sugar thermometer to measure the temperature of the sugar solution, boil until 118°C is reached.

3 Meanwhile aerate the egg whites to a stiff peak on an electric machine.

4 Keeping the egg whites whisking, add the boiled sugar solution in a steady stream.

5 Continue whisking until the meringue is firm.

6 When the meringue is cool remove from the machine and check the consistency to form stiff peaks.

7 The finished meringue should hold its own shape.

CHEF'S TIP Egg whites and sugar are both hygroscopic (water-attracting) ingredients. Consequently, meringue becomes soggy when refrigerated or stored in a high-humidity environment. This also explains the problem called 'weeping' or 'sweating', in which beads of moisture form on all surfaces of the meringue. Sweating is a particular problem for meringues in which the sugar is inadequately dissolved in the egg whites, and for high-moisture pie fillings such as lemon meringue pie.

Step-by-step Process

1. Place the sugar, water and cream of tartar in a saucepan and carefully bring to the boil and heat to 118°C.

2. Meanwhile aerate the egg whites to a stiff peak.

3. Keeping the egg whites whisking, add the boiled sugar solution in a steady stream.

4. Continue whisking until the meringue is firm.

5. When the meringue is cool remove from the machine and check the consistency to form stiff peaks.

6. The finished Italian Meringue holding its own shape. This is now ready for immediate use.

Crème Anglaise

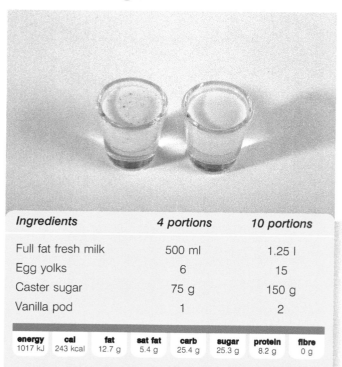

Ingredients	4 portions	10 portions
Full fat fresh milk	500 ml	1.25 l
Egg yolks	6	15
Caster sugar	75 g	150 g
Vanilla pod	1	2

energy	cal	fat	sat fat	carb	sugar	protein	fibre
1017 kJ	243 kcal	12.7 g	5.4 g	25.4 g	25.3 g	8.2 g	0 g

METHOD OF WORK

1   Place the milk into a heavy-bottomed saucepan with one tablespoon of the sugar (this will help to prevent the milk from scalding).

2   Split the vanilla pod in half lengthways and scrape the seeds from within the pod into the milk. Add the vanilla pod too. Slowly bring the milk to the boil.

3   Meanwhile, using a whisk beat the egg yolks and caster sugar together in a large bowl until pale in colour.

4   At boiling point, remove the milk from the heat and carefully pour it onto the egg yolk mixture, stirring constantly.

5   Return this mixture to the saucepan and cook on a low heat, stirring continuously with a wooden spoon until the sauce thickens enough to coat the back of the spoon. Draw a finger down the back of the spoon to see if an impression has been formed.

6   Alternatively, use a digital thermometer and ensure that the sauce has been cooked to 85°C.

7   Remove the saucepan from the heat and strain through a fine strainer into a chilled bowl to help prevent the sauce from cooking further and thus overcooking the eggs. Chill in the refrigerator until required or serve warm.

Steps

1.

2.

Vanilla soufflé

Ingredients	4 portions	10 portions
Full fat fresh milk	125 g	300 g
Caster sugar (1)	25 g	80 g
Flour	25 g	60 g
Butter	15 g	40 g
Egg yolk (1)	1	1
Whole egg	1	1
Egg yolk (2)	3	5
Egg whites	6	10
Caster sugar (2)	25 g	25 g
Vanilla pod	1	2

energy	cal	fat	sat fat	carb	sugar	protein	fibre
884 kJ	211 kcal	10.9 g	4.6 g	19.5 g	14.7 g	10 g	0.2 g

METHOD OF WORK

1   Lightly coat the soufflé moulds twice with some soft butter. Coat the butter in the soufflé moulds with caster sugar and tap out the surplus.

2   Place the milk into a heavy-bottomed saucepan with the vanilla. Split the vanilla pod in half lengthways and scrape the seeds out, adding this to the milk alongside the remaining pod.

3   Bring the milk to the boil and meanwhile mix together the whole egg, the first quantity of egg yolk, flour, butter and first quantity of caster sugar together in a stainless steel bowl.

4   Add the boiled milk to the egg yolk mixture and stir thoroughly until the mixture is smooth.

5   Return to a clean saucepan and stir continuously with a wooden spoon over a gentle heat to cook out the mixture so that it thickens.

6   Allow to cool slightly before adding the second amount of egg yolks to this preparation.

7   Preheat an oven to 200°C.

8   Aerate the egg whites with the second amount of caster sugar and then carefully fold into the pastry cream preparation.

9   Place the soufflé mixture into the prepared moulds, filling to the top of each one. Level off the tops of each soufflé and run a finger around the edge of each mould to help the soufflés to rise when baking.

10 Place the soufflés onto a baking sheet and place into the preheated oven for ten minutes before reducing the temperature to 190°C and cooking for a further ten minutes depending on the size of the soufflés being cooked.

11 Remove from the oven and dust with icing sugar and serve immediately.

CHEF'S TIP Adding a pinch of cream of tartar to the egg whites will help with the stability of the aeration process.

Raspberry soufflé

Ingredients	4 portions	10 portions
Full fat fresh milk	125 g	300 g
Caster sugar (1)	25 g	80 g
Flour	25 g	60 g
Butter	15 g	40 g
Egg yolk (1)	1	1
Raspberry purée	45 g	95 g
Whole egg	1	1
Egg yolk (2)	3	5
Egg whites	6	10
Caster sugar (2)	25 g	25 g
Fresh raspberries	to garnish	to garnish
Raspberry coulis	25 g	50 g

energy	cal	fat	sat fat	carb	sugar	protein	fibre
938 kJ	224 kcal	10.9 g	4.6 g	22.5 g	17.6 g	10.3 g	0.7 g

METHOD OF WORK

1 Lightly coat the soufflé moulds twice with some soft butter. Coat the butter in the soufflé moulds with caster sugar and tap out the surplus.

2 Place the milk into a heavy-bottomed saucepan and bring to the boil and meanwhile mix together the whole egg, the first quantity of egg yolk, flour, butter and first quantity of caster sugar together in a stainless steel bowl.

3 Add the boiled milk to the egg yolk mixture and stir thoroughly until the mixture is smooth.

4 Return to a clean saucepan and stir continuously with a wooden spoon over a gentle heat to cook out the mixture so that it thickens. Mix in the raspberry purée.

5 Allow to cool slightly before adding the second amount of egg yolks to this preparation.

6 Preheat an oven to 200°C.

7 Aerate the egg whites with the second amount of caster sugar and then carefully fold into the pastry cream preparation.

8 Place the soufflé mixture into the prepared moulds, filling to the top of each one. Level off the tops of each soufflé and run a finger around the edge of each mould to help the soufflés to rise when baking.

9 Place the soufflés onto a baking sheet and place into the preheated oven for ten minutes before reducing the temperature to 190°C and cooking for a further ten minutes depending on the size of the soufflés being cooked.

10 Remove from the oven and dust with icing sugar, carefully place the raspberries on top of each soufflé and spoon a little warmed raspberry coulis over them. Serve immediately.

Coffee and date pudding with ice cream

Coffee and date pudding with a rum and raisin ice cream

Ingredients	6 portions	12 portions
Medjool dates (stoned and chopped)	175 g	350 g
Water	300 ml	600 ml
Bicarbonate of soda	1 tsp	2 tsp
Unsalted butter	50 g	100 g
Caster sugar	175 g	350 g
Whole eggs	2	4
Soft white flour	165 g	330 g
Baking powder	10 g	25 g
Strong espresso coffee	6 tsp	12 tsp
Toffee sauce		
Double cream	300 ml	600 ml
Light muscovado sugar	50 g	100 g
Black treacle	2 tsp	4 tsp
Unsalted butter	30 g	60 g
Rum and raisin ice cream		
Pâte à bombe	180 ml	360 ml
Raisins	100 g	200 g
Dark rum	100 g	200 g
Water	30 ml	60 ml
Caster sugar	30 g	60 g
Fresh milk	120 ml	250 ml
Double cream	120 ml	250 ml

energy	cal	fat	sat fat	carb	sugar	protein	fibre
3804 kJ	922 kcal	53.7 g	31.9 g	95.7 g	75.4 g	8.8 g	1.8 g

METHOD OF WORK

1   Butter individual pudding moulds twice and preheat an oven to 180°C.

2   Place the dates and the water into a heavy-based saucepan and bring to the boil. Continue to boil for four minutes then remove from the heat and add the bicarbonate of soda and coffee. Leave to stand.

3   Cream together the butter and sugar until light in colour and with a soft, fluffy texture. Gradually add the eggs, mixing continuously.

4   Combine the dates and water with the creamed butter mixture and fold in the flour and baking powder.

5   Pour the mixture into the prepared moulds and bake for approximately 30 minutes or until the pudding is just firm to the touch.

6   To make the sauce, place the cream, sugar, treacle and butter into a saucepan and bring to the boil. Simmer for three minutes and pass through a chinois. Reserve warm.

7   To make the ice cream, wash the raisins in warm water and then place in a saucepan with the dark rum, sugar and water. Slowly bring to the boil and remove from the heat and cover with plastic film. Leave to cool and macerate for 24 hours before using.

8   Make the pâte à bombe and set aside. Place the milk and cream in a saucepan and bring to the boil, then leave to cool over a bain-marie of iced water. Combine with the pâte à bombe and pour into an ice cream machine to churn. Halfway through the freezing process add the raisins and some of the dark rum liquor to taste. Continue to churn and freeze.

9   To serve, de-mould the puddings into and spoon the sauce over each. Serve with the ice cream.

Queen of puddings

Ingredients	10 portions	20 portions
Full fat milk	1.25 l	2.5 l
Vanilla flavour	a few drops	a few drops
Whole eggs	9	18
Caster sugar (1)	160 g	320 g
Génoise or Madeira cake crumbs	250 g	500 g
Egg whites	3	6
Salt	pinch	pinch
Caster sugar (2)	175 g	350 g
Raspberry or apricot Jam	100 g	200 g
Icing sugar	25 g	55 g

energy	cal	fat	sat fat	carb	sugar	protein	fibre
1706 kJ	405 kcal	12.2 g	5.7 g	64.2 g	58.6 g	12.8 g	0.3 g

METHOD OF WORK

1 Preheat an oven to 180°C.

2 Place the milk in a saucepan with the vanilla and warm slightly.

3 Mix together the eggs and the first quantity of caster sugar and then add the warmed milk.

4 Lightly butter an appropriate pudding dish (2 × 25 cm dishes for ten portions) and pass the custard base through a fine chinois.

5 Place the cake crumbs onto the base of each pudding dish equally. Distribute the custard mix between each pudding dish.

6 Set each dish into a bain-marie, half filled with warm water. Place in the preheated oven and cook to set the custard for approximately 35 minutes.

7 Remove from the oven and allow to cool.

8 Whisk the egg whites and salt in a clean, stainless steel bowl to a stiff peak. Whisk in half of the second quantity of caster sugar and then fold in the remainder.

9 Warm the jam in a small saucepan and then pour over the top of the set custard.

10 Place the meringue into a piping bag with a 'chibouste' or a plain tip and decorate the top of the puddings with the meringue.

11 Dust the meringue with the icing sugar and then place into a hot oven to lightly brown the meringue. Serve.

Apple and thyme crumble

Apple and thyme crumble with mascarpone ice cream and salted caramel sauce

Ingredients	4 portions	8 portions
Caster sugar	50 g	100 g
Butter	60 g	120 g
Ground almonds	55 g	110 g
Soft white flour	60 g	125 g
Bramley apples	3	6
Clear honey	25 g	50 g
Fresh thyme	1 sprig	2 sprigs
Unsalted butter	25 g	50 g
Sultanas	10 g	20 g
Salted caramel sauce		
Water	100 g	200 g
Granulated sugar	60 g	120 g
Double cream	100 g	200 g
Fleur de sel	2 g	4 g
Mascarpone ice cream		
Caster sugar	75 g	150 g
Egg yolks	3	6
Fresh full fat milk	250 g	500 g
Mascarpone	150 g	300 g

energy	cal	fat	sat fat	carb	sugar	protein	fibre
4764 kJ	1135 kcal	62.3 g	33.7 g	138.5 g	127.3 g	13.6 g	13.8 g

METHOD OF WORK

1   Preheat an oven to 180°C.

2   To make the crumble, mix the sugar with the butter. Incorporate the ground almonds and the flour and rub together to create a crumbly texture. Spread the mixture onto a baking sheet lined with a silicone baking mat and bake for 15 minutes. Remove from the oven and set aside.

3   Wash, peel and cut the apples into 1 cm dice. In a shallow pan, cook the honey, butter and thyme to a light caramel. Add the sultanas and then add the apples. Place a cartouche of baking paper over the top and continue to cook until the apples are soft to the touch but still retain their shape.

4   Put the cooked apple mixture into the base of a 6 cm stainless steel ring placed onto a silicone baking mat on a baking sheet. Place the crumble on top and return to the oven for 15 minutes to warm through and colour.

5   For the salted caramel sauce, place the water and sugar in a heavy-based saucepan and cook to a caramel. Deglaze carefully with the double cream and add the fleur de sel. Re-boil and pass through a fine chinois. Reserve warm for service.

6   For the mascarpone ice cream, beat together the egg yolks and sugar. Meanwhile, place the milk and half of the mascarpone into a saucepan and bring to the boil. Add to the egg yolk mixture and mix well. Return to the saucepan and cook to 85°C, stirring continuously. Pass through a fine sieve and chill over a bain-marie of iced water. Add the remaining mascarpone and freeze in an ice cream machine.

7   To serve, place the crumble onto the service plate and spoon the salted caramel sauce around it. Set a quenelle of the ice cream to the side and decorate accordingly.

CHEF'S TIP   Always ensure that customers are aware of the nut content in the crumble topping for this recipe. Alternatively, the ground almond content can be replaced with flour and the butter content slightly increased.

SOURCING   With added interest in producing food locally there is a great provenance to honey, it is a very place-specific product. Bees fly no more than three miles from their hive so it is absolutely a local food. The geographic region in which honey is produced also influences a honey's essence. Soil and climate are the most effective elements of provenance. An in land clover honey may differ noticeably from coastal clover honey because these regions' climates and soils are dissimilar.

Crêpe soufflé

Ingredients	4 portions	10 portions
Crêpes		
Soft white flour	120 g	250 g
Caster sugar	10 g	30 g
Good quality salt	3 g	5 g
Whole eggs	2	4
Fresh full fat milk	400 ml	700 ml
Orange and vanilla sauce		
Sweet white wine	300 ml	650 ml
Oranges	2	4
Vanilla	1 pod	2 pods
Caster sugar	50 g	100 g
Unsalted butter	70 g	150 g
Double cream	30 ml	70 ml
Vanilla soufflé centre		

energy	cal	fat	sat fat	carb	sugar	protein	fibre
2156 kJ	516 kcal	25.3 g	14.9 g	51.9 g	26.4 g	10.1 g	2 g

METHOD OF WORK

1   Preheat an oven to 220°C.

2   To prepare the **crêpes**, combine the flour, salt and sugar and slowly beat in the eggs. Stir in one-third of the milk and beat to a smooth paste. Add the rest of the milk and leave to rest in a refrigerator for one hour before using.

3   Stir the batter and pass through a chinois. Add a little sunflower oil to a crêpe pan and heat. Ladle a little of the batter and cook for approximately one minute on each side with very little colour. Place each cooked crêpe in between small sheets of silicone paper to retain the soft texture and refrigerate until needed.

4   To prepare the orange and vanilla sauce, add the wine, sugar and split vanilla pod to a saucepan and reduce by half. Zest and squeeze the juice from the oranges and reserve to one side. Add the double cream and cubed unsalted butter to the reduced liquor, whisk and cook until the fats emulsify into a sauce. Add the orange juice and reserve warm.

5   Prepare the vanilla soufflé mixture.

6   Pipe or spoon the soufflé mixture onto the middle of each crêpe. Fold each crêpe into quarters and pipe any remaining mixture into the cavities. Place onto a baking tray.

7   Bake in the preheated oven for approximately five minutes until well risen.

8   Serve immediately by dusting each crêpe soufflé with icing sugar and place into the centre of a plate. Decoratively serve the orange and vanilla sauce with the crêpe soufflé.

Kirsch soufflé with griottine compote

Ingredients	4 portions	10 portions
Full fat fresh milk	125 g	300 g
Caster sugar (1)	25 g	80 g
Flour	25 g	60 g
Butter	15 g	40 g
Egg yolk (1)	1	1
Vanilla macaroons	8	20
Kirsch	100 ml	200 ml
Whole egg	1	1
Egg yolk (2)	3	5
Egg whites	6	10
Caster sugar (2)	25 g	25 g
Griottines in Kirsch	100 g	200 g
Cherry coulis	75 g	150 g

energy	cal	fat	sat fat	carb	sugar	protein	fibre
1368 kJ	326 kcal	11 g	4.6 g	34 g	29.2 g	10.3 g	0.2 g

METHOD OF WORK

1 Lightly coat the soufflé moulds twice with some soft butter. Coat the butter in the soufflé moulds with caster sugar and tap out the surplus.

2 Place the milk into a heavy-bottomed saucepan and bring to the boil and meanwhile mix together the whole egg, the first quantity of egg yolk, flour, butter and first quantity of caster sugar together in a stainless steel bowl.

3 Add the boiled milk to the egg yolk mixture and stir thoroughly until the mixture is smooth.

4 Return to a clean saucepan and stir continuously with a wooden spoon over a gentle heat to cook out the mixture so that it thickens. Mix in a little of the Kirsch.

5 Allow to cool slightly before adding the second amount of egg yolks to this preparation.

6 Preheat an oven to 200°C.

7 Aerate the egg whites with the second amount of caster sugar and then carefully fold into the pastry cream preparation.

8 Place two vanilla macaroons in the base of each soufflé dish and macerate with the remaining Kirsch.

9 Place the soufflé mixture into the prepared moulds, filling to the top of each one. Level off the tops of each soufflé and run a finger around the edge of each mould to help the soufflés to rise when baking.

10 Place the soufflés onto a baking sheet and place into the preheated oven for ten minutes before reducing the temperature to 190°c and cooking for a further ten minutes depending on the size of the soufflés being cooked.

11 Meanwhile, heat the Griottines with the cherry coulis and reserve warm to one side.

12 Remove from the oven and dust with icing sugar, carefully spoon the griottine compote on top of each soufflé. Serve immediately.

Clafoutis Limousin

Ingredients	4 portions	15 portions
Griottines or tinned black cherries	45 g	100 g
Whole eggs	2	4
Caster Sugar	35 g	80 g
Fresh milk	160 ml	360 ml
Kirsch	15 ml	25 ml
Soft flour	35 g	80 g
Icing sugar	20 g	30 g

energy	cal	fat	sat fat	carb	sugar	protein	fibre
638 kJ	151 kcal	3.4 g	1.2 g	23.8 g	17.5 g	5.4 g	0.3 g

METHOD OF WORK

1 Using a stainless steel mixing bowl, beat the eggs and sugar together and gradually add the milk and Kirsch.

2 Sieve the flour and whisk into the egg mixture. Pass through a fine chinois and set aside.

3 Preheat an oven to 190°C.

4 Place the griottines into flat dishes (sur le plat) and cover with the batter.

5 Bake in the preheated oven for approximately 15 minutes until the mixture has set and slightly risen.

6 Serve warm dusted with the icing sugar around the edges of the dish.

CHEF'S TIP Omelette soufflé au Grand Marnier may be prepared with any type of flavouring, spirit or liqueur. It is essential that is served immediately and any delay can result in the omelette collapsing.

Omelette soufflé au Grand Marnier

Ingredients	4 portions	10 portions
Orange or vanilla macaroons	8	20
Grand Marnier	50 ml	120 ml
Egg yolks	4	9
Caster sugar	175 g	350 g
Egg whites	6	12
Cream of tartar	pinch	pinch

energy	cal	fat	sat fat	carb	sugar	protein	fibre
1187 kJ	281 kcal	5.3 g	1.5 g	46.8 g	46.8 g	6.9 g	0 g

METHOD OF WORK

1 Preheat the oven to 185°C.

2 Cut the macaroons into quarters and macerate with the Grand Marnier.

3 Place the egg yolks into a stainless steel bowl with the caster sugar and whisk to a thick, creamy texture. Mix in the prepared macaroons.

4 Whisk the egg whites with the pinch of cream of tartar to a stiff peak.

5 Fold the aerated egg whites into the egg yolk mixture.

6 Reserve a little of this mixture in a piping bag with a star tube. Place the remainder of the mixture into an oval dish that has been buttered and smooth and mould quickly with a palette knife to an oval shape.

7 Pipe a scroll across the top of the moulded preparation. Place into the oven for 15 minutes to bake.

8 Dredge with icing sugar and return to the oven to glaze and colour. Finish with a little additional icing sugar and serve.

Cold lemon soufflé with candied lemon

Ingredients	4 portions	10 portions
Gelatine	5 leaves	10 leaves
Egg yolks	3	6
Caster sugar	110 g	260 g
Lemon juice and finely grated zest	2 lemons	4 lemons
Egg whites	3	6
Whipping cream	200 ml	500 ml
Finely sliced candied lemon	4	10
Crème Chantilly	50 g	150 g

energy	cal	fat	sat fat	carb	sugar	protein	fibre
1741 kJ	417 kcal	28.5 g	16.5 g	36.1 g	35.5 g	6.5 g	1 g

METHOD OF WORK

1 Prepare small ramekin dishes by attaching a strip of silicone paper to the outside of the dish so that it extends 2 cm above the rim.

2 Soak the gelatine leaves in cold water.

3 Place the lemon zest and juice with the egg yolks and the sugar into a stainless steel mixing bowl.

4 Place the bowl over a bain-marie of simmering water (not exceeding 90°C) and whisk continuously to thicken and aerate the mixture.

5 Add the gelatine and mix in until it has dissolved. Remove from the heat and continue to beat until cool.

6 Lightly whisk the whipping cream to the ribbon stage.

7 Stiffly aerate the egg whites.

8 Fold in the cream to the lemon mixture and then the egg whites.

9 Pour into prepared dishes and leave to set in a refrigerator for one hour.

10 To serve, remove the paper border from the sides of the soufflé. Pipe small rosette of crème Chantilly on top of each soufflé and decorate with the candied lemon.

SOURCING Purchasing small lemons will not give the optimal amount of freshly squeezed lemon juice. Instead purchase large lemons which feel heavy as this in an indication the lemon is ripe and full of juice.

Vanilla brûlée with passion fruit cream

Vanilla brûlée with passion fruit cream and basil poached pineapple

Ingredients	4 portions	8 portions
Coconut biscuit		
Egg whites	40 g	80 g
Caster sugar	60 g	125 g
Desiccated coconut	75 g	130 g
White rum	6 g	12 g
Zest of lime	1 lime	2 limes
Passion fruit cream		
Passion fruit pulp	30 g	50 g
Lime juice	3 g	7 g
Vanilla	½ pod	1 pod
Caster sugar	30 g	60 g
Whole egg	33 g	65 g
Unsalted butter	50 g	100 g
Vanilla brûlée		
Egg yolks	27 g	55 g
Full fat milk	35 g	70 g
Double cream	90 g	180 g
Caster sugar	23 g	45 g
Vanilla pod	½	1
Gelatine	2 leaves	4 leaves

Basil poached pineapple		
Water	500 ml	1 l
Caster sugar	150 g	300 g
Fresh basil	11 g	22 g
Sliced pineapple with the core cut out (6 cm × 3 cm)	4 slices	8 slices
Assembling the dessert		
White chocolate acetate square	4	8
Crème Anglaise flavoured with lemon	60 ml	120 ml

energy	cal	fat	sat fat	carb	sugar	protein	fibre
4762 kJ	1132 kcal	50.5 g	28.1 g	164.5 g	157.5 g	14.3 g	8.5 g

METHOD OF WORK

1   Preheat an oven to 210°C.

2   To make the coconut biscuit, mix the egg whites and sugar together and add the coconut, white rum and lime zest.

3   Place between two sheets of silicone paper and roll out as thinly as possible. Put into a freezer to set and then cut individual discs out of the sheet.

4   Place the discs onto a baking sheet lined with a silicone baking mat. Bake for two minutes then reduce the oven temperature to 170°C for a further seven minutes.

5   To make the passion fruit cream, place the passion fruit pulp, lime juice and vanilla into a small saucepan and bring to the boil.

6   Mix together the eggs and sugar. Add the boiled passion fruit to the eggs and mix well. Return to the saucepan and cook out the mixture to 85°C as for a crème Anglaise. Immediately cool the passion fruit cream over a bain-marie of iced water.

7   Slowly beat the softened butter into the passion fruit cream. An electric mixer will ensure that the butter emulsifies with the passion fruit cream. Reserve in a refrigerator for later use.

8   To make the vanilla brûlée, preheat an oven to 90°C. Mix all the ingredients together except the gelatine. Pour this into an ovenproof dish and bake in the oven for 60 minutes or until the brûlée has just set.

9   Soften the gelatine in some cold water and drain. Remove the brûlée from the oven and place into a food blender immediately with the gelatine and process to a soft, cooked liquid. Pour the liquid into individual small moulds (preferably flexible silicone moulds) and freeze.

10 When frozen, de-mould and leave to defrost on a tray in a refrigerator.

11 To make the basil poached pineapple, place the water, sugar and basil into a saucepan and bring the contents to the boil.

12 Place the slices of pineapple into a high-sided tray and pour over the basil syrup and cover with plastic film. After the syrup has cooled, put the pineapple into a refrigerator and leave to macerate for 24 hours.

13 To serve, set the coconut biscuit in the centre of the serving plate. Place the pineapple slice on top and position the vanilla brûlée on top of the pineapple.

14 Quenelle the passion fruit cream onto the top of the brûlée.

15 Finish with the chocolate motif and spoon the lemon crème Anglaise around the plate.

> **CHEF'S TIP** The method of producing the vanilla brûlée departs from the classical method because of the need to ensure that the brûlée is set sufficiently to support the quenelle. This is an example of changing the method of preparation and recipe to suit the requirements of a particular dish.

Terrine of two chocolates

Ingredients	1 terrine	2 terrines
White chocolate mousse		
White chocolate	200 g	400 g
Whipping cream	300 ml	600 ml
Gelatine	2 leaves	3 leaves
Grand Marnier	15 ml	25 ml
Dark chocolate mousse		
Dark chocolate	200 g	400 g
Whipping cream	300 ml	600 ml
Additional preparations		
Sheet of Japonaise (40 cm × 20 cm)	1 sheet	2 sheets
Fresh raspberries for decoration	3	6
Candied lemon zest	5 g	10 g
Chocolate curls for decoration	2 per portion	2 per portion

energy	cal	fat	sat fat	carb	sugar	protein	fibre
1946 kJ	469 kcal	40.1 g	18.6 g	21.9 g	14.5 g	5.3 g	0.1 g

METHOD OF WORK

1 Line individual terrine moulds with plastic film. Carefully cut four strips of Japonaise slightly smaller than the base of each mould. Place one strip in the bottom of the terrine mould.

2 Melt the white chocolate in a bain-marie to no more than 45°C. Meanwhile, half whip the cream. Soften the gelatine in cold water and squeeze out. Melt the gelatine with the Grand Marnier.

3 Fold the white chocolate into the whipped cream to create a smooth mixture and add the melted gelatine.

4 Deposit the white chocolate mousse into the lined terrine mould half way up. Put in a refrigerator to set.

5 Melt the dark chocolate and whip the second quantity of whipping cream in the same way. Combine the two ingredients carefully to a smooth mousse and deposit on top of the set white chocolate mousse.

6 Place in a refrigerator to set for two hours.

7 To serve, remove the chocolate terrine from the mould and set on a serving plate. Decorate with the raspberries, chocolate curls and candied lemon zest.

> **CHEF'S TIP** Milk chocolate can be used as an alternative to white chocolate, but gelatine will not be required to set the mousse because of the presence of cocoa solids. Jaconde sponge or hazelnut Génoise could be used instead of Japonaise.

Almond cake

Almond cake with fig ice cream and a red fruit soup

Ingredients	4 portions	8 portions
Almond cake		
Double cream	120 g	240 g
Raw almond paste	90 g	180 g
Egg yolks	60 g	120 g
Egg whites	90 g	180 g
Caster sugar	45 g	90 g
Fig ice cream		
Pâte à bombe	180 ml	360 ml
Fresh figs	200 g	400 g
Dried figs	50 g	100 g
Raspberry purée	70 ml	140 ml
Double cream	120 ml	250 ml
Red fruit soup		
Red fruit berries (such as raspberries, blackberries, redcurrants and strawberries)	500 g	1 kg
Caster sugar	25 g	50 g
Vanilla	1 pod	3 pods

energy	cal	fat	sat fat	carb	sugar	protein	fibre
2845 kJ	682 kcal	47.5 g	23.1 g	55.9 g	53.2 g	11.9 g	6.3 g

METHOD OF WORK

1   Prepare individual moulds by brushing with melted butter and lining with silicone paper unless using rubber non-stick moulds. Ensure the silicone paper is 3 cm higher than the ring. Brush butter onto the inside of the silicone paper. Place the moulds onto a baking sheet lined with a silicone baking mat. Preheat an oven to 180°C.

2   Place the double cream, raw almond paste and egg yolks into a food blender and mix the ingredients together for a few seconds. Remove from the blender and place the almond mixture in a mixing bowl.

3   Create a meringue with the egg whites and caster sugar.

4   Carefully fold in the meringue to the almond mixture a little at a time to maintain the aeration as much as possible.

5   Pour the almond batter into the moulds to two-thirds full and bake in the oven for ten minutes.

6   To make the fig ice cream, place the fresh figs, dried figs and raspberry purée into a food blender and liquidize.

7   Combine the fig purée with the pâte à bombe and mix in the double cream.

8   Freeze in an ice cream machine.

9   To make the red fruit soup, place the fruit, sugar and split vanilla pods into a stainless steel bowl and cover tightly with plastic film.

10   Place the bowl onto a saucepan of simmering water and turn the heat down low. Maintain this for two hours; the heat generated will cause the fruit to shed its juices.

11   Put the fruit through a chinois without squeezing. Reserve the juice warm for service.

12   To serve, place the warm almond cake in the centre of a bowl and spoon the fruit soup around it. Finely chop a fresh fig and place into the soup. Set a quenelle of the fig ice cream on top of the almond cake and decorate as required.

Passion fruit mousse cake

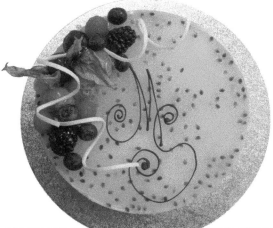

Ingredients	1 mousse cake	3 mousse cakes
Passion fruit purée	280 ml	575 ml
Caster sugar	15 g	30 g
Lemon juice	½ lemon	1 lemon
Gelatine	6 leaves	12 leaves
Egg whites	120 g	240 g
Caster sugar	150 g	300 g
Water	50 g	100 g
Whipping cream	280 ml	575 ml
Dacquoise disc	1 × 16 cm	3 × 16 cm
Biscuit jaconde	1 strip	3 strips
Glaze		
Passion fruit juice with seeds	20 g	40 g
Stock syrup	100 ml	240 ml
Gelatine	2½ leaves	3 leaves

energy	cal	fat	sat fat	carb	sugar	protein	fibre
1216 kJ	290 kcal	14.9 g	8.9 g	36.8 g	35.9 g	4.4 g	0.1 g

METHOD OF WORK

1 Soften the gelatine in cold water and squeeze out the excess water once softened. Melt the gelatine in a bain-marie.

2 Prepare a 22 cm torten ring by lining the sides with the biscuit jaconde and placing the disc of dacquoise in the base.

3 Mix together the passion fruit purée, smaller quantity of sugar, lemon juice and melted gelatine. Leave to half set in a refrigerator.

4 Create an Italian meringue with the egg whites, larger quantity of sugar and water.

5 Softly aerate the whipping cream to a ribbon stage. Fold in the cream to the passion fruit purée and then gradually incorporate the meringue.

6 Set into the prepared torten ring and place in the refrigerator to set for two hours.

7 To make the glaze, soften the gelatine in cold water and warm up the stock syrup with the passion fruit juice. Add the gelatine and allow it to melt, and then cool the syrup to 30°C.

8 Quickly apply the glaze using a large palette knife. Return to the refrigerator to set. De-mould the ring when required for service and decorate as required.

CHEF'S TIP   This recipe can be adapted to use other forms of fruit purées, such as banana, raspberry, cassis, mango and strawberry.

Strawberry Bavarois with a soft strawberry centre

Ingredients	4 portions	8 portions
Strawberry purée	125 g	250 g
Lemon juice	15 g	25 g
Stock syrup	125 g	250 g
Gelatine	3 leaves	6½ leaves
Whipping cream	250 g	500 g
Soft centre		
Strawberry purée	125 g	250 g
Stock syrup	100 g	200 g
Lemon juice	5 g	10 g
Dacquoise disc	4 small discs	8 small discs
Biscuit Jaconde	4 strips	8 strips
Glaze		
Strawberry purée	20 g	40 g
Stock syrup	100 ml	200 ml
Gelatine	2½ leaves	5 leaves

energy	cal	fat	sat fat	carb	sugar	protein	fibre
2711 kJ	646 kcal	32.6 g	17.1 g	86 g	79 g	7.5 g	2.7 g

METHOD OF WORK

1 To make the soft fruit centre, mix together the strawberry purée, stock syrup and lemon juice. Pass through fine chinois and pour into small cylindrical moulds that will easily fit inside the moulds to be used for the fruit Bavarois. Place in the freezer to freeze.

2 Prepare the individual moulds by lining the coloured biscuit Jaconde three-quarters up the side of the mould. Place a small disc of dacquoise on the base.

3 Soak the leaf gelatine in cold water to soften and bloom.

4 Place the strawberry purée, stock syrup and lemon juice into a saucepan and warm through to approximately 60°C.

5 Add the gelatine and pass through a fine chinois. Leave to begin to set.

6 Whisk the cream to soft peaks and when the strawberry purée has a similar consistency to the whipped cream fold the two components together.

7 Pour a little of the Bavarois into the base and up the sides of the mould. Position a frozen strawberry cylinder inside the so that the Bavarois mixture encases it.

8 Finish by filling the Bavarois to the top of the mould. Set in a refrigerator.

9 To serve, create the glaze by softening the gelatine in water and heating the stock syrup and strawberry purée. Add the gelatine to strawberry syrup and mix in well. Pass through a fine chinois and cool to 30°C.

10 Spread on top of each of the bavarois and set before removing from the moulds.

11 Serve with an appropriate decoration and accompaniment.

Individual raspberry Charlotte Russe

Ingredients	4 portions	10 portions
Raspberry purée	125 g	250 g
Lemon juice	15 g	25g
Stock syrup	125 g	250 g
Gelatine	3 leaves	6½ leaves
Whipping cream	250 g	500 g
Biscuit à la Cuillère mix		
Egg yolks	5	10
Caster sugar	120 g	240 g
Egg whites	4	8
Soft flour, sieved	120 g	240 g
Dacquoise disc	4 small discs	10 small discs

energy	cal	fat	sat fat	carb	sugar	protein	fibre
2925 kJ	697 kcal	34.3 g	17.5 g	88.4 g	65.8 g	12.9 g	2.1 g

METHOD OF WORK

1 Preheat an oven to 220°C.

2 To prepare the biscuits à la Cuillère place the egg yolks and two-thirds of the caster sugar in a stainless steel bowl and whisk until pale and creamy.

3 Whisk the egg whites with the remaining caster sugar until stiff.

4 Fold in a quarter of the meringue mixture to the yolk mixture.

5 Gently fold in the sieved flour, followed by the remaining meringue. Prepare two baking sheets with silicone paper.

6 Place three-quarters of the mixture into a piping bag with a 1 cm plain tube and pipe diagonal fingers of the mixture approximately 9 cm long next to each other so that when they are baked they will join together to create a collar to wrap inside each charlotte mould.

7 The final quarter of the mixture should now be added to a piping bag with a 1 cm tube. On a separate baking sheet lined with silicone paper, stencil the amount of discs that are required to the size of the charlotte mould used. Pipe the mixture decoratively into these stencils by piping a small bulb of mixture from the perimeter of the disc and pulling it toward the centre. Repeat this pattern to create a small flower design.

8 Dust the tops of the Biscuits à la Cuillère with icing sugar and bake in the preheated oven for approximately ten minutes.

9 When baked, remove from the paper and allow to cool on a wire rack.

10 Prepare the individual charlotte moulds by lining the inside with a measured strip of the biscuit à la cuillère, to the top of the mould.Place a small disc of dacquoise on the base.

11 Soak the leaf gelatine in cold water to soften and bloom.

12 Place the raspberry purée, stock syrup and lemon juice into a saucepan and warm through to approximately 60°C.

13 Add the gelatine and pass through a fine chinois. Leave to begin to set.

14 Whisk the cream to soft peaks and when the raspberry purée has a similar consistency to the whipped cream fold the two components together.

15 Pour the Bavarois into the mould.

16 Finish by carefully positioning the disc of biscuit à la cuillère on top of the mould. Set in a refrigerator.

17 To serve, remove the Charlotte from the mould and decorate with some berries on top, dusted with a little icing sugar.

Riz à l'Impératrice

Ingredients	4 portions	10 portions
Raspberry jelly	200 ml	400 ml
Fresh milk (1)	250 ml	500 ml
Vanilla extract	To taste	To taste
Caster sugar (1)	40 g	75 g
Short grain rice	40 g	80 g
Egg yolks (1)	1	2
Butter	10 g	25 g
Whipping cream	75 ml	150 ml
Crystallized fruits	40 g	75 g
Fresh milk (2)	125 ml	250 ml
Egg yolks (2)	1	3
Caster sugar (2)	30 g	75 g
Leaf gelatine	2 leaves	4 leaves
Crème Chantilly	100 g	200 g

energy	cal	fat	sat fat	carb	sugar	protein	fibre
2142 kJ	510 kcal	23.5 g	13.8 g	71.5 g	65.8 g	6.5 g	1 g

METHOD OF WORK

1 Place the milk in a saucepan and add the vanilla and sugar. Bring to the boil.

2 Rain in the washed rice, stir constantly until it reboils, cover with a lid and cook slowly in the oven at 175°C for approximately one hour until the rice is tender. Stir occasionally.

3 Remove the rice from the oven, add the yolks and butter and mix in well. Allow to cool and fold in the crystallized fruits that have been cut into small dice.

4 Place the second quantity of milk into a saucepan with some vanilla extract and warm on a low heat.

5 Mix together the second quantities of egg yolks and caster sugar, add the milk slowly, stirring in well. Return the mixture to the pan and cook out gently, stirring with a wooden spoon until the mixture thickens and coats the back of the spoon.

6 Soak the gelatine in cold water to soften and bloom. Add to the hot custard and stir until the gelatine has dissolved. Pass through a fine chinois into a chilled bowl and cool down.

7 Place the cream into a basin and whip to soft peaks. Fold into the cold custard upon setting point.

8 Add the custard mixture to the prepared rice and mix in thoroughly, but gently.

9 Pour the rice mixture into glasses and place into the refrigerator to set.

10 Melt the jelly and carefully pour on top to cover each rice dish. Set in a refrigerator.

11 To serve, pipe the crème Chantilly on top and decorate accordingly.

Bavarois rubané
(ribboned Bavarois)

Ribboned Bavarois with chocolate, vanilla and pistachio layers.

Ingredients	4 portions	10 portions
Bavarois base		
Fresh milk	400 ml	1 l
Egg yolks	3	8
Caster sugar	75 g	200 g
Leaf gelatine	6	14 leaves
Whipped cream	300 ml	800 ml
Additional flavours		
Split vanilla pod	1 pod	3 pods
Dark chocolate (70% cocoa)	40 g	90 g
Pistachio paste	to taste	to taste

energy	cal	fat	sat fat	carb	sugar	protein	fibre
2118 kJ	509 kcal	39.7 g	20.6 g	30 g	26.7 g	10 g	0 g

The ribboned Bavarois can consist of any number of colours and flavours, however pink or red (strawberry or raspberry), white (vanilla) and chocolate are the usual flavour combinations. On this occasion, we have combined chocolate, vanilla and pistachio.

METHOD OF WORK

1   Soak the gelatine leaves in cold water for approximately ten minutes to soften, then drain and squeeze to remove excess water.

2   Bring the milk to the boil and mix together the egg yolks and caster sugar.

3   When the milk has boiled, removed from the heat and mix carefully with the egg yolks and sugar mixture. Pour into the saucepan and return to the stove, stirring constantly while heating the mixture to 83°C or until it has cooked and coats the back of a wooden spoon. The mixture should not be allowed to boil.

4   Add the softened gelatine and stir in until dissolved.

5   Strain through a sieve or chinois and divide the mixture into equal portions in three separate bowls. Allow to cool, stirring occasionally.

6   Flavour each bowl with the required flavouring. Add the vanilla to the first by scraping the seeds out into the mixture. For the second, ensure that the chocolate has melted fully and add to the slightly warm egg mixture before it has completely cooled. For the third bowl add the pistachio paste until you are satisfied that the flavour and colour are correct.

7   When the vanilla mixture is cold, fold in a third of the whipped cream and pour into the selected moulds that you are using for the dessert. Allow to almost set in a refrigerator and then repeat the process with the chocolate mixture. Allow this to almost set also and then repeat this process once more for the pistachio mixture.

8   Allow to completely set in a refrigerator and remove from the mould when ready for service. Decorate as required with some crème Chantilly.

Blackberry and raspberry gratin

Ingredients	6 portions	12 portions
Grand Marnier or Kirsch	50 ml	100 ml
Blackberries	110 g	220 g
Raspberries	110 g	220 g
Caster Sugar	50 g	100 g
Dacquoise (cut into 1 cm cubes)	300 g	600 g
Crème Chibouste	250 g	500 g
Icing sugar	40 g	90 g

energy	cal	fat	sat fat	carb	sugar	protein	fibre
868 kJ	205 kcal	3.6 g	1.3 g	37.5 g	30.2 g	3.5 g	1.1 g

METHOD OF WORK

1 Macerate the Grand Marnier or Kirsch with the berries and caster sugar for one hour.

2 Place the Dacquoise cubes in the base of the dishes and then equally distribute the macerated fruits over.

3 Spoon over the fruit the crème Chibouste and dust with icing sugar.

4 Place into a preheated oven at 240°C for three minutes before finishing under a hot salamander to glaze the top.

5 Serve warm.

Cappuccino crème brûlée

Ingredients	4 brûlée	8 brûlée
Double cream	350 ml	700 ml
UHT milk	125 ml	250 ml
Strong espresso coffee	50 ml	100 ml
Tia Maria	2 tbsp	4 tbsp
Large egg yolks	6	12
Caster sugar	75 g	150 g
Demerara sugar	50 g	100 g
Vanilla foam		
Fresh full fat milk	120 ml	240 ml
Icing sugar	10 g	20 g
Vanilla	½ pod	1 pod
Powdered albumin	2 g	4 g

energy	cal	fat	sat fat	carb	sugar	protein	fibre
2994 kJ	721 kcal	56.5 g	32.5 g	42.2 g	42.2 g	8 g	0 g

METHOD OF WORK

1 Preheat an oven to 140°C.

2 Place the cream and milk into a heavy-based saucepan and bring to the boil. Add the espresso coffee and Tia Maria.

3 Beat together the egg yolks and sugar until pale. Pour the boiled mixture onto the egg yolks and mix well.

4 Pass the liquid through a fine chinois and pour into prepared coffee cups. Place the cups in a bain-marie and bake in the preheated oven for approximately 50 minutes or until the brûlée is set. To test, the brûlée should be slightly wobbly and springy to the touch and the core temperature should read at least 80°C.

5 Remove from the oven and cool in a refrigerator.

6 To serve, sprinkle the Demerara sugar on top and caramelize with a blowtorch.

7 For the foam, place the milk, sugar, vanilla seeds scraped from the pod and the dried albumin into a bowl. Using a hand blender, froth the milk quickly and spoon onto the top of the brûlée, dust with cocoa powder and pipe a little cappuccino milk design on top and serve immediately.

 **VIDEO CLIP** Brûlée

Pistachio and white chocolate dome

Ingredients	4 portions	10 portions
Bavarois base		
Fresh milk	400 ml	1 l
Egg yolks	3	8
Caster sugar	75 g	200 g
White chocolate	60 g	120 g
Pistachio paste	To taste	To taste
Leaf gelatine	6	14 leaves
Whipped cream	300 ml	800 ml
Additional elements		
Dacquoise disc	4 discs	10 discs
Lemon cream	60 g	120 g
Glaze		
Stock syrup	120 ml	240 ml
Gelatine	2½ leaves	5 leaves

energy	cal	fat	sat fat	carb	sugar	protein	fibre
3059 kJ	731 kcal	43.4 g	23.9 g	76.8 g	75.6 g	13.4 g	0.5 g

METHOD OF WORK

1   Soak the gelatine leaves in cold water for approximately ten minutes to soften, then drain and squeeze to remove excess water.

2   Bring the milk to the boil and mix together the egg yolks and caster sugar.

3   When the milk has boiled, remove from the heat and mix carefully with the egg yolks and sugar mixture. Pour into the saucepan and return to the stove, stirring constantly while heating the mixture to 83°C or until it has cooked and coats the back of a wooden spoon. The mixture should not be allowed to boil.

4   Add the softened gelatine and stir in until dissolved. Add the melted white chocolate.

5   Strain through a sieve or chinois and add the pistachio paste. Allow to cool, stirring occasionally.

6   Fold in the whipped cream and pour two-thirds into the selected dome moulds that you are using for the dessert. Allow to almost set in a refrigerator and then pipe a little lemon cream into the centre, repeat the process with the remaining bavarois mix and fill to 3 mm from the top.

7   Place a disc of the Dacquoise on the base and press in slightly. Allow this to set in a refrigerator.

8   To make the glaze bring the syrup to the boil and soften the gelatine. Squeeze the water from the gelatine and dissolve in the heated syrup. Allow to cool to 30°C.

9   To serve, remove the Bavarois from the mould and place onto a wire rack. Pour over the glaze and place back in a refrigerator to set. Decorate with the chocolate motifs.

Petit chocolate délice cake and caramelized hazelnuts

Ingredients	24 individual cakes
Base	
Toasted hazelnuts	100 g
Caster sugar	100 g
Good quality milk chocolate	150 g
Délice	
Full-fat milk	140 ml
Double cream	325 ml
Eggs	2
Good-quality dark chocolate, minimum 60 per cent cocoa solids	340 g
Caramel hazelnuts	
Caster sugar	225 g
Hazelnuts, shells removed, lightly toasted in a dry frying pan	80 g
To serve	
Cocoa powder	8 tbsp
Chocolate motifs	
Chocolate glaze	

energy	cal	fat	sat fat	carb	sugar	protein	fibre
1301 kJ	313 kcal	22.7 g	6 g	22.4 g	15 g	5.7 g	2.4 g

METHOD OF WORK

1   For the base, cook the hazelnuts and sugar in a pan until caramelization begins. Turn onto a baking tray lined with baking paper and leave to cool. Roughly blend in a food processor and slowly add the melted milk chocolate. Mix to a paste in a mixing bowl.

2   Line a baking tray with a sheet of greaseproof paper, then transfer the praline mixture onto it. Cover the chocolate-praline mixture with a second sheet of greaseproof paper, and then roll the mixture out until it measures at least 14 cm × 20 cm/5½ in × 8 in and is 0.5 cm/¼ in thick.

3   Remove the top sheet of greaseproof paper, then cut individual discs out to create the base of the dessert.

4   Meanwhile, for the délice, heat the milk and cream in a saucepan and heat gently over a medium heat until it just reaches boiling point.

5   Whisk the eggs in a bowl.

6   As the milk and cream mixture comes to the boil, pour it over the eggs, and then whisk the mixture constantly until smooth and thick.

7   Stir in the chopped chocolate and whisk again until the chocolate has melted and the custard is smooth.

8   Pour in the chocolate délice mix to almost fill each dome mould. Gently tap the sides of the mould to release any trapped air bubbles, then smooth the surface using a palette knife. Place the discs on top. Chill in the fridge for six hours, or until completely set.

9   Meanwhile, for the caramel hazelnuts, heat the caster sugar in a pan over a low heat, stirring occasionally until golden-brown and caramelized. Remove from the heat and set aside to cool slightly. (NB: The caramel is cool enough when a cocktail stick dragged across its surface leaves an imprinted trail.)

10   Spear each hazelnut onto a cocktail stick, and then dip the hazelnuts into the caramel until coated. Leave to cool and set on some silicone paper and store in an airtight container for service.

11   To serve, warm the outside of the mould to loosen the délice and turn out.

12   Heat the top of the délice very quickly using a chefs' blow torch to make the surface glossy. Dust the délice finely with the cocoa powder.

13   Drop a teaspoonful of the chocolate glaze over the dessert and decorate with the caramelized hazelnuts and chocolate motifs.

Garnishes and decorations

Piped chocolate in sugar

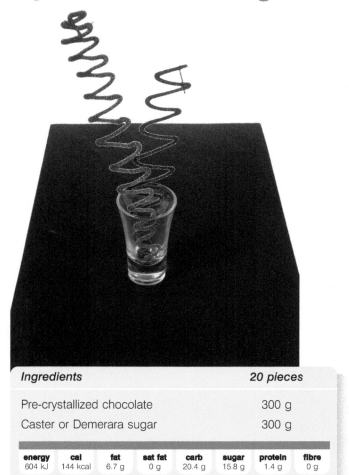

Ingredients	20 pieces
Pre-crystallized chocolate	300 g
Caster or Demerara sugar	300 g

energy	cal	fat	sat fat	carb	sugar	protein	fibre
604 kJ	144 kcal	6.7 g	0 g	20.4 g	15.8 g	1.4 g	0 g

METHOD OF WORK

1 Evenly spread the sugar onto a tray.
2 Using a small piping bag, pipe the chocolate into your required design onto the sugar.
3 Leave to harden before removing and using as a decoration.

Hazelnut sugar spike

Ingredients	makes 8
Caster sugar	125 g
Hazelnuts, shells removed, lightly toasted in a dry frying pan	8

energy	cal	fat	sat fat	carb	sugar	protein	fibre
1287 kJ	307 kcal	16.7 g	1.3 g	34.9 g	34.1 g	6.3 g	2.2 g

METHOD OF WORK

1 Heat the caster sugar in a pan over a low heat, stirring occasionally until golden-brown and caramelized. Remove from the heat and set aside to cool slightly. (Note: The caramel is cool enough when a cocktail stick dragged across its surface leaves an imprinted trail.)
2 Spear each hazelnut onto a cocktail stick, and then dip the hazelnuts into the caramel until coated. Stick a little adhesive putty onto the underside of a shelf or cupboard above a work surface and secure the cocktail stick into the putty, so that the caramel drips off the hazelnut and creates a tail. (Note: Place a baking tray or sheets of greaseproof paper underneath the hazelnuts to catch any caramel that drips.)
3 Set the caramel hazelnuts aside to cool and harden for at least 30 minutes.

Iced Madagascan chocolate parfait

Ingredients	4 portions	8 portions
Egg yolks	25 g	50 g
Caster sugar	30 g	60 g
Fresh full fat milk	45 g	90 g
Madagascan dark chocolate (66%)	65 g	130 g
Whipping cream	75 g	150 g
Caramelized hazelnuts		
Hazelnuts (toasted, skins removed and halved)	55 g	110 g
Demerara sugar	15 g	30g
Good-quality salt	to taste	to taste
Warm water	a little	a little
Caramel salt and spice sauce		
Caster sugar	75 g	150 g
Liquid glucose	45 g	90 g
Double cream	350 g	700 g
Fleur de sel	2 g	4 g
Vanilla	1 pods	3 pods
Star anise	2	4
Cinnamon stick	½	1
Cardamom seeds	1 g	3 g
Decorative items		
Thin chocolate discs	4	8
Piped chocolate sticks	4	8
Vanilla ice cream	4 quenelles	8 quenelles
Decorative chocolate	4	8

energy	cal	fat	sat fat	carb	sugar	protein	fibre
4530 kJ	1092 kcal	88.2 g	35.4 g	65.9 g	40.1 g	11.4 g	1 g

METHOD OF WORK

1 To prepare the chocolate parfait, place the milk into a heavy-based saucepan and bring to the boil. Meanwhile, beat together the egg yolks and sugar.

2 Pour the milk onto the egg yolks and mix well then return to the saucepan. Stirring constantly, cook the egg mixture to 85°C.

3 Melt the Madagascan chocolate and combine with the cooked out egg custard. Cool to 30°C in a refrigerator.

4 Carefully whisk the cream to aerate it to a ribbon stage. Gently fold in the cream to the chocolate mixture. Transfer the parfait mixture into individual moulds (preferably flexible silicone moulds so it is easier to remove the frozen parfait) and freeze.

5 To make the caramelized hazelnuts, preheat an oven to 120°C. Toss the hazelnuts in a shallow pan with just enough warm water to make the nuts slightly sticky. Add the sugar and salt to taste and bring to the boil ensuring that the sugar coats the nuts. Turn the nuts out onto a baking sheet lined with silicone paper then place in the oven and bake for 30 minutes. Remove from the oven and cool. The hazelnuts should be totally dry and crunchy after cooling. If not, return to the oven and bake longer. Store tightly covered in an airtight plastic container ready for service.

6 To make the caramel salt and spice sauce, infuse the fleur de sel, split vanilla pods, star anise, cinnamon and cardamom seeds in the cream for at least two hours, covered in a refrigerator.

7 Place the sugar in a heavy-based saucepan and heat. When the sugar begins to melt add the glucose. Continue cooking until a caramel has been reached. Deglaze the caramel with the infused cream and spices.

8 Bring back to the boil, pass through a fine chinois and cool.

9 To serve, turn out the frozen chocolate parfait onto the prepared chocolate disc and position it onto the serving plate. Deposit some of the caramelized hazelnuts in the centre of the chocolate parfait and around the plate. Spoon the caramel sauce onto the plate and finish with the quenelle of vanilla ice cream and chocolate decorations.

CHEF'S TIP Madagascan chocolate is generally renowned for its fruity character and dark bitter flavour, so it is an ideal single-origin chocolate to use for this recipe. However, it can be replaced by alternative dark chocolates, but they will need to have a strong, bitter flavour.

Iced parfait of strawberries

Iced parfait of strawberries, lavender ice cream, champagne granite and strawberry salad

Ingredients	4 portions	8 portions
Strawberry parfait		
Caster sugar	150 g	300 g
Glucose	15 g	30 g
Strawberry purée	3 tbsp	5 tbsp
Egg whites	3	6
Egg yolks	3	6
Caster sugar	75 g	150 g
Strawberry purée	125 g	250 g
Whipped cream	175 ml	350 ml
Dacquoise biscuit	4 small discs	8 small discs
Lavender ice cream		
Lavender flowers or seeds (edible)	1 tsp	2 tsp
Caster sugar	60 g	120 g
Fresh full fat milk	230 ml	460 ml
Egg yolks	3	6
Double cream	50 ml	100 ml
Strawberry champagne salad		
Washed and hulled strawberries	125 g	250 g
Champagne	75 g	150 g
Champagne Granite		
Stock syrup	50 g	90 g
Champagne	200 g	350 g

energy	cal	fat	sat fat	carb	sugar	protein	fibre
3438 kJ	820 kcal	36.9 g	18.9 g	104.5 g	102.3 g	11.8 g	1.9 g

METHOD OF WORK

1   To prepare the strawberry parfait, create an Italian meringue with the larger quantity of caster sugar, glucose, smaller quantity of the strawberry purée and the egg whites, cooking to 118°C (soft ball stage).

2   Over a bain-marie at approximately 90°C, whisk the egg yolks and smaller quantity of sugar. Slowly add the larger quantity of strawberry purée and cook out. Remove from the heat and carry on whisking to cool and aerate the mixture. When cool fold in the whipped cream and then the meringue.

3   Prepare individual ring moulds with a small disc of Dacquoise in the base. Pour the parfait into the moulds and freeze.

4   To prepare the lavender ice cream, grind the lavender into the sugar and beat with the egg yolks.

5   Bring the milk and cream to the boil. Pour the boiled milk onto the egg yolk mixture, stir well and return to the saucepan. Cook out to 85°C, stirring constantly.

6   Pass through a fine chinois and cool over a bain-marie of iced water. Churn in an ice cream machine.

7   For the champagne granite; combine the champagne and stock syrup. Pour into a shallow dish and place in a freezer to freeze for at least one hour. Every five minutes mix with a fork to encourage the growth of large ice crystals.

8   For the champagne strawberry salad, cut the strawberries into brunoise and carefully combine them with the Champagne at the last moment. Leave to one side for service.

9   To serve, create some red coloured 'bubble' sugar for decoration. Present the de-moulded parfait in the centre of the plate with a quenelle of the lavender ice cream on top. Spoon the **compôte** around the plate with some of the granite and place the bubble sugar on top of the overall dessert.

Almond, rum and prune ice cream

Ingredients	4 portions	8 portions
Fresh full fat milk	570 ml	1140 ml
Double cream	160 g	320 g
Milk powder	40 g	75 g
Softened marzipan	50 g	100 g
Caster sugar	80 g	160 g
Glucose	40 g	80 g
Egg yolks	3	6
Rum	25 ml	50 ml
Prunes, de-stoned	50 g	100 g

energy	cal	fat	sat fat	carb	sugar	protein	fibre
2335 kJ	561 kcal	32.8 g	18.2 g	52.8 g	48.4 g	11.9 g	0.5 g

METHOD OF WORK

1 Steep the prunes in the dark rum for at least two days before making this ice cream, sealed in an airtight jar.

2 Place the milk, cream, milk powder and softened marzipan into a saucepan and slowly heat. At 45°C, add the liquid glucose and bring to the boil.

3 Beat the sugar and egg yolks together and pour the boiled milk onto the yolks. Return to the pan and cook the mixture, continuously stirring until 85°C has been reached. Pass through a fine chinois into a bowl.

4 Chill quickly over a bain-marie of iced water. Add the rum and chopped prunes, churn in an ice cream machine.

CHEF'S TIP Ice cream quickly absorbs the flavours of other ingredients stored alongside it. Ensure that a plastic container with a good seal is used for storage. Once ice cream has been made and frozen it is best to use it within a week.

Yoghurt and mascarpone ice cream

Ingredients	4 portions	8 portions
Caster sugar	125 g	250 g
Water	80 ml	160 ml
Mascarpone	100 g	200 g
Fresh full fat milk	85 ml	175 ml
Natural yoghurt	50 g	100 g
Glucose	20 g	40 g
Ice cream stabilizer	3 g	5 g

energy	cal	fat	sat fat	carb	sugar	protein	fibre
1167 kJ	278 kcal	13.1 g	8.7 g	39.5 g	37.2 g	2.9 g	0 g

METHOD OF WORK

1 Place the sugar and water in a heavy-based saucepan over medium heat. Use a clean and wet pastry brush to remove any sugar clinging to the sides of a pan.

2 Bring the syrup to the boil, skim off any foam and simmer briskly for seven minutes. Do not allow to colour. Immediately remove from the heat and pour into a stainless steel bowl to cool.

3 When the syrup is completely cold, combine it with the remaining ingredients.

4 Pour the mixture into an ice cream maker and process according to the manufacturer's instructions to freeze into an ice cream.

Sous vide vanilla ice cream

Ingredients	4 portions	8 portions
Ice cream		
Caster sugar	90 g	180 g
Egg yolks	5	10
Vanilla pods	1	2
Fresh full fat milk	240 g	480 g
Double cream	240 g	480 g
Skimmed milk powder	35 g	75 g
Syrup base	110 g	220 g
Granulated sugar	350 g	700 g
Egg whites	4 g	8 g
Water	500 ml	1 l
Liquid glucose	100 g	200 g

energy	cal	fat	sat fat	carb	sugar	protein	fibre
2598 kJ	624 kcal	41.2 g	23.4 g	56.8 g	54.3 g	9.5 g	0 g

METHOD OF WORK

Syrup base

1 Heat 690 g sugar with water and bring to the boil. Add the liquid glucose and bring back to the boil.
2 Whisk egg whites and the remaining sugar together.
3 Add the egg whites to the boiling syrup, leave for 30 seconds before removing from the heat and cooling. This will **clarify** the syrup base and a foamy scum will appear on the top of the syrup. Skim the top and place in a sealed, clean plastic container for further use.

Ice cream

1 Whisk the egg yolks and the sugar together until pale and creamy.
2 Boil the cream, milk, skimmed milk powder and vanilla pods in a heavy based saucepan, then pour over the egg yolks then add the sweet base syrup. Mix well for one minute using a whisk.
3 Put the contents into a sous vide cooking bag, carefully seal and place into the preset water bath at 84°C for 20 minutes.
4 Remove from the water bath.
5 Leave for five minutes in iced water then leave in a refrigerator for 24 hours before churning in an ice cream machine.

Honeycomb ice cream

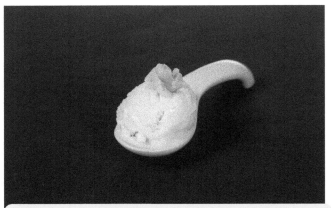

Ingredients	4 portions	8 portions
Ice cream		
Caster sugar	90 g	180 g
Egg yolks	5	10
Vanilla pods	1	2
Fresh full fat milk	240 g	480 g
Double cream	240 g	480 g
Skimmed milk powder	35 g	75 g
Syrup base	110 g	220 g
Granulated sugar	350 g	700 g
Egg whites	4 g	8 g
Water	500 ml	1 l
Liquid glucose	100 g	200 g
Honeycomb pieces	60 g	120 g

energy	cal	fat	sat fat	carb	sugar	protein	fibre
2619 kJ	630 kcal	46.3 g	26 g	45.9 g	45.6 g	9.6 g	0 g

METHOD OF WORK

Syrup base

1 Heat 690 g sugar with water and bring to the boil. Add the liquid glucose and bring back to the boil.

2 Whisk egg whites and the remaining sugar together.

3 Add the egg whites to the boiling syrup, leave for 30 seconds before removing from the heat and cooling. This will clarify the syrup base and a foamy scum will appear on the top of the syrup. Skim the top and place in a sealed, clean plastic container for further use.

Ice cream

1 Whisk the egg yolks and the sugar together until pale and creamy.

2 Boil the cream, milk, skimmed milk powder and vanilla pods in a heavy based saucepan, then pour over the egg yolks then add the sweet base syrup. Mix well for one minute using a whisk.

3 Put the contents into a sous vide cooking bag with half of the quantity of honeycomb pieces, carefully seal and place into the preset water bath at 84°C for 20 minutes.

4 Remove from the water bath.

5 Leave for five minutes in iced water then leave in a refrigerator for 24 hours before churning in an ice cream machine with the remaining honeycomb pieces.

Olive oil ice cream (using a Pacojet)

Ingredients	4 portions	8 portions
Fresh full fat milk	150 g	300 g
Double cream	65 g	125 g
Caster sugar	65 g	125 g
Leaf gelatine	½ leaf	1 leaf
Egg yolks	1	3
Cornflour	3 g	5 g
Extra virgin olive oil	55 g	110 g
Salt	½ g	1 g

energy	cal	fat	sat fat	carb	sugar	protein	fibre
1288 kJ	310 kcal	25.2 g	8.7 g	19.7 g	19 g	2.3 g	0 g

METHOD OF WORK

1   Bring the milk, cream and half of the sugar to the boil in a heavy based sauce over a medium heat.

2   Soften the gelatine in cold water and add to the boiled milk and cream mixture, whisking constantly.

3   Remove from the heat and pass through a fine chinois.

4   In a stainless steel bowl, whisk together the egg yolk, remaining sugar and the cornflour until light and double in volume.

5   Combine the strained milk with the yolk mixture into another saucepan and slowly bring to the boil, stirring constantly. Cook the mix until it slightly thickens.

6   Strain, once again, into a bowl and whisk in the olive oil. Season with salt and leave to mature for four hours in a refrigerator.

7   Pour the mixture into a Pacojet canister and freeze for another four hours.

8   Process the ice cream in the Pacojet for one full cycle and serve.

CHEF'S TIP   This recipe can be made using a normal ice cream machine. At point 7, simply pour the prepared ice cream mix into an ice cream machine instead.

CHEF'S TIP   What is a Pacojet? Pacojet is a professional kitchen appliance that makes it easy to prepare high-quality dishes while saving time, labour and reducing food waste. Chefs worldwide use the Pacojet to produce mousses, sauces, sorbets and ice creams. The high-precision Pacojet blade spins at 2000 rpm, shaving a micro-thin layer off the top of the frozen food, resulting in an ultra-smooth texture. Unused beaker contents remain frozen solid to be used later at your convenience.

Praline iced soufflé
(soufflé glacé au praline)

Ingredients	4 portions	10 portions
Water	50 ml	80 ml
Granulated sugar	80 g	170 g
Egg yolks	4	8
Egg whites	3	5
Whipped cream	190 ml	500 ml
Praline (crushed)	55 g	120 g

energy	cal	fat	sat fat	carb	sugar	protein	fibre
1681 kJ	403 kcal	27.6 g	13.5 g	33.7 g	33.1 g	7.2 g	0.6 g

METHOD OF WORK

1. Prepare the moulds (usually ramekin dishes 8 cm in diameter) with strips of acetate or silicone paper that have been measured to sit approximately 3 cm higher than the rim of the mould that has been used. If using silicone paper, this may need to be folded twice to produce a structure strong enough to hold the mixture. Place the acetate or paper around the outside of the mould so that there are no gaps between it and the mould. To hold the collar firmly in place secure with a strip of adhesive tape.

2. To prepare the pâte à bombe base for this recipe mix and bring the granulated sugar and the water slowly to the boil. Using a sugar thermometer as a guide cook the sugar solution to 121°C.

3. Carefully pour the hot sugar syrup onto the egg yolks while whisking continuously to aerate the mixture. Once all of the sugar has been added, keep whisking until it has cooled down and the mixture stands in soft peaks.

4. Aerate the egg whites in a separate bowl to create stiff peaks and ensure that the whipped cream is also correctly aerated ready for combining the preparations.

5. Fold in the whipped cream and the crushed praline to the pâte à bombe preparation.

6. Carefully fold in the aerated egg whites in two incorporation stages.

7. Fill the moulds to the top by piping the mixture into the moulds. Smooth the top with a small palate knife and place each filled mould onto a baking tray to place into a freezer.

8. The freezing process takes approximately five hours, depending on the inside temperature of the freezer being used.

9. Remove the acetate or paper band carefully from the iced soufflé. The soufflé is usually kept in the mould (although it can be de-moulded and presented alternatively) and decorated with crème Chantilly, according to the style of the chef and a main ingredient used to flavour the dessert.

CHEF'S TIP When the iced soufflé is frozen, just before service scoop out some of the centre and fill the central well with fresh strawberries. These can be lightly sauced with a little strawberry coulis and decorated with whipped cream. This classical dish is called soufflé Glacé Hericart.

Fromage frais sorbet

Ingredients	4 portions	8 portions
Fromage frais	200 g	400 g
Lemon juice	18 g	36 g
Sorbet syrup	175 g	350 g
Sorbet syrup		
Water	2.1 l	
Granulated sugar	2.25 kg	
Glucose	270 g	

energy	cal	fat	sat fat	carb	sugar	protein	fibre
2625 kJ	617 kcal	4 g	2.8 g	151.6 g	120.1 g	3.1 g	0 g

METHOD OF WORK

1 To make the sorbet syrup, place the water, sugar and glucose in a saucepan and bring to the boil. Simmer for two minutes and strain into a sterilized plastic container. Leave to cool and refrigerate for use.

2 Place the fromage frais, sorbet syrup and lemon juice together in a bowl and mix well together.

3 Pass through a fine chinois and churn in an ice cream machine.

CHEF'S TIP Use this sorbet syrup recipe as the base for all fruit sorbets. Use at a ratio of 1 kg fruit purée to 550 g sorbet syrup.

Apple and basil sorbet

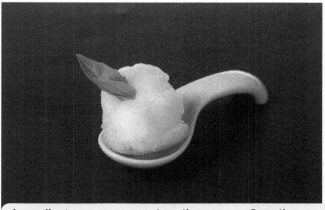

Ingredients	4 portions	8 portions
Green apple (such as Granny Smith)	140 g	280 g
Lemon juice	90 g	190 g
Caster sugar	110 g	225 g
Fresh basil leaves	5 g	10 g
Water	140 g	280 g
Milk powder	7 g	14 g

energy	cal	fat	sat fat	carb	sugar	protein	fibre
563 kJ	132 kcal	0.1 g	0 g	34.1 g	34.1 g	0.8 g	0.7 g

METHOD OF WORK

1 Working quickly cut the apples into pieces and place into a deep freezer (to prevent them turning brown).

2 Combine the water, sugar and milk powder together in a saucepan. Place on a medium heat and bring to the boil.

3 Pass the syrup through a fine chinois and chill to 4°C.

4 Chop the fresh basil and mix with the lemon juice.

5 Place the syrup and frozen apples into a blender and purée. Pass through a fine chinois then add the basil and lemon juice.

6 Place the mixture into an ice cream machine to freeze.

CHEF'S TIP It is important that the apples are frozen as quickly as possible to prevent discolouration. The citric acid found in lemon juice will also help to retain the natural colour of the apple. Always use the green skin of the apple to help with the flavour and colour of the sorbet.

Chocolate sorbet

Ingredients	4 portions	8 portions
Whipping cream	250 g	500 g
Fresh milk	500 ml	1 l
Caster sugar	50 g	100 g
Cocoa powder	100 g	200 g
Dark chocolate (70%)	15 g	30 g

energy	cal	fat	sat fat	carb	sugar	protein	fibre
1829 kJ	439 kcal	33.8 g	19.9 g	25 g	20.9 g	10.6 g	7 g

METHOD OF WORK

1 Combine the cream and milk in a saucepan and place on a medium heat.

2 Add the sugar and cocoa powder. Stir in well and bring the liquid to the boil.

3 Remove from the heat and stir in the chopped chocolate. Pass through a fine chinois and leave to cool then freeze in an ice cream machine.

Strawberry sorbet

Ingredients	4 portions	8 portions
Ripe strawberries	140 g	280 g
Lemon juice	10 g	20 g
Caster sugar	110 g	225 g
Leaf gelatine	½ leaf	1 leaf
Water	140 g	280 g
Liquid glucose	7 g	14 g

energy	cal	fat	sat fat	carb	sugar	protein	fibre
527 kJ	124 kcal	0 g	0 g	32.5 g	31.7 g	0.4 g	0.4 g

METHOD OF WORK

1 Place the strawberries into a food blender with the lemon juice and process to a puree. Soften the gelatine in cold water.

2 Combine the water, sugar, glucose and liquid glucose together in a saucepan. Place on a medium heat and bring to the boil.

3 Pass the syrup through a fine chinois and chill to 4°C.

4 Place the syrup and strawberries into a blender again, and purée. Pass through a fine chinois.

5 Place the mixture into an ice cream machine to freeze.

Chocolate sauce

Ingredients	makes 1 kg	makes 2 kg
Water	710 ml	1425 ml
Caster sugar	400 g	800 g
Cocoa powder	60 g	110 g
Cornflour	20 g	40 g
Dark chocolate	125 g	250 g
Single cream	135 ml	275 ml

energy	cal	fat	sat fat	carb	sugar	protein	fibre
473 kJ	112 kcal	3.8 g	1 g	19.5 g	16.9 g	1.1 g	0.7 g

METHOD OF WORK

1   Bring the water to the boil with the caster sugar.

2   Mix together the cocoa powder and the cornflour. Add the boiled sugar solution and return to the pan to cook out the mixture.

3   Chop the dark chocolate into small pieces and add to the mixture.

4   Stir continuously to melt the chocolate into the liquid. Ensure that the chocolate does not burn on the base of the saucepan.

5   Add the single cream and adjust the consistency.

6   Strain through a fine chinois.

7   Use as required.

CHEF'S TIP   This sauce can be stored in bulk in a refrigerator in a covered container. A little at a time can be taken to use either hot or cold.

Fruit coulis

Ingredients	4 portions	10 portions
Fresh fruit (such as raspberries, strawberries or redcurrants)	800 g	1.7 kg
Stock syrup	200 ml	425 ml
Lemon juice (optional)	1 lemon	2 lemons

energy	cal	fat	sat fat	carb	sugar	protein	fibre
812 kJ	190 kcal	0.3 g	0.1 g	47.8 g	46.3 g	2.3 g	5.3 g

METHOD OF WORK

1   Carefully wash the fruit. Place into a food blender with the strained lemon juice and the stock syrup.

2   Purée the fruit mixture for approximately a minute until a smooth purée has been obtained.

3   Pass the purée through a fine chinois or muslin cloth and correct the consistency by adding more stock syrup or puréed raspberries.

4   The coulis is now ready for use, and will keep for three–four days in a refrigerator. Alternatively it can easily be frozen.

SOURCING   Many varieties of fresh fruit are available all year in almost every part of Europe, because of the excellent transportation and storage facilities. For the greatest nutritional value and flavour, however, choose fruits at the peak of their freshness.

Also, between 20 and 30 per cent of the global warming caused by human activity is caused by our food and agriculture systems. Buying more sustainable ingredients is not just the right thing to do ethically, it makes good business sense because more customers are demanding that sustainable and seasonal foods are used.

Muscat wine sabayon

Ingredients	4 portions	10 portions
Egg yolks	3	8
Caster sugar	70 g	170 g
Water	50 g	125 g
Muscat (sweet white wine)	75 g	200 g
Vanilla	½ pod	1 pod

energy	cal	fat	sat fat	carb	sugar	protein	fibre
538 kJ	128 kcal	3.9 g	1.1 g	19.4 g	18.4 g	2.1 g	0 g

METHOD OF WORK

1 Pour some water into a heavy-based saucepan large enough to hold a round-based mixing bowl on top. Heat the water on a stove to 45°C.

2 Combine the egg yolks, sugar, water, scraped seeds from the vanilla pod and Muscat wine in the mixing bowl. Place onto the saucepan of heated water on a low heat.

3 Whisk continuously using a balloon whisk for about 12 minutes. Ensure that the water temperature for the bain-marie does not exceed 90°C.

4 The mixture will aerate and a ribbon consistency should be obtained. The internal temperature of the sabayon should be 50°C with a smooth, aerated and light texture.

5 Use the sabayon while it is still warm. Serve as an accompaniment to a dessert such as a tart or as the main part of a dessert, in a wine glass with freshly picked strawberries and a biscuit à la cuillère.

CHEF'S TIP This sabayon can be served cold, but it would be best to stabilize the aeration by adding a leaf of softened gelatine. Alternative alcohols can be used to create different flavoured sabayons, such as Marsala and eaux de vie.

Coconut foam

Ingredients	6 portions	15 portions
Coconut milk (tinned)	250 ml	500 ml
Yoghurt	80 ml	175 ml
Whipping cream	30 ml	60 ml
Icing sugar	40 g	75 g
Desiccated coconut	30 g	60 g
Gelatine	1½ leaves	3 leaves

energy	cal	fat	sat fat	carb	sugar	protein	fibre
674 kJ	162 kcal	13.5 g	10.6 g	8.9 g	8.8 g	1.8 g	0.4 g

METHOD OF WORK

1 Soften the gelatine leaves in cold water.

2 Add the desiccated coconut to the coconut milk and bring to the boil in a saucepan. Reduce the liquid by half. Add the gelatine and melt into the hot coconut milk.

3 Mix together the reduced coconut with the yoghurt, cream and icing sugar.

4 Pass the mixture into an aeration canister. Chill in a refrigerator.

5 Charge the canister with two gas cartridges and use as required.

CHEF'S TIP The coconut elements can be replaced with a fruit purée and an alternative liquid, such as mint-flavoured syrup.

Chocolate foam

Ingredients	6 portions	15 portions
Dark chocolate – melted	150 g	300 g
Water	70 g	140 g
Syrup base (see sous vide vanilla ice cream recipe)	80 g	160 g
Gelatine leaf	1	2

energy	cal	fat	sat fat	carb	sugar	protein	fibre
784 kJ	188 kcal	11.2 g	0 g	19.9 g	10.9 g	2.6 g	0 g

METHOD OF WORK

1 Soften the gelatine leaves in cold water.
2 Warm the water and the base syrup together.
3 Add the melted chocolate and the gelatine. Mix together and pass through a fine chinois.
4 Pass the mixture into an aeration canister. Chill in a refrigerator for one hour.
5 Charge the canister with two gas cartridges and use as required.

Raspberry foam

Ingredients	6 portions	15 portions
Raspberries	250 g	500 g
Water	50 g	100 g
Syrup base (see sous vide vanilla ice cream recipe)	50 g	100 g
Gelatine leaf	1	2
Lemon juice	A few drops	A few drops

energy	cal	fat	sat fat	carb	sugar	protein	fibre
168 kJ	39 kcal	0.1 g	0 g	9.4 g	8.6 g	0.8 g	1 g

METHOD OF WORK

1 Soften the gelatine leaves in cold water. Warm the gelatine with a little of the water.
2 Puree in a food processor the raspberries, water, gelatine, syrup and lemon juice.
3 Pass through a fine chinois. Pass the mixture into an aeration canister. Chill in a refrigerator for one hour.
4 Charge the canister with two gas cartridges and use as required.

Caramel foam

Ingredients	4 portions	8 portions
Caster sugar	40 g	80 g
Water	1 tbsp	2 tbsp
Egg yolks	2 large	4 large
Double cream	180 ml	360 ml
Full fat milk	3 tbsp	4 tbsp
Gelatine	½ sheet, softened	1 sheet

energy	cal	fat	sat fat	carb	sugar	protein	fibre
1248 kJ	302 kcal	27.3 g	16.1 g	11.9 g	11.9 g	2.6 g	0 g

METHOD OF WORK

1 Combine the sugar and water in a small saucepan and cook, without stirring, over medium heat until the sugar has dissolved and the caramel turns a light golden brown.

2 Meanwhile, whisk the egg yolks together in a bowl. Heat the cream and milk together until hot.

3 Remove the caramel from the heat and whisk in the cream mixture. Whisk the mixture over low heat until any lumps of caramel have completely dissolved and the caramel is smooth.

4 Gradually whisk the caramel into the egg yolks, and return to the saucepan. Cook the sauce over low heat until it reaches 84°C. Remove from the heat and add the gelatine, whisking until it dissolves.

5 Strain through a fine-mesh sieve into a bowl and chill in an ice bath, then refrigerate until ready to use. Take the caramel foam out of the refrigerator and transfer it to a siphon and charge with gas for use.

Chocolate jelly

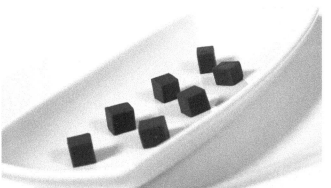

Ingredients	6 portions	15 portions
Milk or dark chocolate	135 g	275 g
Water	55 g	115 g
Gelatine leaf	1	2

energy	cal	fat	sat fat	carb	sugar	protein	fibre
532 kJ	128 kcal	10.1 g	0 g	7 g	0 g	2.4 g	0 g

METHOD OF WORK

1 Soften the gelatine leaves in cold water. Warm the gelatine with a little of the water.

2 Ensure the chocolate is either chopped into small pieces or is purchased in callets.

3 Bring the water to the boil, remove from the heat and melt the chocolate into the water. Add the softened gelatine and ensure that the mixture is smooth and completely melted.

4 Strain through a fine chinois and set into a rectangle mould and chill in a refrigerator.

5 Serve as required.

Sous vide poached Victoria plums

Ingredients

Plums, halved and stones removed	500 g
Unrefined caster sugar	100 g
Water	200 ml
Sprigs of lavender (optional)	6

energy	cal	fat	sat fat	carb	sugar	protein	fibre
614 kJ	144 kcal	0.1 g	0 g	37.3 g	37.3 g	0.8 g	2 g

METHOD OF WORK

1   Heat the water bath to 80°C.

2   Wash the plums, cut them in half and remove the stones.

3   Place all the ingredients in a vacuum bag and seal the pouch on medium vacuum.

4   Place the plums in the preheated water bath and cook for ten minutes.

5   Remove the fruit pouch and cool in ice water for 20 minutes.

6   Let the fruits infuse for one hour before use.

CHEF'S TIP   This recipe can be used for a variety of different fruits, although the cooking time may alter.

Guest Chef

Pain perdu, with soft fruits, olive oil and crème fraiche ice cream

Chef *John Crowe*

Centre *North West Regional College (Northern Ireland)*

In the past this recipe was a way of using up 'lost bread' (pain perdu), but has been updated by using a rich buttery brioche instead. The soft fruits warmed and infused with the basil provide a Mediterranean feel, enhanced by the nutty almond flavour of the olive oil in the ice cream. Many countries around the world have their version of this recipe and its can be traced back to Roman times.

Ingredients for 2 portions

Ingredient	Amount
Brioche	
Plain flour	562 g
Salt	11 g
Butter	395 g
Eggs	7
Milk	100 ml
Sugar	33 g
Yeast	16 g
Pain perdu	
Egg	1
Sugar	50 g
Millk, cream	100, 100 ml
Vanilla	¼ pod
Butter	50 g
Ice cream	
Milk	500 ml
Crème fraiche	250 g
Sugar	150 g
Eggs yolks	5
Olive oil	250 ml
Vanilla pod	½ pod
Fresh fruits	
Strawberries	50 g
Raspberries	50 g
Blackberries	50 g
Mango	1
Blackcurrants	50 g
Basil	3 leaves
Stock syrup	50 g

METHOD OF WORK

Brioche

1 Add yeast to milk with sugar, cover and set aside in a warm place. Next melt the butter and add to the flour, mix well. Then add egg, mix again and finally add the culture. Place in a bowl and allow to prove overnight. Weigh in 600 g batches, knead until smooth, place in greased loaf tins, cover and allow to prove again for approx. 50 minutes. Bake at 190°C with 40 per cent humidity for 30 minutes.

Ice cream

2 Infuse milk and vanilla. Combine egg yolks and sugar and whisk until thick and pale. Gradually add infused milk and vanilla onto egg yolks and sugar slowly and incorporate well. Once liquid has come to the boil again pass on to crème fraiche and olive oil, mix well. Then chill and churn. Store in a clean sealed container in freezer.

Fruit preparation

3 Wash and pat dry all berries and store in plastic container. Peel and dice ripe mango and reserve. Warm fruits in a small pan with a little stock syrup, add chiffonade of basil and allow to infuse. Be careful to only warm and not cook or stew fruits.

To cook

4 Slice the brioche and pass through beaten egg, milk and cream. Fry on both sides in a knob of unsalted butter until golden brown.

To finish

5 Place the fried brioche on the plate, heap the warmed fruits over and top with ice cream and serve.

ASSESSMENT OF KNOWLEDGE AND UNDERSTANDING

To test your level of knowledge and understanding, answer the following short questions. These will help to prepare you for your summative (final) assessment.

Quality identifications

1 Explain the importance of selecting the correct type, quality and quantity of ingredients when producing an ice cream.

2 State the quality points to look for when producing a crepe soufflé.

3 What are the main quality points to consider when purchasing cinnamon for use in a pastry kitchen.

Equipment and materials

1 State two advantages of using an electric mixer for producing a pâte à bombe.

2 Identify the difference between a Swiss and an Italian meringue.

Preparation methods

1 Briefly describe how to produce a vanilla ice cream and state the importance of aging the mix.

2 Explain how pasteurization plays an important part in ice cream making.

Cooking methods

1 State how a crème brûlée is tested in order to see if it is correctly cooked.

2 State the temperature for baking the following:

a Coffee and date pudding;

b French meringue;

c Vanilla soufflé.

3 Identify the critical quality points for the following products:

a Pate a bombe;

b Iced parfait of strawberries;

c Omelette soufflé;

d Lemon cream;

e Swiss meringue.

Recipes

13 Producing cakes, sponges and petit fours

VRQ

Produce biscuits cake and sponges

Produce biscuits cake and sponges

Produce petits fours

NVQ

Prepare, cook and finish complex cakes, sponges, biscuits and scones

LEARNING OBJECTIVES

The aim of this chapter is to enable the reader to develop the necessary complex techniques, knowledge and understanding of the principles in preparing and producing a range of advanced cakes, sponges, biscuits and petit four products.

The emphasis of this chapter is on developing knowledge attained in the previous Professional Chef Level 2 book and perfecting refined, contemporary and advanced techniques. Also included in this chapter is further information on materials, formulas, ingredients and equipment.

At the end of this chapter you will be able to:

● **Identify the main methods of production for advanced cake, sponge, biscuit and petit four products.**

● **Understand the development of flavour and decoration concepts.**

● **Identify each type of complex preparation and finished product at this advanced level.**

● **Comprehend the function of the essential ingredients in the development of complex cakes, sponges, biscuits and petit fours.**

● **Understand the quality points of various complex products.**

● **Prepare, bake and present each type of complex cake, sponge, biscuit and petit four product.**

● **Distinguish the storage procedures of all products.**

● **Identify the correct tools and equipment used in the production of cakes, sponges, biscuits and petit four products.**

Introduction

The term cake has a long history. The word itself is of Viking origin, from the Old Norse word *kaka*. The Greeks invented beer as a leavener, initially frying fritters in olive oil. In ancient Rome basic bread dough was sometimes enriched with butter, eggs and honey, which produced a sweet baked item that was similar to cake. During the Renaissance period, sponges were developed as lighter versions of cake in Europe.

A torte is a rich, sometimes multilayered, cake that can be filled with buttercream, mousses, jams or fruits. Generally, the torte is glazed and decorated. A torte may be made with little to no flour, but instead with ground nuts or breadcrumbs used as the main dry ingredient. The best known of the typical tortes include the Austrian Sachertorte, the German Schwarzwälder Kirschtorte and the many-layered Hungarian Dobos torte.

In recent times, the production and presentation of cakes, gâteaux and torten within Europe and North America has changed significantly. For these types of pâtisserie the emphasis is now on producing individual portions, individually decorated with glazes and fruits or chocolate decorations. There is a trend towards lightness in texture and design of the dessert or cake – the use of biscuit Jaconde, Dacquoise, creams and mousses gives the pastry chef additional opportunities to be more creative.

Unusual flavours and combinations are now being used in conjunction with sophisticated presentations, and influences from the Eastern and Indian regions and the Caribbean are now mixed with more traditional and classical European styles. This chapter explains the various base components used in the production of modern-style and classical cakes, biscuits, sponges and petit fours.

The use of fats in bakery and cake production

Fats that are solid at room temperature (e.g. butter) have a propensity to be derived from animal sources. There are, however, a few exceptions, such as hydrogenated vegetable shortenings, cocoa butter and some tropical fats, which are derived from plants. Fats that are liquid at room temperature are referred to collectively as 'oils'. These tend to originate from plants, such as olives, maize, nuts and seeds. Oils can be chemically processed into solid form (hydrogenated), which will increase their shelf life.

Fats perform many different functions in baking; an example of this is that they provide flavour. They also create tenderness in the baked product by coating the strands of gluten present in batters, sponge and dough. Fats add moisture and a rich quality that will help to increase the shelf life of many products. When creamed together with sugar, fats can also hold a great amount of air, and when used jointly with other leaveners (such as baking powder) this will help baked goods to rise.

Solid fats with a high melting point will help to provide flakiness to pastes and laminated dough products, such as croissants and puff pastry, by creating distinct fine layers of fat between sheets of dough. Fats can also impart flavour when used for frying, such as deep frying of doughnuts and beignets.

Choosing an appropriate fat to use for a particular recipe will make a big difference to the result. One of the main points of consideration is the fat's plasticity. The greater the plasticity of a fat (e.g. vegetable shortening), the less pleasant it may be to eat because it will tend to leave a coating on the tongue. This is because highly plastic fats have a higher melting temperature. Butter is plastic at a cool room temperature, but once refrigerated it becomes harder and less plastic. Vegetable shortening will still have a good degree of plasticity even when refrigerated, which makes it easier to use in some laminated recipes.

> **CHEF'S TIP** The ability of a fat to hold its own shape at room temperature but still have the capacity to be moulded is known as 'plasticity'.
>

Butter and vegetable shortening are both capable of holding air and are therefore good to use as creaming agents. When creaming, butter should always be soft enough to be beaten and therefore trap air. This happens best at temperatures between 19°C and 21°C. The flavour and colour of butter make it the most desirable fat for use in the production of cakes, biscuits and sponges. Vegetable shortening will hold more air than butter because it contains less water, but it has the drawbacks of a lack of colour and flavour and a slightly greasy feel on the tongue during eating.

> **CHEF'S TIP** Hydrogenated vegetable shortenings are liquid oils that have undergone the chemical process of hydrogenation, which changes the oil to a solid. This gives the added benefit of a longer shelf life.
>

When producing cakes and sponges, fat has five major roles in baking as outlined below. How well it will perform each of these functions depends largely on the temperature at which the fat just begins to melt. The roles of fat are as follows.

SHORTENING

Fat weakens or 'shortens' a dough, cake or pastry by weakening its gluten network, resulting in the baked product being softer, breaking easily and having a more tender mouth feel.

CREAMING

Fat can trap air during beating and mixing, producing a batter that consists of masses of tiny air bubbles trapped within droplets of fat. This is very important in cake baking in which it is these air bubbles that expand during baking forming a light, airy structure.

LAYERING

In puff pastry fats which are soft over a wide temperature range are used. These can be spread between pastry layers and will separate them during cooking giving a layered pastry.

FLAVOUR

Usually the fats used should have a bland flavour to prevent them from changing the flavour of the finished product, but occasionally fats are chosen on the basis of a particular flavour which they may impart, such as butter.

In addition, the fat needs to be able to form an emulsion with the other ingredients in a batter during the cake or sponge production.

Storage of fats

Solid fats absorb odours and strong flavours and therefore need to be stored correctly in the refrigerator, away from strongly flavoured ingredients. They can also be frozen for several weeks. Liquid fats will turn rancid more quickly and should be stored in airtight containers in a dark, cool and dry area. The longer a fat is stored, the greater the chance of it turning rancid. Liquid fats can be stored in a refrigerator; however, they can turn semi-solid at these cooler temperatures and must be brought back to room temperature before use.

The use of eggs in bakery and cake production

Fresh shell eggs are undoubtedly best for most cuisine and bakery purposes. However, the time required for cracking the eggs, the inevitable waste, the mess caused by egg shells and the ever-present possibility of the inclusion of a stale egg in a mixing all highlight the benefits of using good brands of pasteurized eggs.

The primary risk associated with eggs is food-borne illness caused by *Salmonella enteritidis* bacteria. *Salmonella enteritidis* is a dangerous bacterium that can be transferred to humans through ingestion of raw or undercooked eggs. Egg products include whole eggs, whites, yolks and various blends with or without non-egg ingredients that are processed and pasteurized and may be available in liquid, frozen and dried forms. This is achieved by heating the products to a specified temperature for a specified period.

THREE MAIN COMPONENTS OF FRESH EGGS

Shell – calcium carbonate	12%
White – protein: **albumen**	58%
Yolk – protein: lecithin	30%

The average weight of an egg is 50 g. Eggs have various uses in cookery, especially in the pastry section:

- Eggs are used as moistening agents.
- They absorb a large quantity of air when manipulated (whisked).
- They act as enriching agents in food products, giving better structure, flavour and appearance.
- Egg yolk coagulates at 65–71°C.
- Egg white denatures at 60–65°C.

Basic composition of eggs

Both egg white and egg yolk contain a large proportion of water, some protein, fats and minerals, but in slightly different quantities.

	EGG YOLK	EGG WHITE	WHOLE EGG
WATER	50–50.5%	86–87%	73–75%
PROTEIN	16–16.5%	12–12.5%	12–14%
FAT	31–32%	0.25%	10–12%
MINERALS	0.8–1.5%	0.5–0.6%	0.8–1.5%

Storage of eggs

Fresh eggs should be stored in a cool but not too dry place, refrigeration at 2–3°C is ideal. Egg shells are porous and so eggs will absorb strong odours.

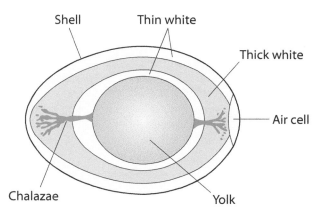

When an egg is stored, the thick white gradually absorbs moisture and therefore thins down. The yolk, in turn, absorbs moisture and begins to spread. Eventually the water will evaporate from the egg through its porous shell and is replaced by air. Since water is heavier than air, fresh eggs will be heavier than stale ones.

Frozen eggs

The use of frozen eggs is becoming more widespread due to fears of contamination of fresh eggs and the issue of wastage. There were initially problems with some imported frozen eggs, which were contaminated with *Salmonella* and other food poisoning bacteria. To overcome this, legislation was introduced stating that all eggs to be frozen must first be pasteurized.

Pasteurized frozen eggs must be defrosted gently before use. Immerse the can in cold running water until defrosted. When defrosted, remove the eggs from the can, thoroughly mix and then bring to room temperature. On no account should eggs be defrosted by the application of heat or the eggs will be denatured and lose their efficiency. Once defrosted, pasteurized eggs should be used without delay as, like all forms of egg, they are an extremely good medium for the growth of bacteria.

The aeration process in bakery, cakes and sponges

There are four methods of aeration used in the preparation of cakes, biscuits, sponges and bakery items such as pâte à Savarin. These are:

1 *panary* – yeast;
2 *chemical* – baking powder;
3 *physical* – whisking and beating;
4 *combination*.

Panary aeration

In 1859, the French scientist Louis Pasteur discovered that dough is aerated by living microorganisms, which convert sugar into carbon dioxide (CO_2). This is the principle behind panary fermentation, which is brought about by the action of enzymes in yeast and flour. Fermentation in breads and dough is dealt with in Chapter 11, but it is also a prime concept in baked products, for instance; pâte à Savarin.

Panary aeration is fermenting yeast; note how tiny bubbles of carbon dioxide (CO_2) are interspersed during fermentation

The initial gas production during panary fermentation comes from the breakdown of simple sugars present in the flour or in other added ingredients. Further glucose is made available by the conversion of other carbohydrates in the flour by specific enzymes. The gas is held within the structure of the gluten network, which gradually becomes more elastic during the fermentation process, and so the dough rises. Two by-products of this fermentation process are acids and alcohol, which make a contribution to the overall dough flavour.

When in the oven, gas production is accelerated until the yeast is killed by the heat, at which point activity ceases. The expansion of air and gas and the pressure of water vapour cause an increase in volume, which is maintained by the coagulation of all the proteins present as baking continues.

Chemical aeration

Historically, cakes originated from the practice of using up surplus ingredients – sugar (probably in the form of honey), fats or oils – by adding them to fermented dough. This produced a rich and pleasant range of finished goods.

This basic method continued to be used until the introduction of chemical aeration, when it was discovered that certain chemicals would give off gas when mixed with moist ingredients and then heated.

An examination of old recipe books shows that chemical aeration was known and in use many centuries ago.

Certainly, bicarbonate of soda has been in use for over 200 years, and before that pearl ash, a pure form of potash obtained from deteriorating wood and vegetable matter, was used. It was discovered that if potash was added to gingerbread dough it would become aerated during storage before baking. Potassium carbonate obtained from residues of beet sugar refining was another known aerating chemical.

Bicarbonate of soda

Old recipe books also refer to muriatic acid, now known as hydrochloric acid. When mixed with bicarbonate of soda, the resulting reaction releases carbon dioxide and leaves a residue of sodium chloride (common salt).

A mixture of tartaric acid and bicarbonate of soda then came into favour, tartaric acid in turn being superseded by cream of tartar. Cream of tartar, however, was much more expensive than tartaric acid and more of it is necessary for a given amount of bicarbonate of soda. This mixture is known as baking powder.

CHEF'S TIP If too much baking powder is used in a recipe the flavour of the cake will become quite salty as the sodium residue builds up.

Baking powder may be produced by combining one part bicarbonate of soda with two parts cream of tartar. Efficient baking powder should liberate the maximum amount of gas during baking. It must also be harmless and should not be unpleasant in taste or aroma.

Carbon dioxide generated by the chemical reaction becomes entangled in the gluten and albumin framework of a cake. This holds the gas and expands until the proteins coagulate, at which point the aerated structure becomes comparatively rigid.

The baking powder has a delayed action – only a small amount of carbon dioxide is given off when the liquid ingredients are added. The majority of the gas is released when the mixture is heated, therefore cake and pudding mixtures will not lose their ability to rise if they are not cooked immediately.

Suggestions on using baking powder:

- Mix the baking powder thoroughly with the flour.

- Replace the lid tightly on the tin after use.

- Measure accurately.

- Do not slam the oven door in the early stages of cooking.

- Excess baking powder causes a cake to collapse in the middle and dumplings to break up.

- Insufficient baking powder results in a close, heavy texture.

CHEF'S TIP Over time the shelf life of baking powder is shortened because it absorbs moisture from the air, which weakens it. A quick test to determine whether baking powder is still active is to mix a little of it with some malt vinegar. If the powder is active it will fizz.

Physical aeration

Beating particular mixtures of ingredients will cause air to become incorporated into the mixture, resulting in a baked product with a light texture. This is known as physical aeration. Two principal bakery ingredients are capable of holding air when beaten: fats and eggs. It is probable that eggs were the first ingredient aerated in this way, but animal fats can also be made much lighter by beating, particularly when blended with other ingredients, such as sugar.

Aerated egg whites create a fine foam with small bubbles of air

Beating eggs denatures the protein content by breaking it down into smaller fragments and allows air to be trapped. As the aeration of the egg continues, the denatured protein surrounds the air bubbles and locks in the air, preventing it from escaping. This process helps in the production of cakes and sponges by creating a lightness and leavens the cake (makes it rise) as it bakes.

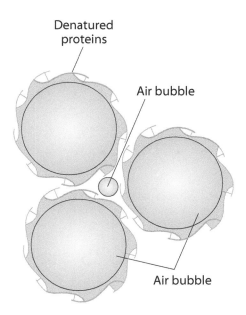

Denatured proteins

Air bubble

Air bubble

When beaten, egg white can hold more air than either whole egg or egg yolk, and for this reason it is the ideal medium for meringues, soufflés and royal icing.

Short pastry is also lightened by physical aeration, but to a lesser extent. Air is introduced either when the fat is rubbed in to the flour or when the fat and sugar are beaten prior to mixing into the flour.

Incorporating egg foams into other ingredients

It is important to properly incorporate egg foams into other ingredients such as biscuits à la Cuillère or biscuit Jaconde by folding them in with a rubber spatula. Folding is a gentle way of blending light, foamy ingredients into heavier ones. If the egg foams are mixed in too harshly, the air trapped within the protein network will escape as will the ability to leaven (or rise) the finished product. Some chefs fold ingredients in with gloved hands instead of a rubber spatula to maintain more control over the mixing process.

Combination method

A simple example of a combination method is that used for Croissants and Danish pastry, when butter is laminated into fermented dough. This combines panary aeration with aeration by lamination.

The combination of physical and chemical aeration is quite common. A mixture of fat, sugar and eggs is beaten during the first stages of production. The aeration is then supplemented by the addition of baking powder during the later stages.

An example where panary and chemical aeration are combined is the fermented scone. This is made using a preliminary yeast fermentation which is then incorporated with other ingredients to which baking powder has been added.

Combination of panary aeration and lamination create a strong structure but light and airy at the same time for croissants

Preventing cakes collapsing after baking

The bubbles in a baked sponge are closed so that no air can get in or out. As the cake cools, the steam inside the bubbles condenses and changes back into moisture. As this process gathers pace, a cake can begin to collapse. The cake is generally more cooked around the edges and therefore has a stronger structure. The sides of the baking tin will also lend support to the cake.

However, the cake can collapse in the middle unless we change the structure so that air can come back into the bubbles to replace the condensed steam. Dropping the cake, from a height of 30 cm onto a work surface passes a shock wave through the bubble walls and allows some of them to break, converting the cake from a closed to an open cell structure. Now air is able to get into the broken bubbles and the cake will not collapse.

Problem solving with sponge cakes using chemical aeration

Usually there is no way to rescue a failed sponge once it has been baked, but the guide shown will be able to provide a cause and explanation alongside a potential remedy.

PROBLEM	CAUSE AND EXPLANATION	SOLUTION
Cake does not rise	Insufficient or inactive baking powder used. All the baking powder reacted before the cake started to bake. Mixture too wet and the bubbles of carbon dioxide are not able to lift the cake during baking.	Check the 'best before' date of the label of the baking powder packet. Make sure the correct quantity of baking powder is accurate scaled. The cake mixture may have been left standing, or it may have been too acidic. Try not to leave the basic prepared mixture standing before baking. If the mixture is acidic (tastes sour) then add a little bicarbonate of soda or baking powder. Far too much liquid used in the cake mix.
Cake rises too much and spills over the sides of the baking tin	Mixture is too soft. Too much baking powder used.	Too much liquid used in the cake mix. Use less liquid or baking powder in the recipe.
Cake collapses as soon as it is removed from the oven	Proteins are not sufficiently coagulated (i.e. cake not baked for long enough or at high enough temperature).	Cook for a longer time and/or at a higher temperature.
Cake collapses in the middle	Cake cooked on the outside but not in the centre – cooking time is too short and cooking temperature is too high.	Increase cooking time and reduce the oven temperature.
Top of the cake is well browned but the inside is undercooked	Cake baked at too high temperature.	Use a cooler oven temperature.
Cake dried out or becomes stale very quickly	Baking temperature too high. Cake baked for too long or a lack of fat content in the recipe.	Ensure fat is added to the recipe. If necessary, bake for a shorter time or in a cooler oven.

Problem solving with sponge cakes using physical aeration

Génoise sponge cakes do not use a raising agent such as baking powder, but rather the bubbles are made before the cake is placed in the oven to bake. The bubbles are in the form of an egg foam and the other ingredients are carefully added to the stiff foam so as not to break down the aeration created.

The best sponge cakes will be those with the most and the smallest bubbles when baked. Since all the bubbles in this type of cake are created by beating the eggs and sugar together, the amount of small bubbles will be many. However, the egg foams will be stiffer when they contain smaller bubbles and stiffer foams will create finer textured cakes.

Close up of a fine textured sponge cake made with an egg foam

PROBLEM	CAUSE AND EXPLANATION	SOLUTION
Cake collapses in the oven	The bubbles in the foam collapse before the egg proteins coagulated during baking. Possible causes are; the fat broke down the egg foam or the foam was not stiff enough in the first place.	The cake mixture may have been left to stand after the fat was added and before it was put into the oven. Or, the oven may not have been pre-heated enough before baking of the cake was undertaken. Ensure the cake is placed immediately into the oven as soon as the fat has been added to the cake mixture. The egg foam needs to be very stiff before the flour and fats are incorporated. Ensure that it is beaten for long enough and beat over a bowl of hot water to aid aeration.
Cake does not rise	The mixture is so stiff that the bubbles cannot expand.	The mixture that goes into the baking tin should be just about pourable. If too much flour is added it may become overly stiff. Use less flour.
Cake rises too much and overflows the baking tin	Too much mixture was placed into the baking tin. Or, the mixture was not stiff enough.	Use a larger tin or less mixture. Beat the eggs longer, or add a little more flour to stiffen the mixture.
Cake collapses as soon as it is removed from the oven	The egg proteins have not coagulated during the baking process – the cooking time is too short or the oven temperature is too low.	Bake the cake at a higher oven temperature for a longer time.
Cake collapses in the middle	The outside of the cake is cooked and the centre is not, because the oven is too hot.	Bake at a lower temperature. Make sure to 'drop' the cake as soon as it is removed from the oven.
Top of the cake is well browned but the inside is undercooked	Cake baked at too high temperature.	Use a cooler oven temperature.
Cake dried out or becomes stale very quickly	Baking temperature too high. Cake baked for too long or a lack of fat content in the recipe.	Ensure fat is added to the recipe. If necessary, bake for a shorter time or in a cooler oven.

> **CHEF'S TIP** Sugar increases the viscosity or 'thickness' of the whole eggs so that the speed of beating required to denature the proteins is achievable with an electric mixing machine. Warming the eggs over a bowl of hot water will achieve aeration whilst whisking with a balloon whisk.

The use of dried fruit in bakery and cakes

Many types of fruit are available dried. Whereas fruit in its natural state is bursting with fresh, sweet juices, when dried it changes character completely. It becomes dense, concentrated in flavour and often not particularly attractive to look at, being wrinkled and leathery.

Dried fruit is an excellent source of dietary fibre, and although much of the moisture has been removed, most of the nutrients found in the fresh fruit are retained (apart from vitamin C). Dried fruit is higher in calories, volume for volume, than fresh fruit. When rehydrated, the nutritional value of the dried fruit approximates that of fresh fruit. Some fruits absorb larger volumes of liquid than others: tree fruits such as apples and pears increase by between three and five times their volume after soaking, vine fruits such as currants and raisins by about twice their volume.

Dried fruits also have the capacity to take on additional flavours when rehydrated, such as from fruit juices, alcohol, spices and tea. This is especially valuable when producing fruit cakes. Not all dried fruit is soaked before use. Fruits such as dates, figs and raisins can be eaten as they are.

Before using dried fruits in cake recipes it is best to wash them then soak them in the required flavoured liquid. The fruit can be soaked for long periods of time, especially for rich fruit cakes for weddings and Christmas festivals, where the richness and moisture of the fruit will help to prolong the shelf life of the actual cake. Dried fruits are often purchased in packs and can make very good winter fruit salads or compôtes.

Fruit cakes

In the UK, fruit cakes come in many varieties, from soft and light to rich and moist. The traditional Christmas cake is a round fruit cake covered in marzipan and then in white satin or royal icing. In Yorkshire, a fruitcake is often served accompanied with cheese. One type of cake that originated in Scotland is the Dundee cake. This is a fruit cake that is decorated with almonds. A popular story is that Mary Queen of Scots did not like cherries in her cakes, so the Dundee cake was first made for her, as a fruit cake that used almonds and not cherries.

In the Bahamas, not only is the fruit cake drenched with rum, but the ingredients are too. All of the candied fruit, walnuts and raisins are placed in an enclosed container and are soaked with the darkest variety of rum, anywhere from two weeks to three months in advance. The cake ingredients are mixed, and once the cake has finished baking, dark rum is poured onto it while it is still hot.

A square Dundee cake decorated with almonds and candied orange slices

Essential equipment used in cake production

SPRING LOADED BAKING TINS

These types of baking tins help to release the baked cakes, quickly and efficiently. The non-stick versions are fine, but it is usual for the tins to be lined with baking parchment to aid the release of the cake where possible.

SILICONE BAKING MOULDS

Silicone baking moulds have made a huge impact on the bakery and pastry kitchen. This enables chefs to produce a variety of different shaped cakes, gâteaux, mousses and confections. They are both freeze and bake stable and very easy to clean.

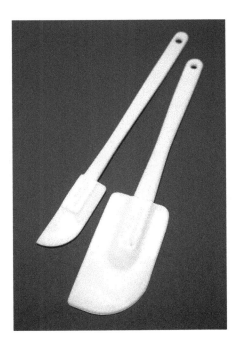

PLASTIC SPATULAS

Spatulas are an over-looking equipment item, and essential for smoothing out cake mixture into baking tins and scraping the sides of mixing bowls to ensure there is no wastage of ingredients during the production process and that they are all incorporated successfully into the cake mix.

ELECTRONIC-DIGITAL WEIGHING SCALES

It is important for all ingredients to be weighed out as accurately as possible. Digital scales will weigh out wet and dry ingredients to the nearest gram. By ensuring all commodities are accurately scaled significantly reduces the chances of error in the production process.

Recipes

Rich fruit cake

Ingredients	1 × 20 cm round cake	1 × 30 cm round cake
Soft flour	180 g	360 g
Dark brown muscovado sugar	180 g	360 g
Unsalted butter	180 g	360 g
Washed currants	225 g	450 g
Washed sultanas	225 g	450 g
Seedless raisins	90 g	200 g
Glacé cherries	50 g	100 g
Mixed peel	150 g	300 g
Ground almonds	75 g	150 g
Eggs	3	6
Mixed spice	5 g	10 g
Nutmeg	2 g	5 g
Ground mace	2 g	5 g
Good quality salt	2 g	5 g
Zest and juice of lemon	1 lemon	2 lemons
Brandy	75 ml	150 ml
Sherry	50 ml	100 ml
Dried fruits and nuts for decoration	100 g	175 g
Apricot glaze	55 g	80 g

energy	cal	fat	sat fat	carb	sugar	protein	fibre
2922 kJ	696 kcal	29.8 g	13.4 g	97.4 g	93.7 g	9.4 g	4.7 g

METHOD OF WORK

1. First line the baking tin with a double layer of greaseproof parchment. Then clean and prepare the fruit, halve the cherries.
2. Mix all the fruit together with the lemon juice, zest and alcohol. This mixture can be left for about one week in advance of making the cake, covered in a sealed plastic container.
3. Sift the flour and spices together.
4. Beat the butter until soft and light. Add the sugar to create a good aeration. Gradually incorporate the egg.
5. Stir in the ground almonds and fold in the flour and spices.
6. Add the fruit with the liquid and mix well together. Transfer to the baking tin.
7. It is extremely important to follow the correct recipe balance. Preheat an oven to 140°C. Put a tray containing one pint of water into the oven; this will create steam within the oven and help the cake rise evenly. Remove the tray of water half way through the baking process. The cake should be cooked after three-and-a-half-four hours.
8. Leave the cake in the tin for one day. Add a soaking mixture of rum and sherry every two days for one week. Wrap the cake in wax paper and place in an airtight container. The cake should be mature after three weeks.
9. Decorate with dried fruit and nuts and finish by brushing hot apricot glaze over the top and sides of the cake. Decorate the side of the cake with a collar (as shown in the photograph).

CHEF'S TIP To calculate the size of cake required, eight portions are generally cut from each 450 g of finished cake.

Step-by-stpe: Decorating the cake with icing

1. Select the correct sized board to present the cake. Trim the top of the cake to create a level surface.

2. Knead the marzipan (if required) and pin out so that it is at least 8 cm larger than the actual cake. Brush some boiled apricot jam over the cake to completely seal it.

3. Carefully roll up the marzipan and lay it over the cake.

4. Manipulate the marzipan so it completely covers the cake and creates a protective skin.

5. Leave the marzipan to dry for at least 24 hours before attempting to cover with the cover paste (icing). Using the same method, cover the cake with the cover paste, but brush a little alcohol onto the marzipan to help the cover paste to adhere. Smooth out any creases using a special smoothing paddle or the palm of your hand.

6. Using a piping bag with a small (number one) plain tube, pipe small decorative sequences over the cake using royal icing.

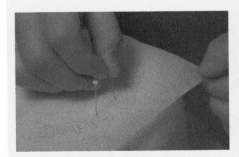

7. Write the name of the person that the cake is for (or the message for the cake) onto some silicone paper. Carefully place this onto the top of the cake and using a small pin, prick the outline of the words directly onto the cake to form a guide to pipe over.

8. Pipe over the guide marks using royal icing.

9. Finish off with a pre-made decorative motif or flowers as desired.

Separated egg sponge

Ingredients	1 small baking sheet or 12 individual discs	2 small baking sheets or 24 individual discs
Fresh eggs	4	8
Soft flour	110 g	220 g
Caster sugar	110 g	220 g
Vanilla flavour	a few drops	a few drops

energy	cal	fat	sat fat	carb	sugar	protein	fibre
384 kJ	91 kcal	1.8 g	0.5 g	16.3 g	9.8 g	2.9 g	0.3 g

METHOD OF WORK

1 Line a baking sheet (35 cm × 25 cm × 2 cm deep) with silicone paper or a silicone baking mat. Preheat an oven to 200°C.

2 Separate the eggs. Aerate the egg yolks with two-thirds of the caster sugar and the vanilla essence in a bowl until stiff and almost white in colour.

3 Meanwhile, warm the remaining caster sugar in the oven for a few minutes until hot to touch.

4 Aerate the egg whites with the warmed caster sugar to a stiff peak.

5 Mix in a little of the aerated egg whites to the yolk mixture.

6 Carefully fold in the sieved flour and then the remainder of the egg whites. At this stage you must fold in very carefully using a plastic spatula so as not to knock the air out of the preparation.

7 Pipe the mixture onto the prepared baking sheet in fingers (biscuit à la cuillère), individual discs or spread onto the sheet and use as a base for gâteaux.

CHEF'S TIP Replace one-third of the flour with potato flour to make the finished sponge soft and flexible for use as a Swiss roll.

Flourless chocolate sponge

Ingredients	2 × 20 cm round cake tins	4 × 20 cm round cake tins
Egg yolks	5	10
Cocoa powder	40 g	80 g
Caster sugar (1)	55 g	110 g
Egg whites	5	10
Caster sugar (2)	75 g	150 g
Vanilla flavour	a few drops	a few drops

energy	cal	fat	sat fat	carb	sugar	protein	fibre
516 kJ	123 kcal	4.3 g	1.6 g	17.7 g	17.1 g	4.3 g	1.4 g

METHOD OF WORK

1 Prepare the cake tins with silicone paper or line a baking sheet with silicone paper or a silicone baking mat. Preheat an oven to 200°C.

2 Whisk the egg yolks and the smaller quantity of caster sugar to a sabayon stage over a bain-marie of hot water (softly aerated).

3 Create an aerated foam with the egg whites and the larger quantity of caster sugar.

4 Sieve the cocoa powder and carefully fold in to the egg yolk sabayon with some vanilla flavour.

5 Gently fold in the egg white foam and then deposit onto the prepared baking sheet or cake tins.

6 Bake in the oven until the chocolate sponge contracts from the sides and it feels springy to the touch. Remove from the oven and cool on a wire rack.

7 Cut into desired shapes and use or freeze until required.

CHEF'S TIP This sponge recipe can be used for desserts, gâteaux and cakes. To freeze the sponge; simply wrap in baking parchment and then plastic film to protect it from frosting.

Biscuit Jaconde

Ingredients	2 large baking sheets	4 large baking sheets
Chocolate stencil paste		
Icing sugar	50 g	100 g
Unsalted butter	50 g	100 g
Egg whites	55 g	105 g
Soft flour	40 g	80 g
Cocoa powder	10 g	20 g
Alternative stencil colour		
Coloured Stencil paste		
Icing sugar	50 g	100 g
Unsalted butter	50 g	100 g
Egg whites	55 g	105 g
Soft flour	50 g	100 g
Powdered colour		
Biscuit		
Icing sugar	190 g	375 g
Ground almonds	190 g	375 g
Whole eggs	250 g	500 g
Soft flour	50 g	100 g
Melted butter	40 g	75 g
Egg whites	130 g	260 g
Caster sugar	25 g	50 g

energy	cal	fat	sat fat	carb	sugar	protein	fibre
828 kJ	198 kcal	10 g	2.8 g	23.2 g	14.3 g	5 g	1.1 g

CHEF'S TIP Biscuit Jaconde is a flexible, highly moisturized biscuit designed to be used decoratively in association with cakes, torten, mousses, bavarois and other entremets.

VIDEO CLIP Using a silk screen to make a biscuit Jaconde.

METHOD OF WORK

1 Line a baking sheet (45 cm × 35 cm × 2 cm deep) with a silicone baking mat. Preheat an oven to 240°C.

2 To make the stencil paste, beat the icing sugar and the softened butter. Add the egg whites and fold in the sieved flour (and cocoa powder or powdered colour). Mix all ingredients to a smooth paste.

3 To create the frieze effect, spread the stencil paste using a decorative template, silk screen, rake or free-hand onto the baking sheet lined with a silicone baking mat. Freeze the baking sheet until the stencil mixture is hard.

4 To make the biscuit, pass the icing sugar and ground almonds through a sieve twice.

5 Whisk the sieved mixture with the whole eggs to a ribbon stage on an electric mixing machine.

6 Sieve the flour.

7 Create a stiff foam with the egg whites and caster sugar.

8 Fold the sieved flour into the sabayon of eggs and almonds and then fold in the melted butter. Carefully fold in the aerated egg whites.

9 Thinly spread the biscuit mixture over the frozen stencil paste (about 5 mm).

10 Bake at 240°C for about five minutes. The biscuit should be moist, springy to the touch and on no account dry.

11 Remove from the oven, cool, carefully remove from the silicone baking mat. Store wrapped in cling film in a refrigerator and use as required.

CHEF'S TIP Other colours can be achieved in the stencil paste. Just replace the cocoa powder with 20 g soft flour and add the appropriate coloured/flavoured paste. See the alternative stencil recipes in the biscuit Jaconde recipe to choose from.

CHEF'S TIP A textured effect can be produced by liberally sprinkling chopped pistachio nuts, hazelnuts, poppy seeds or desiccated coconut over the silicone baking mat before carefully spreading on the biscuit mixture.

Dacquoise

Ingredients	4 × 20 cm discs	8 × 20 cm discs
Egg whites	220 g	440 g
Caster sugar	80 g	160 g
Hazelnut tant-pour-tant	190 g	380 g
Almond tant-pour-tant	170 g	340 g

energy	cal	fat	sat fat	carb	sugar	protein	fibre
579 kJ	138 kcal	6.3 g	0.5 g	17.8 g	17.4 g	3.6 g	0.9 g

METHOD OF WORK

1 Line a baking sheet with a silicone baking mat. Preheat an oven to 180°C.

2 Create an aerated foam with the egg whites and the caster sugar.

3 Carefully combine both tant-pour-tant preparations into the meringue using a plastic spatula to maintain as much aeration as possible.

4 Place into a disposable piping bag with a plain tube and pipe discs on to the baking sheet.

5 Bake in the oven for approximately 20 minutes.

CHEF'S TIP Tant-pour-tant is a French pastry term for equal quantities of two dry ingredients. In this case it is equal quantities of ground nuts and icing sugar, which are sifted together *twice* to aerate and combine the two ingredients.

Heavy Genoese sponge

Ingredients	2 trays or 1 × 20 cm baking ring	4 trays or 2 × 20 cm baking rings
Butter or cake margarine	225 g	450 g
Caster sugar	225 g	450 g
Whole eggs	5	10
Soft flour	250 g	500 g
Cornflour	30 g	60 g
Baking powder	10 g	20 g
Vanilla	to taste	to taste
Good-quality salt	3 g	5 g

energy	cal	fat	sat fat	carb	sugar	protein	fibre
813 kJ	194 kcal	10.7 g	6.3 g	22.6 g	12 g	2.8 g	0.4 g

METHOD OF WORK

1 Line the baking trays (15 cm × 8 cm × 5 cm deep) or 20 cm baking rings with silicone paper. Preheat an oven to 180°C.

2 Beat the fat with the sugar to a light aerated consistency. Add the salt and vanilla.

3 Slowly add the eggs, clearing the mixture each time before adding another quantity. Sieve together the flour, baking powder and cornflour.

4 Fold in the sieved flour, baking powder and cornflour.

5 Deposit into the moulds and place in the oven to bake for approximately 40 minutes.

6 Remove from the oven when baked and place onto a wire cooling rack.

CHEF'S TIP This recipe is used for heavy sponge cakes such as fondant dips or for decorated cakes.

Schweizwein torten

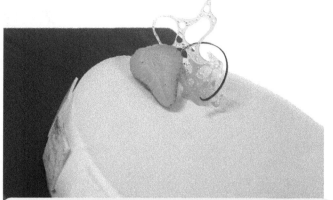

Ingredients	1 × 20 cm torten ring	2 × 20 cm torten rings
Sweet wine mousse		
Sweet white wine	250 ml	500 ml
Caster sugar	70 g	140 g
Egg yolks	4	8
Whipping cream	250 ml	500 ml
Orange zest	1 orange	2 oranges
Gelatine	5 leaves	10 leaves
Vanilla	½ pod	1 pod
Neutral glaze		
Light stock syrup	200 ml	400 ml
Gelatine	2 leaves	4 leaves
Additional ingredients		
Sweet paste (pâte sucrée)	100 g	200 g
Almond flavoured separated egg sponge	1 × 16 cm disc	2 × 16 cm disc
Sieved raspberry jam	100 g	200 g
Mixed prepared fresh fruits (e.g. strawberry, raspberry, fig, orange segments)	250 g	500 g

energy	cal	fat	sat fat	carb	sugar	protein	fibre
2295 kJ	546 kcal	20.9 g	10.9 g	79.2 g	59.3 g	9.2 g	1.6 g

METHOD OF WORK

1 Cut out a 16 cm diameter circle of the rolled out sweet paste. Dock the paste and lay onto a baking tray lined with silicone paper. Bake blind. Remove from the oven and leave to cool.

2 Soften the gelatine in cold water.

3 Spread the disc of sweet paste with the sieved jam and place in the base of the torten ring.

4 Place a circle of the almond flavoured sponge on top, then add the mixed fruit. At this stage you can place a collar of biscuit Jaconde around the side of the torten if required.

5 Whisk the orange zest, caster sugar and egg yolks over a bain-marie to create a light aeration. Meanwhile, warm the wine in a saucepan to 80°C. Slowly add to the egg yolk while whisking continuously to form a sabayon.

6 Add the softened gelatine and make sure it is dissolved completely into the sabayon.

7 Remove from the bain-marie and slowly whisk until the mixture has cooled down. Place into the refrigerator to half set.

8 Whip the cream to a ribbon stage and carefully fold into the sabayon. Pour into the torten ring and set in a refrigerator for at least two hours.

9 Make the neutral glaze by warming the stock syrup and adding the softened leaves of gelatine. Ensure that the gelatine has completely melted; cool down over a bain-marie of cold water.

10 When the torten has completely set and the glaze has cooled sufficiently, glaze the top of the torten and refrigerate for another 15 minutes. Remove the torten from the ring and serve with a raspberry coulis.

Sacher torte

Ingredients	1 × 20 cm round cake tin	2 × 20 cm round cake tins
Sponge		
Butter	105 g	210 g
Caster sugar	75 g	150 g
Egg yolks	3	6
Melted dark chocolate	40 g	80 g
Soft flour	100 g	200 g
Baking powder	5 g	10 g
Ground almonds	25 g	50 g
Cocoa powder	30 g	30 g
Egg whites	3	6
Caster sugar	30 g	60 g
Chocolate glaze		
Fresh milk	100 g	210 g
Double cream	75 g	150 g
Icing sugar	50 g	100 g
Water	50 g	100 g
Liquid glucose	50 g	100 g
Dark chocolate	375 g	750 g
Additional ingredients		
Apricot jam	100 g	200 g
Dark rum or kirsch	25 ml	50 ml
White chocolate, melted (optional)	50 g	75 g

energy	cal	fat	sat fat	carb	sugar	protein	fibre
2972 kJ	713 kcal	45.8 g	12.5 g	64.9 g	36.2 g	10.8 g	1.8 g

METHOD OF WORK

1 Line the baking tins with silicone paper. Preheat an oven to 180°C.

2 To make the Sacher sponge, cream the butter and the larger quantity of caster sugar together to aerate. Slowly add the egg yolks and the melted dark chocolate.

3 Sift together the baking powder, flour, ground almonds and cocoa powder twice. Incorporate into the creamed chocolate butter preparation.

4 Create a meringue with the smaller quantity of caster sugar and the egg whites. Carefully fold this into the chocolate preparation. Deposit the mixture into the prepared tins and place into the oven to bake.

5 Remove from the oven when fully cooked and turn out onto a wire cooling rack.

6 To make the Sacher glaze, place the milk, water, icing sugar, cream and glucose into a saucepan and slowly bring to the boil.

7 Meanwhile, melt the chocolate in a bain-marie.

8 Remove the boiled cream liquid from the stove and add the melted chocolate. Mix together to a silky smooth consistency. Pass through a fine sieve and leave to cool to 20°C.

9 To prepare the base, cut the chocolate sponge into three equal layers. Macerate each layer with the alcohol and brush the surface with some boiled apricot jam thinned with a little of the alcohol. Reassemble the layers and place onto a cake board. Brush the remaining apricot glaze over the Sacher sponge.

10 With the glaze at the correct temperature (nearly at setting point), ladle the glaze over to completely cover the sponge.

11 Leave to set. Using a little of the chocolate glaze pipe the name 'Sacher' on top of the torte and decorate with a little chocolate. Alternatively use a little melted white chocolate to pipe the name 'Sacher'.

CHEF'S TIP In 1832, Prince Wenzel von Metternich charged his personal chef with creating a special dessert for several important guests. The head chef, having taken ill, let the task fall to his 16-year-old apprentice, Franz Sacher, then in his second year of training in Metternich's kitchen. While the torte created by Sacher on this occasion is said to have delighted Metternich's guests, the dessert received no immediate further attention. Sacher completed his training as a chef and ultimately settled in his hometown of Vienna where he opened a specialty delicatessen and wine shop.

Sacher's eldest son Eduard carried on his father's culinary legacy, completing his own training in Vienna with the Royal and Imperial Pastry Chef at the Demel bakery and chocolatier, during which time he perfected his father's recipe and developed the torte into its current form. The cake was first served at the Demel and later at the Hotel Sacher, established by Eduard in 1876. Since then, the cake remains among the most famous of Vienna's culinary specialties.

In the early decades of the twentieth century, a legal battle over the use of the label 'The Original Sacher Torte' developed between the Hotel Sacher and the Demel bakery. Eduard Sacher completed his recipe for Sacher torte while working at Demel, which was the first establishment to offer the 'original' cake. Following the death of Eduard's widow Anna in 1930 and the bankruptcy of the Hotel Sacher in 1934, Eduard Sacher's son (also named Eduard Sacher) found employment at Demel and brought to the bakery the sole distribution right for an Eduard-Sacher-Torte.

Over the next few years, both parties waged an intense legal war over several of the dessert's specific characteristics, including the change of the name, the second layer of jam in the middle of the cake, and the substitution of margarine for butter in the baking of the cake. In 1963 both parties agreed on an out of court settlement that gave the Hotel Sacher the rights to the phrase 'The Original Sachertorte' and gave the Demel the rights to decorate its tortes with a triangular seal that reads Eduard-Sacher-Torte.

December 5 is National Sachertorte Day.

Japonaise

Ingredients	2 × 20 cm discs or 30 piped biscuits	5 × 20 cm discs or 90 piped biscuits
Egg whites	5	10
Caster sugar (1)	150 g	300 g
Ground hazelnuts	150 g	300 g
Cornflour	25 g	50 g
Caster sugar (2)	60 g	120 g

energy	cal	fat	sat fat	carb	sugar	protein	fibre
265 kJ	63 kcal	2.8 g	0.2 g	8.5 g	7.6 g	1.5 g	0.4 g

METHOD OF WORK

1 Line a baking sheet with a silicone baking mat. Preheat an oven to 160°C.

2 Mix together the hazelnuts, cornflour and the smaller quantity of caster sugar (2).

3 Create a stiff foam with the larger quantity of caster sugar (1) and the egg whites.

4 Carefully fold in the dry mix to the egg white foam and quickly pipe onto the prepared baking sheet into discs or small piped rosettes for biscuits.

5 Place in the oven to bake for approximately 15–20 minutes. Remove from the oven to cool. When nearly cooled cut out the required shapes or discs. When the Japonaise has totally cooled down it will dry out similar to a meringue.

CHEF'S TIP Keep any excess Japonaise and reduce to crumbs in a blender. Keep in an airtight container and use for decorating various gâteaux (e.g. gâteau succès).

Dobos torte

Ingredients	1 × 20 cm round torte	2 × 20 cm round torte
Dobos biscuit		
Butter	120 g	240 g
Icing sugar	120 g	240 g
Vanilla flavour	to taste	to taste
Whole eggs	100 g	200 g
Soft flour, sieved	120 g	240 g
Dobos buttercream		
Pasteurized whole eggs	150 g	300 g
Caster sugar	175 g	350 g
Glucose	15 g	30 g
Water	150 ml	300 ml
Unsalted butter	320 g	640 g
Dark chocolate (70%)	50 g	100 g
Caramel		
Water	90 ml	150 ml
Granulated sugar	250 g	500 g
Unsalted butter	10 g	25 g
Glucose	20 g	40 g
Additional ingredients		
Roast, chopped hazelnuts	120 g	240 g

energy	cal	fat	sat fat	carb	sugar	protein	fibre
4023 kJ	964 kcal	59.8 g	30 g	102.8 g	74.3 g	9.5 g	1.6 g

METHOD OF WORK

1 Preheat the oven to 180°C.

2 To prepare the Dobos biscuit; cream the butter and the icing sugar together until pale and add the vanilla flavour. Beat in the whole eggs, a little at a time, and carefully fold in the sieved soft flour.

3 Spread the biscuit paste onto a baking sheet lined with silicone paper or a Sil-pat baking mat. Place in the oven to bake until light golden in colour. Approximately 15–20 minutes.

4 Remove from the oven and peel off the silicone. Whilst still slightly warm, cut out seven 20 cm discs. Leave on a wire rack to cool.

5 To prepare the Dobos buttercream; add the water and sugar to a clean, heavy based saucepan and bring to the boil. Add the glucose and continue boiling to 118°C.

6 Meanwhile, begin aerating the eggs in an electric mixing machine (using the whisk attachment). Slowly pour the boiled sugar solution into the aerated eggs with the machine still whisking. Add all of the sugar solution and continue whisking until the egg mixture is just slightly warm.

7 Cut the butter into small cubes and begin adding the butter to the egg mixture, a little at a time. Add the melted chocolate and beat thoroughly, ensuring that the butter and chocolate has been fully incorporated into the mixture.

8 Using six discs of the Dobos biscuit, layer them with the buttercream between each disc and around the sides and top, keeping the surface of the buttercream as smooth as possible.

9 Mask the sides of the torte with the chopped hazelnuts.

10 To prepare the caramel; add the water and sugar to a heavy based saucepan and bring to the boil. Add the glucose and wash down the sides of the saucepan with a clean cold water to prevent sugar crystals from forming during the cooking process.

11 When a light amber caramel colour has been achieved, remove from the heat and plunge the base of the pan into cold water to halt the cooking process. Add the butter carefully and ensure that it is fully incorporated into the caramel by 'swirling' the pan. Do not be tempted to stir the butter in otherwise sugar crystals may form.

12 Pour the butter caramel onto the remaining disc of Dobos biscuit and allow to nearly set before cutting into portions with a sharp knife brushed with a little vegetable oil to prevent it sticking to the caramel. Leave the caramel segments to cool and fully set.

13 Pipe the remaining buttercream on top of the torte to denote each portion and then position a caramel segment on each piped buttercream rosette.

Opera

Ingredients	20 slices	40 slices
Biscuit Jaconde	3 sheets (60 cm × 9 cm each)	6 sheets (60 cm × 9 cm each)
Espresso coffee (strong)	40 g	80 g
Stock syrup	40 g	80 g
Dark Rum	10 g	20 g
Coffee buttercream		
Fresh milk	300 g	600 g
Caster sugar (1)	125 g	250 g
Coffee, diluted with a little water	10 g	20 g
Egg yolks (pasteurized)	125 g	250 g
Caster sugar (2)	125 g	250 g
Unsalted butter	1000 g	2000 g
Italian meringue	250 g	500 g
Chocolate ganache		
UHT Whipping cream	400 g	800 g
Dark chocolate (60%)	500 g	1000 g
Unsalted butter, softened	100 g	200 g
Additional ingredients		
Chocolate glaze	250 g	500 g

energy	cal	fat	sat fat	carb	sugar	protein	fibre
2496 kJ	602 kcal	51 g	22 g	31 g	19.6 g	5.8 g	0.1 g

METHOD OF WORK

1   To prepare the chocolate ganache, bring the UHT cream to the boil and chop the chocolate into very small pieces. Pour the boiled cream onto the chocolate pieces and begin mixing using a whisk to create and emulsion between the cream and the chocolate as the chocolate begins to melt.

2   Add the butter and beat in well. Leave to one side and prepare the remaining commodities.

3   To prepare the coffee buttercream, bring the milk to the boil with the first quantity of caster sugar (1). Mix the egg yolks with the second quantity of caster sugar (2). Add the coffee to taste.

4   Pour the milk onto the egg yolks and mix well to incorporate all the ingredients. Pour into a clean, heavy based saucepan and cook out to 85°C (as for a crème Anglaise).

5   Strain through a fine chinois and cool to 30°C.

6   Slowly beat in the butter to the coffee flavoured custard and mix until smooth.

7   Fold in the Italian meringue, adjust the flavour if necessary and set aside for further use.

8   To construct the Opera; mix together the stock syrup, Espresso coffee and dark rum. Brush the first layer of biscuit Jaconde and layer with a thin coating of chocolate ganache before layering the coffee buttercream on top.

9   Brush another biscuit Jaconde with the coffee syrup and place this on top of the buttercream. Add another coating of chocolate ganache on top.

10   The final sheet of biscuit Jaconde should be brushed with the syrup and placed on top and set in a refrigerator for at least 30 minutes.

11   Apply a coating of the chocolate glaze and once again leave to set before trimming and cutting into slices approximately 8 × 3 cm. Pipe the word *Opera* on each slice.

Pear and chocolate mousse cake

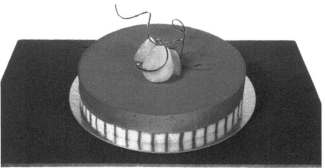

Ingredients	1 × 20 cm round cake tin	2 × 20 cm round cake tins
Pear compôte		
Poached pears	550 g	1150 g
Unsalted butter	50 g	100 g
Caster sugar	100 g	200 g
Vanilla	½ pod	1 pod
Pear liqueur	25 g	50 g
Nougatine		
Caster sugar	75 g	150 g
Pectin (optional)	1 g	2 g
Glucose	25 g	50 g
Butter	75 g	125 g
Flaked almonds	50 g	100 g
Dark chocolate mousse		
Melted dark chocolate	350 g	550 g
Whipping cream (half whipped)	480 g	680 g
Additional ingredients		
Flourless chocolate sponge (see recipe on page 462)	2 discs	4 discs
Biscuit Jaconde (3 cm wide strip to fit the circumference of the torten ring; see recipe on page 463)	1 strip	2 strips
Cocoa powder	50 g	100 g
Chocolate decoration as required		

energy	cal	fat	sat fat	carb	sugar	protein	fibre
3198 kJ	770 kcal	61.6 g	24.2 g	45.5 g	28.9 g	8.5 g	2.5 g

METHOD OF WORK

1 For the compôte, take the pears that have been poached in syrup and cut into 5 mm dice. Melt the butter in a heavy-based pan then add the sugar and the split vanilla pod. Cook until a light caramel starts to appear and then add the pears and a little of the syrup. Cook for a further three–four minutes to evaporate most of the liquid. Add the alcohol and flambé then set aside to cool for later use.

2 For the nougatine, warm all the ingredients together in a saucepan and then roll the contents between two sheets of silicone paper. Remove the top sheet and bake in the oven until golden brown. Cut discs out of the nougatine when it has cooled a little.

3 For the dark chocolate mousse, melt the chocolate at 50°C. Combine with a little of the semi-whipped cream then mix together with the rest of the cream.

4 In a stainless steel torten ring, place the first disc of chocolate sponge in the base and moisten with a little extra liqueur. Place a disc of the nougatine on top. Wrap a strip of the biscuit jaconde around the inside of the ring. Half fill the torten with the chocolate mousse. Place the second chocolate sponge disc on top and spoon the compôte of pears over the disc. Finally fill the torten ring to the top with the chocolate mousse.

5 Leave to set in a refrigerator for at least two hours. Dust the top with the cocoa powder for decoration before removing the torten ring.

6 Serve with a crème Chantilly.

Strawberry and lemon mousse cake

Ingredients	1 × 20 cm torten ring	3 × 20 cm torten rings
strawberry and lemon mousse		
Egg yolks	90 g	180 g
Water	90 g	180 g
Milk powder	30 g	60 g
Strawberry puree	50 g	80 g
Glucose	20 g	40 g
Lemon zest	3 lemons	6 lemons
Gelatine	10 leaves	20 leaves
Water	60 g	120 g
Lemon juice	180 g	360 g
Whipping cream (half whipped)	300 g	600 g
Italian meringue		
Egg whites	90 g	180 g
Caster sugar	90 g	180 g
Glucose	40 g	80 g
Water	40 g	80 g
Strawberry gel		
Strawberry purée	350 ml	700 ml
Gelatine	4 leaves	8 leaves
Water	25 ml	50 ml
Chopped fresh strawberries	100 g	200 g
Neutral glaze		
Stock syrup	320 g	600 g
Gelatine	4 leaves	8 leaves
Additional ingredients		
Dacquoise discs	1 × 18 cm	3 × 18 cm
Strip of decorated biscuit Jaconde	1 strip	3 strips
Decoration as required		

energy	cal	fat	sat fat	carb	sugar	protein	fibre
1777 kJ	423 kcal	19.4 g	10.5 g	57.7 g	52.1 g	8.2 g	2 g

CHEF'S TIP   A classical pâte à bombe recipe is to beat cooked sugar (118°C) and egg yolks over a bain-marie to a sabayon stage. This modern version for the lemon mousse recipe has the addition of water, glucose and milk powder to stabilize the egg yolk content. Cooking to 85°C will ensure that the eggs cook out completely without splitting the mixture.

METHOD OF WORK

1   To prepare the lemon and strawberry pâte à bombe base for the mousse, place the egg yolks, water, strawberry puree, glucose, lemon zest and milk powder into a stainless steel saucepan and whisk while cooking out on the stove to 85°C.

2   Meanwhile, make the meringue to the Italian method by boiling the sugar, water and glucose to 121°C. Aerate the egg whites using an electric mixing machine until firm. Slowly stream the cooked sugar into the egg whites while beating on the machine. Continue to beat at a low speed until all the sugar has been incorporated and the meringue has cooled.

3   Melt the gelatine in a bain-marie of hot water and add to the lemon mixture. Fold the lemon and strawberry pâte à bombe into the meringue.

4   Carefully fold the lemon juice into the half whipped cream. Fold in all the ingredients together to create the lemon and strawberry mousse.

5   Bring the second quantity of strawberry purée to the boil. Soften the gelatine in the water and add to the hot purée. Strain onto the chopped strawberries and set in 150 mm diameter rings.

6   Bring the stock syrup to the boil. Add the softened gelatine off the heat. Pass through a sieve and cool until required for glazing.

7   Lay the disc of dacquoise in the base of the torten ring. Position the biscuit Jaconde around the side of the mould. Add some of the lemon mousse to cover the base. Turn out the strawberry gel and place into the centre. Cover with the lemon and strawberry mousse, filling to the top of the ring. Refrigerate for two hours.

8   Remove the torten ring and glaze. Set up in the refrigerator once again and decorate as desired.

Chocolate velvet cakes

Ingredients	16 individual cakes	32 individual cakes
Golden caster sugar	200 g	400 g
Whole egg	180 g	360 g
Sunflower oil	200 ml	400 ml
Bitter cocoa powder	50 g	100 g
Soft flour	180 g	340 g
Baking powder	8 g	16 g
Salt	¼ tsp	½ tsp
Freshly cooked beetroot	300 g	600 g
Vanilla extract	to taste	to taste
Vanilla buttercream	300 g	650 g

energy	cal	fat	sat fat	carb	sugar	protein	fibre
1594 kJ	382 kcal	24.4 g	8.1 g	38.4 g	24.9 g	4.1 g	1.6 g

METHOD OF WORK

1   Preheat an oven to 180°C.
2   Aerate the eggs and the caster sugar to a thick sabayon consistency.
3   Puree the beetroot in a food blender with a little of the oil.
4   Carefully add the oil to the egg mixture whilst whisking vigorously in a slow, but steady stream, similar to making mayonnaise.
5   Sift the flour, cocoa powder, baking powder and salt together.
6   Fold in the dry ingredients before adding the vanilla and then the pureed beetroot.
7   Pipe the mixture into cupcake moulds and place in the oven to bake for 20 minutes.
8   Remove from the oven and leave to cool.
9   Finish with a rosette of buttercream and an appropriate decoration.

Gateau succès

Ingredients	1 gateau	2 gateaux
Caster sugar (1)	140 g	280 g
Full fat milk	20 g	40 g
Almond tant-pour-tant	180 g	360 g
Egg whites	180 g	360 g
Caster sugar (2)	85 g	170 g
French buttercream flavoured with praline and coffee	250 g	500 g
Toasted nibbed almonds	100 g	200 g
Melted chocolate	50 g	70 g

energy	cal	fat	sat fat	carb	sugar	protein	fibre
2369 kJ	566 kcal	33.3 g	11.4 g	61.6 g	58.9 g	8.7 g	2 g

METHOD OF WORK

1   Preheat an oven to 130°C.
2   Aerate the egg whites with the second amount of caster sugar (2) to stiff peaks.
3   Carefully fold in the remaining caster sugar (1) and the almond tant-pour-tant.
4   Finally fold in the milk and transfer to a piping bag.
5   Pipe three 20 cm discs onto some silicone paper on a baking sheet.
6   Place into the oven to bake for two hours.
7   Remove from the oven and peel away the silicone paper carefully before cooling on a wire rack.
8   Sandwich together the three discs of biscuit succes with the buttercream.
9   Coat the sides and the top with the remaining buttercream creating a smooth finish.
10   Coat the sides of the gateau with the nibbed almonds and finish by piping the word *Succès* on the top in chocolate.

Blueberry muffins

Ingredients	10 muffins	20 muffins
Soft flour	300 g	600 g
Caster sugar	155 g	310 g
Baking powder	1 tsp	2 tsp
Bicarbonate of soda	½ tsp	1 tsp
Salt	2 g	4 g
Fresh full fat milk	250 ml	500 ml
Eggs	2	4
Vanilla extract	to taste	to taste
Unsalted butter, melted	85 g	170 g
Blueberries	80 g	160 g

energy	cal	fat	sat fat	carb	sugar	protein	fibre
1104 kJ	263 kcal	9.4 g	5.4 g	40.7 g	18.7 g	5 g	1.1 g

METHOD OF WORK

1   Preheat an oven to 180°C.
2   Sieve together the flour, baking powder, bicarbonate of soda, salt and half of the caster sugar.
3   Mix together the milk and the eggs with the vanilla.
4   Make a well in the centre of the dry ingredients and add the milk mixture, mixing continuously.
5   Continue mixing until the batter is smooth.
6   Add the melted butter and mix well to incorporate it.
7   Carefully add the berries, taking care not to bruise them.
8   Spoon the batter into muffin cases, filling up to two-thirds full and sprinkle the tops with the remaining sugar.
9   Bake in the oven until the muffins are golden brown on top and bounce back when lightly pressed to test cooking.
10   Turn out onto a wire rack to cool down and serve.

CHEF'S TIP Madeleines can be flavoured with lemon, orange or lime simply by using the finely grated zest in the mix. Other alternative flavours can be rose water, vanilla, nutmeg or cinnamon.

Madeleines

Ingredients	8	20
Unsalted butter	80 g	160 g
Whole eggs	2	4
Caster sugar	80 g	160 g
Ground almonds	40 g	80 g
Soft flour	80 g	160 g
Almond extract	to taste	to taste
Icing sugar	50 g	100 g

energy	cal	fat	sat fat	carb	sugar	protein	fibre
926 kJ	221 kcal	12.5 g	5.8 g	24.8 g	17.4 g	3.6 g	0.7 g

METHOD OF WORK

1   Preheat an oven to 180°C.
2   Melt the butter in a pan and slowly cook it until a light nut-brown colour has been achieved (do not let the butter burn).
3   Leave the butter to cool for a few minutes and then carefully drain off the fat leaving the residue behind.
4   Whisk the eggs and sugar together using an electric mixing machine. Aerate to soft peaks.
5   Combine the flour and ground almonds together before gradually folding into the egg mixture.
6   Carefully add the nut-brown butter and the almond extract to the mixture and then leave to stand for an hour to rest.
7   Lightly grease a **Madeleine** mould and spoon the mixture into the prepared mould.
8   Bake for approximately nine minutes until the tops are springy to the touch.
9   Keep in the moulds for a couple of minutes to cool slightly and then remove onto a wire rack, dust with icing sugar if required and serve.

Raspberry financiers

Ingredients	25–30 petit fours	50–60 petit fours
Butter	120 g	240 g
Vanilla extract	To taste	To taste
Almond tant-pour-tant	160 g	320 g
Icing sugar	140 g	280 g
Soft flour	85 g	170 g
Baking powder	2 g	4 g
Invert sugar	20 g	40 g
Egg whites	225 g	450 g
Raspberry eau de vie	10 g	20 g
Fresh raspberries	25–30	50–60

energy	cal	fat	sat fat	carb	sugar	protein	fibre
383 kJ	91 kcal	4.8 g	2.2 g	10.8 g	8.6 g	1.5 g	0.3 g

METHOD OF WORK

1. Preheat an oven to 200°C.
2. Melt the butter in a pan and slowly cook it until a light nut-brown colour has been achieved (do not let the butter burn).
3. Leave the butter to cool for a few minutes and then carefully drain off the fat leaving the residue behind.
4. Mix together the almond tant-pour-tant, icing sugar, flour and baking powder.
5. Aerate the egg whites to a peak.
6. Beat the butter, invert sugar, eau de vie and vanilla into the dry ingredients.
7. Carefully fold in the egg whites.
8. Three quarter fill the moulds with the mixture and place a raspberry in the centre of each one.
9. Bake for between eight–ten minutes until golden.
10. Glaze with a little apricot or neutral glaze whilst still warm. Leave to cool before serving.

Lemon tuilles

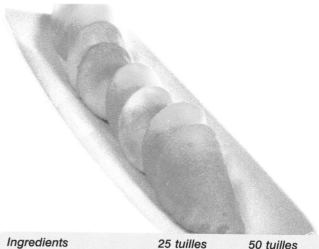

Ingredients	25 tuilles	50 tuilles
Lemon zest	2 lemons	4 lemons
Icing sugar	85 g	170 g
Melted butter	60 g	120 g
Egg whites	70 g	140 g
Soft flour	85 g	170 g

energy	cal	fat	sat fat	carb	sugar	protein	fibre
185 kJ	44 kcal	2 g	1.3 g	6.2 g	3.6 g	0.6 g	0.2 g

METHOD OF WORK

1. Preheat an oven to 220°C.
2. Beat together the icing sugar, egg whites, melted butter and the finely grated lemon zest.
3. Mix in the flour and place the tuille mixture into a refrigerator to chill and set up. This can take approximately one hour.
4. Using a template spread the mixture onto a baking sheet lined with a silicone baking mat.
5. Place in the oven and bake until the tuille begins to colour to a golden brown.
6. Remove from the oven and manipulate over a rolling pin into the classical tuille shape.

VIDEO CLIP   Orange tuilles

CHEF'S TIP   Alternative flavours can be used, such as vanilla, cinnamon, orange, hazelnut and almond. Simply add the flavour to this basic recipe.

Classic tuilles

Ingredients	25 tuilles	50 tuilles
Caster sugar	500 g	1 kg
Glucose	50 g	100 g
Melted butter	250 g	500 g
Flaked almonds	250 g	500 g
Water	200 ml	400 ml
Soft flour	150 g	300 g
Pistachio nuts	100 g	200 g

energy	cal	fat	sat fat	carb	sugar	protein	fibre
1109 kJ	266 kcal	16 g	5.9 g	28.2 g	22.6 g	3.6 g	1.5 g

METHOD OF WORK

1   Preheat an oven to 200°C.

2   Place the sugar, glucose, water, butter and almonds in a saucepan and bring to the boil, stirring constantly.

3   Remove from the heat and stir in the sieved flour. Ensure that the flour is incorporated thoroughly.

4   Put into a bowl and cool, and then place in a refrigerator to chill down.

5   Place well-spaced piles of the mixture (approximately one teaspoon) on baking sheets lined with silicone paper. Flatten thoroughly.

6   Sprinkle with the pistachio nuts and place in the oven. Bake until golden brown.

7   Remove from the oven and cool for approximately one minute, then shape over a rolling pin and allow to cool.

Almond biscotti

Ingredients	2 × 500 g logs	4 × 500 g logs
Unsalted butter	125 g	250 g
Caster sugar	225 g	450 g
Whole eggs	1	3
Aniseed	4 g	8 g
Lemon zest	½ lemon	1 lemon
Almond flour	to taste	to taste
Soft flour	850 g	1.7 kg
Good quality salt	5 g	10 g
Baking powder	7 g	15 g
Flaked almonds	85 g	170 g
Vanilla flavour	to taste	to taste

energy	cal	fat	sat fat	carb	sugar	protein	fibre
1122 kJ	266 kcal	8.3 g	3.6 g	43.4 g	12.6 g	5.3 g	1.7 g

METHOD OF WORK

1   Preheat an oven to 180°C.

2   Cream the butter and the caster sugar together. Add the egg to the creamed mixture and beat together. Add all the flavourings and mix well.

3   Sift the flour, salt and baking powder. Gradually combine with the creamed butter.

4   Fold in the almonds.

5   Scale off at 500 g each and roll into thin baguette shapes.

6   Bake in the oven on a baking tray lined with silicone paper for 20 minutes. Remove from the oven and slice thinly while still slightly warm.

7   Place the slices back into the oven (or until they have reached a golden colour). Turn and bake for a further eight minutes.

8   Cool on a wire cooling rack and store in an airtight container.

Fruit loaf

Ingredients	2 × 450 g loaves	4 × 450 g loaves
Strong white flour	450 g	900 g
Fresh yeast	15 g	30 g
Caster sugar	50 g	100 g
Salt	3 g	6 g
Warm milk	150 ml	300 ml
Whole egg, beaten	1	2
Unsalted butter	50 g	100 g
Ground cinnamon	2 tsp	4 tsp
Ground ginger	1 tsp	2 tsp
Dried apricots	50 g	100 g
Dried figs	50 g	100 g
Sultanas	50 g	100 g
Glace cherries	50 g	100 g
Flaked almonds	50 g	100 g
Orange, zest and juice	1	2

energy	cal	fat	sat fat	carb	sugar	protein	fibre
641 kJ	152 kcal	4.4 g	1.7 g	25.5 g	8.5 g	4 g	2.3 g

METHOD OF WORK

1 Preheat an oven to 220°C.

2 Cut the dried fruits into smaller sized pieces where necessary. Soak the dried fruits in the orange juice for about 30 minutes, then sieve, reserving the juice.

3 Blend the flour with the fresh yeast in a mixing bowl.

4 Add the caster sugar and salt to the flour-yeast mixture and continue to add the spices and soaked fruit and mix well.

5 Make a well in the centre and pour in the warm milk, reserved orange juice, the beaten egg and the melted butter.

6 Mix everything together to form a dough. If the dough is too dry, add a little more warm water; if it's too wet, add a little more flour.

7 Gently knead the dough on a lightly floured surface until the dough becomes smooth and springy. Transfer to a clean, lightly greased bowl and cover loosely with a clean, damp tea towel. Leave in a warm place to rise until doubled in size – this will take about one hour depending on how warm the room is.

8 Carefully turn the dough over and fold onto itself a couple of times. Grease the loaf tins. Scale off the dough at 450 g each and leave to rest for ten minutes under the cloth.

9 Use a little flour to help you shape each half into a smooth oval, then pop them into the tins. Cover both loosely with a clean, damp tea towel and leave to prove in a warm place for about 30 minutes.

10 Sprinkle with a few additional flaked almonds.

11 Place in the preheated oven to bake for 20–25 minutes, before removing from the oven and leaving the loaves to cool in the tins before turning out and glazing with a little apricot glaze.

Scones

Ingredients	Makes about 20	Makes about 40
Soft flour	500 g	1000 g
Baking powder	17 g	34 g
Salt	2 g	4 g
Diced butter	100 g	200 g
Caster sugar	100 g	200 g
Fresh full fat milk	250 ml	500 ml
Sultanas	60 g	120 g
Egg wash		
Egg yolks	2	4
Milk	10 ml	20 ml
Caster sugar	2 g	4 g

energy	cal	fat	sat fat	carb	sugar	protein	fibre
699 kJ	166 kcal	5.4 g	3.1 g	26.6 g	8.4 g	3.2 g	0.8 g

METHOD OF WORK

1 Sift the flour, baking powder, sugar and salt into a bowl.

2 Using just your fingertips, rub the butter into the flour mixture until a sandy texture has been achieved.

3 Add the sultanas and the milk and mix well. Once the dough begins to form together, turn out on to a lightly floured surface and knead gently until it forms a smooth, soft dough.

4 Wrap it in baking parchment and chill for one hour.

5 Preheat the oven to 200°C.

6 Roll the dough out on a lightly floured surface to 2.5 cm thick and cut into rounds with a 5 cm cutter. Place on a baking tray lined with baking parchment.

7 For the egg wash, mix the ingredients together in a small bowl and brush the tops of the scones twice.

8 Bake for ten minutes until golden brown. Do not over-bake them or they will be dry.

9 Serve them warm with Devonshire clotted cream and homemade strawberry jam.

Griddle scones

Ingredients	12 scones	24 scones
Soft flour	225 g	450 g
Bicarbonate of soda	1 tsp	2 tsp
Cream of tartar	2 tsp	4 tsp
Butter	25 g	50 g
Caster sugar	25 g	50 g
Fresh milk	150 ml	300 ml

energy	cal	fat	sat fat	carb	sugar	protein	fibre
402 kJ	95 kcal	2.2 g	1.3 g	16.5 g	3 g	2.2 g	0.6 g

METHOD OF WORK

1 Preheat a griddle or heavy-based frying pan and lightly oil the surface.

2 Sift the flour, bicarbonate of soda and cream of tartar into a bowl and rub in the butter.

3 Gradually stir in the sugar and the milk to form a soft paste.

4 Divide the paste in half and lightly knead on a lightly floured surface.

5 Roll each piece out to 1 cm thick and cut out individual scone rounds. Place them onto the prepared griddle and cook for about five minutes per side, until the scones are evenly brown. Place onto a wire rack to cool.

6 Serve as quickly as possible with jam and cream accompaniments.

CHEF'S TIP Wholemeal flour can replace the white flour in this recipe, although a little extra milk will be required to balance the overall consistency of the finished paste.

Fondant fancies (petit four sized)

Ingredients	Makes about 25	Makes about 50
Pre-prepared fondant	250 g	500 g
Clear, unflavoured stock syrup	50 g	75 g
Colour (optional)	to taste	to taste
Alcohol or flavouring (optional)	to taste	to taste
Heavy Génoise	**1 medium sized square sheet**	**1 large square sheet**
Apricot jam	100 g	200 g
Marzipan	150 g	300 g
Melted chocolate	50 g	80 g

energy	cal	fat	sat fat	carb	sugar	protein	fibre
522 kJ	124 kcal	2.8 g	0.6 g	23.9 g	20.7 g	1.6 g	0.2 g

METHOD OF WORK

1   Knead the marzipan until soft and then roll it out with a little icing sugar so that it will cover the square sponge.

2   Ensure the sponge is trimmed so that the depth is 2.5 cm.

3   Brush the top of the sponge with hot apricot jam and place this side onto the rolled out marzipan. Trim the sides of the marzipan and turn the sponge over so that the top is now coated with the marzipan.

4   Chill in a refrigerator for 30 minutes.

5   Cut the sponge into 2.5 cm squares and line on a wire rack.

6   Heat the fondant over a warm bain-marie, stirring constantly to thin down and slightly melt the icing. Do not heat it over 38°C; otherwise the glossy sheen of the fondant will be lost.

7   If the fondant is too thick for using, slowly add a few drops of the stock syrup and stir in. Continue this procedure until the correct consistency is achieved.

8   Add the flavouring and colouring at this stage if required.

9   Apply the warm fondant by pouring it over the individual sponge pieces or by dipping them into it.

10 Finish by decorating with the melted chocolate using a piping bag, dress and serve.

French buttercream

Ingredients	Makes about 250 g	Makes about 500 g
Caster Sugar	125 g	250 g
Water	40 g	60 ml
Egg Yolks	45 g	90 g
Softened, unsalted butter	150 g	300 g
Vanilla extract	2 g	4 g

energy	cal	fat	sat fat	carb	sugar	protein	fibre
734 kJ	177 kcal	13.7 g	8.2 g	13.2 g	13.2 g	0.8 g	0 g

METHOD OF WORK

1   Combine the sugar and the water in a clean, heavy based saucepan (preferably copper). Let the sugar dissolve for a few minutes before bring to the boil.

2   Continue to boil whilst constantly monitoring the temperature using a sugar thermometer. The sugar solution should eventually reach 115°C before removing it from the heat.

3   Whilst the sugar is boiling; using a mixing machine with a whisk attachment, beat the egg yolks at a fast speed for two minutes.

4   After the sugar has reached the correct temperature, slowly pour a thread of the hot liquid into the egg yolks whilst whipping the yolks on a medium speed.

5   Continue to add all of the sugar solution and continue to whip the yolks until the mixture is completely cooled and the yolks are pale and thickened.

6   Whisk in the butter, a little at a time on the machine. Finally beat in the vanilla. If the buttercream is too soft, place in a refrigerator to firm it up.

Fruit gelatine based glaze

Ingredients	Makes about 300 g	Makes about 600 g
Gelatine leaves	4 leaves	8 leaves
Caster sugar	90 g	180 g
Water	60 g	120 g
Glucose	30 g	60 g
Fruit Puree	150 g	300 g

energy	cal	fat	sat fat	carb	sugar	protein	fibre
142 kJ	33 kcal	0 g	0 g	8.5 g	7.5 g	0.3 g	0.2 g

METHOD OF WORK

1   Soften the gelatine leaves in cold water.
2   Place the sugar, water and glucose into a saucepan and heat until the sugar has dissolved. Remove from the heat and stir in the softened gelatine.
3   Add the fruit puree and mix well.
4   Strain the mixture through a Chinois or fine strainer.
5   Pour over the top of a cake or dessert and quickly spread to the edges with a palette knife. One 300 g batch will make enough for a large 20 cm cake.

Chocolate glaze

Ingredients	Makes about 600 g	Makes about 1200 g
Fresh milk	100 g	210 g
Double cream	75 g	150 g
Caster sugar	50 g	100 g
Water	50 g	100 g
Glucose	50 g	100 g
Chopped dark chocolate	375 g	750 g

energy	cal	fat	sat fat	carb	sugar	protein	fibre
377 kJ	91 kcal	6.6 g	0.8 g	6.8 g	2.5 g	1.3 g	0 g

METHOD OF WORK

1   Place the sugar, milk, cream and glucose into a saucepan and heat until the sugar has dissolved. Bring to the boil and remove from the heat.
2   Add the dark chocolate and mix well.
3   Strain the mixture through a chinois or fine strainer.
4   Pour over the top of a cake or dessert and quickly spread to the edges with a palette knife. 1200 g is enough to coat 4 × 20 cm cakes.

Apricot glaze

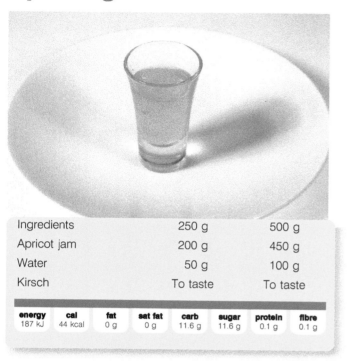

Ingredients	250 g	500 g
Apricot jam	200 g	450 g
Water	50 g	100 g
Kirsch	To taste	To taste

energy	cal	fat	sat fat	carb	sugar	protein	fibre
187 kJ	44 kcal	0 g	0 g	11.6 g	11.6 g	0.1 g	0.1 g

METHOD OF WORK

1   Boil together the water and the apricot jam.
2   Pass through a fine sieve.
3   Flavour with a little Kirsch.
4   The glaze should be re-boiled before use.

Guest Chef

Yorkshire Parkin with apple and cheese curd ice cream

Chef *Richard Walsh*
Centre *Calderdale College*

Yorkshire parkin is a traditional sticky ginger cake that contains oats and treacle. It is widely eaten across Yorkshire in the autumn months but traditionally around bonfire night. This parkin contains barley wine made by the Barearts brewery in Todmorden, West Yorkshire. The ice cream is based on the flavours of another traditional dish the Yorkshire curd tart. It is made from cheese curd and currents and flavoured with rose water.

Ingredients

Ingredient	Amount
For the parkin	
Oatmeal, ground	100 g
Plain flour	110 g
Caster sugar	110 g
Ground ginger	1 tsp
Baking powder	1 tsp
Unsalted butter	55 g
Black treacle	150 g
Barley wine	125 ml
Egg, medium	1
For the curd	
Whole milk	250 ml
Rennet, vegetarian	5 drops
For the ice cream	
Whole milk	200 ml
Egg yolk	2
Caster sugar	80 g
Currants	20 g
Cheese curd (above)	100 g
Rose water	5 ml
Jelly	
Apple juice	125 ml
Agar-agar	7.5 g
Garnish	
Braeburn apple	1
Popping candy	5 g

METHOD OF WORK

Parkin

1   1 Preheat the oven to 150°C. Sieve all the dry ingredients into a bowl. Warm the treacle and butter in a pan and add to the dry ingredients. Add the egg and thoroughly mix. Pour into 150 ml non-stick pudding basins. Bake in the oven for approximately 20 minutes.

Curd

2   Warm the milk to 37°C, add the rennet and leave to separate for about one hour. Pass through a muslin cloth and squeeze gently.

Ice cream

3   Heat the milk in a saucepan. Whisk the egg yolks and sugar in a bowl. Add half the hot milk to the egg yolks and mix thoroughly. Pour back in to the saucepan.

4   Stir with a wooden spoon over a low heat until it becomes thick and coats the back of the spoon. Add the curd and stir.

5   Pass through a chinois and allow too cool. Pour into an ice cream mixer, add the currants and churn until frozen.

Jelly

6   Warm the juice and agar-agar together in a saucepan. Bring to the boil and occasionally stir. Boil for three minutes. Pour into a tray to a thickness of 1 cm. Place in the fridge to set.

7   Peel and dice the apple into 1 cm cubes and sauté in butter.

To finish

8   Serve the parkin warm and present with the other elements and honey pearls. Garnish with apple crisps and sprinkle a little popping candy over the ice cream.

ASSESSMENT OF KNOWLEDGE AND UNDERSTANDING

You have now learned about the use of the different types of complex cakes, sponges, biscuits and scones and how to produce some varieties utilizing an array of commodities and techniques.

To test your level of knowledge and understanding, answer the following short questions. These will help to prepare you for your summative (final) assessment.

1 Explain the importance of selecting the correct type, quality and quantity of ingredients when producing a Sacher torte.

2 State the quality points to look for when producing a separated egg sponge.

3 State two advantages of using an electric mixer for aeration and what technique you would need to use if there is not one available.

4 State which two fats are ideal for aeration and creaming.

5 Explain the term 'foam'.

6 Briefly describe how to produce a separated egg sponge.

7 Explain how the aeration of egg helps to create a light texture in a sponge.

8 State three roles that fat plays in baking cakes.

9 Explain the difference between a Génoise sponge and a heavy Génoise sponge.

10 Identify the critical quality points for the following baked products:

a griddle scones

b classic tuilles

c Dacquoise.

Recipes

Chocolate 14

VRQ

Produce petits fours

Produce display pieces and decorative items

NVQ

Prepare, process and finish complex chocolate products

Cocoa pods before harvest

A variety of cocoa pods after harvesting by hand

Cocoa flower

Cocoa

The cocoa tree grows in warm and humid climates around the equator. Plantations can be found in the tropical rainforests of Africa, Asia and Latin America. Africa produces the largest proportion of the world harvest today, providing up to 65 per cent of the world's cocoa. The tree itself is quite fragile and needs other tall-growing plants, such as palm trees or banana plants, to give it protection from strong winds and the burning sun. Some cocoa trees are harvested for up to 100 years, but after 30 years the harvest for each tree diminishes. Cocoa farmers are now encouraged to plant other crops such as banana, rubber, palm trees and other fruits to help substitute their income and to help soil regeneration and give shade to the cocoa trees.

There are three principal varieties of cocoa, although many hybrids have been produced by chocolate companies over the years.

- Criollo – known as 'the king of cocoa' due to its exceptional flavour qualities, but is the most fragile variety. It is a smaller pod (fits into the palm of the hand), is rounded in shape, usually composed of shades of green and yellow, and is very sensitive to disease, which is why some farms are moving to Forastero types and hybrids.

- Forastero – this is a stronger type that is easier to cultivate and produces larger yields of cocoa. It has a stronger and more bitter flavour than the criollo and is usually blended with other varieties. It is a longer size, rougher textured outside shell, larger overall pod and is usually shades of greens, yellows, reds and purple.

- Trinitario – this is a cross-breed of the criollo and forastero types and gives a strong but refined flavour. Hybrids such as trinitario are produced to help resist against disease, increase the supply to demand of cocoa production and increase the actual bean size per pod (therefore increasing yield), and better control of quality. The grafting process produces a hybrid.

VIDEO CLIP   Barry Callebaut Factory and Academy: types of chocolate

Harvesting takes place as and when the pods are ready and this is always undertaken by hand because of the delicate nature of the process. After the pods have been gathered, the outer shell is opened and the pulp is removed. The cocoa beans are then extracted from the pulp and left to ferment for up to seven days. The average yield per tree is 1–1.5 kg cocoa beans.

The pulp and beans inside the cocoa pod

Fermentation is important for developing colour and flavour in the beans. Fermentation can last two days, which produces a lower quality yield, but some fermentation processes go on for up to six or seven days. The beans are taken to the fermentation area where they are placed into large wooden, slatted vats. Some are lined with banana leaves which can help the fermentation process further. By day two of the fermentation process, the moisture content is up to 65 per cent which is then reduced to between 6 and 11 per cent upon drying. The smell during the process of fermentation is highly acidic, vinegar scented, strong and pungent.

The cocoa beans drying after fermentation

After the fermentation, the beans are spread out to dry naturally in the sun for up to seven days. They are turned regularly to stop the fermentation process. Different methods of drying can be used:

- Drying beans on a cement roof that has heat from a wood fire oven in the room underneath the concrete drying chamber. This can result in a slightly smoky flavour to the chocolate.

- Drying the beans on a wood slatted base, with a moveable roof that can be slid on and off very easily to protect from rain.

Many farms have drying chambers to reduce the moisture of the beans to under 8 per cent. Drying time depends on the weather, but an average of five to seven days is normal.

The beans are graded either locally or in the factory. Dried beans are placed onto a special board and then cut in half to reveal the inside of the bean. Well fermented beans, six–seven days and then well dried, are coloured dark brown with no mould. They almost resemble a roasted bean in appearance. Mouldy beans would make the cocoa butter taste rancid. Mould occurs due to too much moisture content in the bean with a poor fermentation process. The grading measurement of the beans is on a scale of one–four in Central America. Africa including the Ivory Coast is one–three.

Before the cocoa beans can be processed into chocolate, beans from various origins are blended according to the requirements of the recipe. The cocoa bean shells are removed and the beans are broken down into 'nibs', which are then roasted to increase the flavour of the cocoa.

The roasted cocoa nibs are then ground. The heat produced during this procedure melts the cocoa butter, which is removed by being pressed out. The cocoa solids will now be formed into a dry cake and used as the base ingredient in the production of chocolate or processed into a fine cocoa powder.

The next stage in chocolate making is conching, whereby the cocoa solids and cocoa butter are slowly mixed in tanks over a period of time. This develops the flavour of the chocolate and breaks down the particles into a smooth texture. Further ingredients are then added: cocoa butter, sugar, vanilla and soya lecithin. The chocolate is then tempered and set into blocks or drops, which are then packaged for storage and distribution.

Couverture is the term used for chocolate in which the fat content is pure cocoa butter. In family or bakers' chocolate the cocoa fat content is replaced by a vegetable-based fat. This has a detrimental effect on the texture and hardness of the chocolate but makes the product cheaper to purchase and easier to use. When used for making chocolates, decorations or moulded chocolates, couverture first has to go through a process of tempering called 'pre-crystallization'.

Melting chocolate

Dark, milk and white couverture all contain cocoa butter. When the chocolate is warmed, the fat crystals in the cocoa butter melt and the chocolate becomes liquid. This starts to occur at 25°C, but cocoa butter contains a variety of fat crystals, some of which will not melt until a temperature of 37°C has been reached. To make sure that the mass of chocolate is totally melted it is common practice to heat the chocolate to 45°C.

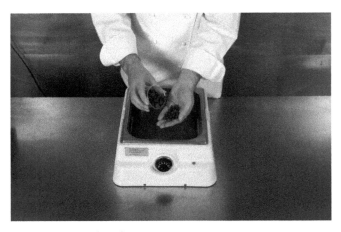

Dark couverture chocolate

The following practices must be applied when melting chocolate:

1   Ensure that the chocolate does not come into direct contact with the heat source otherwise it may burn.

2   Use a dry bain-marie or chocolate melting pot to prevent the chocolate coming into contact with moisture.

If storing melted chocolate for a long period of time, it is important to stir the chocolate regularly to prevent the cocoa butter rising to the surface.

VIDEO CLIP Pre-crystallization

Pre-crystallizing chocolate

If chocolate has been melted at 45°C then poured into a mould and left to set without further processing, the following will occur:

● The chocolate will take a long time to harden.

● When the chocolate has eventually hardened it will have a grainy structure and a greyish colour.

● The chocolate will stick to the mould.

The reason for this is that as the chocolate cools, crystals form in the cocoa butter, but these crystals are unstable. Cocoa butter actually contains six different forms of crystal, but only one is stable. It is this form of crystal that makes chocolate hard and shiny with a deep and even colouring. The chocolate will also turn out of the mould easily.

There are several different techniques used to pre-crystallize chocolate; crystals can be created in melted chocolate through manipulation and temperature control or by adding chocolate that already contains the stable crystal.

Tabletop pre-crystallizing

It is preferable to use a marble or a granite worktop, which will retain heat better than stainless steel.

1   Melt the chocolate to 45°C.

2   Stir well.

3   Pour two-thirds of the chocolate onto the work surface. Leave the remaining chocolate in the bain-marie.

4   Spread the chocolate over the work surface, moving it around with a palette knife and a scraper. This movement cools down the chocolate mass evenly. The chocolate will begin to thicken as it cools. This is an indication the stable crystals are forming.

5   At 27°C the chocolate will be too thick to process and use. Return it to the bain-marie and mix together well with the remaining warm chocolate.

This will create the right amount of stable crystals throughout the chocolate, which is now ready to use as required.

> **CHEF'S TIP**   Time, temperature and movement are the three essential factors in this method. If the chocolate is too thick after pre-crystallizing, simply raise the temperature by 1°C to re-melt some of the stable crystals.

It is easy to focus on just the temperature when preparing chocolate. This will not guarantee that there are sufficient stable crystals present in the chocolate. Pre-crystallizing is a form of 'tempering', in other words bringing the chocolate to a certain temperature. However, if the chocolate is just left to cool down to 32°C after melting, it will have been tempered but not pre-crystallized. Without the stirring and moving around of the chocolate required to form the crystals, the result will be a chocolate that hardens slowly, is dull and sticks in the mould.

The seeding method

This method uses ready-to-use pre-crystallized chocolate callets or small pieces of chopped chocolate block, which are added to the chocolate being processed.

1   Melt the chocolate to 45°C.

2   Stir well.

3   Add 15–20 per cent of callets or chopped chocolate block and stir well into the melted chocolate; these pieces contain the stable cocoa crystals. They will slowly melt and cool down the mass. When the chocolate reaches its correct processing temperature, stir well again; it will be completely pre-crystallized.

4   If all the crystals melt quickly before the correct temperature has been reached, just add a small extra quantity and stir in well until the correct temperature has been obtained.

> **CHEF'S TIP**   To test if the chocolate if ready, dip the tip of a palette knife into the melted chocolate. It should harden within five minutes and have a nice sheen. If you have too few crystals the chocolate will not harden. If you have too many crystals the chocolate will not have a sheen.

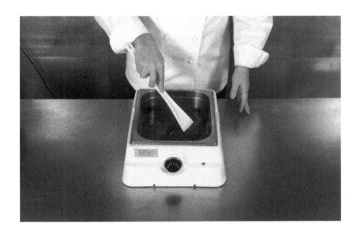

Stirring the callets into the melted chocolate mass

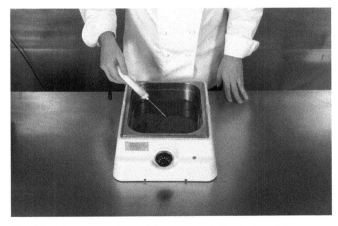

Checking the temperature of the pre-crystallized chocolate

Temperature control for chocolate

The ideal processing temperatures after melting and pre-crystallization are different for the three different types of chocolate (dark, milk and white). This is attributed to their different compositions; for instance, the higher the quantity of milk fats (milk and white chocolate), the lower the processing temperature.

Irregular cooling can create a dull appearance and a soft structure in the finished chocolate. The ideal temperature to cool and harden chocolate is 10–15°C. A refrigerator with air circulation set to this temperature range is ideal for setting chocolate.

Dark chocolate processing temperature is 31–32°C
Milk chocolate processing temperature is 30–31°C
White chocolate processing temperature is 28–29°C

Shelf life and storage of chocolates

The ideal temperature for storing chocolate is 12–20°C, and the temperature should not fluctuate. At higher temperatures the chocolate becomes soft and will lose its sheen, and at lower temperatures it may be affected by condensation. Chocolate that has been stored at a lower temperature should, when required for use, be left to acclimatize in its original packaging for a few hours until it reaches ambient temperature.

> **CHEF'S TIP** The ideal room temperature when working with chocolate is 20°C.
>

Chocolate is sensitive to humidity and easily absorbs smells and flavours. It is also liable to oxidization if it is exposed to light, direct sunlight and air for too long.

Therefore, chocolate should be stored in a cool, dry place, completely sealed from light and air. Always ensure that the packaging is resealed after using.

> **CHEF'S TIP** Cocoa solids contain naturally occurring antioxidants. Since white chocolate contains no cocoa solids, it lacks these antioxidants and so will be more susceptible to oxidation than other chocolates.
>

Finished products are also very sensitive to temperature, foreign smells, flavours, light, air and humidity and to the effects of time and transportation. Typical changes that can occur during storage of chocolate products include:

● Fat bloom – a thin layer of fat crystals on the surface of the chocolate. The chocolate loses its sheen and a soft, milky white bloom appears on the surface, giving the finished chocolate an unattractive appearance. Fat bloom is caused when fats in the chocolate crystallize or when the fats in the ganache/filling migrate to the chocolate layer. The appearance of fat bloom can be delayed by storing the chocolate at a constant temperature of 10–15°C.

● Sugar bloom – in contrast to fat bloom, sugar bloom creates a rough, coarse layer on top of the chocolate. Sugar bloom is mainly caused by condensation, which can form on the surface of chocolate if storage temperatures are too low or if the chocolate is left in a refrigerator for too long. This moisture will dissolve the sugar within the chocolate and when the moisture evaporates, the sugar re-crystallizes on the surface. Avoid rapid changes of temperature to help prevent this occurrence.

> **CHEF'S TIP** Chocolate should be stored in a well-ventilated area with no strong odours. Always ensure that the packaging is secure.
>

If the storage time for chocolate can be kept short, the quality of the product will be much better. Each type of chocolate will have a different shelf life, which is measured from the initial production date and is shown on the packaging. Because of the milk fat solids present in white and milk chocolate, these have shorter shelf lives than dark chocolate. Chocolates that contain a filling need special consideration. Chocolates made with cream or butter fillings have a very short storage life (the recipes shown in this chapter have a shelf life of one week), provided they are stored in ideal conditions. The substitution of cream or butter with alternative ingredients (such as light sugar solutions) will help to increase shelf life.

Moulding hollow figures

Moulded hollow figures or Easter eggs can be made using one or more different types of chocolate. The chocolate first has to be pre-crystallized and is then poured into a mould and cooled down.

Most chocolatiers and chefs work with polycarbonate moulds because they are easy to maintain, are quite strong and will give a good end result. Metal moulds are also available, but are used less and less due to their price and weight. PVC moulds are also popular. They are flexible, allowing the chocolate shapes to be turned out quickly, and cheap, but they can scratch easily and will often break.

There are two basic forms of moulds:

- Single moulds – sometimes referred to as half moulds, the chocolate is poured into the mould, cooled and then removed from the mould. The chocolate halves are then joined together.

- Double moulds – these are made up of two half moulds linked together to form one mould. The chocolate is poured into the mould and cooled. The moulded shape is then removed by unfastening the two half moulds and prising them apart.

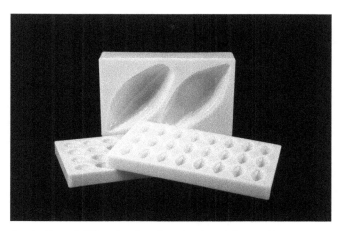

A selection of different polycarbonate chocolate moulds

Before moulding figures, the moulds must be thoroughly cleaned and then polished with cotton wool, and they must be at room temperature.

The chocolate must be pre-crystallized and the various pieces of equipment, such as palette knives, plastic spoons, stainless steel trays, silicone paper and wire cooling racks, should be prepared in advance.

Step-by-step: Producing a small moulded figure

1. Clean and polish the mould with cotton wool or a soft clean cloth.

2. Pour the pre-crystallized chocolate into the mould. Tap the back of the mould to remove any air bubbles and swirl the chocolate around to create an even layer of chocolate, then pour any excess out of the mould.

3. Scrape the setting chocolate from the surface of the mould and place into a refrigerator at 12°C for at least 20 minutes.

4. After cooling, check to see if the chocolate figures are ready to come out of the moulds. If the chocolate has crystallized it should have contracted slightly away from the inside of the mould.

5. Tap the edges of the mould gently and remove the moulded chocolate halves.

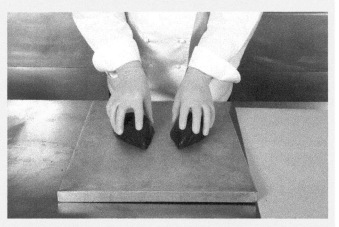

6. Lay two halves, with the open sides down, onto a warm stainless steel tray to melt the chocolate. Stick the halves together immediately. Press together and hold for a few seconds.

7. The finished figures can then be presented or wrapped in decorative packaging ready to be sold.

Small chocolate display pieces

Chocolate designs can be relatively simple and still be creative and eye-catching. Learning a few uncomplicated decorative techniques will equip the chef to be able to produce striking chocolate display pieces for banquets, festivals or dinners or just for fun.

The moulding techniques explained in this chapter can easily be transferred to create Easter eggs, chocolate bars or other moulded pieces. However, the following techniques will further enhance any display, and can also be used in the decoration of desserts.

Step-by-step: Creating acetate curls

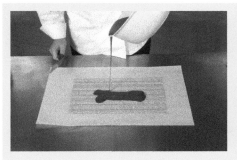

1. Lay a sheet of acetate on a sheet of plastic film on a work surface. Pour some pre-crystallized chocolate onto the acetate and spread it over the surface evenly.

2. Leave the chocolate to begin to set. While the chocolate is still pliable and not fully hardened, quickly make curved cuts from the inside of the acetate to the edge, without cutting through the acetate.

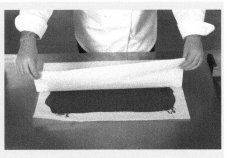

3. Place a sheet of silicone paper over the acetate.

4. Quickly roll up the acetate before the chocolate sets. Leave to harden for approximately 15 minutes.

5. When the chocolate is set, carefully unravel the acetate sheet. The chocolate curls will break off where the cuts were made.

6. The finished curls ready for use.

VIDEO CLIP Decorative acetate work

Flat cutting

This is a technique used to create different forms and shapes. The items produced can be used as decoration, as bases for decoration pieces or combined to create figures.

Step-by-step: flat cutting

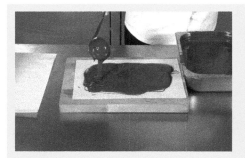

1. Pour some pre-crystallized chocolate onto some silicone paper on a wooden board.

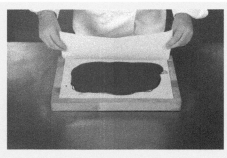

2. Place a top sheet of silicone paper over the chocolate trying not to capture any air pockets.

3. Smooth out and turn over the chocolate to regulate the cooling and setting of the chocolate. Repeat this process every 60 seconds or so.

4. Using a ruler for measuring and straight edges cut any shapes required with a sharp scalpel.

5. Leave the chocolate to fully set and then carefully peel away the silicone paper from the cut shapes.

Display figures and show pieces

CHRISTMAS DISPLAY

The techniques discussed above have been utilized to create the small display piece shown here. The composition of the piece is a small moulded, coloured sphere, moulded mini stamens of chocolate, acetate decorations and a flat cut triangle base and tree. The base has been assembled and then lightly sprayed with chocolate to give a soft matt finish. The tree has also been sprayed with chocolate ad also green cocoa butter to give a two-tone effect and therefore depth to the chocolate display.

The presented coils of chocolate have been moulded and coloured.

LIME GREEN FLOWER

To create a flower:

1   Pre-crystallize white chocolate.

2   Dip the end of a small kitchen knife into the chocolate then imprint the chocolate onto a strip of silicone paper to create 'petals'. Repeat about 30 times.

3   Lay the strip of 30 petals into a small tuile mould to give them a rounded shape.

4   Spray the petals using a green cocoa butter at 45°C.

5   Begin fixing the petals around the centre of a small moulded sphere, working your way around the sphere towards the base.

6   Leave to set and spray once more with a lime green colour.

RED FLOWER ON A SPHERE

Assembling this display piece also uses some of the techniques discussed in this chapter:

1   Flat cut the base into a triangle and join together with melted chocolate and fix the spheres in the centre of the base, maintaining the balance of the piece.

2   Spray the piece with fluid chocolate if desired.

3   Add the acetate curls around the larger sphere.

4   Create a small flower using the acetate technique and creating petals that have been joined together on top of the sphere. On this occasion it has been sprayed with red cocoa butter.

VIDEO CLIP   Finishing a decorative display

COPEAUX, CIGARETTES AND SHAVINGS OF CHOCOLATE

To create these elements follow the steps below:

1   Using pre-crystallized chocolate thinly spread the chocolate onto a marble slab into a rectangular shape.

2   Work the chocolate until it just sets and immediately make slicing cuts with a large healed chopping knife.

3   The blade is required to be at an angle of 45° and the slice action should be quick and in one motion.

Recipes

Honey and cinnamon moulded chocolates

Ingredients
	40–50 chocolates
Dark chocolate (minimum 60% cocoa)	250 g
Milk chocolate (minimum 32% cocoa)	250 g
Double cream	250 g
Clear honey	80 g
Cinnamon	2 sticks or 20 g powder
Pre-crystallized dark chocolate	50 g
Pre-crystallized white chocolate for moulding	1 kg

energy	cal	fat	sat fat	carb	sugar	protein	fibre
916 kJ	220 kcal	15.3 g	5.9 g	18.3 g	14.4 g	3.1 g	0 g

VIDEO CLIP Moulding

METHOD OF WORK

1   Place the double cream in a saucepan with the cinnamon and bring to the boil. Remove from the heat and leave to infuse for 15 minutes.

2   Melt the dark and milk chocolates together and add the cinnamon-infused cream. Blend well with a whisk.

3   Add the honey and allow the ganache to cool.

4   Prepare the chocolate moulds by polishing well with cotton wool to ensure there are no marks, dust or remaining chocolate.

5   Take a little pre-crystallized dark chocolate and using a plastic disposable glove, dip a finger into it. Rub some chocolate into each mould and leave to set.

6   If desired, at this stage a fine spray of coloured cocoa butter can be applied to build up a pronounced presentation of the finished chocolate. Leave to set.

7   Using the pre-crystallized white chocolate, fill the moulds. Shake out any air bubbles in the chocolate.

8   Pour out the excess chocolate and make sure all the edges and corners in the mould have been covered.

9   To leave a clean finish, remove any remaining chocolate from the top and the edges using a palette knife.

10   Invert the mould onto a wire rack or silicone paper for four minutes. Scrape off any remaining chocolate that has dripped down the mould and leave to harden for a few minutes.

11   Place the ganache into a disposable piping bag and pipe into the centre of each chocolate shell. Take care not to pipe too much ganache into the chocolate shell; it is best to leave a 2 mm gap from the top. Make sure the ganache is not too warm otherwise it will melt the chocolate shell. Leave the filling to solidify.

12   To close the chocolates, put a small amount of the pre-crystallized white chocolate onto the mould and spread over each moulded ganache chocolate. Scrape off any excess chocolate and leave to set at 10°C for 30 minutes.

13   Tap the moulds gently onto a sheet of paper and carefully turn out the chocolates.

CHEF'S TIP   Wear gloves when removing chocolates from the mould to avoid fingerprints.

Step-by-step: Creating chocolate moulds

1. Spraying the coloured cocoa butter onto the moulds using a small, clean pastry brush

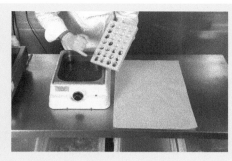

2. Rubbing pre-crystallized dark chocolate into each mould

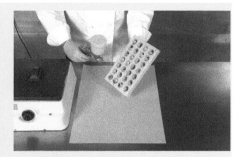

3. Spraying the yellow coloured cocoa butter into the mould using a compressed air spray gun

4. Filling the mould with pre-crystallized white chocolate

5. Pouring out the excess chocolate and tapping the sides the help remove the excess chocolate

6. Inverting the mould onto the wire rack to help remove any excess chocolate

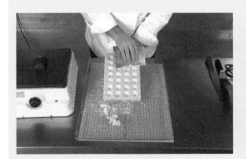

7. Scrapping off the excess chocolate that has begun to crystallize

8. Piping the chocolate filling into the set chocolate shells

9. Scraping off the excess chocolate after closing off the moulds

Raspberry moulded chocolates

Ingredients	40–50 chocolates
Dark chocolate (minimum 64% cocoa)	300 g
Raspberry purée	150 g
UHT cream	125 g
Caster sugar	10 g
Invert sugar	25 g
Unsalted butter	60 g
Alcohol (framboise or kirsch)	15 g
Pre-crystallized dark chocolate (minimum 64% cocoa) for moulding	1 kg

energy	cal	fat	sat fat	carb	sugar	protein	fibre
796 kJ	192 kcal	15.5 g	1.6 g	10 g	1 g	2.9 g	0.1 g

METHOD OF WORK

1   Melt the dark chocolate.

2   Place the raspberry purée, caster sugar and invert sugar into a saucepan and bring to the boil. Using a sugar thermometer, continue cooking the purée to 104°C.

3   Add the UHT cream carefully and stir in. Incorporate into the dark chocolate and add the alcohol. Leave to cool.

4   When cool, beat in the softened unsalted butter.

5   Follow the method for moulding the chocolates in the previous recipe, but using the dark chocolate.

CHEF'S TIP   Invert sugar is created by mixing basic sugar syrup with a small amount of acid, such as lemon juice or cream of tartar. This will break down the sugar (sucrose) into two simple sugars (fructose and glucose) and so reduce the size of the sugar crystals. Adding this to the chocolate filling recipe will help to create a smoother texture in the product.

Step-by-step: Creating the filling and the moulding

1. Boiling the raspberry puree

2. Adding the raspberry cream mixture onto the dark chocolate

3. Blending the ingredients together to form a stable emulsion

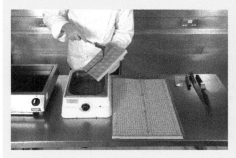

4. Filling the cocoa sprayed chocolate mould with dark chocolate

5. Pouring out the excess chocolate and tapping the base of the moulds with the handle of the palette knife

6. Remove the excess chocolate by sliding the edge of the metal scraper

7. After the raspberry filling has been added and set, cap off the chocolates with some dark chocolate

8. Carefully position the patterned acetate over the pre-crystallized chocolate

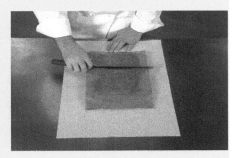

9. Run a palette knife over the acetate to remove excess chocolate and leave to set before peeling away and demoulding the chocolates

Vanilla chocolate truffles

Ingredients	40–50 chocolates
Dark chocolate (minimum 70% cocoa)	400 g
Whipping cream	325 g
Milk chocolate (minimum 36% cocoa)	200 g
Invert sugar	40 g
Unsalted butter	50 g
Vanilla	1 pod
Pre-crystallized dark chocolate (minimum 64% cocoa) for dipping	1 kg
Cocoa powder	500 g

energy	cal	fat	sat fat	carb	sugar	protein	fibre
1140 kJ	275 kcal	22.1 g	3.8 g	13.5 g	1.2 g	5.6 g	3.1 g

METHOD OF WORK

1   Melt the dark and milk chocolate together.

2   Bring the cream to the boil with the split vanilla pod. Remove from the heat and leave to infuse for five minutes.

3   Pour the infused cream onto the chocolate and add the invert sugar. Combine the ingredients well.

4   Beat in the softened unsalted butter when cold.

5   Fill a disposable piping bag with the truffle filling and pipe out small truffle shapes onto silicone paper. Leave to harden for at least three hours in a refrigerator.

6   Dip the individual truffles into the pre-crystallized dark chocolate. Shake off any excess chocolate.

7   Immediately place the truffles into a container filled with cocoa powder and roll until completely covered with a fine layer of the powder.

CHEF'S TIP   Alternatively, the truffles can be rolled in sieved icing sugar or small chocolate shavings for different effects. Other flavours can also be added to the chocolate ganache, such as praline, coconut, orange zest, Grand Marnier and aniseed.

Salted caramel chocolates

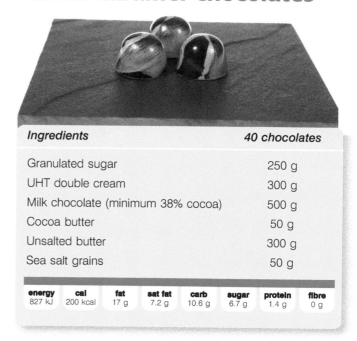

Ingredients	40 chocolates
Granulated sugar	250 g
UHT double cream	300 g
Milk chocolate (minimum 38% cocoa)	500 g
Cocoa butter	50 g
Unsalted butter	300 g
Sea salt grains	50 g

energy	cal	fat	sat fat	carb	sugar	protein	fibre
827 kJ	200 kcal	17 g	7.2 g	10.6 g	6.7 g	1.4 g	0 g

METHOD OF WORK

1   Caramelize the sugar and reduce with the cream. Cool for a few seconds.

2   Add the milk chocolate and mix in the cocoa butter.

3   Once cold, beat in the butter.

4   Mould the chocolates using a similar technique for moulded chocolates as explained earlier in this chapter.

5   Place a few grains of sea salt in the moulds before piping the caramel ganache on top.

6   Set the ganache and cap off the chocolates with some more pre-crystallized chocolate.

7   Set and demould.

Pralines

Ingredients	40–50 chocolates
Milk chocolate (minimum 38% cocoa)	100 g
Praline paste	220 g
Pure hazelnut paste	50 g
Unsalted butter	50 g
Pre-crystallized milk chocolate (minimum 38% cocoa) for moulding	1 kg

energy	cal	fat	sat fat	carb	sugar	protein	fibre
756 kJ	182 kcal	13.8 g	0.7 g	11.7 g	3.6 g	3.1 g	0.3 g

METHOD OF WORK

1 Melt the milk chocolate to 40°C.
2 Add the praline paste and the hazelnut paste.
3 Blend together to form a smooth paste and beat in the softened butter.
4 Prepare the moulds using the pre-crystallized milk chocolate, as described previously. An alternative is to marble with a little pre-crystallized white or dark chocolate to create an interesting design.
5 Pipe the praline filling into the prepared moulds and finish by topping off and leaving to set.

Malakoff

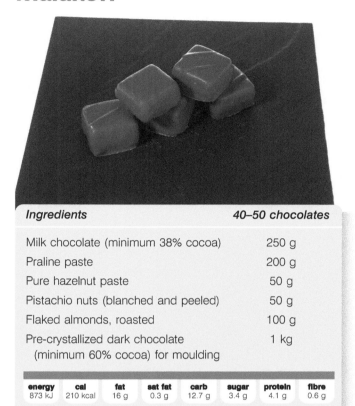

Ingredients	40–50 chocolates
Milk chocolate (minimum 38% cocoa)	250 g
Praline paste	200 g
Pure hazelnut paste	50 g
Pistachio nuts (blanched and peeled)	50 g
Flaked almonds, roasted	100 g
Pre-crystallized dark chocolate (minimum 60% cocoa) for moulding	1 kg

energy	cal	fat	sat fat	carb	sugar	protein	fibre
873 kJ	210 kcal	16 g	0.3 g	12.7 g	3.4 g	4.1 g	0.6 g

METHOD OF WORK

1 Melt and pre-crystallize the milk chocolate and mix in the praline paste.
2 Add the flaked almonds and pistachio nuts.
3 Mix the nuts in and pour into a tray lined with silicone paper, to a depth of 1.5 cm.
4 Set the mixture in a cool area at about 12°C.
5 Turn out of the tray and cut the slab into even chocolate sizes (1.5 cm squares).
6 Dip the squares into the pre-crystallized dark chocolate and set upon a plain sheet of acetate to set.
7 Store in an airtight plastic box, in a cool place without light or temperature fluctuations.

Step-by-step: How to dip chocolates

1. Brush some pre-crystallized chocolate on one side of the set chocolate ganache.

2. Cut the set chocolate into the required shape and size.

3. Place the chocolates into the pre-crystallized dark chocolate and ensure it has fully submerged into it.

4. Using a chocolate dipping fork, remove the set chocolate and tap the fork on the top of the chocolate surface to remove excess chocolate.

5. Tap the sides of the bain-marie to remove any further excess chocolate.

6. The finished chocolates having been set.

Chocolate lollipops

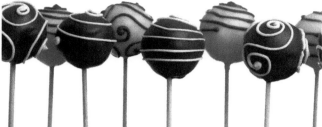

Ingredients	40–50 chocolates
Milk and dark chocolate shells (minimum 38% and 60% cocoa)	40–50
Chocolate truffle centre (see recipe for chocolate truffles on page 498)	300 g
Lollipop sticks	40–50
Pre-crystallized dark, milk and white chocolate for moulding	1 kg

energy	cal	fat	sat fat	carb	sugar	protein	fibre
610 kJ	147 kcal	10.9 g	1.5 g	9.9 g	4 g	2.5 g	0.2 g

METHOD OF WORK

1 Pipe the chocolate truffle mixture into the milk and dark chocolate shells. Leave to half set before positioning a lollipop stick upright in each one of them.

2 Leave to fully set.

3 Dip each lollipop into a pre-crystallized chocolate and leave to set once more by place each stick upright into a polystyrene block.

4 Pipe chocolate decorations over the set coating before serving.

Chocolate tuiles

Ingredients	50 tuiles
Icing sugar	300 g
Soft flour	100 g
Cocoa powder	100 g
Egg whites	250 g
Melted butter	200 g

energy	cal	fat	sat fat	carb	sugar	protein	fibre
286 kJ	68 kcal	3.8 g	2.3 g	8 g	6.3 g	1 g	0.6 g

METHOD OF WORK

1 Preheat an oven to 220°C.

2 Mix the dry ingredients together well in a food processor.

3 Mixing on a slow speed, gradually add the egg whites, and then the melted butter.

4 Pipe onto silicone baking mats in small bulbs approximately 2 cm in size.

5 Place in the oven to bake for a few minutes.

6 Quickly remove from the oven and shape in a tuile mould or over a rolling pin.

Gianduja macaroons

Ingredients 40 macaroons

Egg whites	200 g
Sieved icing sugar	480 g
Ground almonds	280 g
Vanilla extract	To taste
Gianduja	
Lightly roasted and skinned hazelnuts	100 g
Icing sugar	100 g
Milk or dark couverture	100 g

energy	cal	fat	sat fat	carb	sugar	protein	fibre
551 kJ	131 kcal	6.4 g	0.4 g	16.7 g	15.5 g	2.7 g	0.8 g

METHOD OF WORK

1 To make the macaroons; aerate the egg whites until stiff, add very quickly the vanilla.

2 Rain in a mixture made of the sifted icing sugar and the ground almonds, fold in well.

3 Pipe on a baking sheet coated with silicone paper put onto another baking sheet. Stand for 20 minutes at room temperature before baking in a preheated oven at 250°C immediately dropped to 180°C, for ten to 12 minutes, with the oven door ajar.

4 When baked, pour a little water in the silicone paper, remove the macaroons and cool on a wire rack.

5 To make the gianduja; grind down the nuts and icing sugar in a Thermomix or food blender. Add the chocolate and mix in well. Pour onto a sheet of silicone paper to set.

6 Break into pieces after it has set and place into the Thermomix or food blender again and blend until very smooth. You can repeat this process until a really fine paste has been achieved.

7 Pipe the gianduja onto one side of a macaroon and place the other on top to sandwich it together.

CHEF'S TIP By using a Thermomix, you can melt the chocolate at the same time as mixing the nuts and sugar.

Ingredient	Amount
Chocolate box	
White, milk or dark melted chocolate	800 g
Strawberry mousse	
Double cream	350 ml
Caster sugar	75 g
Egg yolks	4
Strawberry pulp coulis	250 ml
Fresh mint	
Gelatine leaves	3
To finish	
Strawberry coulis	150 ml
Small strawberries hulled	16
Fresh mint sprigs	8

Guest Chef

Chocolate box filled with a Kentish strawberry mousse

Chef Tom Hall

Centre (college) Carshalton, Surrey

This dish combines a classic, formal dark chocolate box construction with a fresh strawberry mousse. The strawberries are locally grown in nearby Kent. Half of English strawberries originate in Kent and there are over five different varieties in season from May to October. Strawberries are good for you too as they contain more vitamin C than oranges.

METHOD OF WORK

Mousse

1 Soak the gelatine in cold water until soft.

2 Place the fruit coulis in to a pan and half the sugar, bring to the boil, and simmer for 20 minutes until reduced by half. Remove from the heat and allow to cool. Add the gelatine and stir in until completely dissolved then strain.

3 Whisk the egg yolks and the remaining sugar over a bain-marie until thick and creamy, fold in the fruit coulis and allow to cool.

4 Whip the cream until it holds, carefully fold in the fruit coulis and place the mix into a clean bowl. Cover, place into a fridge and allow to set.

5 Place into a piping bag and keep chilled until required.

Chocolate box

6 Evenly spread out the melted chocolate and allow to set, cut out four equal sides 7 cm × 3.5 cm and two ends 3.5 cm × 3.5 cm.

7 Using a little melted chocolate place the box together, keeping one side for the lid. Keep in a cool place.

To finish

8 Carefully place the box on to a plate and pipe the strawberry mousse into the box, top with the strawberries a mint, carefully place the lid on top dust with icing sugar, finish with a little fruit coulis or chocolate lattice.

ASSESSMENT OF KNOWLEDGE AND UNDERSTANDING

You have now learned about the use of chocolate and how to produce a variety of chocolates and decorations utilizing an array of commodities and different chocolate types.

To test your level of knowledge and understanding, answer the following short questions. These will help to prepare you for your summative (final) assessment.

1   Name the fat used in the production of couverture chocolate.

2   Identify the quality points to look for when using couverture.

3   Explain why we need to pre-crystallize couverture.

4   Identify and explain one technique for pre-crystallizing (tempering) couverture.

5   Identify the difference between milk and white chocolate and why they have different processing temperatures.

6   State the ideal refrigeration temperature for setting chocolate.

7   Identify two pieces of essential equipment that may be used to make chocolates and describe their use.

8   State the general melting temperature for chocolate.

9   Describe the effect that invert sugar has on ganache.

10 Explain the correct procedure for melting chocolate.

11 Describe the procedure for moulding hollow chocolate figures.

12 Describe how to store white chocolate to prevent it from losing its sheen.

13 State the factors that can affect the shelf life of chocolates after preparation.

Sugar and marzipan based products and decorative items

15

VRQ

Produce petits fours

Produce display pieces and decorative items

NVQ

Prepare, process and finish marzipan,
  pastillage and sugar products

LEARNING OBJECTIVES

This chapter describes how to prepare a variety of marzipan, pastillage and small sugar decorative pieces and decorations using some technically advanced skills and presentation expertise. It will also describe how to prepare, process and finish marzipan, pastillage and sugar items required for Level 3.

The aim of this chapter is to enable the reader to develop the necessary complex techniques, knowledge and understanding of the principles in preparing and producing a range of advanced marzipan items, pastillage and sugar products.

The emphasis of this chapter is on developing knowledge attained in the previous Professional Chef Level 2 book and perfecting refined, contemporary and advanced techniques. Also included in this chapter is further information on materials, formulas, ingredients and equipment.

At the end of this chapter you will be able to:

- **Understand how to cook sugar and isomalt.**

- **Understand how to prepare marzipan.**

- **Understand how to prepare pastillage.**

- **Understand the importance of temperature control for cooking sugar.**

- **Identify the various skills required to prepare and present a range of marzipan, pastillage and sugar confections.**

- **Identify the important storage techniques.**

- **Recognize a range of advanced techniques for presentation.**

Introduction

Sugar confectionery has a long and widespread history. Honey was the first source of sugar and was used to conserve fruits, herbs and grains. The ancient Chinese and Egyptians coated fruits, flowers, grains and plants with honey and served them as sweet treats. The Greeks and Romans also used honey to conserve raisins and other fruits. The Roman Empire, which influenced cookery techniques across Europe, introduced the first confiture (or preserved fruit) recipes.

Honeycomb

Sugar cane was first discovered in the South Pacific, where the sweet juice was extracted by pressing it from the cane. Sugar manufacturing began in the Eastern Mediterranean as the trade routes between Asia and western regions slowly developed. The Arabs appear to have been the first to use sugar to create confections such as almond paste.

Sugar confections developed rapidly after they were first introduced to the Europeans. During the crusades, Europeans came in contact with many new ingredients, including various spices and sugar cane. The chefs to the noble courts and royalty began to experiment with sugar and candy making, and recipes for sugar bonbons had appeared by the 16th century. Candies were developed and given as precious gifts for weddings, birthdays and religious festivals. They were mainly reserved for the upper classes because sugar was so rare and expensive at this time.

The further development of sugar confections expanded when sugar became more available and the price began to fall due to the new large sugar plantations in Europe's colonies and to the later discovery of beet sugar. By the 18th century, bonbons were being made by many artisans in Europe. In France, the confiseurs were known as *marchands de plaisirs* (pleasure sellers) and their bonbons were made with flowers, essences, oils and spices.

Today, most sugar confections are made in factories, although modern candies have developed from the long tradition of artisan candy making. Confiseurs can still be found in well structured pastry kitchens, where they provide a selection of bonbons and produce basic pastry ingredients such as marzipan, raw almond paste, pralines, fondants and nougatine.

Sugar confectionery preparations

Most of the bases made by confectioners are also available as finished products under a range of different brand names. Today, most hotels, restaurants, caterers and even pastry shops will purchase them to help save time and improve consistency of the final product. However, it is crucial for a professional chef to have the knowledge and the skills to produce them. Creating these bases will produce finished products that are fresher and more individual than products made with industrially produced bases.

VIDEO CLIP A sugar artist at work.

Marzipan (almond paste)

Marzipan is a paste made of ground almonds (or almonds mixed with other nuts) and cooked sugar. Trimoline and sorbitol (used as stabilizers) and flavourings can also be added. This is a primary ingredient that is widely used in any pastry kitchen. Marzipan is also used in a number of sugar confections.

Raw almond paste

A paste made of ground almonds and sugar, This is a primary ingredient in the production of various cakes, such as pound cakes, sponges and pain de gênes.

Praline

This paste made of caramelized sugar and roasted hazelnuts, praline is a primary ingredient in various pastry products, used to flavour candies or as a filling in chocolates and cakes.

Fondant

A cooked sugar syrup that is re-crystallized by mechanical agitation, it can be flavoured and coloured as required. In the past fondant was used extensively in sugar confections. Today it is mainly used for glazing or covering pastries, sweets, cakes and choux pastries.

Nougatine

Nougatine is a mixture of caramelized sugar with glucose and nuts. Unsalted butter and fresh vanilla can be added to improve the flavour. To protect it against humidity, a drying agent, such as powdered pectin, can be added. In the pastry kitchen it is used in mousses, ice creams, croquembouche and many chocolate fillings.

Caramelized nuts

Caramelized, sugar-coated roasted nuts are used for a few sugar confections, but mainly in industrially produced candies or candy bars. They are also used in mousses, cakes and ice creams and in chocolate making.

Sugar syrups

These have many different purposes in candy making, and may be used either as part of the recipe or in a finishing process (dipped, crystallized, powdered or glazed). The most important characteristic of sugar syrups is their sugar density. This can be determined using a saccharometer or a refractometer and is measured in degrees Baumé or degrees Brix. Measuring sugar density is very important in the production of sorbets and sauces to help control the freezing process and consistency of a sauce.

Invert sugar

Inverted or invert sugar syrup is a mixture of glucose and fructose; it is obtained by splitting sucrose into these two components. Compared with its foundation, sucrose, inverted sugar is sweeter and its products tend to remain moister and are less prone to crystallization. Inverted sugar is therefore valued by bakers and pastry chefs, who refer to the syrup as *trimoline* or invert syrup. In technical terms, sucrose is a disaccharide, which means that it is a molecule derived from two simple sugars (monosaccharides). In the case of sucrose, these monosaccharide building blocks are fructose and glucose.

Inverted sugar syrup can be made by adding 1 g of citric acid or ascorbic acid per kilogram of sugar. Cream of tartar (1 g per kilogram) or fresh lemon juice (10 ml per kilogram) may also be used. The mixture is boiled for 20 minutes to obtain a temperature of 114°C, and will convert enough of the sucrose to effectively prevent crystallization, without giving a noticeably sour taste. Invert sugar syrup may also be produced without the use of acids or enzymes by thermal means alone: two parts granulated sucrose and one part water simmered for five to seven minutes will convert a modest portion to invert sugar. Invert sugar is produced or used in the following products:

1   Honey – is principally a mixture of glucose and fructose, giving it similar properties to invert syrup. This gives it the ability to remain liquid for long periods of time.

2   Jam – produces invert sugar during extensive heating under the action of the acid in the fruit.

3   Golden syrup – is syrup of approximately 56 per cent invert syrup, 44 per cent sucrose.

4   Fondant – filling for chocolates is unique in that the conversion enzyme is added, but not activated before the filling is enrobed with chocolate. The very viscous filling then becomes less viscous with time, giving the creamy consistency desired.

Sugar confectionery

Candies have been classified into groups based on a specific ingredient or a specific technique. Collectively they are called sugar confections or sugar candies (*bonbons de sucre*).

Cooked sugars

A sugar solution (often with the addition of glucose) is cooked until enough water evaporates to ensure the hard setting of the bonbon. These candies can be moulded, cut or pressed. Sugar and glucose syrups are both unflavoured and colourless, so the chef can be very creative in the choice of flavours and colours to be added. Examples of cooked sugars are lollipops and bonbons.

Caramels

These are composed of sugar, water, milk, glucose and butter. The sugar is usually caramelized with the liquid content and then re-cooked to the desired temperature and colour. They are produced from light brown to darker shades, depending on the strength of flavour being sought. After cooking and cooling, they are cut and wrapped. Nuts or other flavours can be added. Among the most famous found in Europe are caramels with salted butter from Brittany and toffees from the United Kingdom. Chewy caramels, hard caramels and toffees all belong in this family.

Nougats

The term 'nougat' is derived from the Latin word *nugatum* (of nuts), and the first Roman recipe was recorded by Apicius made using nuts, honey and eggs. Nougat was first seen in Marseille and has become popular and famous throughout the south-eastern areas of France.

There are four types of nougats in France:

- Nougat de Montélimar – 28–30 per cent almond content.
- Honey nougat – minimum 20 per cent honey content.
- Nougat Provençale – 25 per cent honey with almond, coriander, hazelnuts and aniseed.
- Black nougat – the same as Provençale but not aerated or caramelized.

The addition of egg whites or gelatine allows air to be incorporated to increase the volume and makes a difference in the texture between the different types of nougat that are available. Sugar and honey are cooked and mixed with egg whites or gelatine. Roasted nuts, dried or candied fruits and spices can be added and the nougats are cut when cold and set. Sometime the nougat is set in between sheets of rice paper (which is edible).

Dragées

These take their name from the popular almonds covered with honey favoured by the Greeks called *tragemata*. The first mention of dragées is found in the archives of the French town of Verdun (1220 AD). The technique used is to cover a whole nut or other filling in regular layers of sugar that are made hard and smooth. The centre can be made of whole nut, chocolate, nougat, marzipan or fondant. Dragées used to be made by hand, but today they are mainly produced industrially in factories, although some specialist patisseries and chocolatiers still make dragées today. The dragées are slowly covered with sugar syrup (maintained at a constant temperature) in a revolving pan until crystallization takes place. They are traditionally used in Europe at celebrations of baptism and weddings.

the art of confiture. Fruit purées, sugar (a minimum of half the purée weight), glucose and pectin are cooked to a required temperature. Pectin is added to help set the jellies and citric acid is mixed in prior to casting to ensure the setting of the pectin. Fruit jellies can be moulded and cut after cooling. They are usually covered with granulated sugar or crystallized in saturated sugar syrup.

Gums

Gums are centuries old, and in the past were used as medicines. They are made using gum Arabic, a natural vegetable substance. Purified, powdered and diluted in warm water, the gum is added to sugar syrup and glucose and then flavoured and coloured as required. Bonbons are then cast in starch moulds and when set are crystallized in sugar syrup before serving.

Liquorice

Liquorice candies are made using a substance extracted from the root of the liquorice plant. This plant was valued in the Middle Ages as an aid in digestion, and at the end of the 17th century an Englishman was the first to use it to create a confection. The roots are cleaned and crushed before being heated in water. The solution is purified, filtered and concentrated to obtain the final flavouring. There are two kinds of liquorice: a hard type, made of liquorice, sugar syrup, glucose and gum Arabic, and a soft type, in which wheat flour and powdered sugar are added to liquorice flavouring and the candy is pushed through a machine to form strings or ribbons.

Turkish delight

Turkish delight or lokum is a family of confections based on a gel of starch and sugar. Premium varieties consist largely of chopped dates, pistachios and hazelnuts or walnuts bound by the gel; the cheapest are mostly gel, generally flavoured with rosewater or lemon. The confection is often packaged and eaten in small cubes dusted with icing sugar or powdered cream of Tartar, to prevent clinging.

Jams, fruit preserves, marmalades and jellies

These are generally produced from whole or pieces of fresh fruits and are set with the aid of pectin. Marmalades are made from strained fruit purées such as Seville oranges. Jellies are made from strained fruit juice. The preparation of fruit preserves today often involves adding commercial or

Fruit jellies

These delicacies are among the oldest candies and were introduced from the Far East along with candied fruits and natural pectin as a gelling agent, although sugar or honey may be used. Before World War II, fruit preserve recipes did not include pectin, and many artisan jams today are made without this. The ingredients used and how they are prepared determine the type of preserves; confits, jams, jellies and marmalades are all examples of different styles of fruit preserves that vary based upon the ingredients used.

1 Confit – taken from the French verb *confire,* 'to preserve', is most often applied to preservation of pork and duck by cooking them in their own fat or oils and allowing the fats to set. However, the term can also refer to fruit or vegetables which have been seasoned and cooked with honey or sugar until the mixture has reached a jam-like consistency.

2 Conserves – often the making of conserves can be a delicate process because the balance between cooking, or sometimes steeping fruit in a hot sugar solution for just enough time to allow the flavour to be extracted may break down the fruit structure. Overcooking the fruit will break down the proteins and dissolve the fruit. This process can also be achieved by spreading crystal sugar over raw fruit in layers, and leaving for several hours to saturate the fruit. At this point, the heating of the resulting mixture should be carefully undertaken to setting point. As a result of this minimal cooking, some fruits are not particularly suitable for making into conserves, because they require cooking for longer periods to avoid issues such as tough skins.

Candied fruit

Fruit or citrus fruit peel is dipped into a sulphur bath before being blanched in hot water and candied in a sugar solution. The sulphur lightens the original colour of the fruit and kills any bacteria that could later cause fermentation. Blanching is a crucial step. If the fruit is not blanched enough it may dry out and impart an unpleasant colour or in the case of citrus peel a bitterness that is too overpowering. If it is blanched too much, the fruit may become too soft and will result in a compôte texture being produced where the fruit structure breaks down. The fruit is soaked in a hot sugar solution, which rises slightly in density over time, to reach the centre of the fruit and so preserve it.

Sugar-coated fruit (fruits déguisés)

Fresh, dried or candied fruits, nuts or fruits shaped out of marzipan are covered in a protective shell of either crystallized sugar or cooked (coloured and flavoured) sugar.

Fudge

This is a soft caramelized and crystallized sugar confection with added cream or butter fat. It is usually cut into squares and served in many different flavour combinations, such as vanilla, chocolate, coffee or rum and raisin.

In forming a type of fondant to create fudge, it is not easy to keep all vibrations from the stirring action and seed crystals from causing rapid crystallization to large crystals. Consequently, milk fat and corn syrup are often added. Corn syrup contains glucose, fructose (monosaccharides) and maltose (disaccharide). These sugars interact with the sucrose molecules. They help prevent premature crystallization by inhibiting sucrose crystal contact. The fat also helps inhibit rapid crystallization. Controlling the crystallization of the supersaturated sugar solution is the key to smooth fudge. Initiation of crystals before the desired time will result in fudge with fewer, larger sugar grains. The final texture will have a grainy mouth feel rather than the smooth texture of high quality fudge.

One of the most important attributes of fudge is its texture. The end-point temperature separates hard caramel from fudge. The higher the peak temperature, the more sugar is dissolved and the more water is evaporated, resulting in a higher sugar-to-water ratio. Before the availability of cheap and accurate thermometers, cooks would use the ice water test, also known as the cold water test, to determine the saturation of the confection. Fudge is made at the soft-ball stage, which varies by altitude and ambient humidity from 113 to 116°C.

Supersaturated sugar solution

A supersaturated solution contains more dissolved crystallized sugar than it should, according to the compound's solubility. In the case of sugar about 211 g will dissolve in 100 ml of water. The first key to preparing supersaturated solutions lies in the temperature of the water. Solubility is temperature-dependent; more sugar will dissolve in hot water than will dissolve in cold water. The second key to preparing supersaturated solutions lies in preventing the excess sugar from crystallizing as the solution cools. In general, rapid cooling aids the formation of supersaturated solutions, whereas slow cooling helps the crystallization process.

Rock candy crystals are made entirely of sugar. The crystals form when a supersaturated solution of sugar and water and grows on a seed, such as a string or lollipop stick. Crystals grow through a process known as nucleation. When enough of a soluble material (in this case sugar) is dissolved in a solution, a few molecules of that material will eventually come together and form a bond. This is known as a protocrystal and it becomes a site on which nucleation can take place. Once enough sugar molecules attach to the protocrystal, it will be too large to remain dissolved and come out of the solution. At this point, the crystal continues to grow until equilibrium is reached between the sugar molecules in the crystal and those still dissolved in the solution.

TO CREATE CRYSTALLIZED SUGAR STICKS

1. Bring a saucepan containing 100 ml water to a boil.

2. Add 211 g of granulated sugar slowly while stirring with a plastic or wooden spoon until no more sugar will dissolve.

Continue stirring while heating until all sugar has dissolved. Add more water as needed if all the sugar will not dissolve.

3. Using a sugar or digital thermometer cook the solution to 107°C or measure the solution to 74° Brix (sugar content of an aqueous solution), with a refractometer. Add food colouring if desired. Turn off the heat after the solution reaches the required allow it to cool.

4. Pour the solution into small plastic cups and place a lollipop stick into each one and suspend in the sugar mixture. Cover with plastic film.

5. Allow the sticks to remain in the mixture for several days until the desired formation of sugar crystals adheres to the sticks.

6. Remove the sticks and leave to dry on a wire rack for 24 hours before using.

The components of sugar

Raw sugar cane

Sucrose, the main constituent of cane and beet sugar, is one of a number of natural sweeteners used in the professional kitchen. These sweeteners form part of a larger group of commodities known as carbohydrates. Carbohydrate molecules are made up from atoms of carbon, hydrogen and oxygen and are arranged as chains of simple sugars:

- Monosaccharides – a single sugar unit, such as glucose or fructose.

- Disaccharides – are made up of two joined monosaccharides, for example sucrose, lactose or maltose.

- Polysaccharides – These are long chains of monosaccharides and form starches.

Sucrose is the most common sugar in our diet and consists of one molecule of glucose and one of fructose. Glucose syrups are created by breaking down starch molecules found in wheat, maize and potatoes. The polysaccharides are broken down by heating the starch with an acid. When sugar (sucrose) is heated with an acid present (such as cream of tartar or lemon juice) a process called 'inversion' takes place. The sucrose is split evenly into fructose and glucose, which is termed 'invert sugar'. An invert sugar is sweeter than a sugar solution and will have a similarly small crystal size. Invert sugar inhibits crystal formation.

Syrups and treacles are dissolved invert sugars that have been heated to develop the characteristic flavours. Treacles have added molasses. They are used in a range of baked goods and confectionery including toffees and liquorice. Low calorie sugars and sweeteners are often made of maltodextrin with added sweeteners. Maltodextrin is an easily digestible synthetic polysaccharide consisting of short chains of glucose molecules and is made by the partial

hydrolysis of starch. The added sweeteners are often aspartame, saccharin, stevia or sucralose

Cooking sugar

When boiling sugar it is important to observe the correct procedures and rules to prevent the sugar re-crystallizing.

VIDEO CLIP Boiling sugar for catering

Step-by-step: Boiling sugar for catering

1. Ensure cleanliness of the equipment and the ingredients at all stages of the boiling process. A copper pan or stainless steel saucepan should be cleaned with an acid (lemon juice or vinegar) and scouring material (salt) and rinsed under cold water to ensure absolute cleanliness. All other equipment should be scrupulously cleaned. The sugar thermometer should be placed into cold water and brought to the boil on a stove to ensure that it is clean. Have all ingredients weighed and to hand. Dissolve the sugar in the water completely over a low heat before boiling.

2. If scum forms on top of the sugar solution during boiling, remove it using a spoon or strainer (this could be the impurities from the actual sugar). Repeat until no more scum forms.

3. Add the glucose or invert sugar at 104°C.

4. When the sugar solution begins to boil, brush the insides of the hot pan with a brush and clean cold water. This will help to prevent any crystallization building on the sides of the pan.

5. Boil the sugar rapidly and continuously measure the temperature using a sugar thermometer.

6. Cook the sugar to the required stage and arrest the cooking by dipping the base of the saucepan into some iced water for eight–ten seconds. Wipe the base of the saucepan dry and use the sugar as required.

Measuring the density of sugar solutions

Many different types of pâtisserie, dessert and confectionery items require the use of a sugar solution, such as sorbets, ice creams and preserved fruits. The density of a sugar solution is measured using a saccharometer, and the units of measurement used are either degrees Baumé or degrees Brix.

The Baumé scale is a pair of hydrometer scales developed by French pharmacist Antoine Baumé in 1768 to measure density of various liquids. The unit of the Baumé scale has been notated variously as *degrees Baumé*, *B°*, *Bé°* and simply Baumé. One scale measures the density of liquids heavier than water and the other, liquids lighter than water. The Baumé of distilled water is 0.

Degrees Brix (symbol °Bx) is the sugar content of an aqueous solution. One degree Brix equals 1 g of sucrose in 100 g of solution and represents the strength of the solution as percentage by weight. If the solution contains dissolved solids other than pure sucrose, then the °Bx only approximates the dissolved solid content. The °Bx is traditionally used in the wine, sugar, fruit juice and honey industries.

When measuring a solution to determine density, always ensure that the temperature of the sugar solution to be tested is 20°C. This is because the density changes with temperature. Place the sugar solution into a suitable container, a 500 ml measuring jug is ideal, and place the saccharometer into the solution. Take the reading where the scale on the side of the saccharometer meets the surface of the solution. The density of the sugar solution can be adjusted as required: add thicker syrup at the same temperature to increase the density or add water to decrease the density. A refractometer can also be used which gives an exact reading by measuring the light depth within the solution.

The following chart is designed to give the chef a working reference of the sugar to water ratios required to produce certain degrees of density. Although this book concentrates on degrees Baumé, the Brix measurements are included below.

WEIGHT OF SUGAR TO BE ADDED TO 450 ML WATER	DENSITY REQUIRED	DENSITY REQUIRED
GRAMS	BAUMÉ: B°	BRIX: °Bx
51	5.6	10
74	7.8	14
100	10.0	18
144	13.3	24
204	17.0	31
255	20.0	36
317	22.5	41
480	28.0	51
742	33.5	62
1010	37.1	69
1083	40.0	75

During the sugar boiling process the water evaporates and so the solution becomes denser, which will result in the solution setting firm when cold. The thicker the sugar solution, the more the temperature increases, and it is by reading the changes in temperature that we can determine the physical change in the sugar solution. The chart below shows the changes that occur at different temperatures and the use of the sugar solution at each stage. The solution can be tested by dropping a small amount from a clean spoon into a bowl of very cold water and then quickly examining it or picking it up with the fingers to check the setting consistency.

TEMPERATURE: °C	NAME OF DEGREE	HOW TO TEST	USES
104	Boiling	Look for agitation of liquid surface	
107	Thread	At this relatively low temperature there is still a lot of water left in the syrup. Take a little of the solution between the thumb and finger and separate them to form an elastic thread of sugar	Stock syrup and some icings
110	Pearl	The thread formed by pulling the sugar solution may be stretched. When a spoon is dipped into the syrup and then raised, the syrup runs off in drops	Jelly, candies and some icings
113	Soufflé	The syrup spins a 5 cm thread when dropped from a spoon	Delicate sugar candy and syrup
115	Feather	The film of sugar can be blown into feather-like pieces	Jams and confiture

TEMPERATURE: °C	NAME OF DEGREE	HOW TO TEST	USES
118	Soft ball	A small amount of syrup dropped into chilled water forms a soft, flexible ball, but flattens after a few moments in the fingers	Fudge, fondant, pâte à bombe, Italian meringue and classic butter creams
121	Hard ball	The sugar concentration is much higher, which means less moisture in the sugar solution. Syrup dropped into chilled water may form into a ball that holds its shape on removal. The ball will be firm, but its shape can still be changed by squashing it.	Nougat, marshmallows
132–138	Soft crack	At this stage, the moisture content is low. Syrup dropped into chilled water separates into hard but pliable threads. They will bend slightly before breaking	Rock sugar
138–155	Hard crack	At these temperatures, there is almost no water left in the sugar solution. Syrup dropped into chilled water separates into hard, brittle threads that break when bent	Can be poured and pulled to make presentation displays
170	Light caramel	The sugar solution turns amber due to caramelization. The sugar is beginning to break down and form many complex compounds that contribute to a rich flavour	Sauces and glazes
178–180	Dark caramel	A darker caramelization has now occurred	Dessert decorations

Decorative sugar work

Health and safety issues

A chef or sugar artist must always be aware that boiling sugar can cause severe burns. The appropriate protective clothing should always be worn and oven cloths should be used at all times when pouring hot sugar. It is always wise to have a container of iced water nearby when working with sugar, in case a burn on the fingers or hands occurs. Quickly plunging the burned area into iced water will reduce the pain and stop the heat burning through the layers of skin.

Care should always be taken to prevent any accidents during the cooking of sugar. All pre-preparation should be undertaken before the actual cooking of the sugar takes place. This will ensure that you remain with the cooking sugar at all times to oversee the cooking process and tend to the sugar as it cooks. Many chefs and sugar artists now use protective gloves when working with sugar at high temperatures.

The preparation required for sugar work

The following equipment should be prepared and ready for use before any cooking of sugar takes place.

SAUCEPANS FOR BOILING SUGAR

Although it is commonly assumed that copper pans are essential for the boiling of sugar, this is not entirely true. The pan used must have a heavy base and be capable of being cleaned thoroughly; stainless steel, enamel and copper are all suitable. The pan should be thoroughly cleaned using a mild acid and an abrasive and rinsed thoroughly with cold water and left to drip dry before using.

MARBLE SLAB

A marble slab or granite work top will be required for certain sugar work techniques. Before using, it should be washed with a light detergent, which will help prevent the sugar from sticking. It should then be rinsed, dried and very lightly oiled; any standard cooking oil is suitable for this purpose. Using too much oil may result in the sugar sticking to the marble.

CUTTING EQUIPMENT

A metal scraper and heavy knife (or a palette knife) is needed for turning sugar prior to pulling. A pair of scissors is also required for cutting the sugar after pulling.

CLEAN PASTRY BRUSHES

A brush is required to clean the sides of the sugar pan with cold water during cooking. A separate brush should be kept for this purpose. Pastry brushes used for egg wash or general use are not suitable for this as they can contaminate the sugar.

LEAF AND PETAL MOULDS

These come in many shapes and sizes and are useful for producing sugar leaves efficiently.

HEAT LAMP

This is essential if no oven is available to keep the sugar warm. Suitable lamps can be obtained at most specialist culinary suppliers.

STORAGE CONTAINERS

Containers should be airtight. Before use, silica gel or lime crystals should be placed in the bottom and they should be lined with foil. Containers are used to store sugar work until ready for use. Any leftover sugar can be vacuum packed and used at a later date.

Additives used in sugar work and confectionery

ASCORBIC ACID

Ascorbic acid (vitamin C) is an antioxidant and is used to conserve the colour of a product (for example, poached fruits).

TARTARIC ACID

This acid is found in many types of fruit, but it is always extracted industrially from grapes. The crystals are large and clear. One part of boiling water dissolves two parts of tartaric acid. Tartaric acid enhances flavours and brings tartness. It is also an antioxidant, so it improves colours and aromas. This is added to sugar to help prevent the sugar from crystallizing and to aid the shine of pulled sugar decorations. Tartaric acid can affect the hygroscopic ability of sugar and make sugar slightly more likely to attract moisture. Tartaric acid at 5°C before the end of the cooking process.

CITRIC ACID

Usually extracted from lemons, citric acid is used with cream of tartar in fondants or cooked sugar to make them softer and more pliable. It is also used to stabilize the albumin in whipped egg whites. During the cooking process of sugar it should be added at the beginning of the cooking process.

AGAR-AGAR

Also called Japanese isinglass, agar-agar is derived from seaweeds found in the Pacific and Indian oceans. It expands in cold water but does not dissolve. It only dissolves in boiling water after a certain amount of cooking. Agar-agar is used in bonbons, jellies and even jams. The powdered form is the easiest to use.

PECTINS

Pectin is a gelling agent found in fruits. It is usually extracted from crushed apples but is also derived from citric fruit rinds. Pectin is used in powder form in gums, fruit jellies and jams. It maintains the moisture in gum candies and fruit jellies. Adding an acid such as citric, lactic or tartaric to a recipe using pectin causes the pectin to set:

1 Pectin NH – is used in fruit glazes and fruit fillings; its gelling effect is reversible by heating and it holds well on fruit.

2 Pectin (medium rapid set) – is especially well-suited for making fruit preserves and jellies; setting does not occur too rapidly, thereby increasing the time a product can be worked, for example casting fruit jellies in individual starch or Flexipan moulds.

3 Yellow pectin – is used in fruit jellies; its gelling effect is not reversible by heating. When using this pectin, it should be 1–2 per cent of the overall weight of the mix.

GUMS

These are neutral substances derived from trees. There are several varieties of gum of which three are used in sugar confections:

● gum Arabic;

● gum tragacanth;

● fruit-tree gum.

Dissolved gums provide an elastic consistency. Gums dissolve slowly in cold water but quickly in boiling water. The alcohol contained in gums is forced to evaporate, making the product thicker and gummier, until it finally solidifies into a transparent mass that shows no traces of crystallization.

CHEF'S TIP Sweetening power is a measure of how much (in percentage) a substance will increase the sweetness of the product that it is being added to.

GELATINE

Colourless when pure, gelatine is extracted from the bones and cartilage of animals. It is used in sugar confections to set whipped pastes and jelly candies. Bringing gelatine to the boil will not destroy its gelling property, but boiling the gelatine for an extended amount of time will reduce its gelling power. Gelatine is bloomed (softened) in cold water and will absorb from five to ten times its weight in water.

SORBITOL

This is used to stabilize moisture and prevent mould and bacterial growth and as a sweetener in low-sugar or sugarless desserts. Sorbitol prevents the drying of cakes, macaroons and sponges. It also helps to preserve freshness and flexibility in almond paste, ganache, praline paste and fruit jellies. Sorbitol has a solid content of 95 per cent and a sweetening power of 55 per cent.

DEXTROSE

A form of pure glucose (99.5 per cent), supplied as a fine white powder. Dextrose is used as a stabilizer and as an anti-crystallizing agent in ice cream and sorbets, and it has many uses in baking. It has a solid content of 95 per cent and its sweetening power is 70 per cent.

GLUCOSE

A monosaccharide sugar produced by the breaking down of starch found in potato, wheat or maize. It is used as an anti-crystallization agent in the cooking of sugar.

SODIUM BICARBONATE

Also known as baking soda, sodium bicarbonate is a salt that acts as a leavening agent and conserving agent. It is used to raise the boiling point of a liquid, and therefore speed up the boiling process.

ISOMALT

Isomalt is a natural sugar substitute derived from sugar beet. Isomalt is an odourless, white, crystalline substance containing about 5 per cent water. Isomalt is used in sugar sculptures and is preferred by some pastry chefs and sugar artists because it will not crystallize as quickly as cooked sugar. It will therefore maintain its shine and structure better in humid conditions than cooked sugar.

Marzipan

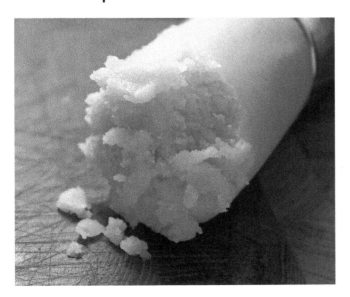

Marzipan has been used for centuries by pastry chefs all over the world. It is a favoured delicacy in many European countries and can be used in baking, confectionery, biscuits, breads, gâteaux, torten and cakes. Marzipan is a sweet, pliable mixture of almonds and sugar. It is sometimes tinted with food colouring and modelled into a variety of decorative shapes.

Recent studies into the history of marzipan have shown that *marci panis* has had a long and complex journey. During the 13th century in such places as Venice, Naples, Sicily and Provence various spices and sweets were presented in thin wooden boxes. These boxes were called *mazaban* and eventually this word must have extended its meaning to cover its contents. In other languages this became *marzipan* (German), *marchpane* (English), *marzapane* (Italian) or *massepain* (French).

Marzipan is now known to have originated in Asia, where the delicate almond/sugar mixture was served at the sultan's table as the crowning of a meal. Through Arabian rule, marzipan reached Spain and Portugal, and during the crusades it spread through the rest of Europe via the largest trading port of the area, Venice.

Once in Europe, marzipan was produced in the early days by the apothecaries; it was well known as a remedy into the 18th century. In the 14th century, marzipan was used for artistic creations and figurines modelled by hand. Lübecker marzipan was first mentioned in the city's guild rolls in 1530. Lübeck's reputation as the City of Marzipan and its dominance in the production of marzipan was established after 1800. Much of this dominance was due to new production technology being introduced and the marzipan houses of the area being able to source the highest quality ingredients from around the world while still keeping to traditional recipes.

VIDEO CLIP   Moulding a marzipan rose

Lübecker marzipan

Lübecker marzipan has a great tradition and is world-renowned. Among the many companies that have set the standards for this type of marzipan, two stand out: Carstens and Niederegger. But there are distinguishing elements that mark Lübecker marzipan from other marzipans.

The basic elements of marzipan are a marzipan paste and sugar. Marzipan paste is generally 75 per cent almonds and 25 per cent sugar, the almonds being roasted and blended together with the sugar. It is the relative proportions of marzipan paste and sugar that helps to determine the flavour and quality of Lübecker marzipan. A Lübeck Fine Marzipan contains up to 90 parts marzipan paste to ten parts sugar.

Marzipan legislation

For a paste to be classified as a marzipan or almond paste it must not have less than 23.5 per cent dry almond content and not less than 75 per cent of the remaining content should be sugar. This standard does not, however, apply to items such as cake decorative figures and petit fours. With the high cost of almonds, other cake covering pastes are beginning to be used in place of traditional marzipan in some areas of confectionery. These have an almond content of less than 23.5 per cent and so cannot be called marzipan.

Decorative marzipan figures

Making animals, flowers and objects is quite easy to do with marzipan or sugar paste as these mediums are soft and pliable and allow plenty of time to work the shapes and figures without the pastes hardening too quickly. For most figures, using marzipan is the best medium to use as the soft, malleable texture means it can be sculpted, manipulated and smoothed as much as is required. It can also be sprayed with colour using an airbrush and lacquered to create a shine and protect the item using a food grade varnish which protects it from humidity and drying out.

CATERPILLAR

1   Roll out a piece of coloured marzipan to create the main tail, slightly thicker at one end. Create grooves in the tail section as shown in the next figure.

2   Using a modelling tool create two eye sockets in a small ball of coloured marzipan to create the head.

3   Five smaller balls of marzipan can be modelled to create two small ears, two small antennae and a nose. The eyes are piped with white royal icing and then over-piped with black icing to create the pupils of the eyes.

4   The green hair and small lettuce leaf are moulded in a silicone leaf mould.

5   Assemble the caterpillar by coiling the tail and mounting the head on top. Attach the elements of the head and cut a slot for the mouth, opening it slightly with the modelling tool. Finish with the hair, lettuce leaf and a decorative flower.

Components for the production of the caterpillar

TEDDY BEAR

1   Make a large ball out of the coloured marzipan for the body.

2   Form four medium cylinders for the two arms and two legs.

3   Gently press on the ends of the legs with your fingers to create the feet. Do the same to create small paws to the arms.

4   Using a paintbrush, wet the undersides with a little previously boiled water and attach the arms and legs to the body.

5   Using half the amount of marzipan that you used to create the body, make another ball for the head. Hollow out the eye sockets using a modelling tool, extend the nose slightly and cut to slightly split the nose. Place a small, different coloured nose on top. Create the mouth at this stage too.

6   Pipe some royal icing into the eye sockets. Once it is dry pipe the dark pupils with black royal icing.

7   For the ears, make a small, flattened ball out of the marzipan. Cut it in half with a knife, trying not to distort the shape. Use a modelling tool to curve the ears and adhere to the head.

8   Finish by adding a small red marzipan heart so that the teddy bear is holding it.

ROSE AND LADYBIRD

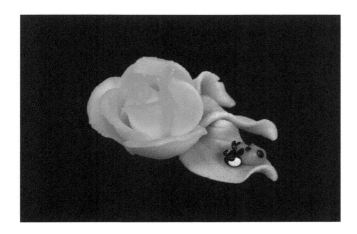

1   Create a rose using red marzipan and three green leaves.

2   Set these together onto a small disc of marzipan and leave to dry for thirty minutes.

3   Create a small ladybird by moulding a red ball and creating a mark down the back. Add smaller discs of black marzipan to create the distinctive ladybird marking and pipe the eyes onto the front with two small antennae over the top made from marzipan.

Pastillage

Pastillage is a flexible paste composed of icing sugar, cornflour, gum tragacanth or gelatine, water and lemon juice. Egg white and glucose may also be used in pastillage, but these are not strictly necessary. Pastillage is one of the easiest decorative mediums to work within the pastry kitchen and can be moulded, coloured, cut, shaped and modelled. When allowed to dry it sets with a matt finish and a brittle, crisp hardness, and it can be brushed and smoothed to create a clean textured finish. Once set, pieces can be joined together with royal icing to form a display piece.

VIDEO CLIP Pastillage

Pastillage is easy to handle and does not require specialist equipment or storage arrangements. The main ingredient is icing sugar to which a little cornflour is added to aid the drying process. The setting agent is either gum tragacanth or leaf gelatine (gelatine is often used as gum tragacanth can be difficult to incorporate), the egg white acts as a binding agent and also gives shine, and the lemon juice, if used, bleaches the sugar, giving it a high white definition.

Preparation of pastillage

Cleanliness is essential. Dirt, dust, oil and grease and soiled and stained hands are to be avoided at all costs.

● A marble slab or a clean wooden board can be used for preparing small quantities of paste; larger quantities may require an electric mixing machine.

● Use a stainless steel bowl; aluminium will discolour the paste during the mixing process.

● Use a dough hook so as not to aerate the mixture.

1   Sift all the dry ingredients through a fine nylon sieve.

2   Soak the gelatine or gum tragacanth in the water.

3   Add the glucose if used and melt over a bain-marie.

4   Strain the melted ingredients into the sieved dry ingredients and mix well until a fairly firm but not dry paste is formed.

5   Knead this well to improve the consistency and whiteness of the paste.

Holding

Once the mass is ready to work with, it should be placed in a covered container to prevent it drying out. Use a clean damp cloth to cover the paste. If the paste is to be kept for prolonged periods it should be wrapped with several layers of plastic film and placed in the refrigerator, where it will last for up to seven days. It must be kneaded before use.

Consistency

For general use the pastillage should feel like a lightly worked short paste. It should feel elastic and flexible in consistency. It should also be easy to roll out, but not so wet that it will stick to the working surface or so dry that it will crack when rolled out.

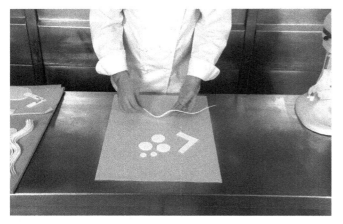

It is important that all the cut shapes are measured precisely and have dried thoroughly

Adding colour

Food colours may be carefully added to obtain the required shade. Always remember to colour a sufficient amount of the mass to finish the project; trying to match the colour or shade will not be easy. Always try to use delicate or pastel shades. Harsh or deep colours do not always work well with this medium. Marbling effects may be achieved by carefully blending one or more colours, but do not overwork the paste.

The pastillage may be painted after it is dried, using edible water-based colour or standard food colour, to obtain stronger or more specific effects. If pastillage is to be painted it should be dried slowly to prevent the edges from curling. Before beginning to paint on the pastillage, lightly scrape its surface with the blade of a knife (or sometimes glass-paper) to make sure that it is perfectly smooth. Be sure to place the sheet of pastillage on several layers of kitchen towelling to prevent it from breaking.

If the surface of the pastillage is to be painted with food colouring, rather than artist's paint, it should first be glazed in the oven with a coating of gelatine dissolved in water. This glazing creates an impermeable coating on the surface of the pastillage, otherwise the surface acts like a blotter and may cause the colours to bleed and run into each other.

Ensure that the pastillage is smooth and clean of blemishes before spraying or painting with colour

If colour is to be applied to large flat surfaces it is often best to spray the colour using an airbrush connected to a compressor or gas canister. Always try out the colour on a small piece of pastillage to ensure that the correct shade and technique are being used.

Handling

It is best to estimate the amount required for the task at hand and to only use that amount; this will avoid drying out a large piece. The pastillage should preferably be worked on a wooden board to prevent rapid drying out, and the warmth of the hand can be used to render the pastillage soft and workable.

Rolling out

Pastillage is normally rolled out on a smooth flat surface that has been finely dusted with cornflour; this can be achieved using a 'dusting dolly'. Dusting with cornflour prevents the paste sticking. To ensure the smoothest surface, the paste can be rolled out on toughened glass, marble or polished slate.

> **CHEF'S TIP**   A 'dusting dolly' is a square of muslin cloth into which an amount of cornflour has been placed; this is then tied at the top with string to form a loose bag to finely dust the cornflour.

A separate rolling pin should be reserved for this purpose as rolling pins generally have dents and scratches and so will not give a perfect finish. Textured and different finishes can be achieved by the use of specialized or shaped rollers.

Cutting

A clean, neat cut is essential to the finish of pastillage. A sharp blade should be used, such as a scalpel. Pastry cutters can be used, as well as pastry wheels or any other sharp object that will cut. A direct downward guillotine cut is best; the action of dragging the blade should be avoided as this can crease the pastillage. Always cut out more pieces than are required to allow for breakage.

Drying out

Pastillage cut-outs will dry naturally in a dry atmosphere in approximately one hour, but the drying process can be speeded up by the use of an oven with a low setting. Ultimately, the drying time will be governed by the thickness of the paste. The paste should not be handled until completely dry, but it will need to be turned over to ensure it will dry out effectively.

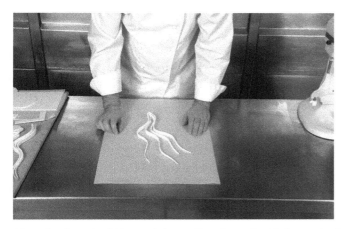

All rough edges should be sanded smooth and you should always check that that the pieces fit together first before adhering them

Decoration

Before assembling, any blemishes or rough edges can be sanded smooth with very fine grade glass-paper. The dried pastillage may be coloured, as previously described. Royal icing can be used as a decorative medium as well as glue for joining the pastillage pieces; it can enhance the careful and fine work of the chef. Avoid heaviness of decoration at all times; remember, less is always better.

Recipes

Boiled marzipan

Ingredients	900 g marzipan	2 kg marzipan
Caster sugar	400 g	1 kg
Water	240 ml	600 ml
Ground almonds	300 g	750 g
Egg white (lightly beaten)	1 egg	2½ eggs
Almond flavour (optional)	to taste	to taste
Icing sugar	100 g (approximately)	225 g (approximately)

energy	cal	fat	sat fat	carb	sugar	protein	fibre
643 kJ	153 kcal	6.7 g	0.5 g	21.8 g	21.5 g	2.6 g	1 g

METHOD OF WORK

1 Place the sugar into a clean pan with the water and cook to 118°C (soft ball stage) and observe all the sugar boiling rules.

2 Remove the pan from the heat and carefully add the almonds and flavour if required.

3 Add the lightly beaten egg white then return to the heat to cook for a further two minutes, stirring constantly.

4 Place the paste into an electric mixing machine with a paddle attachment and slowly beat, adding a little icing sugar, to create a smooth consistency to the paste.

5 Turn the paste out onto a marble work surface and knead until smooth and cool. Wrap the marzipan well in plastic film and store in a dry, cool area.

Raw marzipan *(Pâte d'amande cru)*

Ingredients	700 g marzipan	1.6 kg marzipan
Icing sugar	450 g	1 kg
Ground almonds	250 g	600 g
Egg white (lightly beaten)	2 eggs	5 eggs
Additional icing sugar	50 g (approximately)	100 g (approximately)

energy	cal	fat	sat fat	carb	sugar	protein	fibre
741 kJ	176 kcal	7 g	0.6 g	27.1 g	26.5 g	2.9 g	1.1 g

METHOD OF WORK

1 Sift the icing sugar and ground almonds together twice and place into a clean stainless steel bowl.

2 Make a well in the centre and add the lightly beaten egg white. Stir together to form a smooth paste.

3 Turn out onto a clean work surface and knead until smooth. Add the additional icing sugar if the paste is initially too wet. Wrap the marzipan well in plastic film and store in a cool area, such as a refrigerator.

Marzipan déguisés

Ingredients	10 déguisés	20 déguisés
Cooked marzipan	50 g	100 g
Dried dates	10	20
Cointreau or kirsch (to flavour the marzipan)	to taste	to taste
Colour	as required	as required
Granulated sugar	250 g	500 g
Liquid glucose	30 g	60 g
Water	50 g	100 g

energy	cal	fat	sat fat	carb	sugar	protein	fibre
578 kJ	136 kcal	0.7 g	0.1 g	33.8 g	32.5 g	0.4 g	0.2 g

METHOD OF WORK

1 Flavour and colour the marzipan as required.

2 Cut an incision lengthways into the date and remove the stone if still inside. Stuff the dates with small pieces of the marzipan and remould to their original shape. Leave to dry out for at least one hour.

3 Boil the sugar and water together, adding the glucose at 104°C. Cook the sugar solution further to 156°C and then immediately arrest the cooking by plunging the pan into a bowl of cold water for ten seconds.

4 Carefully dip the dates into the hot sugar and leave to set on a lightly oiled marble worktop or a silicone baking mat.

5 Keep in a dry, airtight container until required.

Lemon and almond marzipan bonbons

Ingredients	35 bonbons	70 bonbons
Granulated sugar	350 g	700 g
Liquid glucose	40 g	80 g
Water	100 g	200 g
Skinned whole almonds	350 g	700 g
Cooked marzipan	175 g	325 g
Sugar syrup (at 30 °Bx)	100 g	200 g
Trimolene	30 g	60 g
Blanched lemon zest	1 lemon	2 lemons
Unsalted dry butter	60 g	120 g
Crystallization syrup (saturated sugar solution)		
Granulated sugar	1375 g	2725 g
Water	500 g	1000 g

energy	cal	fat	sat fat	carb	sugar	protein	fibre
1278 kJ	302 kcal	7.2 g	1.3 g	61.3 g	59.1 g	2.5 g	1.2 g

METHOD OF WORK

1   Boil the sugar and the water, adding the liquid glucose at 104°C. Continue boiling until 119°C has been reached.

2   Grind the almonds to a powder using a food blender, then slowly pour in the hot sugar solution and blend for 30 seconds.

3   Add the marzipan, trimoline and the syrup at 30B° and continue mixing for another five minutes using an electric mixing machine with the paddle attachment.

4   Add the blanched lemon zest, and when the mixture is cold add the unsalted dry butter. Roll into small, evenly sized bonbons.

CHEF'S TIP   Cover the candissoire with a paper that will absorb the humidity (not silicone paper), if you notice a delay in the crystallization process. The size of the crystals on the paper will be the size they are on the candies.

METHOD OF FINISHING

Very clean equipment and utensils are needed for this task.

1   Place the sugar and the water into a clean saucepan and slowly bring to the boil, stirring to dissolve the sugar solids.

2   Skim the sugar syrup just before it comes to the boil to remove any impurities. When the sugar boils, clean the sides of the saucepan with a clean brush and clean water. Skim off any impurities as it boils.

3   Boil the syrup for one minute, then cover with plastic film and allow to cool down without stirring, to prevent any premature crystallization.

4   Place the bonbons to be candied on a wire rack that fits in a shallow tray (candissoire). Ensure the bonbons do not touch each other so that they can be evenly coated. Pour the sugar syrup over the bonbons very slowly (to help obtain small crystals) until the syrup reaches the top of the bonbons.

5   Invert a rack over the bonbons if needed to keep them in place and leave them in the candissoire at room temperature until the syrup has cooled to about 40°C.

6   Cover the candissoire with baking parchment. Do not move the container in which the bonbons are crystallizing otherwise the crystals will shift and start growing on other parts, rather than on the actual bonbons.

7   Let the bonbons crystallize for 17–20 hours, or more, depending on how dry the surrounding environment is. When the crystals reach the desired size, drain the bonbons on the bottom of the rack for one hour and remove them to a clean rack to dry until they are not sticky (this can take up to six hours). Keep the bonbons in an airtight container in the refrigerator at 5°C until required.

CHEF'S TIP   A candissoire is a metal tray with a grill or wire rack inserted inside. This is to allow the elements that require to be soaked in a sugar solution to be covered and the sugar solution is collected in the base.

Vanilla fudge

Ingredients	30–40 pieces	80–100 pieces
Granulated sugar	225 g	450 g
Soft brown sugar	225 g	450 g
Liquid glucose	110 g	225 g
Unsalted butter	110 g	225 g
Double cream	140 ml	280 ml
Vanilla extract	to taste	to taste

energy	cal	fat	sat fat	carb	sugar	protein	fibre
428 kJ	102 kcal	4.7 g	3 g	16 g	14.6 g	0.1 g	0 g

METHOD OF WORK

1 Place all the ingredients into a large, clean saucepan and place on a medium heat. Boil steadily to 118°C. Remove from the heat.

2 Using a clean wooden spoon, stir constantly until the boiled mixture begins to grain.

3 Pour into a shallow tray that is lightly oiled (or lined with silicone paper) and allow to cool and set completely.

4 When set, cut into squares.

CHEF'S TIP Derivatives of this recipe include:
Coffee – add diluted instant coffee to taste
Chocolate – add dark couverture (minimum 68 per cent cocoa solids) at the mixing stage. Do not add the chocolate earlier or it may burn the cocoa.

Rum and raisin fudge

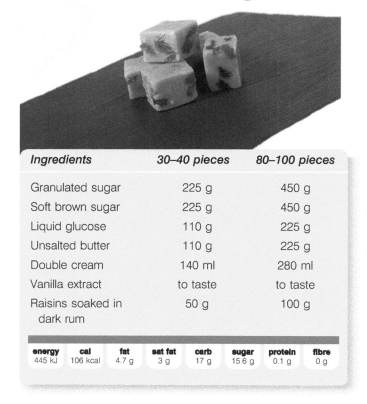

Ingredients	30–40 pieces	80–100 pieces
Granulated sugar	225 g	450 g
Soft brown sugar	225 g	450 g
Liquid glucose	110 g	225 g
Unsalted butter	110 g	225 g
Double cream	140 ml	280 ml
Vanilla extract	to taste	to taste
Raisins soaked in dark rum	50 g	100 g

energy	cal	fat	sat fat	carb	sugar	protein	fibre
445 kJ	106 kcal	4.7 g	3 g	17 g	15.6 g	0.1 g	0 g

METHOD OF WORK

1 Place all the ingredients apart from the raisins into a large, clean saucepan and place on a medium heat. Boil steadily to 118°C. Remove from the heat.

2 Using a clean wooden spoon, stir constantly until the boiled mixture begins to grain. Drain the raisins from the rum and add the raisins to the fudge mix.

3 Pour into a shallow tray that is lightly oiled (or lined with silicone paper) and allow to cool and set completely.

4 When set, cut into squares.

Pâte des fruits (cassis and apricot)

Ingredients	1 small slab (18 × 18 cm)	1 large slab (36 × 36 cm)
Cassis purée	425 g	850 g
Apricot purée	250 g	500 g
Powdered pectin	20 g	40 g
Caster sugar	75 g	150 g
Granulated sugar	750 g	1.5 kg
Liquid glucose	175 g	350 g
Tartaric acid	5 g	10 g
Water	3 g	5 g

energy	cal	fat	sat fat	carb	sugar	protein	fibre
1588 kJ	373 kcal	0.1 g	0 g	98.8 g	91.8 g	0.5 g	1 g

METHOD OF WORK

1 Place the purées together in a clean heavy-based saucepan. Mix the powdered pectin with the caster sugar and whisk into the fruit purées. Bring to the boil.

2 Add the granulated sugar and the glucose. Stirring constantly, bring the temperature of the boiling mixture to 107°C.

3 Dissolve the tartaric acid in the water and add to the cooked fruit paste.

4 Line the bottom of a frame with silicone paper and pour the fruit paste into the frame. Leave to cool.

5 Remove from the frame, peel off the silicone paper carefully then cut the set fruit into 2.5 cm squares and roll in granulated sugar.

CHEF'S TIP Derivatives of this recipe include different fruit purées, simply replace the cassis purée or both the apricot and cassis purée with the chosen fruit purée substitute.

Nougat Montélimar

Ingredients	30 pieces	60 pieces
Granulated sugar	210 g	420 g
Clear honey	60 g	120 g
Water	50 g	100 g
Liquid glucose	60 g	120 g
Egg whites	25 g	50 g
Glacé cherries	30 g	60 g
Blanched pistachio nuts	30 g	60 g
Flaked almonds	20 g	30 g
Chopped hazelnuts	20 g	30 g

energy	cal	fat	sat fat	carb	sugar	protein	fibre
240 kJ	57 kcal	1.3 g	0.1 g	11.4 g	10.5 g	0.6 g	0.2 g

METHOD OF WORK

1 Bring the sugar and water to the boil in a heavy-based saucepan. Add the honey and the liquid glucose at 107°C. Skim off any impurities that reach the surface of the boiling sugar solution.

2 Boil to 137°C. Meanwhile, aerate the egg whites to soft peaks and slowly pour in the hot syrup while still beating. Continue beating until the mixture becomes firm.

3 Warm the cherries and nuts in an oven for a few minutes and carefully combine into the cooked meringue mixture.

4 Pour the mixture into a shallow tray lined with rice paper. Place a further sheet of rice paper on the top of the nougat and weigh down with a flat board.

5 Leave to set for 24 hours before turning out and cutting into small pieces.

6 Store in an airtight container if not required immediately.

Cooking and using Isomalt for display

ingredients

Isomalt	1 kg
Water	100 g

METHOD OF WORK

1 Place the isomalt and water into a heavy-based saucepan and leave for ten minutes. Bring to the boil and clean the sides of the pan with clean cold water.

2 Continue to boil to 170°C. Add the colour at the correct temperature, if required.

3 Use the cooked isomalt in the same way as a normal cooked sugar solution. It can be poured or pulled as usual.

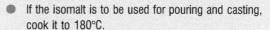

CHEF'S TIP

● If the isomalt seems too brittle or too hard to work with, reduce the boiling time by reducing the water content or lower the cooking temperature to 160°C.

● If the isomalt is too soft or sticky to work with, increase the boiling time to evaporate more of the water content.

● If the isomalt is to be used for pouring and casting, cook it to 180°C.

PRE-PREPARATION

● If coloured isomalt sugar is required, colouring should be prepared prior to the cooking of the sugar.

● Prepare a lightly oiled clean marble slab or a cleaned and dried silicone baking mat.

● Have a sugar heat lamp or a preheated oven (to 150°C) to keep the isomalt warm.

● Prepare an airtight, deep plastic container lined with silica gel for storage of the isomalt.

Sugar candy lollipops

Ingredients	10 lollipops	20 lollipops
Isomalt	100 g	200 g
Granulated sugar	350 g	700 g
Liquid glucose	150 g	300 g
Water	160 g	340 g
Appropriate colour	as required	as required
Lemon, orange, lime and strawberry flavourings	as required	as required

energy	cal	fat	sat fat	carb	sugar	protein	fibre
973 kJ	229 kcal	0.3 g	0 g	59.9 g	52.9 g	0.1 g	0.1 g

METHOD OF WORK

1   Place the isomalt, granulated sugar, glucose and water in a heavy-based saucepan and boil to 140°C.

2   Add the colour and flavouring and continue boiling until 155°C has been reached. Arrest the cooking by plunging the base of the saucepan into cold water for a few seconds.

3   Pour the candy solution into lightly oiled individual stainless steel heart moulds on a silicone baking mat and leave to cool slightly. Remove the rings and push lollipop sticks into each candy as required.

4   Leave to fully set and cool down. Remove from the silicone mat and store in an airtight container.

Milk chocolate caramels

Ingredients	45 caramels	90 caramels
Double cream	350 g	700 g
Cubed sugar	200 g	400 g
Liquid glucose	200 g	400 g
Trimolene	50 g	100 g
Milk couverture (minimum 38% cocoa solids)	120 g	240 g
Cocoa paste (100% cocoa solids)	60 g	120 g
Unsalted butter	40 g	80 g

energy	cal	fat	sat fat	carb	sugar	protein	fibre
433 kJ	104 kcal	6.7 g	3.1 g	11 g	7.8 g	0.5 g	0 g

METHOD OF WORK

1   Boil together the cream, sugar, liquid glucose and trimoline in a heavy-based saucepan to 118°C.

2   Add the cocoa paste, couverture and butter and stir in well off the heat.

3   Pour the mixture into a lightly oiled shallow stainless steel tray and leave to cool and set.

4   When it is cool enough, remove carefully from the tray and cut into 2.5 cm slabs. Store in an airtight container before use.

Vanilla macaroons

Ingredients	40 macaroons	80 macaroons
Icing sugar	300 g	600 g
Ground almonds	75 g	150 g
Egg whites	90 g	185 g
Granulated sugar	85 g	180 g
Liquid glucose	45 g	90 g
Water	35 g	70 g
Egg whites	85 g	180 g
Vanilla	to taste	to taste

energy	cal	fat	sat fat	carb	sugar	protein	fibre
231 kJ	55 kcal	1.1 g	0.1 g	11.2 g	10.6 g	0.8 g	0.2 g

METHOD OF WORK

1   Preheat an oven to 210°C.

2   Mix together the icing sugar, ground almonds and the larger quantity of egg whites to a paste.

3   Meanwhile, bring the sugar and the water to the boil in a heavy-based saucepan. Add the glucose at 104°C and continue boiling until 118°C has been reached.

4   Whisk the smaller quantity of egg whites to a soft peak. Slowly pour the boiled sugar syrup into the whisked egg white. Continue whisking until cold to create an Italian meringue.

5   Carefully fold in the meringue into the ground almond mixture. Add the vanilla at this stage. Place the mixture into a piping bag with a plain tube.

6   Pipe the macaroons onto a silicone baking mat and let them dry for 30 minutes at room temperature.

7   Place the macaroons into the oven. After three minutes reduce the heat to 170°C and bake for a further six minutes.

8   Remove the macaroons from the oven and place onto a wire rack to cool. Carefully remove the macaroons when they are cool. Pipe a little butter cream, ganache or apricot jam onto the underside of a macaroon and then stick two macaroons together.

CHEF'S TIP   To store the finished macaroons is it important to place them into an airtight container and store in a refrigerator.

Strawberry macaroons

Ingredients	40 macaroons	80 macaroons
Icing sugar	300 g	600 g
Ground almonds	75 g	150 g
Egg whites	90 g	185 g
Granulated sugar	85 g	180 g
Liquid glucose	45 g	90 g
Water	35 g	70 g
Egg whites	85 g	180 g
Red colour		

energy	cal	fat	sat fat	carb	sugar	protein	fibre
231 kJ	54 kcal	1.1 g	0.1 g	11.2 g	10.6 g	0.8 g	0.2 g

METHOD OF WORK

1   Preheat an oven to 210°C.

2   Mix together the icing sugar, ground almonds and the larger quantity of egg whites to a paste.

3   Meanwhile, bring the sugar and the water to the boil in a heavy-based saucepan. Add the glucose at 104°C and continue boiling until 118°C has been reached.

4   Whisk the smaller quantity of egg whites to a soft peak. Slowly pour the boiled sugar syrup into the whisked egg white. Continue whisking until cold to create an Italian meringue.

5   Carefully fold in the meringue into the ground almond mixture. Add the red colour at this stage. Place the mixture into a piping bag with a plain tube.

6   Pipe the macaroons onto a silicone baking mat and let them dry for 30 minutes at room temperature.

7   Place the macaroons into the oven. After three minutes reduce the heat to 170°C and bake for a further six minutes.

8   Remove the macaroons from the oven and place onto a wire rack to cool. Carefully remove the macaroons when they are cool. Pipe a little strawberry butter cream onto the underside of a macaroon and then stick two macaroons together.

Florentines

Ingredients	70 florentines	150 florentines
Unsalted butter	150 g	300 g
Caster sugar	200 g	400 g
Clear honey	50 g	100 g
Double cream	100 g	200 g
Mixed peel	100 g	200 g
Chopped walnuts	100 g	200 g
Flaked almonds	200 g	400 g
Pistachio nuts	100 g	200 g
Raisins	50 g	100 g
Tempered dark couverture	500 g	1000 g

energy	cal	fat	sat fat	carb	sugar	protein	fibre
490 kJ	118 kcal	9.1 g	1.9 g	7.5 g	5.2 g	1.9 g	0.5 g

METHOD OF WORK

1 Preheat an oven to 200°C.

2 Place the butter, sugar and cream into a heavy-based saucepan and bring to the boil. Add the clear honey at 104°C and continue boiling to 115°C.

3 Remove from the heat and add all the nuts and fruit. Stir in well and pour the mixture onto a silicone baking mat. Place another mat on top and spread the mixture evenly between the two mats. Place in a freezer.

4 When the mixture has just frozen, cut out 2.5 cm discs and place onto a baking tray lined with a silicone baking mat.

5 Place into the oven and bake for 12 minutes.

6 When the Florentines are baked they may spread a little. Let them cool before cutting them back to the required shape using a plain cutter.

7 Dip the base of each Florentine into the melted chocolate and set on an embossed plastic chocolate mat until the chocolate has set.

8 Reserve in an airtight container until service.

Vanilla marshmallows

Ingredients	50	100
Granulated sugar	600 g	1200 g
Egg whites	3	6
Gelatine leaves	16 leaves	32 leaves
Water	130 g	260 g
Vanilla extract	to taste	to taste

energy	cal	fat	sat fat	carb	sugar	protein	fibre
209 kJ	49 kcal	0 g	0 g	12.6 g	12.6 g	0.4 g	0 g

METHOD OF WORK

1 Place the sugar in a heavy based and clean saucepan with the water and bring to the boil.

2 Skim off any impurities.

3 Soak the leaves of gelatine in some cold water.

4 Continue to boil until the sugar solution reaches 140°C.

5 When the sugar is 10°C away from reaching its objective temperature, begin to aerate the egg whites to a stiff peak.

6 Gradually add the boiled sugar to the egg whites as if making an Italian meringue.

7 Drain the water from the gelatine and add the gelatine to the hot sugar and egg white mixture whilst it is still hot.

8 Add the vanilla.

9 When the gelatine has thoroughly melted and been beaten into the mixture, turn out into a tray dusted with cornflour.

10 Sieve a little further cornflour on top. Leave to set.

11 When set, cut into small cubes and roll in a mixture of icing sugar and cornflour (three parts icing sugar to one part cornflour).

Turkish delight

Ingredients	25	50
Caster sugar	225 g	450 g
Water	250 g	500 g
Icing sugar	50 g	100 g
Lemon juice	2 g	4 g
Cream of tartar	2 g	4 g
Cornflour	75 g	150 g
Rose water	to taste	to taste
Grenadine	2 g	4 g

energy	cal	fat	sat fat	carb	sugar	protein	fibre
232 kJ	54 kcal	0 g	0 g	14.3 g	11.5 g	0 g	0 g

METHOD OF WORK

1   Create an icing sugar and cornflour mix similar to the version used in the previous recipe for marshmallows using three parts icing sugar and one part cornflour.

2   Dust a moulding tray or a normal baking tray with straight sides with the cornflour/icing sugar mixture.

3   Pour half of the water into a heavy based saucepan and add the sugars. Bring to the boil and then add the lemon juice. Skim any impurities off the top of the sugar solution once it reaches boiling point.

4   Reduce the heat and cook until 115°C has been achieved. Remove from the heat.

5   In a separate saucepan, mix the cornflour and cream of tartar with the remaining water and cook over a medium heat until the mixture begins to thicken, stirring all the time.

6   Carefully pour the hot sugar solution into the thickened cornflour and return to the heat. Stir continuously over a low heat for approximately one hour.

7   To test if the mixture is ready take a little onto a frozen plate and check to see if the mixture sets to a gum consistency.

8   Add the flavour and Grenadine, mix in well

9   Pour the mixture into the mould or baking tin and leave to set for at least 12 hours.

10   Cut into squares after it has set and roll in a mixture of the icing sugar and cornflour. Store in an airtight container between layers of baking parchment.

Candied orange peel with chocolate

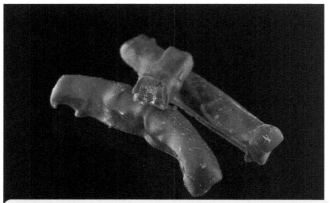

Ingredients	10 oranges
Caster sugar	1000 g
Water	600 g
Oranges	10
Caster sugar	100 g each day
Liquid glucose	20 g on final day
Dark chocolate (68% minimum cocoa solids)	1000 g

energy	cal	fat	sat fat	carb	sugar	protein	fibre
886 kJ	211 kcal	9 g	0 g	31.9 g	25.5 g	2.2 g	0.5 g

METHOD OF WORK

1   The oranges must be blanched first. Dip the whole oranges, one by one into hot, but not boiling, salted water. Remove the oranges after sixty seconds and refresh in running cold water.

2   Cut the peel from the oranges and slice into strips, approximately 8 cm in length and 1 cm in width.

3   On the first day; bring the caster sugar and water to the boil to achieve 20°Baumé or 36°Brix. Place the drained orange peel immediately into the hot sugar solution, remove from the heat and allow to rest for 24 hours. Place a grid or silicone paper cartouche on top to ensure that all the peel is submerged.

4   On the second day; drain the orange peel and add 100 g of caster sugar to the remaining sugar solution and heat to 22°Baumé or 40°Brix. Pour the syrup over the peel and rest for another 24 hours.

5   Repeat this process for another ten days, as below:

   a.   3rd day add 100 g caster and increase to 24°Baumé or 44°Brix.
   b.   4th day add 100 g caster and increase to 24°Baumé or 44°Brix.
   c.   5th day add 100 g caster and increase to 26°Baumé or 47°Brix.
   d.   6th day add 100 g caster and increase to 26°Baumé or 47°Brix.
   e.   7th day add 100 g caster and increase to 28°Baumé or 51°Brix.
   f.   8th day add 100 g caster and increase to 28°Baumé or 51°Brix.
   g.   9th day add 100 g caster and increase to 30°Baumé or 54°Brix.
   h.   10th day add 100 g caster and increase to 30°Baumé or 54°Brix.
   i.   11th day add 100 g caster and increase to 32°Baumé or 58°Brix.

6   By the 12th day instead of adding 100 g caster sugar, add 20 g liquid glucose and heat the sugar solution to 34°Baume or 62°Brix. The peel should marinate in this sugar solution for another four days, covered with a cartouche.

7   Remove the peel and drain on a wire rack to dry and create a dry sugar coating.

8   Pre-crystallize the chocolate and dip each strip of peel into the chocolate completely coating it and leave to set on a sheet of silicone paper.

9   Serve as a petit four.

Brandy snap biscuits

Ingredients	25	50
Icing sugar	125 g	250 g
Butter	85 g	155 g
Golden syrup	65 g	125 g
Soft flour	65 g	125 g

energy	cal	fat	sat fat	carb	sugar	protein	fibre
261 kJ	62 kcal	2.8 g	1.8 g	9.3 g	7.2 g	0.3 g	0.1 g

METHOD OF WORK

1   Preheat the oven to 190°C and line two baking sheets with baking parchment.

2   Put the caster sugar, butter and golden syrup in a small saucepan and cook over a low heat, stirring occasionally, for three–four minutes until all of the ingredients have melted and are blended together.

3   Remove the pan from the heat and put it in iced water for 60 seconds to arrest the cooking, stirring the mixture continuously, until cool, and remove from the water bath. Stir in the flour.

4   Drop small teaspoonfuls of the brandy snap mixture onto each baking sheet, spacing well apart. Bake for five–six minutes until golden and remove from the oven leaving to cool slightly.

5   Using a palette knife, lift the brandy snaps and gently mould them into small baskets (as shown) or roll them around a small wooden doweling rod to create petit fours. Leave to cool for one–two minutes before removing and using.

6   Store in an airtight container for further use.

CHEF'S TIP It is important to store these dipped fruits in a dry, airtight container. Sugar is hygroscopic and so will attract moisture in damp or cold environments. Dipped fruits are usually made at the last moment before being served.

Sugar-dipped fruit (*Fruits glacés*)

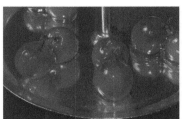

Ingredients	20 dipped fruits	40 dipped fruits
Cube sugar	240 g	480 g
Liquid glucose	20 g	40 g
Water	70 g	140 g
Fruits to be dipped		
Grapes	as required	as required
Cherries	as required	as required
Mandarin orange	as required	as required
Strawberries	as required	as required

energy	cal	fat	sat fat	carb	sugar	protein	fibre
233 kJ	55 kcal	0 g	0 g	14.6 g	14 g	0.1 g	0.1 g

METHOD OF WORK

1   Prepare the fruit carefully, taking care not to bruise or cut the skins or membranes. Any leakages of liquid from the fruit will immediately begin to break down the sugar once the fruit has been dipped and will result in re-crystallization. Cherries and grapes should be cut into pairs and kept on the stalk.

2   Place the fruit onto a wire rack and place on top of an oven or a warm place to dry their surfaces for at least 30 minutes.

3   Bring the sugar and water to the boil in a heavy-based saucepan. At 104°C, add the liquid glucose. Continue boiling to 155°C (hard crack stage). Remove from the heat and arrest the cooking.

4   Dip the fruit into the sugar. Use a small set of tweezers to avoid burning the fingers. Ensure each fruit is fully dipped and that no part of the fruit is left without a covering of sugar.

5   Quickly transfer the dipped fruits onto a lightly oiled, clean marble slab or a silicone baking mat to set.

Pastillage

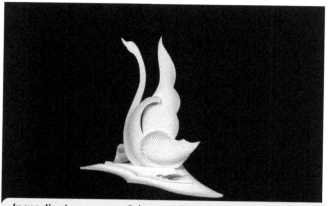

Ingredients	2 kg pastillage	3.5 kg pastillage
Icing sugar	1750 g	3300 g
Cornflour	100 g	200 g
Gelatine	6 leaves	12 leaves
Liquid glucose	60 g	120 g
Water	130 g	260 g
Lemon juice	¼ lemon	½ lemon

energy	cal	fat	sat fat	carb	sugar	protein	fibre
1986 kJ	465 kcal	0 g	0 g	123.7 g	115.1 g	0.4 g	0 g

METHOD OF WORK

1   Sift the icing sugar and cornflour together.
2   Soften the gelatine leaves in the water and melt in a warm bain-marie together with the glucose and lemon juice.
3   Add the liquid to the dry ingredients and work together.
4   Knead on a clean surface until a soft paste has been achieved.
5   Wrap in a clean damp cloth and plastic film. Use as required and as directed in the section of this chapter, 'Preparation of pastillage'.

Fondant

Ingredients	500 g of fondant	1 kg of fondant
Granulated sugar	480 g	960 g
Water	125 ml	250 ml
Cream of tartar	1 tsp	2 tsp

energy	cal	fat	sat fat	carb	sugar	protein	fibre
406 kJ	95 kcal	0 g	0 g	25.2 g	25.2 g	0 g	0 g

METHOD OF WORK

1   Bring the sugar and water to the boil in a heavy-based saucepan. Add the cream of tartar at 104°C.
2   Continue boiling until 115°C has been obtained.
3   Pour the sugar solution on a very lightly oiled marble slab.
4   Splash the surface of the sugar with a little cold water and let the temperature drop to 100°C. Agitate the sugar with a clean spatula. The mass will become thicker as it cools and as the agitation continues.
5   When the sugar solution has become stiff and hard to work, knead by hand into a smooth, plastic paste.
6   Cover with plastic film or polythene to prevent skinning and use as required.

CHEF'S TIP   Convenience fondant is often used in the pastry kitchen because it is reliable, consistent and saves time. Fondant can be used for cooking in place of sugar – it has the advantage of already having undergone a degree of inversion.

Poured sugar *(sucre coulé)*

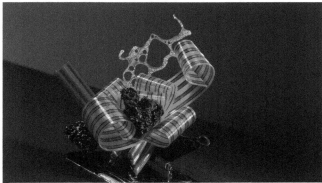

Ingredients

Granulated or cubed sugar	750 g
Liquid glucose	150 g
Water	400 g

energy	cal	fat	sat fat	carb	sugar	protein	fibre
366 kJ	86 kcal	0 g	0 g	22.9 g	21.2 g	0 g	0 g

PRE-PREPARATION

- If you require an opaque finish, mix chalk powder or titanium powder with an equal amount of water and blend to a paste.

- Prepare the powder colour as required and ensure that you have enough to maintain the required depth of colour (such as black – pictured).

- Prepare a few drops of tartaric acid.

- Prepare any moulds (stainless steel moulds will need lightly oiling to prevent the sugar sticking).

METHOD OF WORK

1   Place the sugar and water in a heavy-based saucepan and leave for ten minutes. Bring to the boil and skim off any scum from the surface then add the glucose. Clean the sides of the pan with clean cold water and boil to 105°C, then remove from the heat, cover with plastic film and stand until required.

2   If the sugar solution is required immediately, continue to boil to 133°C (soft crack).

3   Add the chalk/titanium paste if required and boil to the final temperature of 155°C (hard crack). Add the colour just before the final temperature is reached and add two spots of tartaric acid as it reaches the temperature.

4   Arrest the cooking of the sugar. Pour into the prepared moulds in a continuous stream. Gently remove any air bubbles with a small gas blowtorch by running the flame carefully over the surface of the sugar. Leave to cool and set before carefully removing from the moulds ready for assembling.

5   Join the sugar pieces together using any leftover molten sugar (cooked to hard crack stage) as glue. Ensure that no fingerprints are left on the surface of the sugar pieces and always protect the sugar from coming into contact with moisture.

6   Temperatures for adding colour to poured sugar:
   i.   white and blue colour 145°C
   ii. all other colours 147°C
   iii. clear and opaque sugar 150°C.

CHEF'S TIP   While boiling the sugar, do not stir. Keep the sides of the saucepan and the thermometer continuously washed down with the cold clean water to re-dissolve any sugar crystals that have formed.

Step-by-step for poured sugar

1. The sugar has cooked and has been coloured with the black colouring. Check that the sugar has reached the required temperature and that all equipment is prepared and ready for use, especially the frame or mould that the sugar is being poured into.

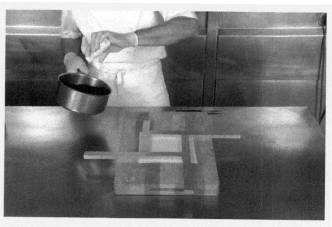

2. Adding a little silver colouring to the sugar at the last minute, shaking in to give a two-colour effect to the finished poured piece.

3. Pouring the sugar carefully into the frame, ensure that the sugar fully floods the frame and does not escape.

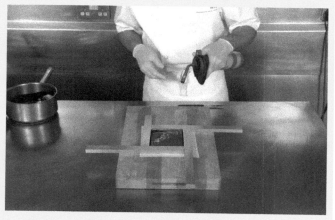

4. Using a blow torch run the flame over the surface of the molten poured sugar to remove any air bubbles. Leave to set and cool before removing the frame.

Rock sugar *(Sucre roché)*

Ingredients

Granulated or cubed sugar	480 g
Royal icing	30 g
Water	180 g

energy	cal	fat	sat fat	carb	sugar	protein	fibre
426 kJ	100 kcal	0 g	0 g	26.6 g	26.6 g	0 g	0 g

PRE-PREPARATION

- If coloured rock sugar is required, colouring should be added to the royal icing.
- Preheat an oven to 120°C.
- Prepare the royal icing.
- Prepare a suitable baking dish lined with foil.

METHOD OF WORK

1. Place the sugar and water in a heavy-based saucepan and leave for ten minutes. Bring to the boil and skim off any scum from the surface.
2. Boil the sugar to 138°C and remove from the heat.
3. Dip the pan in cold water to arrest the cooking of the sugar.
4. Add the royal icing and mix in quickly. The sugar will now increase in volume.
5. Quickly pour into the prepared baking tray. Place into the preheated oven for ten minutes to harden.
6. Remove from the oven and leave to cool and dry out for 12 hours.
7. Turn out the sugar and remove the tin foil before shaping as required, cutting with a small fretsaw or serrated knife.
8. Sprayed colours can be added after the sugar has dried out.

Bubble sugar

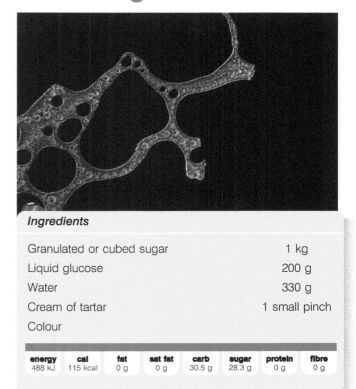

Ingredients

Granulated or cubed sugar	1 kg
Liquid glucose	200 g
Water	330 g
Cream of tartar	1 small pinch
Colour	

energy	cal	fat	sat fat	carb	sugar	protein	fibre
488 kJ	115 kcal	0 g	0 g	30.5 g	28.3 g	0 g	0 g

METHOD OF WORK

1. Cook the water and sugar to boiling point. Add the glucose and boil to 150°C. Add the colour just before the cooking has completed.
2. Pour the cooked sugar onto a silicone mat and leave to set.
3. Break into pieces and blend to a powder in a food processor.
4. Sieve the sugar dust onto a silicone baking mat (different colours of sugar will create a different colour effect).
5. Place another silicone mat over the top and place into a pre-heated oven at 185°C. The sugar should begin to melt and bubble.
6. Remove from the oven and leave to set before breaking into the required size needed.

CHEF'S TIP Do not attempt to use the rock sugar too early after removing from the oven as it will still retain a little moisture. It must be allowed to dry out completely before carving/cutting in desired shapes. This type of sugar is used to give a rocky effect to an overall display.

Spun sugar *(Sucre voile)*

Ingredients

Granulated or cubed sugar	1 kg
Liquid glucose	200 g
Water	330 g

energy	cal	fat	sat fat	carb	sugar	protein	fibre
488 kJ	114 kcal	0 g	0 g	30.5 g	28.3 g	0 g	0 g

PRE-PREPARATION

- If coloured spun sugar is required, colouring should be prepared before the cooking of the sugar.

- Prepare two wooden rods (rolling pins will do) by covering them in foil and positioning them so that they protrude over the edge of the work surface by about 10 cm.

- Place plenty of paper sheets on the floor directly underneath the wooden rods to catch any excess sugar.

- Prepare an airtight, deep plastic container lined with silica gel for storing the spun sugar.

CHEF'S TIP The colder the sugar solution when spun, the more wire-like the consistency of the set sugar will be and the longer the shape will hold.

METHOD OF WORK

1   Place the sugar and water into a heavy-based saucepan and leave for ten minutes. Bring to the boil on a medium heat and add the liquid glucose at 104°C. Add any colour at 145°C.

2   Increase the heat and boil the sugar solution to 155°C. Arrest the cooking of the sugar in a bowl of cold water for a few seconds.

3   Let the sugar solution stand for two–three minutes until it becomes slightly cooled.

4   Dip a whisk with the ends removed (to provide makeshift wire strands) into the sugar solution. Flick the sugar quickly, back and forth over the two prepared rods. Continue to spin the sugar until enough has been collected between the two rods.

5   Collect up all the spun sugar and store until required. The spun sugar will not last for more than two days in optimum storage conditions.

Step-by-step: Spun sugar

1. Prepare the equipment by ensuring all areas are covered with tin foil and that three rolling pins are placed between 40 and 50 cm apart from each other to catch the sugar.

2. Begin spinning the molten sugar across the three rolling pins using a cut-down wire balloon whisk to create the fine strands of sugar.

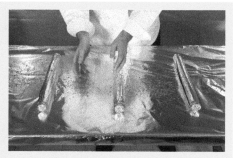

3. Begin to gather up the spun sugar when it has set and there is enough to be used. Roll it up and use as required.

Pulled sugar *(Sucre tire)*

Ingredients

Granulated or cubed sugar	1 kg
Liquid glucose	200 g
Water	330 g
Tartaric acid	10 drops

energy	cal	fat	sat fat	carb	sugar	protein	fibre
488 kJ	114 kcal	0 g	0 g	30.5 g	28.3 g	0 g	0 g

PRE-PREPARATION

● If coloured pulled sugar is required, colouring should be prepared before the cooking of the sugar.

● Prepare a lightly oiled clean marble slab or a cleaned and dried silicone baking mat.

● Have a sugar heat lamp or a preheated oven (to 150°C) to keep the pulled sugar warm.

● Prepare an airtight, deep plastic container lined with silica gel for storing the pulled sugar.

● Special plastic sugar gloves can be used when pulling the sugar if required.

METHOD OF WORK

1   Place the sugar and water in a heavy-based saucepan and leave for ten minutes. Bring to the boil and skim off any scum from the surface then add the glucose. Clean the sides of the pan with clean cold water and boil to 105°C, then remove from the heat, cover with plastic film and stand until required.

2   If the sugar solution is required immediately, continue to boil to 133°C (soft crack). Add the tartaric acid. Add the colour at the correct temperature, if required.

3   Boil to the final temperature of 155°C (hard crack) and add two spots of acid as it reaches the temperature. Arrest the cooking briefly.

4   Pour the sugar on the prepared work surface. Using a lightly oiled palette knife fold the edges of the poured sugar back into the centre. Ensure that no hard pieces of sugar are allowed to form. Continue to do this until the sugar mass stops spreading. The aim is to keep a uniform heat throughout the sugar mass and prevent any cool areas forming.

5   Handle the sugar mass by holding the sugar with one hand and pulling with the other. Fold it over and continue to use this technique until the sugar forms a shine and becomes smooth. Keep the sugar mass moving to maintain the temperature and to prevent it from setting. If the sugar begins to crack, it is ready.

6   Place the sugar mass on a silicone baking sheet under a sugar lamp or at the mouth of the preheated oven. The sugar must be turned over every so often to maintain an even heat throughout the mass.

7   Any pieces of pulled sugar not required for use can be cooled down, sealed in a vacuum bag and stored in an airtight plastic container with a little silica gel placed in the base.

8   Various shapes and designs can now be produced to create a centrepiece or decoration.

CHEF'S TIP   If the sugar appears sticky during the pulling process this will be because too much glucose was added or the sugar was not cooked to the correct temperature. If the pulled sugar begins to grain (crystallize), this may be because it has been manipulated too much.

Step-by-Step: Creating a pulled sugar ribbon

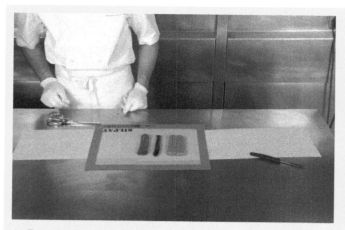

1. Ensure all the equipment is ready and close at hand. Place your selected colours of pulled sugar onto a silicone mat in the order that your ribbon will be presented.

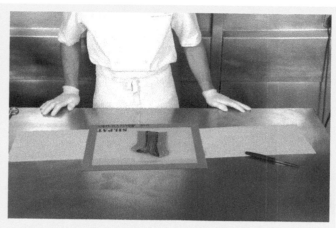

2. Merge the colours in strips so that they adhere to each other. Maintain the temperature and the flexibility of the sugar.

3. Cut the sugar in half and then adhere each piece side by side to create a thicker ribbon starting point.

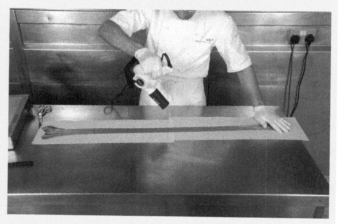

4. Stretch the sugar into a ribbon and maintain the temperature to keep the gloss and flexibility.

5. Cut the ribbon into smaller lengths for further moulding into loops.

6. The cut ribbon is shaped into loops for the finished piece to be assembled.

Blown sugar *(Sucre soufflé)*

Ingredients

Granulated or cubed sugar	1 kg
Liquid glucose	200 g
Water	330 g
Cream of tartar	1 small pinch

energy	cal	fat	sat fat	carb	sugar	protein	fibre
488 kJ	115 kcal	0 g	0 g	30.5 g	28.3 g	0 g	0 g

PRE-PREPARATION

- If coloured blown sugar is required, colouring should be prepared before the cooking of the sugar.

- Prepare a lightly oiled clean marble slab or a cleaned and dried silicone baking mat.

- Have a sugar heat lamp or a preheated oven (to 150°C) to keep the blown sugar warm.

- Prepare an airtight, deep plastic container lined with silica gel for storage of the blown sugar and have a sugar pump ready.

- Special plastic sugar gloves can be used when handling the sugar if required.

METHOD OF WORK

1 Place the sugar and water into a heavy-based saucepan and leave for ten minutes. Bring to the boil and skim off any scum from the surface, then add the glucose. Clean the sides of the pan with clean cold water and boil to 105°C, then remove from the heat, cover with plastic film and stand until required.

2 If the sugar solution is required immediately, continue to boil to 133°C (soft crack). Add the small pinch of cream of tartar. Add the colour at the correct temperature, if required. Boil to 151°C and arrest the cooking of the sugar immediately.

3 Follow the method for pulled sugar until you have a mass of sugar that is really to be blown.

4 Take a ball of pulled sugar that is elastic and uniform in temperature. Place a finger into the centre of the sugar ball and insert the tube of the sugar pump. Firmly press the edges of the sugar around the end of the tube so that it sticks.

5 Gently blow in the air so that the sugar ball begins to inflate. If the sugar is not uniformly warm, the warmer parts will expand more than the cooler parts. Constantly regulate the heat under a sugar lamp.

6 Use the fingers to manipulate and control the shape of the sugar while air is blown into it.

7 Once the desired shape has been achieved, blow cool air on the shape with a fan or hair-drier to set the shape quickly. Remove the tube using a hot knife or scissors.

Step-by-step: Blowing sugar straws

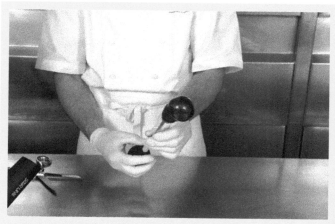

1. Begin by attaching the air pump tube to a piece of pulled sugar and begin pumping to slowly blow the sugar a little at a time. Be carefully not to pump too hard or the sugar will deform.

2. Stretch the sugar as it becomes hollow with the air being slowly blown into it.

3. Fold the sugar on itself twice and carefully adhere the hollow straws together. Leave to cool down slightly being careful to regulate the temperature so as to prevent hot and cold spots on the sugar.

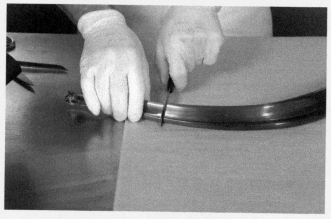

4. Cut sections of the straws with a hot knife being careful not to crack the fragile sugar.

5. The finished straws are cooled and kept until ready for assembly.

Step-by-step: Assembling a small sugar display

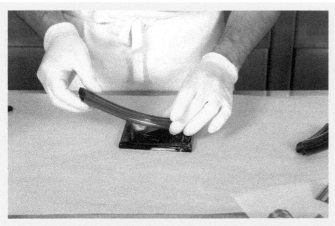

1. Using some molten sugar as glue, adhere the first sugar straw onto the poured sugar base. Use gloves to prevent fingerprints marking the shiny sugar.

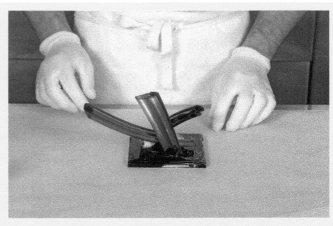

2. Add the other straw sugar pieces and ensure that the sugar glue is well set and cooled before moving onto the next stage.

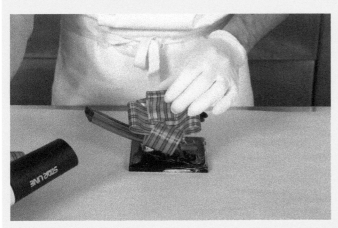

3. Begin assembling the sugar ribbon.

4. Move the sugar piece to help with the assembly and finish the ribbon. Once again ensure that each of the pieces are fully set before adding a further one.

5. Gently add the rock sugar.

6. Finally add the bubble sugar to finish the sugar display piece.

Nougatine

Ingredients

Granulated sugar	500 g
Water	200 g
Glucose	100 g
Flaked almonds	375 g

energy	cal	fat	sat fat	carb	sugar	protein	fibre
481 kJ	115 kcal	5.2 g	0.4 g	15.9 g	14.5 g	2 g	0.8 g

METHOD OF WORK

1 Place the water and sugar into a heavy based saucepan and bring to the boil. Add the glucose and cook to a light caramel following all the usual cooking precautions.

2 Remove from the heat and stir in the flaked almonds.

3 Pour onto a silicone baking mat and place another one on top.

4 Roll out to create thin nougatine and whilst still warm, cut out shapes as required.

Praline

Ingredients

Granulated sugar	500 g
Water	200 g
Whole, blanched almonds	180 g
Whole, blanched hazelnuts	180 g

energy	cal	fat	sat fat	carb	sugar	protein	fibre
248 kJ	59 kcal	2.7 g	0.2 g	8.2 g	7.7 g	1.1 g	0.5 g

METHOD OF WORK

1 Place the water and sugar into a heavy based saucepan and bring to the boil. Cook to a light caramel.

2 When the caramel is even in colour, add the two nut types, remove from the heat and stir in.

3 Deposit onto a silicone baking mat and allow to cool and set.

4 Break into pieces and store in an airtight container.

CHEF'S TIP This can be used as flavouring for creams, ice creams, pastries and desserts. Simply place in a food blender to grind to a powder and use. This recipe uses both hazelnuts and almonds to give a balanced flavour, however praline can be produced using hazelnuts only.

Guest Chef

Lavender, vanilla and white chocolate fudge

Chef *Greg Cheeseman*
Centre *Suffolk New College*

Using lavender in white chocolate fudge allows a light perfume to merge with the white chocolate. This soft fudge is then dipped into tempered white chocolate and finished with dried lavender bud.

Ingredients

Ingredients	Amount
Caster Sugar	500 g
Butter	250 g
Double cream	350 ml
Golden syrup	250 g
Vanilla pod	1
White chocolate	250 g
Lavender Edelweiss	1 tsp
White chocolate	500 g
Lavender buds – crystallized	1 tsp

METHOD OF WORK

1   Bring caster sugar, butter, double cream and golden syrup to a slow boil and cook to 121°C.
2   Remove from the heat and add the white chocolate, vanilla seeds and lavender.
3   Pour into a 30 cm × 15 cm tray lined with greaseproof paper.
4   Cut and dip into tempered white chocolate and sit on a cooling rack.
5   Lightly sprinkle crystallized lavender buds over the top of the fudge and cool until set.

ASSESSMENT OF KNOWLEDGE AND UNDERSTANDING

You have now learned about the use of sugar in confectionery and how to produce a variety of sugar-based sweets and decorations utilizing an array of commodities and different techniques.

To test your level of knowledge and understanding, answer the following short questions. These will help to prepare you for your summative (final) assessment.

1   State how glucose is produced and why it is used in confectionery.

2   State the temperature at which glucose is added to a sugar solution for cooking.

3   Identify the reason for pulled sugar being sticky during the pulling process.

4   Explain the importance of using a hygrometer.

5   Explain how a sugar pan should be cleaned prior to use.

6   Describe the correct procedure for cooking a sugar solution for pulled sugar.

7   Explain how to prepare three pieces of equipment before pulling sugar.

8   State the procedure for preparing sugar for boiling.

9   State how to store sugar decorations to prevent them from losing colour and absorbing moisture.

10 Name the agent which will help to keep the sugar decorations dry.

11 State two health and safety precautions when handling sugar

12 State the difference between fondant, nougatine and praline.

Food innovation: New ingredients, techniques and product development

NVQ

Contribute to the development of recipes and menus

Hydrocolloids

Hydrocolloids can be added to liquids and foods to modify their texture. Gelatine and flour have been used in the kitchen for many years to modify texture: gelatine is used to convert liquids into gels, and flour is a very common thickening agent. More recently, hydrocolloids that have been historically used in the food industry are starting to appear in the kitchen, although agar-agar and carrageenan have been used for many years in Asian and Irish cooking respectively. These additives,

HYDROCOLLOID	SOURCE
Agar-agar	Seaweed
Carrageenan (Iota and Kappa)	Seaweed
Sodium alginate	Seaweed
Gelatine	Animal protein
Gellan gum	Micro bacterial fermentation
Xanthan gum	Micro bacterial fermentation
Methylcellulose	Cellulose
Guar gum	Seeds of the guar plant
Locust bean gum	Seeds of the carob tree

whose functions in the food industry include preventing moisture migration in pies, creating the pimento gel that is used to stuff olives, and creating identically shaped onion rings, are now creeping into the kitchen. Today, experimental chefs are trying them out to create more innovative textures in their cooking, such as fake caviar, hot ice-cream and fluid gels.

Despite what many people think, these ingredients are derived from natural sources. With the exception of gelatine, which is a protein, hydrocolloids are polysaccharides. See bottom of previous column for a list of the most common hydrocolloids found in the kitchen along with their source.

Hydrocolloids as thickening and gelling agents

Hydrocolloids hydrate in water, forming associations with the water molecules and restricting their subsequent movement. This is how they thicken solutions, and in certain situations the hydrocolloid molecules will start to form a network with each other, trapping the water molecules completely and therefore forming a gel.

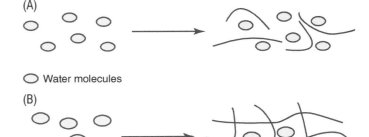

(A)

○ Water molecules

(B)

Diagram 1. To show how hydrocolloids act as thickening (A) and gelling (B) agents.

Unlike the traditional gelling and thickening agents of gelatine and flour, these new hydrocolloids have the ability to thicken and form gels at very low concentrations, offering economic benefit to the food industry. They also offer the advantage of being suitable for vegetarians and people with gluten intolerance.

The following terms are relevant when discussing gels:

● Thermo-reversible – gels that change their structure on heating, but go back to their original structure on cooling. Most hydrocolloid gels melt on heating, whereas methylcellulose forms thermo-reversible gels that set when heated and melt when cooled.

● Syneresis – occurs when liquid seeps out of a gel over time.

Hydrocolloids as moussing and emulsifying agents

If a molecule contains both hydrophobic (water hating) and hydrophilic (water loving) groups, it is able to act as an emulsifier. When fat and water is mixed in the absence of an emulsifier, the fat droplets will slowly find each other and coalesce, and due to their lower density compared to water they will rise to the surface of the mixture, separating out from the water. In the presence of an emulsifier, the hydrophobic groups on the molecule will interact with the fat droplets, while the hydrophilic groups interact with the water molecules. This helps to stabilize the emulsion and prevents it from separating over time.

This property also allows an emulsifier to act as a mousse stabilizer. In a mix of water and air, the hydrophilic groups on the molecule associate with the water molecules, leaving the hydrophobic parts, which hate to interact with the water, to form a network around the air bubbles, stabilizing them and prevent the air water mix from separating out.

> **CHEF'S TIP**   Avoid the addition of fat when making water based mousses, since the fat will tend to interact with the hydrophobic parts of the mousse stabiliser more strongly than the air, destabilizing the mousse.

> **CHEF'S TIP**   Gelatine contains both hydrophobic and hydrophilic parts – why not try using gelatine to create egg free mousses, or replace it with the egg yolk in mayonnaise to create egg free emulsions.

Which hydrocolloid to use?

All of the different hydrocolloids have slightly different properties, and it is important to understand what each of them can do to maximise their benefit in the kitchen.

> **CHEF'S TIP**   While hydrocolloids do hydrate in water, they need to be properly dispersed to ensure that they associate with the water molecules rather than clumping together. Proper dispersion can be achieved in several ways:
> - Fully agitating the liquid with a hand blender to create a vortex while adding the powder.
> - Pre-blending the hydrocolloids with a bulking agent such as sugar or maltodextrin before adding to the liquid.
>
> Since most hydrocolloids act as thickening agents, and some directly act as moussing agents, agitating the liquid with a hand-blender can cause air bubbles to get stably trapped within the solution, so often the solution will need to be left to stand for a few hours before being used to allow the air bubbles to escape.

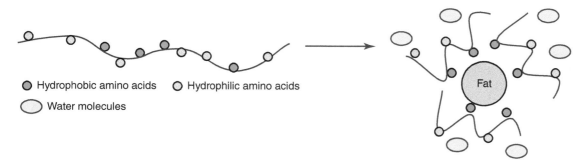

Diagram 2. To show how molecules containing hydrophobic and hydrophilic parts can stabilize emulsions

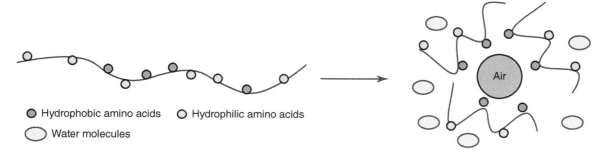

Diagram 3. To show how molecules containing hydrophobic and hydrophilic parts can stabilize mousses

AGAR-AGAR

Agar-agar is a useful gelling agent, and will cause liquids to gel at low concentrations (less than 1 per cent).

Solutions with agar need to be heated to near boiling in order to fully dissolve the agar – gels will form on cooling.

Agar-agar is a versatile gelling agent and offers good stability with acidic ingredients.

The gel is thermo-reversible, so it will melt on heating but will reform on subsequent cooling.

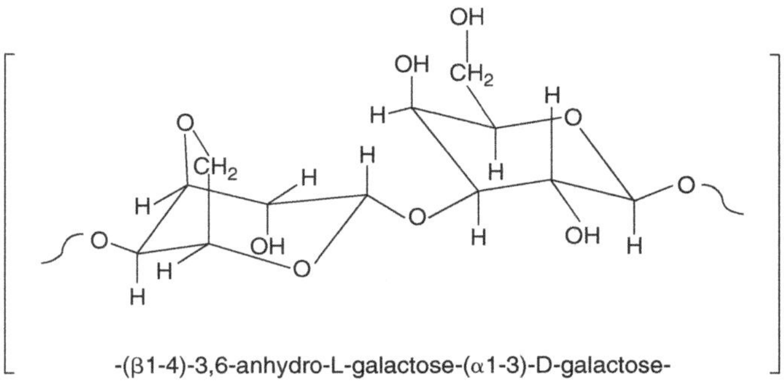

-(β1-4)-3,6-anhydro-L-galactose-(α1-3)-D-galactose-

Diagram 4. The structural unit of agar. ("Food Stabilisers, Thickeners and Gelling Agents" edited by Alan Imeson. Agar Chapter by Alan Imeson, p.38, John Wiley & Sons, October 2009, copyright © 2010 Blackwell Publishing Ltd.)

CARRAGEENAN (IOTA AND KAPPA)

Two main forms of carrageenan with gelling properties exist: kappa carrageenan forms brittle gels, whereas iota carrageenan forms more elastic gels. The two can be mixed to form more intermediate textures. Carrageenans are often used in milk-based applications because it interacts with milk proteins allowing gels to be formed at lower concentrations. The addition of locust bean gum makes kappa carrageenan gels stronger, more elastic and less prone to syneresis. Lambda carrageenan also exists, but is not able to form gels.

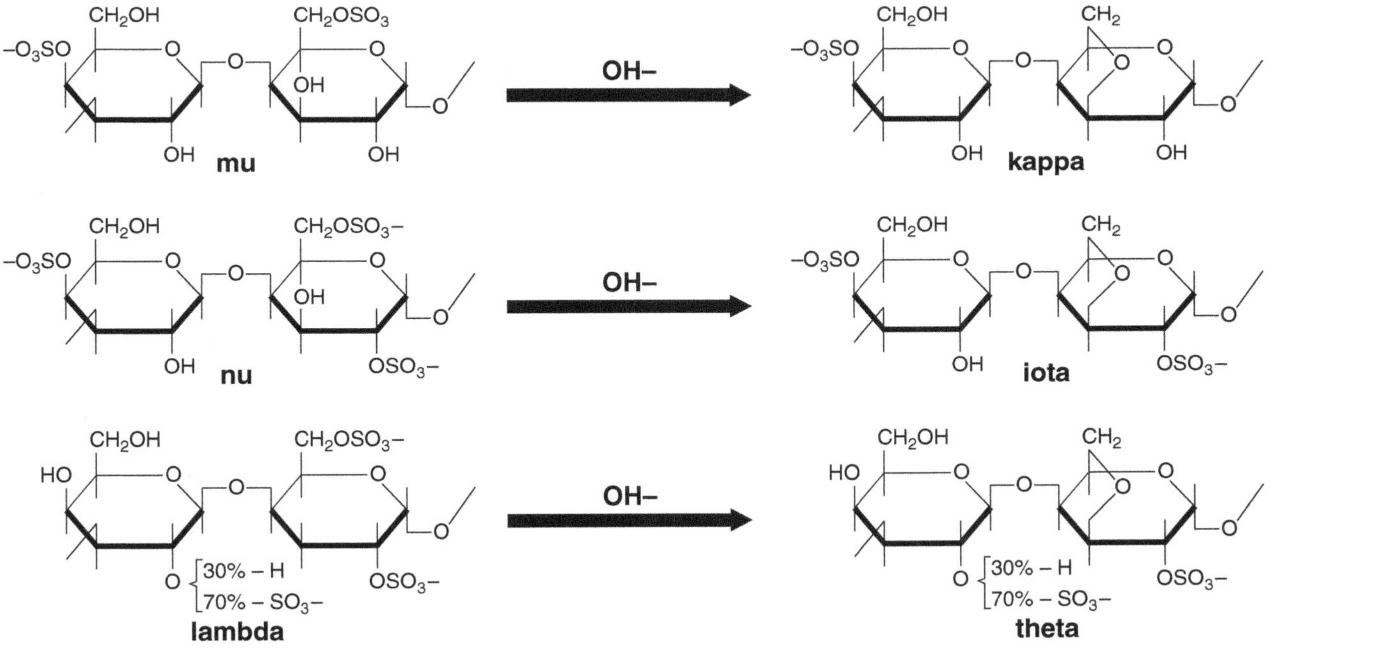

Diagram 5. The structures of primary carrageenans. ("Food Stabilisers, Thickeners and Gelling Agents" edited by Alan Imeson. Carrageenan Chapter by William R. Blakemore and Alan R. Harpell, p.78, John Wiley & Sons, October 2009, copyright © 2010 Blackwell Publishing Ltd.)

To hydrate, disperse the carrageenan in cold water or milk while mixing thoroughly and heat until completely dissolved (usually above 60°C but this depends on the exact type of carrageenan).

The gels are thermoreversible, and melt on heating but will regel on cooling.

SODIUM ALGINATE

Sodium alginate is a very effective thickening agent, and when added to liquids it imparts thickness without the need for heating (although thorough mixing is required). In the presence of calcium ions, the sodium alginate will gel. Therefore, solutions of sodium alginate are often pipetted into a solution of a calcium salt such as calcium chloride or calcium lactate in order to form fake caviar, where the droplet will instantly gel on the outside as it comes into contact with the calcium.

Since sodium alginate is a thickening agent, caviar beads made in this way will have a thickened interior – if a more liquid centre is required, reverse spherification can be used whereby a liquid containing calcium is pipetted into a bath of water thickened with alginate – the bead will gel on the outside but remain liquid inside.

> **CHEF'S TIP** When preparing mixes to use for standard spherification, avoid using dairy products. The calcium present in milk and cream will cause the alginate to set, before the solution can be pipetted into the calcium bath.

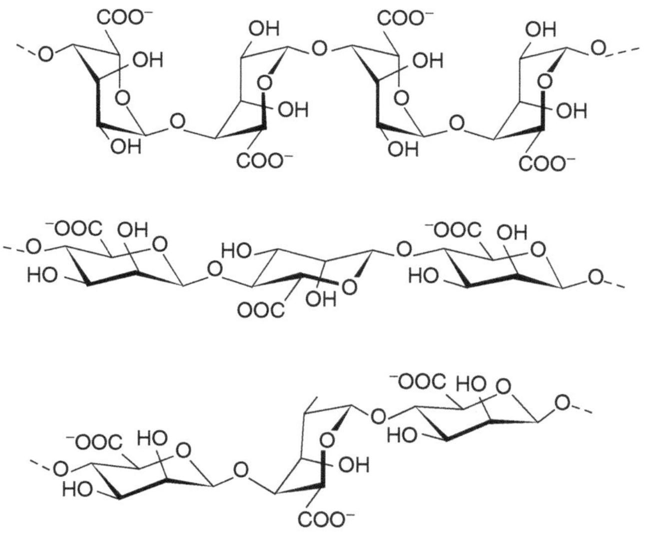

Diagram 6. Block structures in alginates. ("Food Stabilisers, Thickeners and Gelling Agents" edited by Alan Imeson. Alginates Chapter by Trond Helgerud, Olav Gåserød, Therese Fjæreide, Peder O. Andersen and Christian Klein Larsen, p.53, John Wiley & Sons, October 2009, copyright © 2010 Blackwell Publishing Ltd.)

GELATINE

Gelatine has excellent mouth-feel properties because it melts at 37°C, so when you place it in your mouth it melts, giving a great melt-in-the-mouth sensation. It also has better flavour release properties compared to the more gummy hydrocolloids, which are harder to break down in the mouth. Gelatine hydrates in cold water but must be heated to dissolve. Gelatine can be dissolved in a small portion of a recipe's liquid and then stirred into the remaining liquid so that the entire batch does not have to be heated.

It is a thermo reversible gel, which melts on heating and re gels on cooling.

METHYLCELLULOSE

Methylcellose is derived from cellulose but it has been modified in a certain way to add hydrophobic groups onto the structure. This gives it some unique properties:

● Due to having both hydrophobic and hydrophilic groups, methylcelluloses are very effective emulsifiers and moussing agents

● Solutions containing methylcellulose form a gel when they are heated (opposite to most gelling agents), and melt back to a liquid on cooling.

Due to the presence of the hydrophobic groups, methylcellulose is difficult to hydrate, so it is recommended that the hydrocolloid is added to hot liquids and then cooled while stirring, to ensure proper hydration and dissolution.

A large number of different types of methylcellulose exist, which vary in their chain length (which affects viscosity) and their level of substitution (which affects their gelling and melting temperatures). Because methylcellulose solutions gel on heating, solutions containing this ingredient are often used by chefs to pipette into a hot liquid and will display instant gelation, allowing noodles to be formed in a hot soup for example.

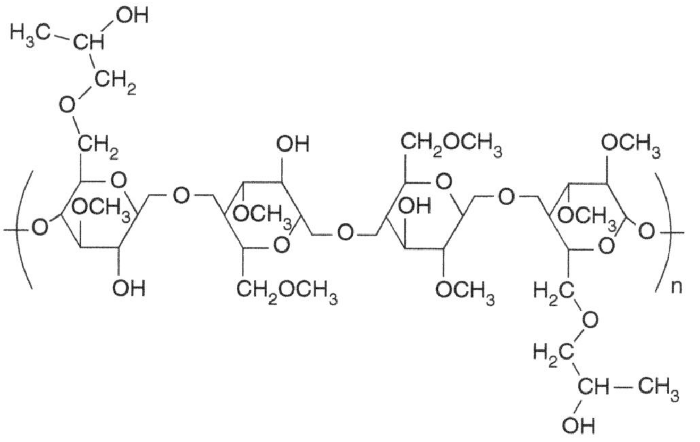

Diagram 7. Idealized structure of hydroxypropylmethyl cellulose. ("Food Stabilisers, Thickeners and Gelling Agents" edited by Alan Imeson. Cellulose Derivatives Chapter by Mary Jean Cash and Sandra J. Caputo, p.102, John Wiley & Sons, October 2009, copyright © 2010 Blackwell Publishing Ltd.)

GELLAN GUM

Gellan gum is a very effective gelling agent that can form gels at extremely low concentrations. When added to liquids and heated, solutions will gel on cooling. If the solution is either agitated (e.g. with a whisk) on cooling, or after cooling, a fluid gel will be formed. This gel will appear like a liquid in terms of its viscosity, yet its gelling properties will allow it to suspend particles, making it a popular ingredient in the food industry, for example in herb containing vinaigrettes.

Gels made of gellan gum offer much better flavour release properties and mouthfeel than the other new gelling agents, yet are sensitive to highly acidic liquids.

(a) Native or high-acyl gellan gum

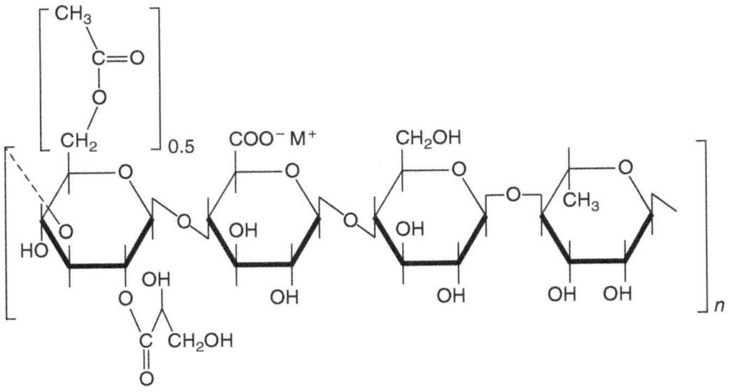

(b) Low-acyl gellan gum

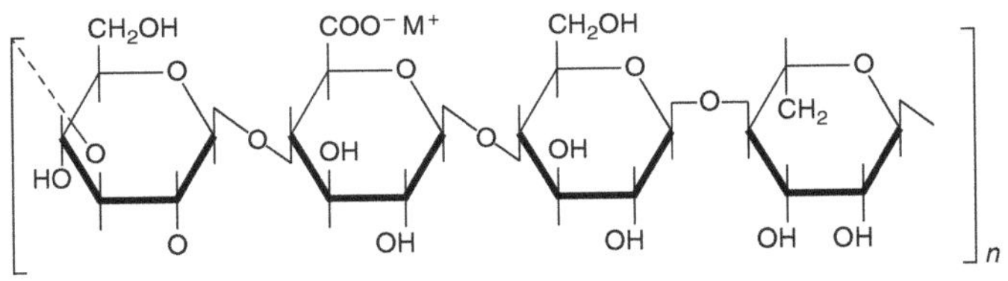

Diagram 8. Primary structure of gellan gum. ("Food Stabilisers, Thickeners and Gelling Agents" edited by Alan Imeson. Gellan Gum chapter by Raymond Valli and Ross Clark, p.147, John Wiley & Sons, October 2009, copyright © 2010 Blackwell Publishing Ltd.)

XANTHAN GUM

Xanthan gum is a useful thickening agent that hydrates in cold water to produce a viscous solution. Solutions thickened with xanthan gum are unique in that they appear fairly thick when they are left alone, but as soon as any force or motion is applied the solution thins. This makes it very useful for making salad dressings and sauces, which can be poured from the bottle as you agitate and therefore thin them, yet thicken up on contact with the plate, allowing for a better thickness and adherence.

Xanthan gum is very stable, and can be added to liquids high in acid and salt. Solutions thickened with xanthan gum can also be heated. It is often used in the food industry as a stabilizer, and is often used to stabilize products like low fat mayonnaise. Xanthan gum forms gels with locust bean gum.

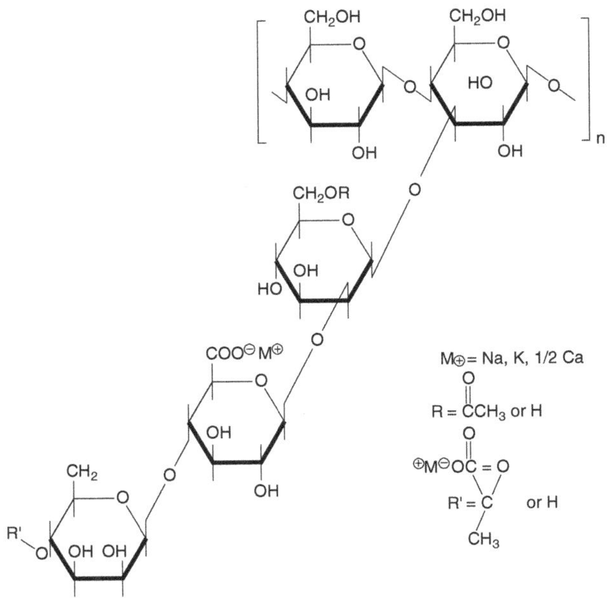

Diagram 9. Primary structure of xanthan gum. ("Food Stabilisers, Thickeners and Gelling Agents" edited by Alan Imeson. Xanthan Gum chapter by Graham Sworn, p.326, John Wiley & Sons, October 2009, copyright © 2010 Blackwell Publishing Ltd.)

GUAR GUM AND LOCUST BEAN GUM

These gums are both very effective thickening agents, but are unable to gel on their own. Guar gum is cold water soluble, and acts in combination with xanthan gum to form very thick solutions. Locust bean gum, as well as thickening when used on its own, forms gels when used with xanthan gum.

> **CHEF'S TIP** When trying out a new gelling agent, start making the gel using water at 1 per cent. If the gel is too strong, slowly reduce the concentration until you find the minimum gelling concentration. Then substitute the water with the ingredient of your choice – if your resulting gel will not set, you know that this is because of the ingredient used.

Non-hydrocolloid texture modifiers

As well as the hydrocolloids, a number of other new ingredients are starting to emerge in the kitchen, which allow the chef to develop different textures. These are briefly described below.

TRANSGLUTAMINASE

This is an enzyme that is able to join any two amino acids together. This therefore allows you to firmly attach different proteins together, either different fishes, different meats or a combination of the two. The powder is simply sprinkled on the meat or fish, and then the other protein source is placed on top. After heating, these two proteins will be firmly attached together.

MALTODEXTRIN

Maltodextrin absorbs oils and fats, so it is used in the kitchen to create powders out of fat based ingredients. Different types of maltodextrin exist, depending on the crop from which they were derived, and each different type has slightly different properties.

SOYA LECITHIN

Soya lecithin is a very effective emulsifier and is often used to stabilise emulsions instead of egg.

Sous vide cookery

While many people think of sous vide cooking as new, it has been around for many years. The concept of preparing food at low temperatures in sealed vessels is one of the oldest forms of cookery. In Hawaii pigs were roasted underground, in China clay pots were used to simmer tough meats, in Mexico they would toss corn **husks** into glowing embers. Cooking *en papillotte*, the traditional French way to prepare food which involves packing food in a parchment paper envelope, was a form of low temperature cooking. The concept of using a plastic film to wrap meats was first used by Chef Georges Pralus in 1967, who was trying to reduce moisture loss and shrinkage on a foie gras terrine.

Sous vide means 'under vacuum', and when cooking sous vide, the food is placed in a bag along with flavourings and often butter, and then vacuum packed to remove all the gas. When vacuum packing meat with bones and vegetables with sharp stalks, care should be taken that the bag is not pierced.

The bag is then placed in a water bath set at a precise temperature (modern water baths are adopted from those used in laboratories, and temperature control is often as precise as 0.1°C). This allows for very controlled cooking, and lets the chef to decide on the precise temperature to cook at depending on the cut of the meat. Meat is less likely to overcook in the water bath and can result in perfectly cooked and juicy meat and fish. Cooking is also more even in the water bath compared to more

conventional ways, for example grilling, which can result in the outer parts of the meat overcooking while the core reaches the desired temperature.

When cooking in a waterbath, ensure that the bags that you are using are suitable for the temperature at which your water is set. Holes and leaks in the bag cause a loss of moisture and flavour compounds, and allow bacteria to move between the food and the water. Different thicknesses of bags are available depending on the use. If the intention is to freeze the vacuum packed product, ensure that the bag is suitable for this purpose.

Sous vide offers other advantages in cooking – the water soluble flavours will remain locked in the bag and not move into the cooking water, retaining flavour in the product being cooked; and the food produced can be healthier because fat is not required for cooking.

The sous vide technique is often used without cooking – because the process removes oxygen, spoilage bacteria are less like tu grow in the vacuum bag so the food can last longer. Fats and other components of the foods are less likely to oxidize in the oxygen free environment, and discolouration of meats can be prevented. Vacuum packing is therefore often used to extend the shelf life of products. Vacuum packed foods that are kept in the freezer do not lose moisture to the air, so the process prevents freezer burn.

While most bacteria cannot grow in the absence of oxygen, some very dangerous bacteria like *Clostridium botulinum* can actually survive and grow in anaerobic conditions (i.e. when there is no oxygen present). Therefore, care must be taken to prevent the introduction, and therefore subsequent growth, of this bacteria. Users of the sous vide method of cooking should be fully trained and have a comprehensive knowledge of food hygiene and a detailed understanding of sous vide techniques.

Another specialized sous vide technique is called compression. When porous fruits such as pineapple and melon are vacuum packed, their texture becomes dense and 'meaty'. Sometimes, sous vide can be used to give a food a specific shape, so that when it is cooked for a short period of time, it sets in this shape while the inside stays raw, so it can be cooked by a different method later.

The sous vide technique is ideal for marination. Normal vacuum sealer bags cannot be used with liquids, since it prevents the bags from sealing. Chamber vacuum machines are essential when the meat is to be packed with liquids and marinades.

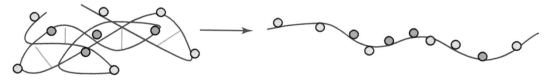
Diagram 10. To show the denaturation of proteins.

Cooking meat with sous vide

As explained in Chapter 7, meat is made up of muscle tissue, connective tissue and fat, and the proteins responsible for the changes in meat texture on cooking are located within the muscle tissue and the connective tissue.

Connective tissue can be seen as the harness of the meat, connecting individual cells and tissues together. The more force that a muscle exerts when the animal is alive, the more connective tissue it needs for reinforcement. So the more an animal uses its muscle fibres, the more the connective tissue is built up. Collagen also thickens and toughens as the animal ages, leading to tougher meat.

Proteins are made up of long chains of amino acids, which either have hydrophobic (water hating) or hydrophilic (water loving) side chains. In raw meat, the proteins in the muscle tissue exist as three-dimensional bundles. These individually separated bundles allow light to pass through the bundles, making the meat translucent.

As meat is heated up, the proteins within the meat unwind into long strands (see diagram 10). These long strands no longer let the light through, which is why the meat starts to go opaque. This process is called denaturation.

This initial denaturation step is associated with the release of water that was held by the bound proteins, which keeps the meat juicy.

On further heating, the proteins start to form bonds with each other, or coagulate. This helps keep the released water trapped within the meat structure.

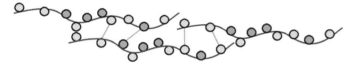

Diagram 11. To show the coagulation of proteins

However, as the meat is heated to a higher temperature, the protein network starts to squeeze the water molecules out of the meat, making the meat dry. This is why hard-boiled eggs become rubbery, and overcooked meat becomes dry. This is referred to as syneresis.

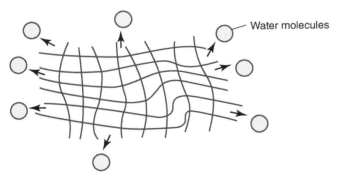

Water molecules

Diagram 12. To show the squeezing out of water from protein network at higher temperatures

As meat is heated to between 50 and 60°C, the proteins in the muscle tissue start to denature and form their coagulated network, releasing and then trapping the water, resulting in firm and juicy meat. Furthermore, at these temperatures the enzymes responsible for tenderizing meat during hanging increase in activity. Low temperature cooking allows meat to stay in this zone resulting in meat being tender.

As the temperature increases to between 60 and 65°C, the protein network continues to strengthen, and starts to squeeze out water over time. At these temperatures, the collagen in the connective tissue starts to denature and shrink – exerting a new pressure on the muscle cells which cause them to squeeze out even more water. Meat can lose up to a sixth of its volume of water at this point and become tough and dry.

However, meat with a high collagen content needs to be cooked at temperatures greater than 70°C for the collagen in the tough cuts of meat to be broken down into gelatine.

This therefore provides the chef with a paradox – we enjoy meat when it is tender and juicy rather than tough and dry, so we want to minimize moisture loss due to over coagulation of the meat proteins, while maximizing the conversion of tough connective tissue collagen to gelatine. Unfortunately this is not easy to do. Minimizing over coagulation and moisture loss means cooking meat quickly. Turning collagen to gelatine requires prolonged cooking at 70°C and above, so there is no ideal cooking method for all meats – the cooking method must be adjusted to the meat's toughness. Tender cuts are best heated rapidly just to the point that their juices are in full flow. Tough cuts are best heated for a prolonged period at higher temperatures to allow the tough collagen to soften, even if this results in the proteins themselves drying out. Tough cuts of meat often have higher fat levels, and the melting of fat at these higher temperatures helps further lubricate the meat, to some extent offsetting the drying out that occurs due to the proteins squeezing out the water.

CHEF'S TIP   Look back at Chapter 7, which discusses the different types and cuts of meat on an animal. Thinking about how much the animal uses its muscle, and therefore how much collagen will be present, suggest recommended cooking temperatures for the different cuts of meat.

Cooking fish sous vide

When cooking meat, the squeezing out of the juice is exaggerated by the connective tissue proteins contracting, putting pressure on the muscle cells forcing the water out. Fish connective tissue is weak, and unlike in animals where it builds up with age and muscle use, fish connective tissue is repeatedly built up and broken down, and dissolves at 50–55°C. Fish collagen therefore doesn't play the same critical role in fish cookery, because its squeezing power is relatively weak and it collapses before coagulation is well underway. Where meats begin to shrink from coagulation and major fluid loss at 60°C and becomes dry by 70°C, most fish shrink at 50°C and begin to become dry at around 60°C. In general fish is firm but still moist when cooked to 55–60°C. Some dense-fleshed fish, including tuna and salmon are especially succulent at 50°C, when they are still slightly translucent and jelly like.

In animals, the muscles and muscle fibres are quite long, but in fish, the muscle fibres are very short. Therefore, as the connective tissue breaks down on cooking, the fish, unlike meat, separates into distinct flakes.

Cooking vegetables sous vide

Non-green vegetables are normally cooked in the water bath at temperatures of 85°C and above – at these temperatures the cell walls weaken as the pectin holding the cell walls together starts to degrade. The vegetables become tender without being overcooked or losing flavour.

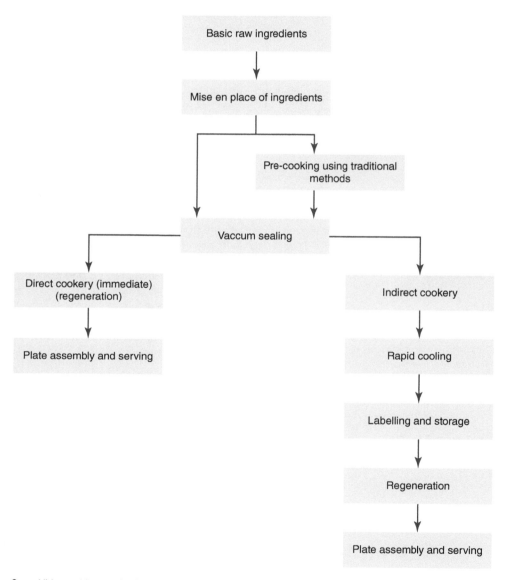

Sous Vide cooking methods

Safety in sous vide

All meat is essentially contaminated, especially at the surface. To reduce the bacteria to a safe level, the FSA recommends that you cook food until the core temperature reaches 75°C. However, if meat is going to be cooked for longer times, the FSA appreciates that lower temperatures are also acceptable, provided that the below times are followed:

● 60°C for a minimum of 45 minutes

● 65°C for a minimum of ten minutes

● 70°C for a minimum of two minutes.

Note: these temperatures correspond to the core meat temperature, not the water bath temperature

With sous-vide cooking, care must be taken during the preparation and handling to ensure that any growth of bacteria is reduced to a minimum, and that any contamination is avoided. Under ideal conditions, bacterial counts can double every 20 minutes. In a mere 12 hours, a single bacterium may multiply exponentially into a colony of millions.

Therefore, the following safety guides should be followed:

● Use the freshest meat possible (start of life).

● Keep all meat cold (<3°C) before cooking.

● Cook immediately post vacuum sealing or else cool down to <3°C first.

● After cooking, eat immediately or quickly chill to 1°C and hold at <3°C.

● Ensure the water bath has reached the required temperature before the food is added.

As an extra precautionary measure, sous vide items within walk in coolers may be stored in covered storage containers with alternating layers of ice in order to maintain strict temperature control. A walk-in fridge is typically accessed several times per hour, which can raise the ambient temperature along with everything inside. Since sous vide bags are packaged and hermetically sealed, there is no certain way of guaranteeing the core temperature of the product is kept cool unless it is buried in ice at all times.

Where the food is to be consumed directly, this is called 'direct cooking'. Where the food is going to be consumed at a later date, this is referred to as 'indirect cooking'. The diagram on page 554 outlines the difference between the two.

By identifying critical control points and establishing hurdles to microbial growth, all of the safety concerns related to vacuum packaging and sous-vide cooking may be virtually eliminated or significantly reduced. Below are examples of vacuum packing/sous-vide HACCP matrices that have been produced in order to ensure these measures are implemented correctly. Note, these are examples only and your own HACCP plan must be developed and approved by your HACCP team or Environmental Health officer before sous-vide cookery can be performed.

STORAGE	HAZARDS	CONTROLS	CRITICAL LIMITS	MONITORING PROCEDURES	CORRECTIVE ACTIONS
Purchase	Foods contaminated with food poisoning bacteria or toxins or foreign bodies	Only purchase from reputable suppliers on nominated list. Freshest highest quality ingredients used to significantly lower initial microbial levels		Audits done on suppliers frequently	Complete supplier's comments procedure on the intranet
Delivery CCP	Growth of food poisoning bacteria or toxins in foods	Chilled deliveries to be accepted only at below 5°C, but for best practice aim for below 3°C	<8°C is the legal limit, but for best practice aim for below 3°C	Check temperature of food on arrival and document on the food delivery log	Reject chilled food if above 8°C and record action on a food delivery log
	Contamination risk due to faulty packaging	No damaged packaging		Visual check of condition of packaging	Reject food where it is not protected, is in damaged or dirty packaging, is visibly contaminated or you think it is unsafe
	Cross contamination risks through mixing raw, cooked and ambient	Raw and cooked food should be separate. Ambient dry goods foodstuffs decanted and vac pac at this stage if required			
	Contamination due to condition of vehicle or driver or presence of pests	Clean vehicle and driver and delivery vehicle free from pests		Visual checks of the delivery vehicle	Record action on a food delivery log

STORAGE	HAZARDS	CONTROLS	CRITICAL LIMITS	MONITORING PROCEDURES	CORRECTIVE ACTIONS
	Other food contaminated by soiled outer wrapping	Decant raw/ cooked food from contaminated external wrappings. Clean storage containers			
	Inadequate shelf life	Foods accepted within shelf life		Check date coding and sufficient shelf life remaining	Ambient goods that are to be vac packed must be clearly labelled with supplier name/ manufacturer's expiry date on new vac pac bag with company labels. Reject foods if out of date and document on food delivery log
Preparation CCP	Growth of pathogenic bacteria	Limit time food prepared at room temperature. Properly scheduled production		Visual monitoring of staff practices, cleanliness of equipment, worktops, utensils, etc	If the food has been left too long at ambient temperature then dispose of immediately
	Bacterial contamination from • Surfaces • Equipment • Food handlers	Ensure food contact surfaces are cleaned and sanitized before use Use cleaned and sanitized equipment. Use clearly defined worktop/chopping boards Correct personal hygiene standards. Food should not be directly handled, food grade gloves to be worn at all times Wash all fruit, vegetable and salad items in company approved anti-bacterial wash.			Correct supervision/ retraining of staff. Dispose of any contaminated foods

STORAGE	HAZARDS	CONTROLS	CRITICAL LIMITS	MONITORING PROCEDURES	CORRECTIVE ACTIONS
Blast chill CCP	Bacterial growth due to higher temperature before vacuum packaging	Chill food down to ensure below 5°C, but for best practice aim for below 3°C, prior to vacuum packing	<5°C but for best practice aim for below 3°C	Temperature check food prior to vac packing	Re-examine decanting procedures. Re-train staff
Vacuum packing CCP	Bacterial contamination	Vacuum packing machine must be thoroughly cleaned and sanitized before use. Separate machines to be used for cooked and raw		Visual check of vacuum packing machine and completion of cleaning schedule	Re-train staff

STORAGE	HAZARDS	CONTROLS	CRITICAL LIMITS	MONITORING PROCEDURES	CORRECTIVE ACTIONS
	Damaged bags or physical contamination	Only bags approved for vacuum packing should be used. The bags should be stored in a clean dry environment to protect them from contamination		Visual checks of condition of bags	Dispose of any damaged bags and do not use
	Incorrect sealing of bags during vacuum. (Subsequent growth of bacteria)	Every packet must be suitably and sufficiently sealed with a tight fit around the food. The integrity of the heat seal should be checked on every bag. Packs must be checked for no air access, air or leaks. Manufacturer's guidelines to be followed. Staff trained in the use of the vac pack machine		The integrity of the heat seal must be checked on every bag. All packs should also be checked for no air access and leaks Regular maintenance of the machine by approved company to ensure correct working. Close monitoring of staff	If packet not properly sealed discard package and re-vacuum with new package
Storage CCP	Growth of anaerobic bacteria in vacuum packed product	Chilled foods to be stored below 5°C, but for best practice aim for below 3°C	<5°C but for best practice aim for below 3°C	Check fridge and freezer temperatures twice daily and record on equipment temperature record	Adjust or repair equipment or if temperature not maintained where possible move to another chilled unit
		Bags should not be tightly packed to ensure air circulation		Visual check to ensure correct storage	
		Food products should be clearly labelled and dated with date of vacuum and use by date. Ensure correct stock rotation Ensure food stored in a manner to protect packaging from any damage during storage. Ensure raw and high risk food is stored separately		Visual checks to ensure no out of date food stored Daily visual checks to ensure correct storage of food	Discard any foods that are out of date have been contaminated Re-train staff
Cook		Re-heating so core is above danger zone temperatures		Protein items i.e. meat, fish and poultry to be probed to ensure minimum temperatures achieved	Discard and do not serve foods that have not reached minimum temperatures

New product launch

Launching a successful new food product is not straightforward, and takes time and resource. Many new products that are launched by food companies and retailers fail, and are removed from the supermarket shelves soon after launch due to low sales and high waste, and often this is because insufficient time has been spent on the development process.

The first, and most important, step in new product development is in identifying the market opportunity. A full review of the current market offering to identify opportunities and gaps, as well as detailed customer insights, is essential. What you may think of as an essential addition to a product range may not be what your customers think, and knowledge of current best sellers, as well as previous failed products, will give a good indication of what might work, and what might not. Furthermore, understanding the profile of the shopper, their demographic, other products that they buy and how often, all provide valuable data on which to structure your development ideas.

Once the concept has been agreed, extensive benchmarking is often useful to understand what are the key factors that need to be considered when developing that type of food product. For example, how are similar products packaged? What are the important claims (for example nutritional claims, use of sustainable ingredients).

The next stage is the development of the product, and ensuring that the concept prototype delivers in all aspects of flavour, as well as fully meeting the original concept brief. Once this has been agreed, a full analysis of ingredients should be carried out. By changing levels and qualities of different components within the product will help show which ingredients are vital to flavour delivery, and in which quantity they are needed. If the doubling of a single ingredient has no impact on product flavour or product perception, then this finding can result in a cost saving.

Once a decision on the product has been finalized and agreed, and the costs approved, the next step is to produce it in a factory. This involves closely working with the manufacturer who will make the product. How does a factory sample match the prototype? How do they differ? What can be done to make the factory sample more similar? What are the key steps in the process that determine quality, since these are the points that need close monitoring during manufacture?

Once the product has been trialled and approved, scale up studies are required. This ensures that when large quantities of this product are made to meet demand, the quality parameters are not affected.

Final stages in product development include analysis – nutritional analysis, validation of any claims being made, generation of microbiological data to provide information about the product life and confirmation of the packaging.

Once the product has launched, the process doesn't stop. Key bits of data, such as sales, waste, customer purchase behaviour, all need to be monitored, since they provide invaluable feedback for future product development and launches.

CHEF'S TIP Think of a new product that you want to develop. Why do you think it is needed? What similar products exist? How might you get the customer insights? Why might it fail?

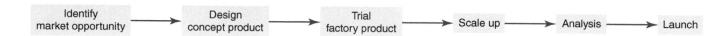

Flow chart outlining the product development process

Guest Chef

Stuffed fillet of Gloucester old spot, tortellini of pear and goat's cheese with Tewkesbury mustard foam

Chef *Mark Hyde-Catton*

Centre (college) *Gloucestershire College*

The Gloucester old spot pig was bred in the local cider and perry orchards by the dairy farms, which helped with the selection of the other local ingredients from Gloucestershire for the dish; the Blakeney red pear from the Forest of Dean, still grown and used by local cider makers today; Cerney Starter goats' cheese, which won silver at the 2011 British Cheese Awards, and Tewkesbury Mustard. The sous vide method helps retain the pork tenderloin's colour and moisture and tenderizes the meat.

Ingredients	Amount
Pork tenderloin	
Old spot pork loin	800 g
Black pudding	350 g
Thyme	3 sprigs
Old spot smoked streaky bacon	250 g
Salt and pepper	to taste
Tortellini of pear and goat's cheese	
Fresh pasta dough	150 g
Cerney starter cheese	70 g
Blakeney red pear (brunoise)	70 g
Rosemary (chopped finely)	1 sprig
Sugar	1 tsp
Butter	10 g
Water	1 tbsp
Tewkesbury mustard foam	
Tewkesbury mustard	2 ½ tsp
Shallots	100 g
Brandy	90 ml
Chicken stock	250 ml
Double cream	120 ml
Butter (diced)	50 g
Salt and pepper	to taste

METHOD OF WORK

Pork tenderloin

1 Remove excess fat and skin from the tenderloin. Slice the pork lengthways to make a pocket, blend the black pudding and thyme, then stuff the tenderloin with it.

2 Place a sheet of cling film on the work surface and lay out bacon, overlapping the slices slightly, to the length of the tenderloin, cover with cling film, bat out to even thickness, remove top cling film, season the bacon.

3 Place stuffed loin across the bacon ends using the cling film tightly roll up the loin so it is wrapped in the bacon.

4 Place the tenderloin into a vacuum bag, and vacuum seal. Place in a water bath at 64°C and cook for 90–120 minutes.

Tortellini

5 Prepare the tortellinis (five per portion). Place half the pear dice into a saucepan with the butter and water and cook down to a puree, and then add the remaining pear and cook for three minutes; cool.

6 Blend the cheese until smooth; then fold in the pear mixture.

7 Roll out the pasta dough and cut out circles approximately 5 cm in diameter.

8 Place filling in the middle of circles, brush around edges of circles with water, fold over and seal. Cook in salted water while meat is resting.

9 Remove loin from bag. Heat some oil in a frying pan and sear the tenderloin until golden, remove from pan and allow resting for five–ten minutes before carving.

10 Return the pan to heat; sweat shallots, deglaze with brandy, flame and reduce. Add the stock and reduce by half, add mustard, mix until smooth, add cream and bring to boil and season.

11 Strain sauce, and whisk in the cold diced butter until emulsified (monte), place in a gas charger or foam with hand blender.

To finish

12 Place sliced pork on top of a broad bean **cassoulet** or some vegetable mash, placing five tortellini evenly spaced around the plate, spooning some foam sauce on top and around them.

ASSESSMENT OF KNOWLEDGE AND UNDERSTANDING

You have now learned about the use of new ingredients and techniques that are used in cooking, as well as understanding the process of product development.

To test your knowledge and understanding, answer the following short questions:

1 What does the term thermoreversible mean when referring to gels?

2 What two methods can you use to ensure proper hydration of hydrocolloids in water?

3 What are the two different types of carrageenans that gel, and what gel textures do they provide?

4 What ingredients should you avoid using when making an alginate base for spherification?

5 What are three unique properties of methylcelluloses?

6 At what temperature does a gelatine gel melt?

7 Name three gums that can be used to thicken liquids

8 What does transglutaminase do?

9 What bacteria is of major concern when using sous vide?

10 What happens to proteins as you heat them?

11 At what temperature does collagen significantly start to break down into gelatine?

12 What safety guides should be followed when cooking sous-vide?

13 Above what temperature do sous-vide vegetables need to be cooked?

14 Outline the main stages involved in product development

Prepare, cook and finish healthier dishes

NVQ

Prepare, cook and finish healthier dishes

LEARNING OBJECTIVES

The aim of this chapter is to enable you to develop skills and implement knowledge in the preparation and cookery principles of healthy dishes and eating. This will also include materials, ingredients and equipment.

At the end of this chapter you will be able to:

● Identify each variety of healthy eating dish and technique.

● Understand how to cook dishes to maintain their maximum nutritional value.

● State the quality points of various commodities and dishes.

● Prepare ingredients following a healthier concept and using appropriate skills.

● Have a concise knowledge of preparing and cooking a range of healthier derived dishes.

● sporting and entertainment stadia;

● hospitals;

● care and residential homes;

● schools, colleges and universities;

● armed forces;

● workplace catering.

Government guidelines for healthy eating

Nutritional requirements vary depending on a person's age, gender and occupation. However, between the ages of 19 and 50 the dietary requirements do not vary a great deal. Recommended intakes of food are expressed in terms of DRVs (dietary reference values), which are tailored to certain population groups. This term replaces RDA (recommended daily allowance).

Achieving a balanced diet

Food provides the essential fuel and raw materials that the body requires. The fuel is converted into energy to maintain body temperature, and the raw materials are used in growing tissues and in the repair of internal organs and systems. Our food composition is broadly made up from carbohydrates, proteins, fats, vitamins, mineral salts and fibre, and a balanced diet should contain all of these nutrients in the correct proportions. The lack of any of these foods in our diet can affect the body's overall performance and can lead to poor health, low energy levels, lack of growth in the early years and poor response to healing from wounds or illness.

If certain foods are consumed in excess the body will build up layers of fat, leading to increased weight and imbalanced chemical levels within the body's system, such as increased levels of sugar or salt. This can lead to diabetes, high blood pressure or thyroid inactivity or overactivity.

The hospitality industry provides catering services for an overwhelming majority of the population through a variety of services:

● restaurants;

● hotels, hostels;

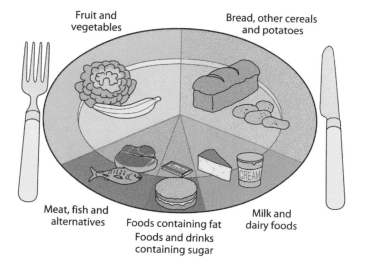

The Balance of Good Health

For a healthy diet, the Food Standards Agency suggests that we should aim to:

● Choose lean meat, and trim off the fat and any skin.

● Eat more fish; try to eat fish at least twice a week.

● Grill, bake, poach, boil, steam or microwave instead of frying or roasting.

● Reduce the sugar in our diets.

- Reduce the use of salt when cooking; do not add salt to cooked and served food at the table and be more aware of the salt content of ready-prepared foods.

- Try to drink at least six–eight cups of water a day, or more if you exercise.

The Balance of Good Health

The *Balance of Good Health* (based on UK Government guidelines) divides foods into five food groups and shows how much of each group we should eat each day. It is a useful way of checking whether your diet is healthy and balanced. The five food groups are as follows:

- Bread, cereals and potatoes – up to two servings per day

- Fruit and vegetables – five servings per day.

- Meat, fish and alternatives – up to two servings per day.

- Milk and dairy – up to three servings per day.

- Foods containing fat and foods containing sugar – one small serving per day.

New recommendations about our diet are issued on a yearly basis, after Government has produced a basic report on the public's health based on nutritional values and food trends.

Protein

Proteins are active and sensitive substances that have many intrinsic uses and values. Chefs can take advantage of proteins by using various culinary techniques to change their structure (such as aerating egg whites).

Proteins are made up from chains of amino acids. Most amino acids can be produced by the body, but there are some that can not: these are referred to as 'essential amino acids' as they must be included in our diet. It is important that we understand what food types are protein based. The chart below indicates the types of protein sources available:

PROTEIN COMMODITIES
Meat
Game
Poultry
Fish
Eggs
Milk, cream, cheese
Peas
Beans
Nuts
Seeds
Wheat flour

Fats

Fats provide the body with energy and certain important vitamins. They are also sources of essential fatty acids which the body cannot produce. Fats can be derived from both vegetable and animal sources.

It is recommended that lower fat alternatives should be used wherever possible, and that smaller quantities of foods containing saturated fats or trans fats should be eaten and replaced with foods high in unsaturated fats. Another recommendation is to increase the intake of omega 3 fatty acids, which are found in foods such as oily fish.

Animal fats are saturated fats. These fats can cause raised levels of cholesterol in the blood, increasing the likelihood of developing heart disease. Some animal fats also contain vitamins A and D. Examples of some commodities high in saturated fats are ready-prepared meat products, meat pies, sausages, hard cheeses, butter, lard, pastry, some cakes and shortbreads.

The effects of trans fats (partially hydrogenated fats) on our health are similar those of saturated fats, with emerging evidence suggesting that they may actually be worse. Some hydrogenated fats, such as some margarines (which are liquid oils turned into solid fats), also contain trans fats. This type of fat is increasingly found in ready-meals.

Unsaturated fats are a healthy alternative and provide the body with essential fatty acids. The unsaturated fats found in oily fish may further help to prevent heart disease. Products such as oily fish, avocados, nuts and seeds, sunflower oil, rapeseed oil, olive oil and vegetable oil all contain unsaturated fats.

Carbohydrates

Carbohydrates are produced by all plants and animals for the purpose of storing chemical energy. Simple sugars and starch are energy stores, while pectin and cellulose are the plant's structural materials where carbohydrates can also be found.

Sugars are the simplest carbohydrates. Some sugars are small single molecules (monosaccharides), while others are made up of two or more simple sugar molecules joined together. Glucose and fructose are monosaccharides, while sucrose (normal table sugar) is a disaccharide made up of one glucose molecule and one fructose molecule. The following chart describes the characteristics of sugars commonly used in the kitchen:

SUGAR	CHARACTERISTICS
Glucose	Also known as dextrose. A simple sugar (monosaccharide) found in many fruits and honey. Pastry chefs may use this as corn syrup in the kitchen. Compared with sucrose, glucose is less sweet
Fructose	Also known as levulose. It is also found in fruits and honey. It is metabolized by the body more slowly than normal sugar and therefore is preferable for use for diabetics. It is the sweetest of all common sugars
Sucrose	This is common table sugar. It is extracted from sugar cane and from sugar beet. Sucrose can be broken down into two simple sugars (fructose and glucose) by heating it with some acid. This is known as inversion and the resulting mass is called an invert syrup. This syrup is useful in sugar work and candy making because it helps to limit the extent of sugar crystallization
Lactose	This is found in milk. It is a disaccharide made up of glucose and galactose. It is much less sweet than sucrose
Maltose	This is found in wheat and flours and is much less sweet than sucrose

Honey contains fructose

Lactose is the sugar found in milk

The body uses sugars as a source of energy to fuel the activity of cells and to provide the building blocks of growth. This is why we have taste receptors that register the presence of sugars and why our brains attach pleasure to a sweet taste sensation. Sweetness is a sign that a food is high in calories.

Polysaccharides are molecules made up of chains of simple sugars. By far the most important polysaccharide is starch. Starch is found in plants, including all cereals, such as rice, flour and grains, and also potatoes and pulses, such as lentils. Starch-based foods are rich in insoluble fibre and contain valuable nutrients. They form an important part of a healthy diet.

Vitamins

Vitamins are chemical substances naturally found in food groups and are very important to the health of the body. Maintaining the correct balance of vitamins in the body is important to our overall health and growth. The main vitamin groups are:

- Vitamin A – found in dairy products, fish oil and green vegetables.
- Vitamin B – found in yeast, meat and cereals.
- Vitamin C – found in fresh fruit, green vegetables and potatoes.
- Vitamin D – found in dairy produce and oily fish.

Minerals

Minerals such as iron and salt are required by the body to help maintain health. However, too much of any particular mineral may result in bad health, and this is reflected in the Government's guidelines for daily salt intake. Important minerals include:

- Calcium – found in dairy products, fish and bread.
- Iron – found in meat, green vegetables and fish.
- Salt – found naturally in meat, fish and eggs.

Ensuring the quality of ingredients

Labels on packaged food now contain a lot of information about the product purchased and its ingredients, such as:

- the name of the commodity;
- its weight or volume content;
- an accurate list of ingredients used to produce the commodity in order of weight;
- a 'use by' date for perishable food or a 'best before' date;
- allergy information;
- storage recommendations;
- the name and contact details of the manufacturer;
- a production code number for traceability purposes;
- nutrition information.

The variety of commodities available to the modern chef is considerable. A factor affecting the purchase of some produce is the distance that it has travelled. Due to cheaper and increasingly quicker transportation, importing foods from far-away countries is now common practice. However, the length of the passage and the method of storage during transit can greatly affect the quality of the end product.

The best and sometimes the cheapest way of purchasing is to follow the seasonality of foods and to buy as locally as possible. This will help to ensure that commodities are purchased at their freshest and in optimum condition.

Correct storage of produce is important for maintaining its nutritional value; vitamins in particular can be lost if produce is not stored properly. Fruits and vegetables should be stored in cool, dark places or in refrigerated units. They will perish quicker if stored at higher temperatures and direct light will lead to wastage of vital vitamins and minerals.

The healthy preparation of ingredients

This section looks at how to prepare ingredients or dishes to maximize their health value.

Fresh ingredients that are prepared too far in advance of use will begin to lose vital vitamins and minerals. Flavour and moisture will also be lost. It is therefore important that ingredients are only prepared when they are required.

The fibre and starch content in dishes can be increased by simply using wholemeal flour in place of white flour in pastry recipes and using wholemeal pasta and brown rice. The addition of pulses in dishes will also help.

The reduction of salt in dishes is an important issue for health. Avoid the use of preserved ingredients that contain high levels of salt and continually check the labels of commodities that are used to add flavour or enrich specific dishes, such as soy sauce, butter, mustard and Worcester sauce. These commodities can contain high levels of salt and therefore the chef will be able to lower the overall salt content of a dish by omitting or significantly reducing the amount of salt added as seasoning.

Reducing saturated fats in dishes is an important aspect in maintaining a balanced diet. The use of olive, sunflower or seed-based oils in place of butter and margarine is effective. If using oil to fry with, always ensure that the oil is at the correct temperature; oil that is not hot enough will be absorbed into the protein being fried. Always drain on absorbent kitchen paper to remove as much excess fat as possible.

Reducing sugar in dishes is vital for diabetics and good for maintaining a balanced diet. Sugar substitutes have been successfully introduced to help with this aspect of dietary control. Other ways to reduce the sugar content of dishes include:

- using fresh fruit juices when possible;
- reducing the amount of sugar used in the production of desserts;
- using low-sugar preserves;
- using natural sugars such as honey to sweeten desserts.

Using the healthy option

Ensuring that portion sizes are set at an appealing level and not too large will guarantee that a guest will not over-indulge.

Dishes that are grilled, poached, boiled, steamed or baked will not incorporate the oils or fats used to assist other methods of cooking and are therefore immediately healthier.

Lean meats, fresh fish and pulses have low levels of saturated fats and can increase the intake of fibre. They are naturally well flavoured products so to complement them with additional herbs or spices will not compromise their quality or flavour in the finished dish.

To preserve their nutritional value, foods generally need to be cooked quickly and in some cases, such as vegetables, cooked slightly underdone (al dente).

VIDEO CLIP   Using pulses and grains

Ingredient	Amount
Pheasant	1 each
Asparagus	1 bunch
Olive oil	5 g
Rocket	20 g
Salt	5 g
Cream	2 tbsp
Wholemeal flour	200 g
Egg	2 each
Capers	1 tbsp

METHOD OF WORK

1   Make a basic pasta dough using wholemeal flour. Refrigerate.

2   Remove the carcass of the pheasant by following the basic galantine procedure.

3   Remove the legs, discarding any fat, skin, bone and tendons and blitz in the Robot Coupe with a little cream and capers to produce a fine forcemeat. Season and pass through a fine drum sieve.

4   Blanch all the asparagus. Refresh three of the asparagus, and puree the remainder with some boiling water and seasoning until smooth. (A touch of cream may be used.)

5   Open up the galantine, and spread the forcemeat evenly over the flesh side of the pheasant. (Retain a tablespoon of forcemeat as a filling for the tortellini). Remove the tips from three of the asparagus for garnish, and place the spear less asparagus tips on top of the forcemeat.

6   Roll the galantine very tightly into a roulade in clingfilm, and ensure that the sides are tied in knots. Steam until cooked, and chill in a blast chiller until cool.

7   Roll out the pasta dough and make three tortellini per portion, using the forcemeat as a filling and water to seal.

Guest Chef

Galantine of pheasant, served with wholemeal tortellini, asparagus and rocket

Chef *Johannes Keevey*

Centre *Midkent College, Gillingham, Kent*

Kent is well known for its game birds. The galantine is rolled with some of the forcemeat, capers (to substitute salt) and asparagus, then steamed, which is a healthier cooking method. Once cooked, the individual slices will be griddled for heating and presentation purposes with very little olive oil to prevent the slices from sticking and also enhance the flavours. Griddling would also make the dish healthier as the oil will flow away from the pheasant into the grooves. The tortellini will be stuffed with forcemeat made from the legs, and wholemeal flour.

Cooking and finishing

1   Slice the galantine into even slices about 5 mm in width. Lightly brush with olive oil using a fine pastry brush and griddle turning only once per side until heated and grill lines are evident.

2   Cook the tortellini in a chauffante, and lightly brush once out of the water with olive oil.

3   Regenerate the asparagus spears using the chauffante and heat the asparagus purée in a sauce pan.

4   Place three galantine slices on a plate in a triangle formation. Lightly dress rocket in olive oil and place in the middle of the plate. Rest three asparagus spears facing up on the sides of the rocket. Using a teaspoon, place three drops of asparagus puree between the galantine slices.

5   Place the tortellini on the asparagus purée.

SOURCING Wholefoods are foods that are processed or refined as little as possible before they are eaten. They do not have ingredients added to them such as sugar or salt.

Ingredient	Amount
Fillets of Sea Bream (any white fish will work)	2 approx. 150 g each
Coriander	Small bunch
Garlic cloves	2
Grated ginger root	1 tbsp
Red chilli deseeded and chopped	1
Shaohsing rice wine or sherry	1 tbsp
Light soy sauce	2 tbsp
Toasted sesame oil	1 tsp
Sea salt and white pepper	pinch
Jasmine rice Selection of vegetables to stir fry	

Guest Chef

Ginger, chilli and Soy steamed sea bass

Chef Karen Rivers

Centre (college): Petroc Tiverton

For quick healthy dishes using any white fish steaming over a wok is a tasty meal. This dish is suitable for quick lunch or dinner. It is low in fat and high in vitamins/nutrients. I have served it with jasmine rice and stir fry vegetables. If you use gluten free soy sauce, this dish is suitable for coeliacs.

METHOD OF WORK

1 Make the sauce by chopping the garlic finely, place in a bowl with grated ginger and chopped chilli. Add wet ingredients rice wine, soy, sesame oil and seasoning.

2 Add fish to the sauce and leave to marinade for ten minutes.
Place fish on heat proof plate. Place a bamboo steamer over a large wok. Add water to wok, then place the plate of fish into the steamer. Make sure water does not touch the dish.

3 Steam for just five–seven minutes until flesh of fish cooked.

4 Serve with stir fry vegetables and plain boiled jasmine rice.

5 Serve fish over the rice using julienne of fresh spring onion to finish the dish.

ASSESSMENT OF KNOWLEDGE AND UNDERSTANDING

You have now learned about the benefits of healthy eating and an array of commodities and cooking techniques.

To test your level of knowledge and understanding, answer the following short questions. These will help to prepare you for your summative (final) assessment.

Quality identifications

1 List two ways of choosing quality ingredients when writing a menu.

i)

ii)

2 Name three of the five food groups needed to make up a balanced diet, explaining the benefits of each.

i)

ii)

iii)

Cooking methods

1 Identify two ways you can reduce the amount of saturated fat in products when cooking.

i)

ii)

Research task

Below is a classical menu made up of three courses to cater for a banquet event. Using knowledge gained from this chapter, rewrite the menu using healthier ingredients and options. Reflect on and take into consideration all aspects of healthy eating in your answer and the allergies or food issues that can be resolved.

MENU STRUCTURE	HEALTHIER MENU STRUCTURE	REASON FOR CHOICE AND ALLERGY AWARENESS
Starter Prawn cocktail	Starter	
Main course Roast beef, Yorkshire pudding, roast potatoes, glazed carrots and cauliflower cheese	Main course	
Dessert Chocolate mousse	Dessert	

Glossary

00 flour Speciality flour used in pasta making as it has a high gluten content

à la (French) 'In the style of', such as: à la Française (the style of the French)

à la bourgeoisie (French) The style of the family (family style)

à la broche (French) Cooked on a skewer

à la carte (French) Items on the menu that are priced individually and cooked to order

à la Florentine (French) 'In the style of Florence'. Generally refers to dishes served on a bed of spinach and gratinated with sauce Mornay

à la Française In a French style

à la minute (French) Cook food at the last minute

à la Provençal (French) Dishes prepared with garlic and olive oil

à la Russe (French) In the Russian style

à point (French) Food cooked just to the perfect point of doneness: when cooking beef steaks, 'à point' means that a steak is cooked medium

abats (French) Offal

acetic acid A natural organic acid present in vinegar and citrus juices

acidulate To give a dish or liquid a slightly acidic, tart or piquant taste by adding some lemon juice, vinegar, fruit juice. Also, one can acidulate fresh cream by adding lemon juice to get sour cream.

acidulated water Water to which a mild acid, usually lemon juice or vinegar, has been added to prevent sliced fruits (especially apples and pears) and peeled or cut up vegetables (such as artichokes and salsify) from turning dark during preparation

additives, food Substances added to food to maintain or improve nutritional quality, food quality and freshness. Additives are strictly regulated. Manufacturers must prove the additives they add to food are safe

agar-agar An extract of seaweed from the Indian and Pacific Oceans. When dissolved in water, it will set into a jelly on cooling. Often used as a vegetarian substitute for gelatine

ageing A term used to describe the holding of meats at a temperature of 1–4°C for a period of time to break down the tough connective tissues through the action of enzymes, thus increasing the tenderness

agneau (French) Lamb

al dente Italian for 'to the tooth': refers to the firm but tender consistency of a perfectly cooked piece of pasta

albumen The protein portion of the egg white, comprising about 70 per cent of the egg. Albumen is also found in animal blood, milk, plants and seeds

almond paste A confectionery preparation consisting of ground almonds mixed with a sugar solution to form a paste. Sometimes referred to as marzipan it can be a raw paste or a cooked paste

aloyau de boeuf Sirloin of beef

amandine (French) Prepared with or garnished with almonds

ambient temperature Room temperature

amuse bouche This is a pre-starter or mouth pleaser given as an opening for the coming menu

Anglaise (French) English style

antioxidants Substances that inhibit the oxidation of meat, vegetables and fruit. They help prevent food from becoming rancid or discoloured

Apicius Marcus Gavius Apicius, born around 25 AD, is credited with writing cookery books and devising recipes. His book *Cuisine in Ten Books* was used as a reference work for several centuries

appareil A mixture of different ingredients to be used in a recipe

aromates A mixture of herbs and spices used to increase or bring out flavours in a dish

arrowroot The starch extracted from the stems of certain tropical plants. A fine, white powder, it is used to thicken sauces and soups and certain desserts

ascorbic acid Vitamin C

aspic Clear savoury jelly

au blanc (French) Meaning 'in white'. Foods, usually meats, that are not coloured during cooking

au bleu 1. A term for the cooking method for trout: 'Truite au bleu. The fish is taken from a fish tank, killed, gutted, trussed and slid into boiling court bouillon. The fish skin is not washed. This gives a characteristic silver blue finish to the finished dish. 2. A steak cooked very rare

au four Baked in the oven

au gratin (French) Food topped with a sauce and cheese or breadcrumbs, then baked or glazed under a salamander

au jus (French) Served with natural juices

au lait (French) With milk

au naturel (French) Food that is cooked simply, with little or no interference in its natural appearance or flavour

au vin blanc (French) Cooked with white wine

bacteria Micro-organisms that can cause food poisoning

baguette A French bread that is formed into a long, narrow cylindrical loaf. It usually has a crisp brown crust and light, chewy interior

bain marie (French) Water bath used to cook or store food

bake To cook in an enclosed oven

baking powder A raising agent consisting of bicarbonate of soda and cream of tartar. It is commonly used in the baking of cakes

ballotine A prepared meat, poultry, game or fish dish where the flesh is boned out, rolled and tied before cooking whole; sometimes stuffed with a farce or mousseline

bard To wrap meat, poultry or game with bacon or pork fat. The bard will render during cooking and impart succulence and flavour

barquette Boat-shaped pastry case or mould

baste To pour drippings, fat- or stock over food while cooking

Baumé The Baumé scale is a hydrometer scale developed by French pharmacist Antoine Baumé in 1768 to measure density of various liquids. Notated variously as degrees Baumé, B°, Be°, Bé°, Baumé

bavarois A cold dessert made from a cooked egg custard set with gelatine and lightened with whipped cream

beard The common name for the hair-like filaments that shellfish such as oysters and mussels use to attach themselves to rocks. They must be trimmed before the shellfish are prepared

beat To introduce air into a mixture using a utensil such as a wooden spoon, fork or whisk, in order to achieve a lighter texture

beurre blanc A sauce made with reduced alcohol or vinegar and shallots into which butter is whisked

beurre fondue Melted butter

beurre manié A raw mixture of flour and butter in equal quantities used as a thickening agent

beurre noir Black butter; can be served with skate wings and brains

beurre noisette Nut-brown butter served with fish meunière

bicarbonate of soda An alkaline powder: used to soften water for cooking vegetables and is one of the main ingredients of baking powder

blanch To place foods in boiling water or oil briefly, either to partially cook them or to aid in the removal of the skin (e.g. nuts, tomatoes). Blanching also removes the bitterness from citrus zests

blend To mix together ingredients, usually of different consistencies, to a smooth and even texture, utilizing a utensil such as a wooden spoon or blender

blind bake To bake pastry without a filling. Metal weights or dried beans are usually used to keep the pastry from rising

blinis Pancakes made from buckwheat flour and yeast

boil To bring a liquid to boiling temperature and to maintain it throughout the cooking time

boil rapidly Food is submerged into boiling liquid over a high heat and the bubbling state is maintained throughout the required cooking period. This method is also used to reduce sauces by boiling off the liquid and reducing it to a concentrated state

bouchee A small puff pastry case with high sides and a hollow middle

bouillon 1. Any broth made by cooking vegetables, poultry, meat or fish in water. The strained liquid is the bouillon, which can form the base for soups and sauces. 2. A salt paste used as a stock

bouquet garni A faggot of herbs and aromatic vegetables, usually parsley, thyme, bay leaf, carrot, leek and celery, tied together and usually dangled into a stockpot on a string. These herb bundles give the stew, soup or stock an aromatic seasoning. The bouquet garni is removed before serving

braise A cooking method where food (usually meat) is first browned in oil and then cooked slowly in a liquid (wine, stock or water)

bresoala Beef cured in a wine-rich brine. It is then air dried and sliced very thinly for service

Brillat-Savarin Jean-Anthelme (1755–1826): French gastronome and author of the famous book *Physiologie du Goût*

brine A strong solution of water and salt used for pickling or preserving foods

Brix The Brix scale was originally developed by Adolph Brix. Degrees Brix (symbol °Bx) is a measurement of the mass ratio of dissolved sugar to water in a liquid. It is measured with a saccharometer, which shows the density of a liquid. It largely replaced the Baumé scale in the early 1960s

broil The American term for browning under the grill

brunoise 1 mm dice

buffet A buffet is a meal where guests serve themselves from a variety of dishes set out on a table or sideboard

butterfly To cut food (usually meat or seafood) leaving one edge joined and then open it out like the wings of a butterfly

buttermilk Milk product that is left after the fat is removed from milk to make butter

calorie Unit of energy; 1 calorie = 3.968 btu = 4.1868 joules. The heat required to raise the temperature of 1g of water by 1°C

canapé A base of bread, pastry, vegetable or porcelain onto which savoury food is placed as a pre-dinner appetiser or as part of a light buffet

caper The flower bud of a shrub that is native to eastern Asia and is widespread in hot regions of the world. Capers are pickled in vinegar or preserved in brine

caramelise To allow the surface sugars of food to caramelise, giving a characteristic Amber colour and aroma

carbohydrate There are three major groups of carbohydrates which are found in fresh fruits, vegetables and cereals: sugars (e.g. sucrose, fructose, glucose), starches and cellulose

Carême Marie-Antoine (1784–1833): 'The king of chefs and chef of kings.' Commenced his career as a pastry chef and was a personal chef to Tallyrand, the future King George IV and Tsar Alexander I. Responsible for many ground-breaking changes in the preparation and presentation of food and classical cuisine. Author of many books, including *L'Art de la Cuisine*

Caroline A savoury mini éclair that can be served hot or cold with a filling on buffets

carpaccio Originally, paper thin slices of raw beef with a creamy sauce, invented at Harry's Bar in Venice. In recent years, the term has come to describe very thinly sliced vegetables, raw or smoked meats and fish

carte du jour Menu of the day

carving Slicing or cutting items, usually for customers or in front of customers

casserole   To cook in a covered dish in the oven in liquid such as stock or wine

cassoulet   A classic French dish from the Languedoc region consisting of white beans and various meats (such as sausages, pork and preserved duck or goose)

caul   Also known as crepinette (lamb) or crepin (pork), it is a thin, fatty membrane that lines the stomach cavity of pigs or sheep. It resembles a lacy net and is used to wrap and protect foods such as pâtés, ballotines, etc. The fatty membrane melts during cooking. It should be soaked in slightly salted water before use

chapelure   Dried fresh breadcrumbs

charcuterie   (French) cured or smoked meat items

chaud   (French) Hot

chef   (French) A culinary expert. The chief of the kitchen

chef de garde manger   (French) The person in charge of the cold meat department

chef de partie   (French) 'Chief of the section', a chef who leads a team of assistants in a section

chemiser   To line or coat a mould with a substance (either sweet or savoury)

chiffonade   (French) 'Made from rags'. A small chopped pile of thin strips of an ingredient, usually raw but sometimes sautéed

chine   Removal of the backbone on a cut of meat such as a rack of pork

chinois   A metal conical strainer used for straining

clamart   Any dish that contains peas or pea purée

clarified butter   Clarified by bringing to the boil until it foams and then skimming the solids from the top or straining through muslin before use

clarify   To clear a cloudy liquid by removing the sediment

clouté   An onion studded with cloves and bay leaf

coagulate   To solidify protein with heat

coat   To cover with a thin film of liquid, usually a sauce

coat the spoon   When a substance is rendered thin/thick enough so that when a wooden or metal spoon is inserted into it and taken out, the substance leaves a thin film 'coating the spoon'

cocotte   A fireproof dish usually made from porcelain

coddling   Cooking just below the boiling point, for example coddled eggs

collagen   White connective tissue that gelatinises with long slow cookery

collop   Small thin slices of meat, poultry or fish, but mainly refers to slices across the tail of lobster

commis chef de partie   (French) A qualified chef who is an assistant to a chef de partie

compôte   Stewed fruit

compound salad   A salad with more than one main ingredient

concassé   Coarsely chopped, e.g. tomato concassé

concassé a cuit   A cooked small dice of peeled tomatoes

confit   A method of preserving meat (usually goose, duck or pork) whereby it is lightly cured and slowly cooked in its own fat. The cooked meat is then packed into a crockpot and covered with its cooking fat, which acts as a seal and preservative. Confit can be stored in a refrigerator for up to six months

consommé   Clear soup

coquille   (French) Shell

cordon   A dish that is surrounded by a thin line of sauce

Cordon Bleu   (French) 'Blue ribbon'. A term used to describe high quality household cookery

correct   To adjust the seasoning and consistency of a soup or sauce

coulis   Fine purée of fruit

coupe   A rounded dish of varying size. Often used classically for presenting an ice cream based dessert with accompaniments such as fruit, salads and biscuits

court bouillon   A cooking liquor made by cooking mirepoix in water for about 30 minutes then adding wine, lemon juice or vinegar. The broth is allowed to cool before the vegetables are removed

couverture   A type of chocolate used for the preparation of cakes, confectionery and a variety of desserts; containing at least 35 per cent cocoa butter and a maximum of 50 per cent sugar

cream   The process where sugar and softened butter are beaten together with a wooden spoon until the mixture is light, pale and well blended. This process may also be carried out with a hand-held mixer or in a food processor

crecy   Any dish that contains carrots

crêpe   (French) Pancake

crimp   To seal the edges or two layers of dough using the fingertips or a fork

croquembouche   A decorative cone-shaped presentation of choux buns glazed with caramel, usually placed on a base of nougatine and decorated with pulled sugar ribbons and flowers

cross-contamination   The transfer of pathogens from contaminated food to uncontaminated food

croute   A bread or pastry base that is used to hold sweet or savoury items

croûtons   Shaped bread that is fried or toasted to accompany soups, entrées or as a base for canapés

crudites   Raw vegetables, served with a dip

curdle   When a liquid or food, such as eggs, divides into liquid and solids, usually due to the application of excess heat or the addition of an acid such as lemon juice

curing   The preservation of food items, using acidic liquids, salt or marinating

cut in   To incorporate fat into a dry ingredient, such as flour, by using a knife and making cutting movements in order to break the fat down

cutlet   A cut of lamb or veal from the loin with the rib bone attached

dariole   small mould used to cook individual portions of food, e.g. summer pudding

darne   A cut of round fish on the bone

daube   A slow-cooked stew, usually of beef in stock with vegetables and herbs. Traditionally cooked in a sealed daubiere

debone   To remove bones from meat, fish or poultry

deep fry   The process of cooking food by immersion in hot fat or oil in a deep pan or electric fryer to give a crisp, golden coating

deglaze   To add liquid such as wine, stock or water to the bottom of a pan to dissolve the caramelized drippings so that they may be added to a sauce, for added flavour

degrease   Skim the fat from food, e.g. stock

demi glace   A thick, intensely flavoured, glossy brown sauce that is served with meat

desalting   The removal of salt from foods. Food is soaked in cold water or washed under running water to dissolve the salt. Some foods such as salt cod require long, overnight soaking

détrempe   A mixture of flour and water for making a dough or a puff paste

diced   Cut into cubes

disgorge   To soak meat, poultry, game, offal in cold water to remove impurities

dock   To prick or spike a raw pastry base using a metal pastry tool such as a fork or a specialised pastry docker

doria   Food cooked with or garnished with cucumbers

dorure   Glazing with an egg mixture on raw pastries and dough before baking to produce an attractive coloured finish

dredging   To coat with dry ingredients, such as flour or breadcrumbs

drizzle   To drip a liquid substance, such as a sauce or dressing, over food

'dry' butter   European-style butter, with a fat content of 82 per cent or above, available in specialty pastry shops. It is used widely in the production of puff pastry and confectionery because it has reduced moisture content

drying off   The removal of excess moisture from foods during cooking. Not to be confused with drying or reducing. An example of drying off is when potatoes are placed over a low heat after having been drained in order to dry them off before mashing

durian   an oval fruit weighing up to 5kg. The flesh is cream coloured and textured and has a distinctive putrefying odour. It is found in Southeast Asia

dusting   To sprinkle with sugar or flour.

duxelle   Minced mushrooms and shallots cooked until dry

Ecossaise   (French) Scottish

eggwash   Beaten egg used to coat food as a glaze or as a binding agent

elastin   Yellow connective tissue that does not break down during cooking

emincé   (French) Cut fine, or sliced thinly

emulsify   The blending of two liquids that would not naturally combine into each other without agitation. The classic examples are oil and water, French dressing and mayonnaise

en croute   Cooked in pastry, e.g. beef Wellington

en papillote   (French) Cooked in a folded greaseproof bag

enrober   To completely cover a food item with a liquid

entrecôte   A steak cut from the boned sirloin

entrée   (French) A main course of meat or poultry that is not baked or roasted

entremet   The sweet course. An entremet is usually a dessert of some distinction and can be presented with a showpiece (usually made from sugar or chocolate). Can be hot but are usually cold or iced and in the form of a layered gateau which is glazed to conceal its contents

escalope   (French) A thinly sliced, boneless, round cut of meat that is batted until very thin

espagnole   Basic brown sauce

étuvée   French term to describe the slow stewing of a main ingredient (usually vegetable based)

farce   (French) Forcemeat or stuffing

farci   Stuffed

feuilletage   Puff pastry

flake   To separate segments naturally, e.g. cooked fish into slivers

flambé   Ignite alcohol on a dish, e.g. crêpe Suzette or Christmas pudding

fleurons   Crescent-shaped puff pastry used to garnish fish dishes

flute/fluting   Used in pastry or biscuit making as a decoration. Pies and tarts are fluted around the edge by pinching the pastry between the forefinger and thumb to create v-shaped grooves

fold   To gently combine lighter mixtures with heavier ones usually using a metal spoon or spatula in a cutting or slicing 'J' movement whilst slightly lifting the utensil

forcemeat   Ground meat or meats mixed with seasonings, used for stuffing

frangipane   A pastry cream used in the preparation of various desserts, cakes and sweets. It is an almond based cream that was derived from the Italian Marquis Muzio Frangipani, who invented a perfume for scenting gloves based on bitter almonds. This inspired pastry chefs of the time to make an almond-flavoured cream, which was named 'frangipane'

freezer burn   Food that is left uncovered in the freezer desiccates and becomes unusable

friand   A small puff pastry case filled with sausage meat, minced meat, ham or cheese, baked in the oven and served as an hors d'oeuvre

friandise   (French) A small delicacy, e.g. petit fours or small sweets

fricassée   A white stew where the meat or poultry is cooked in the sauce

fritture   Deep fat fryer

froid   (French) Cold

fromage   (French) Cheese

fume   (French) Smoked

fumet   A liquid obtained by reducing a stock or cooking liquid that can be added to a sauce to enhance the flavour

galantine   A dish made from poultry, game, pork, veal or rabbit usually incorporating stuffings. The flesh is boned out and the whole meat (with the skin intact) is rolled and pressed into a symmetrical or sometimes a cylindrical shape. Galantines can also be made using fish

galette   A flat round cake of variable size, can be sweet or savoury based

game   Name given to wild feathered and furred animals hunted in certain seasons

ganache   A flavoured chocolate-based cream used to decorate desserts, fill cakes and make petit fours

garnish   To decorate. Also refers to food used as decoration

gastrique   A reduced mixture of vinegar and sugar used in the preparation of sauces and dishes with a high degree of acidity. For example, tomato sauce

gastronomy   The art of good eating and appreciation of fine food and drink

gelatine   A colourless substance extracted from the bones and cartilage of animals. Supplied in powder or leaf form, it will dissolve into warm liquids and set the liquid when cooled. Widely used for making desserts

gingerbread   A type of cake. British gingerbread is made using ginger and treacle and the French version, pain d'épice, contains honey and a variety of spices

glacé   Crystallized fruits in a syrup or liqueur

glaze   To give a food a shiny appearance by coating it with a sauce or similar substance, such as aspic, sweet glazes or boiled apricot jam

glucose   A clear simple sugar made by heating starch with an acid. Used in the production of jam and syrups, and also extensively used by the pastry chef in sugar work

goujons   Small strips cut from a fillet of flat fish, often panéd or dipped in batter and then deep fried

gourmet   (French) Food connoisseur

grate   To reduce a food to very small particles by rubbing it against a sharp, rough surface, usually a grater or zester

grease   To cover the inside surface of a dish or pan with a layer of fat, such as butter, margarine or oil, using a brush or kitchen paper

grill   1. To cook foods with radiated heat. 2. Cooking equipment that radiates heat from below, e.g. barbecue

hacher   To cut very finely (often with a mincing machine).

hanging   Hanging meat from a hook at a controlled temperature to facilitate ageing (see *ageing*)

hors d'oeuvres   Small dishes served as the first course of the meal

hummus   A Greek dish made from cooked chickpeas crushed with sesame oil; usually accompanies hors d'oeuvres

husk   The tough outer casing of wheat, barley and rye. The French expression of *farine de gru* is used for wholemeal flour

icing   A preparation of icing sugar used to coat cakes and confectionery

infusion   The process of steeping an aromatic substance in a cool or warm liquid until the liquid has absorbed the flavour

iron   An essential mineral that is found in food sources such as liver, red meat, spinach and egg yolks

jardiniere   Batons of vegetables

jelly   A cold dessert made of fruit juice, wine or liqueur to which sugar and gelatine have been added

julienne   (French) A cut of meat, poultry or vegetables, which has the same dimensions as a match

jus   (French) 'Juice', usually refers to the natural juice from meat

jus lie   (French) Thickened gravy

knead   A process where dough is made smoother, softer and more elastic by applying gentle pressing and stretching actions to it. One end of the dough is secured by the heel of one hand and stretched away then pulled back over the top. In bread making, two hands are used

knocking back   To release pockets of gas in fermented dough before shaping and proving

lait   (French) Milk

larding   Larding is fat cut into strips and inserted into meat using a special needle. Used to add moisture to meat

lardons   Bacon that is cut into small batons

levain   (French) A dough that is used to make bread rise

legumes   (French) Dried beans, peas, lentils, etc.

liaison   A binding agent made up of egg yolks and cream, used for enriching soups and sauces

Lyonnaise   Refers to dishes accompanied by sautéed onions

macédoine   A neat dice of mainly vegetables which measure 1/2cm square

macerate   To soak a fruit in a liqueur or wine. This softens the fruit while releasing its juices and the fruit absorbs the macerating liquid's flavours

madeleine   A small cake shaped like a rounded shell

marinade   A mixture of wet and/or dry ingredients used to flavour or tenderise food prior to cooking

marinate   To let food stand in a marinade (such as a liquid, dry cure or paste) before cooking. Some marinades add

flavour, while those that contain acids or enzymes help to tenderise, e.g. made with fruits such as lemon, mangos papaya or kiwi fruits, or with wine, vinegar or yoghurt

marquise   A chocolate dessert, a type of rich mousse that can be served chilled or iced

Melba toast   Thin triangular pieces of crisp toast, classically served with pâté

menthe   (French) Mint

minced   Ground or chopped, usually refers to meat, fish or poultry

mirepoix   A mixture of diced aromatic vegetables, e.g. carrots, onions, celery and leek

mise en place   Basic preparation prior to cooking

miso   A Japanese condiment of fermented soya

monosodium glutamate   A type of salt used as a flavour enhancer

monte au beurre   Addition of butter to create an emulsion of cooking liquor and butter

mousse   A sweet or savoury preparation that has a very light consistency

nage   An aromatic court bouillon in which shellfish are cooked. Dishes prepared in this way are often called 'à la nage'

nape   To cover an item with either a hot or cold sauce

navarin   A brown stew of mutton or lamb

noir   (French) Black

noisette   A cut from a boned loin of lamb

nori   An edible scented seaweed used in Japanese cookery. Used as a powder, or pressed and dried for wrapping around sushi

nouilles   (French) Noodles

nutrients   The essential parts of food that are vital to health

oenology   The study of wines

oeuf   (French) Egg

offal   The edible internal organs of an animal

open sandwich   A sandwich that has a base only

organic farming   A farming method which aims to maintain natural farming methods of growing crops or maintaining livestock without the use of chemicals

palatable   Pleasant to the taste and edible

panache   A selection of vegetables or fruits

panada   A paste of various bases, either bread, flour or potato, used to thicken or bind products

pané à la Francaise   Passed through seasoned milk and seasoned flour. Used as a coating for fried foods

pané à la Aiglaise   A coating of flour, eggwash and breadcrumbs

papillote   (French) Cooked in foil or parchment paper to seal in flavour, then served and cut open at the table

parboil   To cook partially by boiling for a short period of time

parfait   (French) 'Perfect', a smooth pâté or iced dessert which can be sliced leaving an even and consistent appearance

pass   Push liquids or solids through a sieve

pâtes   (French) 'Paste'. 1. Pâté is either a smooth or coarse product made from meat, poultry, fish, vegetable, offal or game that has been blended and cooked with cream, butter and eggs. 2. Pate is different base pastry products: sweet, short, lining, puff, choux

pathogen   Micro-organism that can cause food poisoning

pâtisserie   Sweet or savoury pastries and cakes, generally baked in the oven

paupiette   Rolled and/or stuffed fillet of flat fish

pavé A square or diamond-shaped piece of meat, poultry or fish, but can also be referred to pastry or cakes

paysanne Vegetables cut into thin slices

pectin A natural gelling agent found in plants and is abundant in certain fruits, such as apples, quinces, redcurrants and lemons. Pectin is an important ingredient when making jams and jellies

pesto Rustic Italian dressing made with basil, garlic, olive oil and pine nuts

petit (French) Small.

petit four A small biscuit, cake or item of confectionery, usually served after dinner with the coffee

petit pois (French) Small peas

pipe To shape or decorate food using a forcing bag or utensil fitted with a plain or decorated nozzle

piquante A dish or sauce that is sharp to the taste

pluche Small tips of salad leaves or herbs used as a garnish

poach To cook food in hot liquid over a gentle heat with the liquid slightly below boiling point

pressing To apply pressure to items to help shape or remove excess moisture, e.g. terrines to help them keep an even layering or sweatbreads to remove excess liquid

prove To allow yeast dough to rise

purée A smooth paste of a particular ingredient or a soup that is passed through a sieve

quenelle A poached dumpling, mousseline or cream presented in an oval shape. Classically made of veal or chicken

ragout A stew of meat or vegetables

ramekin Individual or small ceramic round baking dish.

rasher Thin slice of bacon

rechauffer Reheat food for service

reduce To concentrate the flavour of a liquid by boiling away the water content

refresh To plunge food into, or run under, cold or iced water after blanching to prevent further cooking.

roast To cook food in an oven or on a spit over a fire with the aid of fat

roux Fat and flour mixture used to thicken sauces and soups; can be cooked to white, blond and brown colours

rubbing in The incorporation of fat into flour. Butter is softened and cubed then gently rubbed into the flour between the thumb and forefinger, lifting the mixing at the same time. When the fat is fully incorporated the mixture resembles fine breadcrumbs

salad tiède A salad with the addition of warm or hot ingredients

salamander A small contact grill and poker used to brown or gratin foods, or a term to describe an overhead grill

salami An Italian charcuterie product made of ground pork or beef

sauté Cook quickly in shallow fat

savouries A small after-meal dish or item as an alternative to a dessert or cheese

savoury sorbet A flavoured water ice using savoury ingredients such as tomatoes

scald To heat a liquid, usually milk, until it is almost boiling, at which point very small bubbles begin to form around the edge of the pan

score To make shallow incisions with a small knife

seal To caramelize the outer surface of meat

sear To brown the surface of food in fat over a high heat before finishing cooking by another method, in order to add flavour

season to taste Usually refers to adding extra salt and pepper

sec (French) Dry

shallow fry To cook in oil or fat that covers the base of a shallow pan

shred To tear or cut food into thin strips

sift To pass a dry ingredient, such as flour, through a sieve to ensure it is lump free

simmer To maintain the temperature of a liquid at just below boiling

simple salad A salad with only one main ingredient, e.g. tomato salad

skim To remove impurities from the surface of a liquid, such as stock, during or after cooking

skin To remove the skin from meat, fish, poultry, fruit, nuts and vegetables

slice To cut food, such as bread, meat, fish or vegetables, into flat pieces of varying thickness

smoking Hot or cold method of curing and flavouring food using wood, herbs or spices

soak To immerse in a liquid to rehydrate or moisten a product

sorbet A smooth frozen ice made with flavoured liquid-based ingredients, such as fruit juices

sous chef (French) 'Under chief', second to the head chef

steam To cook food in steam, over rapidly boiling water or other liquid. The food is usually suspended above such liquid by means of a trivet or steaming basket, although in the case of puddings the basin actually sits in water

steep To soak food in a liquid such as alcohol or syrup until saturated.

stir fry To fry small pieces of food quickly in a large frying pan or wok, over a high heat, using very little fat and constantly moving the food around the pan throughout cooking, keeping it in contact with the hot wok

stock A cooked, flavoured liquid that is used as a cooking liquor or base for a sauce

sweat To cook gently in a little fat without colour

table d'hôte A set menu at a set price

terrine A dish used to cook and present pâté

thumbing up Producing an edge all the way around the top of a flan by pinching in with the thumb and forefinger

timbale A small high-sided mould

tronçon A cut of flat fish on the bone

truss To tie up meat or poultry with string before cooking

vegan Someone who will not eat any animal product

vegetarian Someone who will not eat meat or fish but will eat animal products such as milk, eggs and cheese

velouté (French) A sauce made with stock and a blond roux, finished with a liaison of cream and yolks

viande (French) Meat

whip To beat an item, such as cream or egg whites, to incorporate air

whisk To beat air into a mixture until soft and aerated

zester A hand-held tool with small, sharp-edged holes at the end of it, which cuts orange, lemon or grapefruit peel into fine shreds

Index